GLOBAL CORPORATE FINANCE:
Text and Cases

Second Edition

GLOBAL CORPORATE FINANCE:
Text and Cases

Second Edition

SUK H. KIM
University of Detroit Mercy

SEUNG H. KIM
St. Louis University

KOLB Kolb Publishing Company
4705 S.W. 72 Ave.   Miami, Florida 33155
(305) 663-0550   FAX (305) 663-6579

Library of Congress Catalog Card Number 92-75221

ISBN: 1–878975–21–8 — Text Only
      1–878975–26–9 — Complete Package which includes:
                Text
                Student Resource Manual
                Software

The cover photograph was provided by NASA.

Revised October 1993.

Kolb Publishing Company
4705 S.W. 72nd Avenue   Miami, Florida 33155
(305) 663-0550   FAX (305) 663-6579

Preface

Global Corporate Finance can be used in international finance and investment courses at universities, company management development programs, and management institutes. We especially aimed to make this book clear, readable, and practical. It is hoped that readers will be motivated to seek out additional knowledge and courses in order to expand their understanding of international corporate finance. Our overriding goal was to give them a collection of all the basic tools and techniques of international financial analysis without a complex treatment of theoretical financial concepts. With that aim in mind, this text introduces, develops, and illustrates all areas of international finance in sufficient detail so that students may understand both what is important and what to focus on.

The last section of *Global Corporate Finance* has a number of short cases designed to illustrate major points in key chapters. Three cases are projected from actual situations. The other eight are real cases that deal with controversial problems and situations in international corporate finance. This case–study approach allows instructors to use a "hands–on" orientation. They can use cases for homework assignments or class discussions. All chapters have end–of–chapter questions. In addition, key chapters contain end–of–chapter problems. All end–of–chapter problems are tied or keyed to the numerical examples presented in each chapter. Both end–of–chapter questions and end–of–chapter problems are designed to help the student understand important concepts and topics in international corporate finance. Another strong point of this book is a quick reference glossary with 400 key terms.

A *Student Resource Manual* is an integral part of the learning package for the text. Each chapter of this manual includes: a listing of chapter objectives, a detailed chapter outline, a listing of key terms and concepts with definitions, and multiple choice questions. In addition, the manual comes packaged with *Skeleton* outlining software and *STUDY!* multiple–choice– questioning software.

Finally, a comprehensive Instructor's Manual is available for adopters of *Global Corporate Finance.* The Instructor's Manual contains a complete set of ancillary materials: chapter objective, chapter outline, answers to end–of–chapter questions, solutions to end–of–chapter problems, a test bank of 400 multiple–choice questions, and transparency masters for a set of lecture notes and key tables and figures.

Those instructors who want their students to possess practical, job–oriented international financial skills will find that this book speaks to their needs. Corporate recruiters often criticize business schools for turning out graduates who cannot contribute immediately. At the core of their criticism is their belief that students are educated in various theories, but little emphasis is placed on developing skills. That criticism should not apply to the adopters of this book because its chief purpose is the development of requisite skills in global finance.

Suk H. Kim
University of Detroit Mercy

Seung H. Kim
St. Louis University

Contents

Part Two
International Monetary Environment   39

3   The Balance of Payments   41

Part Three
Financing International Transactions   199

8   International Financial Markets   201

9   International Banking and Country Risk   226

10   Financing Foreign Trade   251

Part Six
Case Problems in
Global/Corporate Finance   463

Part One
Introduction

Part One of this text consists of Chapters 1 and 2 and is an overview of global finance. Chapter 1 discusses some contemporary issues, environmental differences, and implications of global competition for the finance function. Contemporary issues such as the U.S.-Canada Free Trade Agreement, the integration of Europe, and the dissolution of the Soviet Union are expected to create great opportunities and complex risks for multinational companies. Two major functions of finance—investment and financing—share some environmental differences, such as types of risk and conflict of interest. Financial management is undergoing fundamental change due to the two major sets of external forces: (1) the globalization of competition in factor and product markets; and (2) the deregulation and integration of world financial markets. Chapter 2 examines motives for world trade and foreign investment. Most textbooks for finance are written as though the world stops at the borders of a country. Most finance courses are taught in that way too. Recent statistics, however, indicate the growing importance of world trade and foreign investment. Hence, it is important to understand the economic basis for these activities.

1

Introduction

Although business operations in countries across the globe have existed for centuries, the world has recently entered an era of unprecedented activity in the areas of worldwide production and distribution. In the 1990s the world reached a climax in this drama of economic change. No one can deny the effects of these changes on our hopes for peace and prosperity: political and economic freedom in Eastern Europe; the emergence of market-oriented economies in Asia; the creation of a single European market; and reduction of national trade barriers. As global integration advances amid intensified international competition, the United States, Japan, and Germany are expected to lead the world toward a system of free trade and open markets.

There are also many examples of the growing importance of international operations for individual companies. Mobil Oil, Texaco, Gulf Oil, Dow Chemical, Coca-Cola, and American Express earn more than 60 percent of their total operating profits in international operations. Multinational companies, such as Mobil Oil, British Petroleum, IBM, American Express, and Sony do business with more than 50 countries around the world. World trade exceeded $5 trillion in 1992. U.S. exports and imports have increased more than ten times in the last two decades.

By the same token, global corporate finance has also become increasingly important as it serves world trade and foreign investment. International earning assets for the Bank of America, for example, represent more than half of its total earning assets. Citibank maintains more than 250 overseas branches in over 100 countries. Simply stated, each nation is economically related to other nations through a complex network of international trade, foreign investment, and international loans.

This chapter has four major sections. The first section discusses major differences between multinational companies and purely domestic companies from a financial manager's point of view. The second section explains new economic developments. The third section describes the implications of global competition for the finance function. The fourth section gives an overview of the book.

Goals, Agency Theory, and Environmental Differences

Management is motivated to achieve a number of objectives, some of which conflict with each other. Such conflicts arise because the firm has a number of constituents, such as stockholders, employees, customers, creditors, and suppliers whose desires do not necessarily coincide with each other. It is management's responsibility to satisfy such differing desires. Hence, the conflicting objectives confronting management raise the problem of setting priorities.

The commonly accepted objective of a firm is to maximize stockholder wealth, as reflected by stock price. The stock price reflects the market's evaluation of the firm's prospective earnings stream over time, the riskiness of this stream, the dividend policy, and quality aspects of the firm's future activities. However, when multinational companies attempt to maximize their overall company value, they face various constraints, such as large agency costs and environmental differences.

Management versus Stockholders

We may think of managers as agents of the owners. Stockholders delegate decision-making authority to managers on the grounds that the agents will act in the stockholders' best interest. However, it has often been argued that the objectives of managers may differ from those of the firm's stockholders. Because the stockholders of most multinational companies today are well diversified, the control of these companies is separated from ownership. This situation allows managers to act in their own best interest rather than in the best interest of the stockholders. Thus, some managers are more likely concerned with their own welfare, such as their own income, power, self-esteem, and prestige. The welfare of managers, therefore, could be increased by management decisions that in fact tend to lower stockholder wealth.

To ensure that managers act in the best interest of the stockholders, the managers must be monitored and rewarded with appropriate incentives. Such incentives could include stock options, bonuses, and perquisites. Monitoring can be done by reviewing management perquisites, auditing financial statements, and limiting management decisions. It is reasonable to assume that managers will undertake actions relatively consistent with stockholder wealth maximization because over the long run, their own goals, including survival, will largely depend on the value of the firm.

In this text, we explain the issues and concepts of international finance as though managers act on behalf of the firm's stockholders. Nevertheless, the size of some multinational companies can make it difficult to determine whether all managers make decisions on the basis of this single corporate objective—stockholder wealth maximization on a global basis. For example, financial managers of multinational companies with many subsidiaries may be tempted to make decisions that would maximize the value of their respective subsidiaries at the expense of their parent company. Consequently, the agency costs of assuring that managers try to maximize stockholder wealth can be larger for multinational companies than for purely domestic companies.

Environmental Differences

What are the differences between multinational companies and domestic companies from a financial manager's point of view? An efficient allocation of funds among assets (investment) and an acquisition of funds on favorable terms (financing) are conceptually the same for both types of companies. But, these two types of companies differ because they do business in different environments. International financial managers must understand these differences if they are to succeed in the international environment.

For successful international operations, a manager must have information about environmental factors that affect business operations in foreign countries. U.S. methods should be adjusted to accommodate customs, attitudes, economic factors, and political factors which prevail in the country of operation.

How do management practices in one country differ from those in other countries? In principle, concepts in accounting, economics, finance, management, management information systems, and marketing are as relevant to business management in one country as they are in another country. However, when a business crosses national boundaries, the environment differs for these functions. In other words, multinational financial managers are confronted with various environmental constraints when they attempt to maximize their firm's value on a global basis. The three types of environmental constraints described in this section are (1) types of risk, (2) conflicts of interest, and (3) multiple environments. These constraints are not mutually exclusive, nor do they exhaust the differences we might find in international operations.

Types of Risk. Three major risks in international business operations are political, financial, and regulatory. Political risks range from moderate actions, such as exchange controls, to extreme actions, such as confiscation of assets. Financial risks involve varying exchange rates, divergent tax laws, different interest and inflation rates, and balance-of-payments considerations. Regulatory risks are differences in legal systems, overlapping jurisdictions, and restrictive business practices against foreign companies.

If a company plans to invest heavily in foreign countries, it must consider all of these risks. Business operations which cross national boundaries add dimensions of risk rarely confronted in domestic business operations. Ideally, a company should analyze these risks to understand underlying causal forces so that the company can develop specific measures to handle them.

Conflicts of Interest.

Conflicts of interest may occur for a variety of reasons. Owners, employees, suppliers, and customers may have different national identities. The interests of sovereign national states may be divergent. The goals of multinational companies and host countries may conflict. Some conflicts of interest may exist within a multinational company. Furthermore, the multinational company and the external environment may clash with each other.

Companies tend to have home-country nationals in key positions for foreign operations, but they tend to hire local persons for nonmanagerial positions. Thus, disparities in salaries and wages are inevitable. Most developing countries require multinational companies to hire and train local people for management positions in exchange for local business operations. External conflicts relate to profit-motivated decisions which involve the transfer of funds, production, exports, imports, and employment from one country to another. For instance, a multinational firm's wish for foreign exchange remittances frequently conflicts with a local government's restrictions on these remittances.

Multiple Environments.

In addition to risk and conflict, multinational companies can have operational problems because they operate in several international environments. These environmental diversities require different concepts, analytical methods, and information. So, multinational companies should identify, evaluate, and predict all environmental variables. Some important environmental variables are the form of business organization, different institutional settings, and cultural differences.

New Order of the World Economy

Sweeping economic changes are under way in many forms around the world. These unprecedented developments will shape the world economy in the 1990s and beyond. This section will discuss some of these developments: global economic integration; a tripolar economic system; the emergence of Asian-Pacific Rim economies; economic reforms in Eastern Europe; international joint ventures; countertrade; and volatile exchange rates.

Economic Integration

A global economy may be the next stage in economic history. People have cooperated economically for centuries because they recognized the advantages of working together. Still, recent events have taken a different turn. New intergovernment cooperation is intended to make member countries a single economic unit. The movement toward the global economy has already begun.

Consider the following: the creation of the European Economic Area in 1993 which combined the seven nations of the European Free Trade Association and the 12 nations of the European Community; the 1992 agreement among the United States, Mexico, and Canada to establish a North American Trade Area; and the creation of an informal trading bloc in Asia around the Japanese yen.

We suspect these countries are in the forefront of the global economy because they agreed to reap the benefits of economic integration. They are still separate countries politically, but they become a single economic unit for all practical purposes. A world of one perfectly integrated economy does not exist. Yet, such an economic integration probably comes close in a free enterprise system. In his interview with *The Wall Street Journal*, Edmund Fitzgerald, Chairman of Northern Telecom, said in March 1990: "My company has its headquarters in Canada, but most of its sales are in the United States. It employs about as many Americans as Canadians. A big chunk of its shares are owned by Americans. Whose company is it anyway?"

A Tripolar Economic System

They used to say that when the United States sneezes, the rest of the world catches pneumonia. This old adage no longer is true. In the 1980s, a gradual shift in economic power took place from a single dominant influence of the United States to a tripolar system driven by the United States, Japan, and Germany. Thus, companies that have major operations in North America, Europe, and Asia are far more likely to prosper in the 1990s and beyond than those that do not have operations in all three of these markets. The emergence of this tripolar system will also affect the design of the international monetary system from the 1990s onward. World leaders face a major challenge of designing a system that reconciles multilateralism in an independent world with the multiplicity of other bilateral and regional forums.

This tripolar economic system has recently increased the number of reserve countries. The international monetary system gradually evolved into a series of currency blocs with the joint float of the European Monetary System and the increased use of Special Drawing Rights (SDRs). SDRs are a reserve asset created in 1967 by the International Monetary Fund. To reduce exchange risk, most of the world's central banks diversified their portfolios of reserve assets to include more key currencies and currency blocs than ever before. An increased number of reserve countries would spread the reserve-currency burden more evenly than before and leave the monetary system less vulnerable to attack.

Asian Pacific Rim Economies

As a group, the Asian Pacific Rim economies—Japan, Hong Kong, Indonesia, Malaysia, the Philippines, Singapore, South Korea, Taiwan, and Thailand—achieved the most spectacular economic growth in the 1980s. Rates of growth, sometimes in double digits, shifted wealth from the United States to these Asian countries. Their share of world gross product rose from 6.7 percent in 1965 to about 20 percent in 1989. Their share of total world exports increased from 8 percent in 1965 to about 25 percent in 1989. As recently as 1970, the Asian Pacific Rim was a net debtor and held a modest 15 percent of the world's international monetary reserves. By the late 1980s, it had become a major net supplier of capital, holding 25 percent of global international reserves.

The economic success of the Asian Pacific Rim has been accompanied in each instance by high rates of investment and savings, rapid technological transfer, and expanding international trade. Asian Pacific Rim economies usually invest about 30 percent of their gross domestic product and save about 35 percent of their gross domestic product. North America and Europe these days struggle with economic hard times. But Pacific Rim countries are preparing for their next economic leap, fueled by trade, investment, and technology links among themselves. Still, these countries rely heavily on imported technology.

Economic Reforms in Eastern Europe

Barriers to free markets are coming down. Indeed, the movement toward free markets accelerated dramatically in late 1989 because of the so-called revolution in Eastern Europe. Actually, events marked the end of the Marxist revolution and started a new phase of economic change. In 1990, the United States and its Western allies established a European Bank for Reconstruction and Development for emerging democracies in Eastern Europe. The United States removed its export ban on high-tech products to Eastern European countries in 1990. West Germany and East Germany have been united only since October 1990, but Germany is ready to take a leading role on the world economic stage. The central government structure of the Soviet Union ceased to exist on January 1, 1992. One can say that the Commonwealth of Independent States replaced the Soviet Union in history. There are leadership changes in East-bloc countries, and sweeping economic reforms are already under way in these countries.

Since late 1989, the world has witnessed unprecedented developments in Eastern Europe as these countries move toward democracy and economic reform. The countries have set out on a difficult road for the future economic well-being of their citizens. East-bloc countries are addressing the fundamental question of how some form of market economy can revive growth rates and raise living standards after years of disappointing economic performance by initiating bold and comprehensive plans for economic reform. These countries wish to become part of the global economy by adopting a variety of economic reforms. Furthermore, they are expected to join the European Economic Area in a fully integrated Europe by the end of the 1990s. Consequently, the prophecy made by Chancellor Helmut Kohl that "the 21st century will be the century of Europe" may come true.

International Joint Ventures

An international joint venture is a popular way to crack new markets. For example, American Telephone & Telegraph Company (AT&T) wanted to sell a broad range of computer chips head to head with some of the world's largest chip makers, even though the company does not produce these products. So, in March 1990 AT&T traded with NEC Corporation in Tokyo. AT&T gave NEC some of its computer-aided design technology in exchange for some of NEC's advanced logic chips, a product AT&T does not make but very much wants to sell. In Fall 1991, AT&T announced that it would go country-by-country around Europe to talk about possible mergers, joint ventures, and other forms of alliance. In December 1991, McDonnell Douglas Corp. agreed to sell 40 percent of its commercial aircraft manufacturing operations to Taiwan Aerospace Corp; this deal gave birth to a trans-pacific version of Europe's Airbus Industry's consortium. This type of alliance will probably be a hallmark of business in the 1990s.

Though in existence for over 30 years, this sort of cross-border alliance has skyrocketed in the last few years. New alliances are now crucial if companies are to deal in global markets for a variety of products. Perhaps the most striking example of such an alliance is the decision by the giants Mitsubishi of Japan and Daimler-Benz AG of Germany to discuss joint projects from autos to aircraft. Both companies want to get into new markets and new products. They see each other as the means to the end. This form of joint venture is a worldwide trend. Business executives today think that it is just too expensive to go alone. Upheaval in the Eastern bloc has increased the potential of this new market.

Countertrade

Barter started, perhaps, with a couple of Stone-Age hunters. Their agreement to share the bounty of their daily hunt probably worked well until the day one bagged a rabbit and the other a bear. This sort of trade, commonly known as countertrade, has gained renewed stature in international trade, in spite of the fact that international financial markets have attained unparalleled levels of sophistication. Countertrade refers to international trade arrangements that are variations on the concept of barter.

Britain, France, Italy, and West Germany allowed their companies in the early 1980s to help the Soviet Union build gas pipelines under a countertrade arrangement, in defiance of the United States. In 1987, Boeing sold AWACS aircraft to France, but the aircraft had to be outfitted with French-built Sneema engines. World trade grows faster than world production because of countertrade. No reliable figures about an overall volume are available because of secrecy in this form of trade. But the U.S. Department of Commerce estimates that countertrade accounts for about 20 percent of world trade.

Volatile Exchange Rates

Daily trading volume in foreign exchange markets is now estimated to be $600 billion—about 50 times the average daily volume on the New York Stock Exchange. In early April 1990, D. G. Paris, an economist for Caterpillar Corp., expressed disappointment when the dollar rose 30 percent against the yen from December 1988 to March 1990. He had several good reasons for his position. First, the difference in the exchange rates alone enabled Caterpillar's rival, Komatsu of Japan, to slash costs by a greater percentage than the savings Caterpillar anticipated from a modernization program of $2 billion. Second, Caterpillar needed seven years to reduce operating costs by 20 percent; the company had overhauled virtually all of its U.S. factories for these seven years. As another example, Sony was the victim of a 40 percent increase in the yen against the dollar in 1986. Its *1986 Annual Report* listed impressive accomplishments—new products, production and distribution rationalization, and strong performance by its subsidiaries. But the same report broke bad news: net sales had dropped by 7 percent, operating income by 75 percent, and net income by 43 percent. These days many other companies are at the mercy of foreign exchange rates.

Daily currency fluctuations have become a way of life since 1973, when a predictable international monetary system switched to a volatile exchange-rate system. Exchange rates became even more volatile and less predictable in the 1980s than ever before. Consequently, foreign-exchange risk management has taken on a more crucial role as more and more companies become global in trade and investment. In the 1990s, the international business community is expected to experience dramatic fluctuations and keen competition because this large volume of exchange trading and wide swings in currency values will add considerable uncertainty.

Summary of New Developments

Today the world economy faces many challenges, such as the economic impact of the 1991 Gulf War, the move toward a market-based economy in Eastern Europe, the economic reforms in the Soviet Commonwealth, the world debt problem, the economic problems of the very poorest countries, and the economic downturn in the United States and some other industrial countries. Nevertheless, changes from national economic systems to a global economic system revolutionize many parts of the world as countries eliminate trade barriers. Multinational companies are expected to play a key role in this process because they have the know-how, money, and experience. The trend toward a global economy will undoubtedly remove market imperfections that restrict the international flows of goods, services, and capital. Yet, companies can still benefit from imperfections in national markets for factors of production, products, and financial assets. Highly volatile exchange rates along with 24-hour exchange-market operations may generate complex risks, but they also create great opportunities for multinational companies. Many subsequent chapters of this book discuss these new developments and their implications for multinational companies.

Implications of Global Competition for the Finance Function

The role of the financial manager has expanded in recent years. Instead of merely focusing on the efficient allocation of funds among various assets and the acquisition of funds on favorable terms, financial managers must now concern themselves with corporate strategy. The consolidation of the corporate strategy and the finance function—a fundamental change in financial management—is the direct result of two recent trends: the globalization of competition and the integration of world financial markets facilitated by improved ability to collect and analyze information. For example, financial managers increasingly participate in corporate strategic matters—from basic issues such as the nature of their company's business to complex issues such as target markets.

Global competition requires greater integration between finance and several operating functions. This integration is particularly important for managing macroeconomic risks, such as those which arise from changes in interest rates, exchange rates, and commodity prices. When managing these risks, multinational companies must utilize not only financial hedges based on knowledge of their expected operating responses to price shifts, but they must also use financial perspectives to guide those responses. Furthermore, multinational companies today not only participate in most national markets but also coordinate their activities across these markets to gain advantages of scale and scope on a global basis.

Finance can add value by permitting a company to exploit pricing distortions in financial markets, reduce taxes, and alleviate risks. Their potential contribution to a company's value, however, depends on the type of international strategy pursued by the company. Donald Lessard classifies all multinational companies into three groups: (1) international opportunists—companies that focus on their domestic markets but engage in some international transactions; (2) multi-domestic competitors—companies committed to a number of national markets with substantial value added in each country but with little cross-border integration of activities; and (3) global competitors—companies that focus on a series of national and supranational markets with substantial cross-border integration of activities. Table 1-1 illustrates how these three types of multinational companies differ in their view of five financial functions: evaluation of new investment, funding operations, exchange risk management, output/pricing responses to exchange rate movements, and performance measurement.

Table 1–1
Implications of Global Competition for Finance Function

Nature of Competition

Function	International Opportunist	Multi–domestic Competitors	Global Competitors
Investment Evaluation	Domestic perspective, few "foreign" considerations	Yes/no decision to enter market or change mode to serve local market	Mutually exclusive global choices, currency and tax issues central
Funding Operations*	Meet domestic norms	Meet local norms	Match global competitors' cost of capital
Exchange Risk Management	Focus on exposure of foreign currency contracts	Focus on exposure converting foreign profits into dollars	Focus on exposure of home and foreign profits to competitive effects of exchange rate shifts
Output/Pricing Responses to Exchange Rate Movements	No change in home currency price	No change in local currency price	Change in home and local price to reflect global competitive position
Performance Measurement	Measure all operations in dollars at actual rates	Measure foreign operations in local currency	Measure all operations relative to standard that reflects competitive effects of exchange rate

*The entries in this row reflect typical behaviors of firms. Clearly, firms can, and some do, pursue global cost-minimizing financing strategies regardless of degree of global linkage of operations.

Source: Donald R. Lessard, "Global Competition and Corporate Finance in the 1990s," *Journal of Applied Corporate Finance*, Winter 1990, p. 61.

Organization of the Book

This book has five major parts. Part One (Chapters 1 and 2) examines major environmental differences and motives for both world trade and foreign investment.

Part Two (Chapters 3 through 7) deals with the forces that affect the relative prices of currencies in international markets. These forces include the balance of payments, the international monetary system, and the foreign exchange market.

Part Three (Chapters 8 through 11) describes sources of international finance. One major facet of corporate finance is to raise funds on favorable terms. In the case of global corporate finance, financing involves those sources of funds for international trade and foreign investment.

Part Four (Chapters 12 through 16) discusses the management of assets. The second major facet of corporate finance is the efficient allocation of funds among assets. A decision to invest abroad must take into account various environmental differences, such as disparities in exchange rates, differences in taxes, and differences in risk factors.

Part Five (Chapters 17 through 19) describes techniques for controlling the operations of a multinational company. Accurate financial data are especially important in international businesses because foreign operations are supervised from a distance. Taxation is an important part of international finance because it affects all aspects of multinational operations. Once a company establishes foreign operations, international transfer pricing becomes an important dimension of pricing strategies.

Summary

Political and economic events in the 1980s underscored the growing importance of free trade and open markets to economic growth and prosperity. These events include a trend toward economic integration; a tripolar economic system shared by the United States, Japan, and Germany; a gradual shift of wealth from the United States to the Asian Pacific Rim; economic reforms in Eastern Europe; the increased popularity of international joint ventures; the revival of countertrade; and volatile exchange rates.

Essentially, the concepts of business management are equally applicable to multinational and domestic companies. However, these two types of companies have environmental differences. These differences include taxes, the economic system, the political system, and inflation and interest rates. Thus, the financial manager must know the institutions and environmental conditions in those countries in which his or her company has subsidiaries or affiliates.

There are many indications that the scope of financial management should be expanded for multinational companies. Some forces for this change are increased world trade, increased movement of human and financial resources between countries, growth in the number and size of multinational companies, and improved ability to collect and analyze information. Moreover, most large and many medium-size companies in most countries around the world have international business operations of one type or another. In recent years, it has become clear that even national companies without foreign investment can be significantly affected by events in the international environment.

Questions

1. What is the primary goal of multinational companies? Why is stockholder wealth maximization more important than profit maximization?

2. Discuss the agency problem of multinational companies.

3. In order to achieve the firm's primary goal of maximizing stockholder wealth, the financial manager performs a number of important functions. What are the two major functions of a financial manager?

4. Explain environmental constraints that conflict with the primary goal of multinational companies.

5. The concept of a perfect market depends on a number of conditions. What are these conditions? Would inflation rates, interest rates, and wages among countries be more similar or less similar under conditions of perfect market than under conditions of imperfect market?

6. A growing movement to "buy American" debates the term: what is an "American" car? One of the following cars is made only in the United States. Can you name it? For extra points, match all the cars to their countries of origin.

1. Pontiac LeMans	A. Canada
2. Chevrolet Lumina	B. Korea
3. Mercury Capri	C. Mexico
4. Honda Accord Coupe	D. U.S.
5. Dodge Stealth	E. Japan
6. Mercury Tracer	F. Canada
7. Plymouth Voyager	G. Australia

7. What are the two major sets of external forces which are causing fundamental change in financial management?

8. What are the three major categories of multinational companies classified by Donald Lessard?

References

Aggarwal, R. and L. A. Soenen, "Managing Persistent Real Changes in Currency Values: The Role of Multinational Operating Strategies," *Columbia Journal of World Business*, Fall 1989, pp. 60-7.

"Asia: The Next Era of Growth," *Business Week*, November 11, 1991, pp. 56–62.

The Council of Economic Advisors, *Economic Report of the President*, Washington, D.C.: United States Government Printing Office, February 1990 and February 1992.

Daniels, J. D. and L. H. Radebaugh, *International Business*, Reading, MA: Addison–Wesley, 1992.

Eiteman, D. K. and A. I. Stonehill, *Multinational Business Finance*, Reading, MA: Addison–Wesley Publishing Company, 1992.

Fieleke, Norman S., "The Liberalization of International Trade and Payments in Eastern Europe," *New England Economic Review*, Federal Reserve Bank of Boston, March/April 1991, pp. 41–50.

Lessard, D. R., "Global Competition and Corporate Finance in the 1990s," *Journal of Applied Corporate Finance*, Winter 1991, pp. 59–72.

Madura, J., *International Financial Management*, St. Paul, MN: West Publishing Company, 1992.

Pavel, C. and J. N. McElravey, "Globalization in the Financial Services Industry," *Economic Perspectives*, Federal Reserve Bank of Chicago, May/June 1990, pp. 3–18.

Robock, S. H., K. Simmons, and J. Zwick, *International Business and Multinational Enterprises*, Homewood, IL: Irwin, 1977, Chapter 3.

Root, F. R., *International Trade and Investment*, Cincinnati, OH: South–Western, 1990.

Rose, R. L., "Caterpillar Sees Gains in Efficiency Imperiled by Strength of Dollar," *The Wall Street Journal*, April 6, 1990, p. A1 and p. A10.

Shapiro, A. C., *Multinational Financial Management*, Boston: Allyn and Bacon, 1992.

Wysocki, B., Jr., "Cross–Border Alliances Become Favorite Way to Crack New Markets," *The Wall Street Journal*, March 26, 1990, p. A1 and p. A12.

2
Motives for World Trade and Foreign Investment

Human desires for goods and services are unlimited, yet our resources are limited. Thus, one of our most important tasks is to seek new knowledge necessary to bridge the gap between desires and resources. The traditional concept of economics assumed that we allocate our scarce resources between competing uses in the most economic manner. Robinson Crusoe, for example, would allocate his time for labor between different alternatives in his world. He would use one level site on the uncharted island as either the location for a hut (shelter) or as a vegetable garden (food). Of course, the real world consists of many persons and nations that are interdependent for sociological and economic reasons. Most societies face problems similar to those faced by Robinson Crusoe, but in more complex forms.

The advantages of economic interdependence between persons center mainly on the efficiency of specialization. Specialization of function or division of labor allows each person or nation to utilize any peculiar differences in skills and resources in the most economic manner. There are a number of reasons why specialization produces a greater amount of goods and services:

1. Natural talents among people are different. If intelligent people specialized only in mental tasks while physically strong people specialized only in physical tasks, the total amount of their output would be greater than if each person tried to do both for himself or herself.

2. Even if the natural abilities of two persons are identical, specialization is advantageous because it creates the opportunity for improved skills and techniques through repetition of tasks.
3. The simplification of function through specialization leads to mechanization and the use of large-scale machinery.
4. Personal specialization saves time because one does not have to shift from one task to another.

This book deals with both foreign trade and foreign investment. Because these two types of international transactions are extremely interdependent, Chapter 2 examines motives for foreign trade and foreign investment. The knowledge and understanding of these motives are essential if we are to appreciate the economic dynamics and policy issues of trade and investment flows among nations. Thus, in this important overview, we will discuss key trade and investment theories before we consider them separately in the coming chapters. This chapter also describes global and regional market agreements designed to restore free trade.

Motives for Foreign Trade

The theories of comparative advantage, factor endowments, and product life cycle have been suggested as three major motives for foreign trade.

The Theory of Comparative Advantage

The classical economic theory of comparative advantage explains why countries exchange their goods and services with each other. Here, the underlying assumption is that some countries can produce some types of goods more efficiently than other countries. Hence, all countries are better off if each specializes in the production of those goods which it can produce more efficiently than others and buy those goods which other countries produce more efficiently than it can produce.

Why Comparative Advantage Occurs.
The theory of comparative advantage depends on two elements:

1. Factors of production, such as land, labor, capital, and technology, are unequally distributed among nations.
2. Efficient production of various goods and services requires combinations of different economic resources and different technologies.

For instance, Canada has vast amounts of fertile land resources and relatively few people. In contrast, Japan has little land and abundant skilled labor. Thus, Canada may produce such land-intensive goods as wheat more economically than Japan, while Japan may produce such labor-intensive goods as cameras more economically than Canada.

However, it is important to recognize that the distribution of economic resources and technology can change over time. This change may alter the efficiency of relative production. In the last 10 to 20 years, some developing countries have considerably upgraded the quality of their labor forces and have substantially expanded their stock of capital. Therefore, they now produce such capital-intensive products as steel, machinery, and automobiles. Moreover, some newly developed countries such as Korea, Taiwan, and Singapore now produce such high technology products as computers and word processors.

Example 2-1.   Suppose, for the time being, that the world has two nations (Canada and Japan) and two commodities (wheat and cameras). For a fixed amount of $1,000 in land, labor, capital, and technology, Canada and Japan can produce either of the two commodities in Table 2-1. The optimum product mix in Canada involves 90 bushels of wheat and 3 cameras, while the optimum product mix in Japan contains 50 bushels of wheat and 3 cameras.

It is clear from Table 2-1 that, under full employment conditions, Canada's exchange ratio for the two products is one camera (C) for 30 bushels of wheat (W) or 1C = 30W. Japan's exchange ratio for the two products is one camera for 10 bushels of wheat or 1C = 10W. Thus, Canada has a greater advantage in the production of wheat, whereas Japan has a better advantage in the production of cameras. In other words, these two countries produce both products but at different levels of economic efficiency. If they specialize according to their comparative advantage, Canada must produce only wheat while Japan must produce only cameras. If they trade with each other, larger outputs of both wheat and cameras would be available to both nations because specialization allocates world resources more efficiently.

The exchange ratios for the two products differ in the two countries. This difference becomes the basis for mutually beneficial specialization and trade. Trade requires a new exchange ratio between the two products so that Canada may obtain one camera for less than 30 bushels of wheat and Japan may obtain more than 10 bushels of wheat for one camera. Thus, the terms of trade lie somewhere between 1C = 30W and 1C = 10W or 30W > 1C > 10W. The actual exchange ratio will depend on world conditions of supply and demand. However, assume that the international exchange ratio for the two products is 1C = 20W. The quantities of the two products available to both

Table 2-1
Production Alternatives of Wheat and Cameras

Country	Wheat	Cameras
Canada	180	6
Japan	80	8

Table 2–2
Gains to Both Nations from Specialization and Trade

Country	Before Specialization	After Specialization	Exports (–) and Imports (+)	After Trade	Gains from Trade
Canada	90W	180W	–80W	100W	10W
	3C	0C	+4C	4C	1C
Japan	50W	0W	+80W	80W	30W
	3C	8C	–4C	4C	1C

countries after specialization and trade would be greater than the optimum product mixes before specialization and trade.

Table 2-2 shows the gains of the two nations from specialization and trade. If Canada exports 80 bushels of wheat (out of 180 bushels) for 4 cameras, it would enjoy 100 bushels of wheat and 4 cameras. Hence, Canada would have 10 more bushels of wheat and one more camera than the optimum product mix that existed before specialization and trade. If Japan trades 4 cameras (out of 8 cameras) for 80 bushels of wheat, Japan would enjoy 4 cameras and 80 bushels of wheat. Thus, Japan would enjoy one more camera and 30 more bushels of wheat than its optimum product mix without specialization and trade.

Specialization and trade permit the two countries in our model to obtain a total of 180 bushels of wheat and a total of 8 cameras. It is important to note that the two countries had a total of 140 bushels of wheat and a total of 6 cameras before specialization and trade. Thus, larger outputs of both wheat and cameras are available to the two countries from specialization and trade.

This original 18th-century model of international trade—the theory of comparative advantage—assumes complementary trade. There are no losers in complementary trade. But since the middle of the 19th century, the growth sector in the international economy has been competitive trade between developed countries. Under competitive trade, two countries buy from each other similar goods which both can produce almost equally efficiently. In this type of trade, some countries lose, though overall most will gain. The theory of comparative advantage and subsequent refinements assume perfect competition, free mobility of capital and labor, and ample time for markets to adjust.

The Theory of Factor Endowments

Countries are endowed differently in their economic resources. Thus, Brazil is more efficient in the production of coffee, and the United States is more efficient in the production of computers. Brazil has the soil, weather, and abundant supply of unskilled labor necessary to produce coffee more economically than the United States. The United States possesses the raw materials, facilities, and ample supply of skilled labor necessary to produce computers more efficiently than Brazil.

Differences in these national **factor endowments** explain differences in comparative factor costs between the two countries. Capital costs are lower in the United States than in Brazil because the United States has more capital than Brazil. Labor costs are lower in Brazil than in the United States because Brazil has more labor than the United States. Simply stated, the more abundant the supply of any factor, the lower the cost of the factor.

According to the theory of factor endowments, a country must specialize in the production and export of any good that uses large amounts of abundant factors. It must import those commodities that use large amounts of scarce production factors at home. On the one hand, most developing countries have a comparative cost advantage in the production of labor-intensive commodities. On the other hand, most industrialized countries enjoy a comparative cost advantage in the production of capital-intensive commodities. Thus, specialization and trade could be mutually beneficial if industrialized countries specialize in the production and export of capital-intensive goods and if developing countries specialize in the production and export of labor-intensive commodities.

Product Life-Cycle Theory

All products have a certain length of life. During this life they go through certain stages. A product's life begins with its market introduction; its market grows rather rapidly; its demand reaches maturity; its market declines; and finally, its life ends.

This theory attempts to explain both world trade and foreign investment patterns on the basis of stages in a product's life. In the context of international trade, the product life-cycle theory assumes that certain products go through four stages:

1. A large company introduces a new product in response to some change in the home-country market. After a time lag, this home country establishes itself as an exporter with a monopoly position.
2. Increasing transportation and tariff costs make it less attractive to export the product. Thus, the firm begins to produce its product in some foreign countries. This international production replaces home-country exports in certain foreign markets.
3. Some foreign companies begin to compete in third-country markets. This competition leads to a further reduction in home-country exports.
4. Some foreign companies export the product back to the home country. Many factors such as low labor costs, economies of scale, and government subsidies make it possible for foreign companies to invade the home-country market.

Other Motives for World Trade

Economies of Scale.
Economies of scale occur because of a synergistic effect which is said to exist when the whole is worth more than the mere sum of its parts. This effect has been frequently defined as "2 + 2 = 5." In other words, another important cause of international trade is that costs may fall as outputs expand. Economies of mass production can be realized if each country specializes in a limited number of products in which it has a comparative advantage. Mass production and mass marketing improve skills and technologies. Opportunities to eliminate duplicate facilities occur. There are also opportunities to consolidate the functions of production, marketing, and purchasing. These types of operating economies and improved skills can lead to larger outputs of goods and services even if no differences existed in comparative costs among countries.

Differences in Tastes.
Even if differences in comparative costs among countries and economies of scale were absent, world trade might take place due to differences in tastes. Suppose that both Canada and Japan produce the same amount of fish and meat. If Canadians prefer meat and Japanese prefer fish, then a mutually beneficial export of meat from Japan to Canada and fish from Canada to Japan would take place. Both countries gain from this trade, because the sum total of satisfaction derived from the trade is greater than would be possible under isolated self-sufficiency without trade.

Free Trade versus Protectionism

The possibility of a foreign embargo on sales of certain products and needs of national defense may cause some countries to seek self-sufficiency in some strategic commodities. Political and military questions constantly affect international trade and other international business operations. Conflicts have historically taken place between multinational companies (typically exporters) and host countries (typically importers) over political ideology, national sovereignty, control of key industries, balance of payments, and control of export markets.

Reasons for Protectionism.
There are a variety of arguments for protectionism: (1) national security, (2) unfair competition, (3) the infant industry argument, (4) domestic employment, and (5) diversification.

First, if a country wishes to be a world power, it must maintain key sectors, such as steel, for national security. By maintaining strategic commodities, it is assured of supplies in the event of global conflicts and boycotts.

Second, labor-intensive industries in developed countries argue that low wages in foreign countries constitute unfair competition. In addition to low wages, countries with industrial policies enjoy unfair competitive advantage because of their public policies such as special tax incentives, subsidies, and selected protection to overcome the competition.

Third, the logic of the infant industry argument is that protective measures are essential for newly begun domestic industries to establish themselves. They need time and thus protection to realize the economies of mass production.

Fourth, protection maintains domestic employment and living standards. The costs from unemployment may be higher than the costs of inefficient domestic production for certain products.

Fifth, highly specialized economies, such as Kuwait's oil economy, depend on international markets for incomes. These countries need some protection to diversify the economy if they are to reduce their dependence upon world markets for one or two products.

Forms of Trade Control.   Tariffs, import quotas, and other trade barriers are three primary means of protectionism. Tariffs on imported commodities may be imposed for purposes of revenues or protection. Tariffs are usually modest when they are used to increase revenues. However, tariffs are typically high when they are imposed to protect domestic companies from foreign competition. Although protective tariffs do not eliminate the importation of foreign products completely, they clearly put foreign sellers at a comparative disadvantage. Here, consumers must pay more for foreign goods, thereby reducing their consumption of imported commodities.

Import quotas may also be used to shield domestic producers from foreign competition. They specify maximum amounts of certain products to be imported during a given period of time, usually one year. Import quotas are sometimes more effective than tariffs in reducing the importation of certain products. Even if tariffs are high, certain commodities may still be imported in relatively large quantities. In contrast, low import quotas totally prohibit imports beyond a quota. Hence, it is no wonder why the United States has recently imposed quotas on the importation of certain goods, such as Japanese automobiles, European specialty steel, motorcycles, and textile products.

The general trend around the world since World War II has been to reduce such obvious trade barriers as quotas and tariffs. This trend has compelled governments to replace them with less obvious forms of protection which, according to a survey by Donald Ball and Wendell McCulloch (1985), number over 800. Three major classes of such other trade barriers are:

1. Direct government participation in trade.
2. Customs and other administrative procedures.
3. Technical and health regulations or standards.

First, a government's participation in trade covers export subsidies, countervailing duties, and antidumping regulations; when engaged in these activities, the government prefers national over foreign bidders. Countervailing duties mean additional import duties imposed to offset an export subsidy by another country.

Second, customs and other administrative procedures include customs classification, valuation, and procedures. Import duties imposed on certain products often depend on how they are classified into the tariff schedule and how they are valued by customs authorities. In addition, customs inspectors can discriminate against a good or a country by delaying the importation process.

Finally, technical and health regulations make up the standards which can hinder imports. Governments apply many safety rules and regulations on imports with marking, labeling, packaging, and technical standards. These standards tend to discriminate against imports by imposing greater hardships on foreign than domestic companies.

Nontariff trade barriers can have a significant impact on international trade. For example, Japan is criticized by some countries for its nontariff barriers, such as extremely stringent product standards on imported products. Some economists argue that these barriers are major causes of the lingering U.S. trade deficit with Japan. Others, however, attribute the deficit to Japan's superior quality and production efficiencies based on team-work, emphasis on education, and work ethic.

Summary.   Free trade, based on the principle of comparative advantage, leads to an efficient allocation of resources and a high level of material benefits. But strong arguments for protectionism have been made. They include military self-sufficiency, unfair competition, the infant industry argument, domestic employment, and diversification for stability. Although arguments for protectionism are very popular in many countries, they cannot overshadow the importance of free trade.

Economic Integration

World leaders have recognized that the reduction or elimination of artificial barriers to trade is necessary for expanding world trade. The worldwide postwar efforts to expand foreign trade included elimination of tariff barriers through the General Agreement on Tariffs and Trade (GATT) and stabilization of currencies through the International Monetary Fund. At the same time these efforts went forward on the international level, many countries around the world also pursued economic cooperation at the regional level. Regional economic cooperation is based on the premise that countries in a region connected by historical, geographic, cultural, economic, and political similarities may be able to strike more intensive cooperative agreements for mutually beneficial economic advantages.

General Agreement on Tariffs and Trade

In 1947, 23 countries signed the General Agreement on Tariffs and Trade (GATT) in Geneva. GATT contained four important rules to liberalize world trade: (1) nondiscriminatory trade policies for all member countries; (2) the reduction of tariffs by multilateral negotiations; (3) the elimination of import quotas; and (4) settlement of trade policy disputes through international consultations. Today GATT's 106 members account for more than 80 percent of world trade.

GATT members have held many talks since 1947 to expand and promote world trade. First, GATT members held periodic meetings from 1947 to 1952 to cut specific tariffs. Second, the Kennedy Round (1964-1967) covered across-the-board tariff reductions on industrial products. Perhaps the most important part of the Kennedy Round was to reduce trade barriers between the United States and the European Community. Third, the Tokyo Round (1973-1979) of multilateral trade negotiations discussed the reduction of nontariff barriers. The most important part of these agreements is a series of detailed codes spelling out permissible and nonpermissible "good" behavior by governments in almost all nontariff measures. Fourth, the Uruguay Round (1986-1992) discussed the expansion of trade liberalization to include services, intellectual property rights, and other areas.

Types of Economic Cooperation

There are five major forms of economic cooperation among countries: free trade area, customs union, common market, economic union, and political union.

The free trade-area type of cooperation requires member countries to remove all tariffs among themselves. However, the member nations are allowed to have their own tariff arrangement with nonmember countries. The U.S.-Canadian Free Trade Agreement illustrates the free trade-area type of agreement.

Under the customs-union arrangement, member nations abolish not only internal tariffs among themselves but also establish common external tariffs. The European Community (EC) initially started as a customs union.

In a common market type of agreement, member countries abolish internal tariffs among themselves and levy common external tariffs. Moreover, they allow the free flow of all factors of production, such as capital, labor, and technology. The EC exemplified a common market type of agreement until 1992.

The economic union combines common-market characteristics with harmonization of economic policy. Member nations are required to pursue common monetary and fiscal policies. This means that economic union members have to synchronize taxes, money supply, interest rates, and regulation of capital markets. The present form of the EC represents an economic union.

The political union combines economic union characteristics with political harmony among the member countries. Essentially, countries merge with each other to create a new nation. Thus, it is the ultimate market agreement among nations. In the 1950s, Egypt, Syria, and Yemen formed a political union, but it did not last long. Thus, in its pure form, an example of the political union does not exist. However, a newly created commonwealth of 11 former Soviet republics could be considered a political union.

Regional Economic Agreements

Most current market agreements are organized by geography. Many economists say that the global economy will become increasingly tripolar in the 1990s. They caution that this tripolarity is likely to lead to less trade among the three groups—Europe, North America, and Asia—in favor of increased trade within the individual blocs and regions. Moreover, they argue that the coming emergence of three giant trading blocs will make the GATT simply irrelevant. These three regional blocs account for about 70 percent of the world gross domestic product. Most issues may have to be negotiated bilaterally among the three blocs. The world then will have to find a way to multilateralize the bilateral negotiations among the three regions.

European Economic Area.

Six European countries—Belgium, France, West Germany, Italy, Luxembourg, and the Netherlands—established the European Economic Community (EEC) through the Treaty of Rome in March 1957 to remove trade barriers among the member countries. Since then, the EEC added Denmark, Greece, Ireland, Portugal, Spain, and the United Kingdom. The broad cooperation of this organization is suggested by its current popular name—the European Community (EC). See Table 2–3 for the history of the EC.

According to the 1957 Treaty of Rome, EC member countries agreed to: (1) abolish tariffs, quotas, and other trade restrictions among member countries; (2) impose a uniform tariff on imports from nonmember countries; (3) remove restrictions on movements of capital and labor within the six-nation group, (4) establish a common policy on transportation, agriculture, competition, and business conduct; and (5) coordinate and synchronize member-countries' monetary and fiscal policies; and (6) set up a "social fund" to compensate workers who might experience economic injury due to the integration process.

The 12-member countries created a single market in 1993 through the Single European Act of 1987. The EC identified three general barriers for complete removal: (1) physical barriers such as customs controls and border formalities, (2) technical barriers such as different health and safety standards, and (3) fiscal barriers such as differences in value-added tax rates and excise duties. These goals are identical with those established under the 1957 Treaty of Rome. The EC made 280 regulatory changes to create a genuine single market in Europe.

In 1993, the 12 members of the EC and the seven nations of the European Free Trade Association (EFTA)—Finland, Iceland, Norway, Sweden, Switzerland, Liechtenstein, and Austria—created the European Economic Area (EEA). This union brought Western Europe's 380 million people into the largest trading bloc in the world. The EFTA countries altered

Table 2–3
European Community Milestones

1957	Treaty of Rome established the European Economic Community.
1959	First reduction in EC internal tariffs.
1962	Common agricultural policy established.
1967	Agreement reached on value-added tax system.
1968	All internal tariffs eliminated and a common external tariff established.
1973	United Kingdom, Denmark, and Ireland joined the EC.
1979	European Parliament directly elected for the first time.
1979	European Monetary System went into effect.
1981	Greece joined the EC.
1985	A White Paper on Completing the Internal Market prepared by Lord Cockfield was endorsed by the member-country governments.
1986	Spain joined the EC.
1987	Single European Act came into effect.
1991	EC and EFTA agreed to create the European Economic Area.
1992	Target date for the elimination of all trade barriers among 12 EC countries.
1993	Target date for the elimination of all trade barriers among 19 EEA countries.
1999	Target date for the creation of a single central bank with a single currency for all 19 EEA countries.

their laws to conform to EC directives and regulations. The 19 EEA countries expect to have a single central bank with a single European currency by the end of the 1990s. Then, the existing 19 central banks would become regional banks, much like the 12 Federal Reserve Banks in the U.S. Federal Reserve System.

The EEA poses a formidable challenge to the United States and Japan because it unites 380 million Europeans into a single business market with $6 trillion in purchasing power and 45 percent of world trade. The complete integration of the 19 countries with a single European currency is expected to enlarge the possibility for growth and to keep inflation under control.

The United States and Japan have two major concerns. First, EEA business standards, which are based on 280 regulatory changes, could make it more difficult for non-EEA based companies to market products in Europe. Analysts are concerned that a single European market would become a "Fortress Europe." Second, a single European market makes it more difficult for non-EEA based companies to compete with EEA companies in Europe. Furthermore, Europe's unification and emerging Japanese economic power herald the end of American domination in world financial and consumer markets.

North American Free Trade Area.   On January 2, 1988, President Reagan and Canadian Prime Minister Mulroney signed the U.S.-Canada Free Trade Agreement (FTA), which went into effect on January 1, 1989. The

United States and Canada are each other's most important trading partners. The FTA liberalizes the largest trading relationship in the world (in 1990, the U.S.-Canadian merchandise trade volume of $170 billion vs. the U.S.-Japanese trade volume of $135 billion). Throughout this decade, the FTA will phase out tariffs, liberalize investment laws, and grant "national treatment" to companies on both sides of the border.

Beginning January 1, 1989, the FTA began to: (1) phase out all tariffs over ten years; (2) preserve the basic elements of the 1965 U.S.-Canada Auto Pact; (3) give U.S. wine makers greater access to the Canadian market; (4) remove some restrictions on cross-border investment; (5) guarantee the United States non-discriminatory access to Canadian oil, gas, and uranium; (6) set up the first-ever rules governing trade in services; (7) establish a U.S.-Canada tribunal to settle trade disputes; and (8) bring about additional talks on such difficult issues as trade subsidies in both countries and Canadian domestic rules for automobiles.

The U.S.-Canada Auto Pact of 1965 eliminated tariffs on traded vehicles and automobile parts between the two countries under certain conditions. First, auto companies must produce one vehicle in Canada for each U.S. vehicle sold in Canada. Second, auto manufacturers must have at least 50 percent North American content to receive duty-free access to the U.S. market. Third, all U.S. cars sold in Canada must contain Canadian parts worth 60-75 percent of the car's value.

In August 1992, Canada, Mexico, and the United States agreed to establish a North American Free Trade Area (NAFTA). This proposed union would convert North America into the largest economic union in the world with 360 million people and more than $6 trillion in purchasing power. Business leaders, government officials, and scholars view the NAFTA as a natural trading bloc because of American technology, Canadian resources, and Mexican labor.

Yen Trading Bloc.   The world is swiftly moving toward trading blocs. Former British Prime Minister Margaret Thatcher, in a recent speech, divided trading nations into three groups based on the mark, the dollar, and the yen. Thus, the world's future economic landscape will see that companies compete within the boundaries of trading blocs—whether in Europe, North America, or Asia. Each of these trading blocs is expected to pose its challenges. If Asian countries continue to compete in the world marketplace as single nations, they could lose their competitiveness in the world marketplace. For example, Zenith Electronics Corp. announced in November 1991 that it would move its manufacturing facility in Taiwan to Mexico. With a free trade pact among Canada, Mexico, and the United States, analysts say that Zenith may prove to be one of the first of many U.S. companies to transfer assembly jobs from Asia to Mexico.

Japanese government officials loudly assail regional trading blocs that serve as protectionist trade umbrellas. But they also concede that trading blocs may be an unfortunate but emerging trend. Because they are afraid of

American or European protectionism, Japanese government and corporate strategists have quietly tried to establish a yen bloc linking Japan's economy more closely with the economies of other Asian countries.

The declining U.S. role as the major source of foreign direct investment in Asia reflects a major shift in investment patterns in this region. Much of the new foreign investment funds come from the region itself: from Japan; from the newly industrialized economies of Hong Kong, Singapore, Taiwan, and South Korea; and even from the developing countries themselves. The growing regionalization of foreign direct investment in Asia should increase the possibility that Asian countries might form some sort of their own trading bloc around Japan.

Many Asian leaders view some sort of an informal trading bloc in Asia as a foregone conclusion. Through government aid and private investment, Japanese government and corporate strategists intend to shape and coordinate the economic development of the region. In the early 1980s, Japan initiated a New Asian Industries Development Plan, a blueprint for Japanese industries to set up offshore production in Asia. Implicit in this plan is a division of labor. For example, as Japan sees it, Indonesia will pay special attention to textiles, forest products, and plastics. Thailand will focus on furniture, toys, and die-cast molds. And Malaysia will concentrate on sneakers, copiers, and television picture tubes. Experts see in such strategies the emergence of a regional Asian economy. Meanwhile, European and American executives worry that these strategies may be the foundation stones for a future protectionist trading bloc.

Japanese yen is increasingly being used as a medium of exchange, a unit of account, and a store of value beyond Japan's borders. Many analysts believe that a yen zone will emerge—that is, that the yen will play a role in Asia comparable to that of the German mark in Europe or the U.S. dollar in the world. The use of the yen by Asian economies has dramatically increased in trade and finance. For example, the share of yen-denominated debt of Asian countries has nearly doubled since 1980. In fact, the yen has replaced the dollar as the predominant currency of denomination of Asian debt.

Economic Effects of Market Integration

Tariff and nontariff barriers disrupt the free flow of goods and, therefore, resource allocation. However, any form of market integration reduces discrimination among participating nations even though it often increases discrimination with nonmembers. Since the mid-1950s, countries have established many forms of market integration (such as the GATT, the EEA, and the NAFTA) to generate economic gains. Economists agree that economic integration will lead to the most efficient use of society's scarce resources. Analysts identify two major gains from free trade: allocation efficiencies from comparative advantage and production efficiencies from economies of scale. To achieve allocation efficiency, resources must be apportioned among firms and industries in such a way as to obtain the particular mix of products most wanted by society (consumers). To achieve production efficiency, each product embodied in this optimum product mix must be produced in the least costly way.

First, a more traditional approach depicts a world in which markets are competitive and economies of scale do not exist. In these situations, gains stem from comparative advantage. Production costs vary from country to country because countries have different economic resources such as climate, raw materials, and technology. Thus, a country is better off if it exports those goods which it can produce more cheaply than others and if it imports those goods which other countries can produce more cheaply.

Second, economic integration creates opportunities for economies of scale or synergistic effects. They exist when the combined economies are worth more than the sum of their parts. The reduction of barriers automatically increases total demand. As economic resources shift to the more efficient producers due to increased competition, companies could expand production to take advantage of the larger market. This dynamic change in market size allows companies to spread fixed costs over more and more units of production.

Motives for Foreign Investment

Many companies have been induced to enter into new and profitable markets abroad since World War II. Economic and political forces in the host countries, along with those countries' desire to sell more abroad, are largely responsible for the expansion of direct foreign investment. Companies find it increasingly easier to reach foreign markets through direct investment. More tariff restrictions, more restrictive import quotas, and nontariff barriers have made it very difficult for companies to reach foreign markets solely by exportation. Increasing transportation costs and import duties have sharply increased prices of exported goods, thus reducing the competitiveness of many companies' exports. The product life-cycle theory, the portfolio theory, and the oligopoly model have been suggested as a basis for explaining and justifying foreign investment.

Product Life-Cycle Theory

The theory of product life-cycle explains changes in the location of production. When new products are introduced in home country markets, their sales and profits tend to increase sharply until they reach maturity. Competition increases rapidly as these products approach their maturity point; this competition narrows profit margins. At this stage, companies may utilize foreign manufacturing locations to lower production costs and sustain profit margins.

This theory assumes that larger companies in highly advanced countries have a comparative advantage in new products over the companies in developing nations. But companies in developing countries have a comparative advantage in fabricating mature products. Highly advanced technologies, highly educated labor resources, and abundant capital are essential to develop new products. They are readily available to larger firms in advanced countries. Larger markets and necessary alteration requirements in early production stages are additional reasons why larger companies in the developed areas of the world first introduce new products in the home country markets.

As products become mature, product defects and technological imperfections, inherent in new products, are ironed out so that the method of production becomes standardized. Competition begins to appear during the stage of market growth and becomes highly intensive during the stage of market maturity. At this point, some companies will shift their standardized manufacturing methods to developing countries for a number of good reasons:

1. Standard production methods require many unskilled workers.
2. Most developing countries have an abundant supply of unskilled labor.
3. Labor costs are lower in developing countries than in advanced countries.

Portfolio Theory

The portfolio theory is another rationale for foreign investment. This theory rests on two variables: risk and return. Risk is the variability of returns associated with an investment project. Two projects may have the same long-term average rate of return. But one project may fluctuate widely in annual return while the other may have a stable return. A project whose returns fluctuate widely is said to be more risky than the other whose returns are stable.

Typically, only a few financial variables are known in advance. Business people and investors are, basically, risk averse. Thus, they desire to minimize the overall degree of risk for their investment projects. Fortunately, there are many business situations in which the risks of individual projects tend to offset each other. As a consequence, successful diversification makes it possible for investors to have the risk of a portfolio less than the sum of the risks of the individual projects in the portfolio.

A study by Haim Levy and Marshall Sarnat (1970) indicated that a company is often able to improve its risk-return performance by holding an internationally diversified portfolio. The key element in the portfolio theory is the correlation coefficient between projects in the portfolio. When projects with low degrees of correlation are combined with each other, a company is able to reduce its risk of expected return. The Levy-Sarnat model assumes that foreign investment projects tend to be less correlated with each other than domestic investment projects. The economic cycles of different countries, the United States and Saudi Arabia, for example, do not tend to be totally synchronized. On the other hand, most domestic projects tend to be highly correlated with each other because they depend on the same state of economy.

Oligopoly Model

An oligopoly exists where there are only a few firms whose products are usually close substitutes for one another. Because a few firms dominate a market, each of these firms has a large share of the market. Thus, the policies of one firm have repercussions on the other firms.

The oligopoly model offers a way of explaining why multinational companies invest in foreign countries. The model assumes that business firms make foreign investments to exploit their quasi-monopoly advantages. The advantages of a multinational company over a local company may include technology, access to capital, differentiated products built on advertising, superior management, and organizational scale.

Horizontal investments for foreign production of the same goods in a home market are made to produce operational economies of scale. A horizontal investment may reduce the number of competitors, eliminate duplicate facilities, and expand a firm's operation in an existing product line. Vertical investments for foreign production of raw materials are usually made to control input sources. The control of input sources may make it possible for companies in an oligopolistic industry to raise barriers to the entry of new competitors and to protect their oligopoly position. Some companies make defensive investments to prevent others from getting an unanticipated advantage.

Other Studies of Motives for Foreign Investment

Many foreign investors are motivated by strategic decisions. Although there are numerous sorts of strategic considerations, we can group them into two categories: those from the standpoint of host countries and those from the standpoint of investors.

Lee Nehrt and Dickerson Hogue (1968) suggested that companies invest abroad for several purposes:

1. New markets.
2. Raw materials.
3. Production efficiency.
4. New knowledge.

First, many companies, whose products are at a saturation stage in their home markets, attempt to preserve or expand these markets through foreign manufacturing locations. A subset of the market strategy falls within the context of the product life-cycle theory.

Second, oil companies, mining companies, and lumber companies find it difficult or costly to obtain raw materials at home. Hence, they invest their money abroad to obtain these raw materials.

Third, some production efficiency-oriented companies look for low costs of production, such as low labor costs. This is one of the most important reasons why multinational companies choose countries in Africa, Asia, and South America for their overseas investment.

Fourth, not many companies invest abroad to seek new knowledge because multinational companies tend to have superior knowledge over local companies. However, some companies may desire to dig out news of technical developments in foreign countries through foreign investment.

The National Industrial Conference Board (1969) surveyed a sample of 60 nations and found that many developing countries have various incentive programs for private foreign investments. They include tax incentives, tariff exemptions, financial assistance, remittance guarantees, administrative assistance, protection against competitive investments and imports, and protection against nationalization and political risk. These and other incentive programs would undoubtedly motivate multinational companies to invest in those nations offering them.

Yair Aharoni (1966) studied the process for foreign investment decisions. After surveying 38 American companies which had invested in Israel, he found the following investment motives:

1. Outside proposals such as those from foreign governments.
2. Fear of losing a market.
3. The bandwagon effect, which means that successful foreign operations reported by a company induce competitors to go abroad.
4. Strong competition from abroad in the home market.

In addition to these four motives, the survey also detected a number of auxiliary motives for foreign investment:

1. Utilization of old machinery.
2. Capitalization of know-how; spreading of research, development, and other fixed costs.
3. Creation of a market for components and other products.
4. Indirect return to a lost market through investment in a country that has commercial agreements with these lost territories.

A Synthesis of Foreign Trade and Investment Theories

Traditionally, economists concentrated on trade only at the national levels, while management scholars focused almost exclusively on the behavior of multinational companies. Both groups of scholars thus failed to incorporate trade and investment theories into a single theory of international involvement. This was not a serious problem when foreign trade was largely carried on by intermediaries while producers remained at home. However, multinational companies have recently crossed the confines of individual nation-states to carry on their operations throughout the world. Consequently, motives for foreign trade and investment are too closely interrelated with each other to consider them separately.

Eclectic Theory

Trade and investment theories, which we have described in the previous section, do not explain why the trade-investment pattern of multinational firms differs across countries. To determine cross-country differences in the trade-investment patterns, James Goodnow and James Hanz (1972) compared 100 countries in 59 categories. They grouped 100 countries into three clusters: hot, moderate, and cold. Hot countries are politically stable; they are high in market opportunity, economic development and performance, and cultural unity; however, they are low in legal barriers, physiographic barriers, and geocultural distance. As one moves from hot to cold countries, the government becomes less stable, the markets poorer, the economy less stable, legal and geographic barriers go up, and their cultures differ from the culture of the United States. The study then compared the frequency distribution of market entry modes by 250 U.S. manufacturing firms. It found that, as companies move from a hot to cold country, they depended increasingly on export entry and decreasingly on investment in local production. For the average hot country, exports accounted for 47.2 percent of all entry modes, investments represented 28.5 percent, and other modes amounted to 24.3 percent. In sharp contrast, for the average cold country, exports accounted for 82.6 percent of all entry modes, investments represented 2.9 percent, and other modes amounted to 14.5 percent.

The eclectic theory, associated with John Dunning (1981), attempts to explain a logical link between the international allocation of resources and the exchange of goods between countries. In other words, this theory argues the case for an integrated approach to international economic involvement on the basis of the advantages of both a country's location and a company's ownership. It implies that specific-location advantages favor a host foreign country while specific-ownership advantages favor an investing firm. Thus, the eclectic theory helps explain cross-country differences in patterns of international involvement in multinational companies. The theory holds that specific endowments of both company and country are necessary for international involvement.

Most trade and investment are carried out by individual companies. When a company expands its operations beyond national borders for the first time, it tends to exploit a foreign country's markets through exports. A company favors investment in a foreign country only if it is most profitable for the company to internationalize its advantages in that country. An export-oriented strategy serves a company well for some time. However, to become part of a global market, a company should have a world presence. Because the world presence cannot be sustained by exports alone, the company should invest abroad at some point in time.

A synthesis of foreign trade and investment theories is essential to form a single theory of international economic involvement. The eclectic theory maintains that specific factors of both firm and country are necessary to a company's foreign involvement. This theory brings together the elements of theories for trade and investment in a model that demonstrates how these elements influence a firm's choice of the entry mode best suited to a particular country.

An Integrated Approach

The eclectic theory makes it possible to synthesize foreign trade and investment theories into a single theory of international economic involvement. On the one hand, the theories of comparative advantage and factor endowments explain foreign trade in terms of specific endowments of a country. On the other hand, the theories of product life-cycle, portfolio, and oligopoly explain foreign investment in terms of specific endowments of a company. As the eclectic theory indicates, the location of production is influenced mainly by specific-country endowments, but the control and ownership of production are affected mainly by specific-company endowments. Hence, an integrated theory of foreign trade and investment would center on the company that operates in imperfect factor and product markets within the world economy of dissimilar factor and product markets on the country level.

Summary

Several theories explain the motives for world trade and foreign investment. The theory of comparative advantage and the theory of factor endowments explain why countries exchange their goods and services with each other. The theory of comparative advantage depends on two assumptions. First, economic resources are unequally distributed among nations. Second, efficient production of various products requires combinations of different economic resources and different technologies.

Both the product life-cycle theory and the portfolio theory provide a conceptual rationale for foreign investment. The product life-cycle theory assumes that a country uses foreign manufacturing locations when products approach their maturity point. The portfolio theory maintains that a company invests overseas because internationally diversified portfolios of assets improve risk-return performance.

A synthesis of foreign trade and investment theories is needed to form a single theory of international economic involvement. We can integrate trade and investment theories into a model which demonstrates how these theories influence a firm's choice of entry mode best suited to a particular country. The eclectic theory postulates that specific factors of both firm and country are necessary for a firm's foreign investment. When it is most profitable for a multinational firm to internationalize its oligopolistic advantages in a given foreign country, it will invest in that country; otherwise, it will exploit the country through exports.

Questions

1. Explain the theory of comparative advantage as a motive for foreign trade. What is the logic behind this theory?

2. The theory of product life-cycle is used as a motive for foreign trade as well as a motive for foreign investment. Discuss this theory as a motive for both foreign trade and foreign investment.

3. What is the economies of scale?

4. Describe reasons for trade protectionism.

5. Assume that world leaders attempt to reduce or eliminate artificial barriers to trade through many forms of economic integration. Explain the types of economic cooperation.

6. Briefly describe the European Community and the U.S.-Canada Free Trade Agreement.

7. What are the major benefits of market integration?

8. Why do many companies diversify their operations internationally when there are many opportunities for domestic diversification?

9. Explain the oligopoly model as a motive for foreign direct investment.

10. Lee Nehrt and Dickerson Hogue suggested that companies invest abroad for new markets, raw materials, production efficiency, and new knowledge. Discuss each of these four motives for foreign investment.

11. What is the eclectic theory?

Problems

2-1.   Assume that production possibilities data for the United States and Taiwan are as follows:

		Production Alternatives		
Country	Product	A	B	C
U.S.A.	Clothing	0	30	90
	Food	30	20	0
Taiwan	Clothing	0	20	60
	Food	15	10	0

(a) What is the comparative cost of clothing and food in the United States?
(b) What is the comparative cost of clothing and food in Taiwan?
(c) Identify the product that each country should specialize in according to the comparative advantage.
(d) Assume that both countries decided to specialize in a product according to the comparative advantage. With 1 food = 3.5 clothing terms of trade, the United States exchanges 10 tons of its food for 35 units of Taiwanese clothing. With the assumption that B is the optimum-product mix, prepare a table such as Table 2-2.
(e) With a fixed investment of $10,000, the United States produces more in both clothing and food than Taiwan. Does this mean that specialization and trade do not provide any benefits for the United States?

References

Aharoni, Y., *The Foreign Investment Decision Process*, Boston: Harvard University Press, 1966.

Ball, D. A. and W. H. McCulloch, *International Business*, Plano, TX: Business Publications, Inc., 1985, pp. 74–75.

Bradley, P. J., "Nobel Laureate Modiglani Sees Rise in Protectionism," *IMF Survey*, Washington, DC: International Monetary Fund, March 4, 1991, p. 65 and p. 69.

"Building Blocs," *The Wall Street Journal*, September 21, 1990, pp. R31–R36.

Cohen, D. A., "The United States–Canadian Automotive Trading Relationship and the Legality of the Canadian Duty Remission," *Syracuse Journal of International Law and Commerce*, Fall 1987, pp. 39–63.

Dunning, J. H., *International Production and the Multinational Enterprise*, London: George Allen and Unwin, 1981.

Fieleke, N. S., "Europe in 1992," *New England Economic Review*, Federal Reserve Bank of Boston, May/June 1989, pp. 13-26.

Goodnow, J. D., "Developments in International Mode of Entry Analysis," *International Marketing Review*, Autumn 1985, pp. 17-29.

Goodnow, J. D., and J. E. Hanz, "Environmental Determinants of Overseas Market Entry Strategy," *Journal of International Business Studies*, Spring 1972, pp. 35-50.

Hunter, L. C., "Europe 1992: An Overview," *Economic Review*, Federal Reserve Bank of Dallas, January 1991, pp. 17-27.

Lee, D., "Asia: The Next Era of Growth," *Business Week*, November 11, 1991, pp. 54-59.

Levy, H., and M. Sarnat, "International Diversification of Investment Portfolio," *American Economic Review*, September 1970, pp. 668-75.

Little, J. S., "At Stake in the U.S.-Canada Free Trade Agreement: Modest Gains or a Significant Setback," *New England Economic Review*, Federal Reserve Bank of Boston, May/June 1988, pp. 3-20.

Magee, J. F., "1992: Moves Americans Must Make," *Harvard Business Review*, May-June 1989, pp. 78-84.

The National Industrial Conference Board, *Obstacles and Incentives to Private Foreign Investment*, Volume II, New York: Conference Board, 1969.

Nehrt, L., and D. W. Hogue, "The Foreign Investment Decision Process," *Quarterly Journal of AISEC International*, February/April 1968, pp. 43-48.

Quelch, J. A., R. D. Buzzell, and E. R. Salama, eds., *The Marketing Challenge of 1992*, Reading, MA: Addison-Wesley, 1990.

Stone, N., "The Globalization of Europe: An Interview with Wisse Dekker," *Harvard Business Review*, May-June 1989, pp. 90-95.

Truell, P., "Trading Places in Global Commerce," *The Wall Street Journal* August 14, 1989, p. 1.

Wysocki, B., Jr., "In Asia, the Japanese Hope to Coordinate What Nations Produce," *The Wall Street Journal*, August 20, 1990, p. A1 and p. A4.

Part Two
International Monetary Environment

Part Two (Chapters 3 through 7) deals with the forces that affect the relative prices of currencies in international markets. These forces include the balance of payments, the international monetary system, and the foreign exchange market. Prices of products and investments across national boundaries are expressed in international money. Commercial transactions between countries were once handled under the relatively rigid gold standard. But pursuit of national economic goals—healthy economic growth, full employment, stable prices, and the favorable balance of payments—has led to many changes in the international environment under which business must operate.

3

The Balance of Payments

A country's balance of payments is commonly defined as the record of transactions over a specified period of time between its residents and foreign residents. These transactions include exports and imports of goods and services, cash receipts and payments, gifts, loans, and investments. Residents may include business firms, individuals, and government agencies.

The balance of payments helps business managers and government officials to analyze a country's competitive position and to forecast the direction of pressure on exchange rates. The ability of multinational firms to move money across national boundaries is critical. Multinational companies depend on this ability for exports, imports, payment of foreign debts, and dividend remittances. Many factors affect a firm's ability to move funds from one country to another. In particular, a country's balance of payments affects the value of its currency, its ability to obtain currencies of other countries, and its policy toward foreign investment.

This chapter has three objectives: (1) to define the balance of payments accounts, (2) to discuss the actual balance of payments, and (3) to explain the means for correcting a balance-of-payments disequilibrium.

Double–Entry Accounting

Double-entry bookkeeping, used in accounting for the balance of payments, is similar to those methods used by business firms in accounting for their financial positions. In ordinary business accounting, the amount of each transaction is recorded both as a debit and as a credit. The sum of all debit entries must, therefore, equal the sum of all credit entries. In addition, the total value of the assets used by the firm in business accounting must be equal to the total value of the claims against the assets. Claims against assets are called the liabilities of the firm. A firm may have two classes of liabilities: those due to creditors and those due to stockholders. By accounting convention, a debit entry is used to show an increase in assets or a decrease in liabilities, while a credit entry is used to show an increase in liabilities or a decrease in assets. Because a debit entry is always accompanied by a credit entry, it follows that the value of total assets on the books of a company is always equal to the value of total liabilities.

We can apply these elementary principles to the recording of transactions in the balance of payments. Some hypothetical transactions may illustrate this double-entry approach.

Example 3-1: Merchandise Trade.

An American company sells $30,000 worth of machinery to a British company, and this British firm pays for the machinery in 90 days. In this transaction, a U.S. resident gives up an asset to a resident of the United Kingdom in return for a promise of future payments. The following entries are required to record the transaction: (1) a debit of $30,000 to show the increase in U.S. short-term claims on foreigners and (2) a credit of $30,000 to show the decrease in merchandise (machinery) available to U.S. residents.

Short-term capital	$30,000 (debit)	
Exports		$30,000 (credit)

Example 3-2: Services.

Services represent non-merchandise transactions such as tourist expenditures. Consider an American woman who visits her husband in Japan. She cashes $5,000 worth of U.S. traveler's checks at a Japanese hotel and spends the $5,000 in Japan before returning to the United States. In this case, the United States received travel services from Japan in the amount of $5,000. In return for these tourist services, Japanese banks now have $5,000 worth of dollars. A debit entry of $5,000 is made to reflect U.S. purchases of travel services, and a credit entry of $5,000 is made to record the increase in U.S. liabilities to foreigners.

Tourist services	$5,000 (debit)	
Short-term capital		$5,000 (credit)

Example 3-3: Unilateral Transfer.

This account covers gifts by domestic residents to foreign residents or gifts by a domestic government to foreign governments. Suppose the U.S. Red Cross sends $20,000 worth of flood-relief goods to Chile. The term "transfer" reflects the nature of the transaction: the United States receives nothing in return. This transaction reduces the real assets of the United States (net worth) because the United States sends its goods to Chile. Thus, these transfers should be debited. A sale or unilateral transfer is credited. The flood relief shipments appear in the U.S. balance of payments as follows:

Transfer payments	$20,000 (debit)	
Exports		$20,000 (credit)

Example 3–4: Long–Term Capital.

This account shows the inflow and outflow of capital commitments whose maturity is longer than one year. It covers investments in financial assets with no significant control of real assets. The account also covers investments in real assets or financial assets with significant control of real assets. Assume that an American purchases $5,000 worth of French bonds and pays for it with a check drawn on a Los Angeles bank account. The United States now owns a French bond, while France owns U.S. dollar deposits. Since the acquisition of the French bond increases U.S. portfolio investments in foreign countries, the portfolio investments must be debited. At the same time, the dollar balance, owned by the French, represents an increase in U.S. liabilities to foreigners. Hence, the U.S. short-term capital should be credited. This transaction will appear in the U.S. balance of payments as follows:

Portfolio investments	$5,000 (debit)	
Short-term capital		$5,000 (credit)

Example 3–5: Short–Term Capital.

Short-term capital includes demand deposits, short-term loans, and short-term securities. For example, a 90-day loan by a resident of the United States to a borrower in Canada entails the transfer of short-term capital by the U.S. resident in exchange for a promise from the Canadian borrower to repay at a future date. Suppose that a U.S. bank lends $10,000 to a Canadian firm for 90 days. A debit entry records the increase in U.S. claims on foreigners, and a credit entry records the increase in demand deposits held by foreigners in the U.S. banks.

Short-term capital	$10,000 (debit)	
Short-term capital		$10,000 (credit)

Recording each international transaction on the basis of the double–entry accounting principle is logical. However, we should recognize that the balance of payments is neither an income statement nor a balance sheet. The balance of payments is a sources–and–uses–of–funds statement reflecting changes in assets, liabilities, and net worth during a specified period. In other words, transactions between domestic and foreign residents are entered in the balance of payments either as debits or credits. In dealing with the rest of the world, a country earns foreign exchange on some transactions and expends foreign exchange on others. Transactions that earn foreign exchange are often called credit transactions and represent sources of funds. These transactions are recorded in the balance of payments as credits and are marked by plus signs (+). The following transactions represent credit transactions:

1. Exports of goods and services.
2. Investment and interest earnings.
3. Unilateral transfers received from foreign residents.
4. Investments and loans from foreign residents.

Transactions that expend foreign exchange are sometimes called debit transactions and represent uses of funds. These transactions are recorded in the balance of payment as debits and are marked by minus signs (-). The following transactions represent debit transactions:

1. Imports of goods and services.
2. Dividends and interest paid to foreign residents.
3. Transfer payments abroad.
4. Investments and loans to foreigners.

The Balance of Payments as a Whole

A country incurs a "surplus" in its balance of payments if its credit transactions exceed debit transactions or if it earns more abroad than it spends. On the other hand, a country incurs a "deficit" in its balance of payments if its debit transactions are greater than credit transactions or if it spends more abroad than it earns.

Essentially, analysts focus on those transactions that occur because of self-interests. These so-called autonomous transactions include exports, imports, unilateral transfers, and investments. The arithmetic sum of these autonomous transactions, sometimes called "above-the-line items," represents the balance-of-payments surplus or deficit. A balance-of-payments surplus occurs when autonomous receipts exceed autonomous payments. By the same token, a balance-of-payments deficit takes place when autonomous payments exceed autonomous receipts. On the other hand, compensating transactions occur to account or compensate for differences between international payments and receipts. These compensating items, called "below-the-line items," are used to eliminate international disequilibrium.

The transactions of Examples 3-1 through 3-5 represent autonomous transactions. In Example 3-1, the export of U.S. machinery earns a foreign exchange of $30,000 and is thus a credit. Transactions of Examples 3-2 through 3-5 cause the United States to expend a foreign exchange of $40,000 and are therefore debits. Consequently, the United States has an overall deficit of $10,000 in its balance of payments and must undertake $10,000 worth of compensating transactions to make up the difference. In this case, the compensating transactions of the United States involve sales of its gold, reductions in its balance of convertible foreign currencies, or increases in the balance of the U.S. dollars held by other nations.

Now, for a moment, suppose that the United States has a surplus in its balance of payments rather than a deficit. To account for this surplus in the U.S. balance of payments, U.S. reserves, such as gold and convertible foreign currencies, would increase by $10,000, or the balance of the U.S. dollars held by other nations would decrease by $10,000. These transactions, designed to account for the surplus in the balance of payments, are also called compensating transactions.

Balance-of-Payments Accounts

The balance of payments identifies transactions along functional lines. We may classify balance-of-payments transactions into four major groups:

1. Current account: merchandise, services, and unilateral transfers.
2. Capital account: long-term capital and short-term capital.
3. Statistical discrepancy: errors and omissions.
4. Official reserve account: official reserve assets and foreign official assets.

The Current Account

The current account includes merchandise exports and imports, earnings and expenditures for invisible trade items (services), and unilateral transfer items. Entries in this account are "current" in nature because they do not give rise to future claims. The balance of payments on the current account is the broadest measure of a country's international trade because it includes financial transactions as well as trade in goods and services. A surplus on the current account represents an inflow of funds, while a deficit represents an outflow of funds.

Balance of Merchandise Trade.
The balance of merchandise trade refers to the balance between exports and imports of physical goods such as automobiles, machinery, and farm products. A favorable balance-of-merchandise trade (surplus) occurs when exports are greater in value than imports. An unfavorable balance-of-merchandise trade (deficit) occurs when imports exceed exports. Merchandise exports and imports are the largest single components of total international payments for most countries.

Services.
International trade involves exports and imports of both goods and services. Services include such invisible items as military expenditures, interest and dividends, travel and transportation, plus fees and royalties. A country's purchases of services represent imports with debits recorded. A country's sales of these services to foreigners represent exports with credits recorded. The balance between exports and imports of goods and services is called the balance on goods and services.

Unilateral Transfers.   Gifts and grants are included in the unilateral transfers by both private parties and governments. Private gifts and grants include personal gifts of all kinds, philanthropic activities, and shipments by relief organizations. For example, money sent by immigrants to their families in their native country represents private transfers. Government transfers include money, goods, and services as aids given to other countries. For instance, goods and services, provided by the United States government to other countries as part of a drought relief program, represent government transfers.

The Capital Account

U.S. residents and businesses may choose to invest in foreign countries. Of course, foreigners may engage in similar capital transactions; for example, they may buy real capital assets in the United States, or they may invest in U.S. government securities. The capital account consists of loans, investments, other transfers of financial assets, and the creation of liabilities. Unlike current account entries, entries in the capital account indicate changes in future claims; for instance, loans and their interest should be paid, or dividends on investment should be paid. The capital account covers long-term capital and short-term capital.

Long–Term Capital.   Long-term capital flows represent claims with a maturity of longer than one year. They include direct investments, portfolio investments, and loans. Private flows are characterized by direct and portfolio investments, whereas government flows are characterized by loans.

Direct investments are equity investments such as purchases of stocks, the acquisition of entire firms, or the establishment of new subsidiaries. The U.S. Department of Commerce defines direct investments as investments in either real capital assets or financial assets with a minimum of 10 percent ownership in a foreign firm.

Portfolio investments are purchases of foreign bonds or other financial assets without a significant degree of management control. Desires for return, safety, and liquidity in investments are the same for international and domestic portfolio investors. However, international portfolio investments have additional risks such as changes in exchange rates, wars and revolutions, and expropriations. Portfolio investments in utilities and government agencies are active because the risk of loss in these fields is less than in other fields.

Government long-term flows include loans, financial support in economic development projects overseas, subscriptions to various regional development banks, and participation in other foreign projects either directly or through international institutions. The U.S. government, in particular, makes substantial loans to many nations for economic development. The U.S. Export-Import Bank also extends loans to other nations in order to promote U.S. exports.

Short-Term Capital.

Short-term capital represents claims with a maturity of less than one year. Such claims include demand deposits, short-term loans, and short-term securities. Short-term capital flows are either nonliquid or liquid capital. Nonliquid short-term flows include bank loans and time deposits which are very difficult to liquidate quickly without losses. Liquid short-term flows represent such claims as demand deposits and short-term securities which are easy to liquidate quickly with minimal or no losses.

Some short-term capital flows occur due to changes in the current account or changes in long-term investment. More specifically, these changes may take place because of merchandise trade, service trade, unilateral transfers, and investments. Short-term capital movements, induced by such transactions, are sometimes called compensating or accommodating adjustments. These compensating accounts change only for one reason—to finance other items in the balance of payments. In contrast, other short-term flows are attributable to differences in interest rates among nations and to expected changes in foreign exchange rates. Short-term capital movements caused by such changes are frequently called autonomous adjustments. These autonomous accounts change for purely economic reasons.

Statistical Discrepancy: Errors and Omissions

The balance of payments should always balance in theory because all debits are offset by credits and vice versa. But it rarely does balance in practice for a number of reasons. Balance-of-payments data gathered from many different sources are incomplete and may be interpreted differently by individuals and agencies. Thus, the debits and credits may not balance at the end of a year. This is why the statistical discrepancy is treated as a "plug" item to keep the balance-of-payments accounts in balance. Although this item could be placed anywhere in the balance of payments, it is typically placed close to the short-term capital account because more errors and omissions occur in that account than in other accounts.

The Official Reserve Account

Official reserves are government-owned assets. The official reserve account represents only purchases and sales by official monetary authorities, such as the Federal Reserve System of the United States or the Bank of Japan. Changes in official reserves are necessary to account for the deficit or surplus in the balance of payments.

The official reserve account consists of official reserve assets and foreign official assets. Official reserve assets are composed of gold, convertible foreign exchange, and Special Drawing Rights. The principle convertible currencies are the U.S. dollar, the British pound, the German mark, and the Japanese yen for most countries. Special Drawing Rights (SDRs), sometimes called "paper gold," are rights to draw on the International Monetary Fund

(IMF). At its 1967 meeting in Rio de Janeiro, the 106 members of the IMF adopted a plan to create a new international reserve asset in the form of SDRs. In 1970 SDRs went into use as a supplement to gold and dollars in international reserves of nations. SDRs can be used as a means of international payment.

The official reserve account of a country also includes its liabilities to foreign official holders. These liabilities are sometimes called foreign official assets. U.S. liabilities to foreign official holders, such as foreign central banks, refer to foreign official deposits with U.S. banks and official holdings of U.S. Treasury securities. Foreign governments frequently wish to hold such assets in the United States because of their interest earnings. In recent years, U.S. trade deficits have been financed primarily by increasing official liabilities rather than by transferring official reserve assets abroad.

The official reserve account presents a great difficulty when trying to classify its transactions either as debits or credits. On the one hand, an increase in any of the reserve assets represents a use of funds on a debit entry (–) in the balance of payments. On the other hand, a decrease in any reserve asset indicates a source of funds on a credit entry (+). By the same token, a decrease in any official liability is entered as a debit, and an increase in any official liability is recorded as a credit.

Purchases of foreign exchange and gold (increases in reserve assets) are imports of something the United States did not have before; they are thus recorded as debits. Dollars, likewise, are imported when they are acquired by the United States; so, dollar inflows (decreases in official liabilities) are debit entries. On the other hand, sales of foreign exchange and gold (decreases in reserve assets) are exports of something we are holding in "inventory;" hence, they are recorded as credits. Dollars, by the same token, are exported when they are acquired by foreigners; so dollar outflows (increases in official liabilities) are credit entries. In other words, any transaction which finances the balance–of–payments surplus should be recorded as a debit; any transaction which finances the balance–of–payments deficit should be recorded as a credit.

Measuring the Surplus or Deficit

The operational definition of surplus or deficit is the sum of the above–the–line transactions or autonomous transactions. Surely, a nation's surplus or deficit will vary according to the definition of autonomous transactions. The balance of merchandise trade designates only exports and imports of merchandise as autonomous transactions. Balance on goods and services covers merchandise trade items and services as autonomous items. Balance on current account considers goods, services, and unilateral transfers as autonomous items. Balance on capital account treats current account items and capital flows as autonomous items. A clear definition of autonomous transactions is thus essential if one is to isolate the most probable causes of imbalances before determining what actions government officials should take to remedy these imbalances.

A change in the official reserve account measures a nation's surplus or deficit on its current and capital account transactions by netting official liabilities from official reserve assets. Normally, a surplus will lead to an increase in official reserve assets, while a deficit will cause a reduction in these assets. The only question that might arise is how to treat private holdings of foreign exchange on both sides. Few private citizens of other countries hold Spanish pesetas, Mexican pesos, or Indian rupees. If they receive foreign currency, the foreign currency will be exchanged quickly for their own currency at a commercial bank. The commercial bank, in turn, exchanges the foreign currency at the central bank. At this point, the transaction shows up in the official reserve account.

The exception is a reserve currency, particularly the U.S. dollar. U.S. balance-of-payments deficits have not been matched by net changes in official reserve assets because many billions of dollars have been held by private foreigners—individuals, corporations, and banks for future transactions not only with the United States but also with third countries. For most countries, however, there is a close correlation between balance-of-payments imbalances and net changes in official reserve assets.

The Actual Balance of Payments

The balance-of-payments statement has many formats, because many different organizations collect and present balance-of-payments statistics. A number of international organizations such as the International Monetary Fund (IMF) and the General Agreement on Tariffs and Trade (GATT) compile balance-of-payments data for their member countries and present them in their yearbooks. The U.S. Department of Commerce compiles U.S. balance-of-payments statistics and publishes them in its *Survey of Current Business*.

The World Balance of Payments

The value of world merchandise trade reached a new record of $3.5 trillion in 1990. In its review of the 1980s, the GATT report observes that the volume of world trade increased by 50 percent during the decade, while the value of trade rose by 75 percent. The expansion of world trade averaged 6 percent annually, while the growth of global output averaged 4 percent a year. Hence, the share of production traded increased substantially during the 1980s; this reflects the relative openness of markets and the ongoing integration of the global economy.

Figures 3-1 through 3-3 present a number of interesting statistics for international trade during the 1980s. Figure 3-1 shows that world trade has grown faster than world production throughout the 1980s. As given in Figure 3-2, the three largest economies in the world—the United States, Japan, and Germany—have incurred massive external-account imbalances during the

Figure 3–1
World Trade and Output

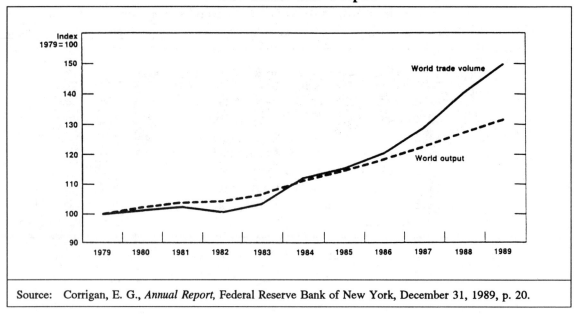

Source: Corrigan, E. G., *Annual Report*, Federal Reserve Bank of New York, December 31, 1989, p. 20.

Figure 3–2
Current Account Balances for the U.S., Japan, and Germany

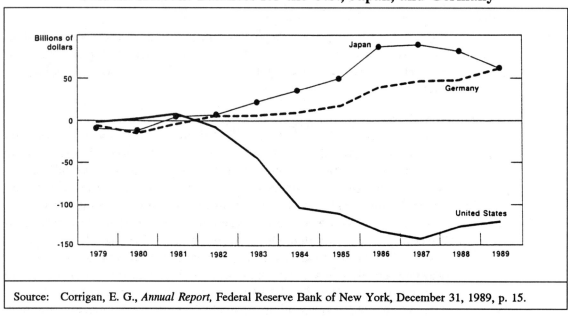

Source: Corrigan, E. G., *Annual Report*, Federal Reserve Bank of New York, December 31, 1989, p. 15.

1980s. Figure 3-3 shows that industrial countries as a group have shown significant external deficits through much of the 1980s.

Figure 3–3
Current Account Deficits for Industrial Countries

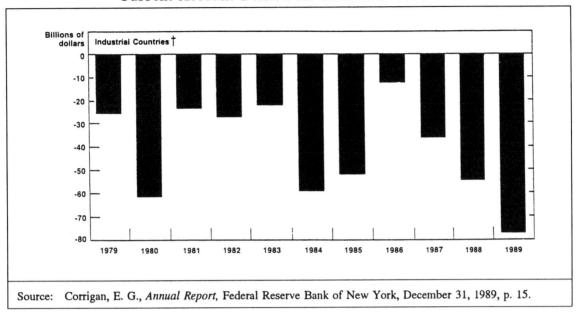

Source: Corrigan, E. G., *Annual Report*, Federal Reserve Bank of New York, December 31, 1989, p. 15.

The U.S. Balance of Payments

Table 3-1 summarizes the U.S. balance of payments figures from 1970–1990. A careful examination of some significant figures in Table 3-1 allows us to develop a fairly clear understanding of U.S. performance, problems, and responses over the last 20 years.

Merchandise Trade.   In 1990, the world's second largest trading nation, the United States, exported $389 billion worth of goods and imported $498 billion worth of goods. Both figures represent about 15 percent of the world total. In 1990, the United States lost its position as the world's largest merchandise exporter to Germany, due to a 16.5 percent increase in the value of the German mark and the unification of the east and west regions.

The U.S. balance on merchandise trade was in surplus during the early 1960s, but from the mid–1960s to the early 1970s, the U.S. merchandise-trade balance moved gradually from surplus to deficit. This movement was interrupted, however, during the worldwide recession of 1974–75. During this time of recession, the United States suffered more economic contraction than most other major trading nations. Thus, the U.S. merchandise-trade balance swung into surplus in 1975, even though there was a sizeable increase in U.S. outlays for imported oil. The surplus proved short-lived because the U.S. balance-of-payments deficit for merchandise trade rose sharply from

The Balance of Payments   **51**

Table 3–1
U.S. Balance of Payments: Selected Accounts
(in billions of dollars)

Year	Merchandise Trade	Services Trade	Unilateral Transfers	Current Account	Statistical Discrepancy
1970	2.6	3.2	-3.5	2.3	-0.2
1971	-2.3	4.7	-3.8	-1.4	-9.8
1972	-6.4	4.7	-4.1	-5.8	-1.9
1973	0.9	10.3	-4.1	7.1	-2.7
1974	-5.5	14.9	-7.4	2.0	-1.5
1975	0.9	14.1	-4.9	10.1	5.9
1976	-9.5	19.0	-5.3	4.2	10.5
1977	-31.1	21.6	-5.0	-14.5	-2.0
1978	-33.9	24.1	-5.6	-15.4	12.5
1979	-27.5	32.7	-6.1	-1.0	25.4
1980	-25.5	34.6	-7.6	1.5	25.3
1981	-28.0	43.8	-7.6	8.2	18.7
1982	-36.4	38.6	-9.2	-7.0	34.4
1983	-67.1	32.6	-9.8	-44.3	9.2
1984	-112.5	20.8	-12.5	-104.2	23.9
1985	-122.1	24.9	-15.4	-112.7	15.3
1986	-145.1	27.6	-15.8	-133.2	11.3
1987	-159.5	30.0	-14.2	-143.7	1.9
1988	-127.0	15.7	-14.9	-126.2	-9.2
1989	-115.9	25.1	-15.5	-106.3	18.4
1990	-108.1	38.3	-22.3	-92.1	63.5

Source: The U.S. Department of Commerce, *Survey of Current Business*, June 1991, pp. 44–45.

1976 through 1987. Three factors had been singled out as leading causes of this six-fold rise in the U.S. deficit for merchandise trade from 1980 to 1987: the strong U.S. dollar, reduced U.S. exports to heavily indebted developing countries, and faster economic growth in the United States than in its major trading partners. This is why there have been many calls for trade protection and why the United States became a net debtor nation in 1986.

However, the merchandise trade deficit began to fall with the rapid expansion of American exports in 1988. The U.S. merchandise trade deficit fell from $160 billion in 1987 to $127 billion in 1988; this was the first drop in the U.S. trade deficit since 1980. The U.S. merchandise trade deficit declined even further to $73 billion in 1991. The devaluation of the dollar, a decline in inflation rates, and an acceleration in the growth of U.S. trading partners all combined to significantly reduce the U.S. trade balance and to strengthen the competitiveness of its products in the world market.

Service Trade. But U.S. exports of services have consistently exceeded its imports of services for the last 20 years. In recent years, increases in exports within each of the major service categories—travel, passenger fares, transportation, royalties and fees, and investment income—have exceeded increases in imports by an appreciable margin. However, recent increases in U.S. imports within two major categories—interest and dividend payments—reduced the U.S. service-trade surplus from 1981 to 1988. The U.S. service-trade surplus has increased again since 1989, but this trend is not expected to last long.

The United States has recently paid for its huge trade deficit by foreign loans and direct foreign investment. The growth of net capital into the United States has been expanded by a parallel expansion of the U.S. trade deficit. This growth is a reflection of increased foreign investment in U.S. securities and real capital assets.

Service transactions have played a crucial role in lowering the U.S. trade deficit, but this has tended to escape our attention for several reasons. First, some service-trade categories reflect transactions which rarely come to mind when the topic is trade. Second, service items have remained a relatively minor part of overall trade volume. Third, international trade negotiations have tended to focus on barriers to merchandise trade.

Current Account. The U.S. current account was in surplus until 1970. Since 1970, surpluses fell drastically, leading ultimately to substantial deficits. In fact, the U.S. current-account deficit exceeded $14 billion in 1977 and 1978. But the United States registered some surplus in its balance of payments on the current account in 1980 and 1981. Once again, the surplus was short-lived because the current-account deficit rose sharply from 1982 through 1987. The current-account deficit increased from $7 billion in 1982 to $144 billion in 1987. Most of this increase was attributable to the merchandise-trade deficit. But the current-account deficit has declined since 1988 as the result of the falling merchandise-trade deficit.

Statistical Discrepancy. "Statistical discrepancy" was called "errors and omissions" until 1976, when that label, with its somewhat embarrassing connotation, was officially dropped. This item has become uncomfortably large in some years. For example, when the Commerce Department tallied the two sets of reports for 1990, it found a record $64 billion "statistical discrepancy," up from $18 billion in 1989. At a time when considerable analytical interest is focused on the availability of capital, the large statistical discrepancy makes it difficult to determine whether the supply of foreign capital to the United States has indeed been reduced.

A plus figure reflects an inflow of funds, and a minus figure reflects an outflow of funds. No one knows exactly what the discrepancy means, except that it may constitute a sort of barometer for such things as political unrest, crime, sloppy paper work, or deception among central banks.

The discrepancy may be due to unreported foreign funds coming to the United States for investment in some form of asset. Some analysts believe that many affluent foreigners—particularly those from politically unstable countries—move large sums of money into this country without government knowledge because they perceive the United States as a safe political haven. Some observers also fear that this movement may cause the Federal Reserve System of the United States to underestimate the amount of credit expansion.

Another important factor affecting the discrepancy of increasing payments is the role of currency trading. Increased trading in foreign currencies, in combination with the flexible exchange system, undoubtedly introduces larger errors in payments figures. Analysts believe that certain countries, such as Japan and Germany, may deliberately underestimate the number of dollars held by their central banks in order to avoid pressure from the U.S. government to reduce exports to the United States. On the other hand, some poor countries, according to analysts, may deliberately underestimate the amount of their dollar holdings in order to obtain low-interest loans from such organizations as the IMF.

Sloppy work is another factor. Most data on the balance of payments depend on personnel in banks and other business offices to complete federal forms. Unfortunately, these persons sometimes make multimillion dollar mistakes.

Net Capital Flows to the U.S.   Table 3-2 shows net U.S. assets abroad [increase/capital outflow (-)] and net foreign assets in the United States [increase/capital inflow (+)] from 1980 to 1990. Net capital flows to the United States increased from -$28 billion in 1980 to $167 billion in 1987. The net capital flows from abroad increased because prospects for domestic investment had been sufficiently positive to make investment in the United States more attractive than investment elsewhere. U.S. banks and other

Table 3–2
Net Capital Flows to the U.S.
(in billions of dollars)

Year	U.S. Assets Abroad	Foreign Assets in U.S.	Net Flows to U.S.
1980	-86.1	58.1	-28.0
1981	-111.0	83.0	-28.0
1982	-124.5	93.8	-30.7
1983	-56.1	84.9	+28.8
1984	-31.1	102.6	+71.5
1985	-27.7	130.0	+102.3
1986	-92.0	130.0	+38.0
1987	-62.9	229.8	+166.9
1988	-86.1	221.5	+135.4
1989	-128.6	216.6	+87.9
1990	-57.7	83.3	+25.6

Source: The U.S. Department of Commerce, *Survey of Current Business*, June 1991, pp. 44–45.

entities decided to invest less abroad and more in the United States, and foreigners decided to do the same. These large net capital flows to the United States had some positive, short-term effects on the U.S. economy. The net investment flows from abroad increased the pool of savings in the U.S. economy; they reduced the U.S. interest rates; they enabled the U.S. economy to grow faster than otherwise would have been the case; and they reduced the U.S. inflation rate.

However, the net capital flows to the United States tumbled from $167 billion in 1987 to $26 billion in 1990, raising alarm on Wall Street and elsewhere. The dramatic decrease in net capital flows to the United States indicates that the United States may have more trouble than expected in pulling out of the recession. Some economists say that the falloff in foreign investment was a major factor behind the dollar's 17 percent fall against European currencies in 1990. The Securities Industry Association called the figures "sobering news."

U.S. International Investment Position

Balance of payments is a flow concept because it measures the economic activities of a country over a one-year period. International investment position is a stock concept because it summarizes a country's assets and liabilities on a given date. Table 3-3 shows the international investment position of the United States from 1982 to 1990. The U.S. net overseas investment evolved steadily from $6 billion in 1919 to $141 billion in 1981. This long-term increase in the U.S. net investment position has decreased dramatically since 1982. In 1986 the United States became a net debtor nation for the first time since World War I. Its foreign debt reached $412 billion in

Table 3–3
International Investment Position of the United States
(in billions of dollars)

Type of Investment	1982	1983	1984	1985	1986	1987	1988	1989	1990
U.S. Assets Abroad	1100	1114	1105	1174	1319	1463	1534	1673	1764
Government assets	217	203	190	206	229	251	230	253	256
Private assets	883	911	915	968	1090	1212	1304	1420	1508
Foreign Assets in U.S.	737	829	941	1109	1393	1598	1840	2112	2176
Government assets	189	194	200	202	242	283	322	337	367
Private assets	548	635	741	907	242	1315	1518	1775	1809
Net Position	363	285	164	65	-74	-135	-306	-439	-412

Note: Portfolio investment position at market value and direct investment position at current cost.
Source: The U.S. Department of Commerce, *Survey of Current Business*, June 1991, p. 26.

1990. This is about one-third the combined total debt of some 110 developing countries. Huge trade and budget deficits, caused by major shifts in macroeconomic policy in the first half of the 1980s, turned the United States from creditor to debtor.

Net international investment positions themselves are not particularly meaningful. This is why many economists look at four broad categories of the international investment position: short-term position, long-term position, government sector, and private sector. In other words, analysts break down international investment holdings into several categories so that they can draw policy implications from each category about the liquidity status of a country.

Short-term foreign assets in the United States such as bank deposits and government securities are meaningful because foreigners can withdraw these holdings at very short notice. If they fear capital losses from further depreciation of the dollar or if interest rates decline, foreign investors may turn away from dollar-denominated short-term assets. Such actions by foreign investors can endanger the stability of the U.S. financial system. Foreign official assets in the United States are also significant. If foreign monetary authorities decide to liquidate their holdings of U.S. government securities, the financial strength of the dollar will fall. Long-term investments such as long-term corporate securities and direct investment are less important because they respond to basic economic trends and are not subject to erratic withdrawals.

Increased Economic Interdependence

The growing economic interdependence of the United States and other countries is reflected in expanding international trade and capital flows. U.S. imports of goods and services increased from less than 5 percent of total demand on average in the 1960s to more than 11 percent on average in the 1980s. U.S. exports of goods and services increased from just 6 percent of domestic production on average during the 1960s to nearly 11 percent on average during the 1980s.

International financial markets have also grown dramatically over the past decade. Capital flows abroad helped to finance investment expenditures in the United States. These flows respond quickly in 24-hour financial markets to differences in short-term interest rates and other developments across countries. Because capital movements are sensitive to differences in policy, the globalization of financial markets has increased the interdependence of national economic policies.

The globalization, innovation, and deregulation of financial markets have reduced the cost of financial transactions and improved the allocation of investment internationally. But these same forces have also increased volatility in financial markets and introduced highly complex elements of risk.

Japanese International Transactions

Current and Capital Account Overview

Table 3-4 shows figures for broad categories of Japan's international transaction flows for 11 years from 1980 to 1990. Japan has experienced substantial current-account surpluses since 1981. These surpluses have increased from $5 billion in 1981 to $87 billion in 1987, approximately 4 percent of Japan's gross national product. The rapid rise in Japan's current-account surplus has caused its net long-term capital outflows to increase sharply. However, Japanese net long-term investments have been consistently greater than the current-account surpluses. The net long-term capital outflows which arise from both portfolio and direct investments have been generally accompanied by net short-term capital flows.

During the 1980s Japan became the world's largest capital exporter. Its net long-term capital outflows rose from $10 billion in 1981 to $137 billion in 1987. As the world's largest capital exporter, Japanese investors have been leading acquirers of U.S. securities and other types of assets. In the 1980s Japanese capital outflows have increased for a number of reasons: (1) a large excess of domestic savings over domestic investments in Japan, (2) rising trade and budget deficits in the United States, and (3) the financial market liberalization in Japan.

Table 3–4
Japanese International Transactions
(billions of dollars)

	1980	1981	1982	1983	1984	1985	1986	1987	1988	1989	1990
Current Account Balance	-10.7	4.8	6.9	20.8	35.0	49.2	85.8	87.0	79.6	57.2	37.0
Long-Term Capital, net	2.3	-9.7	-15.0	-17.7	-49.7	-64.5	-131.5	-136.5	-130.9	-89.2	-56.1
Short-Term Capital, net	16.3	8.7	-1.5	-3.5	13.3	9.9	56.9	95.7	64.0	29.4	11.2
Bank-related	13.1	6.4	0.0	-3.6	17.6	10.8	58.5	71.8	44.5	8.6	9.8
Other	3.1	2.3	-1.6	0.0	-4.3	-0.9	-1.6	23.9	19.5	20.8	1.3
Official Reserves, net	-4.9	-3.2	5.1	-1.2	-1.8	-0.2	-15.7	39.2	-16.2	12.8	12.8
Official Non-Reserves, net	0.2	-1.1	-0.2	-0.4	-0.5	1.7	2.0	-3.0	0.7	11.9	0.7
Errors & Omissions	3.1	0.5	4.7	2.1	3.7	4.0	2.5	-3.9	2.8	-22.0	-15.4

Source: Glick, R., "Japanese Capital Flows in the 1980s," *Economic Review*, Federal Reserve Bank of San Francisco, Spring 1991, p. 20.

Trade Friction Between the U.S. and Japan

Japan's closed-door policy refused commerce with the Western world until the mid-19th century. Then on July 18, 1853, Commodore Matthew Perry sailed into Tokyo Bay with a fleet of four warships and demanded that the Japanese government sign an agreement with the United States. Perry returned the following February to Tokyo Bay and backed these demands with even more warships. These events, framed by a show of force, persuaded Japan to sign a treaty with the United States. Under this treaty, Japan agreed to open two ports to the Americans.

Now, 140 years later, the United States hopes to accomplish a similar feat. It has charged in recent years that Japan maintains unfair trade barriers to generate large trade surpluses. In a show of economic force, the United States, on May 25, 1989, designated Japan as the worst trading partner under Super 301 of the 1988 Trade Act. Super 301 was designed to identify "priority practices," which include major barriers and trade-distorting practices. Under these criteria, the United States identified three Japanese practices in May 1989: government procurement of super computers, government procurement of satellites, and standards and codes for wood products. Japan was subject to tough retaliation unless it removed its barriers within 12 months. In March 1990, Japan agreed to remove its barriers to these products as part of a comprehensive trade agreement with the United States.

As economic studies show, trade restrictions rarely benefit a country. In support of this belief, the United States has a strong tradition of free trade. Yet, U.S. imports under protection of quotas and "voluntary" import restrictions have risen from 10 percent in 1980 to more than 20 percent today; the percentage of U.S. imports under protection was only 8 percent in 1975. In recent years, tariffs have increased mostly in the textile, footwear, steel, motorcycle, ceramic tile, shipbuilding, and other industries. Congress passed the Omnibus Trade and Competitiveness Act in 1988, which set up a timetable for action against those countries judged to have unfair barriers to U.S. trade. The so-called Super 301 gave the President of the United States authority to retaliate against countries with a consistent pattern of unfair trade practices against the United States. Super 301 expired in 1991, but Congress has recently threatened to reintroduce it, unless the U.S. trade deficit with Japan decreases quickly.

Table 3–5 underscores the reasons for U.S. trade protectionism. The U.S. total trade deficit increased from $25 billion in 1980 to $160 billion in 1987, an increase of 540 percent. Its trade deficit with Japan has increased from $7 billion in 1980 to $57 billion in 1987, an increase of 714 percent. Japan is a source of the U.S. largest bilateral trade deficit. Access to the U.S. market is crucial to Japan because the United States has been its number one export market for many years. The United States takes about 35 percent of Japan's total exports; Japan accounts for about 40 percent of the U.S. trade deficit.

Table 3–5
U.S. and Japanese Merchandise Trade Balances
(in billions of dollars)

| Year | United States | | Japanese |
	Overall Balance	Balance with Japan	Overall Balance
1980	–25.5	–7.3	–10.7
1981	–28.0	–13.6	8.7
1982	–36.4	–17.1	6.9
1983	–67.1	–19.7	20.5
1984	–112.5	–33.9	33.6
1985	–122.1	–46.6	46.1
1986	–145.1	–59.1	82.7
1987	–159.5	–57.1	79.7
1988	–127.0	–53.1	77.6
1989	–115.9	–49.1	64.3
1990	–108.1	–42.7	52.4

Source: The U.S. Department of Commerce, *Survey of Current Business*, various issues, and Japan Economic Institute of America.

Causes of the Trade Imbalance. Some U.S. politicians argue that the huge U.S. trade deficit with Japan arose solely because of unfair Japanese trade practices. In their view, Japanese trade practices directly threaten the world trading system, which in the last 45 years has brought prosperity to both countries. Japanese officials, on the other hand, point to the low U.S. savings rate, the budget deficit, and poor training standards as major causes of the U.S. trade deficit. The truth is, of course, somewhere in the middle of these positions. Economic relations between the two nations in recent years have become increasingly important. In spite of that notion, their relations have become severely strained. Japan's role in the world economy grew, and the United States became concerned about its international economic position.

Japan has felt U.S. protectionist pressures for the past two decades. Nonetheless, it has taken full advantage of the open U.S. market but without reciprocity. U.S. measures against Japanese exports surged, and Japan's reaction to the U.S. pressure has recently strained the relationship between the two close allies. The United States has demanded that Japan open its market to U.S. products, restrain Japanese export growth in the U.S. market, and invest in the United States. Simultaneously, U.S. companies have used unfair trade laws to harass Japanese exporters. Unfortunately, these measures have been only modestly successful.

The Japanese take the U.S. reaction seriously and lobby hard to offset the protectionist mood in the United States. But they see different reasons for the

U.S. mounting trade deficit with Japan. They contend that: (1) the U.S. government deficit is too high; (2) U.S. companies are short-term profit-oriented; (3) U.S. business executives do not try to learn the normal Japanese style of doing business in Japan; and (4) after-sale services of American companies are poor. All over the industrialized world, politicians and critics complain about Japan's massive trade surpluses. The Japanese, obsessed by foreign criticism of their trade practices and surpluses, sometimes charge that these complaints result from racism and cultural prejudice.

Adversarial Trade.   The original 18th-century model of international trade, known as the theory of comparative advantage, assumes complementary trade. Some countries can produce some goods more efficiently than other countries. Therefore, all countries benefit if they specialize in producing goods which they can produce more efficiently than others and if they buy those goods which other countries can produce more efficiently. In other words, there are no losers in complementary trade. Since the middle of the 19th century, the growth sector in the international economy has been competitive trade between developed countries. Under competitive trade, two countries buy from each other similar goods that both can produce almost equally efficiently. In this type of trade, some countries lose, though most will gain.

Still, some researchers such as Peter Drucker (1986) say that Japan practices adversarial trade, only selling but not buying. Thus, some American critics charge that "our rich friend Japan bankrolls America and underwrites Europe, but does not want us in the family business." In adversarial trade both sides lose—the buyer immediately and the seller later, within a decade or so. Based on the adversarial trade model, the successful seller eventually destroys the buyer's industry and purchasing power because the seller's goods displace the goods produced by the manufacturers of the buying country. First, buyers can pay only if they have an income. Second, the seller in adversarial trade may lose more in the long run than the buyer. Sellers may be unable to prevent it because they have no defense against a buyer's retaliatory actions. Sellers cannot counteract by stopping their purchases because they do not purchase the buyer's products.

Undoubtedly, the United States could manage without importing Japanese manufactured goods at fairly low cost; and so could Western Europe. Japan would face a major depression without exports to the United States. Also, Japan has the world's largest-ever surplus for liquid funds. Correction of the trade imbalance will impose costs on the United States and on countries, such as Japan, that have become "addicted" to the U.S. market.

Solutions.   Japan's success in American markets and complaints by U.S. firms about difficulties in penetrating Japanese markets have prompted charges of unfair Japanese trade practices. But recent U.S. pressure has forced Japan to remove most trade barriers to imports of U.S. manufacturers.

Several other avenues to open Japanese markets are being pursued in the United States. Some barriers, such as Japan's ban on rice imports, are the subject of multilateral trade negotiations in the GATT. Furthermore, the United States and Japan had held bilateral trade discussions under Super 301 of the 1988 Trade Act since May 1989. When Japan refused to yield to U.S. Super 301-based unilateral pressures, the two countries in early September 1989 entered into the so-called "Structural Impediments Initiatives" negotiations. Under this political compromise, both the United States and Japan agreed to remove their "structural barriers" to international trade and investment.

In March 1990, the United States and Japan reached a historical agreement on their trade issues. Japan agreed to: (1) shorten to 18 months the time it takes for a foreign firm to open a store in Japan; (2) eliminate obstacles and inefficiencies in the goods distribution system that make it hard for foreigners to get their products into stores; (3) increase enforcement of antitrust laws; and (4) boost government spending on public works projects. In return, the United States agreed to: (1) reduce the capital gains tax to encourage investment in the U.S. business; (2) strengthen the Gramm-Rudman Act, which requires reductions in the federal deficit; and (3) allow owners of Individual Retirement Accounts to use that money for buying a first home, to stimulate the economy. Consequently, on April 28, 1990, the Bush Administration, despite heavy pressure from business groups and members of Congress, dropped Japan from the list of unfair traders under Super 301.

In November 1991, Japan launched a program designed to correct international trade imbalances by boosting its imports. The program consisted of four parts:

1. Tax incentives to Japanese importers of manufactured goods that increase the value of imports by at least 10 percent from a base year.
2. Elimination or reduction of tariffs.
3. A $100 million budget for programs that promote imports.
4. Low-interest loans for facilities considered necessary for expansion of imports and for foreign corporations making direct investments in Japan.

Trends in the U.S.–Japanese Trade. In 1987, Americans imported $84 billion worth of goods from Japan and exported $27 billion worth of goods there. The next year, American exports to Japan rose by almost $10 billion, but Japan's sales here grew by less than half that. That meant a U.S. export rise of 33 percent and a Japanese export rise of 6 percent. The same thing happened in 1989: American exports to Japan rose by 18 percent, whereas Japan's exports to the United States rose by 5 percent. And in 1990, Japan's exports to the United States actually declined in a development hardly noted here. In contrast, American exports again rose—this time by 8 percent, to $46 billion. If these trends continue, the U.S. trade deficit with Japan will disappear in a foreseeable future. However, the U.S. government is not too happy about this progress because Japan's share of the U.S. trade deficit has actually increased from 36 percent in 1987 to 47 percent in 1990.

How to Restore International Equilibrium

Some countries, such as the United States, have had deficits for many years. But their compensating transactions cannot be maintained indefinitely. Hence, some adjustments must be made to correct the balance-of-payments deficit. International equilibrium may be restored in three ways: price mechanism, income mechanism, and public controls.

Price Mechanism

In international finance, price mechanism refers to exchange rates. Exports and imports between countries with different units of money introduce a new economic factor called the **foreign exchange rate**. The foreign exchange rate is the rate of exchange between a country's currency and a foreign currency. An equilibrium exchange rate occurs at the point where demand equals the supply for foreign exchange. At the equilibrium exchange rate, there would be no tendency for the exchange rate to rise or to fall. Debit and credit items in the balance of payments cause demand and supply for foreign exchange. Thus, equilibrium for a foreign exchange rate also implies some form of equilibrium in the balance of payments.

The exchange rate is a special price because it is the relationship between all domestic prices and all foreign prices. Consider the exchange rate between the U.S. dollar and the Japanese yen. A change in the exchange rate would alter the prices of all American products for Japanese people and the prices of all Japanese products for Americans. Such changes in an exchange rate could cause the relative attractiveness of American exports and imports to change in such a way that it would restore equilibrium in the U.S. balance of payments.

The price mechanism restores international equilibrium through changes in interest rates and commodity prices. Assume that the United States is the deficit country and that Japan is the surplus country. In this case, money tends to move from the United States to Japan in order to finance the U.S. deficit. Unless the Federal Reserve System of the United States counteracts these flows, money supply in the United States will decrease. A decrease in the U.S. money supply will push U.S. interest rates up. In Japan, the money supply will increase. Such an increase in money supply will push Japanese interest rates down. The new relative yield will encourage capital flows from the surplus country (Japan) to the deficit country (the United States). Such a reverse movement of money will help to bring the U.S. payments into balance.

If prices are flexible in both countries, commodity prices in the United States will fall because its deficit implies a decrease in demand for American products. In contrast, commodity prices in Japan will rise because its surplus means an increase in demand for Japanese products. Such a change in relative prices will stimulate the demand for American products and curb the demand for Japanese products, thereby restoring the balance in the United States.

The operation of freely fluctuating exchange rates, as reflected by changes in interest rates and commodity prices, is supposed to correct the U.S. balance-of-payments deficit automatically. However, it is also possible that a fluctuation of exchange rates may be insufficient to correct the original deficit. The ability of the price mechanism to correct the balance-of-payments deficit depends on the responsiveness of quantity demanded to change in prices, i.e., the price elasticity for imported products. If price elasticities for traded goods are high, the price mechanism will increase extensively the exports of a deficit country and the imports of a surplus country. Such a change in exports and imports will restore international equilibrium. But if the price elasticities for traded goods are low, the price adjustment may be insufficient to correct the balance-of-payments deficit.

Income Mechanism

The equilibrium level of income exists where the aggregate quantity demanded (spending) equals the aggregate quantity supplied (income). In an open economy, the equilibrium condition is explained in the following way:

$$C + I + G = C + S + T + (Ex - Im) \qquad (3\text{-}1)$$

where:

C = consumption
I = investment
G = government purchases of goods and services
S = savings
T = taxes
Ex = exports
Im = imports

It is important to recognize that the left-hand side of Equation 3-1 represents an aggregate spending, and its right-hand side represents an aggregate income. If exports exceed imports, domestic spending is smaller than domestic income. If imports exceed exports, domestic spending is larger than domestic income. When the excess of imports over exports is extremely large or continues too long, the obvious remedies would be an increase in income or a reduction in spending.

Income changes in one country affect other countries. An increase in U.S. imports means more export sales for Japan. This has an expansionary effect in the Japanese economy; thus, Japan will increase its imports. If Japan buys more goods and services from the United States as a result of its increased income, the United States will find its exports increasing. An increase in U.S. exports will eliminate part of its original deficit caused by rising imports. At the same time, increased exports by Japan means more imports by the United States. Such an increase in U.S. imports means a reduction in U.S. income. After a time, the United States will reduce its consumption and imports because of its reduced income. Reduced imports by the United States will eliminate part of the original increase in Japanese exports. When these two forces are combined—the increase in exports by the deficit country (the United States) and the decrease in exports by the surplus country (Japan)y—international equilibrium will be restored between the two nations.

Income changes also tend to restore international equilibrium because they affect interest rates on domestic investment in capital assets. Investment in capital assets, such as plants and equipment, tends to increase as interest rates fall. Because capital flows from the deficit country to the surplus country, interest rates in the United States start to increase. An increase in U.S. interest rates reduces U.S. investment in assets. As a result of its reduced investment in capital assets, the United States will find its national income and imports falling. The reverse is true in Japan where declining interest rates will raise investment in capital assets. An increased investment in assets will, in turn, push Japanese income and its imports to rise. This mechanism operates as long as there is a surplus or a deficit. It could eventually eliminate international disequilibrium.

The income mechanism, like the price mechanism, is supposed to correct the U.S. balance-of-payments deficit automatically. But it is also possible that a fluctuation of income may be insufficient to correct an original deficit. In a fashion similar to price elasticity, income elasticity measures the relative change in quantity demanded for a given percentage change in income. If income elasticities for traded products are high, an income mechanism will restore the balance-of-payments disequilibrium automatically. Because income elasticities for certain products are low, an income mechanism may be insufficient to correct the balance-of-payments imbalances.

Public Control

Most leading economists and leaders of commercial nations have applauded pleas for liberal trade and automatic adjustment policies. Nevertheless, free trade among nations and automatic adjustment mechanisms have recently faced their most serious challenge. Governments have two major reasons for their balance-of-payments controls. First, they may find their international reserves inadequate to finance their deficits. Second, the free fluctuation of exchange rates may be insufficient to eliminate international disequilibrium completely.

In general, there are two types of public controls: foreign exchange controls and trade controls. Think, for a moment, of a case in which increased Mexican imports create a shortage in its foreign exchange. Under exchange controls, the Mexican government would force its exporters and other recipients to sell their foreign exchange to the government or to designated banks. Then, the government would allocate this foreign exchange among the various users of foreign exchange. In this way, the Mexican government restricts Mexican imports to an amount of foreign exchange earned by Mexican exports. Thus, imports under exchange controls are less than they would be under free market conditions.

When governments are faced with a serious payment deficit, they may manipulate exports and imports through tariffs, quotas, and subsidies. High tariffs on imported goods and import quotas by Mexico would reduce Mexican imports. On the other hand, the Mexican government may subsidize certain Mexican exports to make them competitive in world markets and to increase the volume of Mexican exports. Special taxes on foreign direct investments by Mexican firms tend to reduce Mexican capital outflows.

Summary

The balance of payments summarizes all international transactions between residents of a country and residents of foreign countries during a specified period. The systematic record of these international transactions requires pre-established principles. These principles include rules or procedures, such as the double-entry accounting rule, and definitions of terminology, such as the current account.

Double-entry accounting records each transaction as both a debit and a credit of equal amount. Increases in assets and decreases in liabilities or net worth constitute debits (uses of funds). On the other hand, decreases in assets and increases in liabilities or net worth represent credits (sources of funds). Some international transactions, such as exports or imports, occur due to purely economic reasons. These transactions are called autonomous transactions. Such transactions as sales of gold or increases in foreign debt take place to account for differences between international payments and receipts. These transactions are often called compensating transactions.

Some countries have had deficits for many years. These deficits cannot indefinitely be financed by compensating transactions. The balance-of-payments deficit can be corrected by means of freely fluctuating exchange rates, changes in income, and government controls. The first two methods are supposed to correct international disequilibrium through changes in interest rates, commodity prices, and income. Government controls, such as exchange and trade controls, can be used to alleviate or correct the balance-of-payments deficit.

Questions

1. What are the three major components of the current account?

2. Briefly describe the capital account.

3. If a country has a deficit on its current account, what are the consequences for the country's balance of payments on its capital account? Assume that the country practices a flexible exchange-rate system.

4. What is the role of the statistical discrepancy in the balance of payments? What are the major causes for the statistical discrepancy?

5. Most developing countries (excluding oil-exporting countries) have incurred huge balance-of-payments deficits for many years. What alternatives are available to these countries for dealing with their balance-of-payments problems?

6. The U.S. merchandise trade deficit rose sharply from 1980 to 1987. Discuss some reasons for such a dramatic increase in the U.S. merchandise trade deficit.

7. Briefly explain why net capital flows to the United States have decreased dramatically since 1989.

8. What is the major difference between the balance of payments and the international investment position? When did the United States become a net debtor nation for the first time since World War I? Explain why the United States became a net debtor nation.

9. Explain the reasons that Japan became the world's largest capital exporter during the 1980s.

10. What is adversarial trade? Why do both sides (the buyer and the seller) lose in adversarial trade?

11. Assume that there are huge balance-of-payments imbalances between two countries: the United States (deficit country) and Japan (surplus country). Explain how the price-income mechanism can restore international equilibrium.

12. List and discuss some reasons why the price-income mechanism does not work fully.

References

The Council of Economic Advisors, *Economic Report of the United States*, Washington, DC: U.S. Government Printing Office, 1985, 1990, and 1992.

Drucker, P. F., *The Frontiers of Management: Where Tomorrow's Decisions Are Being Shaped*, New York: Truman Talley Books, 1986.

Feldstein, M., ed., *International Economic Cooperation*, Chicago: The University of Chicago Press, 1989.

Fieleke, N. S., *What Is the Balance of Payments?* Boston: Federal Reserve Bank of Boston, 1985.

Fieleke, N. S., "International Payments Imbalances in the 1980s," *New England Economic Review*, Federal Reserve Bank of Boston, March/April 1989, pp. 1–14.

Glick, R., "Japanese Capital Flows in the 1980s," *Economic Review*, Federal Reserve Bank of San Francisco, Spring 1991, pp. 18–31.

Heller, R., "Improving America's Competitiveness," *Economic Review*, Federal Reserve Bank of Richmond, March/April 1989, pp. 17–20.

Hipple, F. S., "Multinational Companies and International Trade: The Impact of Intrafirm Shipments on U.S. Foreign Trade 1977–1982," *Journal of International Business Studies*, Third Quarter 1991, pp. 495–504.

International Monetary Fund, *Balance of Payments Manual*, Washington, DC: IMF, 1976.

Orr, J., "The Trade Balance Effects of Foreign Direct Investment in U.S. Manufacturing," *Quarterly Review*, Federal Reserve Bank of New York, Summer 1991, pp. 63–76.

Rosensweig, J. A., and P. D. Koch, "The U.S. Dollar and the Delayed J-Curve," *Economic Review*, Federal Reserve Bank of Atlanta, July/August 1988, pp. 1–15.

Seringhaus, F. H. R., and G. Botschen, "Cross-national Comparison of Export Promotion Services: The Views of Canadian and Austrian Companies," *Journal of International Business Studies*, First Quarter 1991, pp. 115–34.

The U.S. Department of Commerce, *Survey of Current Business*, various issues.

The United States International Trade Commission, *Operation of the Trade Agreements Program*, Washington, DC: USITC, July 1991.

4

The International Monetary System

The international monetary system consists of laws, rules, institutions, instruments, and procedures which involve international transfers of money. These elements affect foreign exchange rates, international trade and capital flows, and balance-of-payments adjustments. Foreign exchange rates determine prices of goods and services across national boundaries. These exchange rates also affect international loans and foreign investment. Hence, the international monetary system plays a critical role in the financial management of multinational business and economic policies of individual countries.

A multinational company's access to international capital markets and its freedom to move funds across national boundaries are subject to a variety of national constraints. These constraints are frequently imposed to meet international monetary agreements on determining exchange rates. Constraints may also be imposed to correct the balance-of-payments deficit or to promote national economic goals.

A successful exchange system is necessary to stabilize the international payment system. To be successful, an exchange system should meet three conditions:

1. Balance-of-payments deficits or surpluses by individual countries should not be too large or prolonged.
2. Such deficits or surpluses should be corrected in ways that do not cause unacceptable inflation or physical restrictions on trade and payments for either individual countries or the world.
3. The maximum sustainable expansion of trade and other international economic activities should be facilitated.

Theoretically, continuous balance-of-payments deficits and surpluses cannot exist around the world. Under a system of freely flexible exchange rates, a foreign exchange market clears itself in the same way a competitive market for goods does. Just like every commodity price, each exchange rate moves to a level where demand and supply are equal. Under a system of fixed exchange rates, central banks or other designated agencies buy and sell on the open market to absorb surpluses and to eliminate deficiencies of foreign currencies at the fixed exchange rates.

This chapter has three major sections. The first section presents a history of the international monetary system, from the gold standard of the late 19th century to the hybrid exchange system that prevails today. The second section examines new developments since the breakdown of the Bretton Woods System. The third section discusses proposals for further international monetary reform.

The Pre-1914 Gold Standard

In the pre-1914 era, most of the major trading nations accepted and participated in an international monetary system called the gold standard, using gold as a medium of exchange and a store of value. The gold standard had a stable exchange rate. During this period before World War I, a nation's monetary unit was defined as a certain weight of gold.

If pure gold bars (or **bullion**) were used everywhere as a medium of exchange, no foreign exchange rate problem would exist. As long as there was a guarantee of its purity and weight, the shape of the gold metal would not matter. For instance, the purchase of an airplane in the United States would simply require payment in gold at a price expressed in ounces of gold, and the purchase of a truck in Russia would require the same kind of payment.

However, the gold standard had practical problems. Gold bars are inconvenient to carry, and their purity and precise weight are difficult to determine. Consequently, it became customary for a state to mint a coin with a specified number of ounces of gold. Such gold coins carried the seal of the state, thus guaranteeing the gold's purity and weight. With gold coins as an exchange medium, international trade would resemble domestic trade but with two minor problems. First, conversion problems would arise if two countries used different systems of weight, e.g., the United States, ounces and the United Kingdom, grams. Nevertheless, a table of conversion would solve this problem. Second, a similar problem would occur if the United States chose to make its dollar coin with 1/12 ounce of gold while England chose to make its pound coin with 1/3 ounce of gold. These two currencies could have an exchange rate of $4 to £1 because the pound would be four times as heavy as the dollar.

Since gold coins were inconvenient to carry for spending purposes, governments issued paper certificates that could be converted into gold. The gold standard required that each nation define its monetary unit in a certain quantity of gold. The rate stipulated in its definition of the monetary unit must then be used to convert certificates into gold, and gold into certificates. Another condition for the gold standard is that each nation must allow gold to be freely exported and imported. The definition of the monetary unit in terms of gold by each nation would establish an exchange rate between the different countries, for example, $4 to £1. For all practical purposes, the free flow of gold between nations would result in fixed exchange rates.

Gold Export and Import Points

In the pre-1914 era, central banks redeemed legal tender (paper money) for bullion at fixed rates per ounce of gold. In this system, the exchange rate between any two different currencies was virtually fixed, fluctuating only between the gold export and import points.

The dollar price of pound sterling and the transportation cost of gold determined the range within which exchange rates could fluctuate. In terms of gold, a pound sterling was once worth $4. This amount was called the par value of the pound or the mint par of the pound. In earlier days, ocean transport was the only way of moving gold from one nation to another. This transportation, moreover, was slow and costly. Assume that it cost 5 cents to ship 1/3 ounce of gold either way across the Atlantic Ocean. No one in the United States would pay more than $4.05 for £1. Nor would an Englishman pay more than £1 for $3.95. Whenever the dollar price of sterling rose above $4.05 or fell below $3.95, an arbitrage transaction would take place. Arbitrage involves the purchase of something in one market and its sale in another market to take advantage of discrepancies between prices prevailing at the same time in different markets.

Americans would, in the situation we have been discussing, pay up to $4.05 for £1 rather than buy and export 1/3 ounce of gold to obtain that pound. It would cost them $4 for the 1/3 ounce of gold and 5 cents to ship it to England for £1. When the dollar price of sterling rose above the $4.05, gold would begin to flow out of the United States. This $4.05 exchange rate is called the gold export point. On the other hand, Englishmen would accept as little as $3.95 in exchange for £1. They could buy 1/3 ounce of gold in England for £1 and resell it in the United States for $4. The exchange rate would fall to the $3.95 before gold would flow into the United States because it would cost the Englishmen 5 cents to send gold to the United States to be exchanged for $4. This $3.95 exchange rate is called the gold import point.

As long as Americans could obtain pound sterling through the acquisition and export of gold for no more than $4.05 per pound, there was no reason for the exchange rate to increase beyond that point. By the same token, there was no reason for the exchange rate to fall below $3.95. Thus, it was possible for the exchange rate to fluctuate only between the gold export and import points. The spread between the mint par ($4 per £1) and each of the two gold points represented such costs as shipping, insurance, and interest. Some of these costs were matters of approximate estimates, and some others changed from time to time. Hence, the spread was neither constant or accurate. Still, the limits of exchange rate fluctuation under the gold standard typically remained close to par value.

London's Dominance in International Finance

The gold standard as an international monetary system worked adequately before World War I because of London's dominance in international finance. The keystone of the system was confidence in the stability of the British financial system. London was the financial center for almost 90 percent of world trade which was organized around sterling as the sole reserve currency. Such commercial transactions as factoring receivables and discounting bills from all corners of the world took place in London. Sterling was convenient because it was universally used and convertible into gold at the Bank of England. Trade and loans were denominated in sterling rather than gold.

The Bank of England backed sterling with an unbelievably small amount of gold reserve, estimated at 2 or 3 percent of the total money supply. The Bank of England maintained this small gold reserve because it manipulated the bank rate to safeguard the gold stock. The bank rate was the rate at which the Bank of England rediscounted commercial paper. Gold outflows increased the bank rate, thus attracting short-term deposits into London. Gold inflows were met by decreases in the bank rate. Such manipulations produced unmatched stability in the capital markets. More specifically, from January 1876 to July 1914, the bank rate moved rather narrowly around an average somewhat above 3 percent; never in that period did it stand at or above 5 percent for longer than 26 consecutive weeks.

The Gold Standard and International Adjustments

If member countries of the gold standard follow those rules described in the previous section, any deficits or surpluses in the balance of payments should be automatically corrected through the gold flow mechanism without any adjustment of exchange rates. The only variations in exchange rates would occur as the result of changes in the cost of shipping from one country to another. Thus, the flow of gold would do more than fix exchange rates.

To clarify this point, let us assume that the United States imports more from England than it exports to England. To settle the U.S. deficit, gold will flow from the United States to England, and this will increase the dollar price of pounds up to the $4.05 export point. The loss of gold by the United States reduces its bank reserves, amount of money in circulation, and credit availability. Everything else being equal, this contributes to a decline in aggregate demand, national income, and price level in the United States. The opposite occurs in England. A British gain in gold expands its bank reserves, national income, and money supply. Aggregate demand and the price level are thereby increased. Under these circumstances, American goods become less expensive, while British goods become more expensive. Thus, the United

States will reduce its imports of expensive British goods and increase its exports of inexpensive homemade goods. In contrast, England will find the amount of its expensive exports falling and its imports of inexpensive American goods rising. The result of the price-level mechanism reduces, through the flow of gold, the U.S. deficit and decreases the British surplus until equilibrium in international trade is established. Equilibrium would be established at those relative prices which keep exports and imports in balance. Income changes will produce the same result. As Americans' income falls, they purchase fewer British goods. As Britons' income increases, they buy more American goods.

The gold standard has three advantages:

1. It provides the stability of exchange rates.
2. It promotes freedom of trade and capital movements.
3. It provides an automatic balance-of-payments mechanism.

However, the gold standard has some disadvantages:

1. An efficient adjustment mechanism requires central bankers to forego their monetary policies to promote full employment without inflation.
2. The stability of exchange rates under the gold standard is too rigid to take care of major upheavals such as wars, revolutions, and widespread disasters.
3. Central banks need to maintain large international reserves to defend a fixed exchange rate.

Monetary Disorder: 1914–1945

The gold standard, as an international monetary system, worked well until World War I interrupted trade patterns and ended the stability of exchange rates for currencies of major industrial countries. The value of currencies fluctuated fairly widely in terms of gold during World War I and in the early 1920s. After World War I, the United Kingdom was not the world's only major creditor nation; the United States started to emerge as a leading creditor, too.

Several attempts were made to restore the gold standard during the 1920s. The United States returned to the gold standard in 1919, the United Kingdom in 1925, and France in 1928. However, these attempts failed, mainly because of the Great Depression of 1929–1932 and the international financial crisis of 1931.

International monetary chaos in the 1920s began with the insolvency in early 1931 of Kredit-Anstalt, a branch banking institution in Austria. Sterling was devalued in 1933; then the U.S. dollar was devalued in January 1934 with the now famous peg of $35 per ounce of gold. These actions by the United Kingdom and the United States overvalued, with respect to the pound and the dollar, the currencies of the "gold bloc" countries (France, Switzerland, the Netherlands, Belgium, Italy, and Poland). Belgium abandoned the gold standard in March 1935, and the rest of the "gold bloc" countries followed suit in September 1936.

In other words, country after country devalued their currencies to stimulate their exports. Governments also resorted to exchange controls in an attempt to manipulate their net exports. Of course, with the onslaught of World War II, hostile countries used foreign exchange controls to finance their war effort.

Fluctuating Exchange Rate and International Adjustments

World War I ended the stability of exchange rates for currencies of major trading nations. The international monetary system of the 1930s presented a mixture of widely fluctuating exchange rates and exchange rates maintained by exchange controls.

Fluctuating exchange rates are rates of foreign exchange determined in the market by supply and demand, without government intervention on how far rates can move. When exchange rates are not controlled by governments, the foreign exchange market closely approaches the theoretical model of pure competition. This model puts the entire adjustment burden on one homogeneous product—the exchange rate. In addition, the number of buyers and sellers is so large that no single buyer or seller can significantly affect the exchange rate. Any force that shifts the supply or demand curve—for instance, inflation, economic growth, interest rate changes, or balance-of-payment surpluses or deficits—will shift the exchange rate. If these forces create a disequilibrium, market forces are allowed to correct the disequilibrium by adjusting the exchange rate. For example, supply and demand for a nation's exports and imports cause minor changes in its exchange rate around a central equilibrium value. Thus, this system relies on automatic mechanisms to correct disequilibrium in the balance of payments. Although governments do not attempt to prevent fundamental changes in the exchange rate between their own currency and other currency, they typically attempt to maintain orderly trading conditions in the market.

In the floating system, exchange rates are free to fluctuate in response to changes of supply and demand. Proponents of fluctuating exchange rates argue that this system automatically and quickly corrects balance-of-payments disequilibria. If a country experiences a balance-of-payments deficit, the external value of its currency will automatically fall and depreciate. This currency depreciation could encourage exports and discourage imports, thereby correcting the original deficit. Hence, it is not surprising to find that many countries have frequently permitted their currencies to depreciate significantly in order to stimulate exports and to lower imports.

Critics of fluctuating exchange rates argue that the exchange rates under a pure version of this system are highly unstable and that such risks likely discourage the flow of world trade. Supporters of fluctuating exchange rates, on the other hand, contend that there is no reason to believe that this would be the case, because changes in the exchange rate would reflect basic economic conditions. However, we cannot deny that fluctuating exchange rates would significantly complicate the pricing mechanism of goods and services in world trade. This complication may add to the risk of foreign trade, thus leading to a reduction in the volume of world trade.

The Bretton Woods System: 1945–1973

The international monetary disorder of the 1930s justified the relative rigidity of the postwar par value system designed at Bretton Woods in 1944. The monetary system from the end of World War II to 1973 was a system of fixed exchange rates on a modified gold standard called the gold exchange standard. Under this system, each currency was fixed by government action within a narrow range of values relative to gold or some currency of reference. The U.S. dollar was used most frequently as a reference currency to establish the relative prices of all other currencies.

At the end of World War II, the leading nations of the free world recognized that the reconstruction of the world economy would depend on establishing a workable international monetary system. At the international conference in Bretton Woods, New Hampshire in 1944, they agreed to establish a new monetary order which centered on the International Monetary Fund (IMF) and the International Bank for Reconstruction and Development (World Bank). The IMF provides short-term balance-of-payments adjustment loans, while the World Bank makes long-term development and reconstruction loans.

The basic purpose of this new monetary system was to facilitate the expansion of world trade and to use the U.S. dollar as a standard of value. The Bretton Woods Agreement produced the following three propositions:

1. The stable exchange rates under the gold standard before World War I were desirable, but there are certain conditions which make adjustments in exchange rates necessary.
2. The performance of fluctuating exchange rates had been unsatisfactory.
3. Certain conditions require government controls over international trade, even though government controls during 1931–1945 had deterred the expansion of world trade and investment.

The Bretton Woods Agreement emphasized the stability of exchange rates by adopting the concept of fixed but adjustable rates. The keystones of the system were that no provision was made for the United States to change the value of gold at $35 per ounce and that each country was obligated to define its monetary unit in terms of gold or dollars. While other currencies were not required to exchange their currencies for gold, U.S. dollars remained convertible into gold at $35 per ounce. Thus, each country established par rates of exchange between its currency and the currencies of all other countries. Each currency was permitted to fluctuate within plus or minus one percent of par value by buying or selling foreign exchange and gold as needed. However, if a country's currency became too weak to maintain par value, it could devalue its currency up to 10 percent without formal approval by the IMF.

Breakdown of the Bretton Woods System

Depreciation and appreciation occurred rarely before 1971, thanks to the fixed exchange-rate system administered by the IMF. The key elements of the Bretton Woods system were the stable value of the U.S. dollar in terms of gold and its convertibility into gold, at least for foreign central banks. The late 1940s marked the beginning of large deficits in the U.S. balance of payments. By 1971, the U.S. payments deficit exploded. America's chronic payments deficits turned into a spectacular dilution of U.S. gold and other reserves during the 1960s and early 1970s. Hence, many people were not surprised to observe that the dollar had to be devalued in 1971 and again in 1973. Moreover, on August 15, 1971, President Nixon, in a famous speech designed to deal with U.S. inflation and international monetary problems, stated that the United States had decided to:

1. Suspend the conversion of dollars into gold.
2. Permit the dollar to float in relation to other currencies.
3. Impose a 10 percent surcharge on most imports.
4. Impose direct controls on wages and prices.

All of these actions were taken without prior consultation with the IMF.

The Smithsonian Agreement.   From August to December 1971, most major currencies were permitted to fluctuate. U.S. dollars fell in value against a number of major currencies. Several countries caused major concern by imposing some trade and exchange controls. It was feared that such protective measures might become sufficiently widespread to limit international commerce. In order to solve these problems, the world's leading trading countries, called the "Group of Ten," produced the Smithsonian Agreement on December 18, 1971. This agreement established a new set of parity rates, called central rates because they lacked the approval of the IMF. This "Group-of-Ten" consisted of the United States, Belgium, England, France, Germany, Italy, Japan, the Netherlands, Sweden, and Switzerland.

Although U.S. dollars were not convertible into gold, they were still defined in terms of gold. The other nine currencies were defined in terms of either gold or the dollar. The United States agreed to devalue the dollar from $35 per ounce of gold to $38 in return for promises from other members to upvalue their currencies relative to the dollar by specified amounts.

Currencies were permitted to fluctuate over a wider band than in the past in order to maintain market exchange rates relatively close to the central rates without constant government intervention. Although a currency was allowed to fluctuate 2.25 percent from the central rates without government intervention, it could fluctuate by as much as 9 percent against any currency except the dollar. Because a currency was permitted to fluctuate up to 2.25 percent on either side of the central rate, its total fluctuation against the dollar could be as much as 4.5 percent. Let us assume for purposes of illustration that Japan upvalued the yen by 4.5 percent against the dollar and that Italy devalued the lira by 4.5 percent against the dollar. Under these circumstances, these two currencies (yen and lira) would change by 9 percent against one another.

Proponents of the Smithsonian Agreement argued that a wider band would allow countries to maintain: (1) the discipline that they would expect from the fixed exchange-rate system and (2) greater freedom and a smoother adjustment process of flexible exchange rates. Although the Agreement was a historical event in international monetary affairs, it failed to reduce speculation. Government controls on foreign exchange, likewise, did not decrease. For all practical purposes, the Agreement came to an end in March 1973, because most "Group of Ten" countries allowed their currencies to float according to market forces. Thus, the system of pegged but adjustable rates, based on the 1944 Bretton Woods Agreement, collapsed.

The Post–1973 Dirty Floating System

Daily exchange-rate changes have become a way of life since March 1973, when the Bretton Woods Agreement collapsed. Moreover, since then, exchange rates have become much more volatile and less predictable due to a number of unexpected events affecting international monetary order. The most important events include the oil crisis of late 1973, loss of confidence in the U.S. dollar between 1977 and 1978, the second oil crisis in 1978, formation of the European Monetary System in 1979, diversification of monetary reserves by central banks since 1979, the surprising strength of the U.S. dollar between 1981 and 1985, a rapid decline in the value of the U.S. dollar between February 1985 and 1988, the surprising strength of the U.S. dollar between January and June 1989, the end of the Marxist revolution in 1990, the dissolution of the Soviet Union in December 1991, and the creation of a single European market in 1993.

From the end of World War II to 1973, international business and multinational corporations operated under a fixed exchange system. Since 1973, most industrial and many developing countries have permitted their currencies to float with frequent government intervention in the exchange market. This monetary system is known by various terms, such as free float, managed float, dirty float, partial float, and others on a primarily market-determined exchange rate. Governments have frequently intervened to maintain orderly markets and to keep their average exchange rate at a level desirable by their economic policy.

Because the Bretton Woods Agreement was based on the system of fixed exchange rates, the IMF had to change its Articles of Agreement in order to permit floating exchange rates. The Jamaican Agreement of 1976 formalized the existing system of floating exchange rates. Important IMF member countries held a series of negotiations during 1973-1976, leading to an agreement to change some of the Bretton Woods Agreement. The Board of Governors of the IMF approved these changes in April 1976, and they went into effect two years later. This amendment legalized the existing system of floating exchange rates and permitted each member to peg or to float the value of its currency. The amendment also terminated the par value system based on gold. Thus, the fixed exchange system based on the Bretton Woods Agreement officially ended in 1976, though, practically speaking, it had died in 1973.

As part of a move to greater flexibility, the IMF allowed member countries to have an exchange-rate arrangement of their choice, as long as they properly communicate their arrangement to the IMF. Each year the IMF receives information from its member countries and classifies each country into one of three broad categories: (1) currencies that are pegged to a single currency or to a composite of currencies, (2) currencies whose exchange rates have limited flexibility, and (3) currencies whose exchange rates are more flexible. Table 4-1 shows exchange-rate arrangements of 151 currencies as of January 1992.

Multiple Exchange Rates

Most IMF member countries conduct all of their foreign exchange transactions at a single unitary exchange rate. But a number of member countries maintain dual exchange rates applicable to different transactions. Moreover, a few other member countries employ complex arrangements involving three or more exchange rates for various sets of transactions. Approximately 20 countries maintain multiple exchange rates for most of the time.

The IMF Executive Board's review of how member countries used multiple exchange rates found that multiple currency practices had entailed high economic costs and distorted resource allocations; furthermore, they hindered medium-term balance-of-payments adjustments.

Unification of exchange rates in multiple rate systems is a basic objective of the IMF. The IMF believes that multiple exchange-rate practices should be eliminated for three reasons. First, multiple exchange rates are detrimental to the economies of those countries that maintain them. Second, multiple exchange-rate systems are harmful to other countries because they can involve discrimination, export subsidization, and undue differentiation between classes of imports and other international transactions. Third, multiple exchange rates are difficult to administer because they require frequent changes in the list of transactions allocated to each market.

In the Articles of Agreement for the IMF, Section 3 of Article VIII, states that "no member shall engage in multiple currency practices except as authorized under this Agreement or approved by the IMF." The IMF's policy on multiple currency practices is flexible, pragmatic, and responsive to a country's circumstances. But the IMF has granted its approval of multiple

Table 4–1
Exchange Rate Arrangements

Currency pegged to					Flexibility Limited in terms of a Single Currency or Group of Currencies		More Flexible		
US Dollar	French Franc	Other currency	SDR	Other composite	Single currency	Cooperative arrangements	Adjusted according to a set of indicators	Other managed floating	Independently floating
Afghanistan	Benin	Bhutan (Indian Rupee)	Burundi	Algeria	Bahrain	Belgium	Chile	China, P.R.	Australia
Angola	Burkina Faso	Kiribati (Australian Dollar)	Iran, I. R. of	Austria	Qatar	Denmark	Colombia	Costa Rica	Bolivia
Antigua & Barbuda	Cameroon	Lesotho (South African Rand)	Libya	Bangladesh	Saudi Arabia	France	Madagascar	Ecuador	Brazil
Argentina	C. African Rep.	Swaziland (South African Rand)	Myanmar	Botswana	United Arab Emirates	Germany	Mozambique	Egypt	Bulgaria
Bahamas, The	Chad	Yugoslavia (deutsche mark)	Rwanda	Cape Verde		Ireland	Zambia	Greece	Canada
Barbados	Comoros	Seychelles		Cyprus		Italy		Guinea	Dominican Rep.
Belize	Congo			Czechoslovakia		Luxembourg		Guinea-Bissau	El Salvador
Djibouti	Côte d'Ivoire			Fiji		Netherlands		Honduras	Gambia, The
Dominica	Equatorial Guinea			Finland		Spain		India	Ghana
Ethiopia	Gabon			Hungary		United Kingdom		Indonesia	Guatemala
Grenada	Mali			Iceland				Korea	Guyana
Iraq	Niger			Israel				Lao P.D. Rep	Haiti
Liberia	Senegal			Jordan				Mauritania	Jamaica
Mongolia	Togo			Kenya				Mexico	Japan
Nicaragua				Kuwait				Pakistan	Lebanon
Oman				Malawi				Portugal	Maldives
Panama				Malaysia				Sao Tome & Principe	Namibia
St. Kitts & Nevis				Malta				Singapore	New Zealand
St. Lucia				Mauritius				Somalia	Nigeria
St. Vincent and the Grenadines				Morocco				Sri Lanka	Paraguay
Sudan				Nepal				Tunisia	Peru
Suriname				Norway				Turkey	Philippines
Syrian Arab Rep.				Papua New Guinea				Viet Nam	Romania
Trinidad and Tobago				Poland					Sierra Leone
Yemen, Republic of				Solomon Islands					South Africa
				Sweden					United States
				Tanzania					Uruguay
				Thailand					Venezuela
				Tonga					Zaire
				Uganda					
				Vanuatu					
				Western Samoa					
				Zimbabwe					

Classification Status	1985	1986	1987	1988	1989 QI	1989 QII	1989 QIII	1989 QIV	1990 QI	1990 QII	1990 QIII	1990 QIV	1991 QI	1991 QII	1991 QIII
Currency pegged to															
US Dollar	31	32	38	36	31	32	32	32	30	28	25	25	27	26	25
French Franc	14	14	14	14	14	14	14	14	14	14	14	14	14	14	14
Other Currency	5	5	5	5	5	5	5	5	5	5	5	5	5	5	5
of which: Pound Sterling	(1)	(–)	(–)	(–)	(–)	(–)	(–)	(–)	(–)	(–)	(–)	(–)	(–)	(–)	(–)
SDR	12	10	8	8	8	7	7	7	7	7	7	6	6	6	6
Other currency composite	32	30	27	31	31	32	32	34	34	35	37	35	34	34	33
Flexibility limited vis-à-vis a single currency	5	5	4	4	4	4	4	4	4	4	4	4	4	4	4
Cooperative arrangements	8	8	8	8	8	9	9	9	9	9	9	10	10	10	10
Adjusted according to a set of indicators	5	6	5	5	5	5	5	5	4	4	3	5	5	5	5
Managed floating	21	21	23	22	25	24	25	21	23	21	23	23	22	22	23
Independently floating	15	19	18	17	19	18	18	20	21	23	26	25	27	28	29
Total	149	151	151	151	151	151	152	152	152	151	154	154	155	155	155

End of Period

Source: *International Financial Statistics*, Washington, DC: IMF, January 1992, p. 22.

exchange-rate systems on a temporary basis and only when two conditions exist. First, a country must adopt a well-conceived plan to bring about the unification of the exchange-rate system during a specific and brief period.

Second, it must implement measures that will help eliminate the need to rely on such a system.

What Is Ahead for the 1990s?

There are many important reasons why international monetary relations in the 1990s and beyond are likely to change along a number of fronts. The emergence of a tripolar economic system—in which global economic power is shared by the United States, Japan, and Germany—will affect the design of the international monetary system in the 1990s. The political rebirth of Eastern Europe, the economic integration of Western Europe in 1993, the volatility of the present floating-rate system, and a gradual shift of economic power from the United States to Japan present many opportunities and challenges for the international monetary system.

A new single European currency is expected to replace the current European Monetary System (EMS) by the end of the 1990s as the EC completes its economic integration. Then the IMF may decide to use a simplified basket of three currencies to determine its SDR's (Special Drawing Rights) daily valuation: the U.S. dollar, the Japanese yen, and the new single European currency. The movement toward joint floating and other cooperative exchange arrangements will probably continue. Even some nations that do not belong to a currency group will begin to cooperate in determining their economic objectives to a greater extent than in the past. The United States is expected to continue taking a more active part in the management of its exchange rates than it did during the term of the Bretton Woods system.

There may be further reforms to control the stock of international reserves available to IMF members. These reforms include an increased use of SDRs as a means of payment among member governments, the possibility of substitution accounts to promote the diversification of international reserve holdings, and the introduction of government regulation in the Eurocurrency financial markets. As innovations in communications and transportation continue to bring nations closer, it will be necessary for the international monetary system to maintain its flexibility and diversity in order to stabilize the growth of the world economy until the IMF adopts a new monetary system.

International Policy Coordination

The world economy has become more integrated in recent decades among industrial countries. For example, international trade has increased almost two times as fast as world output in the last two decades. The ratio of trade to gross domestic product (GDP) has doubled during the past 30 years for G-7 countries, which have accounted for two-thirds of global GDP in recent years. Even more spectacular is the increased mobility of capital in the past 15 to 20 years. The foreign liabilities of industrial country banks, for instance, have increased 11-fold since 1973, and this pace of expansion was more than double that of their total liabilities.

Recognition of the increasingly integrated global economy and dissatisfaction with exchange rate swings have triggered calls for more consistent and compatible policies among major industrial countries. Since 1985, these countries have strengthened the process for international coordination of policies.

Since 1975, the leaders of the seven largest industrial economies have met in annual economic summits to discuss economic issues of common concern. Over time, recognition of the growing integration of financial markets and shared concerns have led to the realization that further policy cooperation could be mutually beneficial.

The divergence of economic policies and performance among major industrial countries after 1982 contributed to the sharp rise in the value of the dollar and to the emergence of large trade imbalances. In 1985, finance ministers and central bankers from the United States, Japan, Germany, the United Kingdom, and France (collectively called the G-5) met in New York. They agreed to work to strengthen the process for coordinating macroeconomic policies, to bring down the value of the dollar, and to reduce trade imbalances. In 1986, the G-5 together with Canada and Italy (the G-7) initiated regular meetings of their finance ministers and central bank governors. The purpose of the G-7 meetings is to promote more consistent and compatible economic policies among members so that they can work toward global growth with low inflation, reduced trade imbalances, and greater exchange-rate stability. In their recent meetings on January 20 and 21, 1991, in New York, these ministers and governors reaffirmed their support for economic policy coordination.

The arguments in favor of policy coordination stress that the effects of one country's policies spill over to other countries. This spillover is especially true for the larger industrial economies such as the G-7. Coordination can improve domestic policy decisions by helping policymakers to consider the global implications of their actions.

Such a coordination process has two main elements. First, the G-7 has instituted a regular, high-level dialogue on economic policy, performance, and objectives. Second, the G-7 has developed economic indicators to provide a framework for multilateral surveillance of their economies and help monitor the international effects of national policies. This process is supplemented through frequent additional discussions in other forums, notably the IMF, the Organization for Economic Cooperation and Development (OECD), and the Bank for International Settlements (BIS).

The International Monetary Fund

The IMF was created as a weak kind of central banks' central bank at the Bretton Woods conference to make the new monetary system feasible and workable. Its major purpose was to assist members that would have structural trade problems or currencies highly unstable in value. The IMF permitted its deficit members to buy with their local currencies some of its own holdings of convertible currencies. These deficit countries were expected to buy back, with gold or other convertible currencies, the local currencies they had sold to the IMF after they had improved their balance of payments. Thus, the IMF's major weapon is the power to declare its members ineligible to utilize its holdings of international reserves.

The IMF was created in 1944 by 30 countries, but today it consists of 151 countries. Article I of the IMF Articles of Agreement clearly set forth its objectives as follows: (1) to promote international monetary cooperation; (2) to facilitate the balanced growth of international trade; (3) to promote exchange stability; (4) to eliminate exchange restrictions; and (5) to create standby reserves.

The IMF established rules and procedures to keep participating countries from going too deeply into balance-of-payments deficits. Those countries with short-term payments difficulties could draw upon their reserves. The amount of such reserves was defined in relation to each member's quota. This quota was determined on the basis of such factors as trade, national income, and international payments. Up to 1976, each member was required to subscribe 75 percent of its quota in its own currency and 25 percent in gold, known as **gold tranche**. However, since 1976, each member has been required to contribute 75 percent of its quota in its own currency and 25 percent in SDRs or convertible currencies.

These quotas for IMF members are reviewed at least every five years to determine whether quotas should be increased to accommodate the growth of the world economy. The Board of Governors of the IMF approved its latest resolution to increase quotas in May 1991, and this resolution became effective at the end of 1991. The latest increases in quotas expanded the size of the IMF by 50 percent, to SDR 135.2 billion.

Germany and Japan share second place in terms of size of quota after the United States, followed by France and the United Kingdom which have equal quotas. Voting power of 151 members is determined by 250 "basic votes," plus 1 vote for each SDR 100,000 of quota. Because of its large quota, the United States still holds close to 20 percent of total votes. Table 4-2 gives new quotas valued in SDRs and quota shares.

IMF members borrow by exchanging their own currencies for convertible currencies of other member countries. A member country may draw, virtually at will, 100 percent of its quota from the IMF at any time; the 100 percent of its quota is called the **reserve tranche**. A country could borrow beyond this amount up to an additional 100 percent of its quota; this 100 percent is called the **credit tranche**. Thus, a member country could conceivably borrow 200 percent of its quota in convertible currencies. But in order to borrow more than 100 percent of its quota, a member must accept restrictions imposed by the IMF to ensure that steps are being taken to correct the borrower's currency problems.

Source: *IMF Survey: Supplement on the Fund*, August 1991, p. 4.

Table 4–2
Fund Quotas as of January 1992
(in millions of SDRs)

Member	Current	Proposed	Member	Current	Proposed	Member	Current	Proposed
Afghanistan	86.7	120.4	Grenada	6.0	8.5	Pakistan	546.3	758.2
Algeria	623.1	914.4	Guatemala	108.0	153.8	Panama	102.2	149.6
Angola	145.0	207.3	Guinea	57.9	78.7	Papua New Guinea	65.9	95.3
Antigua and Barbuda	5.0	8.5	Guinea-Bissau	7.5	10.5	Paraguay	48.4	72.1
Argentina	1,113.0	1,537.1	Guyana	49.2	67.2	Peru	330.9	466.1
Australia	1,619.2	2,333.2	Haiti	44.1	60.7	Philippines	440.4	633.4
Austria	775.6	1,188.3	Honduras	67.8	95.0	Poland	680.0	988.5
Bahamas, The	66.4	94.9	Hungary	530.7	754.8	Portugal	376.6	557.6
Bahrain	48.9	82.8	Iceland	59.6	85.3	Qatar	114.9	190.5
Bangladesh	287.5	392.5	India	2,207.7	3,055.5	Romania	523.4	754.1
Barbados	34.1	48.9	Indonesia	1,009.7	1,497.6	Rwanda	43.8	59.5
Belgium	2,080.4	3,102.3	Iran	660.0	1,078.5	St. Kitts & Nevis	4.5	6.5
Belize	9.5	13.5	Iraq	504.0	864.8	St. Lucia	7.5	11.0
Benin	31.3	45.3	Ireland	343.4	525.0	St. Vincent & Grenadines	4.0	6.0
Bhutan	2.5	4.5	Israel	446.6	666.2	Sao Tome & Principe	4.0	5.5
Bolivia	90.7	126.2	Italy	2,909.1	4,590.7	Saudi Arabia	3,202.4	5,130.6
Botswana	22.1	36.6	Jamaica	145.5	200.9	Senegal	85.1	118.9
Brazil	1,461.3	2,170.8	Japan	4,223.3	8,241.5	Seychelles	3.0	6.0
Burkina Faso	31.6	44.2	Jordan	73.9	121.7	Sierra Leone	57.9	77.2
Burundi	42.7	57.2	Kampuchea, Democratic	25.0	25.0	Singapore	92.4	357.6
Cameroon	92.7	135.1	Kenya	142.0	199.4	Solomon Islands	5.0	7.5
Canada	2,941.0	4,320.3	Kiribati, Republic of	2.5	4.0	Somalia	44.2	60.9
Cape Verde	4.5	7.0	Korea	462.8	799.6	South Africa	915.7	1,365.4
Central African Rep.	30.4	41.2	Kuwait	635.3	995.2	Spain	1,286.0	1,935.4
Chad	30.6	41.3	Lao People's Dem. Rep.	29.3	39.1	Sri Lanka	223.1	303.6
Chile	440.5	621.7	Lebanon	78.7	146.0	Sudan	169.7	233.1
China	2,390.9	3,385.2	Lesotho	15.1	23.9	Suriname	49.3	67.6
Colombia	394.2	561.3	Liberia	71.3	96.2	Swaziland	24.7	36.5
Comoros	4.5	6.5	Libya	515.7	817.6	Sweden	1,064.3	1,614.0
Congo, People's Rep.	37.3	57.9	Luxembourg	77.0	135.5	Syrian Arab Republic	139.1	209.9
Costa Rica	84.1	119.0	Madagascar	66.4	90.4	Tanzania	107.0	146.9
Côte d'Ivoire	165.5	238.2	Malawi	37.2	50.9	Thailand	386.6	573.9
Cyprus	69.7	100.0	Malaysia	550.6	832.7	Togo	38.4	54.3
Denmark	711.0	1,069.9	Maldives	2.0	5.5	Tonga	3.25	5.0
Djibouti	8.0	11.5	Mali	50.8	68.9	Trinidad and Tobago	170.1	246.8
Dominica	4.0	6.0	Malta	45.1	67.5	Tunisia	138.2	206.0
Dominican Republic	112.1	158.8	Mauritania	33.9	47.5	Turkey	429.1	642.0
Ecuador	150.7	219.2	Mauritius	53.6	73.3	Uganda	99.6	133.9
Egypt	463.4	678.4	Mexico	1,165.5	1,753.3	United Arab Emirates	202.6	392.1
El Salvador	89.0	125.6	Morocco	306.6	427.7	United Kingdom	6,194.0	7,414.6
Equatorial Guinea	18.4	24.3	Mozambique	61.0	84.0	United States	17,918.3	26,526.8
Ethiopia	70.6	98.3	Myanmar	137.0	184.9	Uruguay	163.8	225.3
Fiji	36.5	51.1	Nepal	37.3	52.0	Vanuatu	9.0	12.5
Finland	574.9	861.8	Netherlands	2,264.8	3,444.2	Venezuela	1,371.5	1,951.3
France	4,482.8	7,414.6	New Zealand	461.6	650.1	Viet Nam	176.8	241.6
Gabon	73.1	110.3	Nicaragua	68.2	96.1	Western Samoa	6.0	8.5
Gambia, The	17.1	22.9	Niger	33.7	48.3	Yemen, Republic of	120.5	176.5
Germany	5,403.7	8,241.5	Nigeria	849.5	1,281.6	Yugoslavia	613.0	918.3
Ghana	204.5	274.0	Norway	699.0	1,104.6	Zaire	291.0	394.8
Greece	399.9	587.6	Oman	63.1	119.4	Zambia	270.3	363.5
						Zimbabwe	191.0	261.3

Special Drawing Rights

The Bretton Woods system assumed adequate reserves. These reserves consisted of gold and key currencies such as dollars and pounds. Various developments such as GATT and EC caused a rapid increase in trade and foreign investment in the postwar period. But monetary gold stocks had remained virtually constant since the end of World War II. Key reserve currency countries, such as the United States, England, and France, ran large deficits. Although these deficits increased the world's monetary reserves, these additional reserves were not enough to sustain the continued expansion of world trade. Furthermore, huge deficits by these key reserve–currency countries raised a credibility gap. Speculators and central bankers began to doubt whether the reserve–currency countries could continue to convert their currencies into gold (in the case of dollars) and dollars (in the case of non–dollar reserve currencies). Another problem was that the reserve currency countries could not continue to incur large deficits forever. The correction of these deficits would mean the contraction of the world's monetary reserves and the eventual reduction of world trade.

The IMF had been concerned about the lack of growth in gold holdings and about the consequent growth in international reserves, which was slower than world trade. To solve these problems, an agreement was reached at the 1967 Rio de Janeiro meeting of the IMF to create SDRs as another reserve asset. SDRs became an international reserve asset on July 28, 1969, when more than the required 85 percent of IMF members approved the plan. The basic idea was to manage the stock of SDRs in such a way that world monetary reserves would grow in line with world trade.

SDRs were created in a world of fixed exchange rates that reflected fixed par values of currencies in terms of gold or the dollar. The SDRs were initially given a par value of $1 = one SDR or, equivalently, 35 SDR = one ounce of gold, when the official gold price was $35 per ounce. The values of all other currencies in terms of SDRs were determined through their value in terms of gold. Two subsequent devaluations of the dollar raised the gold price to $42.22 per ounce and the dollar value of one SDR to $1.20635.

The dollar devaluation and the advent of floating exchange rates caused the SDR's value, relative to other currencies, to fluctuate along with the dollar. On June 28, 1974, the IMF introduced a system under which the value of an SDR was based on a weighted value of a "basket" of 16 major currencies. These 16 currencies were the currencies of those nations that each represented at least 1 percent of world trade during the 1968–1972 period. The countries' weights in the basket reflected their shares in world trade. But the trade weights of the other 15 countries were scaled down to raise the dollar's weight to 33 percent because of the dollar's importance in world finance.

In a step to further enhance the attractiveness of the SDR, the IMF began on January 1, 1981, to use a simplified basket of five currencies for determining its daily valuation. This decision established percentage weights for the five currencies of 43 percent for the U.S. dollar, 20 percent for the deutsche mark, 17 percent for the Japanese yen, and 10 percent each for the French franc and the pound sterling. These weights were applied using market exchange rates on August 23, 1991, to calculate the amount of each currency that determines the value of the SDR. These currency amounts (see column 1 in Table 4-3) remain the same from day to day.

Although the number of currencies in the SDR basket has been reduced from 16 to five currencies effective January 1, 1981, the method of calculating the U.S. dollar/SDR exchange rate remains the same. Currency amounts

Table 4–3
SDR Valuation on August 26, 1991

Currency	Currency Amount (1)	Exchange Rate (2)	U.S. Dollar Equivalents (3)
Deutsche marks	0.4530	1.74780	0.259183
French francs	0.8000	5.93500	0.134794
Japanese yen	31.8000	136.96000	0.232185
Pounds sterling	0.0812	1.67980	0.136400
U.S. dollars	0.5720	1.00000	0.572000
		SDR = US$1.00	1.334562
		US$ = SDR1.00	0.749310

Column 1: The currency components of the SDR basket.

Column 2: Exchange rates in terms of currency units per U.S. dollar except for the pound sterling, which is expressed in U.S. dollars per pound.

Column 3: The U.S. dollar equivalents of the currency amounts in Column 1 at the exchange rates in Column 2—that is, Column 1 divided by Column 2.

Source: *IMF Survey: Supplement on the IMF*, September 1991, p. 8.

making up the SDR basket are converted into U.S. dollar equivalents, using market exchange rates. These U.S. dollar equivalents (carried to six decimal places) are then added, and the reciprocal of this total is rounded to six significant figures to establish the SDR value of the U.S. dollar. The same total is rounded (also to six significant figures) to determine the U.S. dollar value of the SDR. Table 4–3 shows the computation process of these two values using exchange rates on August 23, 1991.

The market rates used in this calculation are the midpoints between buying and selling rates at noon in the London foreign exchange market, including the rate for the Japanese yen previously obtained from the Tokyo market. The rates used would be from New York at noon whenever the London market is closed. If both the London and New York markets are closed, the rates from the Frankfurt market would be used.

As in the past, once the U.S. dollar/SDR exchange rate has been determined, the rate for any other currency in terms of the SDR is calculated, using the U.S. dollar/SDR exchange rate and the market rate for the currency in terms of the U.S. dollar. The market rates used in the calculation of these rates are so-called "representative" rates which are defined by the IMF. The composition of the SDR valuation basket was last revised in 1991. The amounts of currencies and the list of the currencies in the basket will be revised every five years, unless the IMF's Executive Board decides otherwise.

SDR rates for more than 40 currencies are made available to the public each day. Several wire services carry these rates every day; they are published twice monthly in the *IMF Survey*. Daily newspapers and financial periodicals

Table 4–4
Currency Units per SDR

Currency	16	17	20	21	JANUARY 22	23
Deutsche mark	2.24685	2.25245	2.23482	2.24033	2.23571	2.24128
French franc	7.66135	7.6895	7.6325	7.63547	7.62467	7.64668
Japanese yen	177.916	177.215	174.228	173.524	174.272	173.587
Pound sterling	0.788747	0.788688	0.782266	0.78185	0.780166	0.781786
U.S. dollar	1.3878	1.38612	1.40847	1.40733	1.41054	1.40784
Argentine austral	...	...	...	...	...	...
Australian dollar	1.86758	1.87136	1.89234	1.87569	1.87847	1.86791
Austrian schilling	15.814	15.8364	15.727	15.7607	15.7191	15.7763
Bahrain dinar	0.521813	0.521181	0.529585	0.529156	0.530363	0.529348
Bangladesh taka	53.8466	53.7815	54.6486	54.6044	54.729	54.6242
Belgian franc	46.2068	46.4974	46.0358	46.0197	46.0788	46.1807
Brazilian cruzeiro	1636.22	1666.25	1692.42	1707.09	1726.99	1739.81
Canadian dollar	1.59972	1.5982	1.61988	1.62364	1.62861	1.62986
Colombian peso	987.225	986.737	1003.35	1003.16	1006.03	1004.73
Danish krone	8.70081	8.75404	...	8.66634	8.67129	8.69904
Ecuadoran sucre	...	...	...	...	...	...
Finnish markka	6.08689	6.15715	6.08741	6.08248	6.09212	6.10439
Guatemalan quetzal	...	...	...	...	...	...
Indian rupee	35.9302	35.9275	36.4957	36.5066	36.428	36.5036
Indonesian rupiah	2775.6	2772.24	2815.53	2814.66	2821.08	2815.68
Iranian rial	92.3	92.3	92.3	92.3	92.3	92.3
Iraqi dinar	0.431408	0.430886	0.437833	0.437479	0.438477	0.437637
Irish pound	0.841142	0.845195	0.840175	0.839846	0.838908	0.841205
Italian lira	1694.25	1697.84	1685.09	1686.09	1682.67	1687.15
Kuwaiti dinar	0.402795	...	0.406752	0.406423	...	0.406739
Libyan dinar	0.383929	0.383929	0.383929	0.383929	0.383929	0.383929
Malaysian ringgit	3.76413	3.74876	3.78949	3.7829	3.78603	3.76851
Maltese lira	0.445293	0.445311	...	0.443771	0.444293	0.44361
Mexican peso	...	...	...	...	...	...
Nepalese rupee	59.2591	59.1873	60.1417	60.093	60.2301	60.1148
Netherlands guilder	2.52302	2.53605	2.51891	2.51912	2.5164	2.52355
Norwegian krone	8.82266	8.86978	8.78533	8.77892	8.78484	8.80322
Omani rial	0.533609	0.532963	0.541557	0.541118	0.542353	0.541314
Pakistan rupee	34.3365	34.295	34.8479	34.8197	34.8992	34.8324
Portuguese escudo	194.757	194.726	193.086	193.169	192.804	193.254
Qatar riyal	5.05159	5.04548	5.12683	5.12268	5.13437	5.12454
Saudi Arabian riyal	5.19731	5.19102	5.27472	5.27045	5.28247	5.27236
Singapore dollar	2.28848	2.28585	2.29651	2.29718	2.30186	2.29943
South African rand	3.90457	3.90743	3.92255	3.91164	3.9234	3.92298
Spanish peseta	142.261	142.576	141.568	141.252	141.174	141.529
Sri Lanka rupee	59.2591	59.1596	60.0853	60.0367	60.1736	60.0444
Swedish krona	8.17206	8.219	8.14025	8.13015	8.13599	8.1528
Swiss franc	1.99635	1.99116	1.97679	1.98504	1.97969	1.98717
Trinidad and Tobago dollar	5.9129	5.90574	6.00096	5.99611	6.00978	5.99828
U.A.E. dirham	5.09461	5.08845	5.17049	5.16631	5.17809	5.16818
Venezuelan bolívar	86.0089	86.1474	...	87.4304	87.6298	87.6732

Source: *IMF Survey*, February 3, 1992, p. 47.

also publish the SDR rates for major currencies. Table 4-4 shows the currency units per SDR for 45 currencies from January 16 to January 23, 1992.

Use of SDRs

Members with a need for balance of payments may use SDRs to acquire foreign exchange in a transaction with designation, that is, where another member, designated by the IMF, provides the currency in exchange for SDRs. The IMF designates members to provide the currency in exchange for SDRs on the basis of the strength of their balance of payments and reserve positions. However, a member's obligation to provide currency does not extend beyond the point at which its holdings are three times its total allocations.

The IMF has the authority to extend the range of official holders of SDRs beyond its member countries and the IMF's General Resources Account. It has designated, as of July 31, 1991, 16 organizations as prescribed holders. Each of these institutions can acquire and use SDRs in transactions and operations with other prescribed holders and with any of the IMF's 151 member countries. Prescribed holders have the same degree of freedom as IMF members to use SDRs for a variety of international transactions.

IMF members may also use SDRs in a variety of voluntary transactions and operations by agreement among themselves and with prescribed holders. More specifically, IMF members and prescribed holders buy and sell SDRs both spot and forward; borrow, lend, or pledge SDRs; use SDRs in swaps and in settlement of financial obligations; or make donations (grants) with SDRs.

In addition, SDRs have been used increasingly to settle financial obligations and to make loans since the IMF authorized these and other uses following the Second Amendment of the Articles of Agreement in 1978. Prescribed holders have been particularly active in these types of SDR transfers. Prescribed holders of SDRs use the SDR as a unit of account, extend some loans in the form of SDRs, and accept SDRs in loan repayments and interest payments. Other operations of this type have included debt-service payments by a prescribed holder to participants in its area; the use by a prescribed holder of a currency deposit with a participant's central bank to obtain SDRs from the participant; and the use of SDRs by a regional development bank to service interest payments on a large capital loan made earlier by a member government. The widened scope of SDR operations has proved useful also as a means of settlement in those cases where the respective parties do not maintain banking relationships with each other.

SDR Interest Rate

Since August 1, 1983, the interest rate on the SDR has been determined weekly by reference to a combined market interest rate. This rate is the weighted-average interest rate in specified short-term obligations in the money markets of the same five countries whose currencies are included in the SDR calculation basket. The interest rates used are the rates on these obligations calculated on the basis of a single reference day. These interest rates are weighted by the same number of currency units used in the calculation of the value of the SDR. Having gone into effect on May 1, 1981, the rate of interest on the SDR was raised from 80 percent to 100 percent of the combined market rate and rounded to the nearest two decimal places. Table 4–5 shows that the rate of interest on the SDR was 7.50 percent for the week beginning August 26, 1991.

A member with holdings of SDRs in excess of its allocations earns net interest on those excess holdings, and a member with holdings below its

Table 4–5
SDR Interest Rate Calculation
August 26, 1991

Currency	Currency Amount (1)	Interest Rate (2)	Exchange Rate per SDR (3)	Product (4)
Deutsche marks	0.4530	9.3075	0.43122500	1.8182
French francs	0.8000	9.7600	0.12667000	0.9890
Japanese yen	31.8000	7.2600	0.00546228	1.2611
Pounds sterling	0.0812	10.3708	1.26368000	1.0642
U.S. dollars	0.5720	5.5500	0.74614800	2.3687
SDR interest rate				7.50

Column 1: The currency components of the SDR basket.
Column 2: Short-term interest rates on specific domestic obligations, as of Friday, August 23.
Column 3: Exchange rates as of August 23, expressed in terms of SDRs per currency unit.
Column 4: Product of Columns 1 through 3.

Source: *IMF Survey: Supplement on the IMF*, September 1991, p. 9.

allocations pays net charges at the same rate on its net use of SDRs. Payments of interest and charges are, therefore, self–balancing; that is, the net charges payable by net users are exactly sufficient for the payment of net interest to those who hold SDRs above their allocations, the payment of interest to the IMF's General Resources Account, and the payment of interest to prescribed holders. Interest is credited and charges debited at the end of each of the IMF's financial quarters. As the IMF is required to pay interest in full to each holder at that time, additional SDRs must be created if charges on allocations are not paid in full.

On April 30 of each year, an assessment is levied on each participant in proportion to its net cumulative allocations to cover the expenses of conducting the business of the SDR Department. The rate of assessment for the financial year ended April 30, 1991, was 0.0172629 percent of net cumulative allocations.

The SDR as an International Reserve

The SDR is an international reserve asset created by the IMF and allocated to its members to supplement existing reserve assets. The IMF has allocated a total of SDR 21.4 billion in six allocations since the SDR was created in 1970. As of April 30, 1991, holdings of SDRs by member countries amounted to 3.6 percent of their total non–gold reserves.

The SDR as a Unit of Account.

The SDR is used as a unit of account or as a basis for the unit of account by a number of international and regional organizations. The SDR has also been used to denominate private financial instruments. However, the market for private SDR deposits is still limited. The use of the SDR as a unit of account is explained, in part, by the fact that the value of the SDR tends to be more stable than that of any single currency in the basket, since it is a weighted average of the exchange rates of the five major currencies in which the prices of goods and services in international trade are denominated.

The SDR as a Currency Peg

As of January 1992, six of the IMF's member countries had pegged their currencies to the SDR. The value of the members' currency under such arrangements is fixed in terms of the SDR and then set in terms of other currencies by reference to the SDR value of the other currencies as published by the IMF.

The European Monetary Union

Many attempts to establish monetary unions across national borders have failed, but a few successful unions still exist today. A monetary union is a formal arrangement in which two or more independent countries agree to fix their exchange rates or to employ only one currency to carry out all transactions. One of the most ambitious efforts to date is now under way in the European Community (EC), whose 12 members strive toward a European Monetary Union (EMU). When full union is achieved by the end of the 1990s, these countries will carry out transactions with one currency through one central bank under one monetary policy. This section presents a history of the European monetary system, from the snake within a tunnel of the 1970s to the EC's recent moves in the direction of monetary union.

The Snake within a Tunnel

In May 1972, the European Community (EC) agreed to allow its currencies to fluctuate a maximum of 2.25 percent against one another, while permitting a 4.5 percent fluctuation against other currencies. This system became known as "a snake within a tunnel." The snake was the narrower band of 2.25 percent permitted among the EC countries and the tunnel was the wider band of 4.5 percent allowed by the Smithsonian Agreement.

England, Ireland, and Denmark joined the EC in 1973. This was followed by a series of international monetary crises such as the devaluation of the U.S. dollar in February. In mid-March, the values of all major currencies were permitted to fluctuate according to market forces. Thus, the tunnel was gone in March 1973, but EC countries had tried to maintain the snake. Some of these attempts had been short-lived. For instance, France, after withdrawing from the snake and rejoining it several times, finally abandoned the snake in March 1976. Many causes of conflict between domestic economic goals and exchange stability had intensified domestic pressures on many other participating countries to abandon the snake. The number of participating countries in the snake fell to six by late 1978: the German mark, the Dutch guilder, the Norwegian krone, the Belgian franc, the Danish krone, and the Luxembourg franc. The three main initial members of the snake—England, France, and Italy—had abandoned it some years earlier.

The European Currency Unit

Serious problems had raised questions about the snake's survival. The sharp decline in the exchange rate of the U.S. dollar during the second half of 1978 further bolstered the desire of European countries for exchange stability. On December 5, 1978, the European Council adopted a resolution to establish the European Monetary System (EMS) which went into effect on March 13, 1979. The EMS is a complex exchange rate and intervention system combined with large credit facilities. The institutional arrangements of the EMS include (1) a currency basket, (2) an exchange rate mechanism with rules of intervention, and (3) several credit facilities.

First, the European Currency Unit (ECU) is the cornerstone of the EMS. The ECU is used as the denominator for the exchange rate mechanism, that is, as the basis for a "divergence indicator" to show when one currency diverges from the average of the other participating currencies. The ECU is also used as the denominator for operations under both the intervention and credit mechanisms. The value of an ECU is a weighted average value of a basket of all EC currencies. Each currency's weight is decided by the relative importance of that country's economy in the total EC output and the overall share of that country's trade in the total intra-EC trade. Weights are normally revised every five years. Table 4-6 provides the current composition of the ECU. On June 28, 1974, the value of the basket was equal to one SDR, but these two values have developed differently since then. The difference between the two values reflects a difference in their composition.

Second, the ECU is based on a fixed, but adjustable, exchange-rate system. Each participating currency has a central rate in terms of ECUs. These central rates determine a grid of bilateral central rates. Participating currencies are allowed to fluctuate within a margin of plus or minus 2.25 percent (6 percent for Italy and Spain) from their bilateral central rates. Italy and Spain are allowed to fluctuate their currency up to 6 percent on either side of their bilateral central rates. EC member countries have frequently realigned exchange rates within the EMS to reflect changes in European currency markets. Table 4-7 compares individual currencies within the exchange rate mechanism of the EMS. The second column of figures shows conversion rates per dollar with an exception of the pound sterling, which is expressed in dollars per pound. The third column of figures shows conversion rates per the ECU.

Table 4-6
Composition of the ECU

Currency	Weight (%)
Drachma (Greece)	0.7
Escudo (Portugal)	0.8
Franc (Belgium/Luxembourg)	8.1
Franc (France)	19.3
Guilder (Netherlands)	9.6
Krone (Denmark)	2.5
Lira (Italy)	9.7
Mark (Germany)	30.4
Peseta (Spain)	5.2
Pound sterling (Britain)	12.6
Pound (Ireland)	1.1

Table 4-7
European Monetary System Rates as of July 1, 1991

Currency	Spot Rate	ECU
Belgian franc	37.33	42.0674
French franc	6.1855	6.9705
Guilder	2.0565	2.3175
Krone	7.0035	7.8923
Lira	1356.00	1528.08
Mark	1.8265	2.0583
Peseta	114.02	128.490
Pound sterling	1.6155	0.6976
Pound	1.4650	0.7692

Third, to facilitate compulsory intervention, EMS participants created short-term and medium-term financing facilities. A short-term facility provides short-term financing for temporary balance-of-payments deficits. A medium-term facility is also available for balance-of-payments assistance, but its use is subject to certain conditions.

The EMS has successfully maintained a zone of monetary stability within the EC since its establishment in 1979. Now, the EMS faces new opportunities and challenges because of the single market program in Europe. Competition, allocation efficiency, and evolution within the financial sector are expected to remove capital restrictions, improve the allocation of economic resources, and expand financial services. On the other hand, the financial integration of the EC creates some challenges: the ability to deal with country-specific shocks, the impact of monetary independence, the operation of fiscal policy, and the design of a new single monetary unit.

Recent Moves Toward European Monetary Union

Although EC countries established a treaty for an economic and monetary union, they were unwilling to embrace any major commitment to this goal before the late 1980s. The Madrid summit in June 1989 unanimously adopted the first phase of a three-phase plan by Jacques Delors, President of the European Commission, to push the EC toward the economic and monetary union.

The first phase calls for closer cooperation between member governments in economic and monetary policy. Phase Two foresees the establishment of new EC institutions, including the European System of Central Banks. Phase Three would institute a single currency and a single monetary policy decided and implemented by the EC central bank.

The EC is in Phase One now. At the October 1990 summit in Rome, EC's heads of state approved a text to establish a timetable for the final two phases. During the second phase, which would start on January 1, 1994, the EC would establish a new institution to strengthen the coordination of monetary policies, to develop the instruments and procedures needed for the future conduct of a single monetary policy, and to oversee development of the ECU. Within three years from the start of the second phase, the European Commission and the council of the new monetary institution will report on progress made so that provisions can be arranged for the start of the third phase.

In December 1991, EC leaders reached a milestone agreement on the Maastricht Treaty to create a monetary and political union by 1999. Under their accord, EC leaders agreed to establish a single European currency by January 1, 1999, with a common monetary policy established by an independent European Central Bank. In several stages starting in 1996, EC countries that meet tough economic standards will throw out their currencies and join the single currency. In addition to the single currency, the EC also took steps to bolster the Western Union, the nine-nation defense organization, as the main arm of a common EC defense policy. It agreed to give greater powers to the European Parliament. Eventually, the agreement's biggest impact may be in such areas as foreign policy and defense.

September 1992 Currency Crisis in Europe

The Treaty of Maastricht, named after the provincial Dutch town that hosted the EC summit in mid-December 1991, signalled to many that there was no turning back on the road to European unity. Europe's plans for economic union, however, have been in distress since September 1992 because world currency markets were racked by some of the most turbulent trading in memory amid the chaos surrounding the apparent breakdown of the European Monetary System (EMS). Although the roots of the currency crisis lay in Germany's high interest rates, Britain took center stage. The crisis began when Norman Lamont, Chancellor of the Exchequer, announced on September 16 that Britain would withdraw from the EMS. Table 4-8 shows the chronology of the pound sterling's crisis that eventually mushroomed into full fledged currency turmoil in Europe.

Table 4-8
Chronology of Sterling Crisis

London Time	
8:30 a.m.	London's FTSE (Financial Times Stock Exchange) stock index opens down 28.2 points, as the pound opens a hair above its EMS floor of 2.778 German marks.
9:00 a.m.	Bank of England intervention fails to boost pound, as traders dump sterling for marks.
9:30 a.m.	FTSE index plummets nearly 50 points. German Bundesbank and the French central bank join Bank of England to prop up sterling.
10:45 a.m.	Pound falls below EMS floor. Bank of England intervenes again in a desperate effort to stave off a rise in interest rates.
11:00 a.m.	After conferring with Prime Minister John Major, Chancellor Norman Lamont decides the only medicine to revive the pound is an interest-rate rise.
11.01 a.m.	Two percentage point interest-rate rise announced, to 12%.
11:13 a.m.	FTSE down 79 points; begins slow rise.
12:00 p.m.	FTSE down 52 points.
12:30 p.m.	Pound still below EMS floor. Government warns it may raise interest rates further.
2:30 p.m.	Government announces another three percentage interest-rate rise, to 15%.
4:30 p.m.	FTSE up 8 points at close.
7:30 p.m.	Britain suspends participation in EMS and postpones second interest-rate hike, leaving interest rates at 12%.
7:32 p.m.	Chancellor Lamont announces that the EC's monetary committee will meet "urgently" in Brussels later in the evening to consider how stability can be restored to foreign-exchange markets.
7:39 p.m.	Pound falls another three pfennings against the mark, to 2.70 marks, nearly 8 pfennings below its EMS floor.
8:29 p.m.	Prime Minister Major recalls Parliament from its summer recess; it will convene September 24.

Source: *The Wall Street Journal*, September 17, 1992, p. A7.

Pressures leading to this turmoil had built up for several months since the Danes, in a referendum on May 1992, narrowly opposed ratification of the Maastricht Treaty. Europe's once solid money system suddenly fell into turmoil. Britain and Italy both suspended their currencies from the EMS after the value of the pound and the lira fell below the floor set by that system. Britain, Italy, and Spain then devalued their currencies. Iceland, Spain, and Portugal reimposed limited controls on capital flows. As shown in Table 4–9, European currency fluctuations against the U.S. dollar from September 11 to September 18 ranged from as little as 4 percent for the Belgian franc to as much as 12 percent for the Italian lira. Sweden, not an EMS member, increased its key lending rate to 500 percent to defend the informal link between its krona and the mark.

Currency traders and analysts estimate that Europe's major central banks lost $6 billion in their futile attempt to support weak currencies in September 1992. British, French, German, Italian, and Spanish central banks together spent approximately $150 billion to assist the pound, franc, lira, peseta, and krona. Even with an affirmative French vote on the Maastricht Treaty in the referendum of September 20, many analysts doubt whether the movement toward monetary, economic, and political union will continue.

Causes of the Crisis.   At the center of this recent turmoil in currency markets is Germany's Bundesbank. To control inflation caused by Germany's own reunification, the German central bank raised interest rates in recent years. Germany's problems can be dated to mid–1990, when West Germany handed East Germans one powerful west mark for each east mark. This action was followed by commitments from Bonn to invest heavily in the rehabilitation of East Germany and to finance a Russian troop withdrawal from Germany.

Table 4–9
Europe's Markets After a Frantic Week

Country	Representative Short–Term Interest Rate	Ten–Year Government Bond Yield	Currency Gain/Loss vs. U.S. Dollar 9/11–9/18/92
Belgium	9.37%	8.63%	–3.94%
Britain	9.88	9.06	–9.71
Denmark	15.00	9.14	–4.58
France	10.38	8.58	–4.31
Germany	8.75	7.45	–3.70
Italy	16.75	13.97	–12.21
Spain	14.75	12.06	–11.52
United States	3.25	6.40	—

Source: *The Wall Street Journal*, September 21, 1992, p. C1.

These events resulted in an inflation rate of almost 4 percent, high by German standards. The German Bundesbank sought to control the inflation with a single instrument, short-term interest rates pegged between 8 and 9 percent. In other words, Germany's tight-money policy posed enormous problems for Europe's weaker economies, none of which would impose their high interest rates if their currencies were not tied to the mark by the exchange-rate system. Governments of countries such as Britain, Italy, and Spain faced a difficult choice: either raise interest rates or spend huge sums of money required to boost their currencies to the agreed-upon levels. In fact, these countries had used both approaches for some time, but they were too little and too late to save the EMS.

Results of the Crisis.   Those September actions on European currencies uncovered fundamental weaknesses in the plan for a united Europe, but the actions also increased chances for stability and growth. The currency crisis of September paved the way for lower German interest rates. If the chaos pushes Germany to lower interest rates, it would prove to be a balm for Europe's wounded economies. A decline in German interest rates also would reduce interest rates in other European countries as well. These salutary effects would occur because most European countries have high interest rates and low inflation. There may be some multiple expansions in European markets in 1993 due to interest-rate reductions and expectations of improved earnings.

Certainly, Europe will attempt to put its EMS back together again. It is possible that all the pre-September 16 members of the EMS could reestablish the system at new parities based on defensible market values. For the foreseeable future, though, the economic fundamentals of European countries remain too diverse to maintain the pre-September 16 system. Moreover, the United Kingdom and/or Denmark may not ratify the Maastricht treaty.

The centerpiece of the Maastricht treaty—the creation of a single European currency governed by a single European central bank—may have to be revised. Instead of all 12 EC nations joining in such a system by 1999, Europe's core countries—Germany, France, the Netherlands, Belgium, and Luxembourg—may press ahead faster, but with a scaled down version of a single currency at the exclusion of others. The group might set up its own central bank or it might rely on the Bundesbank. This idea of a two-speed or two-tier system would then leave other EC countries behind, but they could join as their economies strengthened, just as the practice is in the European Common Market.

Proposals for International Monetary Reform

What are the essential elements of international monetary reform? How might the United States deal with its internal and external imbalances? And what are the economic challenges that face the EC? These are questions addressed by many economists who press for international monetary reform. They suggest that countries should share each other's intentions in their economic plans and that a coordinating group of countries should jointly make projections of key economic variables.

The reader would suspect by now that the Bretton Woods system had three basic defects: (1) pegged parities, (2) dollar disequilibrium, and (3) inadequate international reserves. Some important reforms introduced to solve these problems include SDRs, the Smithsonian Agreement, the snake within a tunnel, and the European Monetary System. Nevertheless, these reforms are now inadequate to maintain orderly markets.

Volatile Exchange Rates

When major industrial countries abandoned the fixed exchange-rate system in 1973 in favor of a floating rate system, they saw their decision as a

Figure 4–1
Exchange Rate Volatility Under Fixed
and Floating Exchange Rates

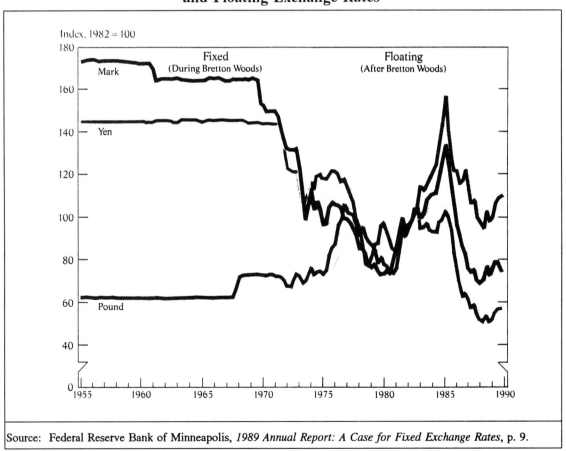

Source: Federal Reserve Bank of Minneapolis, *1989 Annual Report: A Case for Fixed Exchange Rates*, p. 9.

triumph for the free market. Many economists expected exchange rates to be fairly stable under the flexible exchange-rate system. They also expected that the flexible exchange-rate system would reduce national trade imbalances. Figure 4-1 shows that three major exchange rates have been more volatile since 1974. Other major exchange rates show similar patterns. Figure 4-2 shows that the trade imbalances of four major industrial countries have been larger and more persistent since 1974. Other major industrial countries have experienced similar trade imbalances.

Figure 4-2
Trade Imbalances of Four Nations Under Fixed and Floating Exchange Rates

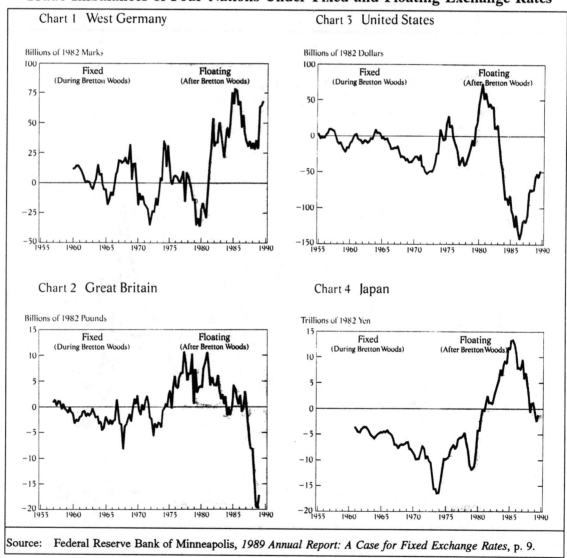

Source: Federal Reserve Bank of Minneapolis, *1989 Annual Report: A Case for Fixed Exchange Rates*, p. 9.

Table 4–10
Large Six–Month Percentage Changes in Major Exchange Rates

Pound–Dollar Ending Date	Rate Size (%)	Mark–Dollar Ending Date	Rate Size (%)	Yen–Dollar Ending Date	Rate Size (%)
July 1981	25.1	Feb. 1986	-22.6	Feb. 1986	-27.8
June 1981	-25.0	June 1981	19.9	Oct. 1978	-23.6
Feb. 1986	18.4	Aug. 1985	-17.8	April 1979	21.6
Sept. 1975	16.6	Oct. 1978	-17.4	March 1978	-17.7
May 1989	16.0	Jan. 1974	16.8	Dec. 1987	-17.4
Dec. 1987	-15.1	Nov. 1986	-15.7	Oct. 1982	16.5
Oct. 1976	13.8	Sept. 1984	15.5	Sept. 1980	-16.3
March 1983	13.5	Feb. 1975	-15.4	May 1989	15.9
July 1979	-13.4	Dec. 1987	-14.6	April 1983	-15.7
Oct. 1978	-13.2	June 1988	14.1	July 1981	15.7
May 1987	-12.4	Dec. 1989	-14.0	Sept. 1986	-15.7
Jan. 1978	-11.6	May 1989	13.5	April 1987	-14.6
Sept. 1988	10.9	March 1978	-13.2	Jan. 1974	12.7
Dec. 1973	10.6	Sept. 1975	12.7	Feb. 1980	12.7
		Aug. 1983	11.2		
		March 1980	10.8		

Source: Joseph A. Whitt, Jr., "Flexible Exchange Rates: An Idea Whose Time Has Passed?" *Economic Review*, Federal Reserve Bank of Atlanta, September/October 1990, pp. 9-11.

Table 4-10 shows the dates and sizes of large moves—defined as 10 percent over a period of six months in the pound-dollar, mark-dollar, and yen-dollar exchange rate. During the years since the breakdown of the Bretton Woods Agreement, the dollar-pound rate has moved more than 15 percent in a six-month period six times. By contrast, under the Bretton Woods Agreement, the pound-dollar rate had experienced only one large change of 15 percent during the decades of the 1950s and 1960s.

Large exchange-rate movements have also occurred for other major currencies during the period of flexible exchange rates. In some respects, these rates have shown even more volatility than the pound-dollar rate. The mark-dollar rate has experienced eight separate cases of movement more than 15 percent in six months. The yen-dollar rate has moved more than 15 percent in a six-month period 11 times. In contrast, the mark and the yen showed even less movement during the 1950s and 1960s than the pound. The mark had two noticeable changes—revaluations of 4.88 percent in 1961 and 8.88 percent in 1969; the yen was virtually unchanged during these two decades.

Exchange rates are said to be volatile when changes in the exchange rates are unpredictable. Exchange rates have been highly variable under the flexible exchange-rate system. Variability itself may not be a serious problem, if the changes in exchange rates were predictable. Even if quite large, predictable changes in exchange rates would not impede international trade or capital flows, because companies could take account of the predicted changes in the exchange rate by adjusting the agreed-on prices. Since 1973, exchange-rate volatility has been magnified because exchange rates have been more flexible than some other indicators, such as wages, prices, and interest rates. There has been widespread concern in recent years over the volatility in exchange rates, with much of this concern stemming from the adverse effects of exchange-rate volatility on international trade and capital flows.

This concern has been reinforced by massive trade imbalances of the four largest economies in the world—the United States, Japan, Germany, and the United Kingdom—after the Bretton Woods Agreement. In other words, the costs of flexible exchange rates have been greater than expected. Consequently, there is a growing consensus that the world should return to stable but flexible policy rules. These and other problems have recently increased the need for further international monetary reform. Proposals for further international monetary reform may be divided into two broad categories: proposals for greater flexibility and other proposals.

Proposals for Greater Flexibility

A system of additional flexibility or even a system of freely flexible exchange rates has been suggested to restructure the current international monetary system so that deficit countries might solve their payments problems. It seems reasonable to assume that fixed exchange rates, which existed under the gold standard before World War I, are now practically impossible. Moreover, fixed but adjustable exchange rates could not accommodate highly diversified modern economies almost one-half of a century after the Bretton Woods Agreement. Countries differ too much in price levels, wage costs, monetary policies, and international capital flows to keep fixed exchange rates.

A Wider Band.   A wider band has been frequently suggested as an alternative to the present international monetary system. The Bretton Woods Agreement allowed a band of 2.25 percent, and the Smithsonian Agreement approved a band of 4.5 percent. Proponents of this wider band would like to see the band expanded further. They argue that a wider band would allow central banks to enjoy freedom for independent monetary policies.

Crawling Peg.   The crawling peg is another proposal. It would provide for regular modification of par value according to an agreed upon formula. Under this system, a country would permit its currency to appreciate or depreciate slowly rather than fight to maintain a band of certain percentages around par value. The crawling peg would provide relatively stable exchange rates for those nations which consider this stability essential for international transactions. Balance-of-payments problems would also be self-adjusted through the international price mechanism rather than through exchange controls, restrictions on growth of national income and employment, price controls, or other unpopular internal policies.

Crawling Band. Another key proposal is the crawling or gliding band; it combines a wider band and a crawling peg. In other words, this proposal compromises the area between the inflexible exchange rates of the gold standard and a system of completely fluctuating exchange rates. Each parity level would be adjusted upward or downward as a moving average of the actual exchange rates that could fluctuate within a wider band: (1) Within one year the exchange rate parity would be allowed to move a predetermined maximum, say, 2 percent. This 2 percent is called an annual crawling. (2) This slowly crawling peg would be surrounded by a wider band within which the actual exchange rate can fluctuate. Let's refer to Example 4-1 to see how the crawling band works.

Example 4-1. Assume: (1) the dollar-pound parity begins at $4.00 in 1990; (2) the parity can move up to 2 percent each year; (3) the actual exchange rate is permitted to float within 2.5 percent on either side of the parity; and (4) British costs rise faster than American.

Figure 4-3 shows how the crawling band might work. Even if the IMF permits a wider band of 5 or 6 percent, pegging the dollar-pound parity at

Figure 4-3
Hypothetical Crawling Band

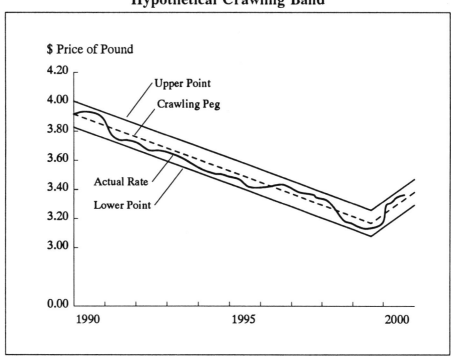

$4.00 per pound would eventually lead to huge English deficits and American surpluses. This is because England's costs rise faster than America's. However, under the crawling band, the exchange rate is not held within the band as formerly set by the gold points or IMF system. The exchange rates can vary between a lower point of $3.90 ($4.00 - $4.00 x 0.025) and an upper point of $4.10 ($4.00 + $4.00 x 0.025) in 1990. In 1991, with parity moved to $3.92 ($4.00 - $4.00 x 0.02) by the British deficit, the range would be from $3.822 ($3.92 - $3.92 x 0.025) to $4.018 ($3.92 + $3.92 x 0.025). Thus, if the parity is allowed to move by 2 percent per year, it would produce enough flexibility to permit a 20 percent adjustment of exchange rates over a period of ten years. This 20 percent adjustment and a wider band of 5 percent should be sufficient to adjust for the normal differences between England and America in their trends of cost-push inflation.

Other Proposals

A number of proposals ask for the creation of a supercentral institution which would perform the same function for an international economy as the commercial banking system performs for a domestic economy. John Keynes, for instance, proposed the establishment of an International Clearing Union that would create an international money called bancors. Under this system, deficit countries could borrow bancors to finance their deficits.

Robert Triffin, to illustrate another viewpoint, proposed the creation of reserves by an international institution such as the IMF. Under this proposal, surplus countries would be required to deposit a portion of their holdings in key currencies (dollars, SDRs, and yen) in the IMF instead of holding them as monetary reserves. On the basis of these deposits, the IMF could create necessary international monetary reserves through its loans to deficit countries.

Another proposal calls for enlarging the number of reserve countries. To reduce exchange risk, many central banks have recently diversified their portfolios of reserve assets to include Japanese yen, ECUs, SDRs, and gold. An increased number of reserve countries would spread the reserve-currency burden more evenly than before and leave the monetary system less vulnerable to attack. Freely flexible exchange rates, discussed in the earlier part of this chapter, have been frequently suggested to reform the international monetary system. Completely flexible exchange rates have never been tried; it is unlikely they ever will be.

Summary

Financial managers must understand the international monetary system if they are to manage multinational businesses efficiently. Foreign exchange rates determine prices of goods and services that multinational companies buy and sell across national boundaries. These exchange rates also have an impact on foreign investments.

Considered historically, the international monetary system of the late 19th century evolved into the current dirty floating system. The pre–1914 gold standard represents one extreme of the international monetary system. Under this system, the exchange rate for each currency was fixed in terms of gold. The flow of gold restored the balance-of-payments equilibrium. In the case of a deficit, a gold outflow would take place to finance an external deficit. In the case of a surplus, a gold inflow would occur to eliminate an external surplus.

The world experienced international monetary disorder from 1914 to 1945. World War I ended the stability of exchange rates for currencies of major trading partners. The Great Depression of 1929-1932 and the international financial crisis afterwards resulted in international monetary chaos. To summarize the international monetary system from 1914 to 1945, we find a mixture of widely fluctuating exchange rates and exchange rates maintained by exchange controls.

The Bretton Woods Agreement of 1944 marked a new era for the operation of the international monetary system, which was a system of fixed exchange rates based on a revised gold standard, called the gold exchange standard. Each currency was fixed within a narrow range of value in relation to gold or the U.S. dollar. Many member countries were unable or unwilling to abide by the Bretton Woods Agreement because its provisions were complex and because their interests conflicted. Nevertheless, the Bretton Woods Agreement and the activity of the IMF were the main features of the international monetary system from 1945 to 1973.

Two problems raised serious questions about the function of the Bretton Woods Agreement as the international monetary system. First, the growth of monetary reserves was inadequate. Second, effective balance-of-payments adjustments could not be achieved under the Agreement. Attempts to save the Bretton Woods Agreement through the introduction of SDRs and the Smithsonian Agreement failed when the whole system collapsed in 1973. Since 1973, the international monetary system has been characterized by a confusing mixture of freely floating, managed floating, joint floating, and fixed rates.

Questions

1. Some governments and economists have repeatedly suggested that the international monetary system return to a system of fixed exchange rates. Discuss the pros and cons of the fixed exchange-rate system.

2. Why did the U.S. dollar become so weak and the Bretton Woods Agreement fail in 1973?

3. Analysts said that President Nixon's speech delivered on August 15, 1971, was designed to prepare Americans for a multipolar world because

American decline economically and militarily was inevitable. List the decisions announced in this famous speech.

4. Discuss the impact of the two-tiered exchange-rate system on a company's cash flow projections.

5. What are alternative exchange-rate systems?

6. List the objectives of the International Monetary Fund.

7. What are Special Drawing Rights (SDRs)? How is the value of SDRs determined?

8. Briefly explain the snake within a tunnel.

9. When do volatile exchange rates exist?

10. Major industrialized countries have practiced the floating exchange-rate system since 1973. Under the floating rate system, economists expected exchange rates to be fairly stable and trade imbalances to fall. Have these two expectations been realized?

11. Discuss the crawling band as a proposal for international monetary reform.

References

Chriszt, M. J., "European Monetary Union: How Close Is It?" *Economic Review,* Federal Reserve Bank of Atlanta, September/October 1991, pp. 21-7.

Copeland, L. S., *Exchange Rates and International Finance*, Reading, MA: Addison-Wesley, 1989.

Dernburg, T. F., *Global Macroeconomics*, New York: Harper & Row, 1989.

Ernst & Whinney, *Europe 1992: The Single Market*, New York: Ernst & Whinney International, 1988.

Humpage, O. F., "A Hitchhiker's Guide to International Macroeconomic Policy Coordination," *Economic Review*, Federal Reserve Bank of Cleveland, March/April 1990, pp. 3-12.

The International Monetary Fund, *IMF Survey: Supplement on the IMF*, Washington, DC: IMF, September 1991.

The International Monetary Fund, *IMF Survey*, Washington, DC: the IMF, various issues.

Leigh-Pemberton, R., "Europe 1992: Some Monetary Policy Issues," *Economic Review*, Federal Reserve Bank of Kansas City, September/October 1989, pp. 3-8.

Machlup, F., *Plans for Reform of the International Monetary System*, Princeton, NJ: Princeton University Press, 1964.

Parsons, M., "Stabilizing the Present International Payment Systems," in *The International Adjustment Mechanism*, Boston: the Federal Reserve Bank of Boston, 1970, pp. 38-43.

Triffin, R., *Our International Monetary System: Yesterday, Today, and Tomorrow*, New York: Random House, Inc., 1968.

Whitt, J. A., Jr., "Flexible Exchange Rates: An Idea Whose Time Has Passed?" *Economic Review*, Federal Reserve Bank of Atlanta, September/October 1990, pp. 2-15.

The World Bank, *World Development Report 1992*, Washington, DC: The World Bank, 1992.

Yeager, L. B., *International Monetary Relations: Theory, History, and Policy*, New York: Harper & Row Publishers, 1976.

Appendix

AMENDED ARTICLES OF AGREEMENT OF THE IMF

Reform of the international monetary system that began in 1971 following the collapse of the postwar Bretton Woods system was formally completed April 1, 1978, when the Second Amendment to the International Monetary Fund's Articles of Agreement went into force with ratification by the required majority of the 133 member nations.

The Second Amendment contains several major provisions, some of which have been already informally adopted by member nations. Provisions on exchange rate arrangements are based on recognition that the essential purpose of the international monetary system is to provide a framework that both facilitates the exchange of goods, services, and capital among countries and sustains sound economic growth for all nations. In ratifying the amendment, members undertake a general obligation to collaborate with the IMF and with other members to ensure orderly exchange arrangements and promote a stable system of exchange rates. Members are required to promote stability by fostering orderly underlying economic and financial conditions and a monetary system that does not tend to produce erratic disruptions. They must avoid manipulating exchange rates or the international monetary system in order to prevent effective balance–of–payments adjustments or to gain an unfair competitive advantage over other members. Members are free to apply the exchange arrangements of their choice, except that they are not to maintain a value for their currencies in terms of gold. They are required to notify the IMF of the exchange arrangements they intend to apply and of any subsequent changes in these arrangements. The IMF will oversee the international monetary system to ensure its effective operation.

The most important changes with respect to the role of gold in the international monetary system are as follows: (1) gold has been eliminated as the unit of value of the SDR and cannot be used as a common denominator for par values of currencies, even if at some future time par values are introduced; (2) the official price of gold has been abolished and members are free to deal in gold in the market and among themselves without reference to any official price; (3) obligatory payments in gold between the IMF and its members have been abrogated; and the IMF can accept gold only under decisions taken with an 85 percent majority of the total voting power; (4) the IMF will be required to complete the announced program of disposing of a total of 50 million ounces of gold and will have powers to make further gold sales both on the basis of prices in the market and at the official price in effect before the Second Amendment (SDR 35 per ounce); (5) profits beyond the former official price on any such further sales will be placed in a Special Disbursement Account for use in the ordinary operations and transactions of the IMF or for other uses, including balance–of–payments assistance for the benefit of developing members in difficult circumstances.

The modifications in the provisions relating to the Special Drawing Rights (SDR) are intended to help make the SDR the principal reserve asset in the international monetary system. Under the amended Articles: (1) the method of valuing the SDR can be determined by the IMF by a 70 percent majority; (2) participants can enter into transactions by agreement without general or special decisions by the IMF, and transfers of SDRs in such transactions are not subject to the requirement of need to use reserve assets; and (3) the SDR replaces gold in certain payments between the IMF and its members, and its possible use in operations and transactions conducted through the IMF's General Department (formerly the General Account) are to be expanded.

5
The Foreign Exchange Market

The efficient operation of the international monetary system has necessitated the creation of an institutional structure, usually called the foreign exchange market. This is a market where one country's currency can be exchanged for another country's. Unlike the term might suggest, the foreign exchange market actually is not a geographic location. It is an informal network of telephone, telex, satellite, facsimile, and computer communications between banks, foreign exchange dealers, arbitragers, and speculators. The market operates simultaneously at three tiers:

1. Individuals and corporations buy and sell foreign exchange through their commercial banks.
2. Commercial banks trade in foreign exchange with other commercial banks in the same financial center.
3. Commercial banks trade in foreign exchange with commercial banks in other financial centers.

We must first understand the organization and dynamics of the foreign exchange market in order to understand the complex functions of international financial management. This chapter explains the roles of the major participants in the exchange market, describes the spot and forward markets, discusses the theories of exchange rate determination, and examines the roles of arbitragers.

Major Participants in the Exchange Market

The foreign exchange market consists of a spot market and a forward market. In the spot market, foreign currencies are sold and bought for delivery within two business days after the day of a trade. In the forward market, foreign currencies are sold or bought for future delivery.

There are many types of participants in the foreign exchange market: exporters, governments, importers, multinational companies, tourists, commercial banks, and central banks. But large commercial banks and central banks are the two major participants in the foreign exchange market. Most foreign exchange transactions take place in the commercial banking sector. It is also possible to arrange foreign currency transactions in specialized markets such as the black market.

Commercial Banks

Commercial banks participate in the foreign exchange market as intermediaries for customers such as multinational companies and exporters. These commercial banks also maintain an interbank market. In other words, they accept deposits of foreign banks and maintain deposits in banks abroad. Commercial banks play three key roles in international transactions:

1. They operate the payment mechanism.
2. They extend credit.
3. They help to reduce risk.

Operating the Payment Mechanism.
The commercial banking system provides the mechanism by which international payments can be efficiently made. This mechanism is a collection system through which transfers of money by drafts, notes, and other means are made internationally. In order to operate an international payments mechanism, banks maintain deposits in banks abroad and accept deposits of foreign banks. These accounts are debited and credited when payments are made. Banks can make international money transfers very quickly and efficiently by using telegraph, telephones, facsimiles, and computer services.

Extending Credit.
Commercial banks also provide credit for international transactions and for business activity within foreign countries. They make loans to those engaged in international business on either an unsecured or a secured basis. Normally, U.S. banks cannot have branches outside their home state. They also cannot own shares of foreign banking subsidiaries.

However, the Edge Act of 1919 allowed American banks to act as holding companies and to own stock in foreign banks. Thus, American banks can provide loans and other banking services for American-owned companies in most countries around the world. Furthermore, since December 1981, U.S.

banks have been permitted to establish international banking facilities (IBFs) at their offices in the United States. In other words, U.S. banks with IBFs are allowed to accept time deposits from non–U.S. residents free of reserve requirements and many other restrictions. They are also allowed to lend to non–U.S. residents not subject to most U.S. income taxes. Hence, U.S. banks with IBFs, just like Eurobanks, can offer dollar loans and other banking services for U.S. companies in foreign countries.

Reducing Risk.

The letter of credit is used as a major means of reducing risks in international transactions. It is a document issued by a bank at the request of the importer. In the document, the bank agrees to honor a draft drawn on the importer if the draft accompanies specified documents. The letter of credit is advantageous to exporters. Exporters sell their goods abroad against the promise of a bank rather than a commercial firm. Banks are usually larger, better known, and better credit risks than most business firms. Thus, exporters are almost completely assured of payment if they meet specific conditions under letters of credit.

Exchange Trading by Commercial Banks.

Most commercial banks provide foreign exchange services for their customers. But for most U.S. banks, currency trading is not an important activity and exchange transactions are infrequent. These banks look to correspondents in U.S. money centers to execute their orders.

A relatively small number of money center banks conduct the bulk of the foreign exchange transactions in the United States. Virtually all the big New York banks have active currency trading operations. Major banks in Chicago, San Francisco, Los Angeles, Boston, Detroit, and Philadelphia also are active through head office operations as well as affiliates in New York and elsewhere. Thus, all commercial banks in the United States are prepared to buy or sell foreign currency balances for their commercial customers as well as for the international banking activities of their own institutions.

Bank trading rooms share common physical characteristics. All are equipped with modern communications equipment to keep in touch with other banks here in the United States and abroad, foreign exchange brokers, and corporate customers. Over 30 U.S. banks have direct telephone lines with the Federal Reserve Bank of New York. Traders subscribe to the major news services to keep current on financial and political developments that might influence exchange trading. In addition, the banks maintain extensive "back office" support staffs to handle routine operations such as confirming exchange contracts, paying and receiving dollars and foreign currencies, and general ledger accounting. These operations generally are kept separate from the trading room itself to assure proper management and control.

In other important respects, however, no two trading rooms are alike. They differ widely according to the scale of their operations, the roster of their corporate customers, and their overall style of trading. The basic objectives of a bank's foreign exchange trading policy are set by senior management. That policy depends upon factors such as the size of the bank, the scope of its international banking commitments, the nature of trading activities at its foreign branches, and the availability of resources.

Global Market and National Markets.

Banks throughout the world serve as market makers in foreign exchange. They comprise a global market in the sense that a bank in one country can trade with another bank almost anywhere. Banks are linked by telecommunications equipment which allows instantaneous communication and puts this "over-the-counter" market as close as the telephone or the telex machine.

Because foreign exchange is an integral part of the payment mechanism, local banks may benefit from closer access to domestic money markets. They usually have an advantage in trading their local currency. For instance, buying and selling sterling for dollars is most active among the banks in London. Similarly, the major market for Swiss francs is in Zurich; for Japanese yen, in Tokyo. But the local advantage is by no means absolute. Hence, dollar-franc trading is active in London and dollar-sterling trading is active in Zurich. Furthermore, New York banks trade just as frequently with London, German, or Swiss banks in all major currencies as they do with other New York banks.

Foreign exchange is traded in a 24-hour market. Somewhere in the world banks are buying and selling dollars for, say, German marks at any time during the day. Banks in Australia and the Far East begin trading in Hong Kong, Singapore, Tokyo, and Sydney at about the time most traders in San Francisco go home for supper. As the Far East closes, trading in Middle Eastern financial centers has been going on for a couple of hours, and the trading day in Europe is just beginning. Some of the large New York banks have an early shift to minimize the time difference of 5-6 hours with Europe. By the time New York trading gets going in full force around 8 AM, it is lunch time in London and Frankfurt. To complete the circle, West Coast banks also extend "normal banking hours" so they can trade with New York or Europe on one side, and with Hong Kong, Singapore, or Tokyo on the other.

One implication of a 24-hour currency market is that exchange rates may change at any time. Bank traders must be light sleepers so that they can be ready to respond to a telephone call in the middle of the night which may alert them to an unusually sharp exchange-rate movement on another continent. Many banks permit limited dealing from home by senior traders to contend with just such a circumstance.

Central Banks

Central banks, such as the Federal Reserve System of the United States and the Bank of Japan, attempt to control the growth of the money supply within their jurisdictions. They also strive to maintain the value of their own currency against any foreign currency. In other words, central bank operations reflect government transactions, transactions with other central banks and various international organizations, and intervention to influence exchange-rate movements.

Central banks serve as their governments' banker for domestic and international payments. They handle most or all foreign exchange transactions for the government as well as for important public-sector enterprises. They may also pay or receive a foreign currency not usually held in official reserves. For example, the Federal Reserve Bank of New York handles a substantial volume of foreign exchange transactions for its correspondents who wish to buy or sell dollars for other currencies. Moreover, most central banks frequently enter into exchange transactions with international and regional organizations which need to buy or sell the local currency. The most important role of central banks in exchange-market operations is their intervention in the exchange market to influence market conditions or the exchange rate. They carry out intervention operations either on behalf of the country's treasury department or for their own account.

In a system of fixed exchange rates, central banks usually absorb the difference between supply of and demand for foreign exchange in order to maintain the par value system. Under this system, the central banks agree to maintain the value of their currencies within a narrow band of fluctuations. If pressures such as huge trade deficits and high inflation develop, the price of a domestic currency approaches the lower limit of the band. At this point, a central bank is obliged to intervene in the foreign exchange market. This intervention is designed to counteract the forces prevailing in the market. In a system of flexible exchange rates, central banks do not attempt to prevent fundamental changes in the rate of exchange between their own currency and any other currency. However, even within the flexible exchange-rate system, they intervene in the foreign exchange market in order to maintain orderly trading conditions rather than to maintain a specific exchange rate.

Specialized Markets

Foreign exchange transactions take place in a number of specialized markets. Here we discuss three of them: the black market, the currency futures market, and the currency options market.

Black Market.   The black market cannot exist under the freely flexible exchange system, because exchange rates are determined by supply and demand without government intervention. It is important to recognize, however, that more or less stringent official restrictions prevent the free play of the market forces for the great majority of the world's 150-odd monetary units. A black market often exists in countries where currencies are pegged and exchange controls are imposed. When a particular black market is illegal, there is usually a large difference between the official rate and the black market rate. Nevertheless, multinational companies should not operate in the black market, not only because it is illegal, but also because it is not easy to arrange large transfers of money in the black market.

Currency Futures Market. The International Monetary Market (IMM) was established in 1972 by the Chicago Mercantile Exchange to facilitate futures trading in foreign currencies. The IMM was conceived as an extension of an already well-established commodity futures market in which specific quantities of corn, soybeans, and wheat were traded for delivery at specified future dates. This market is a good source of funds for multinational companies, but it is relatively small and inflexible. In spite of its drawbacks, the rapid growth of trading in futures contracts for foreign currencies is one of the most remarkable developments in financial markets in recent years.

Currency Options Market. Another specialized exchange market is the foreign-currency options market. The Philadelphia Stock Exchange started currency options trading in 1983; in addition, some commercial banks have just begun to offer currency options trading. Currency options are traded in standard contracts half the size of the IMM futures contracts. A currency option is simply a contract that gives the holder the right to buy or sell a foreign currency at a specified price during a prescribed period. Currency options do not need to be exercised at maturity, but payment and delivery in futures contracts are required at maturity.

Spot and Forward Exchange Rates

The foreign exchange market employs both spot and forward exchange rates. The spot rate is the rate paid for delivery of a currency within two business days after the day of the trade. Most currency transactions take place in the spot market. The forward rate is the rate to be paid for delivery of a currency at some future date. The exchange rate is established at the time the contract is made, but payment and delivery are not required until maturity. Forward rates are usually quoted for fixed periods of 30, 90, or 180 days from the day of the contract. In some instances, actual contracts in major currencies can be arranged for delivery at any specified date up to one year.

Foreign Exchange Quotation

Most foreign exchange quotations are made in the number of units of local currency required to buy one unit of a foreign currency. Hence, the United States quotes its exchange rates in dollars which can be exchanged for one unit of foreign exchange, for instance, $0.5938/DM. Thus, the quotation "$0.5938/DM" means that we can buy one German mark for $0.5938. The major exception to this practice is England, which quotes its foreign exchange rates in terms of foreign monetary units required to purchase one pound.

Practically all major newspapers in the world, such as *The Wall Street Journal* and the *London Financial Times*, print a daily list of exchange rates. Table 5-1 shows the spot rates for a selected number of currencies which appeared in *The Wall Street Journal* on one recent Thursday. Because there is a one-day time lag between the transactions of foreign exchange and the

Table 5-1
Spot Rates for a Number of Currencies

Currency (1)	U.S. $ Equivalent (2)	Currency per U.S. $ (3)
Argentina (Peso)	.0005405	1850.00
Australia (Dollar)	.7703	1.2982
Austria (Schilling)	.08432	11.86
Brazil (Cruzeiro)	.05669	17.65
Britain (Pound)	1.6790	.5956
Canada (Dollar)	.8428	1.1865
China (Yuan)	.211793	4.7216
Colombia (Peso)	.002298	435.13
France (Franc)	.17484	5.7195
Germany (Mark)	.5938	1.6841
Hong Kong (Dollar)	.13802	7.8110
India (Rupee)	.05921	16.89
Italy (Lira)	.0007988	1251.88
Japan (Yen)	.006925	144.40
Mexico (Peso)	.003690	2710.03
Norway (Krone)	.1534	6.5200
Saudia Arabia (Riyal)	.26681	3.7480
Singapore (Dollar)	.5386	1.8567
South Korea (Won)	.0014854	685.68
Switzerland (Franc)	.6667	1.5000
Thailand (Baht)	.38270	26.13
Venezuela (Bolivar)	.02299	43.50
SDR	1.32559	.75438
ECU	1.21215	—

Source: *The Wall Street Journal.*

report of these transactions, we obtained the Wednesday quotations from the Thursday issue of *The Wall Street Journal*. Column 2 in Table 5-1 shows the amount of U.S. dollars required to buy one unit of foreign currency. Given this amount, we can determine the number of foreign currency units required to buy one U.S. dollar. This conversion can be achieved by simply taking the reciprocal of the given quotation. For example:

$$\$0.5938/DM \text{ is identical with } \$1 = \frac{DM1}{\$0.5938} = DM1.6841$$

In other words, the relationship between U.S. dollars and German marks can be expressed in two different ways, but they have the same meaning: (1) we can buy one German mark for $0.5938, or (2) we can buy 1.6841 German marks for $1.00. Column 3 presents the reciprocals of the exchange rates in Column 2. Column 3 equals 1.0 divided by Column 2.

Cross Rates

Most currencies are quoted against the U.S. dollar, but there are instances where multinational companies should know the exchange rate between two non-U.S. currencies. For example, if a British company needs Canadian dollars to buy Canadian goods, it may want to know the exchange rate between the Canadian dollar and the British pound. Because most currency pairs are not traded actively, their exchange rate is determined through their relationship to a widely traded third currency such as the U.S. dollar. The type of exchange rate desired here is known as the cross rate because it reflects the value of one foreign currency against another foreign currency.

Once we understand how two currencies in an exchange quote can be converted into each other, we can learn how the relationships among three or more currencies are reflected in exchange quotes. The last row in Table 5-2 shows that the dollar price of the British pound is $1.6775 per pound and that the dollar price of the Canadian dollar is $0.84232 per Can$. To determine the price of pounds in terms of Canadian dollars or the price of Canadian dollars in terms of pounds, one must convert both quotations to a common denominator, i.e., the U.S. dollar:

$$\$1.6775/\pounds: \pounds1/\$1.6775 = \pounds0.59613/\$$$

$$\$0.84232/Can\$: Can\$1/\$0.84232 = Can\$1.1872/\$$$

If the prices of dollars are quoted in terms of both pounds and Canadian dollars, we can obtain the price of pounds in terms of Canadian dollars:

$$Can\$/\pounds = \frac{1.1872}{.59613} = Can\$1.9915/\pounds$$

Similarly, we can determine the price of Canadian dollars in terms of pounds:

$$\pounds/Can\$ = \frac{.59613}{1.1872} = \pounds0.50213/Can\$$$

Table 5–2
Key Currency Cross Rates

	Dollar	Pound	Yen	Lira	DMark	FFranc	CdnDlr
Canada	1.1872	1.9916	.00822	.00095	.70394	.20723	. . . .
France	5.7290	9.610	.03966	.00457	3.3970	. . . .	4.8256
Germany	1.6865	2.8291	.01167	.00135	. . . .	.29438	1.4206
Italy	1253.3	2102.3	8.675	. . . .	743.11	218.76	1055.6
Japan	144.46	242.33	. . . .	.11527	85.657	25.216	121.68
U.K.	.59613	. . . .	.00413	.00048	.35347	.10405	.50213
U.S.	. . . .	1.6775	.00692	.00080	.59294	0.1754	.84232

Source: *The Wall Street Journal.*

The exchange rate between two currencies is called the **cross rate** if it is obtained from the rates of these two currencies in terms of a third currency. Table 5-2 shows key currency cross rates.

Forward Exchange Quotation: Forward Exchange Rate

Table 5-3 shows the forward rates for Canadian dollars and German marks along with the spot rates from Table 5-1. The current spot rate and the forward rate may be the same during a period of foreign exchange stability. However, there usually is a difference between the spot rate and the forward rate; this difference is known as the spread.

Forward quotations are made either "outright" or in terms of the spread on the spot rate. Table 5-3 shows that the 90-day outright forward quotation is $0.8344 per Can$ for Canadian dollars and $0.5939 per DM for German marks. The spread is stated in terms of points; one point equals 0.01 percent or $0.0001. Point quotations for the two 90-day forward rates are determined as follows:

Spot or Forward Rate	Canadian Dollars	German Marks
90-day forward rate	$0.8344	$0.5939
Less: spot rate	0.8428	0.5938
90-day forward quote in points	-84	+1

In giving a forward quote for the Canadian dollar, a trader might say "minus 84" or "a discount of 84." For the German mark, the trader would say "plus 1" or "a premium of 1." Thus, when the forward rate is less than the spot rate, it is said to be at a discount. When the forward rate is greater than the spot rate, it is said to be at a premium. Outright quotations are normally used for retail customers of the bank, while point quotations are usually employed for traders.

Table 5-3
Spot and Forward Rates

Spot or Forward Rate	Canadian Dollars	German Marks
Spot rate	$0.8428	$0.5938
30-day forward rate	0.8399	0.5939
90-day forward rate	0.8344	0.5939
180-day forward rate	0.8280	0.5939

Source: *The Wall Street Journal.*

Forward premium or discount is sometimes expressed in terms of the annualized percentage deviation from the spot rate. The premium or discount is computed by the following formula:

$$Premium\ (discount)\ =\ \frac{n\text{--}day\ forward\ rate\ -\ spot\ rate}{spot\ rate}\ \times\ \frac{360}{n} \qquad (5\text{--}1)$$

Applying Equation 5-1 to the 90-day forward quote for Canadian dollars, we obtain:

$$Forward\ discount\ =\ \frac{\$0.8344\ -\ \$0.8428}{\$0.8428}\ \times\ \frac{360}{90}$$

$$=\ -0.0399\ \text{or}\ -3.99\%$$

Applying Equation 5-1 to the 90-day forward quote for German marks, we obtain:

$$Forward\ premium\ =\ \frac{\$0.5939\ -\ \$0.5938}{\$0.5938}\ \times\ \frac{360}{90}$$

$$=\ +0.0007\ \text{or}\ +0.07\%$$

Key Reasons for Forward Exchange Transactions

Actual exchange market participants are banks, companies, individuals, governments, and other financial institutions. However, these participants are called arbitragers, traders, hedgers, or speculators, depending on the purpose of their participation in the exchange market. Arbitragers seek to earn riskless profits by taking advantage of differences in interest rates among countries. Traders use forward contracts to eliminate possible exchange losses on export or import orders denominated in foreign currencies. Hedgers, mostly multinational companies, engage in forward contracts to protect the home-currency value of foreign-currency denominated assets and liabilities. Speculators deliberately expose themselves to exchange risk by engaging in forward contracts in order to make a profit from exchange rate fluctuations.

Individuals and corporations buy and sell forward currencies to provide protection against future changes in exchange rates. So long as we do not have a single world currency, some degree of exchange risk exists in any system. We cannot eliminate some possibility of foreign exchange losses in either the fixed exchange-rate system or the flexible exchange-rate system.

Example 5–1. Assume that an American firm purchases machinery through its U.K. branch for £10,000 with terms of 90 days. Let us also assume that the spot rate for pounds is $1.70 per pound and the 90-day forward rate for pounds is $1.80 per pound. Payment should be made in British pounds 90 days from the day of the shipment.

Actually, there are two alternative ways of payment available to the American firm. First, it could buy pounds in the spot market 90 days from the day of the shipment to pay the credit. If the spot rate for pounds rises to $2.00 during this time, the American firm should spend $20,000 to buy the sum of £10,000. Second, the firm could also buy £10,000 in the forward market for $18,000 to pay the credit on the due date. By so doing, the American firm would avoid the risk of a $2,000 loss ($20,000 - $18,000). However, if the spot rate for pounds declines to $1.50 during this period, the American firm would lose $3,000 ($15,000 - $18,000) under the forward contract.

Speculation in the Foreign Exchange Market

Foreign exchange markets facilitate both commercial and private transactions such as foreign trade, loans, and investments. In addition, they give rise to exchange speculation. The purpose of speculation in the foreign exchange market is to make a profit from exchange-rate fluctuations by deliberately taking an uncovered position. Speculation can be undertaken on both the spot market and the forward market.

Speculating in the Spot Market.
Suppose a speculator anticipates that the spot rate of the German mark will appreciate in 90 days. The speculator will purchase marks at today's spot rate, will hold them for 90 days, and will resell them at a higher rate.

Example 5–2. The present spot rate for marks is $0.4000 per mark. A speculator's expectation of the spot rate for marks in 90 days is $0.4500. If the speculator's expectation proves correct, what would be his dollar profit from speculating $10,000 in the spot market?

With $10,000, the speculator could buy DM25,000 ($10,000/$0.4000) in the spot market, hold them for 90 days, and resell them at $0.4500 per mark for a gross of $11,250 (DM25,000 x $0.4500). As a result, the speculator would earn a net profit of $1,250 or 12.50 percent on the original $10,000 of capital. But spot speculation is risky. If the spot rate declines to $0.3500 during this period, the DM25,000 would have an ending value of $8,750 (DM25,000 x $0.3500) for a net loss of $1,250. Theoretically speaking, no limit exists to the potential profit, but the maximum loss would be $10,000.

A speculator is not locked into an absolute 90-day terminal date but may simply hold it until a date that seems to be most profitable. This is possible because the speculator could close out the position before 90 days or hold it longer than 90 days if his expectation changes after the spot purchase.

Speculating in the Forward Market.
Suppose a speculator anticipates that the German mark's spot rate in 90 days will exceed its 90-day forward rate as quoted today. The speculator buys marks for 90-day future delivery at today's forward rate, waits for 90 days, and then sells the marks spot to close the position.

Example 5–3. The present 90-day forward rate for marks is $0.4300. A speculator's expectation of the spot rate for marks in 90 days is $0.4500. If the speculator's expectation proves correct, what would be his dollar profit from speculating $10,000 in the forward market?

The speculator could buy DM23,256 forward for $10,000 at the forward quotation of $0.4300, receive them in 90 days, and then sell them at the spot rate of $0.4500 for a gross of $10,465. Profit would be $465. The profit of $465 in this case cannot be related to any investment base to determine a rate of return because no capital was invested at the time the contract was entered.

Clearly, there is greater risk for a speculator in forward transaction than in spot transaction. Forward market speculation involves a more remote payment date and a greater chance of unfavorable fluctuations. There are two types of risk here. The first risk is the possibility that foreign exchange rates will fluctuate. The second risk is the possibility that the forward contract will not be carried out. The first risk will affect the speculator only if he carries an open position in the forward contract. The speculator can eliminate this risk by purchasing an offsetting forward contract. Although the speculator has a net position of zero, he still carries the second risk because he stands in the middle.

Theories of Exchange–Rate Determination

In this section, specific attention is given to the theory of foreign exchange-rate determination. This theory is based on a relationship between the money market and the foreign exchange market; this relationship prevails without restrictions imposed by government policy on the extent to which rates can move. Such a free market situation will establish the nature of interrelationships among the money markets and the foreign exchange markets. In other words, we can postulate a simple set of equilibrium relationships that should hold among inflation rates, interest rates, spot rates, and forward rates. This idea, commonly known as the law of one price, is enforced by arbitragers who, by following the famous dictum of "buy low, sell high," prevent all but minor deviations from equality.

There are five major theories of exchange-rate determination:

1. The Theory of Purchasing Power Parity.
2. The Fisher Effect.

3. The International Fisher Effect.
4. The Theory of Interest-Rate Parity.
5. The Forward Rate as an Unbiased Predictor of the Future Spot Rate.

It is important to remember that the economic relationships of these five theories result from arbitrage activities.

Efficient Exchange Markets

Investors make risk-return decisions in the framework of available exchange markets. We base our discussion of the theories of exchange-rate determination on the assumption of efficient exchange markets. Efficient exchange markets exist when exchange rates reflect all available information and adjust quickly to new information. Because exchange markets are highly competitive in such a situation, the market participants buy and sell foreign exchange in a way that eliminates all profits in excess of the minimum required to sustain their continued participation. In other words, the concept of efficient exchange markets depends on three hypotheses:

1. Market prices such as product prices, interest rates, spot rates, and forward rates should reflect the market's consensus estimate of the future spot rate.
2. Investors should not earn unusually large profits in forward speculation. Because exchange-rate forecasts based on market prices are accurate, publicly available forecasts of the future spot rate do not lead to unusual profits in forward speculation.
3. It is impossible for any market analyst to beat the market consistently.

Certainly, these conditions are not completely met in practice. Thus, exchange markets are assumed to be efficient if the conditions are only reasonably met. There are many indications that support the efficient market assumption for international money and exchange markets. First, foreign currencies and other financial assets are traded by companies and individuals who have broad market contacts, sophisticated analytical capabilities, and modern communications. Because new information is widely, quickly, and cheaply disseminated to investors, market prices are rapidly adjusted to reflect significant developments. Second, since 1973 the major trading countries of the world have adopted the system of freely floating rates, and their governmental interference in exchange markets has been minimal.

Market Equilibrium

Exchange rates represent prices of one currency in terms of another currency. In a free market, the rates are determined by the forces of supply and demand, just like other market prices.

Demand for foreign exchange comes from debit items in the balance of payments, such as imports. As the foreign exchange rate falls, the corresponding quantity of the foreign exchange demanded rises. Alternatively, as the exchange rate increases, the corresponding quantity demanded falls. In short, there is an inverse relationship between exchange rate and quantity demanded. This inverse relationship explains why the demand curve for foreign exchange is downward–sloping.

The supply of foreign exchange comes from credit items in the balance of payments such as exports. As the foreign exchange rate falls, the corresponding quantity of foreign exchange supplied falls. As the exchange rate increases, the corresponding quantity supplied also increases. This direct relationship between exchange rate and quantity supplied explains why the supply curve for foreign exchange is upward–sloping.

Figure 5–1 shows the downward–sloping demand curve D and the upward–sloping supply curve S. The intersection of these two curves indicates the equilibrium exchange rate (E1) and quantity (Q1). If the actual exchange rate is below the equilibrium point E1, it will rise because demand exceeds supply. If the actual exchange rate is above point E1, it will fall because supply exceeds demand.

Demand for foreign exchange and its supply could change over time. These changes cause demand and supply schedules to shift upward or downward. For example, an increase in imports of goods priced in foreign

Figure 5–1
Market Determination of Exchange Rates

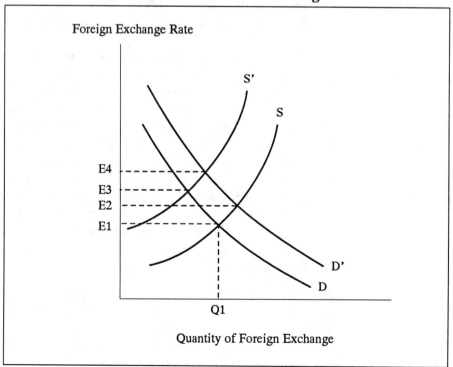

currencies and a rise in prices of such goods may cause a shift of the demand curve for foreign exchange to the right. If the demand curve shifts from D to D', the equilibrium exchange rate rises to E2. In contrast, a decrease in exports of goods priced in foreign currencies and a reduction in prices of such goods may shift the supply curve to the left. If the supply curve shifts from S to S', the equilibrium exchange rate rises to E3. What happens to the equilibrium exchange rate if the demand curve D and the supply curve S shift to D' and S' simultaneously? The equilibrium exchange rate would rise still further, to E4.

The Theory of Purchasing Power Parity

The theory of purchasing power parity (PPP) in its simplest form holds that the exchange rate must change in terms of a single currency so as to equate the prices of goods in both countries. For example, if the prices of Japanese goods rise relative to the prices of U.S. goods, the Japanese yen should depreciate to keep the dollar price of goods in Japan the same as the dollar prices of identical goods in the United States. Otherwise, arbitragers would have an incentive to purchase goods in the United States and sell them in Japan until these prices were again equalized.

The PPP theory has an absolute version and a relative version. The absolute version of the PPP theory maintains that the equilibrium exchange rate between domestic and foreign currencies equals the ratio between domestic and foreign prices. To illustrate, assume that one American dollar can buy two bushels of wheat and that one Dutch guilder can buy one bushel of wheat. In the United States, exchange rates are quoted in terms of dollars required to buy one unit of the Dutch guilder, or the exchange rate is $0.50 per guilder.

The relative version of the PPP doctrine indicates that in the long run, exchange rates reflect the relative purchasing power of currencies. In other words, it relates equilibrium changes in the exchange rate to changes in the ratio of domestic and foreign prices.

Example 5–4.   This time, let us assume that the exchange rate between U.S. dollars and British pounds is $2 per pound. Let us further accept the fact that the United States will have an inflation rate of 10 percent for the coming year and that England will have an inflation rate of 20 percent over the same period.

The PPP theory suggests that the U.S. dollar should increase in value by 10 percent relative to the British pound. The new exchange rate of $1.83 per pound is obtained in this way:

$$\textit{New exchange rate} \; = \; \frac{\$2\,(1+0.10)}{£1\,(1+0.20)} \; = \; \$1.83/£$$

If a country experiences higher inflation rates than its major trading partners, its exports will become more expensive, and its imports will become relatively less costly. This combination will lead a country with higher inflation rates to develop a deficit in its balance of payments. This deficit will put downward pressure on the country's spot rate, because its demand for foreign currency to settle its imports will be greater than other countries' demand for the country's currency for the same purpose. Simultaneously, the additional supply of imports in a country has a depressing effect on its overall price level. Normally, an increased supply of relatively inexpensive imports should reduce the inflation rate in the country. Thus, the PPP theory works on both exchange–rate and relative price levels to restore equilibrium in the balance of payments between countries.

Appraisal of the PPP Theory. The PPP theory not only explains how relative inflation rates between two countries can influence their exchange rate, but it can also be used to forecast exchange rates. It is important to remember that the PPP doctrine is supposed to work well under a freely floating exchange–rate system. With the termination of the fixed exchange–rate system in 1973, the relative price levels and exchange rates in most industrial countries have fluctuated widely. The experience of 1975–1992 indicates that, while movements in dollar exchange rates for some major currencies reflected differences in inflation rates, that was not the case for sharp short–period fluctuations in these rates. In addition, the PPP theory did not work that well for some other currencies.

There are some obvious weaknesses of the PPP theory. First, it assumes that goods are identical across countries and are readily transported for arbitrage purposes. This is not the case for such goods as housing and medical services. The PPP theory, moreover, relies on an index of prices such as the consumer price index. Such an index may be misleading because only traded goods directly affect the balance on goods and services. However, even non–traded goods indirectly affect the price of traded goods through their impact on the overall cost of living and on wage demands.

Second, we must compare a similar basket of goods in each country with its trading partners in order to test the PPP theory. If we try to compare the prices of dissimilar goods, we have to rely on price indexes. It then becomes a question of which index is most reflective of goods traded between countries.

Third, many other factors influence exchange rates besides relative prices. These include relative interest rates, relative income levels, government interference in the foreign exchange market, and multiple currency practices such as the joint floating system of the European Community. Thus, it is difficult to measure the precise magnitude of exchange rate movements attributable to differences in inflation rates.

In spite of these limitations, the PPP theory is quite useful and seems to be valid over the long run. If a country's inflation rate remains higher than that of its trading partners for a long period, that country's currency will tend to depreciate in order to prevent the country from being out of the export market. According to many empirical studies, this fact exists whether it is caused by the PPP theory alone or by a combination of factors.

The Fisher Effect

The Fisher Effect, named after the economist Irving Fisher, assumes that the nominal interest rate in each country consists of a real interest rate and an expected rate of inflation. The real interest rate is determined by the productivity in an economy and a risk premium commensurate with the risk of a borrower. The nominal interest rate embodies an inflation premium sufficient to compensate lenders or investors for an expected loss of purchasing power. Consequently, nominal interest rates are higher when people expect higher rates of inflation and are lower when people expect lower rates of inflation.

The real interest rate is thought to be relatively stable over time. Moreover, in a free market where investors can buy any interest-bearing securities, real interest rates are identical everywhere, but nominal interest rates will vary by the difference in expected rates of inflation. The Fisher Effect asserts that real interest rates are equalized across countries through arbitrage. For example, if expected real rates of interest were higher in Germany than in the United States, capital would flow from the United States to Germany. On the other hand, if real rates of interest were higher in the United States than in Germany, capital would flow from Germany to the United States. This process of arbitrage would continue, in the absence of government intervention, until expected real rates of interest are equalized in both countries.

Appraisal of the Fisher Effect.

Empirical studies have found that most of the variation in nominal interest rates, particularly for short-term government securities, can be attributed to changing inflationary expectations. The hypothesis of the Fisher Effect, based on long-term securities, suffers from an increased financial risk inherent in fluctuations of a bond market value prior to maturity. Comparisons of corporate securities are influenced by unequal creditworthiness of the issuers. In addition, changes in long-term interest rates and changes in inflation rates are not concurrent because long-term rates relative to short-term rates are not that sensitive to changes in prices. However, the Fisher Effect based on long-term maturities has worked fairly well in recent years. First, long-term interest rates, adjusted for inflation, have been relatively stable in most industrial countries since 1980. Second, long-term real rates of interest in most countries have been relatively close together since 1980.

The International Fisher Effect

The International Fisher Effect states that the future spot rate should move in an equal amount but in a different direction to the difference in interest rates between two countries. A future spot rate of a currency with a higher interest rate would depreciate in the long run; a future spot rate of a currency with a lower interest rate would appreciate in the long run.

When investors purchase the currency of a country to take advantage of higher interest rates abroad, they must also consider any possible losses due to fluctuations in the value of the foreign currency prior to maturity of their investment. To clarify this point, assume that interest rates are higher in the United Kingdom than in the United States. In this case, U.S. investors in U.K. securities must be rewarded with a higher interest rate to offset the expected depreciation of a spot rate for the pound when they convert the principal and interest into dollars. U.K. investors in U.S. securities must be rewarded with a higher future spot rate for the dollar to offset the lower interest rate in the United States. In other words, the International Fisher Effect holds that the interest differential between two countries should be an unbiased predictor of the future change in the spot rate.

Short-Run Behavior.   The relationship between interest rates and exchange rates is complex, incorporating numerous behavioral parameters. The short-run behavior of interest and exchange rates, quite contrary to their long-run behavior, shows that a rise in interest rates in a given country is expected to raise the value of that country's currency, and vice versa. In other words, currencies of countries with higher interest rates than the United States tend to appreciate in value against the dollar. Higher interest rates in a given country would raise the value of its currency because higher interest rates could attract capital from investors in other countries. By the same token, currencies of countries with lower interest rates than the United States tend to depreciate in value against the dollar. Hence, the exchange rate moves in the same direction to the difference in interest rates between two countries.

The Theory of Interest-Rate Parity

The movement of short-term funds between two countries to take advantage of interest differentials is a major determinant of the spread between forward and spot rates. According to the interest parity theory, the spread between a forward rate and a spot rate should be equal but opposite in sign to the difference in interest rates between two countries. In a free market, the currency with the higher interest rate would sell at a discount in the forward market; the currency with the lower interest rate would sell at a premium in the forward market. In fact, the forward discount or premium is closely related to the interest differential between the two currencies.

The interest parity theory holds that the difference between a forward rate and a spot rate equals the difference between a domestic interest rate and a foreign interest rate:

$$\frac{n\text{-}day\ F - S}{S} \times \frac{360}{n} = i_d - i_f \qquad (5\text{-}2)$$

where:

$n\text{-}day\ F$ = n-day forward rate
S = spot rate
i_d = domestic interest rate
i_f = foreign interest rate

Example 5–5.   Let us assume four things: (1) the German interest rate = 9 percent; (2) the U.S. interest rate = 7 percent; (3) the spot rate for the German mark = $0.4000; and (4) the 180-day forward rate for the German mark = $0.3960.

In this case, the percentage discount on the 180-day forward rate is equal to the interest rate differential:

$$\frac{\$0.3960 - \$0.4000}{\$0.4000} \times \frac{360}{180} = 0.07 - 0.09$$

$$-0.02 = -0.02$$

German securities would earn 2 percent more than the American securities, but German marks sell in the forward market at a 2 percent discount.

This outcome is brought about by arbitragers who enter into forward contracts to avoid the exchange-rate risk. If interest rates are higher in Germany than in the United States, arbitragers in search of a higher yield could move their funds from the United States to Germany. In order to avoid the exchange-rate risk at maturity, the arbitragers would sell the marks in exchange for dollars in the forward market. Consequently, the forward rate for the German mark with the higher interest rate would depreciate; the forward rate for the U.S. dollar with the lower interest rate would appreciate. Such transactions will continue until the interest differential in favor of Germany is equal to the forward discount for the German mark. Under this condition, there is no incentive for capital to move in either direction because the interest differential is offset by the forward discount.

The Forward Rate and the Future Spot Rate

If speculators think that a forward rate is higher than their prediction of a future spot rate, they will sell the foreign currency forward. This speculative transaction will bid down the forward rate until it equals the expected future spot rate. By the same token, if speculators believe that a forward rate is lower than an expected future spot rate, they will buy a foreign currency forward. This speculative transaction will bid up the forward rate until it reaches the expected future spot rate. Under this condition, there is no longer any incentive to buy or sell a foreign currency forward, because forward rates are unbiased predictors of future spot rates.

Synthesis of Exchange–Rate Determination Theories

In the absence of predictable exchange-market intervention by central banks, an expected rate of change in a spot rate, differential rates of national inflation and interest, and forward premiums or discounts are all directly proportional to each other. Because money, capital, and exchange markets are efficient, these variables adjust very quickly to changes in any one of them. Consequently, the forward rate is the best possible forecaster of the future spot rate.

Example 5–6. Let us assume the following:

1. The spot rate for the German mark: DM1 = $0.4000.
2. The one–year forward rate for the German mark: DM1 = $0.3800.
3. The expected spot rate in one year for the German mark: DM1 = $0.3800.
4. The expected rate of inflation for one year: Germany = 10 percent; U.S. = 5 percent.
5. Interest rates on one-year government securities: Germany = 12 percent; U.S. = 7 percent.

Discuss the relationships among spot rates, forward rates, inflation rates, and interest rates, using these five assumptions.

First, the PPP theory holds that any change in the differential rate of inflation between two countries tends to be offset by an equal but opposite change in the spot rate. A 5 percent higher rate of inflation in Germany is offset by a 5 percent depreciation in the spot rate for the mark. This 5 percent depreciation in the spot rate for the mark is computed as follows:

$$\frac{0.3800 - 0.4000}{0.4000} = -0.05 \text{ or } -5\%$$

Second, the Fisher Effect suggests that real interest rates are identical everywhere and that nominal interest rates will vary by the difference in expected rates of inflation. The real inflation-adjusted interest rate in both countries is 2 percent. The nominal interest rate in Germany (12 percent) is 5 percent higher than the nominal interest rate in the United States (7 percent). This difference is identical to the 5 percent difference in expected rates of inflation between Germany (10 percent) and the United States (5 percent).

Third, the International Fisher Effect states that a future spot rate should move in an equal amount but in the opposite direction to the difference in interest rates between two countries. The 5 percent interest differential in favor of Germany is equal to the 5 percent depreciation in the future spot rate for the mark.

Fourth, the interest parity theory assumes that the spread between the forward rate and the spot rate should be equal but opposite in sign to the difference in interest rates between the two countries. The 5 percent higher rate of interest in Germany is consistent with the 5 percent forward discount for the German mark [(0.3800 − 0.4000)/0.40000 = −5 percent].

Finally, under a freely floating exchange system, the forward rate is an unbiased predictor of the future spot rate. The one-year forward rate of $0.3800 for the mark is identical with the expected spot rate in one year of $0.3800 for the mark. This means that the 5 percent one-year forward discount for the mark is an unbiased predictor that the mark will depreciate by 5 percent over the next year.

Figure 5-2 illustrates these five key theories of exchange-rate determination and their relationships on the basis of Example 5-6: the theory of purchasing power parity (Relationship A), the Fisher Effect (Relationship B), the International Fisher Effect (Relationship C), the theory of interest-rate parity (Relationship D), and the forward rate as an unbiased predictor of the future spot rate (Relationship E). Relationship F does not represent any particular theory, but it has to be true by definition if Relationships A-E are all true. This framework emphasizes the links that exist among spot exchange rates, forward rates, interest rates, and inflation rates.

Figure 5-2
Relationships Among Various Financial Rates

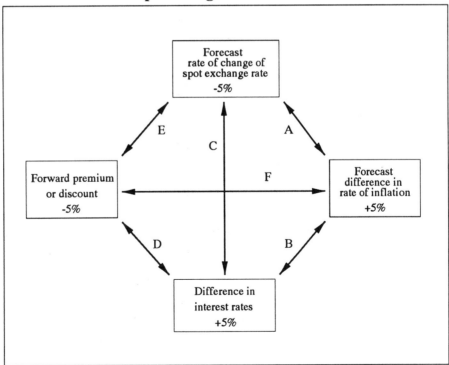

Arbitrages

Arbitrage is the purchase of something in one market and its sale in another market to take advantage of a price differential. Professional arbitragers quickly transfer funds from one currency to another in order to profit from discrepancies between exchange rates in different markets. The process of arbitrage also works through the foreign exchange market to bring interest rates in national markets closer together. Even small discrepancies between the exchange rates and interest rates in different markets would motivate enough arbitrage to eliminate these discrepancies quickly.

Geographic Arbitrage

In principle, the exchange rate for a given currency should be the same in every geographic market. But local demand-and-supply conditions might create temporary discrepancies among various markets. Arbitrage specialists would buy the currency in a market where its price is lower and then sell the currency where its price is higher. If the exchange rate differential is larger than the transaction cost, an arbitrage profit would be made.

Two–Point Arbitrage. A two-point arbitrage is the arbitrage transaction between two currencies. Suppose, for example, that the quotes of the French franc against the U.S. dollar are $0.20 in New York and $0.25 in Paris. The price of francs in terms of dollars is higher in Paris than in New York. An arbitrager could benefit by buying francs with dollars in New York and then selling the francs in exchange for dollars in Paris. Arbitrage tends to wipe out the exchange rate differential that originally triggered it. The purchase of francs in New York would drive the price of francs against the dollar up toward the Paris rate. The sale of francs in Paris would drive the price of francs against the dollar down toward the New York rate. This arbitrage process would continue until the price of francs in terms of the dollar is the same in both markets.

The basic economic principle of "buy low-sell high" dominates the arbitrage transaction of buying and selling currencies in two national money markets. Exchange rates in two different locations must be stated in a given currency if this principle is to be applied in foreign exchange. Thus, the arbitrage process becomes slightly more difficult to understand if exchange rates are quoted in different currencies. Let us restate our previous example in a slightly different way. The price of francs against the dollar is $0.20 in New York. The price of dollars against the franc is FF4 in Paris. The quotes in both locations in terms of $/FF are as follows:

New York	Paris
$0.20/FF (as initially given)	$0.25/FF (1/4)

The franc enjoys a higher price against the dollar in Paris than in New York. This price differential leads to the following transactions in each market.

1. In New York, investors would buy francs and sell dollars.
2. In Paris, investors would sell francs and buy dollars.

A Three-Point Arbitrage.

A three-point arbitrage, commonly known as a triangle arbitrage, is the arbitrage transaction among three currencies. This type of arbitrage can occur if any of the three cross rates is out of line. Consider the possibility that the cross rates of exchange are BF60/$, BF10/SK, and SK3/$. An arbitrager could make a profit of $1. She would buy 60 Belgian francs for $1, then purchase six Swedish kronas for 60 Belgian francs, and finally buy $2 for the six kronas. Such large transactions would strengthen the franc against the dollar, strengthen the krona against the franc, and strengthen the dollar against the krona. This arbitrage process causes some consistent patterns of rates to emerge at which no further arbitrage would be profitable. In other words, the arbitrage will continue until dollars can no longer be bought more cheaply in one market than the price at which they are sold in another market. Currency cross rates such as those given in Table 5-2 can be prepared to ensure that the exchange rates are consistent with each other in all markets.

Covered-Interest Arbitrage

When investors purchase the currency of a foreign country to take advantage of higher interest rates abroad, they must also consider any losses or gains. Such losses and gains might occur due to fluctuations in the value of the foreign currency prior to the maturity of their investment. Generally, investors cover against such potential losses by contracting for the future sale or purchase of a foreign currency in the forward market.

Their actions, aimed at profits from interest rate differentials between countries, lead, in equilibrium, to the condition of so-called interest parity. The interest parity theory says that any exchange gains or losses incurred by a simultaneous purchase and sale in the spot and forward markets are offset by the interest rate differential on similar assets. Under these conditions, there is no incentive for capital to move in either direction because the effective returns on foreign and domestic assets have been equalized.

Figure 5-3 presents a graphic representation of the theoretical relationship between the forward premium or discount and the interest rate differential. The vertical axis represents the interest differential in favor of the foreign currency and the horizontal axis shows the forward premium or discount on that currency. The interest parity line shows the equilibrium state. This chapter ignores transaction costs for simplicity. However, it is important to recognize the fact that transaction costs cause the interest parity line to be a band rather than a thin line. Transaction costs include the foreign exchange brokerage costs on spot and forward contracts as well as the investment brokerage cost on buying and selling securities.

Figure 5–3
Covered Interest Arbitrage

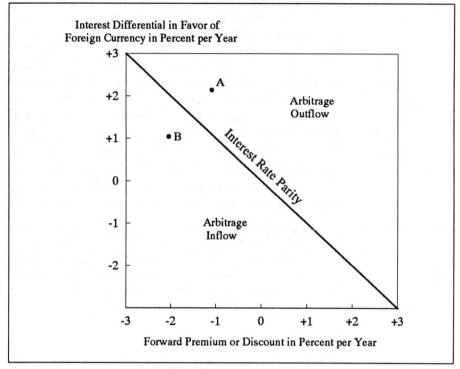

Point A of Figure 5–3 shows that the forward discount for foreign exchange is 1 percent and that the foreign interest rate is 2 percent higher than the domestic interest rate. In this case, the arbitrager could employ the so-called covered-interest arbitrage to make a profit. If the arbitrager buys spot foreign currency with domestic currency and invests the foreign currency in foreign securities, she would earn 2 percent more than if she invested in home-country securities. Because the purchase of foreign currency with domestic currency means a flow of funds out of the country, the arbitrage transaction tends to reduce the money supply.

The arbitrager would have to convert the foreign currency to domestic currency at the end of maturity. The exchange rate may fall before the arbitrager has returned her funds to her home country. For that reason, the arbitrage transaction involves foreign exchange risks. To avoid these risks, she will cover the transaction by selling forward the same amount of the foreign currency at 1 percent discount. The investment protected by forward sales is called covered-interest arbitrage.

Net gain is usually the interest rate differential minus the discount on the sale of foreign currency in the forward market. Thus, this type of capital outflow occurs when the interest rate differential exceeds the forward discount. At Point A, the arbitrager would earn 2 percent more on her investment in foreign securities and lose 1 percent on the repurchase of the domestic currency. The net result is that the arbitrager would make a profit of 1 percent from this covered-interest arbitrage transaction.

Example 5–7. Suppose: (1) the Dutch interest rate = 10 percent; (2) the U.S. interest rate = 8 percent; (3) the spot rate for Dutch guilders = $0.3000; and (4) the 180–day forward rate for Dutch guilders = $0.2985.

The forward discount for the guilder is obtained by using Equation 5-1:

$$Forward\ discount\ =\ \frac{\$0.2985 - \$0.3000}{\$0.3000}\ \times\ \frac{360}{180}\ =\ -0.01\ or -1\%$$

The interest differential is 2 percent (10% - 8%) in favor of the Dutch guilder. The covered-interest arbitrage would work as follows:

1. Borrow dollars in the United States	- 8%
Buy guilders spot with the dollars	
2. Invest the guilders in Dutch securities	+ 10%
3. Sell guilders forward against dollars at a discount	- 1%
Net profit	+ 1%

These transactions would cause four tendencies in foreign exchange markets and money markets:

1. The spot rate of the guilder against the dollar will tend to appreciate as investors buy guilders against dollars.
2. The forward rate of the guilder against the dollar will tend to depreciate as investors sell guilders against dollars.
3. The U.S. interest rate will tend to rise as investors borrow dollars.
4. The Dutch interest rate will tend to fall as investors lend guilders.

The first two tendencies would increase the original forward discount of 1 percent toward the initial interest differential of 2 percent. The last 2 tendencies would reduce the initial interest differential of 2 percent toward the original forward discount of 1 percent. These four tendencies would continue until the forward discount for the guilder equals the interest rate differential in favor of the guilder.

At Point B of Figure 5-3, the foreign interest rate is 1 percent higher than the domestic interest rate. The cost of forward cover (forward discount) is 2 percent. In this case, the arbitrager would sell the foreign currency for the domestic currency, invest this domestic currency in home-country securities, and repurchase the foreign currency in the forward market at a discount. She loses 1 percent on this investment in home-country securities, but she earns 2 percent on the repurchase of the foreign currency. Hence, the arbitrager would make a profit of 1 percent.

Example 5–8.   Suppose: (1) the Canadian interest rate = 10 percent; (2) the U.S. interest rate = 9 percent; (3) the spot rate for Canadian dollars = $0.8500; and (4) the 180–day forward rate for Canadian dollars = $0.8415.

The forward discount for the Canadian dollar is obtained by using Equation 5–1:

$$Forward\ discount = \frac{\$0.8425 - \$0.8500}{\$0.8500} \times \frac{360}{180} = -0.02\ or\ -2\%$$

The interest differential is 1 percent (10% - 9%) in favor of the Canadian dollar. The covered–interest arbitrage would work as follows:

1.	Borrow Canadian dollars in Canada	- 10%
	Buy U.S. dollars with the Canadian dollars	
2.	Invest the U.S. dollars in U.S. securities	+ 9%
3.	Sell U.S. dollars forward at a premium	+ 2%
	Net profit	+ 1%

These transactions would cause four tendencies in foreign exchange and money markets:

1. The spot rate of the Canadian dollar will tend to depreciate as investors sell Canadian dollars against U.S. dollars.
2. The forward rate of the Canadian dollar against the U.S. dollar will tend to appreciate as investors buy Canadian dollars against U.S. dollars.
3. The U.S. interest rate will tend to fall as investors lend U.S. dollars.
4. The Canadian interest rate will tend to rise as investors borrow Canadian dollars.

The first two tendencies would reduce the original forward discount of 2 percent toward the initial interest differential of 1 percent. The last 2 tendencies would increase the initial interest differential of 1 percent toward the original forward discount of 2 percent. These forces will work until the interest rate differential equals the forward discount.

Any point above the interest parity line, such as Point A, has the following two features: (1) the first step of the arbitrage process is to borrow money in the home country, and (2) funds would move from the home country to the foreign country (arbitrage outflow). Any point below the interest parity line, such as Point B, has the following two features: (1) the first step of the arbitrage process is to borrow money in the foreign country, and (2) funds would move from the foreign country to the home country (arbitrage inflow).

The interest parity line of Figure 5–3 identifies the equilibrium position for the relationship between interest rate differentials and forward premiums or discounts. Every point on this line represents a situation in which the interest rate differential equals the forward premium or discount. In this case, arbitragers would have no incentive to transfer funds from one country to the other. However, at any point off the line, there should be an incentive to move funds from one country to another. Such transfer of funds would cause interest differentials or forward premiums (discounts) to move toward the interest parity line.

The theoretical equilibrium position exists only under a free market system. Because there are a variety of artificial barriers and intervention by government authorities in both foreign exchange and money markets, this equilibrium condition hardly exists in practice.

Summary

A major problem of multinational corporations is the fact that cash flows must cross national boundaries. These flows are subject to various constraints imposed by government authorities and exchange-rate fluctuations. Trades in currencies take place in the foreign exchange markets for immediate delivery (spot market) and future delivery (forward market). The foreign exchange market is a worldwide network of telephone and telex communications between banks.

Exchange rates represent prices of one currency in terms of another currency. They are determined by the forces of supply and demand under a free market system. A spot rate is the rate paid for delivery of a currency within two business days after the day of the trade. A forward rate is the rate at which two currencies are to be exchanged at some future date. The forward exchange rate is fixed at the time a contract is made, but payment and delivery are not required until maturity.

The five major theories of exchange-rate determination are the theory of purchasing power parity, the Fisher Effect, the International Fisher Effect, the interest parity theory, and the forward rate as an unbiased predictor of the future spot rate. These five theories illustrate the links that exist among spot rates, interest rates, inflation rates, and forward rates. In efficient exchange markets, spot exchange rates are theoretically determined by the interplay of differential national rates of inflation and interest, and the forward premium or discount.

Essentially, the PPP doctrine and the interest parity theory explain why exchange rates, in the long run, move toward positions of equilibrium in which prices in different countries and their interest rates are the same. This is because arbitragers buy currencies in one market and sell them in another market in order to take advantage of price or interest differentials prevailing at differential national markets. Thus, the process of arbitrage works through the foreign exchange market to bring inflation and interest rates in different markets closer together.

Questions

1. What are the major roles that commercial banks play in international transactions?

2. Can the black exchange market exist in the United States and Japan? How about in the Commonwealth of Independent States and Eastern European countries?

3. What is the cross rate? Why do we have to compute the cross rate?

4. When will a forward exchange contract backfire?

5. List the hypotheses that the concept of efficient exchange markets depends on.

6. Assume that the inflation rate is higher in the United States than in Japan. How should this affect the U.S. demand for Japanese yen, supply of the yen for sale, and equilibrium value of the yen?

7. Discuss some causes for deviations from purchasing power parity.

8. Assume that the interest rate is higher in Italy than in the United States. How should this affect the U.S. demand for Italian liras, supply of liras for sale, and equilibrium value of the lira?

9. Under what conditions will a higher inflation of a country lead to a corresponding increase of its interest rate?

10. If the U.S. trade balance with Germany is expected to improve next year, what is the likely relationship between the forward rate on the German mark and its current spot rate?

11. Assume that the difference between the U.S. interest rate and the Mexican interest rate is 11 percent in favor of Mexico, but the forward discount rate for the Mexican peso is 20 percent. The discrepancy between the interest differential and the forward discount seem to open incentives for arbitrage. Could it be possible to take advantage of the opportunity for covered interest arbitrage?

Problems

5-1 Assume the following exchange rates for a selected number of currencies:

Currency	U.S. $ Equivalent
Brazil (cruzeiro)	0.00900
Britain (pound)	1.9000
Canada (dollar)	0.8500
France (franc)	0.1500
Hong Kong (dollar)	0.200
Italy (lira)	0.001000
Japan (yen)	0.005000
Mexico (peso)	0.0400

(a) Determine the amount of each foreign currency required to buy one unit of the U.S. dollar.

(b) Determine £/FF, FF/¥, and ¥/£.

5-2 Assume the following exchange rates for a selected number of currencies:

Currency	U.S. $ Equivalent
Norway (krone)	5.9000
Saudi Arabia (riyal)	3.5000
South Korea (won)	700.00
Sweden (krona)	5.0000
Switzerland (franc)	2.0000
Venezuela (bolivar)	4.50
Germany (mark)	2.500

(a) Determine the amount of U.S. dollars required to buy one unit of each foreign currency.

(b) Determine KW/SK, SK/DM, and DM/SK.

5-3 Assume: (1) spot rate for Canadian dollars = $0.8089; (2) 180-day forward rate for Canadian dollars = $0.8048; (3) spot rate for German marks = $0.4285; and 180-day forward rate for German marks = $0.4407. Determine the 180-day forward discount or premium on both the Canadian dollar and the German mark.

5-4 Fill in the following blank spaces:

	British Pounds	Swiss Francs	French Francs
Direct (Outright)			
Spot	$2.0787	$0.4108	$0.2008
30-day forward		0.4120	
90-day forward		0.4144	
Points (Spread)			
30-day forward	–13		
90-day forward	–60		
Percentage Discount			
or Premium a Year			
30-day forward			–8.96%
90-day forward			–8.37%

5-5 The following quotations and expectations exist for the German mark:

Present spot rate	$0.5000
90-day forward rate	0.5200
Your expectation of the spot rate in 90 days	0.5500

(a) What is the premium or discount on the forward German mark?

(b) If your expectation proves correct, what would be your dollar profit or loss from investing $4,000 in the spot market? How much capital do you need now to carry out this operation? What are the major risks associated with this speculation?

(c) If your expectation proves correct, what would be your dollar profit or loss from investing $4,000 in the forward market? How much capital do you need now to speculate in the forward market? What are the major risks associated with the speculation?

5-6 An American firm purchases $4,000 worth of perfume (FF20,000) from a French firm. The American distributor must make the payment in 90 days in French francs. The following quotations and expectations exist for the French franc:

Present spot rate	$0.2000
90-day forward rate	0.2200
Your expectation of the spot rate in 90 days	0.2500
U.S. interest rate	15%
French interest rate	10%

(a) What is the premium or discount on the forward French franc? What is the interest differential between the United States and France? Is there an incentive for covered interest arbitrage?

(b) If there is an incentive for covered interest arbitrage, how can an arbitrager take advantage of the situation? Assume: (1) the arbitrager is willing to borrow $4,000 or FF20,000 and (2) there are no transaction costs.

(c) If transaction costs are $100, would an opportunity still exist for covered interest arbitrage?

(d) What alternatives are open to the importer if she wants to cover her transaction against the foreign exchange risk?

(e) Assume that your expectation proves correct and that the importer decides to cover this transaction. What would be the opportunity cost of each alternative? Which alternative is more attractive and why?

(f) Would you advise the American firm to cover its foreign transaction? Why or why not?

5-7   You must make a $100,000 domestic payment in Los Angeles in 90 days. You have $100,000 now and decide to invest it for 90 days either in the United States or in the United Kingdom. Assume that the following quotations and expectations exist:

Present spot rate per pound	$1.8000
90-day forward rate per pound	$1.7800
U.S. interest rate	8%
U.K. interest rate	10%

(a) Where should you invest your $100,000 to maximize your yield with no risk?

(b) Given the U.S. interest rate, the U.K. interest rate, and the spot rate, what would be an equilibrium forward exchange quotation? This equilibrium situation should provide you with no advantage or disadvantage associated with investing in one country or the other.

(c) Given the spot rate, the forward rate, and the U.S. interest rate, what is the equilibrium U.K. interest rate?

References

Adler, M., and B. Lehmann, "Deviations from Purchasing Power Parity in the Long Run," *Journal of Finance*, December 1983, pp. 1471-87.

Brunner, K., and A. H. Meltzer, eds., *Empirical Studies of Velocity, Real Exchange Rates, Unemployment and Productivity*, Carnegie-Rochester Conference 27, 1988.

Chang, C. W., and J. S. Chang, "Forward and Futures Prices: Evidence from the Foreign Exchange Markets," *Journal of Finance*, September 1990, pp. 5-18.

Copeland, L. S., *Exchange Rates and International Finance*, New York: Addison-Wesley, 1989.

Frankel, J. A., and K. A. Froot, "Using Survey Data to Test Standard Propositions Regarding Exchange Rate Expectations," *American Economic Review*, March 1987, pp. 133-53.

Froot, K. A., and J. A. Frankel, "Forward Discount Bias: Is It an Exchange Risk Premium?" *Quarterly Journal of Economics*, February 1989, pp. 139-61.

International Economic Conditions, Federal Reserve Bank of St. Louis, various issues.

Kolb, R. W., ed., *The International Financial Reader*, Miami: Kolb Publishing, 1991.

Krugman, P. R., and M. Obstfeld, *International Economics: Theory and Practice*, Glenview, IL: Scott, Foresman, 1988.

Kubarych, R. M., *Foreign Exchange Markets in the United States*, Federal Reserve Bank of New York, March 1983.

Marrinan, J., "Exchange Rate Determination: Sorting Out Theory and Evidence," *New England Economic Review*, Federal Reserve Bank of Boston, November/December 1989, pp. 39-51.

Mishkin, F. S., "Are Real Interest Rates Equal Across Countries? An Empirical Investigation of International Parity Conditions," *Journal of Finance*, December 1984, pp. 1345-57.

Sternand, J. M., and D. H. Chew, eds., *New Developments in International Finance* (Oxford: Basil Blackwell Ltd., 1988).

Stockman, A. C., "The Equilibrium Approach to Exchange Rates," *Economic Review*, Federal Reserve Bank of Richmond, March/April 1987, pp. 12–30.

Stultz, R. M., "An Equilibrium Model of Exchange Rate Imperfect Information," *Journal of Political Economy*, October 1987, pp. 1024–40.

Whitt, J. A., P. D. Koch, and J. A. Rosenweig, "The Dollar and Prices: An Empirical Analysis" *Economic Review*, Federal Reserve Bank of Kansas City, October 1986, pp. 4–18.

6
Currency Futures and Options

In recent years, financial markets have developed many new products whose popularity has become phenomenal. Measured in terms of trading volume, the growth of these products—principally futures and options—has confused traditional investors. Although active markets in futures and options contracts for physical commodities have existed for many years, these markets for foreign currencies have only recently attracted interest.

Multinational companies normally use the spot and forward markets for international transactions. They also use currency futures, currency options, and currency futures options for various corporate functions. While speculators trade currencies in these three markets for profit, multinational companies use them to cover open positions in foreign currencies.

This chapter is divided into three closely related sections. The first section discusses currency futures. With a currency futures contract, one buys or sells a specific foreign currency for delivery at a designated price in the future. The second section describes currency options. A currency option is the right to buy or sell a foreign currency at a specified price through a specified date. The third section examines currency futures options. A currency futures option is the right to buy or sell a futures contract of a foreign currency at any time for a specified period.

The Currency Futures Market

The Chicago Mercantile Exchange introduced futures trading in foreign currencies through the International Monetary Market (IMM) as an alternative to regular forward contracts offered by commercial banks. The basic mechanics of the IMM are similar to those of well-established commodity futures markets. A commodity futures contract is simply an agreement to buy or sell a specified quantity of a particular commodity for delivery on a future date at a designated price. The evolution of the futures market goes back to the 1860s when the Chicago Board of Trade required the delivery of a specified amount of grain at a particular location within a stated time. Currency futures contracts, however, are for foreign currencies, and they are entered into through a centralized market exchange such as the IMM. Futures trading in foreign exchange began on May 16, 1972. The New York Mercantile Exchange added currency futures in 1978, and the New York Stock Exchange will soon create an exchange devoted solely to currency and financial futures.

The futures market is a good source of funds for multinational companies, but it is relatively small and inflexible. In spite of its drawbacks, the rapid growth of trading in futures contracts for foreign currencies is one of the most remarkable developments in financial markets in recent years. As shown in Table 6-1, the number of currency contracts traded on the IMM increased from 145,000 in 1972 to almost 28 million in 1991.

Table 6-1
Number of Currency Futures Contracts Traded on the IMM
(thousands of contracts)

Year	BP	CD	DM	JY	SF	Other	Total
1972	15	39	19	44	18	10	145
1973	31	29	77	126	22	132	417
1974	14	4	49	7	43	104	221
1975	15	3	55	2	70	56	201
1976	33	17	45	1	37	58	191
1977	79	161	134	82	107	23	586
1978	240	208	401	362	321	26	1558
1979	514	400	451	330	494	30	2219
1980	1264	602	923	575	828	19	4211
1981	1491	476	1655	961	1519	21	6123
1982	1322	1078	1793	1762	2653	82	8690
1983	1615	559	2424	3442	3766	67	11873
1984	1444	346	5508	2335	4130	24	13787
1985	2799	469	6449	2415	4758	22	16912
1986	2701	734	6582	3970	4998	47	19032
1987	2592	915	6037	5359	5268	64	20235
1988	2616	1409	5662	6433	5283	80	21483
1989	2518	1264	8186	7824	6094	116	26002
1990	3410	1409	9169	7437	6525	105	28055
1991	3746	1139	10929	6017	5835	76	27742

Source: Chicago Mercantile Exchange, *The International Monetary Market.*

Futures Market Participants

Futures contracts are deals made now to take place in the future. In a futures contract, the buyer and the seller agree on:

1. A future delivery date.
2. The price to be paid on that future date.
3. The quantity of the currency.

The currency futures market was created for those who use foreign exchange in business. Businesses which deal with international transactions still routinely buy and sell foreign exchange in the spot market. They enter the futures market only to protect themselves against risks from volatile exchange rates. The currency futures contract is like an insurance policy against changes in exchange rates. In practice, most currency-futures contracts are nullified by opposing trades, so futures traders rarely take delivery of a foreign currency; in fact, nearly 98 percent of them are terminated before the delivery.

There are two distinct classes of traders in the currency futures market: hedgers and speculators. Hedgers include multinational companies, importers, exporters, bankers, and brokers that require protection against adverse exchange-rate movements. They expect their profits to come from managerial skills in conducting their business activities, not from incidental fluctuations in exchange rates. Speculators, on the other hand, trade futures strictly for profits; they can make or lose fortunes. A speculator trades currency futures but never uses the currency. The speculator buys and sells currency futures contracts for profit from exchange rate movements.

A hedger may place a contract with another hedger who wishes to cover currency needs in the opposite direction, but the other party to the contract typically is a speculator. Though criticized for greed, the speculator plays a vital role in futures markets by assuming the risk of the hedger. His or her presence not only gives the market liquidity and continuity but also eases entry and exit.

Currency futures trading can take place for hedging or speculation, as well as for arbitrage. In particular, some traders quickly take advantage of any profitable differential, for the same currency, between rates quoted in different markets, such as the spot market, the futures market, and the forward market.

The Futures Market and the Forward Market

Futures contracts are normally available in a pre-determined amount and for one of several specified maturity dates. As Table 6-2 shows, futures contracts are available for eight currencies with contract sizes specified by the IMM. Futures contracts mature on only four days of the year because the maturity dates occur on the third Wednesday of March, June, September, and December.

Table 6–2
Currencies Traded on the IMM and Contract Sizes

Currency	Contract Size	Initial Margin	Maintenance Margin
Australian dollar ($A)	100,000	$1,200	$ 900
British pound (£)	62,500	2,000	1,500
Canadian dollar (Can$)	100,000	700	500
Deutsche mark (DM)	125,000	1,400	1,000
French franc (F)	250,000	700	500
Japanese yen (¥)	12,500,000	1,700	1,300
Swiss franc (SF)	125,000	1,700	1,300
European Currency Unit (ECU)	125,000	2,000	1,500

While the principle of protection against currency price fluctuations is the same in the futures and forward markets, there are two major differences. First, the forward market offers contracts for specific amounts of currencies tailored to particular needs, while the futures market offers only standardized contracts in the predetermined amounts. Take, for example, an importer who wishes to cover accounts payable of DM150,000. He could cover only a portion of the risk in the futures market but could arrange for full coverage with a single contract in the forward market. Second, a forward contract can cover the exact date the foreign currency is needed, but the futures contract has a standardized delivery date. Suppose a multinational company wishes to lift its hedge before the expiration date of the futures contract. It must assume some risk of a currency price fluctuation between the settlement date of the transaction and the delivery date of the contract.

Because multinational companies have specialized needs, they normally prefer the forward contract. Consider IBM, which on April 20 realizes it will need Can$240,000 on May 20 (30 days later). If IBM tries to lock in the future purchase price of Canadian dollars with a futures contract, the closest contract settlement date is the third Wednesday of June. Also, the amount of Canadian dollars needed (Can$240,000) is more than the standardized amount (Can$100,000) specified in the contract. The best IBM can do is to buy two futures contracts (Can$200,000), but the forward market can be tailored to meet the individual needs of multinational companies. IBM can buy a forward contract of Can$240,000 with a maturity date of 30 days from the Bank of America.

Currency futures contracts and forward contracts are acquired for hedging, speculation, or arbitrage. Yet, the futures market is more centralized, standardized, and small customer-oriented than the forward market. The futures market and the forward market differ in notable ways:

1. Because the IMM specifies a maximum daily price range for each day, a participant is not exposed to more than a limited amount of daily price change. But forward contracts have no daily limits on price fluctuations.

2. IMM futures contracts are available for delivery on only one of four maturity dates per year, but banks offer forward contracts for delivery on any date.
3. The futures market offers only standardized contracts in predetermined amounts, but the forward market offers contracts for specific amounts of currencies tailored to specific needs.
4. Futures contracts tend to be smaller than forward contracts.
5. The futures market is regulated by the Commodity Futures Commission, but the forward market is self-regulating.
6. Less than 2 percent of the IMM futures contracts are settled by actual delivery, but more than 90 percent of forward contracts are settled by delivery.
7. Futures trading takes place on organized exchanges, but forward trading is negotiated directly between banks and their clients.
8. The IMM guarantees to deliver the currency on schedule if the seller defaults or to acquire it if the buyer defaults. On the other hand, a bank dealing in the forward market must satisfy itself that the party with whom it has a contract is creditworthy.
9. IMM brokers accommodate speculative transactions, whereas banks generally discourage speculation by individuals.
10. A security deposit (margin) must back every futures contract, but forward contracts do not require any margin payment. Compensating balances are required in most forward contracts.
11. In the forward market, a "spread" between the bank's buy and sell prices sets the commissions of intermediaries. In the futures market, commissions of intermediaries depend on published brokerage fees and negotiated rates on block trades.

How to Read Currency Futures Quotes

The Wall Street Journal and other major newspapers carry currency quotations, though they do not list the newest or least active contracts. The International Monetary Market (IMM) of the Chicago Mercantile Exchange trades in eight currencies. Table 6-3 shows the futures exchange rates for the six active currencies reported in *The Wall Street Journal* on one recent Thursday. Yen prices were the number of U.S. cents per unit of a foreign currency. The other currency prices were the number of U.S. dollars per unit of a foreign currency. Because there is a one-day time lag between the transactions of foreign exchange and the report of these transactions, we obtained the Wednesday quotations from the Thursday issue of *The Wall Street Journal.*

The top, bold-faced line gives the name of the currency, such as German mark; the exchange on which it is traded according to a key in the table, such as the IMM; the size of a single contract, such as 125,000 marks per contract; and the way in which prices are quoted, such as dollars per mark.

The first column gives the months for which delivery of the currency may be obtained. Currency trading takes place in March, June, September,

Table 6–3
Currency Futures

	Open	High	Low	Settle	Change	Life Time High	Low	Open Interest
JAPANESE YEN (IMM) 12.5 – million yen; $ per yen (.00)								
Mar	.6943	.6953	.6928	.6939	+.0030	.8357	.6780	62,846
June	.6956	.6968	.6949	.6957	+.0030	.7530	.6850	2,981
Est vol 24,926; vol Tues 43,974; open int 65,881, –144.								
GERMAN MARK (IMM) – 125,000 marks; $ per mark								
Mar	.5941	.5957	.5921	.5939	+.0059	.6012	.5000	58,276
June	.5938	.5953	.5920	.5938	+.0060	.6007	.5057	4,237
Sept	.5938	.5940	.5928	.5936	+.0060	.5980	.5410	238
Est vol 46,450; vol Tues 51,925; open int 63,147, –1,062.								
CANADIAN DOLLAR (IMM) – 100,000 drs.; $ per Can $								
Mar	.8355	.8397	.8346	.8376	+.0017	.8595	.7890	25,412
June	.8283	.8319	.8276	.8304	+.0018	.8522	.8107	3,422
Sept	.8228	.8260	.8220	.8242	+.0019	.8468	.8100	252
Dec	.8180	.8215	.8180	.8200	+.0030	.8420	.8120	171
Est vol 5,286; vol Tues 3,478; open int 29,318, +74.								
BRITISH POUND (IMM) – 62,500 pds.; $ per pound								
Mar	1.6680	1.6702	1.6620	1.6660	+.0084	1.6668	1.4600	24,107
June	1.6420	1.6444	1.6378	1.6406	+.0082	1.6950	1.4400	2,194
SWISS FRANC (IMM) – 125,000 francs; $ per franc								
Mar	.6685	.6700	.6634	.6655	+.0017	.6744	.5740	36,560
June	.6665	.6682	.6615	.6636	+.0018	.6725	.5850	1,315
Est vol 25,917; vol Tues 25,808; open int 38,741, –773.								
AUSTRALIAN DOLLAR (IMM) – 100,000 drs.; $ per A.$								
Mar	.7606	.7603	.7628	.0063	+.0063	.7854	.7055	3,189
Est vol 323; vol Tues 252; open int 3,248, +87.								

Source: *The Wall Street Journal.*

and December. Futures contracts for German marks were only for March, June, and September; December contracts were excluded because they were not active for the day. The second column gives the opening price of the day. For German marks, prices are in terms of dollars per mark; the .5941 for March delivery means that German marks opened for sale at $0.5941 per mark. The full value of one contract at the open of trading for the day is $74,262.50 (0.5941 × 125,000).

The next three columns tell us the contract's highest, lowest, and closing (settlement) prices for the day. These figures, viewed together, show how volatile the market was during the trading day. After opening at $0.5941 per mark, the mark for March delivery never sold for more than $0.5957 and never for less than $0.5921. Trading finally ended or settled at $0.5939 per mark. A broker uses settlement prices to evaluate portfolios or for deciding whether to call for more margin. Currency futures losses must be settled every day, and profits are credited daily to customer accounts.

The sixth column from the left of the quotation, labeled "change," shows the difference between the latest settlement price and the one for the previous day. A plus (+) sign indicates prices ended higher; a minus (–) sign indicates prices ended lower. The +0.0059 in the change column means that the settlement price of the mark for March delivery on the day was $0.0059 higher than the settlement price on the previous trading day.

The next two columns, second and third from the right of the quotation, show the highest and lowest prices at which each contract month has ever traded. We can see that the German mark for March delivery traded as high as $0.6012 per mark and as low as $0.5000 per mark during the lifetime. The difference between the highest and lowest prices of the mark during the lifetime was $0.1012 (0.6012 – 0.5000). This difference is the range. The range represents the volatility of the currency or the dispersion of individual prices for the currency around its average price. The wider the dispersion, the higher the risk. If the highest price and the lowest price are not widely separated from their neighboring prices, the range may be a good measure of risk. If these two prices are erratic, the range should not be used as a measure of risk because it is unreliable and misleading.

The right-hand column, labeled "open interest," refers to the total number of outstanding contracts; that is, those that have not been cancelled by offsetting trades. This column allows us to see how much interest there is in trading a particular contract. The closest months usually attract the most activity, as we can see from the difference between the March mark (58,276 contracts) and the September mark (238 contracts).

A line at the bottom of each currency quotation gives the estimated number of contracts for the day, the actual trading volume for the preceding day, the total open interest, and the change in the open interest since the preceding day. In other words, Est. vol., vol. Tues., and open interest are total figures for all the months combined for the trading day. For the German mark, the estimated volume for the day (Wednesday) was 46,450; the actual volume on Tuesday (the previous trading day) was 51,925; the total number of the open interests for all of the different contract maturities was 63,147; and the –1,062 shows the number of mark contracts that were subtracted from those outstanding at the end of the previous session.

Market Operations

An agreement to buy a futures contract is a long position, and an agreement to sell a futures contract is a short position. To trade futures, people give their broker an order to enter them into a contract as either a buyer (the long position) or as a seller (the short position), depending on which way they think the market is heading.

Margin Requirements.   Some form of deposit ensures that each party fulfills its commitment; this type of deposit is called the **margin**. The exchanges set a minimum margin for each contract, but brokers often require larger margins from clients. The amount of a futures margin depends on the volatility of the contract value and hence on the risk. Margin levels also vary for hedging and speculating accounts. For example, exchanges and brokerage firms normally require lower margins for hedging accounts because they carry less risk than speculating accounts.

Two basic types of margins are required: the initial margin and the maintenance margin. The initial margin is the amount market participants must deposit into their margin account at the time they enter into a futures contract. Then, on a daily basis, the margin account is debited or credited to protect buyers and sellers against the possibility of contract default. Initial margins for futures contracts typically range between 1 and 3 percent of a contract's face value and are set by the exchanges where the contracts are traded.

The maintenance margin is a set minimum margin customers must always maintain in their account. On any day that market losses reduce funds in the account below the maintenance margin, the broker calls on his customer for an additional deposit to restore the account to the initial margin level. Requests for additional money are known as margin calls. The maintenance margin is usually 70 to 80 percent of the initial margin.

In addition to these two basic types of margins, market participants are required to post performance bond margins. Performance bond margins are financial guarantees imposed on both buyers and sellers to ensure that they fulfill the obligation of the futures contract. In other words, they are required to make or take delivery of the futures contract unless their position is offset before the expiration of the contract. The purpose of a performance bond margin is to provide integrity.

Example 6–1. Lisa George buys mark futures contracts to cover possible exchange losses on her import orders denominated in German marks. She has to put up an initial margin of $2,500. The maintenance margin imposed by the exchange is 80 percent of the initial margin, or $2,000. When would she get a margin call from her broker?

If the spot rate for marks declines, the value of Ms. George's position declines. As long as the decline is less than $500, Lisa George does not need to put up any additional margin. Yet, if the cumulative decline in value comes to $501, her margin account would stand at $1,999. She would get a margin call from her brokerage firm and must restore the account to the initial level of $2,500. Otherwise, the exchange will sell out her position and return any remaining balance in her account.

Speculation in the Futures Market.   Speculation offers potentially large profits or losses due to the highly leveraged nature of futures trading. Because margin requirements average less than 4 percent of the contract's full value, it is possible to control large amounts of currencies with little capital. Speculators deliberately expose themselves to exchange risk by engaging in futures contracts in order to make profits from exchange-rate movements.

Example 6-2.   Kenneth Lee, a speculator, enters into a futures contract for March delivery of 125,000 German marks on February 1. The futures exchange rate of the German mark for March delivery (March 15) is $0.5939 per mark. The margin requirement is 2 percent. His expectation of the spot rate for marks on March 15 is $0.6117. If his expectation proves correct, what would be his rate of return on investment?

Because the margin requirement is 2 percent, Mr. Lee may control this delivery of DM125,000 for $1,484.75 (DM125,000 x $0.5939 x 0.02). He could buy DM125,000 futures for $74,237.50 at the futures quotation of $0.5939, receive them on March 15, and then sell them at the spot rate of $0.6117 for a gross of $76,462.50. Profit would be $2,225. So, he would earn a net profit of $2,225 or 150 percent on the original investment of $1,484.75. Here, the exchange rate would rise by only 3 percent [(0.6117 – 0.5939)/ 0.5939], but the rate of return on investment is 150 percent. Yet, the same leverage could lead to equally substantial losses. If the spot rate declines by 3 percent during this period, Mr. Lee would lose about 150 percent of his investment.

Hedging in the Futures Market.   A single forward contract can arrange for the precise amount and maturity that the bank's customer desires. A single futures contract is available only in a predetermined amount for one of the four maturity dates each year. These two features of the futures market may force multinational companies to assume some risks of coverage and of currency fluctuation because they usually need a specified amount of a currency on a specified date. Still, these risks can be minimized in a properly structured hedge. Prices in the spot and futures markets move in the same direction by similar amounts due to arbitrage transactions between these two markets.

Example 6-3.   On February 1, an American firm imports 5,000 Swiss watches at a cost of 250,000 francs with payment and delivery due on March 1. The Swiss firm, being a tough negotiator, has demanded that the payment be made in Swiss francs upon the delivery of the watches. The exchange rates are $0.6667 per franc in the spot market and $0.6655 per franc in the futures market for delivery on March 15.

Given the costs of marketing the watches, the importer decides that the futures exchange rate is low enough for the company to purchase them and make a profit on the transaction. However, the importer must pay for the watches on March 1, though the expiration date of the futures contract is March 15. The importer can hedge most of its exposure by buying March Swiss franc contracts on February 1 with the intention of lifting the hedge on March 1. Because franc contracts are available from the IMM in units of 125,000, the importer would purchase two March contracts, as given in Table 6-4.

The importer could trade out of the contracts by selling them before receiving a delivery notice. The importer could buy 250,000 francs in the

Table 6-4
Buying Two Franc Futures Contracts
on February 1

	Spot Market	Futures Market for March 15 Delivery
Exchange rate	$0.6667/SF	$0.6655/SF
Cost of SF250,000	$166,675	$166,375
Action taken	None	Buy March 15 contract

futures market for $166,375 on March 15. The only risk that the company still faces comes from the difference in the value of the contract on March 1 and its value on March 15. Assume that by March 1 the following two things would happen: (1) the spot rate appreciates to $0.7658 and (2) the futures rate rises to $0.7650. The importer could close out the franc futures contracts by selling them on March 1, as shown in Table 6-5.

On March 1, the importer purchases 250,000 francs in the spot market for $191,450 and settles its import bill. But, this $191,450 is higher ($24,775) than its original value on February 1 ($166,675); in other words, the exchange loss from the spot transaction is $24,775. The futures contract the company sold on March 1 ($191,250) is higher ($24,875) than the $166,375 the company anticipated in the futures contract it purchased on February 1; in other words, the exchange gain from the futures transaction is $24,875. The $24,875 gain from the futures transaction exceeds the $24,775 loss from the spot transaction. The risk that the importer assumed on February 1 by purchasing two contracts whose maturity did not coincide with the March 1 usage date of the currency resulted in a windfall exchange gain of $100 ($25,875 – $24,775). This $100 gain arose from the difference between the spot rate and the futures rate prevailing on the day the contracts were liquidated. This difference is the **basis**.

The basis, unlike the spot rate itself, is relatively stable and narrows toward zero as the contract moves toward maturity. For example, the basis on February 1 was $0.0012 per franc ($0.6667 - $0.6655), while by March 1 it

Table 6-5
Reversing the Earlier Futures Contracts
on March 1

	Spot Market	Futures Market for March 15 Delivery
Exchange rate	$0.7658/SF	$0.7650/SF
Cost of SF250,000	$191,450	$191,250
Action taken	Buy SF250,000	Sell March 15 contract

had shrunk to $0.0008 ($0.7658 – $0.7650). The degree of uncertainty about the futures price diminishes further as the contract approaches its March 15 expiration date. On March 15, the futures rate, in effect, becomes the spot rate.

In Example 6–3, the difference of $0.0004/SF in the basis between February 1 and March 1 accounted for the windfall exchange gain of $100. This gain might easily have been an exchange loss of a similar amount if the exchange rate of the Swiss franc had depreciated during the same period. The important point is that the importer was protected from any major loss regardless of exchange–rate movements. For example, if the importer had not purchased the futures contract and bought 250,000 francs in the spot market on March 1, the watches would have cost an additional $24,775.

Frequent futures traders may try to coordinate trading between two different markets or two different currencies through a strategy called spread trading. Spread trading means buying one contract and simultaneously selling another contract. They will always make money on one contract and lose money on the other contract. Thus, they may make or lose more money on the one contract than they lose or make on the other, but they are protected from major loss regardless of exchange–rate movements.

The Currency Options Market

The Philadelphia Stock Exchange started currency options trading in 1983; since then, the Chicago Mercantile Exchange and the Chicago Board Options Exchange added currency options trading. Currency options are now traded on exchanges throughout the world, including those in the United States, London, Amsterdam, Hong Kong, Singapore, Sydney, Vancouver, and Montreal. Currency options are currently available in six currencies: British pound, Canadian dollar, German mark, Japanese yen, Swiss franc, and Australian dollar. These currency options are traded in standard contracts half the size of the IMM futures contracts. For example, the pound option contract represents 31,250 units, which is half the 62,500 units represented by the pound futures contract. In addition, a significant amount of currency options are traded outside the organized exchanges. Many banks and other financial institutions have just begun to offer currency options that have exercise prices and exercise dates to meet specific needs of their corporate clients.

Although the size of the options market is still small compared to the futures market, it is growing rapidly. Table 6–6 shows that the number of options contracts for six currencies traded on the Philadelphia Stock Exchange rose from about 728,000 in 1984 to approximately 10 million in 1991.

Basic Terms

Currency options give the holder the right to buy or sell a foreign currency at a designated price in the future. There are two types of options: calls and puts. A currency call option gives the buyer the right, but not the obligation,

Table 6-6

Number of Currency Options Contracts Traded on the PHILL

(thousand of contracts)

Year	BP	CD	DM	JY	SF	AD	Total
1984			728				728
1985	329		1562		325		2216
1986	497	26	2206	865	818		4412
1987	569	49	3126	2251	1053		7048
1988	543	314	2734	2945	1070	7	7613
1989	406	274	3795	3127	1489	23	9114
1990	501	284	3430	3116	1130	27	8488
1991	650	337	5643	2397	998	38	10063

Source: Philadelphia Stock Exchange.

to buy a particular foreign currency at a specified price any time during the life of the option. A currency put option gives the buyer the right, but not the obligation, to sell a particular foreign currency at a specified price any time during the life of the option. The grantor of an option—the writer—must deliver the currency if a holder calls, or he must buy it if it is put to him by a put holder. For this obligation, the writer receives a fee or premium.

The holder of a call option will benefit if the underlying currency's price rises, while the holder of a put option will benefit if it falls. If the currency's price does not change much during the life of the option, the holder of the option loses his entire investment. For this reason, options are risky, but there is a potential for large profits. To buy a foreign currency outright in the spot market, an investor must pay the entire purchase price of the currency, but the price of the option is a small fraction of the price of the underlying currency.

The strike price or the exercise price is the price at which the buyer of an option has the right to buy or sell an underlying currency. Option buyers can decide whether or not to go through with the deal any time up until the expiration date. Options pay no interest and become worthless at expiration unless the price of the underlying currency changes. Only certain expiration dates are available; the exchange, which lists the option, chooses these expiration dates.

Options differ from all other types of financial instruments in the patterns of profit-loss they produce. This is because the holder of an option has the possibility of unlimited profit, but his maximum loss would be limited to the amount of premium paid. The holder has the choice of exercising the option or allowing it to expire unused. The holder will exercise the option only when it becomes profitable. On the down side, the holder can let the option expire and walk away with a loss no more than the premium paid for it. On the other hand, the possibility of unlimited profit or loss exists in the spot market, the forward market, and the futures market. The profit structures for long and short positions in both the forward market and the futures market exactly mirror each other. In other words, the long or short position on an underlying currency produces a one-to-one gain or loss depending on where the spot rate ends up relative to the contracted futures rate. The buyer of a futures contract earns one dollar for every dollar the seller of the futures contract loses, and vice versa.

How to Read Currency Option Quotes

Table 6-7 reflects the closing prices of the options for several currencies reported in *The Wall Street Journal* on one recent Thursday. The top line gives the size of a single contract, such as 31,250 pounds per contract; the name of the currency, such as British pounds; and the way in which prices are quoted, such as cents per pound. Yen prices and yen option prices are the number of 100ths of a cent per unit of a foreign currency. All other currency prices are the number of U.S. cents per unit of a foreign currency.

Table 6–7
Currency Options in Philadelphia Exchange

Option & Underlying	Strike Price	Calls–Last			Puts–Last		
		Feb	Mar	Jun	Feb	Mar	Jun
31,250 British Pounds–cents per unit.							
B Pound	160	8.10	r	r	r	r	r
168.17	165.5	5.24	r	r	0.25	r	r
168.17	165	r	r	r	r	1.85	r
168.17	167.5	r	2.20	r	1.70	3.00	r
168.17	170	r	1.40	r	r	4.55	r
168.17	171.5	0.30	0.84	r	r	r	r
168.17	175	r	r	1.35	r	r	r
6,250,000 Japanese Yen–100ths of a cent per unit.							
JYen	68	r	r	2.36	0.14	r	0.82
69.29	69	0.75	1.05	1.76	0.34	0.63	1.22
69.29	69.5	0.49	r	s	r	r	s
69.29	70	0.30	0.58	1.37	0.93	1.19	r
69.29	70.5	0.15	r	s	r	r	s
69.29	71	0.09	0.34	0.92	r	r	r
69.29	72	0.06	0.14	0.64	r	r	r
Total Call Vol.	47,086	Call open int. 369,838					
Total Put Vol.	23,701	Put open int. 343,124					

r-Not traded. s-No option offered.
Last is premium (purchase price)

Source: *The Wall Street Journal.*

The first column shows the name of the currency, such as B Pound (British pound). The 168.17 listed below B Pound is the closing price of the pound on the Philadelphia Exchange that day; that is, the closing price of the British pound during the day was $1.6817 per pound.

The second column from the left of the quotation shows various strike prices, prices of the underlying currency at which options confer the right to buy or sell. There are seven different strike prices listed for the British pound, which means that there were seven options available for the British pound. These strike prices ranged from $1.60 per pound to $1.75 per pound. Then follow two groups of three prices. The first gives closing prices or premiums for call options at a given strike price valid until each of three different months. The second group gives the closing prices or premiums for put options at a given strike price valid until each of the three months. If a given option is not traded, this column shows an "r" footnote. If the option is not offered, it shows a "s" footnote.

The premium for a pound call option with a strike price of $1.60 and a February settlement date is 8.10 cents. Because the pound option comes in a standardized volume of 31,250 units, the price of this call option per contract is $2,531.25 (0.081 x 31,250). Thus, one call option on the British pound with a strike price of $1.60 and a February settlement date would give the holder the right to buy 31,250 pounds for $50,000 ($1.60 x 31,250). The premium for a pound put option with a strike price of $1.675 and a February settlement date is 1.70 cents. So, an investor can buy this put option for $531.25 (0.017 x 31,250). One put option with a strike price of $1.675 and a February settlement date would give the holder the right to sell 31,250 pounds for $52,343.75 ($1.675 x 31,250).

At the end of the listings is a summary of the trading on the Philadelphia Exchange for the day. Total call volume (47,086) and total put volume (23,701) show the number of options traded that day. Call open interest (369,838) and put open interest (343,124) show the number of options outstanding.

Generally, prices are highest for call options whose strike price is below the spot rate and for put options whose strike price is above the spot rate. The volume of option trading is frequently large relative to trading in the underlying currency. This reflects trading by professionals who make their money on numerous but short-term transactions and by holders of foreign exchange who hedge large blocks with options. Such hedging provides a price protection similar to that offered by currency futures.

Currency Option Premiums

In the case of either a call or a put, the option buyer must pay the option seller (option writer) a premium (price). This premium depends on market conditions, such as supply, demand, and other economic variables. Regardless of how much the market swings, the most an option buyer can lose is the option premium. He deposits the premium with his broker, and the money goes to the option seller. Option buyers are not required to maintain margin (deposit) accounts because of this limited and known risk.

Option sellers, on the other hand, face risks similar to participants in the spot or futures markets. For example, because the seller of a call option is assigned a short position, the risk is the same as for someone who initially bought a foreign currency. The option seller posts margin to demonstrate her ability to meet any potential contractual obligations.

Even though the marketplace is the ultimate determinant of an option premium, there are some basic guidelines traders use to calculate option premiums. In general, an option premium is the sum of intrinsic value and time value; both intrinsic value and time value are influenced by volatility of a strike price and the underlying price.

Intrinsic Value.   Intrinsic value is the difference between the exchange rate of the underlying currency and the strike price of a currency option. A call option has an intrinsic value if the strike price is below the exchange rate of the underlying currency. A put option has an intrinsic value if the strike price is above the exchange rate of the underlying currency.

Any option with an intrinsic value is said to be **in–the–money**. A call option with a strike price less than the current spot rate is said to be in–the–money; a put option with a strike price above the current spot rate is said to be in–the–money. A call option with a strike price above the current spot rate is said to be **out–of–the–money**; a put option with a strike price below the current spot rate is said to be out–of–the–money. When the strike price of any call or put option equals the current spot rate, the option is said to be **at–the–money**. Table 6-8 shows a summary of the intrinsic value of different call and put options.

Time Value.   The second major component of an option premium is time value. Time value is the amount of money that options buyers are willing to pay for an option in the anticipation that over time a change in the underlying spot rate will cause the option to increase in value. In general, the longer the length of time before the settlement date, the higher the option premium. This is because the right to buy or sell something is more valuable to a market participant if she has four months to decide what to do with the option rather than just one month. For example, an expiration date in June has four additional months beyond February for the spot rate to change above or below the strike price.

Table 6–8
Calculating the Intrinsic Value of Currency Options

	Call Option	Put Option
In-the-Money	Spot > Strike	Spot < Strike
At-the-Money	Spot = Strike	Spot = Strike
Out-of-the-Money	Spot < Strike	Spot > Strike

Value of Exchange–Rate Volatility.
Volatility of the underlying spot rate is one of the most important factors which influence the value of the option premium. Volatility measures the change in price over a given period of time. The greater the variability of the currency, the higher the probability that the spot rate will be below or above the strike price. Thus, more volatile currencies tend to have higher option premiums.

Typically, options have positive values even if they are out-of-the money (i.e., zero intrinsic value). Investors will usually pay something today for out-of-the-money options on the chance of profit before maturity. They are also likely to pay some additional premium today for in-the-money options on the chance of an increase in intrinsic value before maturity. Thus, the price of an option is always somewhat greater than its intrinsic value.

Currency Call Options

A currency call option is a contract that gives the buyer the right to buy a foreign currency at a specified price during the prescribed period. People buy currency call options because they anticipate that the spot rate of the underlying currency will appreciate. Currency option trading can take place for hedging or speculation.

Hedging in the Call Options Market.
Multinational companies with open positions in foreign currencies can utilize currency call options. Suppose that an American firm orders industrial equipment from a German company, and its payment is to be made in German marks upon delivery. A German mark call option locks in the rate at which the U.S. company can purchase marks for dollars. Such an exchange between these two currencies at the specified strike price can take place before the settlement date. Thus, the call option specifies the maximum price which the U.S. company must pay to obtain marks. If the spot rate falls below the strike price by the delivery date, the importer can buy marks at the prevailing spot rate to pay for its imports and can simply let its call option expire.

Example 6–4.
Let's see how call options may be used to cover possible exchange losses on import orders denominated in foreign currencies. Assume that on February 1 an American firm has purchased a mainframe computer from a German firm for 625,000 marks; its payment must be made in German marks on June 1. Let us further assume that the premium for a mark call option with a strike price of $0.5000 and a June expiration date is 0.03 cents. Because there are 62,500 units per mark option, the U.S. firm will need 10 call options to buy 625,000 marks. The current spot rate for marks is $0.4900; the U.S. company's bank believes that the spot rate by June 1 will rise to $0.6000.

There are two alternatives available to the U.S. company: do not hedge, or hedge in the options market. If the U.S. company does not want to cover its open position, it would wait for four months, buy marks at the prevailing exchange rate in the spot market, and use these marks to pay for its imports. If the bank's forecast is accurate, the U.S. company would spend $375,000 to purchase 625,000 marks at the spot rate of $0.6000.

The price of 10 mark call options is $187.50 (0.03 cents x 10 options x 62,500 units per contract); on June 1 the U.S. company exercises its right to buy 625,000 marks for $312,500 ($0.500 x 625,000 marks). Consequently, the U.S. firm would spend a total of $312,687.50 ($187.50 + $312,500) to purchase 625,000 marks. By doing so, the American firm would avoid the risk of a $62,312.50 loss ($375,000 - $312,687.50). Still, if the future spot rate for marks remains below the strike price of $0.5000, the U.S. company can let its options expire and buy German marks at the prevailing spot rate when it must pay for its imports. Here the U.S. firm would lose its option premium of $187.50.

Speculating in the Call Options Market.
Individuals may speculate with currency call options based on their expectations of exchange-rate fluctuations for a particular currency. The purpose of speculation in the call options market is to make a profit from exchange-rate movements by deliberately taking an uncovered position. If a speculator expects that the future spot rate of a currency will increase, he makes the following transactions: The speculator will (1) buy call options of the currency, (2) wait for a few months until the spot rate of the currency appreciates high enough, (3) exercise his option by buying the currency at the strike price, and (4) then sell the currency at the prevailing spot rate.

Example 6–5. Suppose that the call premium per British pound on February 1 is 1.10 cents, the expiration date is June, and the strike price is $1.60. Kevin Kim anticipates that the spot rate of the pound will increase to $1.70 by May 1. If Mr. Kim's expectation proves correct, what would be his dollar profit from speculating one pound call option (31,250 units per contract) in the call options market?

Kevin Kim could make a profit of $2,781.25 by making the following trades:

1. Buy call options on February 1   -$0.0110 per pound
2. Exercise the option on May 1   -$1.6000 per pound
3. Sell the pound on May 1   +$1.7000 per pound
4. Net profit as of May 1   +$0.0890 per pound
5. Net profit per contract   £31,250 x $0.0890 = $2,781.25

Kevin Kim does not need to exercise his call options in order to make a profit. Currency call option premiums rise and fall as exchange rates of their underlying currency rise and fall. If call options become profitable, their premiums will rise. They can be sold on an exchange just like any foreign currency itself. So a call option holder such as Mr. Kim can save the expense and bother of taking possession of the currency and selling it.

Graphic Analysis of a Call Option Price.

Figure 6-1 shows the typical relationship between the market value of a call option and its intrinsic value. Up to the point where the strike price equals the spot rate, time value increases as the spot rate increases, but the market value exceeds the intrinsic value for all spot rates. Call options have positive values even if they are out-of-the-money because they have time value. It is also important to note that the intrinsic value of a call option becomes zero whenever the strike price exceeds the spot rate.

Currency Put Options

A currency put option is simply a contract that gives the holder the right to sell a foreign currency at a specified price during a prescribed period. People buy currency put options because they anticipate that the spot rate of the underlying currency will depreciate.

Multinational companies with open positions in foreign currencies can employ currency put options to cover such positions. Consider an American company which has sold an airplane to a Japanese firm and has agreed to receive its payment in Japanese yen. The exporter may be concerned about

Figure 6–1
Market Value of a Call Option

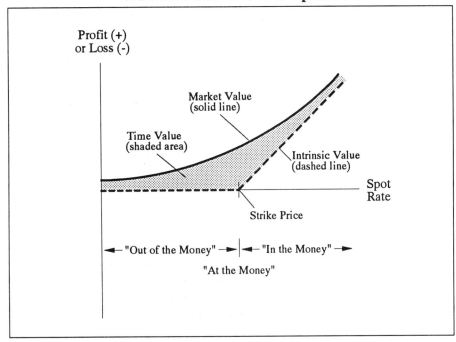

the possibility that the yen will depreciate when it is scheduled to receive its payment from the importer. To protect itself against such a yen depreciation, the exporter could buy yen put options, which would enable it to sell yen at the specified strike price. In fact, the exporter would lock in the minimum exchange rate at which it could sell Japanese yen in exchange for U.S. dollars over a specified period of time. On the other hand, if the yen appreciates over this time period, the exporter could let the put options expire and sell the yen at the prevailing spot rate.

Individuals may speculate with currency put options based on their expectations of exchange rate fluctuations for a particular currency. For example, if speculators believe that the German mark will depreciate in the future, they can buy mark put options, which will entitle them to sell marks at the specified strike price. If the mark's spot rate depreciates as expected, they can buy marks at the spot rate and exercise their put options by selling these marks at the strike price.

Speculators do not need to exercise their put options in order to make a profit. They could make a profit from selling put options because put option premiums fall and rise as exchange rates of the underlying currency rise and fall. The seller of put options has the obligation to purchase the specified currency at the strike price from the owner who exercises the put option. If speculators anticipate that the currency will appreciate, they might sell their put options. But if the currency indeed appreciates over the entire period, the put option will not be exercised. On the other hand, if they expect that the currency will depreciate, they will keep their put options. Then they will sell their put options when the put option premiums go up.

Profit–Loss Profiles of Options.   Figure 6-2 presents "profit-loss profiles" which trace the relationship between the exchange rate at expiration of the contract and the net gain (loss) to the trader.

Assume that the call premium per British pound is $0.04, the strike price is $1.50, and the contract matures in two months. The vertical axes of Figures 6-2(a) and 6-2(b) measure profit or loss for the call option trader at different spot rates (horizontal axes) for the pound at the time of maturity. For the buyer of a call option on the pound, the loss is limited to the price originally paid for the option. The entire price ($0.04) would be lost if the spot rate is $1.50 or less. The call option holder would earn $0.04 at $1.54, but this gain is offset by the $0.04 premium. Thus, this point ($1.54) is called the **break–even point**. The call option holder would realize a one-to-one gain (unlimited profit) at any spot rate above $1.54. For the seller of a call option, the gain is limited to the premium originally charged for the option. The entire premium ($0.04) would be earned if the spot rate is $1.50 or less. The call option seller would suffer a one-to-one loss at any spot rate above $1.54.

Assume that the put premium per British pound is $0.06, the strike price is $1.50, and the contract matures in two months. Figures 6-2(c) and 6-2(d) show profit-loss profiles of a put option trader. The buyer of a put option would obtain a one-to-one gain at any rate below $1.44 but only up to the point where the profit-loss profile of the put option holder intercepts the

Figure 6–2
Profit–Loss Profiles for an Option Trader

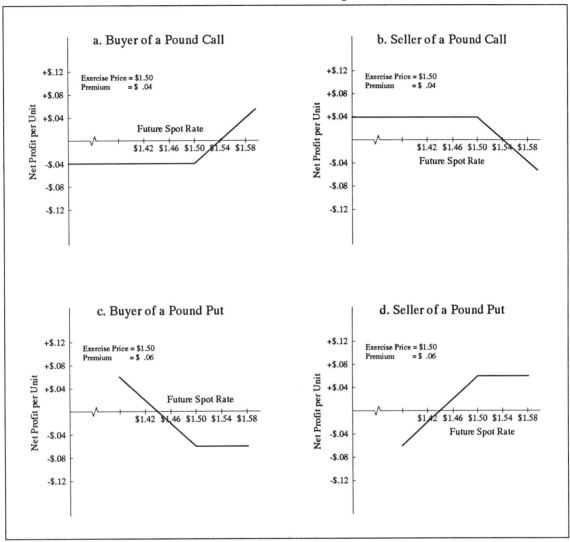

a. Buyer of a Pound Call

Exercise Price = $1.50
Premium   = $ .04

b. Seller of a Pound Call

Exercise Price = $1.50
Premium   = $ .04

c. Buyer of a Pound Put

Exercise Price = $1.50
Premium   = $ .06

d. Seller of a Pound Put

Exercise Price = $1.50
Premium   = $ .06

vertical axis. The break-even spot rate of $1.44 is the price at which the holder neither gains nor loses on exercise of the option: this is the point where the gain of $0.06 is offset by the premium of $0.06. The holder would lose money at spot rates above $1.44, but the loss is limited to the premium originally paid for the option. The profit-loss profile of the put option seller, Figure 6-2(d), is the mirror image of the profit-loss profile for the buyer of a put option.

Futures Options

The Chicago Mercantile Exchange introduced currency futures options or currency options on futures in January 1984. Currency futures options do not reflect the options on the underlying currency itself, but they reflect the options on the futures contract of that currency. They were originally established for the German mark, but they are now available for the British pound, Canadian dollar, Japanese yen, and Swiss franc.

Currency futures options give the holder the right to buy or sell a foreign currency at a designated price in the future. There are two types of currency futures options: currency futures calls and currency futures puts. A currency futures call option gives the buyer the right, but not the obligation, to buy a particular currency futures contract at a specified price any time during the life of the option. A currency futures put option gives the buyer the right, but not the obligation, to sell a particular currency futures contract at a specified price any time during the life of the option. Table 6-9 shows futures positions after options have been exercised.

Quotations of currency futures options are similar to those of currency options and appear near the related options listings. Table 6-10 presents the closing prices of the futures options for the British pound and the Swiss franc which appeared in *The Wall Street Journal* on one recent Thursday. These quotations are divided into calls and puts; then they are divided into different maturities and strike prices.

Multinational companies with open positions in foreign currencies can use currency futures options to cover such positions. Individuals may speculate with currency futures options based on their expectation of exchange-rate movements for a particular currency. Those who believe the futures prices are too low could buy call options on futures. Those who believe the futures prices are too high could buy put options on futures.

If a call futures option is exercised, the holder gets a long position in the underlying futures contract plus a cash amount equal to the current futures price minus the exercise price. If a put futures option is exercised, the holder gets a short position in the underlying futures contract plus a cash amount equal to the exercise price minus the current futures price.

Table 6-9
Futures Positions After Option Exercise

	Call Option	Put Option
Buyer Assumes	Long Futures Position	Short Futures Position
Seller Assumes	Short Futures Position	Long Futures Position

Table 6–10
Currency Futures Options

BRITISH POUND (IMM) 62,500 pounds; cents per pound

Strike	Calls–Settle			Puts–Settle		
Price	Feb–c	Mar–c	Jun–c	Feb–p	Mar–p	Jun–p
1625	4.20	4.88	—	0.12	0.82	—
1650	2.14	3.18	3.92	0.54	1.62	4.80
1675	0.78	1.90	2.94	1.68	2.80	6.26
1700	0.20	1.04	2.20	—	4.40	—
1725	0.06	0.52	1.58	—	—	—
1750	—	0.26	—	—	—	—

Est. vol. 90, Tues vol. 450 calls, 882 puts

Open Interest Tues; 9,359 calls, 12,701 puts

SWISS FRANC (IMM) 125,000 francs; cents per franc

Strike	Calls–Settle			Puts–Settle		
Price	Feb–c	Mar–c	Jun–c	Feb–p	Mar–p	Jun–p
65	1.65	1.98	2.61	0.10	0.45	1.29
66	0.87	1.34	2.05	0.32	0.80	1.71
67	0.36	0.83	1.59	0.81	1.28	2.23
68	0.11	0.50	1.21	1.56	1.93	—
69	0.04	0.29	0.91	—	—	—
70	0.02	0.16	0.68	—	—	—

Est. vol. 4,553; Tues vol. 4,019 calls, 5,434 puts

Open interest Tues; 32,298 calls, 38,681 puts

Source: *The Wall Street Journal.*

Example 6–6. Consider an investor who has a June futures call option on one contract of the British pound (62,500) with a strike price of $1.580. The current futures price of the pound for delivery in June is $1.630. If the investor exercises her option, she would receive $3,125 (62,500 x 5 cents) plus a long position in a futures contract to buy £62,500 in June. If desired, she can immediately close out her long position at no cost; this would leave the investor with the $3,125 cash payoff.

Example 6–7. Consider an investor who has a June futures put option on one contract of the Swiss franc (125,000) with a strike price of $0.65. The current futures price of the franc for delivery in June is $0.55. If the investor exercises her option, she receives $12,500 (125,000 x 10 cents) plus a short position in a futures contract to sell SF125,000. If desired, she can immediately close out her short position at no cost; this would leave the investor with the $12,500 cash payoff.

Summary

Three major instruments of the foreign exchange market are currency futures, currency options, and currency futures options. The three types of contracts are similar because they are all used by those who have specific expectations about future exchange-rate movements. Yet, they differ because: (1) holders of currency futures must buy or sell the currency on the settlement date; (2) owners of currency options have the right to buy or sell the currency at a specified price; and (3) holders of currency futures options have the right to buy or sell the futures on the currency.

These three types of currency contracts are acquired for hedging, speculation, or arbitrage. They appeal to individuals and small companies because they offer only standard contracts in the predetermined amounts and their purchase prices are small. Multinational companies with open positions in foreign currencies can use these three markets to cover such positions as an alternative to the forward market offered by commercial banks.

Questions

1. What are the major differences between forward and futures contracts?

2. What is the most important difference between futures and options contracts?

3. What are the major types of margin with respect to a futures contract? What is the role of margin requirement?

4. How can speculators use currency futures?

5. How can U.S. companies use currency futures?

6. What are the components of an option premium?

7. Why is the price of an option always greater than its intrinsic value?

8. Why cannot the intrinsic value of an option be less than zero?

9. Assume that a company wants to use either a currency option or a forward contract to hedge against exchange rate fluctuations. What are the advantages and disadvantages of currency options in this case?

10. When should a company buy a call option for hedging? When should a company buy a put option?

11. When should speculators buy a call option? When should speculators buy a put option?

12. What are currency futures options?

Problems

6-1   An American company sells yen futures contracts to cover possible exchange losses on its export orders denominated in Japanese yen. The amount of the initial margin is $20,000, and the maintenance margin is 75 percent of the initial margin. The value of the company's position declines by $6,000 because the spot rate for yen has increased.

(a)   What is the dollar amount of the maintenance margin?
(b)   Should the broker issue margin calls to the company?
(c)   What is the amount of additional deposit needed to restore the account to the initial margin level?

6-2   A speculator enters a futures contract for September delivery (September 19) of £62,500 on February 2. The futures exchange rate is $1.6500 per pound. He believes that the spot rate for pounds on September 19 will be $1.700 per pound. The margin requirement is 2 percent.

(a)   If his expectations are correct, what would be his rate of return on investment?
(b)   If the spot rate for pounds on September 19 is 5 percent lower than the futures exchange rate, how much would he lose on the futures speculation?
(c)   If there is a 65 percent chance that the spot rate for pounds will increase to $1.700 by September 19, would you speculate in the futures market?

6-3   On March 20, a Detroit investor decides to invest $1 million in a British three-month certificate of deposit (CD) with an annual yield of 20 percent. He expects that this 20 percent rate of return on the British CD is more than he could have realized by investing in the domestic market. The investor buys British pounds in the spot market and purchases the CD from a British bank. The exchange rates are $2.0000 per pound in the spot market and $2.0050 per pound in the futures market for June delivery (June 20).

(a)   The investor buys enough British pounds in the futures market to cover the principal and accrued interest at the time of maturity. Summarize the transaction.

(b) By June 20, the British pound has depreciated to $1.8500 per pound. Remember that the spot rate and the futures rate become the same by the delivery date. On June 20, the investor decides to close the position by selling British pounds in the spot market and reversing the futures contracts. Summarize the transaction.

(c) Compare the exchange gain (loss) from the futures transaction with the exchange loss (gain) from the spot transaction. What is the windfall profit (net exchange gain)?

(d) If the investor had not hedged his investment, how much exchange loss would he have suffered on the transaction? Remember that the British pound depreciated to $1.8500 on June 20.

6-4 The call premium per British pound on March 1 is $0.04, the expiration date is September 19, and the strike price is $1.80. A speculator believes that the spot rate for the pound will rise to $1.92 by September 19.

(a) If the speculator's expectations are correct, what would be her dollar profit from speculating two pound call options (£62,500)?

(b) If the spot rate were $1.76 per pound when the option expired, would the speculator exercise the option? What would be her loss from this speculation?

6-5 The put premium per British pound on March 1 is $0.04, the settlement date is September 19, and the strike price is $1.80. A speculator anticipates that the spot rate for the pound will fall to $1.72 by September 19. If the speculator's expectations are correct, what would be his dollar profit from speculating two put options (62,500 pounds)?

6-6 A U.S. company has bought 30 personal computers from a British company for 62,500 pounds. Its payment must be made in British pounds 90 days from now. The premium for a pound call option with a strike price of $1.60 and a 90-day expiration date is $0.04 per pound. The current spot rate for pounds is $1.58; the U.S. company expects that the spot rate in 90 days will rise to $1.66. The U.S. company has two alternatives: do not hedge and hedge in the options market. Should the U.S. company choose the call option hedge or no hedge?

6-7 A U.S. exporter is scheduled to receive 125,000 marks in 60 days. The premium for a mark put option with a strike price of $0.50 and a 90-day settlement date is $0.03 per mark. The company anticipates that the spot rate in 90 days will be $0.46. Should the company hedge its accounts receivable in the options market? If the spot rate were $0.51 in 90 days, how would it affect the company's decision?

6-8 The exchange rate for Japanese yen is $0.0069 per yen, and a call option has a strike price of $0.0065. An investor has two yen call options. If the investor exercises the call options, how much profit would she realize?

6-9 The exchange rate for Japanese yen is $0.0069 per yen, and a put option has a strike price of $0.0070. An investor has two yen put options. If the holder exercises the put option, how much profit would he realize?

6-10 On October 23, the closing exchange rate of British pounds was $1.70. Calls which would mature the following January with a strike price of $1.75 were traded at $0.10.

(a) Were the call options in-the-money, at-the-money, or out-of-the-money?
(b) Compute the intrinsic value of the call.
(c) If the exchange rate of British pounds rises to $1.90 prior to the January option expiration date, what is the percentage return on investment for an investor who purchased a call on October 23?

6-11 With reference to Problem 6-10, put options with the same strike price and a January maturity for British pounds were traded at $0.05 on October 23.

(a) Were the put options in-the-money, at-the-money, or out-of-the-money?
(b) Compute the intrinsic value of the put.
(c) If the exchange rate of British pounds falls to $1.65 just prior to expiration, what is the percentage return on investment for an investor who purchased a put on October 23?

References

Chalupa, K. V., "Foreign Currency Futures: Reducing Foreign Exchange Risk," *Economic Perspectives*, The Federal Reserve Bank of Chicago, Winter 1982, pp. 3-11.

The Chicago Board of Trade, *Commodity Trading Manual*, Chicago: Board of Trade of the City of Chicago, 1989.

The Chicago Mercantile Exchange, *Using Currency Futures and Options*, 1987.

Duffie, D., *Futures Markets*, Englewood Cliffs, NJ: Prentice Hall, 1989.

Eitman, D. K., and A. I. Stonehill, *Multinational Business Finance*, Reading, MA: Addison-Wesley, 1992, Chapter 5: Futures and Options Markets.

Fieleke, N. S., "Rise of the Foreign Currency Futures Market," *New England Economic Review*, The Federal Reserve Bank of Boston, March/April 1985, pp. 38-47.

Giddy, I. H., "Foreign Exchange Options," *Journal of Futures Market*, Summer 1983, pp. 145-65.

Giddy, I. H., "The Foreign Exchange Option as a Hedging Tool," in Joel M. Stern and Donald H. Chew, eds., *New Developments in International Finance*, New York: Basil Blackwell Ltd., 1988, pp. 83-93.

Hull, J., *Options, Futures, and Other Derivative Securities*, Englewood Cliffs, NJ: Prentice Hall, 1989.

Kolb, R. W., *Understanding Futures Markets*, Third Edition, Miami: Kolb Publishing Company, 1990.

Madura, J., *International Financial Management*, New York: West Publishing Company, 1992, Chapter 5: Currency Futures and Options Markets.

Shapiro, A. C., *Multinational Financial Management*, Boston: Allyn and Bacon, 1992, Chapter 3: Currency Futures and Options Markets.

Solnik, B., *International Investment*, Reading, MA: Addison-Wesley, 1988.

Van Horne, J. C., *Financial Market Rates & Flows*, Englewood Cliffs, NJ: Prentice Hall, 1990.

7

Foreign Exchange Risk Management

Foreign exchange risk is the risk of loss due to changes in the international exchange value of national currencies. Assume that an American exporter sells airplanes on a three-month credit to Japanese citizens and invoices them in yen. If the yen declines in value relative to the U.S. dollar three months later, the exporter suffers a loss in foreign exchange that may well wipe out the trade gain. If the yen increases in value relative to the dollar, it works to the advantage of the exporter.

So long as we do not have a single world currency, some degree of exchange risk exists in any system. Fluctuations in the value of currency have frequently been quite pronounced in the past. A study by Margaret DeVries shows that during the 20-year period from 1948 to 1968, 96 countries devalued their currencies by more than 40 percent, and 24 countries devalued their currencies by more than 75 percent. This problem has become more complicated for the last two decades because most industrial countries have permitted their currencies to float since 1973. Daily currency fluctuations have become a way of life since then.

This chapter has four major sections. The first section describes three major exchange exposures: translation, transaction, and economic. The second section examines several economic indicators which are widely used to forecast exchange rates. The third section covers some techniques designed to minimize foreign exchange risk.

Foreign Exchange Exposures

Every company faces exposure to foreign exchange risk as soon as it chooses to maintain a physical presence in a foreign country. Foreign exchange exposure refers to the possibility that a firm will gain or lose due to changes in exchange rates. By the same token, a firm faces exposure to exchange risk when it chooses to finance its operations in foreign currencies. Both exchange risks are analyzed in the context of investing and financing decisions. An important task of the international financial manager is to compare potential losses with the cost of avoiding these losses. Three basic types of exchange exposures are translation exposure, transaction exposure, and economic exposure.

Translation Exposure

Companies may wish to translate financial-statement items from a foreign currency into their home currency in order to prepare consolidated financial statements or to compare financial results. The term "conversion" should not be used in this case because this translation process does not involve the actual conversion of one currency into another. Here values of financial-statement items are simply restated.

Translation exposure, sometimes called accounting exposure, measures the effect of an exchange-rate change on published financial statements of a firm. Foreign-currency assets and liabilities that are translated at the current exchange rate are considered to be exposed. In accounting terms, the difference between exposed assets and exposed liabilities is frequently called net exposure. Foreign currency depreciations will result in exchange losses, and foreign currency appreciations will produce exchange gains if exposed assets are greater than exposed liabilities. On the other hand, foreign currency depreciations will lead to exchange gains, and foreign currency appreciations will lead to exchange losses if exposed assets are smaller than exposed liabilities.

Example 7-1.   A U.S. parent company has a single wholly owned subsidiary in France. This subsidiary has exposed assets of 100 million francs and exposed liabilities of 50 million francs. The exchange rate declines from FF4 per dollar to FF5 per dollar.

The potential foreign-exchange loss on the company's exposed net assets of 50 million francs would be $2.5 million:

Exposed assets	FF100 million
Exposed liabilities	– 50 million
Net exposure	FF 50 million

Predevaluation rate (FF4 = $1) FF50 million =	$12.5 million
Postdevaluation rate (FF5 = $1) FF50 million =	-$10.0 million
Potential exchange loss	$ 2.5 million

These translation gains and losses do not involve actual cash flows. They are purely of a paper nature. Some companies are concerned about this risk, because it affects their ability to raise capital, their cost of capital, their earnings per share, and their stock price.

Transaction Exposure

Gains or losses may result from the settlement of transactions whose payment terms are stated in a foreign currency. Transaction exposure measures the effect of an exchange-rate change on outstanding obligations which existed before exchange rates changed but were settled after the exchange-rate change. Transactions which are subject to transaction exposure include credit purchases and credit sales whose prices are stated in foreign currencies, borrowed and loaned funds denominated in foreign currencies, and uncovered forward contracts.

Receipts and payments denominated in foreign currencies are considered to be exposed. If exposed receipts are greater than exposed payments, foreign currency depreciations will cause exchange losses, and foreign currency appreciations will cause exchange gains. On the other hand, if exposed receipts are smaller than exposed payments, foreign currency depreciations will create exchange gains, and foreign currency appreciations will create exchange losses.

Example 7-2.   An American firm sold machinery to a British firm through its U.K. subsidiary for 100,000 pounds with terms of 180 days. The payments must be received in pounds. The spot rate for pounds is $1.70 and the U.S. seller expects to exchange 10,000 pounds for $17,000 when payment is received.

Transaction exposure arises because of the risk that the U.S. exporter will receive something other than $17,000 after the British pound receipts are exchanged for dollars. If the spot rate declines to $1.40 180 days from today, the U.S. exporter would receive only $14,000, $3,000 less than the expected $17,000. However, if the spot rate rises to $1.90 during the same period, the exporter would receive $19,000, an increase of $2,000 over the amount expected. If the U.S. exporter had invoiced in dollars, the transaction exposure would have shifted to the British importer. Unlike translation gains and loses, transaction gains and losses have a direct impact on actual cash flows.

Economic Exposure

Economic exposure measures the impact of an actual conversion on the net present value of expected future cash flows from a foreign investment project. Future effects of changes in exchange rates occur under the general category of economic risk. A multinational company may have established its subsidiary in a country with price stability, readily available funds, favorable balance of payments, and low rates of taxation. These positive features may disappear over time if the economic situation of the country deteriorates. Eventually, the local currency will devalue or depreciate. The subsidiary is likely to face immediate operational problems if it has to pay its imports in hard currencies or if it has borrowed from abroad. Exchange rate changes may also affect such economic factors as inflationary forces, price controls, the supply of loanable funds, and local labor availability.

Economic exposure is a broader and more subjective concept of exposure than either translation or transaction exposure, because it involves the potential effects of exchange-rate changes on all facets of a firm's operations. Economic exposure is difficult to measure but may be more significant than the others, because it relates to the long-term profit performance and hence the value of the firm.

Example 7–3.   For the coming year, a French subsidiary of an American firm is expected to earn 35 million francs after taxes, and its depreciation charge is estimated at 5 million francs. The exchange rate is expected to decrease from FF4 per dollar at present to FF5 per dollar for the next year.

The difference between the first-year cash flows with and without devaluation is computed as follows:

Profit after taxes	FF 35 million
Depreciation	+ 5 million
Cash flows from operation	FF 40 million

Predevaluation rate (FF4 = $1) FF40 million =	$10 million
Postdevaluation rate (FF5 = $1) FF40 million =	-$8 million
Potential exchange loss	$ 2 million

The subsidiary's economic loss is a decline in French francs cash flows equal to $2 million over the next 12 months. The translation loss or the transaction loss is a one-time loss, but the economic loss is an open-ended event. If the anticipated business activity were to stay the same for the next five years, cash flows would decrease by $2 million per year for five years.

Comparison of The Three Exposures

The management of foreign-exchange risk based on translation exposure is basically static and historically oriented. By definition, translation exposure does not look to the future impact of an exchange-rate change that has occurred or may occur. In addition, it does not involve actual cash flows. In contrast, both transaction and economic exposures look to the future impact of an exchange-rate change which has occurred or may occur. These exposures also involve actual or potential cash-flow changes.

Transaction risk and economic risk are the same in kind, but they differ in degree. For example, economic risk is essentially subjective because it depends on estimated future cash flows for an arbitrary time horizon. Transaction risk, on the other hand, is essentially objective because it depends on outstanding obligations which existed before changes in exchange rates but were settled after the changes in exchange rates. Table 7-1 illustrates major differences among these three exposures.

Table 7-1
Major Differences Among Three Types of Exposures

Variables	Translation Exposure	Transaction Exposure	Economic Exposure
Contract	Specific	Specific	General
Duration	A point in time	Period of contract	Project life
Gains (losses)	Easy to compute	Intermediate to compute	Difficult to compute
Gains (losses)	Paper in nature	Actual	Actual
Measurement	Depend on accounting rules	Depend on changes in actual spot rates	Depends on changes in actual spot rates
Hedging	Easy	Intermediate	Difficult
Extent of exposure	Determined by accounting rules	Determined by the nature of contract	Determined by product and factor markets
Value	Book value of assets and liabilities	Contract value of assets and liabilities	Market value of assets
Management of exposure	By the Treasury Department	By the Treasury Department	By all departments

Forecasting Exchange Rates

Because future exchange rates are uncertain, participants in international financial markets can never know for sure what the spot rate will be two months or one year ahead. So, currency forecasts must be made. In other words, the quality of a company's decisions depends on the accuracy of exchange rate projections. If some investors could forecast future spot rates more accurately than the rest of the market, they could make large profits.

Currency Forecasting and Market Efficiency

Banks and independent consultants offer many currency-forecasting services. Some multinational companies have in-house forecasting capabilities. Yet, no one should pay for currency-forecasting services if foreign exchange markets are perfectly efficient. The efficient market hypothesis holds that (1) spot rates reflect all current information, and (2) it is impossible for any market analyst to "beat the market" consistently.

Foreign exchange markets are efficient if the following conditions hold: First, there are many well-informed investors with ample funds for arbitrage opportunities when opportunities present themselves. Second, there are no barriers to movement of funds from one country to another. Third, transaction costs are negligible. Under these three conditions, exchange rates reflect all available information. Thus, exchange-rate changes at a given time must be due to new information alone. Because information, useful for currency forecasting, arrives randomly, exchange-rate changes follow a random walk. In other words, no one can consistently beat the market if foreign exchange markets are efficient.

Financial theorists generally define three forms of market efficiency: (1) weak form efficiency, (2) semi-strong form efficiency, and (3) strong form efficiency. Weak form efficiency implies that all information contained in past exchange-rate movements is fully reflected in current exchange rates. Hence, information about recent trends in a currency's price would not be useful for forecasting exchange-rate movements. Semi-strong form efficiency suggests that current exchange rates reflect all publicly available information, thereby making such information useless for forecasting exchange-rate movements. Strong form efficiency indicates that current exchange rates reflect all pertinent information, whether publicly available or privately held. If this form holds, then even insiders would find it impossible to earn abnormal returns in the exchange market.

Efficiency studies of foreign-exchange markets consist of the statistical tests used, currencies studied, and data bases (time periods) involved. Yet, clear-cut evidence on the efficient market hypothesis is unavailable, because study results are mixed. Nevertheless, all careful studies have concluded that the weak form of the efficient market hypothesis is essentially correct.

Empirical tests have also shown that the evidence of the semi-strong form efficiency is mixed. Almost no one believes that strong form efficiency is valid.

Ian Giddy and Gunter Dufey (1975) suggest that currency forecasting can be consistently useful or profitable only if the forecaster meets one criterion out of the following four:

1. The forecaster has exclusive use of a superior forecasting model.
2. The forecaster has consistent access to information before other investors.
3. The forecaster exploits small but temporary deviations from equilibrium.
4. The forecaster predicts the nature of government intervention in the foreign exchange market.

Forecasting Techniques

Two methods—fundamental analysis and technical analysis—are widely used to forecast exchange rates. Fundamental analysis relies heavily on economic models. Technical analysis bases predictions solely on price information. Fundamental analysis is the useful approach for assessing the fair value of foreign exchange rates. Still, some experts argue that technical analysis may better explain short-run exchange rate fluctuations. This divides analysts into fundamentalists and technicians. Both use quantitative models and qualitative analysis.

Fundamental Analysis.   Chapter 5 identified a series of equilibrium relationships that should exist among spot exchange rates, forward rates, interest rates, and inflation rates. Fundamental analysis or market-based forecasts stem from the economic theories described in Chapter 5—the PPP theory, the Fisher Effect, the International Fisher Effect, and the interest parity theory. Some forecasters believe that forward exchange rates objectively predict future spot exchange rates for major freely floating currencies. Because fundamental analysis has become more sophisticated in recent years, it now depends on computer-based econometric models to forecast exchange rates. These model builders believe that changes in certain economic indicators may trigger changes in exchange rates in the patterns similar to those in the past.

Technical Analysis.   Technical analysis has been applied to commodity and stock markets for many years, but its application to the foreign exchange market is a recent phenomenon. Yet, technical analysis of foreign exchange has attracted a growing audience. This method focuses exclusively on past price and volume movements rather than on economic and political factors. Success depends on whether technical analysts can discover forecastable price trends. Price trends will be forecastable only if price patterns repeat themselves. Charting and trend analyses are the two primary methods of technical analysis. Chartists and tape watchers examine all sorts of charts and graphs to identify recurring price patterns. They will buy or sell certain currencies if their prices divert from past patterns. Trend analysts seek to find price trends through mathematical models so that they can decide whether particular price trends will continue or shift direction.

Key Economic Indicators

Currencies are rarely devalued without prior indication of weakness. Many researchers in this area have attempted to forecast currency devaluation on the basis of key economic indicators. Some of these indicators are balance-of-payments deficits, international monetary reserves, inflation, monetary supply, and exchange spread between official versus market rates. These economic indicators are also used to forecast foreign exchange controls. However, many of these economic indicators depend on little theory or empirical studies behind them. Moreover, they can be used to forecast future exchange rates under the fixed exchange-rate system, but they have little use under the floating exchange-rate system.

The Balance of Payments.

Trends and forecasts for the balance of payments indicate the direction that the value of a currency is to be adjusted. If a country spends more abroad than it obtains from abroad over a sustained period, the possibility of devaluation increases. If the country receives more from abroad than it spends abroad, the probability of upvaluation increases.

In the long run, a balance-of-payments deficit is most unhealthy. A trend toward deficit positions in international trade and investment strongly indicates troubled times ahead. The two factors to be analyzed here are (1) the size and length of a deficit in the balance of payments, and (2) the ability of the country to finance its deficit. Balance-of-payments deficits tend to reduce official reserve assets and to increase official liabilities to foreigners. Thus, countries cannot continue to incur large external deficits without their currency devaluing. As the world is flooded with more and more of a country's currency due to large external deficits over a long period, the value of the country's currency must eventually fall.

International Reserves.

International monetary reserves are assets held by central banks or governments which can be used to settle international payments. They are composed of gold, Special Drawing Rights, and convertible foreign exchange. For most countries, the principal convertible currencies are the U.S. dollar, the British pound, the German mark, the Japanese yen, the Swiss franc, and the French franc.

International reserves reflect the solvency of a country—its ability to meet international obligations. Debt repayment obligations, profit and royalty obligations, and payments of purchases on credit represent international obligations. Continued balance-of-payments deficits decrease international reserves of a country that maintains fixed exchange rates, unless these deficits are offset by increased short-term loans or investment. As international reserves of countries with flexible exchange rates decrease, they are likely to be judged in economic trouble. Both situations increase the likelihood of devaluation or depreciation.

Inflation. Many economic forces link the prices of real assets (inflation rates) with the prices of money (exchange rates). The relationship between inflation rates and exchange rates is provided by the purchasing power parity doctrine. According to this doctrine, currencies of countries with higher inflation rates than the United States tend to depreciate in value against the dollar. By the same token, currencies of countries with lower inflation rates than the United States tend to appreciate in value against the dollar.

Inflation and devaluation may not necessarily have a causal relationship, but they may have a partial correlation. In some cases, both inflation and devaluation occur due to a dramatic increase in the cost of some other factors, such as the cost of imported petroleum. In other situations, their relationship is circular. For example, domestic inflation leads to a price disadvantage for exported goods and a price advantage for imported goods. These two forces cause balance-of-payments problems, which in turn lead to devaluation or depreciation. Interestingly enough, devaluation in its turn raises prices of such essential imports as raw materials or foodstuffs, thereby creating another round of domestic inflation.

Money Supply. Money supply consists of currency in circulation and demand deposits. The classical economic theory assumes that a country should experience an increase in output to match increases in demand at home. Increases in output cause unemployment to fall and the level of real income to rise. Theoretically, all this can happen without inflation. But evidence indicates that wages and other forms of payment tend to increase at a faster rate than output. In this situation, the supply of money grows faster than is warranted by real economic growth. Too much money becomes available to purchase too few goods; prices begin to rise; and eventually, this leads to inflation. Simply stated, inflation is the consequence of a country's spending beyond its capacity to produce. As an economy approaches full employment, any additional increase in money supply can serve only to make prices spiral upward. Some foreign exchange forecasters use the money supply as a timely indicator for price changes and as evidence of exchange-rate changes for maintaining purchasing power parity.

Official versus Market Rates. Many foreign exchange forecasters use the exchange spread between official and market rates as a valid indicator of currency health. Their comparison observes the value that outsiders place on a particular currency. Under a freely flexible exchange system, no spread exists between these two exchange rates. However, some spread is practically inevitable where currencies are pegged and exchange controls are imposed on the convertibility of local currency into hard currencies. In such a situation, one measures the falling confidence in a local currency by checking the widening spread between official and free market rates.

Many underdeveloped countries have exchange controls, but they also have a free market rate for certain types of transactions. Payments for imports, dividend remittances, and some other international fund transfers may be required to be made at an official exchange rate. However, remittances for foreign tourists entering the country or for local residents going overseas may be converted into a hard currency or a local currency at the free market rate. The rise in the spread between official and market rates would serve as an indication of increasing apprehension over the near future. Thus, the increasing excess of a free market rate over an official rate can be used as a valuable piece of evidence to forecast devaluation.

Other Indicators.   A number of exchange-rate forecasting models are available from academic journals or commercial sources. However, the list of factors used in forecasting devaluation or revaluation varies from forecaster to forecaster. In addition to the five economic indicators described previously, such economic factors as government spending, relative interest rates, national incomes, and business cycles have been suggested as variables relevant to exchange-rate forecasting.

Perhaps the most comprehensive list of factors has been provided by Christopher Korth (1972). This list includes: level of reserve assets, sudden imbalance in the balance of payments, level of foreign indebtedness, wide fluctuations in the balance of payments, extraordinary factors such as wars, domestic rate of inflation, anticipated changes in trading partners' economies, exchange and capital controls, importance of the currency in international use, importance of the country in international trade, elasticities of supply and demand for trade and other balance-of-payments items, past history of changes in the value of currency, personal philosophies of high-ranking government officials, economic philosophies of the political party in power, proximity of elections, opinions of bankers and leading businessmen, large forward exchange discounts or premiums, unusually low or high interest rates, significant change in domestic investment and spending, and trend of domestic real estate values.

Translation Exposure Management

Financial statements were intended to present information about the performance, financial position, and cash flows of a company. To meet this purpose, the financial statements of separate entities within a business enterprise are consolidated and presented as though they were the financial statements of a single economic entity. Financial statements are frequently restated or translated from one currency into another to assist the users of the financial statements such as investors and creditors.

Accounting for foreign currency translation is undoubtedly one of the most controversial technical issues facing multinational companies. Many of the problems associated with currency translation come from the fact that foreign exchange rates, used to carry out the translation process, are seldom fixed. Consequently, actual operating results can vary, often markedly, from reported results because of the differences in translation rates employed. This is why foreign currency translation has become even more controversial and important since 1973 when the flexible exchange-rate system was established. This flexible exchange system abolished the old fixed exchange-rate system that was established in 1944 based on the Bretton Woods Agreement.

Translation Rules

If exchange rates have changed since the previous accounting period, the translation of financial statement items denominated in foreign currencies will result in foreign exchange gains or losses. The possible extent of these gains or losses often depends on the rules that govern translation. The four translation methods most widely used by multinational companies are current-noncurrent, monetary-nonmonetary, temporal, and current rate.

Current/Noncurrent Method.   In using the current-noncurrent method, one assumes that financial statement accounts should be grouped according to maturity. Under this method, all current assets and current liabilities of foreign affiliates are translated into the parent currency at current exchange rates. All noncurrent assets, noncurrent liabilities, and owners' equity are translated at historical exchange rates.

Monetary/Nonmonetary Method.   Under this method, monetary assets and monetary liabilities are translated at current exchange rates. Nonmonetary assets, nonmonetary liabilities, and owners' equity are translated at historical rates. Monetary assets include cash, accounts receivable, and notes receivable. Nonmonetary assets include inventory and fixed assets. In general, all liabilities are monetary liabilities.

Temporal Method.   This method produces essentially the same results as the monetary-nonmonetary method under generally accepted accounting principles of historical accounting in the United States. The only difference is that under the monetary-nonmonetary method, inventory is always translated at the historical rate. Under the temporal method, inventory is usually translated at the historical rate, but it could be translated at the current rate if inventory is carried at market prices or replacement cost.

Current Rate Method.   This method is the simplest; all assets and liabilities are translated at the current rate. Existing equity accounts such as common stock and paid-in capital are translated at the historical rate.

Comparison of The Four Translation Methods.   All financial statement items restated in terms of the parent currency are the foreign currency amount multiplied by the appropriate exchange rate. Table 7-2 compares the four translation methods—current-noncurrent, monetary-non-monetary, temporal, and current rate—in terms of the exchange rate for each balance sheet item.

Table 7-2
Exchange Rates Used to Translate Balance-Sheet Items

Balance-Sheet Accounts	Current/ Noncurrent	Monetary/ Non-monetary	Temporal	Current Rate
Cash	C	C	C	C
Receivables	C	C	C	C
Payables	C	C	C	C
Inventory	C	H	H or C	C
Fixed assets	H	H	H	C
Long-term debt	H	C	C	C
Net worth	H	H	H	H

Note: C represents the current rate and H represents the historical rate.

Example 7-4. Assume that a foreign subsidiary of a U.S. multinational company has the following: (1) cash = FC100; (2) accounts receivable = FC150; (3) inventory = FC200; (4) fixed assets = FC250; (5) current liabilities = FC100; (6) long-term debt = FC300; and (7) net worth = FC300. Let us further assume that the historical exchange rate is $2 = FC1, the current exchange rate is $1 = FC1, and inventory is carried at market prices.

Table 7-3 illustrates the effect of each translation method on the balance sheet. Exchange gains or losses are shown here as a separate plug (balancing) account to show how they would be derived. However, in actual practice net worth would be used as a plug figure, or exchange gains and losses would be closed out to retained earnings.

Table 7-3
Comparison of Four Translation Method

Accounts	Foreign Currency	Current/ Noncurrent		Monetary/ Nonmonetary		Temporal		Current Rate	
Cash	FC100	1	$100	1	$100	1	$100	1	$100
Receivables	150	1	150	1	150	1	150	1	150
Inventory	200	1	200	2	400	1	200	1	200
Fixed assets	250	2	500	2	500	2	500	1	250
Total	FC700		$950		$1150		$950		$700
Current debts	FC100	1	$100	1	$100	1	$100	1	$100
Long-term debt	300	2	600	1	300	1	300	1	300
Net worth	300	2	600	2	600	2	600	2	600
Gains (losses)			(350)		150		(50)		(300)
Total	FC700		$950		$1150		$950		$700

Under the current-noncurrent method, an exchange loss of $350 is recorded because current assets are greater than current liabilities. On the other hand, under the monetary-nonmonetary method, an exchange gain of $150 is recorded because monetary liabilities exceed monetary assets. Under the current rate method, the exchange loss is $300 for two reasons: (1) all accounts except net worth are translated at the current exchange rate, and (2) exposed assets are greater than exposed liabilities.

FASB No. 8 and FASB No. 52

The accounting profession has recognized the growing importance of foreign-currency transactions and/or foreign operations. In October 1975, the Financial Accounting Standards Board (FASB) issued its Statement No. 8, *Accounting for the Translation of Foreign Currency Transactions and Foreign Currency Financial Statements*. FASB No. 8 formerly required U.S. companies to translate their foreign-currency financial statements into dollars by applying the appropriate exchange rate to the measurement basis of each account; the appropriate exchange rate may be the historical rate, the current rate, or the average rate. This statement also required companies to show all foreign-exchange gains or losses in their quarterly and annual income statements, regardless of whether these gains or losses were realized or unrealized.

FASB No. 8 was a product of considerable effort, including extensive exposure drafts and discussion memoranda, by the FASB to resolve the translation issue. However, from its inception in Autumn 1975, FASB No. 8 was the subject of extensive debate; most of the criticism centered on recognizing foreign exchange gains or losses. Companies claimed that FASB No. 8 grossly distorted their earnings because of the sharp fluctuations in foreign exchange rates. The FASB issued its Statement No. 52, *Foreign Currency Translation*, on December 7, 1981. FASB No. 52 supersedes FASB No. 8. In 1982, U.S. companies were allowed to utilize either FASB No. 8 or FASB No. 52. Ford used FASB No. 52 in 1982 to exclude its translation loss of about $220 from the income statement. In the same year, General Motors employed FASB No. 8 to include its translation gain of about $384 million in the income statement.

FASB No. 52 requires the use of the current exchange rate in translating foreign-currency financial statements into U.S. dollars. Such translation adjustments are placed directly in stockholders' equity rather than income. Thus, FASB No. 52 has substantially reduced fluctuations in many companies' reported earnings caused by gyrations in foreign exchange rates under FASB No. 8.

Functional Currency.   In this section, two terms are extensively used: parent currency and functional currency. **Parent currency**, sometimes called reporting currency, is the currency of the country where the parent company is located. For example, the parent currency of U.S. based multinational companies is the dollar. The **functional currency**, usually called foreign currency or local currency, is the currency of the country where the foreign operation of a multinational company is located. The functional currency of an entity, as defined in FASB No. 52 (paragraph 39), is "the currency of the primary economic environment in which the entity operates; normally, that is the currency of the environment in which an entity primarily generates and expends cash."

The term "functional currency" was first used in the translation literature in conjunction with FASB No. 52. Functional currency is, in fact, a key feature of FASB No. 52 because it determines the choice of translation method. This feature is very important because the translation method employed determines the translation rate and the disposition of exchange gains and losses. If the foreign currency is determined to be the functional currency, FASB No. 52 is used to carry out the translation process. On the other hand, if the U.S. dollar is deemed to be the functional currency, FASB No. 8 is used to remeasure foreign currency operations in dollars.

Normally, a foreign subsidiary's functional currency is the currency of the foreign country in which it operates and generates net cash flows. For example, a French subsidiary with relatively contained and integrated operations in France would have the franc as its functional currency. Such translation adjustments do not affect cash flows and are not included in net income. Consequently, translation adjustments are placed directly in stockholders' equity. However, if the French subsidiary has some transactions and open account balances denominated in German marks from a German customer, those balances must be restated into francs and gains or losses must be included in the subsidiary's net income before the statements are translated into U.S. dollars during the consolidation process.

The functional currency of an entity is not always identical with the currency of the country in which the foreign operation is located or the currency of the country in which the records are maintained. The dollar is the functional currency and exchange gains or losses must be included in the net income for those foreign operations whose cash flows directly affect the parent's U.S. dollar cash flows on a current basis. Such a situation may occur when the foreign entity is merely an extension of the parent company. In this case, the functional currency is the reporting currency of the parent company. For example, if the Mexican subsidiary of a U.S. parent company received all its raw materials from the United States and resold all its output back to the United States, the U.S. dollar should be the functional currency.

Foreign subsidiaries in countries with runaway inflation are another case in which the reporting currency is used as the functional currency. FASB No. 52 (paragraph 11) states that "the financial statements of a foreign entity in a highly inflationary economy shall be remeasured as if the functional currency were the reporting currency." A highly inflationary economy is defined as one that has cumulative inflation of approximately 100 percent or more over a three-year period. The cumulative inflation for three years is a compounded rate; as a result, an annual inflation rate of about 26 percent produces a cumulative inflation of 100 percent over three years.

In some cases, it is difficult to determine the functional currency of a foreign operation. For example, an entity might have more than one distinct and separable operation, in which case each operation may be considered a separate entity. If those operations are conducted in different economic environments, they may have different functional currencies. If a foreign operation conducts significant amounts of business in two or more countries, the functional currency may not be clearly identifiable. In those instances, the functional currency depends on the economic facts and circumstances pertaining to a particular foreign operation. Thus, multinational companies must evaluate the nature and purpose of their foreign operations to decide on the appropriate functional currency.

Differences Between FASB Nos. 8 and 52. The underlying assumption of FASB No. 8 was that consolidated financial statements should reflect the transactions of the consolidated group as though all operations, including foreign operations, were extensions of the parent's domestic operations. This premise failed to recognize the fact that in many cases the operations of foreign subsidiaries exist in other environments and involve foreign-currency cash flows in those other environments. Thus, the results of accounting after translation did not portray the foreign-currency cash flows.

FASB No. 52 is intended to portray foreign-currency cash flows. Companies using the functional currency approach and the current rate method can maintain compatible income and cash flows before and after translation. Financial summary indicators, such as profit margin, gross profit, and debt-to-equity ratio, are almost the same after translation into the reporting currency as they are in the functional currency. In addition, the volatility of a company's reported earnings should be reduced under FASB No. 52 because its foreign exchange gains or losses are placed directly in stockholders' equity rather than income.

Translation of Foreign-Currency Financial Statements. FASB No. 8 had formally required U.S. firms to use the temporal method from 1976 until the FASB replaced it with FASB No. 52 in December 1981. According to the temporal method, balance-sheet items carried at current or future prices should be translated at the current exchange rate, while balance-sheet items carried at historical prices should be translated at the applicable historical rate. Under this method, sales revenue and operating expenses are translated at the average exchange rate, while cost of goods sold and depreciation are translated at the applicable historical rate. Exchange gains or losses from the translation of the balance sheet should be included in the income statement.

Under FASB No. 52, the current exchange-rate method is used to translate foreign-currency balance sheets from their functional currency into the reporting currency. The current exchange-rate method is the easiest to apply because under this method, all assets and liabilities are translated at the current exchange rate. Only owners' equity is translated at the historical exchange rate. Unlike the controversial FASB No. 8, FASB No. 52 does not require companies to include translation adjustments in net income. Instead, a company will report these translation adjustments separately and accumulate them in a separate component of equity until it sells or substantially liquidates the foreign net investment.

Under FASB No. 52, all income-statement elements are translated in a manner that produces approximately the same result as using the exchange rate in effect on the dates on which these elements are recognized. However, paragraph 12 of FASB No. 52 provides that "because translation at the exchange rates on the dates the numerous revenues, expenses, gains, and losses are recognized is generally impractical, an appropriately weighted average exchange rate for the period may be used to translate those elements."

Example 7–5.

The Canadian subsidiary of a U.S. multinational corporation with a Canadian dollar functional currency started business and acquired fixed assets on January 1, 1992, when the Canadian dollar/U.S. dollar exchange rate was 0.85. Table 7–4 applies the temporal method and the current exchange-rate method to hypothetical financial statements which are affected by 11.8 percent devaluation and revaluation. For devaluation, the exchange rate on December 31, 1992, was 0.75 and the weighted average rate for the period was 0.80. For revaluation, the exchange rate on December 31, 1992, was 0.95 and the weighted average rate for the period was 0.90.

Table 7–4 shows that fluctuations in reported earnings in this example are reduced significantly under FASB No. 52 because we used a single rate in translating balance-sheet items and reported translation adjustments in equity. Under the new standard, moreover, net income of the U.S. parent company is the same as what is expected based on the level of earnings in Canadian dollars.

Under FASB No. 52, a translation loss of $11 is the expected economic effect of the Canadian dollar whose value declined against the U.S. dollar. This translation loss of $11 is reported in the balance sheet as "equity adjustments from translation." On the other hand, FASB No. 8 required the U.S. parent company to report a translation gain of $70 in the income statement.

In contrast, a translation gain of $11 under the new standard is the expected economic effect of the Canadian dollar whose value increased against the U.S. dollar. The gain is placed on the balance sheet directly in stockholders' equity. On the other hand, the old standard requires the U.S. parent company to recognize a translation loss of $58 in the income statement.

Under FASB No. 52, key Canadian-dollar ratios, such as net income to revenue, gross profit, and long-term debt to equity, are maintained after translation from the Canadian dollar to the U.S. dollar. However, these ratios in the Canadian dollar are significantly different from those in the U.S. dollar under FASB No. 8.

Table 7–4
Translation of Foreign Currency Operations
Under FASBs No. 8 and No. 52

| | Canadian Dollars | After Devaluation of Canadian $ | | | | After Revaluation of Canadian $ | | | |
| | | FASB No. 8 | | FASB No. 52 | | FASB No. 8 | | FASB No. 52 | |
		Rates Used	U.S. Dollars	Rates Used	U.S. Dollars	Rates Used	U.S. Dollars	Rates Used	U.S. Dollars
Balance Sheet:									
Cash & receivables	100	.75	75	.75	75	.95	95	.95	95
Inventory	300	.81*	243	.75	225	.91*	273	.95	285
Fixed assets, net	600	.85	510	.75	450	.85	510	.95	570
Total	1000		828		750		878		950
Current liabilities	180	.75	135	.75	135	.95	171	.95	171
Long–term debt	700	.75	525	.75	525	.95	665	.95	665
Common stock	100	.85	85	.85	85	.85	85	.85	85
Retained earnings	20		83		16		(43)		18
Equity adjustments from translation	—		—		(11)		—		11
Total	1000		828		750		878		950
Income Statement:									
Revenue	130	.80	104	.80	104	.90	117	.90	117
Cost of goods sold	(60)	.83*	(50)	.80	(48)	.93*	(56)	.90	(54)
Depreciation	(20)	.85*	(17)	.80	(16)	.95*	(19)	.90	(18)
Other expenses	(10)	.80	(8)	.80	(8)	.90	(9)	.90	(9)
Exchange gain (loss)	—		70		—		(58)		—
Income before tax	40		99		32		(25)		36
Income tax	(20)	.80	(16)	.80	(16)	.90	(18)	.90	(18)
Net Income	20		83		16		(43)		18
Ratios:									
Net income/revenue	0.15		0.80		0.15		negative		0.15
Gross profit margin	0.54		0.52		0.54		0.52		0.54
Long–term debt/equity	5.83		3.13		5.83		15.83		5.83

*Historical rates for inventory, cost of goods sold, and depreciation of fixed assets.

Hedging Translation Exposure

When a devaluation or upvaluation seems likely, a company must determine whether it has an unwanted net exposure to exchange risk. If the company finds an unwanted net exposure to exchange risk, it can use a variety of techniques in order to reduce this net exposure. Adopting particular techniques to protect a net exposure depends primarily on two factors: (1) the potential exchange loss from exchange rate fluctuations and (2) the cost of buying protection against the potential exchange loss. The level of risk as measured by the potential exchange loss can be compared with the cost of providing protection against the foreign exchange loss. Essentially, management's basic objective with any exposure is to minimize the amount of probable exchange losses and the cost of protection.

An arrangement that eliminates translation risk is said to hedge that risk. A hedge is designed to substitute a known cost of buying protection against foreign exchange risk for an unknown translation loss. One can use a variety of techniques to deal with translation exposure. These techniques consist of one major group of hedging devices: a balance-sheet hedge. In order to implement this hedging device, a company must increase hard-currency assets and reduce soft-currency assets at the same time; it should decrease hard-currency debts and increase soft-currency debts. Hard currencies are those currencies which are likely to appreciate; soft currencies are those currencies which are likely to depreciate.

Balance–Sheet Hedge.

Balance-sheet hedges are generally employed to minimize translation exposure. A balance-sheet hedge involves the selection of the currency in which exposed assets and liabilities are denominated so that an exchange-rate change would make exposed assets equal to exposed liabilities. To attain this objective, a company must maintain the same amount of exposed assets and exposed liabilities in a particular currency. A devaluation would affect both types of balance-sheet accounts equally; thus, the company would suffer neither a gain nor a loss.

There are two types of balance-sheet hedges in the event of a devaluation: operations with third parties and intercompany operations. In the context of a subsidiary's relationship with other firms, the reduction of undesirable exposures would involve the following procedures: sell the weak currency forward, reduce local-currency holdings, tighten credit terms to reduce local-currency receivables, increase local-currency borrowing, and delay local-currency payables. These procedures would be reversed for hard-currency assets and liabilities.

When the parent company has several subsidiaries, intracompany accounts can also be used to reduce foreign exchange exposure. These methods include transfer price adjustments, the accelerated payments of dividends and intracompany accounts payable, and the delayed collection of intracompany accounts receivable. These techniques require a multinational company to adopt the following two basic strategies:

1. The company must increase hard-currency assets and decrease hard-currency liabilities.
2. The company must decrease soft-currency assets and increase soft-currency liabilities.

Table 7-5
Basic Hedging Techniques and Their Costs

Depreciation	Costs
Sell local currency forward.	Transaction costs; difference between forward and spot rates.
Reduce levels of local currency and marketable securities.	Operational problems; opportunity cost (loss of higher interest rates on local securities).
Tighten credit (reduce local currency receivables).	Lost sales and profits.
Delay collection of hard currency receivables.	Cost of financing additional hard currency receivables.
Increase imports of hard currency goods.	Financing and holding costs.
Borrow locally.	Higher interest rates.
Delay payments of payables.	Harm to credit reputation.
Speed up dividend and fee remittances to parent and other subsidiaries.	Borrowing cost if funds are not available or loss of higher interest rates if local securities must be sold.
Speed up payment of intersubsidiary payables.	Opportunity cost of money.
Delay collection of intersubsidiary receivables.	Opportunity cost of money.
Invoice exports in foreign currency and imports in local currency.	Lost export sales or lower price; premium price for imports.

Source: Shapiro, A. C., *Multinational Financial Management* Boston: Allyn & Bacon, 1992, p. 216.

Table 7-5 presents a comprehensive list of basic hedging procedures for devaluations and the costs of these hedging procedures.

Transaction Exposure Management

An action which removes transaction risk is said to **cover** that risk. A cover involves the use of forward contracts, a combination of spot market and money market transactions, and other techniques to protect a foreign exchange loss in the conversion from one currency to another. The term "conversion" relates to transaction exposure because the transaction exposure involves the actual conversion of exposed assets and liabilities from one currency to another. If multinational companies decide to cover their transaction exposure, they may select from a variety of techniques:

1. Forward market hedge.
2. Money market hedge.
3. Options market hedge.
4. Swap agreements.

Forward Exchange Market Hedge

A forward exchange market hedge involves a contract and a source of funds to fulfill that contract. The contract permits the exchange of one currency for another at a fixed rate on some future date. The purchase of a forward contract substitutes a known cost for the uncertain cost due to foreign exchange risk caused by the possible devaluation of one currency in terms of another. Although the cost of a forward contract is usually smaller than the uncertain cost, the forward contract does not always assure the lowest cost due to foreign exchange-rate change. The forward contract simply fixes this cost in advance, thus eliminating the uncertainty caused by foreign exchange-rate change. For example, an American company may have a German mark import payable in nine months. The American company can cover this risk by purchasing marks at a certain price for the same date forward as the payment maturity.

A forward exchange market hedge as a source of funds involves funds already available and funds due because of some business operation. An example of funds already available would be pounds held in the United Kingdom for an airplane being built in the United States, payment for the airplane being due in nine months in dollars, and the British company already having bought dollars forward. The available pounds will be utilized to pay the forward contract. An example of funds due because of some business operation would be revenues from an export sale by a British company to the United States billed in dollars. The dollar export proceeds may be committed to fulfill a forward purchase of pounds for dollars.

Money Market Hedge

Like a forward exchange market hedge, a money market hedge involves a contract and a source of funds to carry out that contract. In this case, the contract represents a loan agreement. Assume that an American company has a French franc import payable in 90 days. It may borrow in dollars, convert the proceeds into French francs, buy a 90-day French Treasury bill, and pay the import bill with the funds derived from the sale of the Treasury bill. Of course, it can buy French francs in the foreign exchange spot market when the import bill becomes due.

A money market hedge is similar to a forward market hedge. The difference is that the cost of the money market hedge is determined by differential interest rates while the cost of the forward exchange market approach is determined by forward premium or discount. If foreign exchange markets and money markets are in equilibrium, the forward market approach and the money market approach incur the same cost.

Options Market Hedge

Companies understand that hedging techniques such as the forward exchange market hedge and the money market hedge can backfire or may even be costly when an accounts-payable currency depreciates or an accounts receivable currency appreciates over the hedged period. Under these circumstances, an uncovered strategy might outperform the forward exchange market hedge or the money market hedge. The ideal type of hedge should protect the company from adverse exchange rate movements but allow the company to benefit from favorable exchange rate movements. Currency options contain these attributes. By buying a call option on the foreign currency, the company can lock in a maximum dollar price for its foreign currency accounts payable. By purchasing a put option on the foreign currency, the company can lock in a minimum dollar price for its foreign currency accounts receivable.

Example 7–6.   To see how forward exchange market, money market, and options market hedges may be utilized to protect against transaction exposure, assume that an American firm has sold an airplane to a German firm for 100,000 marks with terms of 90 days. Let us further assume that the spot rate for marks is $0.5233, the 90-day forward rate for marks is $0.5335, the German 90-day interest rate is 10 percent, and the U.S. 90-day interest rate is 17.8 percent. The interest rates are in equilibrium with forward exchange quotations, and this is confirmed by the following computation using Equation 5-2:

$$\frac{n\text{-}day\ F\ -\ S}{S} \times \frac{360}{90} = \text{domestic rate} - \text{foreign rate}$$

$$\frac{\$0.5335\ -\ \$0.5233}{\$0.5233} \times \frac{360}{90} = 17.8\% - 10.0\%$$

$$7.8\% = 7.8\%$$

The U.S. company's bank believes that the spot rate in 90 days will rise to $0.6000, which is higher than the implicit unbiased forecast of $0.5335 that exists in the currency forward quotation. Finally, assume that put options with a three–month settlement date have a strike price of $0.5369 per mark and a premium of $0.01 per mark.

There are four alternatives available to the U.S. company: do not hedge (take the transaction risk), hedge in the forward exchange market, hedge in the money market, or hedge in the options market.

If the U.S. company decides to accept the transaction risk, it would receive 100,000 marks in 90 days and sell them in the foreign exchange market for dollars. If the bank's forecast is accurate, the U.S. company would receive $60,000 ($0.6000 x 100,000 marks) in 90 days. However, that receipt is subject to foreign exchange risk. If the mark should decline to $0.4000, the U.S. company would receive only $40,000, which is $20,000 less than expected. The $40,000 could in fact be insufficient to cover the manufacturing cost of the airplane. On the other hand, if the mark should increase in value even more than the bank's forecast, the U.S. company would receive substantially more than $60,000.

If the U.S. company wishes to hedge its transaction exposure in the forward market, it would sell 100,000 marks in the forward market for $53,350. This is known as a covered transaction in which the U.S. company no longer has foreign exchange risk. In 90 days, the U.S. company would receive 100,000 marks from the German importer, deliver the proceeds to the bank against its forward sale, and receive $53,350. It should be recognized that the certain $53,350 is less than the uncertain $60,000 expected from the unhedged position because the forward market quotation is not identical with the bank's forecast.

In addition to the forward exchange market approach, the U.S. company can also cover its transaction against foreign exchange risk through the money market approach. The money market approach works as follows: (1) borrow 97,561 marks from a Bonn bank at 10 percent per annum (2.5 percent per quarter) in exchange for a promise to pay 100,000 marks (97,561 marks x 1.025); (2) receive $51,054 (97,561 marks x $0.5233) by exchanging the 97,561 marks for dollars at the current spot rate of $0.5233; (3) invest this sum in the U.S. money market at 17.8 percent per annum (4.45 percent per quarter) and receive $53,326 ($51,054 x 1.0445) at the end of three months. This sum should be equal to the sum received in the forward exchange market hedge described earlier. The small difference between these two sums is due to a compounding error.

Finally, the U.S. firm can cover its mark receivables with the put option. The U.S. firm buys put options for a total premium of $1,000 (100,000 marks x $0.01), exercises its options in 90 days, and sells 100,000 marks at a strike price of $0.5369 for $53,690. Thus, the U.S. firm would obtain a net amount of $52,690 ($53,690 − $1,000) in exchange for 100,000 marks at the end of three months. If the spot rate of the German mark should exceed $0.5369 in 90 days, the U.S. firm would let the option contract expire unexercised and convert the 100,000 marks at the prevailing spot rate.

Options Versus Forward Contracts. A forward contract is often an imperfect hedging instrument because it is a fixed agreement to buy or sell a foreign currency at a specified price in the future. However, in many practical situations, companies are not sure whether their hedged foreign currency cash flows will materialize. Consider the situations where: (1) an overseas deal may fall through; (2) a bid on a foreign currency contract may be rejected; or (3) a foreign subsidiary's dividend payments may exceed the expected amount. In such cases, companies may not need the obligation, but the right, to buy or sell a foreign currency at a specified price in order to reduce their exchange-rate risk. Ian Giddy (1983) suggested that companies should use the following general rules to choose between forward contracts and currency options for hedging purposes:

1. When the quantity of a foreign currency cash outflow is known, buy the currency forward; when the quantity is unknown, buy a call option on the currency.
2. When the quantity of a foreign currency cash inflow is known, sell the currency forward; when the quantity is unknown, buy a put option on the currency.
3. When the quantity of a foreign currency flow is partially known and partially uncertain, use a forward contract to hedge the known portion and an option to hedge the maximum value of the uncertain remainder.

Swap Agreements

When exchange rates and interest rates fluctuate too widely, the risks of forward market and money market positions are so great that the forward exchange market and the money market may not function properly. Currency options are available only for a selected number of currencies and are inflexible. In such cases, governments or private traders may use swap arrangements to protect the value of both export sales, import orders, and outstanding loans deominated in foreign currencies. Swaps take many forms, but they can be divided into four general categories: foreign currency swaps, credit swaps, interest-rate swaps, and back-to-back loans.

Currency Swaps. A currency swap is an agreement between two parties to exchange local currency for hard currency at a specified future date. In other words, a company purchases the specified amount of local currency in the foreign exchange market and simultaneously buys a forward contract to sell this amount of local currency for hard currency at a future date. The former transaction is a spot transaction, and the latter transaction is a forward transaction. Thus, the currency swap is a simultaneous spot and forward transaction. This arrangement allows the company to recover the foreign exchange at a predetermined exchange rate.

To see how a currency swap works, assume that a U.S. parent company wants to lend British pounds to its British subsidiary and to avoid foreign exchange risk. The parent company would buy pounds in the spot market and lend them to the subsidiary. At the same time, the parent firm would sell the same amount of pounds in exchange for dollars in the forward market for the period of the loan. The parent company would receive the loan in terms of pounds from the subsidiary at maturity and exchange the pounds with the dollars to close the forward contract. Alternatively, the U.S. parent could enter into a swap agreement with a foreign exchange dealer where they trade dollars for pounds now and pounds for dollars at maturity.

Credit Swap. A credit swap is a hedging device similar to the foreign currency swap. This arrangement is a simultaneous spot and forward loan transaction between a private company and a bank of a foreign country. Suppose that an American company deposits a given amount of dollars in the New York office of a Colombian bank. In return for this deposit, the bank lends a given amount of pesos to the company's subsidiary in Colombia. The same contract provides that the bank would return the initial amount of dollars to the company at a specified date and that the subsidiary would return the original amount of pesos to the bank. By so doing, the American company recovers the original dollar amount of its deposit and the Colombian bank obtains a free hard-currency loan in the United States.

Example 7-7. A subsidiary in France requires the French franc equivalent of $1 million at the current exchange rate of FF4 per dollar, or FF4 million. To obtain FF4 million for the subsidiary in France, the parent must open a $1 million credit in favor of a French bank. The French bank charges the parent 10 percent per annum on the FF4 million made available to the subsidiary and pays no interest on the $1 million that the parent has deposited in favor of the bank. The parent's opportunity cost on the $1 million deposit is 20 percent.

The total cost of this swap consists of the parent's opportunity cost and the interest charge on the local currency loan. The opportunity cost at 20 percent on the $1 million is $200,000, and the 10 percent interest on the FF4 million (FF400,000) is $100,000 at the prevailing rate of FF4 per dollar. Thus, the total swap cost is $300,000 on a loan equivalent of $1 million or 30 percent. This example suggests that a direct loan costs the parent 20 percent while the credit swap costs it 30 percent. The parent cannot choose between these two alternatives solely on the basis of comparative costs because the direct loan is unhedged while the credit swap is hedged. The meaningful comparison of the two lending alternatives requires the parent to explicitly consider foreign exchange fluctuations. The direct loan is 10 percent cheaper only if the exchange rate stays the same.

If the multinational company is unable to predict future exchange-rate changes with a fair degree of accuracy, it may attempt to identify the future exchange rate that equates the cost of the credit swap with the cost of the direct loan, that is, the exchange rate where the multinational company would be indifferent between the two financing alternatives. Assume that this exchange rate is denoted by y. The cost of the direct loan from the parent consists of $200,000y$ = the French franc cost equivalent of the direct loan ($1 million X 20 percent) plus $(1,000,000y - 4,000,000)$ = the potential foreign exchange loss. The cost of the credit swap consists of $200,000y$ = the French franc cost equivalent of the $1 million deposited in favor of the French bank plus 400,000 = the interest paid on the FF4 million loan extended by the French bank at 10 percent per annum. Because the cost of the direct loan and the cost of the credit swap are the same at the exchange rate of y, we obtain:

<u>Direct Loan Cost</u>	<u>Credit Swap Cost</u>

$$200,000y + (1,000,000y - 4,000,000) = 200,000\ y + 400,000$$

$$y = 4.4$$

If the multinational company believes that the foreign exchange rate will not deteriorate to the equilibrium exchange rate of FF4.4 per dollar, it should choose the unhedged alternative that will be less costly. It should select the hedged alternative whenever its subjective assessment indicates that there is a significant chance for the foreign exchange rate to deteriorate beyond FF4.4 per dollar.

Interest Rate Swaps.   Interest rate swaps can be used to alter the exposure of a portfolio of assets or liabilities to interest rate movements. Under interest rate swaps, companies exchange cash flows of a floating rate for cash flows of a fixed rate, or exchange cash flows of a fixed rate for cash flows of a floating rate. Interest rate swaps are actively used when companies have costs of debt that are fixed but revenues that vary with the level of interest rates.

Take the example of a Korean company that borrowed $100 million from the Bank of America a year ago at 9.5 percent. The long-term interest rate in the United States has started to fall and, the Korean company believes that it will continue to fall. To take advantage of this drop in interest rates, the Korean company decides to enter an interest rate swap in dollars. It swaps $100 million with a fixed rate of 9.5 percent for $100 million with a floating rate equal to a six-month SDR rate. In effect, the Korean company is now protected against a downward movement in interest rates. Conversely, a reverse swap is arranged if the Korean company believes that the U.S. interest rate will increase.

Back–to–Back Loans.   Back-to-back loans or parallel loans are arranged by two multinational parent companies in two different countries. Suppose that a U.S. parent has a subsidiary in Japan and that a Japanese parent has a subsidiary in the United States. Let us further assume that each parent wants to lend to its subsidiary in the subsidiary's currency. These loans can be arranged without using the foreign exchange market. The U.S. parent lends the agreed amount in dollars to the American subsidiary of the Japanese parent. In return for this loan, the Japanese parent lends the same amount of money in yen to the Japanese subsidiary of the American parent. Parallel loan agreements involve the same loan amount and the same loan maturity. Of course, each loan is repaid in the subsidiary's currency. The parallel loan arrangement avoids foreign exchange risk because each loan is made and repaid in one currency.

There are a number of variations on this basic swap scheme. A variation may involve blocked funds. Assume that GM and IBM have their subsidiaries in Colombia. The Colombian subsidiary of GM has idle pesos but cannot remit to the United States because of Colombian restrictions on the remittance of funds. On the other hand, the Colombian subsidiary of IBM needs peso loans for expansion. In this case, in Colombia the GM subsidiary lends pesos to the IBM subsidiary, while in the United States IBM lends dollars to GM.

Economic Exposure Management

Companies can easily hedge translation and transaction exposures because these risks are based on projected foreign currency cash flows. However, the scope of economic exposure is broad because it can change a company's competitiveness across many markets and products. A company always faces economic risks from competition. When based in foreign currencies, the risks are long-term, hard to quantify, and cannot be dealt with solely through financial hedging techniques. Thus, international financial managers should assess economic exposure comprehensively. Their analysis should account for how variations in exchange rates influence: (1) a company's sales prospects in foreign markets (product market); (2) the costs of labor and other inputs to be used in overseas production (factor market); and (3) the home–currency value of financial assets and liabilities denominated in foreign currencies (capital market).

Economic exposure management is designed to neutralize the impact of unexpected exchange-rate changes on net cash flows. Diversified operations and financing can reduce economic exposure. They permit the multinational company to react to those opportunities which disequilibrium conditions in the foreign exchange, capital, and product markets present. Moreover, diversification strategies do not require that management predict disequilibrium conditions. Still, they require that it recognize them when they occur. In other words, the primary technique to minimize economic risk is strategic management in choosing product markets, pricing policies, promotion, and investment and financing alternatives.

When managing economic exposure, we resort to maneuvers across functional areas of operations. The functional areas of business operations for manufacturing companies are production, marketing, and finance. Production and marketing are clearly critical because they determine a company's existence—its ability to produce products and to sell them at a profit. But finance is an integral part of total management and cuts across functional boundaries.

Economic exposure management depends on the assumption that disequilibrium conditions exist in national markets for factors of production, products, and financial assets. For example, consider the cases where there are temporary deviations from purchasing power parity and the International Fisher Effect. Companies could observe changed comparative costs, profit margins, and sales volume in one country compared to another.

Diversified Production

Several production strategies can deal with economic exposure when disequilibrium conditions exist: (1) plant location, (2) input mix, (3) product sourcing, and (4) productivity increase.

First, companies with manufacturing facilities in many countries can quickly lengthen their production runs in one country and shorten them in another in line with the changing currency costs of production. Second, well-managed companies can substitute their input mix between domestic and imported inputs, depending on the relative prices of inputs and the degree of possible substitution. Third, well-diversified companies can make shifts in sourcing raw materials, components, and products in accordance with currency value fluctuations. Fourth, companies assaulted by wide swings in currency values can improve productivity by closing inefficient plants, automating production process, and negotiating concessions from unions.

Diversified Marketing

Marketing programs are normally adjusted only after changes in exchange rates. Yet, marketing initiatives under conditions of exchange-rate changes can obtain competitive leverage: (1) product strategy, (2) pricing strategy, (3) promotional options, and (4) market selection.

First, product differentiation, diversification, and deletions reduce the impact of exchange-rate fluctuations on worldwide corporate earnings. Second, prices may be adjusted to cope with the consequences of currency value changes. A pricing strategy is affected by a variety of factors such as market share, profit margin, competition, and price elasticity. Third, the size of promotional budgets for advertising, personal selling, and merchandising could be adjusted to reflect changes in currency values. For example, a devaluation of the Japanese yen may well be the time to increase a U.S. company's advertising budget in Japan. Fourth, a worldwide distribution system enables companies to neutralize the impact of unexpected exchange-rate changes on overall company revenues.

Diversified Financing

On the financial side, additional tools against economic risk are the currency denomination of long-term debt, place of issue, maturity structure, capital structure, and leasing versus buying. For example, LSI Logic, a manufacturer of custom-made microchips based in California, used four financial instruments: (1) equity markets in London and other European markets; (2) Japanese equity through institutional investors such as Nomura Securities; (3)

local Japanese credit markets through its joint venture partners; and (4) Eurobond issue, convertible bonds through Swiss and U.S. securities firms.

Diversified financing sources allow a company to improve its overall financial performance because interest-rate differentials do not always equal expected changes in exchange rates. In addition to taking advantage of unexpected differentials in diversified markets, companies reduce economic risk by matching the mix of currencies in loan portfolios or operating expenses to the mix of currencies in expected revenues.

Summary of Economic Exposure Management

Purely domestic companies do not have as many options for reacting to international disequilibrium conditions as multinational companies. International diversification neutralizes the impact of unexpected exchange-rate changes on corporate new-cash flows. Exchange-rate changes under conditions of disequilibrium are likely to increase competitiveness in some markets and to reduce it in others. However, at least one serious constraint may limit the feasibility of a diversification strategy: companies with worldwide production systems may have to relinquish large economies of scale. However, these companies could still diversify sales and financing sources.

Summary

This chapter has discussed foreign exchange exposures, currency value forecasting, and exchange risk management. Every company faces an exposure to gain or loss from changes in exchange rates as soon as it chooses to finance its operations in a foreign country. Translation exposure occurs when companies translate financial statement accounts from a foreign currency to their home currency. Transaction exposure refers to possible gains or losses which may result from the settlement of transactions whose payment terms are stated in a foreign currency. Economic exposure measures the total impact of exchange-rate changes on a firm's profitability.

Currencies are rarely devalued or revalued without prior indication of their weakness or strength. Many researchers in this area have attempted to forecast currency devaluation or revaluation on the basis of key economic indicators. They include the balance-of-payments deficit, international reserves, inflation, money supply, exchange spread between official versus market rates, and interest rates. The use of such economic indicators depends largely upon the purchasing power parity theory. This theory holds that, in the long run, exchange rates reflect the relative purchasing power of currencies. In other words, it relates equilibrium changes in the exchange rate to changes in the ratio of domestic and foreign prices.

In essence, a hedge or a cover is a type of insurance which provides security against the risk of loss from a change in exchange rates. When a devaluation seems likely, the multinational company must determine whether it has any unwanted net exposure to foreign exchange risk. When the company finds that it has an unwanted net exposure to exchange risk, it can use a variety of techniques to reduce this net exposure. They include balance sheet hedges, forward exchange market hedges, money market hedges, option market hedges, and swaps. These techniques are essentially employed to minimize translation and transaction exposures. Economic exposure can be managed by balancing the sensitivity of revenues and expenses to exchange-rate changes through diversification and strategic planning.

Questions

1. Explain the conditions under which items and/or transactions are exposed to foreign exchange risks.

2. Three basic types of exchange exposure are translation exposure, transaction exposure, and economic exposure. Briefly explain each of these three types of exposure.

3. Describe corporate motives for currency forecasting.

4. Why should no one pay for currency-forecasting services if foreign exchange markets are perfectly efficient?

5. Explain fundamental analysis as a technique for forecasting exchange rates.

6. Explain technical analysis as a technique for forecasting exchange rates.

7. How should appreciation of a company's home currency affect its cash inflows? How should depreciation of a company's home currency affect its cash inflows?

8. How does FASB No. 8 differ from FASB No. 52?

9. What is the basic translation hedging strategy?

10. How will the weakened U.S. dollar affect the reported earnings of a U.S. company with subsidiaries all over the world? How will the strengthened U.S. dollar affect the reported earnings of a U.S. company with subsidiaries all over the world?

11. How could a U.S. company hedge net payables in Japanese yen in terms of forward and options contracts?

12. How could a U.S. company hedge net receivables in Japanese yen in terms of forward and options contracts?

13. Are there any special situations where options contracts are better than forward contracts or vice versa?

14. What are the major problems of economic exposure management?

15. What is the basic purpose of economic exposure management?

16. How do most companies deal with their economic exposure?

Problems

7-1   A U.S. company has a single, wholly owned affiliate in Japan. This affiliate has exposed assets of 500 million yen and exposed liabilities of 800 billion yen. The exchange rate appreciates from 150 yen per dollar to 100 yen per dollar.

(a)   What is the amount of net exposure?
(b)   What is the amount of the translation gain or loss?
(c)   If the Japanese yen declines from 150 yen per dollar to 200 yen per dollar, what would be the amount of the translation gain or loss?

7-2   McDonnell Douglas sold an airplane to Korean Airlines for 840 million won with terms of one year. McDonnell will receive its payment in Korean won. The spot rate for the Korean currency is 700 won per dollar and McDonnell expects to exchange 840 million won for $1.2 million (840 million/700) when payment is received.

(a)   If the spot rate for won rises to 600 won per dollar one year from today, what is the potential transaction gain or loss?
(b)   If the spot rate for won declines to 1000 won per dollar at maturity, what is the potential transaction gain or loss?

7-3   For the coming year, a German subsidiary of an American company is expected to earn an after–tax profit of DM25 million, and its depreciation charge is estimated at DM5 million. The exchange rate is expected to rise from DM2.00 per dollar to DM1.5 per dollar for the next year.

(a)   What is the potential economic gain or loss?
(b)   If the anticipated business activity were to stay the same for the next three years, what would be the total economic gain or loss for three years?

7-4 Assume that a French subsidiary of a U.S. company has the following: (1) cash = FF1,000; (2) accounts receivable = FF1,500; (3) inventory = FF2,000; (4) fixed assets = FF2,500; (5) current liabilities = FF1,000; (6) long-term debt = FF3,000; (7) net worth = FF3,000 and net income before translation gain or loss = FF225. Let us further assume that the historical exchange rate is $0.25 per franc, the current exchange rate is $0.20 per franc, the average exchange rate is $0.225 per franc, and inventory is carried at cost.

    (a) Prepare the balance sheet of the U.S. subsidiary in France.
    (b) Determine the dollar net income without the translation gain or loss.
    (c) Determine the translation gain or loss under FASB No. 8 and FASB No. 52.
    (d) If the functional currency is determined to be the U.S. dollar, which translation method should be used? What kind of impact would it have on the company's net income?
    (e) Compute French franc debt ratio, return on investment, and long-term debt to equity ratio. Compare these ratios with the ratios in dollars under FASB No. 8 and FASB No. 52.

7-5 In 1982, Ford incurred an after–tax loss of $658 million, adopted FASB No. 52, and had a translation loss of $220 million. In the same year, General Motors earned an after–tax profit of $963 million, used FASB No. 8, and had a translation gain of $348 million.

    (a) Why do you think that in 1982, Ford adopted a new accounting rule, FASB No. 52, while GM used an old accounting rule, FASB No. 8?
    (b) What would have been Ford's reported net loss if it used FASB No. 8 instead of FASB No. 52?
    (c) What would have been GM's reported net income if it adopted FASB No. 52 instead of FASB No. 8?

7-6 A U.S. company has bought a number of TV sets from a Japanese company for 100,000 yen. This payment must be made in Japanese yen 180 days from today. The following quotations and expectations exist:

Present spot rate	$0.0050
180–day forward rate	$0.0051
Japanese interest rate	7.00%
U.S. interest rate	11.00%
Highest expected spot rate 180 days hence	$0.0052
Lowest expected spot rate 180 days hence	$0.0046

The U.S. company does not have any idle dollar balances at present, but it expects to have adequate cash in 180 days. Identify the alternatives available for making payment.

7-7 An American firm has just sold merchandise to a British customer for 100,000 pounds, with payment in British pounds three months from now. The U.S. company has purchased from its bank a three-month put option on 100,000 pounds at a strike price of $1.6660 per pound and a premium cost of $0.01 per pound. On the day the option matures, the spot exchange rate is $1.7100 per pound. Should the U.S. company exercise the option at that time or sell British pounds in the spot market?

7-8 Assume that a subsidiary in Germany needs DM500,000 and that a credit swap has been proven to be the least costly hedged alternative. Further assume that the best unhedged alternative is the direct loan from the parent and the cost of the direct loan is 20 percent. The current exchange rate is $0.5000 per DM1. To obtain DM500,000 for the subsidiary in Germany, the parent must open a $250,000 credit ($0.5000 x DM500,000) in favor of a German bank. The German bank charges 10 percent per year on the DM500,000 made available to the subsidiary and pays no interest on the $250,000 deposit that the parent has deposited in the bank.

(a) What is the exchange rate which would make the direct loan and the credit swap equally attractive?
(b) If most market analysts predict that the exchange rate will be $0.200 per mark in 180 days, which alternative would you recommend?
(c) If most market analysts predict that the exchange rate would be $0.300 per mark in 180 days, which alternative would you recommend?
(d) If the German bank should pay 5 percent interest on the $250,000 credit, what is the exchange rate that would make the direct loan and the credit swap equally attractive?

7-9 The current exchange rate of Swedish krona is SKr4 per $1. The Exton Company, the Swedish subsidiary of a U.S. multinational company, has the following balance sheet:

Assets		Claims on Assets	
Cash	SKr 500		
Accounts receivable	600	Accounts payable	SKr 100
Inventory (cost)	400	Notes payable	200
Inventory (market price)	800	Other payables	1,000
Total current assets	SKr 2,300	Total current lib.	SKr 1,300
		Long-term debt	800
Plant and equipment	2,400	Common stock	1,000
Accumulated depreciation	1,400	Retained earnings	200
Net plant and equipment	1,100	Exchange loss or gain	—
Total assets	SKr3,300	Total claims	SKr 3,300

If the krona devalues from SKr4 per $1 to SKr5 per $1, what would be the translation loss (gain) under each of the following methods: current/noncurrent, monetary/nonmonetary, temporal, and current rate?

References

Aggarwal, R., "Corporate Use of Options and Futures in Foreign Exchange Management," *Journal of Cash Management*, November/December, 1989, pp. 61–65.

Chicago Board of Trade, *Commodity Trading Manual*, Chicago: Board of Trade of the City of Chicago, 1989.

Choi, J. J., "Diversification, Exchange Risk, and Corporate International Investment," *Journal of International Business Studies*, Spring 1989, pp. 145-55.

Eckley, R. S., "Caterpillar's Ordeal: Foreign Competition in Capital Goods," *Business Horizons*, March–April 1989, pp. 80-86.

Ford Motor Company, *Annual Report 1982*, Dearborn, Michigan: Ford Motor Company, 1982, pp. 22-35.

General Motors Corporation, *Annual Report 1982*, Detroit: General Motors Corporation, 1982, pp. 17-27.

Giddy, I. H., "The Foreign Exchange Option as a Hedging Tool," *Midland Corporate Finance*, Fall 1983, pp. 32-43.

Giddy, I. H., and G. Dufey, "The Random Behavior of Flexible Exchange Rates," *Journal of International Business Studies*, Spring 1975, pp. 1-32.

Korth, C. M., "The Future of Currency: A Four-Step Procedure for Forecasting Change," *Business Horizons*, June 1972, pp. 67–76.

Lessard, D. R., and J. B. Lighstone, "Volatile Exchange Rates Can Put Operations at Risk," *Harvard Business Review*, July–August, 1986, pp. 107–14.

Levich, R. M., "How the Rise of the Dollar Took Forecasters by Surprise," *Euromoney*, August 1982, pp. 49–61.

Lewent, J. C., and A. J. Kearney, "Identifying, Measuring, and Hedging Currency Risk at Merck," *Journal of Applied Corporate Finance*, Winter 1990, pp. 19–28.

Logue, D. E., and R. J. Sweeney, "White Noise in Imperfect Markets: The Case of the Franc-Dollar Exchange Rate," *Journal of Finance*, June 1977, pp. 761–68.

Maloney, P. J., "Managing Currency Exposure: The Case of Western Mining," *Journal of Applied Corporate Finance*, Winter 1990, pp. 29–34.

Ott, M., and P. T. Veugelers, "Forward Exchange Rates in Efficient Markets: The Effects of News and Changes in Monetary Policy Regimes," *Review*, Federal Reserve Bank of St. Louis, June–July 1986, pp. 5–15.

Rogalski, R. J., and J. D. Vinso, "Price Level Variations as Predictors of Flexible Exchange Rates," *Journal of International Business Studies*, Spring–Summer 1977, pp. 71–82.

Swanson, P. E., and S. C. Caples, "Hedging Foreign Exchange Risk Using Forward Foreign Exchange Markets: An Extension," *Journal of International Business Studies*, Spring 1987, pp. 75–87.

Veazey, R. E., and S. H. Kim, "Translation of Foreign Currency Operations: SFAS No. 52," *Columbia Journal of World Business*, Winter 1982, pp. 17–22.

Wolff, C., "Exchange Rates, Innovations, and Forecasting," *Journal of International Money*, March 1988, pp. 49–62.

Part Three
Financing International Transactions

Part Three (Chapters 8 through 11) describes sources of global finance. One major facet of financial management is to raise funds on favorable terms. In the case of global financial management, this involves those sources of funds necessary to finance world trade and foreign investment. These funds can come from either internal or external sources. Internal sources of funds, such as earnings and depreciation, are the major sources of funds for most multinational companies. But external sources of funds, such as bank loans and Eurodollars, are important as well.

Four main trends in capital flows emerged during the 1980s. First, the scale of capital flows expanded sharply. Second, the removal of capital controls and broader liberalization of financial markets in industrial countries stimulated competition and resulted in a growing integration of domestic and offshore markets. Third, industrialized countries used private capital flows to finance their large current-account and fiscal imbalances. Fourth, capital movements took place largely among industrialized countries, thereby making developing country access to capital markets less certain. Multinational companies should take into account these four trends in financing their international transactions. This is because the trends increased not only the efficiency of global capital markets but also created new systematic risks associated with increased asset-price variability.

8

International Financial Markets

International financial markets are a major source of funds for international transactions. Some countries actively discourage foreign participation in their local markets, but many countries have recently internationalized their financial markets to attract foreign business. The most important international financial centers had been London and New York. These centers used to dominate international financial markets because of political stability and limited government intervention. Tokyo has increasingly become another important financial center since Japan deregulated its financial market in 1984. Tokyo compares favorably with New York and London in three important areas as an international financial center: market size, political stability, and a well-developed telecommunications network.

Recent financial globalization is being driven by advances in data processing and telecommunications, liberalization of restrictions on cross-border capital flows, deregulation of domestic capital markets, and greater competition among these markets for a share of the world's trading volume. This globalization involves both a harmonization of rules and a reduction of barriers that will allow for the free flow of capital and permit all firms to compete in all markets. In other words, financial market imperfections declined because of this global integration of money and capital markets. Yet, there are still excellent opportunities for companies to lower their cost of capital and for investors to increase their returns through international financial markets.

A study by Philip Turner (1991) found that during the 1980s, the world financial system underwent three revolutions all at once: deregulation, internalization, and innovation. Consequently, gross capital flows increased from $100 billion in 1979 to $600 billion in 1989. However, financial globalization is growing rapidly at the intermediary level rather than the customer level. Its effects are felt at the customer level mainly because prices and interest rates are influenced by worldwide economic conditions rather than because direct customer access to suppliers has increased. This chapter examines the three financial markets—Eurocurrency, international bond, and equity—that allow companies to serve customers around the world.

Eurocurrency Markets

The Eurocurrency market consists of banks that accept deposits and make loans in foreign currencies outside the country of issue. These deposits are commonly known as Eurocurrencies. Thus, U.S. dollars deposited in London are called Eurodollars; German marks deposited in Paris are called Euromarks, British pounds deposited in New York are called Eurosterling; and Japanese yen deposited in London are called Euroyen.

Because Eurodollars are the major form of Eurocurrency, the term "Eurodollar" frequently refers to the entire Eurocurrency market. Eurodollars could be broadly defined as dollar-denominated deposits in banks all over the world except the United States. These banks may be foreign banks or foreign branches of U.S. banks. However, many experts narrowly define Eurodollars as dollar-denominated deposits in Western European banks or foreign branches of U.S. banks in Western Europe. Hence, they distinguish between Eurodollars and petrodollars in the Middle East or between Eurodollars and Asian dollars in Hong Kong or Singapore.

Eurocurrency markets are very large, well organized, and efficient. They serve a number of valuable purposes for multinational business operations. Eurocurrencies are a convenient money market device for multinational firms to hold their excess liquidity. They also are a major source of short-term loans to finance corporate working capital needs and foreign trade. In recent years, the so-called "Eurobond markets" have developed as a major source of long-term investment capital for multinational companies.

Creation of Eurodollars

Many multinational companies and governments have learned to use the Eurodollar market as readily as they do the domestic banking system. Major sources of Eurodollars are the dollar reserves of oil-exporting countries, foreign governments or business people preferring to hold dollars outside the United States, foreign banks with dollars in excess of current needs, and multinational companies with excess cash balances. Once Eurodollars come into existence, they can create themselves through the lending and investing activities of commercial banks. Treasury accounts may be used to illustrate such Eurodollar creation.

Example 8–1.   Assume that the International Trading Company holds $1,000 on deposit in a New York bank. If the reserve requirement is 20 percent, the $1,000 deposit will be reflected in the books of the New York bank, the International Trading Company, and the Federal Reserve Bank of New York as follows:

New York Bank

	Deposit of International Trading Company $1000

International Trading Company

Deposit held with New York Bank $1000	

Federal Reserve Bank of New York

	Deposit New York Bank held as part of its reserve requirement $200

Cash flows in a commercial bank involve four major elements of information: (1) currency, (2) institution and location, (3) maturity date, and (4) interest rate. To better understand how bank transfers take place and how Eurodollars come into existence, let us examine a few transactions.

Step 1.   Assume that the International Trading Company decides to transfer its $1,000 deposit from the New York bank to a London bank. Let us further assume that the International Trading Company decides to maintain its dollars in a dollar-denominated 90-day deposit account at the going rate with the London bank. This situation will be reflected in the books of the New York bank, the London bank, and the International Trading Company as follows:

New York Bank

	Deposit of International Trading Company –$1000
	Deposit of London Bank +$1000

London Bank

Deposit held with New York Bank	+$1000	Deposit of International Trading Company	+$1000

International Trading Company

Deposit in New York Bank	-$1000	
Deposit in London Bank	+$1000	

By this step, a Eurodollar deposit has been created. The London bank has now obtained the power to deal in dollars outside the United States. Note, however, that total deposit levels in the United States have not changed; the $1,000 liability of the London bank is matched by its $1,000 deposit in the New York bank. The only change at the New York bank was in the name of the depositor from the International Trading Company to the London Bank.

Step 2. Because the London bank has to pay interest on its 90-day deposit liability to the International Trading Company, it decides to extend a Eurodollar loan of $1,000 to a Paris firm. This loan transaction will be reflected in the books of the London bank and the Paris firm as follows:

London Bank

Dollar loan to Paris firm	+$1000	Dollar deposit of Paris firm	+$1000

Paris Firm

Dollar deposit in London Bank	+$1000	Dollar loan repayable to London Bank	+$1000

Because the New York bank still has $1,000 deposit liability to the London bank, its balance sheet has not changed. But the London bank has increased its deposits and loans by $1,000. This expands the total Eurodollar deposit liabilities of non-U.S. banks to $2,000. The International Trading Company now holds $1,000 of Eurodollars with the London bank and the Paris firm has an additional $1,000 of Eurodollars in the London Bank.

The London bank exhausted its dollar lending capacity. Thus, if the Paris firm had held its dollar deposit with the London bank, the multiple creation of Eurodollars would have stopped. However, if the Paris firm withdraws its dollar deposits from the London bank and deposits it with a Paris bank, the Eurodollar creation process could continue.

Step 3. Assume that the Paris firm withdraws its deposit from the London bank and deposits it in a Paris bank. The following set of T-accounts records the event.

New York Bank

		Deposit of London Bank	-$1000
		Deposit of Paris Bank	+$1000

London Bank

Deposit in New York Bank	-$1000	Dollar deposit of Paris firm	-$1000

Paris Bank

Deposit in New York Bank	+$1000	Dollar deposit of Paris firm	+$1000

Paris Firm

Dollar deposit in London Bank	-$1000		
Dollar deposit in Paris Bank	+$1000		

After Step 3 the amount of Eurodollars is still $2,000, but the Paris bank has obtained Eurodollar deposits that it can lend out. The potential expansion of Eurodollars is infinite in the case where banks do not maintain any reserves against their Eurodollar deposits.

Because there are usually no legal reserves against Eurodollar deposits, we may argue that Eurodollar deposits could expand indefinitely. Who creates this infinite expansion of Eurodollars? Three parties do so jointly: (1) public and private depositors by always keeping their money in non-U.S. banks on deposit, (2) banks by keeping none of their Eurodollar deposits in the form of cash, and (3) public and private borrowers who make it possible for the banks to find Eurodollar loans and attractive earning assets to buy with their excess cash. However, there are a number of checks to this expansion. First, public and private depositors may hold a portion of their money in the form of nondeposit cash. Second, banks may retain a part of their Eurodollar deposits as a liquid reserve. Third, borrowers may convert the dollars borrowed into local currency. This conversion will not only stop the further expansion of Eurodollar deposits, but it may actually reduce the volume of outstanding Eurodollar deposits.

Historical Development of the Eurodollar Market

To understand why the Eurodollar market has grown so rapidly since the 1950s, we ought to review the development of the Eurodollar market starting with its origin. The former Soviet Union and other communist countries started a large volume of transactions in Eurodollar deposits shortly after World War II. East European holders of dollars were afraid to deposit their dollar holdings in the United States because these dollars might become blocked there.

The Eurodollar market originated in the 1950s, supposedly because of the desire of East European banks to leave their dollar deposits in Europe rather than in the United States. But the major reason for depositing in Europe was the strength of the U.S. dollar. In the 1950s, the U.S. dollar emerged as the leading international reserve currency. Thus, the U.S. dollar replaced the British pound as the primary instrument of exchange in the money markets of the world.

The Eurodollar market functions efficiently for the following three reasons: First, the United States imposes no restrictions on nonresident payment or transfers of dollar balances. Foreign governments, individuals, and companies are free to maintain and transfer deposits in U.S. banks. Second, European banks accept Eurodollar deposits and make Eurodollar loans at competitive rates. The absence of reserve requirements and no interest ceilings on Eurodollar time deposits make Eurodollars competitive with American banks. Third, there is a demand for dollar deposits and dollar loans outside the United States. In other words, there are non–Eurobank entities which are willing to deposit dollars in non-U.S. banks and to borrow from such banks for investment purposes.

Causes for Eurodollar Expansion.

Although the basic cause of Eurodollar expansion is efficiency, many writers argue that the market grew as a direct result of monetary controls imposed in the United States and exchange controls imposed in Europe during the 1950s and 1960s. In 1957, British monetary authorities attempted to strengthen their weakening pound by imposing tight controls on English banks lending in sterling to nonresidents of England. The Bank of England encouraged English banks to turn to dollar lending as the only alternative which would permit them to maintain their lending position in international finance.

Interest rate ceilings on deposits in the United States and reserve requirements of the U.S. Federal Reserve Board contributed heavily to the rapid growth of the Eurodollar market. Furthermore, in the mid-1960s American authorities adopted regulations to control capital outflows from the

United States and to reduce the balance-of-payments deficit. Although there are some differences in opinion concerning the impact of these regulations on the growth of the Eurodollar market, many believe that the market grew as a result of the regulations. In other words, these monetary regulations and other events in the 1960s and 1970s contributed to the rapid growth of the market:

1. The Federal Reserve's Regulation Q limited the interest rate that U.S. banks could pay on time deposits. Because the ceilings did not apply to Eurodollar deposits, some U.S. bank depositors pulled their funds out of the United States and invested in high-yielding Eurodollar deposits.
2. By the Federal Reserve's Regulation M, U.S. banks are required to keep a stipulated percentage of their deposits at a Federal Reserve Bank or in vault cash. But Eurobanks are not required to maintain reserves against the dollar deposits they take in.
3. The Interest Equalization Tax of 1963 taxed interest on foreign debts sold in the United States and thus increased the effective cost of borrowing in the United States for foreign borrowers.
4. The Voluntary Foreign Credit Restraints of 1964 imposed restrictions on capital outflows from U.S. banks and corporations.
5. The Office of Foreign Direct Investment Regulations of 1968 imposed controls on U.S.-financed foreign direct investment. This meant that U.S. companies were forced to finance their foreign activities with foreign borrowing.
6. The end of the fixed exchange-rate system based on the Bretton Woods Agreement in 1973 created short-term profit investment opportunities in foreign exchange markets. In other words, the floating exchange-rate system greatly increased both the turnover of dollars and the amount of the dollars held by foreigners.
7. The 1973 and 1979 oil crises provided a few oil exporting countries with resources for investment which far exceeded opportunities in their local markets.

Restrictions imposed by the United States in the 1960s were removed in the early 1970s. Oil exporting countries have not had excess oil dollar reserves in recent years because of the oil glut and lower oil prices. The Financial Institutions Deregulation and Monetary Control Act of 1980 effectively terminated interest rate ceilings on time deposits. Nevertheless, the Eurodollar market has continued to thrive for a number of good reasons. They include: (1) the tendency for central banks to place some of their own excess dollar reserves in the market, (2) the growth of foreign trade and investment, (3) confidence in the U.S. dollar and other key currencies such as the Japanese yen, (4) the growth of the Eurobond market, (5) the huge U.S. trade deficit, and (6) the increased efficiency of the market.

Uses of Eurodollars.

European banks with Eurodollars may use these funds in a number of ways. First, they may redeposit their Eurodollars in other European banks or European branches of a U.S. bank. Second, they may make loans to nonbank users such as multinational companies. These multinational companies use the dollars to meet their dollar obligations or to buy local currencies. Third, they may transfer their dollars to Eurodollars in European branches of a U.S. bank which in turn would lend these funds to the U.S. home office.

Heavy borrowers in the Eurodollar market are governments and commercial banks. Many countries have recently been suffering foreign-loan related problems. Hence, they want Eurodollars to improve their international reserves. U.S. commercial banks have borrowed Eurodollars to rebuild their own reserve position. Many commercial banks rely on Eurodollars to grant credit to exporters and importers. Eurobanks frequently swap Eurodollars with local currencies in order to make loans to domestic companies. In addition, international development banks have been regular borrowers in the market.

Many of the private nonbank borrowers continue to be companies engaged in international operations, such as exporters, importers, and investors. They are attracted by the size of the market and the importance of the U.S. dollar as an international reserve. A second advantage of Eurodollar loans is that the funds raised in the external market have no restrictions about their deployment. In contrast, funds raised in national money markets have some restrictions in almost all cases. Finally, international money markets provide multinational companies with flexibility in many ways such as terms, conditions, and covenants.

The Group of Ten countries, as a whole, are usually the net provider of Eurodollars, but Switzerland accounts for most of the net position. In addition, oil-exporting countries are still substantial providers of funds to the Eurodollar market. European countries outside the Group of Ten, Eastern Europe, and Latin America are the three largest users of Eurodollars. Asian countries such as Hong Kong, Indonesia, and the Philippines are also well-known borrowers of Eurodollars.

Eurocurrency Interbank Market

The Eurocurrency interbank market plays a major role in channelling funds from banks in one country to banks in another country. The interbank market has over 1,000 banks from 50 different countries, with a total market size of $7 trillion. Although transactions in U.S. dollars still dominate the interbank market, there are flourishing interbank markets in German marks, Swiss francs, Japanese yen, British pounds, French francs, and Dutch guilders.

Functions of the Interbank Market.

The Eurocurrency interbank market has at least four related functions. First, the interbank market is an efficient market system through which funds move from banks in one country to banks in other countries. Second, the interbank market gives banks an efficient mechanism to buy or sell foreign-currency assets and liabilities of different maturities in order to hedge their exposure to interest-rate and foreign exchange risks. Third, the interbank market is a convenient source of additional loans when banks need to adjust their balance sheets either domestically or internationally. Fourth, because of this market, banks sidestep regulations on capital adequacy and interest rates prevalent in many domestic banking markets.

Risks of Participating Banks.

Participating banks in the Eurocurrency interbank market face at least five different risks: (1) credit or default risk, (2) liquidity risk, (3) sovereign risk, (4) foreign exchange risk, and (5) settlement risk. First, credit risk is the risk that a borrowing bank may default on its interbank loan. This risk is important because interbank loans and deposits are not secured. Second, liquidity risk is the risk that other banks may withdraw their interbank deposits suddenly. Here, the bank may have to sell off illiquid assets for less than their face value to meet its deposit drain. Third, sovereign risk is the risk that a foreign country may prevent its banks from repaying interbank loans or deposits received from banks in other countries. Fourth, foreign exchange risk is the risk that a bank participant in this market will gain or lose due to changes in exchange rates. Fifth, settlement risk is the risk of a breakdown or nonsettlement on the major wire-transfer systems.

Regulators and analysts have expressed some concern about the stability of this market for two major reasons. First, interbank funds have no collateral. Second, central bank regulations are inadequate. These two factors expose the market to potential "contagion;" problems at one bank affect other banks in the market. This kind of contagion ultimately threatens the market's stability and its function.

Stricter Oversight in the U.S. and Europe.

Concern by regulators and analysts about the stability of the interbank market has been realized since Western regulators seized the Bank of Credit and Commerce International (BCCI) on July 5, 1991. Stung by the collapse of BCCI, bank regulators in the U.S. and Europe are expected to tighten their rules for dealing with multinational banks.

The toughened rules envisioned by bank regulators in the United States and Europe are designed to close a loophole through which BCCI slipped. By basing its holding company—BCCI Holdings (Luxembourg), S.A.—in Luxembourg, which does not supervise holding companies, BCCI was able to avoid uniform regulatory scrutiny. With no regulator looking at BCCI's consolidated operations, fraudulent transactions among BCCI affiliates in 69 countries escaped detection for years.

The magnitude of the losses at BCCI allegedly amassed through incompetence, fraud, and outright theft is incredibly high. At the time of its seizure by Western regulators on July 5, 1991, BCCI had roughly $20 billion worth of deposits in more than a million accounts, mostly in countries without U.S.-style deposit insurance. Thus, BCCI's depositors are expected to lose most of their deposit funds. The Federal Reserve System of the United

Table 8–1
Asset Holdings of Foreign Banks in the U.S. by Country
(in billions of dollars as of December 31, 1990)

Country	U.S. Assets	Percent of Foreign Assets
Japan	$435.5	55.3%
Italy	48.0	6.1
Britain	44.1	5.6
Canada	40.2	5.1
France	37.5	4.8
Switzerland	25.6	3.3
Hong Kong	22.4	2.8
Germany	16.2	2.1
Netherlands	12.8	1.6
Israel	10.3	1.3
Spain	10.3	1.3
Ireland	9.2	1.2
Others	75.1	9.5
Total	$787.2	100.0%

Source: The U.S. Senate Banking Committee.

States is particularly concerned about the BCCI-style risk because, as shown in Table 8-1, foreign banks hold a huge amount of assets in the United States. As of December 31, 1990, foreign banks in the United States held $787.2 billion in assets or 21.3 percent of total U.S. bank assets.

Eurodollar Instruments

The two major types of instruments used in the Eurodollar market are Eurodollar deposits and Eurodollar loans.

Eurodollar Deposits.   Eurodollar deposits are either fixed time deposits or negotiable certificates of deposit. Approximately 85 percent of Eurodollar deposits are in the form of time deposits, while the remaining 15 percent are in the form of negotiable certificates of deposit.

Time deposits are funds being placed in a bank for a fixed maturity at a specified interest rate. In contrast to the U.S. practice, Eurobanks do not maintain checking accounts (demand deposits) for the customers. While maturities of these time deposits range from one day to a few years, most of them have a maturity of less than one year. Time deposits are for fixed periods, but Eurobanks are frequently flexible if the depositor desires to withdraw his or her deposits early.

A certificate of deposit (CD) is a negotiable instrument issued by a bank. In other words, negotiable CDs are formal negotiable receipts for funds left with a bank for a specified period of time at a fixed or floating rate of interest. The important advantage of a CD over a time deposit is its liquidity because the holder of a CD can sell it on the secondary market at any time before the maturity date. Eurobanks issue negotiable CDs to attract idle funds from multinational companies, oil exporting countries, and wealthy individuals.

Negotiable CDs for Eurodollars were first introduced in 1966 by the London branch of First National City Bank of New York (now Citibank). Currently, most major Eurobanks issue negotiable CDs whose safety and liquidity are assured by an active secondary market. The secondary market consists of broker/dealer firms which are members of the International CD Market Association. This association was established in London in 1968 to provide customers with the highest quality of services.

Eurodollar Loans.   Eurodollar loans range from a minimum of $500,000 to $100 million, typically in multiples of $1 million. Their maturities range from 30 days to five or seven years. Short-term Eurodollar financings represent the major part of the Eurodollar lending business. Short-term Eurodollar loans are usually conducted under pre-arranged lines of credit. Under such an arrangement, the Eurobank establishes a maximum loan balance (line of credit) after investigation of its client's credit standing. Although the commitment period is typically one year, advances under a line of credit are normally made against notes with maturities of 90 or 180 days. Lines of credit are renewable after a thorough review process. These short-term Eurodollar loans are usually made on an unsecured basis and repaid at the maturity date.

Eurobanks also provide international concerns with medium-term loans. Two major forms of medium-term Eurodollar loans are revolving Eurodollar credits and Eurodollar term loans. A revolving credit is a confirmed line of credit beyond one year. Under this arrangement, the Eurobank permits its clients to borrow a specified amount of Eurodollars for a specified period, usually three to five years. But actual loans are normally made against renewable notes with maturities of between 90 and 180 days. Eurodollar term loans are a less popular form of medium-term Eurodollar loans than revolving Eurodollar credits. They have such provisions as a revolving feature and an agreed-upon amortization schedule. The interest rate on these term loans is adjusted every six months. Borrowers are usually permitted to prepay the loans on the interest-adjustment date.

Interest Rates.   Two sets of interest rates are Eurodollar-deposit interest rates and Eurodollar-loan interest rates. Eurodollar deposit and loan rates are determined by forces of supply and demand. More specifically, these rates depend on the rates in a corresponding home currency, spot and forward exchange rates, domestic and Eurocurrency rates in other currencies, and the inflation rate in various countries. Many economists have assumed that Eurodollar-deposit rates depend on U.S. money market rates. In other words, U.S. CD rates provide an effective floor for Eurodollar deposit rates.

Interest rates on Eurodollar deposits are usually higher than those on deposits in the United States. Interest rates on Eurodollar loans are generally lower than similar loan rates in the United States. With deposit rates higher and lending rates lower in the Eurodollar market than in the U.S. market, Eurobanks must operate on a narrower margin. A number of factors enable Eurobanks to operate profitably on narrower margins than domestic markets.

Interest rates on Eurodollar deposits may be higher than those on deposits in the United States for a number of reasons:

1. Eurobanks must attract deposits from U.S. banks.
2. Eurodollar deposits are not subject to the interest-rate ceilings that prevail in other countries.
3. Eurobanks, being free of reserve requirements, can lend a larger percentage of their deposits.
4. Eurobanks, not being subject to deposit insurance fees and other regulations, have lower regulatory costs.

Interest rates on Eurodollar loans may be lower than those on loans in the United States for a number of reasons:

1. Eurodollar loans are characterized by high volumes and well-known borrowers; these two features reduce the costs of information gathering and credit analysis.
2. Many Eurodollar loans take place out of tax-haven countries.
3. Eurobanks are not forced to lend money to borrowers at concessionary rates, usually lower than prevailing market rates.
4. Eurobanks are free of reserve requirements, and they can thus lend a large percentage of deposits.
5. Eurobanks have very little or no regulatory expenses such as deposit insurance fees.

Eurobanks usually establish their lending rate at some fixed percentage above the six-month London Interbank Offered Rate (LIBOR). LIBOR is the arithmetic average of the rates at which six major banks in London are willing to borrow a substantial portion of their dollar funds at a certain time during the morning. The development of the LIBOR concept has created a number of imitators: Kuwait Interbank Offered Rate (KIBOR), Singapore Interbank Offered Rate (SIBOR), and Madrid Interbank Offered Rate (MIBOR).

Loans are typically made at a range of 3/4 of 1 to 3 percent above the LIBOR. The actual charge to the Eurodollar borrower depends on such factors as market conditions, maturity, and creditworthiness. In addition, it is a well-established practice in the Eurodollar market to charge a commitment fee of 1/4 to 1/2 percent on the unused portion of the loan.

In the absence of tight controls on international financial transactions, arbitrage and risk differences affect the relationship between rates in the internal market (the U.S. market) and in the external market (the Eurodollar market). An absence of government controls on international capital flows results in arbitrage between internal and external segments of the market for dollar credit. The arbitrage keeps the spread between internal and external rates within a narrow margin.

In general, risks on external dollar deposits are somewhat greater than those on internal dollar deposits. Major risks in the Eurodollar market include (1) removal of nonresident convertibility by the United States, (2) seizure of Eurodollar assets by the authorities where they operate, and (3) refusal of central banks to function as lenders of last resort in the case of Eurobanks.

In addition to arbitrage and risk differences, differences in the institutional structure of the markets influence differences between U.S. rates and Eurodollar rates. These market imperfections occur because of (1) institutional factors, (2) perceptual factors, (3) regulatory restraints such as reserve requirements, and (4) oligopolistic market conditions which stem from barriers to entry in the U.S. banking system.

The Asian Currency Market

In 1968, an Asian version of the Eurodollar came into existence with the acceptance of dollar–denominated deposits by commercial banks in Singapore. Singapore was an ideal location for the birth of the Asian currency market. It had an excellent communication network, important banks, and a stable government. Because the U.S. dollar accounts for most of the foreign currency transaction in Singapore, the term "Asian dollar market" can be used to represent the Asian currency market.

The Asian currency market developed when the Singapore branch of the Bank of America proposed that the monetary authority of Singapore relax taxes and restrictions. The monetary authority accepted these proposals and extended a number of important incentives to foreign banks so that dollar accounts could be held in Singapore. They included: (1) the removal of an existing 40 percent tax on interest payments on foreign currency deposits; (2) the reduction of the tax rate on interest earned from offshore loans; (3) the abolition of stamp duties on CDs and bills of exchange; and (4) the abolition of the 20 percent reserve requirements for Asian Currency Units (ACUs). An ACU is a section within a bank which has authority and separate accountability for Asian currency market operations.

On October 1, 1968, the Bank of America was authorized to start its ACU operations. In 1969, a number of other banks such as the Chartered Bank, Citibank, the Hong Kong and Shanghai Bank, and the United Chase Merchants Bank obtained permission to set up ACUs in Singapore. Since 1969 other leading domestic and foreign banks in Singapore have kept up their own ACUs. ACUs are required to operate within several guidelines:

1. They can accept foreign currency deposits from foreigners without the prior approval of the authorities.
2. They can lend to individuals or companies outside the British Commonwealth countries without the prior approval of the authorities.

3. They cannot lend to residents of Singapore or British Commonwealth countries without the prior approval of the authorities.

In theory, several reasons explain the development of the Asian currency market in Singapore. First, Asian dollar deposits would attract other deposits, increase banking activities, and earn income from these financial services. These earnings would also improve its balance of payments and develop a service-oriented industry. Second, Singapore might obtain a degree of additional political security. The existence of foreign deposits and foreign banks in Singapore might build support for its neutrality and increase its importance as an Asian financial center. Third, the presence of the Asian currency market in Singapore would enhance its publicity and prestige. Fourth, most Southeast Asian countries need large amounts of capital for their economic development. Because Singapore is located at the center of this area, it is a logical place for the development of the Asian currency market.

Currently, approximately 150 banks or other financial institutions have licenses from the Monetary Authority of Singapore to operate ACUs. Most deposits in ACUs are in U.S. dollars, but other foreign currencies such as Swiss francs, Dutch guilders, German marks, and Japanese yen are also accepted. Domestic residents are normally prohibited from participating in the offshore market. Similarly, offshore financial institutions are restricted in their dealings with the domestic market.

There are no taxes on interest paid on foreign currency deposits and no restrictions applied to capital outflows and inflows. Regular foreign currency deposits are accepted in amounts as low as $25,000. Although the minimum deposit maturity is one month, the market offers deposit options of varying maturities. Citibank introduced negotiable CDs in 1970, but the active market for negotiable CDs really developed in 1977 with the issuance of U.S. $25 million, three-year floating rate CDs by the Dai-Ichi Kangyo Bank. Fixed-rate CDs were introduced in 1978 with maturities of six to nine months. Since 1978, numerous issues of both floating-rate and fixed-rate CDs have attracted the attention of investors outside the Asian area.

The Asian currency market is primarily an interbank market. Approximately 80 percent of total loans are made to bank customers and only 20 percent go to nonbank customers. Interest rates for Asian currency loans are based on either the Singapore Interbank Offered Rate (SIBOR) or the London Interbank Offered Rate (LIBOR). The LIBOR was preferred by both banks and customers in the early years of the market's development, but in recent years the SIBOR has been used more frequently. Asian dollar interest rates closely follow those in the Eurodollar market.

The International Capital Market

The international capital market consists of the international bond market and the international equity market. The three largest stock exchanges in terms of total market value are the Tokyo, New York, and London stock exchanges.

Table 8-2
Market Size of the World Stock Exchanges

		Tokyo	New York	London
Number of listed companies	Domestic	1,597	1,633	1,955
	Foreign	119	87	604
Number of listed stocks	Domestic	1,602	2,148	1,968
	Foreign	119	98	766
Number of listed bonds	Domestic	1,340	2,744	2,737
	Foreign	146	217	1,648
Total market value ($billion)	Stocks	4,260	2,903	818
	Bonds	977	1,412	498
Trading value ($billion)	Stocks	2,431	1,543	478
	Bonds	586	9	881

Source: Japan Institute for Social and Economic Affairs, *Japan 1992*, Tokyo: Keizai Koho Center, 1991, p. 76.

The soaring yen and rapid increase in Japanese security prices caused Tokyo to surpass New York in the Spring of 1987 to become the world's largest capital market. As noted in Table 8-2, the Japanese continued to hold the lead in 1990.

The International Bond Market

International, offshore bonds are those bonds which are initially sold outside the country of the borrower. International bonds are either foreign bonds or Eurobonds.

Foreign Bonds.   Foreign bonds are sold in a particular country by a foreign borrower, underwritten by a syndicate of members from that country, and denominated in the currency of that country. The first foreign bond was issued in 1958.

Most large foreign-bond issues had been floated in the United States, Great Britain, and Switzerland. The weakening British pound in the late 1950s reduced the importance of the domestic British capital market for foreign firms. The Interest Equalization Tax (1963-1974) of the United States effectively stopped New York's usefulness as a capital market for new foreign bonds. Thus, international borrowers and investors shifted their activities from the United States to Europe. This shift caused the Eurobond market to develop.

Eurobonds. Eurobonds are underwritten by a multinational syndicate of banks and sold simultaneously in many countries other than the country of the issuing entity. The first Eurobond issue was launched in 1963. Eurobonds are direct claims on leading multinational companies, governments, or governmental enterprises. Hence, they are in many respects very much like domestic bonds. They are sold simultaneously in many countries through multinational syndicates of underwriting banks. These underwriting banks include major European banks, European branches of U.S. banks, Japanese banks, and banks from other financial centers such as Hong Kong.

The Eurobond market is similar to the Eurodollar market in one respect. Both markets are "external" because obligations available in these markets are denominated in foreign currencies outside the country of issue. But there are a number of important differences between the two markets. First, the Eurodollar market is an international money market, but the Eurobond market is an international capital market. Second, the Eurodollar market is a financial intermediation market; major world banks operate as intermediaries between depositors and borrowers of Eurodollars. By contrast, the Eurobond market is a direct market in which investors hold the securities issued by the final borrowers; in other words, Eurobonds are issued directly by the final borrowers.

The Eurobond market has a number of attractive factors. First, interest income earned on Eurobonds is usually not subject to a withholding tax. The absence of this tax makes Eurobonds attractive to those investors who either want to evade taxes or who cannot recover taxes withheld. Second, the Eurobond market is often described as a market free from national regulations. Many countries, including the United States, tend to strictly regulate the access of foreign borrowers to their domestic capital markets. But these countries are often more flexible about securities denominated in foreign currencies and sold to their residents who already possess those foreign currencies. Moreover, disclosure requirements in the international bond market are less stringent than those of the United States.

Market Size of International Bonds

Table 8-3 shows that the size of the international bond market reached $254 billion in 1989. Eurobonds account for approximately 80 percent of the international bond market, whereas foreign bonds account for only 20 percent of the market. Industrial countries are the major borrowers of the international bond market.

Currency Denomination of International Bonds

International bonds are denominated in various currencies: British pound, German mark, Japanese yen, Swiss franc, U.S. dollar, and composite units of currencies. These multiple-currency bonds may be classified as currency-option bonds and currency cocktail bonds.

Table 8–3
International Bond Issues:
Placements by Groups of Borrowers
(millions of U.S. dollars)

	1985	1986	1987	1988	1989
Foreign Bonds	**31,229**	**39,359**	**40,252**	**48,273**	**41,964**
Industrial Countries	19,736	29,161	30,990	37,111	30,576
Developing Countries	1,815	1,790	1,480	2,185	1,795
International Org.	9,350	8,360	17,461	8,307	8,249
Other	327		480	670	1,343
Eurobonds	**136,543**	**87,747**	**140,535**	**178,869**	**212,004**
Industrial Countries	118,194	172,020	125,293	161,190	191,142
Developing Countries	6,681	2,989	2,459	4,074	2,887
International Org.	8,543	10,488	11,320	11,393	13,362
Other	3,124	2,250	1,463	2,213	4,613
International Bonds	**167,772**	**227,106**	**180,786**	**227,143**	**253,967**
Industrial Countries	137,931	201,181	156,283	198,301	221,719
Developing Countries	8,497	4,779	3,939	6,259	4,682
International Org.	17,893	18,848	18,781	19,700	21,611
Other	3,450	2,298	1,783	2,883	5,955

Source: International Monetary Fund, *International Capital Markets: Developments and Prospects,* Washington, DC: IMF, 1990, various pages.

Currency–Option Bonds. The holders of currency-option bonds are allowed to receive their interest income in the currency of their option from among two or three predetermined currencies at a predetermined exchange rate. The original bond contract contains the currencies of choice and the exchange rates. The currency option enhances the exchange guarantee for the investor. Thus, the investor will make some gain if all currencies included in the contract do not depreciate against the desired currency.

Currency–Cocktail Bonds. Currency cocktail bonds are those bonds denominated in a standard "currency basket" of several different currencies. A number of currency cocktail bonds have been developed to minimize or hedge foreign exchange risk associated with single-currency bonds. Some popular forms of such bonds include Special Drawing Rights and European Currency Units, both of which are described in Chapter 4. Currency diversification provided by these bonds can be replicated by individual investors. Thus, currency cocktail bonds have never gained wide acceptance with Euromarket borrowers.

Types of International Bonds

Four types of international bonds are fixed-rate (straight) bonds, equity-related (convertible) bonds, floating-rate notes, and zero-coupon bonds.

Fixed-Rate Bonds.

These bonds have fixed maturities and carry a fixed rate of interest. Fixed-rate bonds are repaid by amortization or in a lump sum at the maturity date. The amortization method refers to the retirement of a long-term debt by making a set of equal periodic payments. These periodic payments include both interest and principal. Or a borrower may retire his or her bonds by redeeming the face value of the bonds at maturity. Under this method, a fixed interest on the face value of the bonds is paid at regular intervals.

Fixed-rate bonds are technically unsecured, debenture bonds because almost all of them are not secured by any specific property of the borrower. Because of this, debenture bondholders become general creditors in the event of default; they look to the nature of the borrower's assets, its earning power, and its general credit strength.

Perhaps the greatest advantage of all types of international bonds for individual investors is that interest income on them is exempt from withholding taxes at the source. Investors must report their interest income to their national authorities, but both tax avoidance and tax evasion are extremely widespread. Official institutions hold a large portion of investment in international bonds and are not liable for tax. Another large class of investors in international bonds consists of private institutions. These private institutions legally avoid tax by being in tax-haven countries.

Equity-Related Bonds.

These bonds are convertible into parent common stock and have become prevalent as the market for fixed-rate bonds has weakened. The conversion price is usually fixed at a certain premium above the market price of the common stock on the date of the bond issue. Investors are free to convert their fixed-income securities into common stock at any time before the conversion privilege expires; the borrowing company is obliged to issue new stock for that purpose.

The convertible provision is designed to increase the marketability of fixed-rate Eurobonds. Convertible bonds provide investors with a steady income and an opportunity to participate in rising stock prices. Thus, their interest rates have been 1.5 to 2 percent below those on fixed-rate bonds. Because international investors are inflation-conscious, they prefer convertible bonds which maintain the purchasing power of money.

Some international bonds are issued with warrants. A warrant is an option to buy a stated number of common shares at a stated price during a prescribed period. Warrants pay no dividends, have no voting rights, and become worthless at expiration unless the price of the common stock exceeds the exercise price. Convertible Eurobonds do not bring in additional funds. When they are converted, common stock increases, and the convertible securities are retired. When warrants are exercised, common stock and cash increase simultaneously.

Floating-Rate Notes.

These notes are frequently called floating-rate bonds. The rate of return on these notes is adjusted at regular intervals, usually every six months, to reflect changes in short-term market rates. Because one of their main objectives is to provide dollar capital for non-U.S. banks, practically all floating-rate notes have been issued in dollars.

Like other international bonds, floating-rate notes are issued in denominations of $1,000 each. They carry a margin of usually 1/4 percent above the LIBOR, and this margin is normally adjusted every six months. The link between the rate of return on floating-rate notes and LIBOR rates is intended to protect the investor against capital loss.

When non-U.S. banks obtain dollars by floating-rate notes, their credit lines with other banks are not eroded as when they obtain dollars in an interbank market or by the sale of CDs to other banks. Because non-U.S. banks usually lend at the floating rate of interest, it makes sense for them to obtain funds on the same basis.

Zero-Coupon Bonds.

Zero-coupon bonds provide all of the cash payment (interest and principal) when they mature. The bond does not pay periodic interest but is sold at a deep discount from its face value. The return to the investor is the excess of the face value over the market price.

Zero-coupon bonds have several advantages over conventional bonds. First, there is immediate cash inflow to the issuing company but no periodic interest to pay. Second, a big tax advantage exists for the issuing company because any discount from the maturity value may be amortized for tax purposes by the company over the life of the bond.

Currency Composition and Market Share.

Table 8-4 shows the currency composition of international bond issues and their percentage breakdown by instrument during the period from 1984 to 1989. In 1989, 52 percent was denominated in U.S. dollars, 9 percent was denominated in Japanese yen, and the remaining 41 percent was denominated in either other single currencies or composite units of currencies. In the same year, the percentage breakdown of the total bond market by instrument was 60 percent for fixed-rate bonds, 7 percent for equity-related bonds, 32 percent for floating-rate notes, and 1 percent for zero-coupon bonds.

The International Equity Market

Besides debt instruments like the Eurodollar and international bond markets, the equity capital market is another important source of financing. The three largest stock exchanges in terms of total market value are in Tokyo, New York, and London. Total market value is the total number of common shares listed on the stock exchange times the market price per share.

Table 8–4
International Bond Issues:
Currency Composition and Market Share

	1984	1985	1986	1987	1988	1989
Currency Composition						
U.S. dollar	0.64	0.61	0.55	0.36	0.38	0.52
Japanese yen	0.06	0.08	0.10	0.15	0.10	0.09
German mark	0.06	0.07	0.08	0.08	0.11	0.06
Other currencies	0.24	0.24	0.27	0.41	0.41	0.33
Total	1.00	1.00	1.00	1.00	1.00	1.00
Portion by Instrument						
Fixed-rate bonds	0.52	0.56	0.62	0.67	0.72	0.60
Equity-related bonds	0.10	0.07	0.12	0.24	0.17	0.07
Floating-rate notes	0.34	0.35	0.22	0.07	0.10	0.32
Zero-coupon bonds	0.04	0.02	0.04	0.02	0.01	0.01
Total	1.00	1.00	1.00	1.00	1.00	1.00

Source: International Monetary Fund, *International Capital Markets: Developments and Prospects,* Washington, DC: IMF, 1990, various pages.

The international equity market has grown dramatically for many reasons. First, global macroeconomic trends have been favorable largely because of good economic prospects in Japan, the United States, and most European countries. Second, the United Kingdom experienced the "big bang" of deregulation on October 27, 1986. Since then, trading volume and market values of listed stocks soared, at least until the stock market crash of October 19, 1987. Third, financial deregulation in Japan has accelerated since 1984 and has helped Japanese institutions recycle their large liquid funds.

The Japanese equity market has had the most spectacular growth. By the end of 1990, the total market value of companies was $4.3 trillion for Japan and $2.9 trillion for the United States. Japan's share of the total world equity market increased from 16 percent in 1980 to 44 percent in 1990. On the other hand, the U.S. share of the total world equity market tumbled from 54 percent in 1980 to 29 percent in 1990. This rapid growth occurred because Japan relaxed financial regulations to allow companies to issue yen-denominated securities.

Financial Deregulation in Japan

Tokyo did not become a global financial center until the mid-1980s, because Japan's financial markets operated in international isolation and under tight regulations. U.S. pressure since 1984 has compelled Japan to accelerate deregulations and to recycle Japan's huge trade surpluses. The United States and Japan agreed in May 1984 on several financial matters. As part of the accord, Japan agreed to promote international use of the yen, deregulate financial markets, and strengthen the yen.

Japan adopted several measures since then to liberalize restrictions on international bank instruments, international bonds, foreign exchange transactions, and purchase of foreign bonds by Japanese residents. In 1985, Japan removed a 20 percent withholding tax on interest paid to foreign bondholders by Japanese companies. The establishment of the Japan Offshore Market in December 1986 promoted both Japanese banks' international activities and foreign banks' access to Japanese markets. Japan has allowed U.S. banks to have securities affiliates in Tokyo since March 1987. In April 1990, Japan eased the way for foreign banks to open branches there—a move that chiefly benefited Citicorp. This move reduced approval time for new branch applications by foreign banks from six months to two months.

Some highlights in the deregulation of the domestic market include: (1) liberalizing interest rate ceilings on deposits; (2) creating new markets open to nonbanks, including certificates of deposit; (3) diversifying interbank markets; (4) diversifying money market operations by the Bank of Japan; (5) removing certain barriers between banking and securities activities. Yet, under current banking regulations, Japanese banks and securities firms are not allowed to engage in each other's kind of business within Japan. Of course, Japanese banks and securities firms can do each other's kind of business in overseas markets.

Foreign financial institutions have gained greater access to Japanese financial markets since 1984 as a result of many liberalizing measures. Foreign financial institutions can now deal in government securities, engage in trust business, and establish securities subsidiaries. They have allowed foreign financial institutions to engage in many lines of business traditionally not permitted to domestic Japanese financial institutions.

For Japanese companies, financial deregulation has created attractive investment opportunities, diverse financing channels, and good profit opportunities. The firms sharply shifted the composition of assets and liabilities in the 1980s compared with the late 1970s: (1) a shift toward money market instruments with deregulated interest rates from deposits with regulated interest rates; (2) a rapid increase in purchases of foreign securities; (3) a shift away from bank borrowing and toward stock and commercial paper; and (4) an increase in foreign bond issues as a method of corporate finance.

Summary

The international financial market consists of the Eurodollar market, the international bond market, and the international equity market. Eurodollars are dollar-denominated deposits in banks all over the world except the United States. The Eurodollar market is the truly international money market undisturbed by the rules and restrictions of any national authority. Eurodollars have become a major source of short-term loans for multinational companies to finance their working capital needs and foreign trade. With the growth in availability of Eurodollars, Eurobanks have begun to extend medium-term Eurodollar loans for multinational companies to finance their medium-term needs.

Although the international bond and equity markets are of a more recent vintage, they parallel the importance of multinational financial management. They mainly facilitate expansion involving fixed asset commitment. Japan's role in the international capital market has become increasingly important in recent years because of its financial deregulation since 1984 and its large trade surpluses.

Questions

1. Explain the globalization of financial markets.

2. How has technology affected the globalization of financial markets?

3. Why has the Eurocurrency market grown so rapidly?

4. If Germany imposes interest-rate ceilings on German bank deposits, what is the likely effect on the Euromark interest rate of this regulation?

5. Why have bank regulators and market analysts expressed some concern about the stability of the interbank market?

6. What is the difference between Eurobonds and foreign bonds?

7. What is the difference between currency-option bonds and currency-cocktail bonds?

8. What factors account for the growth of the international equity market?

9. List some highlights of financial deregulation in Japan.

Problems

8-1 Fill in the following blank spaces with a reserve ratio of 20 percent.

	Acquired Reserves	Required Reserves	Excess Reserves	Amount Bank Can Lend
Bank 1	$100.00	$20.00	$80.00	$80.00
Bank 2				
Bank 3				
Bank 4				
Bank 5				
Bank 6				
Bank 7				
Bank 8				
Bank 9				
Bank 10				
Bank 11				
Bank 12				
Bank 13				
Other banks				
Total amount loaned				

8-2 Assume that a commercial bank has the following simplified balance sheet. The reserve ratio is 20 percent.

Assets		1	2	Liabilities & Net Worth		1	2
Reserves	$44000	___	___	Demand Deposits	$200000	___	___
Securities	76000	___	___				
Loans	80000						

(a) Determine the maximum amount which this bank can safely lend. Show in Column 1 how the bank's balance sheet will appear after the bank has loaned this amount.

(b) By how much has the supply of money changed?

(c) Show the new balance sheet in Column 2 after checks drawn for the entire amount of the new loans have been cleared against this bank.

(d) To what extent will this lending alter the supply of money?

(e) Aside from the leakage of required reserves at each stage of the lending process, there are some other leakages of money from the lending process. List and discuss them.

(f) Assume: (1) an American citizen transfers $2,000 of his deposits from a U.S. bank to a Eurobank, and (2) Eurobanks as a whole keep 5 percent of their Eurodollar deposits in vault cash. Determine the maximum amount of Eurodollar supply that Eurobanks can create on the basis of $2,000.

8-3 (a) A German multinational company acquires $2,000 on demand deposit in a Los Angeles bank. How will the $2,000 deposit be reflected in the books of the Los Angeles bank, the German company, and the Federal Reserve Bank of San Francisco? Assume the reserve ratio is 20 percent.

(b) The German company transfers its $2,000 deposit from the Los Angeles bank to an Italian bank. Moreover, it decides to deposit its $2,000 in a dollar-denominated time deposit account. How will this transaction be reflected in the T-accounts for the Los Angeles bank, the Italian bank, and the German company?

(c) The Italian bank retains $200 of its deposit in the Los Angeles bank and extends a Eurodollar loan of $1,800 to a British firm. What are the transactions to record the loan?

(d) The British firm withdraws its deposit from the Italian bank and deposits it in a London bank. Record the event in the appropriate accounts.

(e) The London bank lends its $1,800 demand deposit to a Swiss firm. How will this loan be reflected in the T-accounts for the London bank and the Swiss firm?

(f) After transaction (e), what is the total amount of Eurodollars?

References

Carlock, C., "An Introduction to the Japanese Stock Market," *A Review of Business & Economic Developments*, Federal Reserve Bank of Richmond, Summer 1990, pp. 8-10.

Doukas, J., "Syndicated Eurocredit Sovereign Risk Assessments, Market Efficiency and Contagion Effects," *Journal of International Business Studies*, Summer 1989, pp. 255-67.

Hirtle, B., "Factors Affecting the Competitiveness of Internationally Active Financial Institutions," *Quarterly Review*, Federal Reserve Bank of New York, Spring 1991, pp. 38-51.

International Monetary Fund, *IMF Survey*, Washington, DC: IMF, March ˉ, 1990.

International Monetary Fund, *International Capital Market: Developments and Prospects*, Washington, DC: IMF, 1991 and 1992.

Jones, R. S., "Japan's Expanding Role in World Financial Markets," *Columbia Journal of World Business,* Fall 1989, pp. 3–9.

Khanna, V., "Global Capital Markets Might Behave Differently in the 1990s, Says BIS Study," *IMF Survey*, Washington, DC: International Monetary Fund, June 24, 1991, pp. 198–201.

Mahajan, A., and D. F. Fraser, "Dollar Eurobond and U.S. Bond Pricing," *Journal of International Business Studies*, Summer 1986, pp. 21–36.

Meek, G. K., and S. J. Gray, "Globalization of Stock Markets and Foreign Listing Requirements: Voluntary Disclosures by Continental European Companies Listed on the London Stock Exchange," *Journal of International Business Studies*, Summer 1989, pp. 315–36.

Melvin, M., *International Money and Finance*, New York: Harper & Row, 1989.

Park, Y. S., "The Economics of Offshore Financial Centers," *Columbia Journal of World Business*, Winter 1982, pp. 31–35.

Pavel, C., and J. N. McElravey, "Globalization in the Financial Services Industry," *Economic Perspectives*, Federal Reserve Bank of Chicago, May/June 1990, pp. 3–18.

Saudagaran, S. M., "An Empirical Study of Selected Factors Influencing the Decision to List on Foreign Stock Exchanges," *Journal of International Business Studies,* Spring 1988, pp. 101–28.

Saunders, A., "The Eurocurrency Interbank Market: Potential for International Crises?" *Business Review,* Federal Reserve Bank of Philadelphia, February 1988, pp. 17–27.

Turner, P., *Capital Flows in the 1980s: A Survey of Major Trends*, The Bank for International Settlements, 1991.

9

International Banking and Country Risk

World banking has grown with the unprecedented expansion of economic activity after World War II because banks have followed customers abroad. Recent events in developing countries have compelled analysts and investors to question international bankers about loans to politically risky countries. For some banks, international lending can be as important as domestic operations. Thus, international banks must reduce the impact of country risk through systematic assessment and management.

This chapter has three major sections. The first section discusses international banking operations. International banks are a major source of capital in international markets. The second section looks at how banks assess unique risks of their foreign operations and how these risks can be incorporated into routine operations. The third section describes major causes of the U.S. foreign debt problem and its burdens on the U.S. economy.

International Banking Operations

International banks perform many vital tasks to help international transactions of multinational companies. They finance foreign trade and foreign investment, underwrite Eurobonds and foreign bonds, borrow and lend in the Eurodollar market, organize syndicated loans, participate in international cash management, solicit local currency deposits and loans, and give information and advice to clients.

International Banking Market

The international banking market consists of the foreign sector of domestic banking markets and the unregulated offshore markets. It has undergone important structural changes over the last decade.

Like domestic banking, international banking involves lending and deposit taking. The primary distinction between the two types of banking lies in their customer bases. Since 1982, international lending and deposit taking have both been growing at roughly 15 percent annually. By 1991, foreign loans and foreign liabilities at the world's banks each totaled more than $7 trillion. The extent, nature, and growth of international banking, however, are not the same in all countries. Nearly half of all foreign banking assets and liabilities are held by banks in the United Kingdom, Japan, the United States, and Switzerland.

Types of Foreign Banking Offices

There are six major types of foreign banking offices: representative offices, correspondent banks, branch banks, subsidiaries, agencies, and banking consortia. The list of alternatives also should include Edge Act Corporations, International Banking Facilities, and export trading companies, which are discussed in later chapters.

Representative Offices.
National banks may establish offices in foreign countries when their parent bank is doing business in these countries or in neighboring countries. They do not have traditional banking functions such as deposits, loans, letters of credit, drafts, and Eurodollar markets.

Representative offices obtain information, give advice, and arrange local contacts for their parent bank's business customers. They help local business executives initiate inquiries about the parent bank's services and introduce visiting executives to local banks. They put clients of parent banks in contact with government officials or local business firms. They also provide their parent bank with credit analysis of local firms and political information about the country.

Correspondent Banks.
Most major national banks maintain correspondent banking relationships with local banks in many major foreign cities of the world. The correspondent banking system is an informal arrangement in which a bank in a country maintains deposit balances with banks in foreign countries and looks to them for services and assistance.

Local correspondent banks accept drafts and honor letters of credit. They also provide credit information. Finally, they collect or pay foreign funds from import or export transactions.

Branch Banks.

Foreign branch banks do not have a corporate charter, board of directors, or shares of common stock outstanding. Thus, they are an operational part of the parent bank; their assets and liabilities are, in fact, those of the parent bank.

Foreign branch banks provide a full range of banking services under the name and guarantee of the parent bank. They attract big local borrowers because legal loan limits depend on the size of the parent bank.

Banking Subsidiaries.

Foreign subsidiary banks have their own charter, their own board of directors, their own stockholders, and their own managers. Yet, a foreign parent bank owns them completely or in major part. They must comply with the laws of the host country.

Because foreign subsidiary banks maintain their status as local institutions with local ownership and management, they are able to attract additional local deposits and have greater access to the local business community. In addition, they are more likely to appeal to the foreign business community than a local bank because they have permanent relations with their foreign part-owner.

Agencies.

Agencies of foreign banks can offer only a limited range of banking services. They cannot accept transaction deposits from residents of their own country, but they must deal exclusively with commercial customers. Their primary function is to finance both exports and imports that originate from companies in their own country. Agencies also actively participate in interbank credit markets and some other loans to companies in their own country.

Consortium Banks.

A consortium bank is a permanent group of banks that handle large international loans. It has its own charter but is a joint venture owned by two or more shareholder-parent banks with usually different nationalities.

Consortium banks develop their business and take customers the parent bank suggests. They arrange global syndicates for large international loans. Syndicates in large international loans spread risk and overcome the inability of a single bank to handle a large loan alone. Consortium banks also underwrite corporate securities and arrange mergers and acquisitions.

Interbank Clearinghouse Systems

Three key clearing systems of interbank fund transfers are: (1) the Clearing House Interbank Payments System (CHIPS), (2) the Clearing House Payments Assistance System (CHPAS), and the Society for Worldwide Interbank Financial Telecommunications (SWIFT). These three systems transfer funds between banks through wire rather than through checks.

The CHIPS is used to move dollars between New York offices of about 120 financial institutions that handle 90 percent of all foreign exchange trades and almost all Eurodollar transactions. The CHPAS began its operation in

1983 and provides services similar to those of the CHIPS. It is used to move funds between London offices of most financial institutions.

The SWIFT was founded in 1973 by European and North American banks. It is an interbank communication network which carries messages for financial transactions. Since 1973 its membership has expanded to include many Asian and Latin American banks. The SWIFT network represents a common denominator in the international payment system and uses the latest communication technology. The network has vastly reduced the multiplicity of formats used by banks in different parts of the world. Banks can execute international payments more cheaply and efficiently than ever before because of the common denominator in the international payment system and the speed of electronic transactions. Currently, 2800 live network users send one million messages daily through the SWIFT; its usage increases at an annual average growth rate of 15 percent. Messages transferred through this system include bank transfers, customer transfers, and special messages. The appendix to this chapter shows currency codes used by the SWIFT network.

International Loans

Large international loans to developing and East-bloc countries have become extremely important for European, Japanese, and U.S. banks. For some banks, international loans have become as important as their domestic banking operations. On the other hand, recent global debt problems have raised serious questions about large loans to developing and East-bloc countries.

Rise of Japanese Banking Operations.
The rising share of U.S. corporate loans booked by foreign-owned banks and the withdrawal of U.S. banks from foreign loans raise concerns about the competitiveness of U.S. banks. Moreover, some recent studies attribute the growth of foreign banks in the United States to the increase in foreign direct investment in providing services to multinational firms from their home countries. This interpretation is applied in particular to Japanese banks, which accounted for 20 percent of all U.S. loans in 1990.

Perhaps the most notable event in international banking has been the rapid growth of Japanese banks. This extraordinary growth can be traced to deregulation in Japan, its banks' high market capitalization, the country's high savings rate, and its large current account surplus. Japanese foreign exchange controls and restrictions on capital outflows were removed in 1980. In addition, U.S. pressure has accelerated financial deregulation in Japan since 1984 and has helped Japanese institutions recycle their large liquid funds. Since then the yen has become an attractive investment currency for private and official holders.

In the past few years, international operations of Japanese banks have increased beyond all expectations thanks to Japan's widening trade surplus and Tokyo's booming capital markets. Individual Japanese banks dominate a ranking of the world largest banks. In 1979, the United States accounted for six of the world's 10 largest banks, but in 1991, the top 10 banks in the world were Japanese. The biggest bloc of foreign banks in the United States is Japanese; they own four of the top ten banks in California. Japanese banks as a group also dominate the international banking market. Japan's share of the world market (total bank assets) increased from 26 percent in 1985 to about 50 percent in 1991. The U.S. share of the world market tumbled from 22 percent in 1985 to about 10 percent in 1991. Fifty-five percent of international banking claims involved fund flows to or from Japan in 1991.

The decline in dollar-based lending reflects U.S. banks' recent caution amid the Third World debt crisis and banking strains at home. Those troubles coincided with an end to certain Japanese restrictions on yen-based loans outside Japan; this change helped produce the surge in global loans denominated in yen.

The International Debt Crisis of 1982–1984.

Developing and East-bloc countries dramatically increased their borrowing from lenders in the Western industrial countries from 1973 to 1982. The total external debt of the non-oil developing countries increased from $130 billion in 1973 to $840 billion in 1982, a 6.5-fold increase. Over this 10-year period, the debt grew at an average compound rate of 20 percent per year. At the outset, few people worried as the external debts of these countries mounted in the 1970s. Several poor countries in Africa experienced difficult servicing problems. Yet, by the early 1980s, more developed borrowers such as Poland, Mexico, Brazil, and Argentina had difficulty in servicing their hugh external debts.

The first major blow to the international banking system came in August 1982, when Mexico announced that it could not meet its regularly scheduled payments to international creditors. Shortly thereafter, Brazil and Argentina were in the same situation. By Spring 1983, about 25 developing countries could not make regularly scheduled payments and negotiated rescheduling with creditor banks. These countries accounted for two-thirds of the total debt owed by non-oil developing countries to private banks. A worldwide recession compounded the lending crisis. It put downward pressure on oil prices and on OPEC's revenues. In 1980, OPEC contributed almost $42 billion to the loanable funds of the international banks, but by 1982, OPEC nations withdrew $26 billion from these loanable funds.

Major Causes of the Debt Crisis.

Officials of the developing countries often argue that the international lending crisis arose solely because of global economic dislocations. Still, policy makers of the creditor countries suggest that mismanagement by the debtor countries caused the crisis. The truth is, of course, somewhere in the middle of these positions.

Several developments in the 1970s turned banks into the predominant suppliers of funds to non-oil developing and Eastern bloc nations. First, there were growth and investment opportunities in these countries because economies began to open and to rise in the second half of the 1960s. Second, the 1973-1974 oil shock accelerated bank loans to these countries when higher oil prices and the subsequent world recession skyrocketed the current account deficit of the borrowing nations. Third, many developing countries began to incur large balance-of-payments deficits during the early 1980s because the worldwide recession of 1979-1982 compelled industrial countries to reduce their imports from developing countries. Fourth, observers argue that capital flight, prompted by political and economic uncertainty, caused the debt crisis. The World Bank estimates that capital flight from Latin-American debtor countries to industrial countries exceeded $70 billion between 1979 and 1982.

Solutions.   The global debt crisis of the early 1980s had come and gone. Lenders, borrowers, the IMF, and the World Bank worked together to overcome this latest crisis through rescheduling, refinancing, additional loans, and restrictive economic policies. True, global debt no longer occupies center stage in the current international monetary and financial debate. Management of the debt crisis since 1982 exemplifies successful international policy coordination. Observers feared that the debt crisis would provoke an international banking crisis and a global depression. Those dire predictions of pessimists in 1982 have not come true in large part because policymakers from the creditor countries, debtor countries, and the multinational financial institutions became actively involved. International banks have remained solvent; international capital markets have continued to function; and the world has not fallen into a default-induced depression.

Still, the economic results of most debtor countries have been poor. Economic development for hundreds of millions of people has halted or reversed. These countries have enjoyed neither sustained economic recovery nor renewed access to international capital markets. Some countries have become so desperate that their governments set a unilateral moratorium on debt services. The international banking community still seems fragile and vulnerable because of the sheer magnitude of the global debt outstanding. As shown in Table 9-1, the external debt of 114 developing countries reached a total of $1,351 billion at the end of 1991. Loans from the world's private banks to more than 100 non-oil developing countries exceeded $530 billion. The number of banks holding this debt ranges from 800 to 1000 which includes most banks in industrial countries. Perhaps 200 large banks account for three quarters of the debt. In the United States, nine banks account for two-thirds of all U.S. bank loans to foreign countries.

The total external debt of these developing countries grew at an average annual growth rate of 20 percent from 1973 to 1982. But the debt grew at an average annual growth rate of only 6 percent during the seven-year period of 1982-1991 (See Table 9-1). Total lending has slowed markedly since 1982 because the interests of international banks and debtor countries changed after the lending crises of 1982-1984. Banks preferred to cut loan exposure, while debtor countries tried to increase hard currency inflows through other channels such as increased exports and foreign investment.

The international lending problem faced attacks on many fronts. First, international banks took steps to reduce their burden of developing-country

Table 9–1
Growth of External Debt
(billion U.S. dollars)

	1982	1984	1986	1988	1991
Total debt, DRS countries*	760	862	1,062	1,182	1,281
Long-term debt	561	688	893	996	1,050
Official sources	202	239	367	453	534
Private sources	359	449	526	543	516
Short-term credit	175	138	126	151	194
Use of IMF credit	24	36	43	35	37
Total debt, other countries	86	81	85	100	70
Total debt, all countries	856	943	1,147	1,282	1,351

* Countries reporting to the World Bank Debtor Reporting System.

Source: The World Bank, *World Debt Tables: 1989–1990*, Washington, DC: The World Bank, December 1991, p. 13.

debts. They increased equity-capital base, raised loan-loss reserves, avoided new loans to developing countries, and sold exposed loans at a big discount to investors.

Second, many debtor countries took steps to alleviate their external debt problems. They have increased exports, reduced imports, attracted more foreign investment, adopted restrictive economic policies, and used debt-equity swaps. In debt-equity swaps, creditors exchange their loans for equity in local companies.

Third, policymakers of the creditor nations, the World Bank, and the IMF have worked together to provide partial debt relief for countries in the most extreme difficulties. Under this plan, a portion of a country's external debt would be forgiven permanently. The country would receive new concessionary loans from commercial banks and international financial institutions if it pursued sound growth and reform-oriented policies. Thirteen official creditors (Belgium, Canada, Denmark, Finland, France, Germany, Italy, Japan, Netherlands, Norway, Sweden, Switzerland, the United Kingdom, and the United States) have canceled a total of $8.7 billion from 1982 to 1990.

Syndicated Loans.   A syndicated loan is a credit in which a group of banks makes funds available on common terms and conditions to a particular borrower. Perhaps one of the important developments in the field of international lending during the 1980s has been the rapid growth of syndicated loans. In the Euromarket, syndicated loans compose almost half of bank lending to nonbank borrowers. Syndication is the device a group of banks adopt to handle large loans that one bank is unable or unwilling to supply. In other words, syndication differs from a direct commercial loan in that several banks participate at the outset. For example, Kuwait signed a $5.5 billion loan accord with 81 banks from 21 countries on December 13, 1991.

This five-year reconstruction deal was described as the largest syndicated loan ever extended to a sovereign borrower.

A syndicated loan must be, therefore, structured and packaged so that it satisfies the demands of the lenders and the needs of the borrowers. This type of loan has become increasingly popular because of (1) the increasing size of individual loans; (2) the need to spread risks in large loans; (3) the attractiveness of management fees; (4) the publicity for participating banks; and (5) the need to form profitable working relationships with other banks.

Evaluation of International Loans.   On the one hand, international loans have some advantages for banks:

1. International loans have been very profitable for many large banks and have had a significant impact on the earnings of such giant banks as Citicorp, Chase Manhattan, and Bank of America.
2. Many banks have improved risk-return performance because they can diversify international loans by country and by type of customer.
3. Developing and East-European countries have traditionally attempted to preserve their high credit standing with international banks.
4. Several safeguards have reduced the risk of international loans. They include credit insurance programs in the lenders's own countries, guarantees by parent companies on loans to affiliates, and guarantees by host governments on loans to private companies within their country.

On the other hand, international loans have many disadvantages for banks:

1. Country risk analysis is extremely complex because it depends on many variables.
2. International bankers recently didn't anticipate dramatic increases in country risk.
3. Some bankers have relaxed their credit standards to compensate for weak domestic and commercial demand for loans.
4. Critics question the ability of debtor countries to service their external debt because many loans are short-term variable loans.
5. If borrowing countries are unable to meet their obligations on time, banks will be forced to roll over their loans indefinitely.
6. The ultimate purpose of some loans is to finance balance-of-payments deficits. This type of loan does not improve the debtor country's ability to generate foreign-exchange earnings.

East-Europe's Hard-Currency Debt.   Table 9-2 shows the net hard-currency debt of each East-European country to the West. Net hard-currency loans to East-European countries by Western banks and governments had increased ten times between 1970 and 1980; they have increased 2.2 times from 1980 to 1989. Many analysts worry that these large foreign debt burdens would increase the pain involved in switching to

Table 9–2
East Europe's Hard–Currency Debt
(in billions of dollars)

Country	1970	1980	1989
Bulgaria	$0.7	$2.7	$9.5
Czechoslovakia	0.6	3.4	6.9
East Germany	1.4	11.8	21.2
Hungary	0.6	7.0	20.6
Poland	1.1	21.9	41.0
Romania	1.6	9.0	1.0
Soviet Union	1.0	4.1	48.0
Total	$7.0	$65.4	$148.2

Source: *The Wall Street Journal*, January 2, 1982, p. 16; and *The Wall Street Journal*, June 27, 1990, p. 18A.

market-based economies—soaring prices, closed factories, unemployment risks, and lower standards of living.

Nevertheless, the world's major commercial banks and many Western governments are reluctant to finance the reconstruction of the ravaged economies of the former Soviet Union and its former satellites. Forty-two nations recently pledged about $12 billion to the new European Bank for Reconstruction and Development, which will lend to emerging market economies in Eastern Europe. But these sums are too small to make any significant difference in the tasks Eastern European countries face in transforming their inefficient economies, modernizing industrial plants, and alleviating enormous pollution problems. Bankers sympathize with the plight of emerging democracies in Eastern Europe and their stated desire to adopt free-market mechanisms. However, these bankers' reluctance to bail out the East bloc reflects their caution amid their Third world debt problems and banking strains at home.

In May 1991, the U.S. government unilaterally agreed to forgive 70 percent of the few billion dollars Poland owes to the United States. The U.S. government made it clear that this debt relief was a special case in its debt strategy. But Western European nations and Japan, which hold most of the debt that Poland owes to foreign governments, are not too happy about that for two major reasons. First, debt relief on government claims could well discourage the intention of the self-help efforts of indebted countries who work diligently to repay their debt. Second, it could also complicate the access of indebted countries to this new official money as the last resort for economic reconstruction. International bankers and Western governments say that given the worldwide shortage of capital, Eastern European countries should strive to make themselves more creditworthy, not less.

Country Risk

Investors concerned about politically risky countries question giving loans to developing and East-bloc nations. Country or sovereign risk refers both to the possibility of default on foreign loans and to unanticipated restrictions of cash flows to the parent country.

There are two major differences between domestic loans and foreign loans. First, because repayment of international loans must go through the exchange market, international banks must assess prospects for exchange rates and for controls on capital flows. Second, a common legal system or an ultimate arbitrator does not exist to settle disputed claims. Under this condition, some debtor countries are unlikely to accept the decisions of Western-oriented international legal frameworks. Thus, country-risk assessment is critical for commercial banks to safeguard their international loans against country risk.

Nature of Country-Risk Assessment

Bank executives refer to two major shocks when they discuss country risk. The first was the oil shock of 1973-1974, which spurred most major banks to create formal and systematic approaches to country risk. The second was the Iran shock, which transformed Iran almost overnight from the highly favorable banking environment into the extremely hostile one; in fact, Ayatollah Khomeini's regime expropriated many foreign banks. The first oil shock caused the increased number of banks to do formal country-risk analysis. The second Iran shock caused banks to pay increased attention to expropriation risk. A recent study by Charles Kennedy (1991) found that during the 1965-1985 period, 287 foreign banks had been nationalized; this number accounted for 24 percent of the total expropriations in all industries which took place during the same period.

Many international bankers have undertaken country-risk analysis for many years. They are now working on a second or third generation of country-risk models. These bankers have modified the original models based on experience and on their knowledge of other banks' procedures. These modified models could result in better decisions by more informed business persons and less risk in international loans than before.

Country risk is nothing more than an assessment of economic opportunity against political odds. Thus, country-risk assessment requires that international bankers analyze political and economic indicators. While political factors reflect a country's willingness to pay its debt, economic indicators measure the country's ability to pay its debt. This means that any rating system of a country's risk must combine both economic and political risks.

Several country-risk assessment models are available in academic journals or from commercial sources. Yet, factors to be considered in country-risk analysis vary from forecaster to forecaster. The country-risk rating system should meet several criteria for use at a bank. First, lending officers should be able to understand and use the system easily. Second, the system should rank all developing countries with foreign loans. Third, the system should have both short-term and medium-term horizons. Fourth, the system should be effective in forecasting which countries are likely to reschedule their debts.

Country-risk assessment provides international banks with many useful purposes. First, it permits international banks to assess relative conditions of diverse countries based on common criteria. Second, because it is based on a common set of criteria, it often offsets individual biases. Third, a country's risk ranking is a useful "straw vote" rating.

How to Assess Country Risk

Country risk is the possibility that borrowers in a country will not honor past obligations. Bank managers must develop a better approach for evaluating country risk. Approaches now depend on the type of borrower such as the host government, an industrial firm, or a private bank. The same variables apply to all three types of clients though the relative weight assigned to each variable may differ considerably. Country risk may be assessed by various debt ratios and general creditworthiness of a country.

Debt Ratios.   Debt burdens vary from one developing country to another. For some countries, external debt and debt-service payments are insignificant both in absolute amounts and in relation to gross national product (GNP) or exports of goods and services. In these countries, therefore, the burden of external debt does not place a hardship on the economy. For other countries, the debt burden is so large that it hampers growth-oriented policies. Developing countries between these two groups are not seriously burdened by their external debt but remain vulnerable.

The World Bank classifies the debt burden of developing countries according to a set of four debt ratios: (1) the ratio of total external debt to GNP, (2) the ratio of total external debt to exports, (3) the ratio of accrued debt service to exports (debt service ratio), and (4) the ratio of accrued interest to exports (interest service ratio).

According to *World Debt Tables: 1991–92* issued by the World Bank, the ratios of many developing countries are extremely high. This report focuses on the policy implications of heavy burdens for two groups: severely and moderately indebted countries. A country is classified as severely indebted if three of the four indicators are above critical values: a debt-to-GNP ratio of 50 percent, a debt-to-export ratio of 275 percent, a debt-service ratio of 30 percent, and an interest-service ratio of 20 percent. A country is classified as moderately indebted if at least three of the four indicators exceed 60 percent of the critical values. Using these ratios, the World Bank identified 27 severely indebted low-income countries, 15 severely indebted middle-income countries, 12 moderately indebted low-income countries, and 17 moderately indebted middle-income countries. Low-income countries are those whose GNP per capita was no more than $600 in 1990, and middle-income countries are those whose GNP per capita was somewhere between $600 and $7,620 in 1990.

Debt ratios must be used carefully when we examine a country's debt situation because debt ratio analysis has its limitations. The four debt ratios used by the World Bank have at least two drawbacks. First, they present the debt situation of a country in a particular reference year. The economic measures of that reference year may not be representative. For example, a temporary rise in commodity prices may increase the value of exports and therefore lower the debt-service ratio, but it will not significantly improve a country's long-term creditworthiness. Second, these ratios are static. The debt ratios developed for a particular country at a given time have little meaning unless they are compared with some standards.

Historical (future) standards and world standards are two criteria used. To analyze the debt situation of a country, we should compare its current ratios with its past or future ratios. A ratio may fluctuate considerably over time, so that sole reliance on a single ratio may at times give a misleading indication of a country's debt situation. When ratios are calculated over several years and compared with one another, analysts may find whether the country's debt situation is improving or worsening.

The second standard that analysts can use to examine a country's debt situation is world average ratios. It is important to remember that countries of the same size with the same income should be compared. The increasing diversity of national economies, the accelerated tempo of changes in technology and product development, and rapid changes in income level have made it extremely difficult to identify a particular country with a given country-group of about the same size. Proper classification by country and size is necessary for ratio analysis because the ratios vary from country to country and from size to size.

Aware of these limitations, the World Bank presents historical ratios by country group with similarities in terms of debt burden and income. It classifies all debt-burdened countries (114) into four country groups: severely indebted low-income countries, severely indebted middle-income countries, moderately indebted low-income countries, and moderately indebted middle-income countries. It also classifies all debt-burdened countries into six regions: Africa, East Asia, Europe, Latin America, North Africa, and South Asia. Table 9-3 shows historical ratios, all developing-country averages, and severely indebted low-income country averages.

Overall–Country Creditworthiness.   The combined impact of economic, political, and other indicators may be used to rate country risk. For example, *Euromoney* country credit ratings are based on views by a cross section of specialists on each country with particular reference to some economic and other factors. The system rates each country's ease of access to international capital markets, the country's ability to use new innovations

Table 9–3
Key Debt Ratios for All Developing Countries

Debt Ratios	1984	1985	1986	1987	1988	1989	1990	1991
All Developing Countries								
Debt to GNP	0.42	0.46	0.50	0.52	0.46	0.43	0.42	0.38
Debt to Exports	1.82	2.09	2.36	2.28	2.00	1.84	1.77	1.76
Debt Service	0.25	0.28	0.30	0.28	0.27	0.22	0.20	0.21
Interest Service	0.15	0.15	0.14	0.12	0.12	0.10	0.09	0.10
Severely Indebted Low–Income Countries								
Debt to GNP	0.54	0.61	0.87	1.19	1.22	1.17	1.13	1.04
Debt to Exports	2.80	3.21	4.57	5.21	4.95	4.80	3.90	4.94
Debt Service	0.27	0.30	0.31	0.22	0.28	0.27	0.24	0.31
Interest Service	0.13	0.13	0.14	0.10	0.14	0.13	0.11	0.14

Source: The World Bank, *World Debt Tables: 1991–92*, Washington, DC: The World Bank, December 1991, p. 120 and p. 148.

and borrowing options, its debt payment record, and its ability to service its external debt. These views based on historical data are supplemented by two subjective risk factors: economic and political. The economic risk factor is the prospective view of economic performance to each country by a panel of economists. The political risk factor is the prospective view of political stability to each country by a panel of political risk specialists.

Table 9-4 presents a portion of *Euromoney's* country risk ratings in September 1991. The lowest ranking countries are those that have experienced war (Kuwait and Iraq), civil unrest (former communist countries), and economic difficulty (Ethiopia and Haiti). The international debt crisis of 1982-1984 has dramatized the importance of country-risk analysis. Thus, we can understand why international bankers have searched for more systematic means of evaluating and managing country risk. They have recently increased resource commitments, employed more qualified analysts, and adopted more sophisticated methods to assess country risk.

Although country risk can never disappear, its systematic assessment and management can significantly decrease its impact. A variety of ratios, country-credit ratings by some consulting companies, and procedures established by an individual bank may be used to reduce the possibility of defaults on foreign loans and interest.

The U.S. Debt Crisis

Most major types of debt in the United States have grown rapidly in recent years. Perhaps the most publicized is the unprecedented size of the U.S. foreign debt. Some analysts say that the U.S. buildup in foreign debt could imperil the stability of the U.S. financial system. They argue that America's heavy external-debt burdens have reduced the ability of financial institutions,

Table 9–4
Country Risk Rankings

Rank in 1991	Rank in 1990	Country	Ratings (0–100)		Rank in 1991	Rank in 1990	Country	Ratings (0–100)	
			1991	1990				1991	1990
1	1	Japan	96	91	120	85	Rwanda	19	37
2	6	Switzerland	95	88	121	76	Yugoslavia	18	42
3	3	Netherlands	95	90	122	118	Haiti	17	19
4	18	Germany	94	83	123	124	Guyana	17	19
5	3	France	94	90	124	130	Sudan	17	15
6	3	Austria	94	90	125	108	Albania	17	27
7	10	USA	93	86	126	123	Lebanon	15	20
8	2	Luxembourg	93	91	127	122	Zaire	15	22
9	10	Denmark	93	86	128	126	Ethiopia	14	19
10	9	Canada	92	86	130	128	Iraq	2	18

Source: *Euromoney*, September 1991, pp. 171–72.

borrowers, and the economy at large to withstand recessions and other types of adversity.

Table 9–5 underscores a new reality. Japan has become a rich uncle, the chief source of foreign capital in the United States. Japanese net overseas investment (net external assets) has climbed from $11 billion in 1981 to $328 billion in 1990. Most of that money has gone to the United States. For instance, Japanese investors have bought about 30 percent of U.S. government securities in recent years.

This dramatic reversal in the U.S. international position has awakened economists and the American public to the significance of global capital flows. As recently as 1982, the United States was the world's largest creditor nation. It was a net creditor nation until February 1985. Within a few years, it had an opposite role, becoming the world's biggest debtor nation. Twin deficits—huge trade and budget deficits in the 1980s—are two major reasons for this shift. Foreign debt has grown at such a breathtaking pace that few people were aware of its potential impact until it was too late. By 1990 the U.S. foreign debt reached $700 billion, which is more than about half the combined total debt of 114 developing countries.

In the early stages of its industrial development, the United States was a net debtor nation. Relying heavily on foreign capital, the United States built up its industries. Yet, this country became a net creditor nation by the end of World War I. Its net overseas investment evolved steadily from $6 billion in 1919 to $141 billion in 1981. The long-term increase in the U.S. net investment position decreased dramatically since 1982. By 1985 the United States became a net debtor nation for the first time since World War I.

Table 9–5
Net Overseas Investment
(in billions of U.S. dollars)

Year	Japan	U.S.
1980	$ 11.5	$106.3
1981	10.9	141.1
1982	24.7	137.0
1983	37.3	89.6
1984	74.3	3.6
1985	129.8	-111.9
1986	180.4	-269.2
1987	240.7	-378.3
1988	291.7	-532.5
1989	293.2	-727.8
1990	328.0	-700.4

Note: Net overseas investment position at book value.

Source: The U.S. Department of Commerce, *Survey of Current Business*, various issues; and Japan Economic Institute of America.

America's investment surplus evaporated as the country amassed huge budget and trade deficits during the 1980s. The rise of foreign investment in the United States prompted calls for Congress to curb foreign purchases of U.S. companies and real estate. The United States was a net debtor nation for most of the 19th century with no bad effects as European capital helped to build railroads and factories. Still, some private economists contend that there is a marked difference between the 19th-century net debtor period and the present. In the last century, America was a developing country and needed foreign capital to become an industrial power. During the 1980s, much of the foreign money had gone to finance Federal and consumer deficits rather than being invested in ways that would boost American productivity.

Causes

What are the major causes of the U.S. foreign debt? Mounting budget and trade deficits are primarily responsible for the U.S. foreign debt. Gross federal debt increased from $906 billion in 1980 to $3.6 trillion in 1991. The current account balance had shifted from a surplus of $1.9 billion in 1980 to a record deficit of $154.0 billion in 1987; the current account deficit fell to $92 billion in 1990.

Major shifts in U.S. macroeconomic policy during the first half of the 1980s caused an unprecedented swing from creditor to debtor status. The Federal budget deficit surged because an expansive fiscal policy, which sharply reduced revenue growth and rapidly increased defense procurement, combined with a restrictive monetary policy that kept real interest rates high. The tax cut of 1981, which many regarded as the biggest in U.S. history, reduced revenue growth. The military buildup in the same year, again regarded as the largest in U.S. history, caused Federal outlays to rise suddenly.

Three factors dramatically increased U.S. trade deficits during the first half of this decade: the strong U.S. dollar, a faster economic growth in the United States than in its major trading partners, and reduced exports to heavily indebted developing countries.

In summary, huge budget and trade deficits, caused by major shifts in U.S. macroeconomic policy in the first half of the 1980s, shifted the United States from creditor to debtor status. We may visualize cause-effect relationships among a series of economic variables as follows: huge budget deficit—>high interest rate—>strong U.S. dollar—>huge trade deficit—>huge U.S. foreign debt.

Burdens

U.S. foreign debt had some positive, short-term effects on the U.S. economy. The net investment inflow from abroad increased the pool of savings in the U.S. economy; it reduced the U.S. interest rates; it enabled the U.S. economy to grow faster than otherwise would have been the case; and it reduced the U.S. inflation rate. Yet, the U.S. foreign debt could create serious, long-term problems: (1) lower living standards, (2) policy constraints, and (3) reduced international influence.

Lower Living Standards.
Living standards could fall as U.S. producers and taxpayers relinquish part of their earnings to pay foreigners interest on loans and dividends on investments. These funds will not be available for personal consumption, savings, or domestic investment, thus draining the purchasing power of the United States.

Policy Constraints.
Foreign investors keep wary eyes on economic developments here. Foreign investors might turn away from dollar denominated assets if they fear capital losses from further depreciation of the dollar or if interest rates decline. This would push the United States into a recession. In other words, a growing foreign debt makes the United States more vulnerable to pressure from foreign investors, thus influencing U.S. interest rates and the value of the dollar. The United States has never been in a position where foreign capital flows are as important as they are now. Economists worry about the effects of the increasing influence of money from abroad because the United States could be held hostage by other countries and might have no control over its own economic future.

Reduced International Influence.
External debt weakens the influence of the United States because a debtor must strive to accommodate its creditors. Private economists say that the U.S. status as the biggest debtor has jeopardized its prestige. This decline in prestige was evident at the 1988 Toronto economic summit at which the United States wielded less influence

in the discussions than Japan. Japan used the economic summit to showcase Japan's growing involvement in global affairs. Japan unveiled a $10 billion foreign-aid package before the meeting that would make Tokyo the world's largest donor. Also, Japan upstaged the world's other major democracies at the 1989 Paris economic summit by announcing a $35 billion dollar program to relieve Third World debt and a $2.25 billion environmental aid package for Third World countries.

Summary

This chapter discussed international banking operations, country risk, and the U.S. foreign-debt problem. Management of international banks is more complex than that of domestic banks. Country-risk analysis illustrates this. Recent events in many debtor countries have brought analysts and investors to question international bankers about loans to politically risky countries. For some banks, international lending can be as important as their domestic operations. Thus, international banks must reduce the impact of country risk through systematic assessment and management.

The unprecedented rise of the U.S. foreign debt since 1985 reveals a new reality. The new reality of the 1980s is a gradual shift of economic power from a single hegemony—the United States—to a tripolar system driven by the United States, Japan, and Europe. The emergency of this tripolar system is likely to affect the international banking system in the 1990s and beyond.

Questions

1. Discuss the types of functions that international banks perform.

2. Discuss the types of foreign banking offices.

3. What factors account for the rise of Japanese banking operations?

4. What are major differences between domestic and foreign loans?

5. What were major causes for the international debt crisis of 1982–1984?

6. Explain the various steps taken by debtor countries and international banks to solve international debt problems.

7. What is syndicated lending? Why do banks sometimes prefer this form of lending?

8. What is country risk? How can we assess country risk?

9. Describe the burdens of the U.S. foreign debt.

References

The Council of Economic Advisers, *Economic Report of the President*, Washington, DC: United States Government Printing Office, 1985, 1989, 1990, and 1992.

Davis, R. R., "Alternative Techniques for Country Risk Evaluation," *Business Economics*, May 1981, pp. 7–15.

Feldstein, M., ed., *International Economic Cooperation*, Chicago: The University of Chicago Press, 1988.

Friedman, M., "Straight Talk About Deficits," *Reader's Digest*, March 1989, pp. 105–7.

Garg, R. C., and R. Aggarwal, "Risk Analysis in Bank Lending to Developing Countries: A Survey of International Bankers," *Issues in International Business*, Spring 1987, pp. 17–24.

George, A. M., and I. H. Giddy, eds., *International Financial Handbook*, New York, John Wiley & Sons, 1983.

The Joint Economic Committee, Congress of the United States, *The Economy at Midyear: A Legacy of Foreign Debt*, August 5, 1987.

Kennedy, C. R., Jr., "International Banking and Expropriation Risk," in Thomas I. Kindel, *Proceedings of the 1991 Conference*, Charleston, SC: Association for Global Business, 1991, pp. 228–38.

Khoury, S. J., *Sovereign Debt: A Critical Look at the Causes and the Nature of the Problem*, Center for International Business Studies, The University of South Carolina, 1985.

Kim, S. H., and S. W. Miller, *Comparative Structure of the International Banking Industry*, Lexington, MA: Lexington Books, 1983.

Lessard, D. R., and J. Williamson, eds., *Capital Flight and Third World Debt*, Washington, DC: Institute for International Economics, 1987.

Morgan, J. B., "Assessing Country Risk at Texas Commerce," *The Bankers Magazine*, May–June 1985, pp. 23–9.

Morris, F. E., "The Changing American Attitude Toward Debt and Its Consequences," *New England Economic Review*, Federal Reserve Bank of Boston, May/June 1990, pp. 33-9.

Park, Y. S., and J. Zwick, *International Banking in Theory and Practice*, Reading, MA: Addison-Wesley Publishing Company, 1985.

Rojas-Suarez, L., "Macroeconomic Discipline, Structural Reforms Can Help Reverse Capital Flight," *IMF Survey*, Washington DC: International Monetary Fund, September 10, 1990, pp. 158-9.

Seth, R., and A. Quijano, "Japanese Banks' Customers in the United States," *Quarterly Review*, Federal Reserve Bank of New York, Spring 1991, pp. 79-82.

Turner, P., *Capital Flows in the 1980s: A Survey of Major Trends*, The Bank for International Settlements, 1991.

The World Bank, *World Debt Tables: 1990–1991*, Washington, DC: The World Bank, 1992.

Zimmer, S. A., and R. N. McCauley, "Bank Cost of Capital and International Competition," *Quarterly Review*, Federal Reserve Bank of New York, Winter 1991, pp. 33-59.

Appendix

Currency Codes Used by SWIFT

Country	Currency	Code
Afghanistan	Afghani	AFA
Albania	Lek	ALL
Algeria	Algerian Dinar	DZD
American Samoa	US Dollar	USD
Andorra	Andorran Peseta	ADP
	Spanish Peseta	ESP
	French Franc	FRF
Angola	Kwanza	AOK
Anguilla	East Caribbean Dollar	XCD
Antigua and Barbuda	East Caribbean Dollar	XCD
Argentina	Austral	ARA
Aruba	Aruban Guilder	AWG
Australia	Australian Dollar	AUD
Austria	Shilling	ATS
Bahamas	Bahamian Dollar	BSD
Bahrain	Bahraini Dinar	BHD
Bangladesh	Taka	BDT
Barbados	Barbados Dollar	BBD
Belgium	Convertible Belgian Franc	BEC
	Common Belgian Franc	BEF
	Financial Belgian Franc	BEL
Belize	Belize Dollar	BZD
Benin	CFA Franc Beac	XOF
Bermuda	Bermudian Dollar	BMD
Bhutan	Ingultrum	BTN
	Indian Rupee	INR
Bolivia	Boliviano	BOB
Botswana	Pula	BWP
Bouvet Island	Norwegian Krone	NOK
Brazil	New Cruzado	BRN
British Indian Ocean Terri.	US Dollar	BND
Brunei Darussalam	Brunei Dollar	BND
Bulgaria	Lev	BGL
Burkina Faso	CFA Franc Beac	XOF
Burundi	Burundi Franc	BIF
Byelorussian SSR	Rouble	SUR
Cameroon	CFA Franc Beac	XAF
Canada	Canadian Dollar	CAD
Cape Verde	Cape Verde Escudo	CVE
Cayman Islands	Cayman Islands Dollar	KYD
Central African Republic	CFA Franc Beac	XAF

Chad	CFA Franc Beac	XAF
Chile	Unidades De Fomento	CLF
	Chilean Peso	CLP
China	Yuan Renminbi	CNY
Christmas Islands	Australian Dollar	AUD
Cocos (Keeling) Islands	Australian Dollar	AUD
Colombia	Colombian Peso	COP
Comoros	Comoro Franc	KMF
Congo	CFA Franc Beac	XAF
Cook Islands	New Zealand Dollar	NZD
Costa Rica	Cost Rican Colon	CRC
Cote D'Ivoire	CFA Franc Beac	XOF
Cuba	Cuban Peso	CUP
Cyprus	Cyprus Pound	CYP
Czechoslovakia	Koruna	CSK
Denmark	Danish Krone	DKK
Djibouti	Dijbouti Franc	DJF
Dominica	East Caribbean Dollar	XCD
Dominican Republic	Dominican Peso	DOP
East Timor	Rupiah	IDR
	Timor Escudo	TPE
Ecuador	Sucre	ECS
Egypt	Egyptian Pound	EGP
El Salvador	El Salvador Colon	SVC
Equatorial Guinea	CFA Franc Beac	XAF
Ethiopia	Ethiopian Birr	ETB
Faeroe Islands	Danish Krone	DKK
Falkland Islands (Malvinas)	Falkland Islands Pound	FKP
Fiji	Fiji Dollar	FJD
Finland	Markka	FIM
France	French Franc	FRF
French Guiana	French Franc	FRF
French Polynesia	CFP Franc	XPF
French Southern Territories	French Franc	FRF
Gabon	CFA Franc Beac	XAF
Gambia	Dalasi	GMD
Germany	Deutsche Mark	DEM
Ghana	Cedi	GHC
Gibraltar	Gibraltar Pound	GIP
Greece	Drachma	GRD
Greenland	Danish Krone	DKK
Grenada	East Caribbean Dollar	XCD
Guadeloupe	French Franc	FRF
Guam	US Dollar	USD
Guatemala	Quetzal	GTQ
Guernsey, C.I.	Pound Sterling	GBP
Guinea	Guinea Franc	GNF
Guinea-Bissau	Guinea-Bissau Peso	GWP
Guyana	Guyana Dollar	GYD
Haiti	Gourde	HTG

Haiti (cont.)	US Dollar	USD
Heard and McDonald Islands	Australian Dollar	AUD
Honduras	Lempira	HNL
Hong Kong	Hong Kong Dollar	HKD
Hungary	Forint	HUF
Iceland	Iceland Krona	ISK
India	Indian Rupee	INR
Indonesia	Rupiah	IDR
Iran (Islamic Republic Of)	Iranian Rial	IRR
Iraq	Iraqi Dinar	IQD
Ireland	Irish Pound	IEP
Isle of Man	Pound Sterling	GBP
Israel	Shekel	ILS
Italy	Italian Lira	ITL
Jamaica	Jamaican Dollar	JMD
Japan	Yen	JPY
Jersey, C.I.	Pound Sterling	GBP
Jordan	Jordanian Dinar	JOD
Kampuchea, Democratic	Riel	KHR
Kenya	Kenyan Shilling	KES
Kiribati	Australian Dollar	AUD
Korea, Democratic People's Rep. Of	North Korean Won	KPW
Korea, Republic Of	Won	KRW
Kuwait	Kuwaiti Dinar	KWD
Laos People's Democratic Republic	Kip	LAK
Lebanon	Lebanese Pound	LBP
Lesotho	Loti	LSL
	Financial Rand	ZAL
	Rand	ZAR
Liberia	Liberian Dollar	LRD
Libyan Arab Jamahiriya	Libyan Dinar	LYD
Liechtenstein	Swiss Franc	CHF
Luxembourg	Convertible Belgian Franc	BEC
	Common Belgian Fran	BEF
	Financial Belgian Franc	BEL
	Luxembourg Franc	LUF
Macau	Pataca	MOP
Madagascar	Malagasy Franc	MGF
Malawi	Kwacha	MWK
Malaysia	Malaysian Ringgit	MYR
Maldives	Rufiyaa	MVR
Mali	CFA Franc Beac	XOF
Malta	Maltese Lira	MTL
Marshall Isl., Repub. Of,	US Dollar	USD
Martinique	French Franc	FRF
Mauritania	Ouguiya	MRO
Mauritius	Mauritius Rupee	MUR

Mexico	Mexican Peso	MXP
Micronesia, Federated States of	US Dollar	USD
Monaco	French Franc	FRF
Mongolia	Tugrik	MNT
Monserrat	East Caribbean Dollar	XCD
Morocco	Moroccan Dirham	MAD
Mozambique	Metical	MZM
Myanmar	Kyat	MMK
Namibia	Rand	ZAR
Nauru	Australian Dollar	AUD
Nepal	Nepalese Rupee	NPR
Neth. Antilles	Netherlands Antillean Guilder	ANG
Netherlands	Netherlands Guilder	NLG
Neutral Zone between Saudi Arabia and Iraq	Iraqi Dinar	IQD
	Kuwaiti Dinar	KWD
	Saudi Riyal	SAR
New Caledonia	CFP Franc	XPF
New Zealand	New Zealand Dollar	NZD
Nicaragua	Cordoba	NIC
Niger	CFA Franc Beac	XOF
Nigeria	Naira	NGN
Niue	New Zealand Dollar	NZD
Norfolk Island	Australian Dollar	AUD
Northern Mariana Islands	US Dollar	USD
Norway	Norwegian Krone	NOK
Oman	Rial Omani	OMR
Pakistan	Pakistan Rupee	PKR
Palau	US Dollar	USD
Panama	Balboa	PAB
	US Dollar	USD
Papua New Guinea	Kina	PGK
Paraguay	Guarani	PYG
Peru	Inti	PEI
Philippines	Philippine Peso	PHP
Pitcairn Island	New Zealand Dollar	NZD
Poland	Zloty	PLZ
Portugal	Portuguese Escudo	PTE
Puerto Rico	US Dollar	USD
Qatar	Qatari Rial	QAR
Reunion	French Franc	FRF
Romania	Leu	ROL
Rwanda	Rwanda Franc	RWF
Saint Kitts and Nevis	East Caribbean Dollar	XCD
Samoa	Tala	WST
San Marino	Italian Lira	ITL
Sao Tome and Principe	Dobra	STD
Saudi Arabia	Saudi Riyal	SAR
Senegal	CFA Franc Beac	XOF

Seychelles	Seychelles Rupee	SCR
Sierra Leone	Leone	SLL
Singapore	Singapore Dollar	SGD
Solomon Islands	Solomon Islands Dollar	SBD
Somalia	Somali Shilling	SOS
South Africa	Financial Rand	ZAL
	Rand	ZAR
Spain	Convertible Peseta Accounts	ESB
	Spanish Peseta	ESP
Sri Lanka	Sri Lanka Rupee	LKR
St. Helena	St. Helena Pound	SHP
St. Lucia	East Caribbean Dollar	XCD
St. Pierre and Miquelon	French Franc	FRF
St. Vincent and the Grenadines	East Caribbean Dollar	XCD
Sudan	Sudanese Pound	SDP
Suriname	Surinam Guilder	SRG
Svalbard and Jan Mayen Is.	Norwegian Krone	NOK
Swaziland	Lilangeni	SZL
Sweden	Swedish Krona	SEK
Switzerland	Swiss Franc	CHF
Syrian Arab Republic	Syrian Pound	SYP
Taiwan	New Taiwan Dollar	TWD
Tanzania United Repub. of	Tanzanian Shilling	TZS
Thailand	Baht	THB
Togo	CFA Franc Beac	XOF
Tokelau	New Zealand Dollar	NZD
Tonga	Pa'anga	TOP
Trinidad and Tobago	Trinidad and Tobago Dollar	TTD
Tunisia	Tunisian Dinar	TND
Turkey	Turkish Lira	TRL
Turks and Caicos Islands	US Dollar	USD
Tuvalu	Australian Dollar	AUD
U.A.E.	UAE Dirham	AED
U.S.S.R.	Rouble	SUR
Uganda	Uganda Shilling	UGX
Ukrainian SSR	Rouble	SUR
United Kingdom	Pound Sterling	GBP
United States	US Dollar	USD
	US Dollar, Next Day Funds	USN
United States Minor Outlying Islands	US Dollar	USD
Uruguay	Uruguayan Peso	UYP
Vanuatu	Vatu	VUV
Vatican City State	Italian Lira	ITL
Venezuela	Bolivar	VEB
Vietnam	Dong	VND
Virgin Islands (British)	US Dollar	USD

Virgin Islands, U.S.	US Dollar	USD
Wallis and Futuna Islands	CFP Franc	XPF
Western Sahara	Moroccan Dirham	MAD
Yemen	Yemeni Rial	YER
Yemen, Democratic	Yemeni Dinar	YDD
Yugoslavia	New Yugoslavian Dinar	YUN
Zaire	Zaire	ZRZ
Zambia	Kwacha	ZMK
Zimbabwe	Zimbabwe Dollar	ZWD

10

Financing Foreign Trade

This book emphasizes financial problems that arise when managing multinational operations. However, the financial manager of a multinational firm must be familiar with certain mechanics of financing foreign trade because most multinational companies are frequently engaged in foreign trade activities.

This chapter consists of three major sections. The first section discusses three basic documents involved in foreign trade: draft, bill of lading, and letter of credit. The second section analyzes the various payment terms of foreign trade. The third section describes the major sources of financing foreign trade.

Basic Documents in Foreign Trade

Three important documents involved in foreign trade are:

1. A draft, which is an order to pay.
2. A bill of lading, which is a document involved in the physical movement of the merchandise by a common carrier.
3. A letter of credit, which is a third party guarantee of the importer's creditworthiness.

Basic Objectives of Documentation

Documentation in foreign trade is supposed to assure that the exporter will receive the payment and the importer will receive the merchandise. More specifically, a number of documents in foreign trade are used to eliminate noncompletion risk, to reduce foreign exchange risk, and to finance trade transactions.

Noncompletion Risk.
The risk of noncompletion is greater in foreign trade than in domestic trade. This is why exporters want to keep title to the goods until they are paid and importers are reluctant to pay until they receive the goods. Foreign trade and domestic trade use different instruments and documents. Most domestic sales are on open account credit. Under this credit, a buyer does not need to sign a formal debt instrument because credit sales are made on the basis of a seller's credit investigation of the buyer. Buyers and sellers are typically farther apart in foreign trade than in domestic trade. Thus, the sellers are seldom able to ascertain the credit standing of their overseas customers. The buyers may also find it difficult to determine the integrity and reputation of the foreign sellers from whom they wish to buy. Much of this noncompletion risk is reduced through the use of three key documents: the draft, the bill of lading, and the letter of credit.

Foreign Exchange Risk.
Foreign exchange risk arises when export sales are denominated in a foreign currency and are paid at a delayed date. In international trade, the basic foreign exchange risk is a transaction risk. Transaction risk is the potential exchange loss from outstanding obligations which existed before exchange rates changed but were settled after the exchange-rate change. Forward contracts, futures contracts, currency options, and currency denomination practices can be used to reduce foreign exchange risk associated with foreign trade.

Trade Financing.
Because all foreign trade involves a time lag, funds are tied up in the shipment of goods for some period of time. Most trade transactions are free of noncompletion and foreign exchange risks due to well-drawn trade documents and forward contracts. Banks are thus willing to finance goods in transit or even prior to shipment. Financial institutions at both ends of the cycle offer a variety of financing alternatives that reduce or eliminate either party's (exporter or importer) working capital needs.

Drafts

A draft or a bill of exchange is an order written by an exporter that requires an importer to pay a specified amount of money at a specified time. Through the use of drafts, the exporter may use its bank as the collection agent on accounts that the exporter finances. The bank forwards the exporter's drafts to the importer directly or indirectly (through a branch or a correspondent bank) and then remits the proceeds of the collection back to the exporter.

A draft involves three parties: the drawer or maker, the drawee, and the payee. The drawer is a person or business issuing a draft. This person is ordinarily the exporter who sells and ships the merchandise. The drawee is a person or business against whom the draft is drawn. This person is usually an importer who must pay the draft at maturity. The payee is a person or business to whom the drawee will eventually pay the funds. A draft designates a person or bank to whom payment is to be made if the draft is not a negotiable instrument. Such a person, known as the payee, may be the drawer himself or a third party such as the drawer's bank. However, this is generally not the case because most drafts are a bearer instrument. Drafts are negotiable if they meet a number of conditions:

1. They must be in writing and signed by the drawer-exporter.
2. They must contain an unconditional promise or order to pay an exact amount of money.
3. They must be payable on sight or at a specified time.
4. They must be made out to order or to bearer.

If a draft is made to order, the funds involved should be paid to the person specified. If it is made to bearer, the funds should be paid to the person who presents it for payment.

When a draft is presented to a drawee, the drawee or his bank accepts it. This acceptance acknowledges in writing the drawee's obligation to pay a sum indicated on the face of the draft. When drafts are accepted by banks, they become bankers' acceptances. Because bankers' acceptances are highly marketable, the exporter can sell them in the market or discount them at his bank. Whenever they are sold or discounted, the seller adds his endorsement on the back of the draft. In the event an importer fails to pay at maturity, the holder of the draft will have recourse for the full amount of the draft from the last endorser.

Drafts are used in foreign trade for a number of reasons:

1. They provide written evidence of obligations in a comprehensive form.
2. They allow both the exporter and the importer to reduce the cost of financing and to divide the remaining cost equitably.
3. They are negotiable and unconditional; that is, drafts are not subject to disputes which may occur between the parties involved.

Types of Drafts.   Drafts can be either sight (demand) drafts or time (usance) drafts. A sight draft is payable upon demand to the drawee-importer. Here the drawee must pay the draft immediately or dishonor it. A time draft is payable a specified number of days after presentation to the drawee. When a time draft is presented to the drawee, she may have her bank accept it by writing or stamping a notice of acceptance on its face. When a draft is drawn on and accepted by a bank, it becomes a bankers' acceptance.

Drafts may also be documentary drafts or clean drafts. Documentary drafts require various shopping documents such as bills of lading, insurance certificates, and commercial invoices. Most drafts are documentary because all these shipping documents are necessary to obtain the goods shipped. The documents attached to a documentary draft are passed on to an importer either upon payment (for sight drafts) or upon acceptance (for time drafts). If documents are to be delivered to an importer upon payment of the draft, it is known as a D/P (documents against payment) draft. If the documents are passed on to an importer upon acceptance, the draft is called a D/A (documents against acceptance) draft.

When a time draft is accepted by an importer, it becomes a trade acceptance or a clean draft. When clean drafts are used in foreign trade, the exporter usually sends all shipping documents directly to the importer and only the draft to the collecting bank. In this case, the goods shipped are surrendered to the importer regardless of payment or acceptance of the draft. The clean draft, therefore, involves a considerable amount of risk. This is why clean drafts are generally used in cases in which there is a considerable amount of faith between the exporter and the importer or in cases in which multinational firms send goods to their foreign subsidiaries.

Bills of Lading

A bill of lading is a shipping document issued to an exporting firm or its bank by a common carrier which transports the goods. It is simultaneously a receipt, a contract, and a document of title. As a receipt, the bill of lading indicates that specified goods have been received by the carrier. As a contract, it is evidence that the carrier is obliged to deliver the goods to the importer in exchange for certain charges. As a document of title, it establishes ownership of the goods. Thus, the bill of lading can be used to insure payment before the goods are delivered. For example, the importer cannot take title to the goods until she obtains the bill of lading from the carrier.

Types of Bills of Lading.
Bills of lading are either straight bills of lading or order bills of lading. A straight bill of lading requires that the carrier deliver the goods to the designated party, usually the importer. It is used when the goods have been paid for in advance; thus, it is not title to the goods. An order bill of lading provides that the carrier deliver the goods to the order of a designated party, usually the exporter. The exporting firm retains title to the goods until it receives payment. Once payment has been made, the exporting firm endorses the order bill of lading. The endorsed document can be used as collateral against loans. It accompanies a documentary draft which requires such other documents as the bill of lading, commercial invoices, and insurance certificates. The procedures to handle these two types of bills of lading are well established. Commercial banks and other financial institutions in almost every country handle these documents efficiently.

Bills of lading can also be either on-board bills of lading or re-ceived-for-shipment bills of lading. An on-board bill of lading indicates that the goods have actually been placed on board the vessel. On-board bills of lading are important because some insurance coverages such as war risk are effective only if goods are on board. By contrast, a received-for-shipment bill of lading merely acknowledges that the carrier has received the goods for shipment but does not guarantee that the goods have been loaded on the vessel. The cargo could sit on the dock for some time before it is shipped. This bill of lading is thus unsatisfactory when seasonal or perishable goods are involved. A received-for-shipment bill of lading can easily be converted into an on-board bill of lading by an appropriate stamp which shows the name of the vessel, the date, and the signature of an official of the vessel.

Finally, bills of lading may be either clean bills of lading or foul bills of lading. A clean bill of lading suggests that the carrier has received the goods in apparently good condition. The carrier does not have any obligation to check the condition of the cargo beyond external visual appearance. On the other hand, a foul bill of lading bears a notation from the carrier that the goods appeared to have suffered some damage before the carrier received them for shipment. Because a foul bill of lading is generally not acceptable under a letter of credit, it is important that the exporter obtain a clean bill of lading.

Letters of Credit

A letter of credit is a document issued by a bank at the request of an importer. In the document, the bank agrees to honor a draft drawn on the importer if the draft accompanies specified documents such as the bill of lading. In a typical use, the importer asks that his local bank write a letter of credit. In exchange for the bank's agreement to honor the demand for payment that results from the import transaction, the importer promises to pay the bank the amount of the transaction and a specified fee.

Advantages of Letters of Credit.
The letter of credit is advantageous to both exporters and importers because it facilitates foreign trade. It gives a number of benefits to exporters. First, they sell their goods abroad against the promise of a bank rather than a commercial firm. Because banks are usually larger and better credit risks than most business firms, exporters are almost completely assured of payment if they meet specific conditions. Second, they can obtain funds as soon as they have such necessary documents as the letter of credit and the bill of lading. When shipment is made, the exporter prepares a draft on the importer in accordance with the letter of credit and presents it to his local bank. If the bank finds that all papers are in order, it advances the funds—the face value of the draft less fees and interest.

Although its major beneficiaries are exporters, the letter of credit also gives a number of benefits to importers. First, it assures them that the exporter will be paid only if he provides certain documents, all of which are carefully examined by the bank. If the exporter is unable or unwilling to make proper shipment, recovery of the deposit is easier from the bank than from the exporter. Second, the letter of credit enables the importer to remove commercial risk to the exporter in exchange for other considerations. Thus, the importer can bargain for better terms, such as a lower price. Moreover, it is less expensive to finance the goods under a letter of credit than by borrowing.

Types of Letters of Credit.   Letters of credit can be irrevocable or revocable. Most credits between unrelated parties are irrevocable. An irrevocable letter of credit can be neither cancelled nor modified by the importer's bank without the consent of all parties. A revocable letter of credit can be revoked or modified by the importer's bank at any time before payment. This letter of credit is used as a means of arranging payment, but it does not carry a guarantee of payment. Most banks do not favor revocable letters of credit; some banks refuse to issue them because they may become involved in resulting litigation.

Letters of credit may also be confirmed or unconfirmed. A confirmed letter of credit is a letter of credit confirmed by a bank other than the issuing bank. An exporter might want a foreign bank's letter of credit confirmed by a domestic bank when the exporter has some doubt about the foreign bank's ability to pay. In this case, both banks are obligated to honor drafts drawn in accordance with the letter of credit. An unconfirmed letter of credit is a guarantee of only the opening bank. Thus, the strongest letter of credit is a confirmed, irrevocable letter of credit. Such a letter of credit cannot be cancelled by the opening bank, and it requires both the opening and confirming banks to guarantee payment on drafts issued in connection with an export transaction.

Finally, letters of credit are either revolving or nonrevolving. A revolving letter of credit is a letter of credit whose duration may revolve weekly or monthly. A $50,000 revolving credit, for example, might authorize an exporter to draw drafts up to $50,000 each week until the credit expires. The revolving letter of credit is often used when an importer must make frequent and known purchases. However, most letters of credit are nonrevolving. In other words, letters of credit are typically issued and valid for a single transaction—one letter for one transaction.

Additional Documents

In addition to the three documents described here—the draft, the bill of lading, and the letter of credit—other documents must generally accompany the draft as specified in the letter of credit. Some additional documents commonly required in international trade are commercial invoices, insurance documents, and consular invoices. These and some other documents are required to obtain the goods shipped; they are also essential to clear the merchandise through customs and ports of entry and departure.

Commercial Invoice. A commercial invoice is issued by the exporter; it contains a precise description of the merchandise, such as unit prices, quality, total value, financial terms of sale, and shipping features. Some shipping features are FOB (free on board), FAS (free alongside), C&F (cost and freight), and CIF (cost, insurance, freight). The commercial invoice may also include some other information such as the names and addresses of both exporter and importer, the number of packages, transportation and insurance charges, the name of the vessel, the ports of departure and destination, and any export or import permit numbers.

Insurance Documents. All shipments in international trade are insured. Most insurance contracts used today automatically cover all shipments made by the exporter. The risks of transportation range from slight damage to total loss of merchandise. In most cases, insurance coverage, provided by the carrier up to the port of destination, is sufficient. But most ocean carriers do not have any responsibility for losses during the actual transportation except those directly attributed to their negligence. Therefore, some form of marine insurance should be arranged to protect both the exporter and the importer. These additional coverages range from such limited coverage as collision, fire, and sinking, to the broad coverage of all risks.

Consular Invoices. Exports to many countries require a consular invoice issued by the consulate of the importing country. The consular invoice provides customs officials with information and statistics for the importing nation. More specifically, a consular invoice is necessary to obtain customs clearance; it also provides customs officials with information necessary to assess import duties. The consular invoice does not carry any title to the goods, and it is not negotiable.

Other Documents. Other documents might be required by the importer or might be necessary in clearing the goods through ports of entry or exit. These documents include certificates of origin, weight lists, packing lists, and inspection certificates. A certificate of origin certifies the country where the goods are grown or manufactured. A weight list itemizes the weight of each item. A packing list identifies the contents of individual packages. An inspection certificate is a document issued by an independent inspection company to verify the contents or quality of the shipment.

A Typical International Transaction

There are many steps and documents in the entire process of completing an international transaction. Each step or document is a subsystem of the entire transaction process which itself is closely connected by a variety of other subsystems. Thus, the successful completion of an international transaction may be viewed as an integral unit of many parts which are directly or indirectly interrelated. A typical international transaction might require the following 12 steps:

1. A Chicago firm desires to import a $1 million shipment of machines from a London firm, thereby inquiring if the London firm is willing to ship under a letter of credit.
2. The London firm indicates its willingness to ship under a letter of credit. Simultaneously, it provides the Chicago firm with such information as prices, credit terms, and so on.
3. The Chicago firm arranges to have its Chicago bank open a letter of credit in favor of the London firm.
4. The Chicago bank issues the letter of credit in favor of the London firm and sends it to the London firm's bank in London.
5. The London firm ships the machines to the Chicago firm through a common carrier that issues an order bill of lading.
6. The London firm prepares a 60-day draft on the Chicago firm in accordance with the letter of credit and presents it to the London bank along with such other documents as the bill of lading, insurance certificates, and commercial invoices. At the same time, the London firm endorses the order bill of lading so that title to the machines goes with the holder of the documents.
7. The London bank forwards the draft and other documents to the Chicago bank for acceptance. When the draft is accepted by the Chicago bank, it becomes a bankers' acceptance. This means that the Chicago bank has promised to pay the draft in 60 days. Alternatively, if the London bank has asked the Chicago bank to accept and discount the draft, the Chicago bank returns cash less a discount fee rather than the bankers' acceptance to the London bank.
8. When the London bank receives the bankers' acceptance, it may sell the acceptance to an investor at a discount or hold the acceptance in its own portfolio.
9. If the London bank has discounted the acceptance with the Chicago bank or has sold it in the local money market, it transfers the proceeds less any fees and discount to the London firm. Another alternative is that the London firm may hold the acceptance for 60 days and present it to the Chicago bank for payment.
10. The Chicago bank notifies the arrival of the documents to the Chicago firm. The Chicago firm signs a promissory note or some other arrangement to pay the Chicago bank for the machines in 60 days. Then the Chicago bank releases the documents so that the Chicago firm can claim the shipment.
11. In 60 days, the Chicago bank receives the funds from the Chicago firm to cover the maturing acceptance.
12. On the same day, the holder of the acceptance presents it to the Chicago bank for payment. Alternatively, the holder of the acceptance may return it to the London bank for collection through normal banking channels.

The Payment Terms of Export Transactions

Because trade competition has become increasingly severe, multinational companies must know how best to finance their foreign trade. The terms and conditions under which foreign trade takes place vary significantly. They range from cash before delivery to sales in a foreign currency with credit terms over one year. Supply and demand conditions at the time of sales determine the actual terms and conditions of any particular transaction. But most foreign transactions involve longer credit terms than domestic transactions.

Countertrade

Countertrade refers to world trade arrangements that are variations on the idea of barter. Modern countertrade covers various international trade arrangements in which part or all payments for purchased goods may be in other goods. It became popular in the 1960s and 1970s as a way for communist countries to finance their international trade without money. In recent years countertrade has gained new stature in international trade. World trade continues to grow faster than world production because of increased countertrade. No reliable figures about the volume of countertrade are available because there is so much secrecy. But in the 1980s countertrade increased within the nonsocialist world. A survey of some 500 U.S. companies by the U.S. International Trade Commission in 1985 found that countertrade accounted for 5.6 percent of their total exports. The same study identified 61 countries that had either imposed or vigorously encouraged this form of trade on U.S. exporters. The countries ranged from developing to industrial nations such as Japan and Canada. The U.S. Department of Commerce estimates that countertrade accounts for about 20 percent of world trade.

This section discusses several forms of countertrade: barter, switch trading, counterpurchase, and compensation agreement.

Barter.   Foreign trade, like domestic trade, is conducted in terms of money. However, foreign trade without money is possible through a barter system. Barter is an exchange of goods between two countries without the involvement of finance. Barter terms are usually arranged between two countries on a bilateral trading agreement. An exporter of one country ships certain goods to an importer of another country and receives goods from the importer in exchange for his shipment.

Of course, individual transactions are made within the framework of intergovernmental trade agreements. Such barter deals are popular among nonmarket countries and between Eastern and Western countries. Barter deals allow countries with a shortage of foreign exchange to obtain their deficit goods in return for their surplus goods. They also permit companies in the foreign currency-short country to obtain goods which they would not otherwise be able to obtain.

Switch Trading.   Payments for exports to the East Bloc and nonmarket countries are often made through clearing units whereby sales are balanced with purchases from other countries. This clearing unit has led to many bilateral trading agreements which try to identify the goods each country will trade and to set overall trade limits. The agreement also requires each country to deposit a certain amount of its own currency in a bilateral clearing account. Sales to each other are then paid out of this clearing account.

The basic purpose of switch trading is to eliminate the imbalance in barter trade between two countries. Unfortunately, one of the countries frequently fails to sell sufficient goods to its trading partner. In this case, a shortage in clearing funds will develop for the deficit country. Hence, one of the countries becomes a creditor, and the other becomes a debtor. When this occurs, the bilateral trading agreement tends to break down.

A breakdown is harmful to both countries, but there are two practical methods to avoid this breakdown. First, the bilateral trading agreement may specify that the debtor country pay amounts in excess of allowable variations in gold or convertible currency to the creditor country. Second, to reconcile the imbalance in barter transactions between them, two countries may agree to utilize a switch trade broker.

Example 10-1.   Assume that Russia has agreed to trade its machinery for Cuban sugar. Russian machinery and Cuban sugar are then given arbitrary unit prices in clearing dollars. The agreement specifies that $1 million in commodities would be exchanged during the following year. By the end of the year, Russia finds that it has accumulated $400,000 in unneeded sugar.

To meet its obligations as well as to dispose of the unwanted goods, Russia may seek the services of a switch trader. It calls one of the switch trade brokers and offers him or her $400,000 worth of sugar in the clearing account at a discount of 30 percent. Once the actual value of the sugar has been ascertained by the broker, she calls sugar dealers who might pick up the credit. Eventually, she finds a buyer who offers 75 percent of the credit. Russia receives 70 percent of its $400,000 credit in hard currency for the unneeded sugar, the broker takes 5 percent on the deal, and the buyer purchases the sugar for $400,000 minus a 25 percent discount. Russia, the broker, and the buyer benefit from the deal, but Cuba may find that it has undersold its sugar in world sugar markets by the unexpected dumping of its own goods.

Counterpurchase.   This form of countertrade typically takes place between a Western industrial country and an Eastern or Third World country. Counterpurchase involves a standard hard-currency export, but the seller agrees to a return purchase with a minimum quantity of specified goods from the buyer. For example, McDonnell Douglas may agree to sell two DC-9's to Poland for $10 million and to buy $2 million worth of Polish coal within a two-year period.

The seller is frequently forced to buy some goods which are not easily marketable in its country. Thus, McDonnell in our example could demand marketable goods or cover its loss by increasing its price. If McDonnell charges 15 percent more for its airplanes, it can buy back a comparable percentage of worthless goods. Another alternative available to McDonnell Douglas is to assign its obligation to other Western companies or export trading companies which may market these counterpurchases more readily.

Compensation (Buy–Back) Agreement.

Under this form of countertrade, the initial seller receives compensation in products that arise out of the original sale. For example, IBM will provide equipment and technology for a personal computer plant to Korea and agree to take full or partial payment in personal computers produced by the plant.

A typical buy-back transaction involves very large expenditures and a long-term time frame for fulfillment. Thus, such an arrangement has attributes that make it an alternative form of direct investment. The value of the buy-back agreement normally exceeds the value of the original sale.

Evaluation of Countertrade.

In theory, countertrade is a movement away from free trade. This form of trade often forces companies such as McDonnell Douglas to set up operations to deal in products very remote from their expertise. Countertrade is also inflexible and involves a limited range of products.

Nevertheless, several reasons have been suggested for the current growth of countertrade. They include: (1) limited access to hard-currency finances; (2) opening of new markets; (3) use of countertrade as an alternative to direct investment; (4) avoidance of trade restrictions; (5) fulfillment of state planning goals; and (6) disposal of surplus and poor quality goods.

Cash Terms

Cash terms may be either COD or CBD. COD terms mean **cash on delivery** of the goods, and CBD terms mean **cash before delivery** of the goods. Under either COD or CBD terms, an exporter does not extend credit. Although credit risk does not exist under either terms, COD terms are accompanied by a risk that an importer may refuse a shipment, while CBD terms avoid all risk. Under CBD terms, an exporter may insist on cash at the time of order or he may specify the time of cash payment prior to shipment. Another possible arrangement is that a part of the payment is made at the time of order, that progress payments are made between the time of order and the time of shipment, and that the final payment is made just before the release of goods to a common carrier.

Cash terms are the exception in these days of severe international competition. An importer does not like cash-type transactions though such transactions are ideal from the exporter's point of view. One reason for this dislike is that an importer is forced to accept all risks in transit, in exchange fluctuations, and in the quality of the goods received. Consequently, the exporter will insist on cash terms only in instances of the importer's poor credit standing or extreme political risks in the importing country. If the sale involves products specially manufactured for the importer, the exporter may demand some kind of advance-payment arrangement.

Consignments

Goods for export may be consigned to a subsidiary, the exporter's own agent, an independent agent, or an import house. Assume that an exporter in New York ships, to an importer in London, 100 cases of quart bottles on a consignment basis. Because the exporter pays all the expenses connected with the shipment, the importer incurs no expenses at the time this shipment is delivered to her warehouse. Actually, the 100 cases of bottles are still on the exporter's inventory. Thus, if the importer should fail, the exporter can demand that all the unsold bottles be returned to him.

Let us further assume that this consignment arrangement has a 10 percent commission on all bottles sold. If the importer sold all of the 100 cases at $50 per case, she would deduct her commission of $500 (100 x $50 x 0.10) and remit to the exporter a dollar draft for $4,500 on a New York bank.

A consignment to an independent agent or an import house has most of the same problems as open account transactions. Hence, this type of operation is usually confined to companies working together very closely or completely trusting each other.

Credit Terms

Most importers are not required to pay for goods before or on delivery but are allowed a short deferment period before payment is made. During this period, the exporter extends one of three types of credit to the importer: (1) open account, (2) notes payable, and (3) trade or bankers' acceptances.

Open Accounts.   Open account credit does not require the importer to sign a formal debt instrument as evidence to the amount that she owes the exporter. The importer simply charges her purchases, much in the same fashion that domestic retail stores extend credit to their customers. Then the importer's account is carried on the books of the exporter like other receivables. This arrangement places the entire financial burden upon the exporter. Because banks usually refuse to advance against accounts receivable, it ties up large amounts of the exporter's capital. In addition, with this arrangement the exporter assumes the risks of foreign exchange blockage and buyer default. Therefore, open account terms are extended only to trusted customers in countries that have no foreign exchange or political problems.

Promissory Notes.   In some export transactions, promissory notes are given instead of open account credit. In this case, the importer is requested to sign a note that evidences her debt to the exporter. Thus, this arrangement makes the importer recognize her debt formally. The note calls for the payment of the obligation at some future date.

Trade Acceptances.

A trade acceptance is a form of short-term financing common in almost all foreign trade activities. In fact, it is the largest source of short-term funds for importers. Under this method of financing, the exporter draws a draft on the importer ordering her to pay the draft at some specified future date. The exporter will not release the goods until the importer accepts the draft. When the importer accepts the draft, it becomes a trade acceptance. When a bank accepts the draft, it becomes the bankers' acceptance.

Summary of Credit Terms.

An exporter can specify the credit terms under which he is willing to extend credit with a foreign export sale. The degree of competition has a strong impact on the actual terms. The exporter may be compelled to grant 60- or 90-day credit even if he would like to be paid immediately after shipment. The shortest credit term is extended when the exporter draws a sight draft on a correspondent bank of the importer's bank. Payment is made to the exporter on demand when the draft is received by the importer or her bank. Longer credit terms are achieved when the exporter draws a time draft, which specifies the time after presentation when the funds must be paid.

When a time draft is used in foreign trade, the exporter may carry the credit for his own account or refinance it through a local bank. Under the latter arrangement, the letter of credit ordinarily specifies who will pay the expenses of financing. Although these expenses may be paid by the exporter or the importer, the ultimate choice depends largely upon the conditions of competition at the time of the transaction.

Sources of Financing Foreign Trade

Banks, private nonbank financial institutions, and governments pool their resources to finance foreign trade. Banks finance foreign trade through trust receipts, bankers' acceptances, and several other methods. Export trading companies, factoring, and forfaiting are also used to finance foreign trade. The Export-Import Bank and the Private Export Funding Corporation are major forces in helping U.S. exporters sell their goods and services to foreign buyers.

Bank Financing

Banks are important lenders to those engaged in international trade. They provide several forms of credit which are convenient to exporters and importers, including trust receipts, bankers' acceptances, loans to exporters, and loans to importers.

Trust Receipts.

A trust receipt establishes that borrowers hold certain goods in trust for the lender. When goods are shipped under a time draft, the importer generally signs a trust receipt that collateralizes the draft by the goods. The document provides that the importer will be the agent of her bank in the sale of the goods. The bank retains title to the goods until the importer has made full settlement. The importer is allowed to sell the goods but must turn the proceeds of the sale over to the bank in payment of the loan. The bank assumes any losses that occur under a trust receipt.

Bankers' Acceptances.

We can best explain how this method of financing operates with the following illustration: Assume that a Detroit firm desires to import a $10,000 shipment of perfumes from a French firm. The French firm is willing to grant a 60-day credit. The Detroit firm may arrange to have its Detroit bank open a letter of credit in favor of the French firm. The letter of credit states that the Detroit bank will honor drafts drawn on the Detroit firm if they are drawn in accordance with detailed terms in the letter of credit. When shipment is made, the French firm prepares a 60-day draft on the Detroit firm and presents it to its French bank. The French bank will advance the franc equivalent of $10,000, less interest and fees, to the French firm. Then the French bank will forward the draft, along with such shipping documents as the bill of lading, to its Detroit correspondent bank which, in turn, will present it to the Detroit firm's bank for acceptance. If all papers are found to be in order, the Detroit bank accepts the draft and it becomes a bankers' acceptance.

Because bankers' acceptances are of very high quality, the French bank can easily arrange its sale and thus recover the funds it advanced. If the French firm did not discount the draft at its French bank, it could sell the draft to an investor at a discount. The Detroit firm obtains the credit it wants, and the risks, with an exception of the accepting bank, are minimal. The credit transaction is completed when, in 60 days, the bankers' acceptance is paid by the Detroit bank, which looks for repayment by the Detroit firm.

Loans to Exporters and Importers.

Bankers' acceptances are a form of bank loan to exporters. Banks can also make loans to exporters by cashing, purchasing, discounting, and collecting drafts. Banks cash drafts if the drafts are denominated in local currency and are drawn on time. They purchase drafts if the drafts are denominated in foreign currencies. In this case, drafts are generally exchanged for local currency at an appropriate exchange rate. They discount drafts if the drafts are denominated in local currency and if the terms of the sales involve time drafts. When banks collect drafts, they simply act as agents for exporters. However, they may lend against either the total or a percentage of the drafts outstanding.

Other Private Financing

Some popular forms of other private financing consist of export trading companies, factoring, and forfaiting.

Export Trading Companies.

In October 1982, President Reagan signed into law the Export Trading Company Act to help small and medium-size firms sell their goods overseas. Originally, the Export Trading Company Act was conceived as the U.S. answer to highly successful Japanese trading companies. Until recently, the great internal market of the United States and its abundant raw materials made it virtually unnecessary for U.S. companies to seek profits from external markets. A 1980 study conducted by the U.S. Department of Commerce found that only 1 percent of U.S. manufacturing companies accounted for approximately 80 percent of the nation's exports. The study also indicated that an additional 20,000 firms could profitably export their products but have not ventured beyond the domestic market because of uncertainties. On the other hand, most Japanese exports are handled by export trading companies; 300 trading companies account for nearly 80 percent of Japanese trade.

The Export Trading Company Act of 1982 removed two major barriers that had long put U.S. exporters at a disadvantage. First, this act allowed bank holding companies, previously barred by Federal regulations from investing in commercial enterprises, to invest in export trading companies. Second, it permitted competing companies to join for export purposes without fear of antitrust ramifications.

Export trading companies engage primarily in two forms of activity: trade intermediation and export outlets for U.S. manufacturing companies. In their role as trade intermediaries, export trading companies can provide small and medium-size firms with comprehensive "one-stop" services, such as market analysis, distribution services, documentation, financing, foreign exchange transactions, transportation, and legal assistance. They can buy products from other U.S. companies and export these products either through their own outlets or to outside distributors.

Factoring.

Factors buy a company's accounts receivable on a nonrecourse basis and thus accelerate the conversion of the company's claims against its customers. They also perform a number of additional functions such as credit checking, bookkeeping, account collecting, and risk bearing. The factor reviews the credit of the borrower's customers and establishes credit limits in advance. The maximum amount of advance against uncollected accounts receivable is established as a percentage of the invoice value. The factor receives an interest charge on the daily balance of advances plus a commission for credit analysis, bookkeeping, collecting accounts, and risk taking.

Exporters may turn to a factor when they have difficulty collecting on open account sales or when their bank is unwilling to collect notes receivable.

Factors' rates on foreign accounts are usually higher than those of banks. Thus, factors are frequently used as a last resort by exporters who need funds badly and/or who have almost no hope for collecting.

The factor's credit investigation of the exporter's customers is relatively quick and inexpensive. For this reason, even if the exporter does not discount his accounts receivable, he can still use the factor's facilities to estimate his prospective accounts' creditworthiness. If the exporter discounts his accounts receivable on a nonrecourse basis, the factor will assume all commercial and political risks of nonpayment. For these services, factors charge a commitment fee of one to two percent and a rate of interest in excess of the prime lending rate.

An exporter's use of factors depends on two considerations. The first consideration is whether the exporter can perform credit evaluation functions as well as the factor. Because large international factors evaluate the same customer for many companies, they build credit files and expertise, allowing them to evaluate credit at a lower cost than the exporter. The second consideration is whether the availability of funds and the interest charged by alternative sources are more attractive than those offered by the factor.

Forfaiting. Because capital goods such as plants and airplanes are quite expensive, the importer may not be able to make payment on the goods within a short period of time. Thus, long-term financing may be required on some international trade of capital goods. The exporter could finance such a sale but may not desire to do so because its credit may extend over several years.

A forfaiting transaction involves an importer that issues a promissory note to pay for the imported goods over a period of three to five years. The notes are extended to the exporter who sells them at a discount to a forfaiting bank. The importer will make semiannual payments during the period to the forfaiting bank. In other words, forfaiting refers to the purchase of financial obligations such as promissory notes without recourse to the exporter. The forfaiting markets, centered in London and Zurich, are largely free of government support, supervision, or regulation.

A typical forfaiting transaction involves four parties: the importer, the exporter, a bank, and the forfaiter. The importer pays the exporter with promissory notes that will mature at set intervals over a several-year period. A bank in the importer's country then guarantees these promissory notes; those notes guaranteed by a bank are usually irrevocable, unconditional, and transferable. The exporter in turn sells the guaranteed paper to the forfaiter at a discount from the face value; the amount of discount depends on the importer's credit rating, the guaranteeing bank's creditability, and interest costs over the paper's lifetime. As the paper matures, the forfaiter or the holder of the paper presents it to the guaranteeing bank for payment.

The forfaiting arrangement allows the exporter to avoid most risks involved in his export sales. However, this financing method has a number of drawbacks. First, the amount of the discount can be quite large. Second, the guaranteeing bank normally charges a substantial fee and places a freeze of equal value on the importer's account. Third, the exporter still faces some risk if the bank guarantor and/or the importer refuse to pay on the ground that the notes have some hidden legal defect.

Government Financing

The United States has several government sources of export financing: Export-Import Bank (Exim Bank), Private Export Funding Corporation, and Foreign Credit Insurance Association.

Export–Import (Exim) Bank.

The Exim Bank was founded in 1934 as an independent agency of the U.S. government. The bank is a financially self-sustaining U.S. government agency set up to promote U.S. exports through a variety of export financing and loan guarantees. The creation of the Foreign Credit Insurance Association (FCIA) in 1963 completed the triad of official loan, guarantee, and insurance offerings demanded by U.S. exporters. Exim Bank officials have fully managed these three basic export-finance programs since the bank took over the FCIA in 1983. Since 1935 the bank has financed about $200 billion worth of U.S. exports.

Exim Bank operations must conform to the following general guidelines:

1. Loans must be used exclusively to finance the export of goods and services of U.S. origin.
2. The bank supplements and encourages rather than competes with private capital in assisting U.S. export transactions.
3. Loans should have reasonable assurance of repayment and related transactions should not adversely affect the U.S. economy.
4. Bank loan rates and terms must be competitive with those of government-supported loans available for exports from these countries whose exporters compete with U.S. exporters.
5. Under the Trade Act of 1974, the Exim Bank cannot finance any project in a nonmarket economy country that restricts free emigration of its citizens.
6. All U.S. goods must be shipped on vessels of U.S. registry when the bank participates as a direct lender.

The Exim Bank was originally created to facilitate trade with the former Soviet Union, but its purpose has been expanded over the years. It now finances U.S. exports through a variety of loan and guarantee programs, such as direct loans, discount loans, cooperative financing facility, and guarantees.

1. Bank long-term loans are granted directly to foreign buyers of U.S. goods and services for terms from five to ten years.
2. The bank issues advance commitments to purchase (discount) eligible bank export debt obligations with an original maturity of one to five years.

3. Under its Cooperative Financing Facility, the bank makes medium-term loans to foreign financial institutions, so that they can make credit available to local buyers of U.S. goods and services.
4. The bank guarantees U.S. banks' revolving credits to foreign banks and offers medium-term guarantees for exporters who seek financing from their commercial banks.

Private Export Funding Corporation (PEFCO).

The PEFCO was created in 1970 at the initiation of the Bankers' Association for Foreign Trade with the support of the U.S. Treasury Department and the U.S. Exim Bank. The basic purpose of the PEFCO was to mobilize private capital in order to finance U.S. exports of big ticket items such as aircraft and power plants. PEFCO's stockholders consist of 54 commercial banks, seven large manufacturers, and one investment banker. All of PEFCO's loans are guaranteed by the Exim Bank and are general obligations to the United States. Thus, the PEFCO itself does not evaluate credit risks of foreign borrowers, economic conditions in foreign countries, and other factors that might affect the collection of its loans. Most PEFCO loans have medium-term maturities of seven years, but some have maturities over 15 years.

Foreign Credit Insurance Association (FCIA).

Most exporters sell under letters of credit, as described in the earlier part of this chapter. In this type of sale, banks assume all risks in export transactions except for transactions under revocable letters of credit. However, importers frequently do not want to open letters of credit because of the cost or difficulty of securing them. At other times, under severe competition, exporters must sell on open account or on draft terms without letters of credit. Under these circumstances an exporter could suffer heavy losses even after carefully examining an importer's creditworthiness. These losses may develop from such situations as expropriation and riots beyond the control of the exporter or the importer.

The governments of most industrial countries have helped their exporters in many ways over the years. Although the U.S. Exim Bank had helped U.S. exporters reduce their risks since 1934, they still lacked the protective umbrella which many of their competitors were enjoying. In the fall of 1961, the Secretary of the Treasury, the Exim Bank, and 50 leading insurance companies organized the Foreign Credit Insurance Association (FCIA).

The FCIA provided credit protection for U.S. exporters. It insured exporters for an agreed percentage of losses from credit risks, whether they were commercial, political, or both. Commercial risks include the failure of an importer before payment and its protracted payment default. Political risks include currency inconvertibility, cancellation of import licenses, expropriation, and war or revolution. But in October 1983, 41 of the original FCIA members withdrew from the association because of heavy commercial losses, particularly in Mexico. Since October 1983, the Exim Bank itself has insured exporters against both commercial and political risks, leaving the FCIA to operate as its marketing and service agent.

The Exim Bank credit protection program for exporters covers short-term cases of up to 180 days and medium-term cases of 181 days to five years. For these two cases there are five standard Exim Bank policies:

1. A short-term comprehensive policy covers 90 percent of the commercial credit losses and 100 percent of the political losses.
2. A short-term political risk policy covers 100 percent of the political losses only.
3. A medium-term comprehensive policy covers 90 percent of the credit losses and 100 percent of the political losses.
4. A medium-term political risk policy covers 100 percent of the political losses only.
5. A combined short-term/medium-term policy covers both short-term and medium-term risks.

Under these five standard Exim Bank policies, 90-100 percent of losses are recoverable if the following conditions are met:

1. All disputes on the loss between the exporter and the importer have been settled.
2. The loss is properly reported within eight months.
3. The exporter was unable to insure the loss under another policy.
4. U.S. labor and materials account for more than half of the value of the shipment.
5. The exporter is not negligent.
6. Payment for the export was supposed to be made in the U.S. dollar.

Summary

This chapter has discussed various documents and operations essential to finance foreign trade. The extension of credit on foreign trade is of critical importance to both parties in a transaction. For exporters, their willingness and ability to extend credit are crucial determinants of sales volume across national boundaries. For importers, their ability to continue operations relies on the lag between payments by their customers and remittances to their foreign suppliers.

The three basic documents used in normal export-import transactions are the draft, the bill of lading, and the letter of credit. A draft is an order written by an exporter that requires the importer to pay a specified amount at a specified time. It involves three parties: the drawer, the drawee, and the payee. The drawer is the person who issues the draft. The drawee is the person against whom the draft is drawn. The payee is the person or business to whom the drawee will eventually pay the funds. Drafts may be either sight or time drafts. A sight draft is payable upon presentation, while a time draft is payable at a specified future date.

A bill of lading is a shipping document issued to the exporting firm by a common carrier that transports the goods. It is simultaneously a receipt, a contract, and a document. Bills of lading may be straight or order bills of lading. A straight bill of lading requires that the carrier deliver the goods to the designated party. An order bill of lading provides that the carrier deliver the goods to the order of a designated party.

A letter of credit is a document issued by a bank at the request of the importer. In the document, the bank agrees to honor a draft which results from an import transaction by a foreign buyer. The letter of credit assures that there will be payments for goods shipped to the importer. Letters of credit may be revocable or irrevocable. They may also be confirmed or unconfirmed.

Some forms of countertrade such as barter and switch trading make international transactions possible without money. However, most transactions across national boundaries are conducted in terms of money. The payment terms of foreign trade include cash terms, consignments, and credit terms, all of which require money. The actual payment terms of exports depend largely upon competitive conditions prevailing at the time of initiating the transaction.

Finally, this chapter has examined a number of sources to finance foreign trade. Banks are important lenders to those engaged in foreign trade. Bank-financing operations include trust receipts, bankers' acceptances, and several other forms of loans. In addition to bank financing, there are several other sources of private financing. The Export Trading Company Act of 1982 allows bank holding companies and other financial institutions to set up trading companies for export purposes. Furthermore, the Act eliminates most U.S. antitrust regulations for companies that want to join together in such enterprises. International factors buy accounts receivable from exporters and then collect them as they become due. Factors also perform such functions as credit analysis, bookkeeping, collecting accounts receivable, and risk taking. Finally, forfaiting can be used to finance capital goods such as power plants and airplanes. Under a typical arrangement, an exporter receives immediate cash by discounting its promissory notes or trade receivables to a forfaiting bank.

The Exim Bank is the only U.S. government agency established solely to facilitate the foreign trade of the United States. It is also a major force for helping U.S. exporters reduce their commercial and political risks. The Private Export Funding Corporation finances U.S. exports of aircrafts and other big ticket items.

Questions

1. What are the objectives of documentation in international trade?

2. What are bills of lading and how do they facilitate trade financing?

3. The basic problem in assessing different forms of export financing is how to distribute risks between the exporter and the importer. Explain the following export financing documents in this respect.
   (a) time draft
   (b) sight draft
   (c) confirmed, revocable letter of credit
   (d) confirmed, irrevocable letter of credit
   (e) cash before delivery
   (f) cash on delivery
   (g) consignment
   (h) open account credit

4. In addition to the draft, the bill of lading, and the letter of credit necessary in foreign trade, other documents must generally accompany the draft as specified in the letter of credit. Such other documents include commercial invoices, insurance documents, and consular invoices. Briefly describe each of these three documents.

5. What is countertrade?

6. What are bankers' acceptances? What are the advantages of bankers' acceptances as an export-financing instrument?

7. What are the major elements of the 1982 Export Trading Company Act? What are the major objectives of the Act?

8. What is the role of a factor in foreign trade? How can a factor aid an exporter?

9. What is forfaiting? List the parties involved in a forfaiting transaction.

10. What is the role of the Export-Import Bank?

11. Describe the role of the Private Export Funding Corporation (PEFCO).

References

Aggarwal, R., "International Business Through Barter and Countertrade," *Long Range Planning*, 22:3, 1989, pp. 75-81.

Choudry, Y. A., M. McGeady, and R. Stiff, "An Analysis of Attitudes of U.S. Firms Toward Countertrade," *Columbia Journal of World Business*, Summer 1989, pp. 31-8.

Czinkato, M. R., "The Business Response to the Export Trading Company Act of 1982," *Columbia Journal of World Business*, Fall 1984, pp. 105-11.

Girling, R. H., *Multinational Institutions and the Third World: Management, Debts, and Trade Conflicts in the International Economic Order*, New York: Praeger Publications, 1985.

Hervey, J. L., "Countertrade: Counterproductive?" *Economic Perspectives*, Federal Reserve Bank of Chicago, January/February 1989, pp. 17-24.

Holden, A. C., "U.S. Official Export-Finance Support: Can American Exporters Expect a Competitive Exim Bank to Emerge?" *Columbia Journal of World Business*, Fall 1989, pp. 33-46.

Korth, C. M., ed., *International Countertrade*, Westport, CT: Quorum Books, 1987.

Lecraw, D. J., "The Management of Countertrade: Factors Influencing Success," *Journal of International Business Studies*, Spring 1989, pp. 41-59.

Mirus, R., and B. Young, "Economic Incentives for Countertrade," *Journal of International Business Studies*, Fall 1986, pp. 27-39.

Organization for Economic Cooperation and Development, *Countertrade: Developing Country Practices*, Paris: OECD, 1985.

Rossman, M. L., "Export Trading Company Legislation: U.S. Response to Japanese Foreign Market Penetration," *Journal of Small Business Management*, October 1984, pp. 62-6.

Rabino, S., and K. Shah, "Countertrade and Penetration of LDC's Markets," *Columbia Journal of World Business*, Winter 1987, pp. 31-8.

Seberger, D. P., "The Banking Provisions of the Export Trading Company Act of 1982," *The Business Lawyer*, February 1984, pp. 475-94.

Stoffel, J., "Why the Export Trading Company Act Failed as ETCs Bomb, Deficits Boom," *Business Marketing*, January 1985, pp. 54-8.

The U.S. International Trade Commission, *Assessment of the Effects of Barter and Countertrade Transactions of U.S. Industries*, Washington, DC: ITC, 1985.

Yoffie, D. B., *International Trade and Competition*, New York: McGraw-Hill, 1990.

11
Financing Foreign Investment

Multinational companies decide first on the nature of their needs for funds; then they seek the funds from many available sources. In addition to the investment in a fixed asset, a foreign investment project may require additional current assets such as accounts receivable and inventories. Consequently, multinational companies must consider various sources of funds for their overseas projects and the decision variables that affect the selection of particular sources.

This chapter examines three major sources of funds for foreign investment: (1) internal sources of funds, (2) external sources of funds, and (3) sources of funds from development banks. First, multinational companies may use internally generated funds such as profits and depreciation charges. If internal sources of funds are insufficient, they may obtain their capital from sources within their home country and/or in foreign countries. In addition to these internal and external sources of funds, development banks provide multinational companies with a variety of financing sources.

Internal Sources of Funds

Internal sources of funds are those funds generated within a parent–affiliate network. They include capital contributions from the parent, loans with parent-company guarantees, funds provided by operations from retained earnings and depreciation, and intersubsidiary funds transfers.

Funds from the Parent

Three major types of funds supplied by the parent are equity contributions, direct loans, and indirect loans under parent company guarantees.

Equity Contributions.

Every new foreign subsidiary must receive some funds in the form of equity to satisfy both authorities in the host country and outside creditors about its solvency. Occasionally, multinational companies decide on expansion funds in the form of an equity investment for their own foreign subsidiary. This part of recapitalization gives the foreign subsidiary an increased capital base to support additional loans. More specifically, equity contributions of cash are used to acquire going concerns, to buy out local minority interests, to set up new foreign subsidiaries, or to expand existing subsidiaries. Although they are a normal way of direct investments, in some developing countries direct equity investments take the form of machinery or technology instead of cash. Some multinational enterprises have acquired a percentage of common stock equity of foreign businesses in exchange for supplying machinery, equipment, tools, and intangibles (patents, engineering, etc.) necessary for manufacturing certain products.

Common stockholders have residual claims on earnings and assets in the event of liquidation. Hence, an equity investment is not very flexible for the investor, but it is most acceptable to the host country and outside creditors. Dividends—the profit remittances derived from equity investments—are heavily taxed when we compare equity contributions with investments derived from other funding alternatives. Normally, dividends from countries to foreign shareholders are subject to local income taxes as well as to withholding taxes. Withholding taxes are incurred when local earnings are distributed abroad as dividends. This explains why many multinational companies are reluctant to make large equity investments in their foreign subsidiaries.

Direct Loans.

Multinational companies may elect to provide investment funds to their foreign operations in the form of intracompany loans instead of increasing their equity contributions. However, the parent company lends money as an owner to its subsidiaries. The intracompany loan usually contains a specified repayment period for the loan principal and earns interest income which is taxed relatively lightly. These two features of intracompany loans compare favorably with an open-ended equity investment which produces profits in the form of heavily taxed dividends.

Parent loans to foreign subsidiaries are usually more popular than equity contributions for a number of reasons. First, parent loans give a parent company greater flexibility in repatriating funds from its foreign subsidiary. In nearly every part of the world, laws make it more difficult to return funds to the parent through dividend payments or equity reductions than through interest and principal payments. Moreover, a reduction in equity is often construed as a plan to leave the country.

Second, tax considerations are another reason for favoring parent loans over equity contributions. In most cases, interest payments on internal loans are tax deductible in the host country, while dividends are not. Moreover, principal payments, unlike dividend payments, do not generally constitute taxable income. Thus, it is possible that both a parent and its subsidiaries will save taxes by using loans instead of equity contributions.

Multinational companies can also provide credit to their subsidiaries not only by making loans but also by delaying the collection of accounts receivable. The amount of credit available through these intracompany accounts is limited to the amount of goods exchanged. Moreover, governments frequently limit the length of the credit term. However, because intracompany accounts involve no formal documents, they are easier to use. In addition, most governments interfere less with payments on intracompany accounts than on loans.

Parent Guarantees.

When foreign subsidiaries have difficulty in borrowing money, a parent may affix its own guarantees. While multinational companies have been traditionally reluctant to guarantee the debts of their subsidiaries, indications are these guarantees will increase. There are a variety of parent guarantees:

1. The parent may sign a purchase agreement under which it commits itself to buy its subsidiary's note from the lender in the event of the subsidiary's default.
2. The lender may be protected on only a part of the specific loan agreement.
3. Another type of guarantee is limited to a single loan agreement between a lender and the subsidiary.
4. The strongest type requires that the lender be protected on all loans to the subsidiary without limits on amount or time.

The types of loans with parent guarantees and the availability of such loans depend largely upon the parent's prestige and credit standing.

Funds Provided by Operations

Once a newly formed subsidiary gets on its feet, retained earnings and depreciation are the major sources of funds. These internal fund flows, coupled with local credits, leave relatively little need for fresh funds from the parent.

Foreign subsidiaries are not always free to remit their earnings in hard currency elsewhere. Many developing countries have problems with their balance of payments and do not have sufficient international reserves. Thus, they restrict repatriation of funds for a specified number of years or to a certain percentage of the net income. These factors frequently force foreign subsidiaries to reinvest their internally generated funds in the host country. An initial project may have to be smaller than actual demand requirements if a company wishes to use these internal fund flows for the expansion of an initial project in later years. If the anticipated expansion is necessary to meet current demand and the normal demand growth, multinational companies would have no difficulty in profitably using the internal fund flows in the host country.

Loans from Sister Subsidiaries

Availability of intersubsidiary credit, in addition to funds from the parent, vastly expands the number of possibilities for internal financing. For example, if a subsidiary in Japan has funds which it does not need immediately, it may lend these funds to a sister subsidiary in Taiwan, and vice versa. However, many countries impose exchange restrictions on capital movements to limit the range of possibilities for intersubsidiary loans. Moreover, the extensive use of intersubsidiary financial links makes it extremely difficult for a parent company to control its subsidiaries effectively.

Nevertheless, many subsidiaries borrow cash from their sister subsidiaries. When there are only a few subsidiaries within a company's family, it is fairly straightforward to arrange intersubsidiary loans. One subsidiary treasurer may negotiate directly with another sister subsidiary treasurer to obtain or give credit. However, a multinational company with many subsidiaries in many countries may prefer to have its central staff handle all excess funds or to establish a central pool of these funds on a worldwide basis under two conditions: (1) if the number of financial relationships does not exceed the capability of the main office to manage them effectively; and (2) if a parent company does not want to lose control over its subsidiaries.

External Sources of Funds

If a multinational company needs more funds than the amount that can be reasonably generated within a corporate family, the parent or its foreign subsidiaries may seek outside sources of funds. Such external sources of funds include joint business ventures with local owners and/or borrowings from financial institutions in the parent country, the host country, or any third country.

Although subsidiaries can borrow directly from outside the host country, most of them borrow locally for a number of reasons:

1. Local debts represent automatic protection against losses from a devaluation of local currency.
2. Subsidiary debts frequently do not appear on the consolidated financial statement issued by a parent as part of its annual report.
3. Some host countries limit the amount of funds that foreign companies can import from outside the host country.
4. Foreign subsidiaries often borrow locally to maintain good relations with local banks.

Commercial Banks

As noted in Chapter 10, commercial banks are a major financial intermediary in trade credit. They are also the most important external source of financing nontrade international operations. The types of loans and services provided by banks vary from country to country, but all countries have some funds available at local banks.

Most of the local loans obtained by subsidiaries are short-term credits from commercial banks. These short-term credits are used largely to finance inventory and accounts receivable. They are self-liquidating loans to the extent that sufficient cash flows are produced to repay the credits as inventories are sold on credit and receivables are collected over the business cycle. The principal instruments used by banks to service a multinational firm's request for a loan are (1) overdrafts, (2) unsecured short-term loans, (3) bridge loans, (4) currency swaps, and (5) link financing.

Overdrafts.   Overdrafts are one of the major short-term credits in Europe and North America. An overdraft is a line of credit which permits the customer to write checks beyond deposits. The bank establishes the maximum amount of such credit based on its analysis of the customer's request, needs, and potential cash flows. The borrower agrees to pay the amount overdrawn and interest on the credit. Although some banks waive service charges for their creditworthy customers, others frequently require service charges and other fees.

Unsecured Short-Term Loans.   Most short-term bank loans for multinational companies to cover seasonal increases in current assets are made on an unsecured basis. The percentages of such loans vary from country to country and reflect variations in individual bank policy and central government regulations. Most multinational firms prefer to borrow on an unsecured basis because bookkeeping costs of secured loans are high and because these loans have a number of highly restrictive provisions. However, some foreign subsidiaries cannot obtain loans on an unsecured basis because they are either financially weak or have not established a satisfactory performance record.

Bridge Loans.   When foreign subsidiaries need short-term funds for only one purpose, they can obtain the funds by signing promissory notes. When they are in the process of obtaining long-term funds, these short-term loans may be renewed. Such short-term renewal loans are frequently called bridge loans, and they are repaid when the permanent financing arrangement is completed.

Currency Swaps.   Currency swaps are agreements to exchange one currency with another for a specified period after which the two currencies are re-exchanged. **Arbi loans** are the best known example of such swaps. An arbi loan is arranged in a country where money is readily available at reasonable rates. It is converted to the desired local currency, but the borrower arranges a forward exchange contract to insure converting the local currency into the foreign currency of original denomination at a specified future date. Thus, arbi loans allow multinational companies to borrow in one market for use in another market and to avoid foreign exchange risks. The cost of arbi loans includes the interest on the loans and the charges associated with the forward exchange contract.

Link Financing.   Link financing permits multinational companies in weak-currency countries to indirectly tap external sources of funds. Commercial banks in strong-currency countries help subsidiaries in weak-currency countries obtain loans by guaranteeing repayment on the loans. These subsidiaries borrow money from local banks or firms with an excess of weak money. Certainly, banks in strong-currency countries require some sort of deposits from a borrower's parent company and the borrower must pay local interest rates. To protect itself against foreign exchange risk, the lender usually hedges its position in the forward exchange market.

Edge Act and Agreement Corporations

Edge Act and Agreement corporations are subsidiaries of American banks which are physically located in the United States, but they engage in international banking operations. The Edge Act of 1919 allows American banks to perform as holding companies and to own stock in foreign banks. Thus, these banks can provide loans and other banking services for American-owned companies in most countries around the world. Edge Act corporations are domestic subsidiaries of banking organizations chartered by the Federal Reserve Board; Agreement corporations are Edge equivalents chartered by individual states. Both types of subsidiaries may perform not only international banking operations, but they may also finance foreign industrial projects through long-term loans or equity participation.

Types of Activities.   Edge Act and Agreement corporations typically engage in three types of activities: international banking, international financing, and holding companies. In their capacity as international banking corporations, Edge Act and Agreement corporations may hold demand and time deposits of foreign parties. They can make loans, but these loans to any single borrower cannot exceed 10 percent of their capital and surplus. They can also open or confirm letters of credit, make loans or advances to finance foreign trade, create bankers' acceptances, receive items for collection, remit funds abroad, buy or sell securities, issue certain guarantees, and engage in foreign exchange transactions.

In their capacity as international financing corporations, Edge Act and Agreement corporations invest in the stock of nonbank financial concerns, development corporations, or commercial and industrial companies. Certainly, such investments require prior specific consent of the Federal Reserve Board or state banking authorities under certain circumstances. Edge Act subsidiaries have financed some foreign finance companies and official development corporations. In most cases, however, they finance commercial and industrial companies directly through loans and equity contributions. The major purpose of such financing activities is to provide promising foreign companies with capital at an early or important stage.

In their capacity as holding companies, Edge Act and Agreement corporations can own shares of foreign banking subsidiaries and affiliates. Member banks of the Federal Reserve System are not permitted to own shares of foreign banking subsidiaries. A foreign banking subsidiary may be more advantageous than a branch for two reasons. First, foreign branches are allowed to carry on only the activities allowed to their parent banks in the United States. Second, certain countries do not permit nondomestic banks to open branches in their territory. In other instances, Edge Act and Agreement corporations have been the instrument through which U.S. banks have acquired equity interests in well-known foreign banks.

International Banking Facilities

Since December 3, 1981, banks in the United States have been allowed to establish international banking facilities (IBFs) at their offices in the United States. IBFs are vehicles that enable bank offices in the United States to accept time deposits in either dollars or foreign currency from foreign customers, free of reserve requirements and of other limitations. Foreigners can also borrow funds from IBFs to finance their foreign investment projects. IBFs have been further strengthened by legislation in New York, California, and other states which exempt them from state and local income taxes. IBFs are located in the United States, but in many respects they function like foreign branch offices of U.S. banks. In other words, the creation of IBFs means the establishment of off-shore banking facilities in the United States similar to other Eurocurrency market centers.

In order to qualify for IBFs, institutions must be depository institutions, Edge or Agreement corporations, or U.S. branch offices of foreign banks which are legally authorized to do business in the United States. These institutions do not require the approval of the Federal Reserve Board to establish IBFs; a simple notification is sufficient. In addition, they are not required to establish a separate organizational structure for IBFs, but they must maintain separate books which would distinguish their offshore business from their domestic business.

IBFs have a number of advantages over bank operations through foreign locations. First, small banks can enter into the Eurocurrency market easily, because they no longer need to establish a foreign office or a domestic subsidiary exclusively for international banking operations. Second, U.S. banks can reduce operating costs because they have more direct control and use existing support services such as personnel and facilities.

IBFs also have several disadvantages when we compare them to off-shore banking centers, caused mostly by regulations that IBFs serve only nonresidents. First, IBFs must receive written acknowledgment from their customers that deposits do not support activities within the United States and that IBF loans finance only operations outside the United States. Second, IBFs are prohibited from offering demand deposits or transaction accounts that could possibly substitute for such accounts now held by nonresidents in U.S. banks. Third, IBFs are also prevented from issuing negotiable certificates of deposits or bankers' acceptances though they can issue letters of credit and undertake repurchase agreements. Fourth, time deposits offered to nonbank foreign residents require minimum deposits and withdrawal of $100,000 to preserve the wholesale nature of the business; they also require a minimum maturity or two business days' notification prior to withdrawal.

Joint Ventures

In a trend that accelerated during the 1980s, companies have begun to link up with former competitors in a vast array of joint ventures. A joint venture is a corporate entity in which two or more parties, for example, a multinational company and several host–country companies, have equity interest. In the past, use of a wholly owned subsidiary was the most common approach to overseas investment because worldwide strategy depended on complete control over all foreign operations. However, more and more host countries require that multinational companies have some local participation. In some situations, multinational companies will seek local partners even when there are no local requirements to do so.

Types of Joint Ventures.
There are three types of international joint ventures. First, two companies form a joint venture to conduct a business in a third country. For example, Ford Motor Company and Toyota Motor Corporation may establish a truck assembly plant in Poland. Second, a multinational company forms a joint venture with host–country companies. For instance, IBM and Hyundai Group of Korea may set up a computer company to produce personal computers in Korea. Third, a multinational company and a local government form a joint venture. For example, Exxon and the Iranian government may establish an oil company for oil extraction in Iran.

Advantages of Joint Ventures.
Many factors may induce multinational firms to enter joint ventures with local partners, other multinational companies, and local governments. These factors include tax benefits, local marketing expertise, more capital, less political risk, and quick acquisition of new technologies.

On the other hand, multinational companies want tight control of their foreign subsidiaries to efficiently allocate investments and to maintain a coordinated marketing plan on a global basis. Dividend policy, financial disclosure, transfer pricing, establishment of royalty and other fees, and allocation of production and marketing costs among plants are just some areas in which each owner has an incentive to engage in activities that could hurt its partners. This is why most multinational companies resist local participation. In fact, there are many cases in which multinational companies have chosen to pull out of foreign countries rather than to comply with government regulations that require joint ventures with local partners.

Guidelines for Adequate Capitalization

Multinational companies are not only able to raise funds in international and national capital markets but also to take advantage of capital market imperfections throughout the world. This comparative advantage should theoretically allow multinational companies to enjoy a lower cost of capital than competing domestic companies. Companies have a number of outside financial options from which to choose to finance their foreign investment projects. These external financial options include banks, government institutions, other types of financial intermediaries, and even the public sector in the host country. To avoid drawbacks inherent in the thin capitalization of foreign investment projects, companies usually seek an optimum capital structure. An optimum capital structure is defined as the combination of debt and equity that yields the lowest cost of capital.

Several ratios can be used to determine an optimum financing mix of debt and equity for overseas projects. George Cassidy (1984) recommends a number of guidelines for companies to develop capitalization strategies for their overseas projects:

1. The investor's own resources should be sufficient to approximately cover the project investment in fixed assets. Outside financing should support investment in net working capital of the unit.
2. The ratio of outside financing to total capitalization of the project (the debt ratio) should generally be about 0.50. Thus, approximately equal amounts of outside debts and equity investments will be employed in the local project.
3. The projected earnings from the overseas project should provide adequate "interest coverage" for its intended outside debt service. To ensure continuing liquidity, these earnings should be a substantial multiple of the project's annual financial costs.

Development Banks

Development banks provide multinational companies with a broad range of financing resources. These banking organizations are established to support the economic development of underdeveloped areas through intermediate and long-term loans. There are three broad groups of development banks: worldwide, regional, and national.

World Bank Group

The World Bank Group is a group of worldwide financial institutions organized after the devastation of World War II to aid economic reconstruction. These institutions include the International Bank for Reconstruction and

Development, the International Finance Corporation, and the International Development Association.

International Bank for Reconstruction and Development.

The International Bank for Reconstruction and Development (IBRD), commonly known as the World Bank, was established at the Bretton Woods conference in 1944 as a companion institution to the International Monetary Fund. Because the major objective of the World Bank was to finance reconstruction and development after World War II, it made certain loans in Europe for reconstruction. It found its resources completely inadequate for this purpose and thus stopped reconstruction loans. However, the World Bank was able to concentrate on lending for economic development because the Marshall Plan provided funds for reconstruction in Europe. The Marshall Plan was the European economic recovery program established by the United States in 1948. The overriding objective of the Plan was to restore the productive capacity of European industry destroyed during World War II. The Plan existed slightly less than four years and channeled more than $10 billion in American aid to Europe.

In recent decades, the World Bank has placed a major emphasis on loans to underdeveloped countries for social infrastructure projects such as irrigation, schools, and roads. This kind of development is essential for future industrialization. Approximately a third of its development loans has gone to electrical power, a third for transportation improvements, and the remaining third for agricultural projects and education. Loans are made only to member governments, government agencies, and private businesses whose loans are guaranteed by their governments.

Because the Bank finances only a portion of project costs, private investors must finance the remaining portion. To encourage the direct participation of private investors in its loans, the Bank has adopted high credit standards:

1. The Bank makes loans only for projects whose cost and revenue estimates are reasonably accurate.
2. When loans are made to private companies, these loans must be guaranteed by their governments.
3. An additional 1 percent is added to the regular interest rate. These funds go into reserve funds to meet losses in the event of default.
4. Member countries are required to pay the unpaid portion of their quotas in the event that funds are needed to meet losses.

Private funds for international investments have increased because the Bank has applied these high standards.

The capital subscribed by member countries represents the basic equity capital for the Bank. Member countries are assigned subscription quotas on the basis of their size and wealth. They must pay 10 percent of their quota when they join the Bank, and the remaining 90 percent of the quota is subject to call. However, a substantial portion of the Bank's capital comes from bonds sold on world markets. Because the Bank applies high credit standards, its bonds usually carry high credit ratings and low interest rates.

The newly established Multilateral Investment Guarantee Agency of the Bank offers various forms of political risk insurance. As one of the largest borrowers in the world, the Bank borrowed a total of $100 billion from 100 countries. Its loans are well-diversified among more than 20 countries. The Bank enjoys the highest credit rating, AAA.

International Finance Corporation. Initially, the World Bank had a number of problems in providing financial assistance to less developed countries. First, all loans had to be guaranteed by governments. Second, the Bank provided only loans. Third, it financed only the foreign exchange requirements for a project and ignored local expenditures or working capital requirements. Fourth, it typically financed only large projects of public importance.

These problems led to the development of the International Finance Corporation (IFC) in 1956 primarily to finance private enterprises in less developed countries through loan or equity participation.

The IFC regards development finance companies and industrial projects as the proper outlets for its limited capital. It assists in establishing development finance companies in areas where there are gaps in the local capital and money markets. It also helps existing development finance companies to expand or reorganize operations. The IFC usually invests in those industrial projects which will contribute to improved foreign exchange positions, increased employment, improved management skills, or the exploration of natural resources. It provides risk capital to companies that require funds in order to expand, modernize, or diversify operations. It also helps to finance new ventures. Ordinarily, it does not invest in such infrastructure projects as hospitals, transportation, and agricultural development.

IFC funds are available for either foreign exchange or local currency expenditures to meet fixed assets or working capital requirements. It makes nonguaranteed loans to private enterprises in less developed countries. Most of these loans have maturities from seven to 12 years. All its investments are made along with private investors, and its financial contribution usually accounts for less than 50 percent of total project cost.

International Development Association. The International Development Association (IDA) was established in 1960 as an affiliate of the World Bank Group to meet the specific needs of less developed countries. IDA loans are designed to finance projects for companies which cannot adhere to loan repayment schedules with conventional terms. Credit terms are generally extended for 50 years with very low or no interest. Repayment begins after a ten-year grace period and can be made in local currencies.

All World Bank members are free to join the IDA, and more than 100 countries have done so. IDA resources are separate from World Bank resources. Nearly 90 percent of the IDA's capital comes from subscriptions of its member countries. The second most important source of its capital is the World Bank's contribution. IDA member countries are classified into two broad categories. Part I countries, which consist of relatively developed countries; and Part II countries, which consist of less developed countries. Part I countries pay all of their subscriptions in convertible currencies, while Part II countries pay only 10 percent of their subscriptions in convertible currencies and the remainder in their own currencies. Certain nonmember countries such as Switzerland and New Zealand have made loans to the IDA on the same terms as the IDA lends to its members.

Regional Development Banks

Regional groups of countries have established regional development banks to promote effective economic development within the member countries. Leading regional development banks are the Inter-American Development Bank, the European Investment Bank, the European Bank for Reconstruction and Development, the Asian Development Bank, and the African Development Bank.

Inter-American Development Bank.
The Inter-American Development Bank (IDB) was founded in 1959 by the United States and 19 Latin American countries to further the economic development of its member countries. IDB loans are available only when private sources are not available on reasonable terms. The IDB usually finances no more than 50 percent of total project cost.

The IDB has three types of activity:

1. With its Ordinary Capital Resources Fund, the Bank makes development loans to both public and private institutions. These loans are earmarked for projects that promote Latin America's economic development.
2. With its U.S. created Social Progress Trust Fund, the Bank makes loans to finance projects with high social value.
3. With its Fund for Special Operations, the Bank makes loans whose terms are much more lenient than those available in the regular money and capital markets. Maturities may be extremely long, repayment may be made in the borrower's currency, or interest rates may be arbitrarily low.

European Bank for Reconstruction and Development.
The European Bank for Reconstruction and Development (EBRD), with $12 billion of capital, was established in 1990 by 42 countries as a development bank for emerging democracies in Eastern Europe. These 42 member countries include the United States, Japan, Russia, and European countries.

The United States with a 10 percent share is the largest single shareholder. Britain, France, Italy, Japan, and Germany each have shares of 8.52 percent. Russia, with a 6 percent share in the bank, is the largest single shareholder among East-bloc countries. All together, European countries hold a major stake in the bank. Share contributions may be made in dollars,

European Currency Units, or yen. All of the shareholders paid in only 30 percent of their capital contributions; the rest of their capital is callable.

European Investment Bank.

The European Investment Bank (EIB) was established in 1958 by members of the European Community. Its resources are used to support the socio-economic infrastructure of the member nations or their basic industries. Most of these loans have maturities from 12 to 20 years. Ordinarily, three or four year intervals are established before loan repayments begin.

The EIB has three types of responsibility:

1. It assists in financing projects which involve two or more member governments. In this case, it plays an important role in coordinating the activities of different national financial agencies.
2. It promotes the potential of economies of scale. It helps specialize or expand the operations of plants or firms in countries with a comparative advantage in certain lines of business.
3. It helps achieve a more uniform and high level of economic maturity within the European Community.

Asian Development Bank.

The Asian Development Bank (ADB) was formed in 1966 by several Asian countries in partnership with the United States, Canada, Britain, Germany, and other European countries. The ADB makes long-term loans to private companies without government guarantees. Some ADB loans go to Asian national banks that reloan to private enterprises through their respective development agencies. Some other ADB loans are used to supply risk capital.

African Development Bank.

The African Development Bank (AfDB) was established in 1964 by the Organization of African Unity. Unlike other regional development banks, the AfDB had, until the early 1980s, excluded nonregional partners in an effort to avoid undue outside influence; thus, it suffered from severe capital limitations, hampering its ability to lend. Since the early 1980s the AfDB has accepted non-African countries as contributing but nonborrowing members. In order to attract commercial bank funds and public debt offerings, the AfDB maintains conservative lending policies and interest rates. Loans are made only to governments or their agencies. Interest rates are similar to commercial rates.

National Development Banks

Many governments in industrial countries have their own development banks to foster international loans and investments. The three leading institutions of the United States are the Export-Import Bank, the Agency for International Development, and the Overseas Private Investment Corporation.

Export-Import Bank (Exim Bank).

The Exim Bank provides investment funds to multinational companies. These funds include long-term direct financing to facilitate the purchase of U.S. goods and services used in industrial projects in foreign countries. In this type of long-term direct financing, the Exim Bank expects a substantial equity participation by the borrower. Moreover, it provides U.S. companies with guarantees on their engineering and feasibility studies, as well as on their technical and construction services, performed abroad. In summary, the Exim Bank is a key source of financing overseas projects when private sources are not available. These projects must be economically justifiable, contribute to the economic development of the country, and improve the country's foreign exchange position.

Agency for International Development.

The Agency for International Development (AID) was established in 1961 to carry out nonmilitary U.S. foreign assistance programs. AID, as an agency of the U.S. State Department, emphasizes assistance to friendly governments or to support programs which will make foreign friends for the United States. As the primary aid agency of the U.S. government, it performs three functions:

1. It administers the government's programs of technical cooperation with less developed countries.
2. It administers the government's economic programs for less developed countries.
3. It carries out special emergency programs as directed by the President of the United States.

Development loans are made to friendly governments, and private companies may borrow these funds from their governments. To prevent a heavy drain of U.S. dollars, loans are usually tied to purchases of U.S. goods and services. Moreover, these funds are generally maintained in the United States and are simply made available for use by recipient countries. All development loans are repayable in dollars and can have a maximum maturity of 50 years, with a grace period of ten years. In making development loans, AID considers the availability of funds at reasonable terms from other free-world sources. Interest rates are usually lower than international money rates.

Overseas Private Investment Corporation.

The Overseas Private Investment Corporation (OPIC) was established in 1969 to take over AID's responsibility for investment insurance and guarantee programs. OPIC became operational in 1971 and is wholly owned by the U.S. Treasury Department. It operates two programs: insurance of U.S. private investments in less developed countries and project financing. More specifically, its insurance programs cover losses from political risks of currency inconvertibility, expropriation, and land-based war to U.S. companies that make investments in friendly developing countries. Its project financing is carried out through an investment guarantee program. This program provides guarantees against losses from commercial and political risks, direct investment funds in dollars or foreign currencies, and a pre-investment survey program.

OPIC combines private business with the U.S. foreign policy objective of encouraging American firms to invest in less developed countries. Thus, it grants insurance and guarantees for projects which are in the best interest of both the United States' and the host country's economy.

Summary

For purposes of expansion, new investment, and day-to-day operations, the international financial manager must be familiar with various sources of internal or external funds. This chapter has discussed three types of internally generated funds: (1) retained earnings and depreciation provided by operations, (2) equity contributions, loans, and credits from the parent company, and (3) loans from sister subsidiaries.

External sources of funds include borrowing from financial institutions in a parent country or abroad, joint ventures with local partners, and development banks. Commercial banks are a major financial intermediary in foreign trade and investment. The upsurge of direct foreign investment by multinational companies since the early 1950s has forced banks to follow their customers overseas. The principal instruments used by banks to accommodate multinational firms' borrowing requests are overdrafts, unsecured short-term loans, bridge loans, arbi loans, and link financing.

The Edge Act of 1919 allowed American banks to act as holding companies and to own common stock of foreign banks. Since then, many Edge Act and Agreement corporations have been established as subsidiaries of American banks to engage in international banking and financial operations. These Edge Act and Agreement corporations provide loans and other banking services to American companies in most countries around the world. In order to help U.S. banks capture a large portion of the Eurocurrency business, the Federal Reserve Board authorized the establishment of U.S. based international banking facilities (IBFs) in 1981. IBFs accept time deposits from foreigners and make loans to foreigners. They have attracted a significant share of Eurodollar business away from other existing centers since 1981. More and more host countries require that foreign companies have local participation. But some multinational firms voluntarily seek local partners because they need tax benefits, local marketing expertise, more capital, and quick acquisition of new technologies.

Development banks provide multinational companies with a variety of financing sources. They are banks established to aid in economic development through equity participation, loans, or some intermediate form of investment. They may be worldwide, regional, or national. The World Bank Group consists of the International Bank for Reconstruction and Development, the International Development Association, and the International Finance Corporation. These worldwide development banks are designed to provide financial support for less developed countries. Regional groups of countries have established regional development banks to promote more effective economic development within the member countries. Five regional lending institutions formed to facilitate development on four continents are the Inter-American Development Bank, the Asian Development Bank, the European Investment Bank, the European Bank for Reconstruction and Development, and the African Development Bank. National development banks perform the same general functions as worldwide and regional development banks.

Questions

1. What are the major types of funds supplied by the parent company to its subsidiaries?

2. Why are parent loans to foreign subsidiaries more popular than equity contributions?

3. What are the internal sources of funds provided by operations? What is the role of internal funds?

4. List the types of loans that local banks provide to foreign subsidiaries for nontrade international operations. Are these local credits used to finance current assets or fixed assets? Why are these loans sometimes called self-liquidating loans?

5. What are the similarities and differences between Edge Act–Agreement corporations and International Banking Facilities?

6. What are advantages and disadvantages of joint ventures?

7. George Cassidy suggested several guidelines which can be used to determine an optimum financing mix of debt and equity for overseas projects. Explain these guidelines.

8. What is the role of development banks? How can multinational companies benefit from these development banks?

9. Describe the role of the European Bank for Reconstruction and Development (EBRD).

References

Baker, J. C., "The IFC and European Banks: Key Factors in Development Aid," *Journal of World Trade Law*, May/June 1980, pp. 262-70.

Bogdanowicz, B., and C. A. Canavan, "The World Bank and the International Private Sector," *Columbia Journal of World Business*, Fall 1986, pp. 31–5.

Cassidy, G. T., "Financing Foreign Investments: The International Capital Markets," in Allen Sweeny and Robert Rachlin, eds., *Handbook for International Financial Management*, New York: McGraw–Hill, 1984, pp. 1–11.

Chrystal, A. K., "International Banking Facilities," *Federal Reserve Bank of St. Louis Bulletin*, April 1984, pp. 5–11.

Franko, L. G., "Use of Minority and 50–50 Joint Ventures by U.S. Multinationals During the 1970s: The Interaction of Host Country Policies and Corporate Strategies," *Journal of International Business Studies*, Spring 1989, pp. 1–18.

Geringer, J. M., and L. Hebert, "Control and Performance of International Joint Ventures," *Journal of International Business Studies*, Summer 1989, pp. 211–34.

Nigh, D., and K. D. Smith, "The New U.S. Joint Ventures in the USSR: Assessment and Management of Political Risk," *Columbia Journal of World Business*, Summer 1989, pp. 39–44.

O'Reilly, A. J., "Establishing Successful Joint Ventures in Developing Nations: A CEO's Perspective," *Columbia Journal of World Business*, Spring 1988, pp. 65–72.

Part Four
Asset Management

Part Four (Chapters 12 through 16) covers the management of assets. The second major facet of financial management is the efficient allocation of funds among various assets. This part describes the management of current assets, financial assets, capital budgeting, and political risks associated with foreign investment. The objective of current asset management is to protect the purchasing power of assets and to maximize the return on investment. The management of current assets is extremely important for the multinational company. Thus, the complicating international factors and approaches for resolving them should be analyzed carefully. National capital markets have recently changed to an integrated global capital market, often followed by widespread international multiple listings of securities. Consequently, investors are starting to realize the enormous potential through international portfolio diversification. Financial management literature on capital budgeting has expanded rapidly in the past decade. As a result, relatively sophisticated techniques exist to analyze how foreign investment decisions are made. Investment decisions affect the value of a company's stock by influencing both the size of the earnings stream and the riskiness of the company. This risk factor in foreign operations takes on a new dimension of importance because it is rarely encountered in domestic business operations.

12
Current Asset Management

The management of current assets and current liabilities constitutes working capital management. The efficient allocation of funds among various current assets and the acquisition of short-term funds on favorable terms are conceptually the same for both multinational companies and domestic companies. However, these two types of companies are different because they do business in different environments. These differences include the impact of currency fluctuations, potential exchange controls, and multiple tax jurisdictions on working capital decisions. In addition, multinational companies enjoy a wide variety of short-term financing and investment opportunities.

Chapters 8-11 discussed various short-term sources of funds in detail. This chapter emphasizes current asset management, which can be viewed as either a static (stock) responsibility or a dynamic (flow) process. The static approach focuses on individual processes such as the composition of various current assets. The important aspect of this approach is how to determine appropriate levels of cash, accounts receivable, and inventories. On the other hand, the dynamic approach focuses on the denomination of liquid funds by currency and the placement of such holdings by country. This flow process places a heavy emphasis on transfers of liquid funds from one geographic location or currency to another. These transfers have many constraints and uncertainties, such as political risks, foreign-exchange rate fluctuations, tax problems, and liquidity considerations.

Basic Concepts of Current Asset Management

The basic objective of current asset management is to determine the optimal amount of investment in various current-asset accounts. This optimal amount of investment in current assets is the level of current-asset holdings that maximizes the overall profitability of a firm. However, there are a variety of economic constraints which make it difficult for multinational companies to achieve the objective of working capital management.

Economic Constraints of Current Asset Management

Because multinational companies operate across national borders, they face regulatory, tax, foreign exchange, and other economic constraints. To achieve a predetermined objective of current assets, the financial manager must give special consideration to these constraints.

Regulatory Constraints.
Regulatory constraints can block dividend repatriation or other forms of fund remittances. This blockage occurs because of restrictions on the international movement of funds and other exchange controls.

Tax Constraints.
Tax constraints limit the free flow of affiliate funds to a parent or to sister affiliates. These may occur because higher taxes on all corporate earnings or extra taxes on dividends may be imposed to curb inflation.

Foreign Exchange Constraints.
Foreign exchange constraints are another limiting factor on fund flows from one country to another. International fund flows involve foreign exchange transaction costs and exchange rate fluctuations.

Summary of Constraints.
Other economic factors such as inflation and interest rates also have an important impact on the international mobility of corporate funds.

There are many elements and issues in international current asset management. Here, we assume that the major tasks of current asset management consist of (1) the ability to transfer funds; (2) the positioning of funds within a multinational firm; (3) arbitrage opportunities; and (4) different channels to move funds.

The Ability to Transfer Funds

A multinational company has the ability to adjust intracompany fund flows and profits on a global basis. This ability is one of the most important advantages that multinational companies enjoy. Financial transactions within a multinational company stem from the internal transfer of goods, services, technology, and capital. Such intracompany flows range from finished goods to intangible items such as management skills, trademarks, and patents. Furthermore, capital investments and direct loans give rise to future flows of dividends, interest, and principal payments. On the other hand, many of the gains by intracompany fund flows derive from some questionable business practices. For example, the amount of gains could depend on a company's ability to take advantage of soft spots in tax laws and regulatory barriers. Consequently, conflicts between multinational companies and their host governments are quite likely.

Positioning of Funds

Another main task of current asset management is to position working cash balances or excess liquidity within a multinational company. The division of funds among various affiliates involves the choice of country and the selection of currency denomination for all liquid funds. In domestic businesses, fund flows among units of a large company confer little or no advantage to a firm. First, financial markets are quite efficient in the sense that the cost of funds reflects the riskiness of a particular investment. If financial markets are highly efficient, independent firms or individual investors can replicate fund transfers among domestic affiliates with little or no additional cost. Hence, internal domestic transfers do not provide a company with any tangible advantage. Second, because all affiliate profits are subject to the same national tax rate, taxes paid by a company should have nothing to do with the operating unit which generates these profits. This assumption will not be true if tax rates differ widely.

The value of intracompany fund flows for multinational companies lies precisely in the fact that there are wide variations in national tax systems and regulatory barriers. In other words, many different types of market imperfections increase the value of internal fund flows among units of a multinational firm. These market imperfections include exchange controls, tax systems, and political factors.

Arbitrage Opportunities

The ability to relocate working cash balances and profits on a global basis provides multinational firms with three different types of arbitrage opportunities: (1) tax arbitrage, (2) financial market arbitrage, and (3) regulatory system arbitrage. First, multinational companies can reduce their overall tax burden by shifting profits from subsidiaries in high-tax countries to subsidiaries in low-tax countries. Second, internal fund transfers may enable multinational firms to circumvent exchange controls, earn higher yields on excess funds, and tap domestically unavailable capital sources. Third, if affiliate profits depend on government regulations or union pressure, multinational companies can disguise true profits through transfer pricing and other intracompany adjustments.

Different Channels to Move Funds

Multinational business operations require a steady flow of funds from parent to subsidiary, from subsidiary to parent, and between subsidiaries. Because these fund flows are unique, we will consider one at a time.

Fund Flows from Parent to Subsidiary.   The largest flow of funds from parent to subsidiary is the initial investment. The subsidiary may also receive additional funds in the form of loans or added investments. The purchase of goods from the parent offers another form of fund flows from parent to subsidiary. This form of fund flows involves transfer pricing, the price on goods sold between related entities.

Fund Flows from Subsidiary to Parent.   The major components of fund flows from subsidiary to parent consist of dividends, interest on loans, principal reduction payments, royalty payments, license fees, technical service fees, management fees, export commissions, and payments for goods received from the parent. The parent does not have total control in the size of the flow of funds because of various external factors, such as foreign exchange controls and tax constraints. For example, many governments impose a withholding tax when dividends are remitted to foreign owners.

Fund Flows from Subsidiary to Subsidiary.   Funds flow from one subsidiary to another when they lend funds to each other or buy goods from each other. Funds from one subsidiary may also be used to establish another subsidiary. When such investments are made, all dividends and principal payments may go directly to the home office. However, it is possible for these two subsidiaries to have cash flows similar to parent company cash flows.

Many factors, such as exchange controls and domestic political pressures, can block dividend repatriation or other forms of fund remittances. If funds are blocked in perpetuity, the value of a foreign project to the parent company is zero. But multinational companies have secretive methods to remove blocked funds, including (1) multilateral netting, (2) leading and lagging, (3) transfer pricing, (4) reinvoicing centers, (5) intracompany loans, (6) payment adjustments, and (7) unbundling fund transfers.

Multilateral Netting.   Large multinational corporations often require a highly coordinated interchange of material, parts, work-in-process, and finished goods among various units because they must handle a large volume of intracorporate fund flows. These crossborder fund transfers involve the foreign exchange spread, the opportunity cost of the float, and other transaction costs such as cable charges. Netting has been frequently suggested as one method of minimizing the total volume of interaffiliate fund flows.

Multilateral netting is an extension of bilateral netting. For example, if subsidiary A purchases $10 million worth of goods from subsidiary B and B in turn buys $11 million worth of parts from A, the combined flows are $21 million. But on a net basis, subsidiary A would pay subsidiary B only $1 million. Bilateral netting would be useless where internal sales are more complex. Think of a situation where subsidiary A sells $10 million worth of goods to subsidiary B, subsidiary B sells $10 million worth of goods to subsidiary C, and subsidiary C sells $10 million worth of goods to subsidiary A. In this case, bilateral netting would be of no use, but multilateral netting would eliminate interaffiliate fund transfers completely.

An accelerated globalization of production, distribution, and finance during the 1980s has created an unusually large volume of intracompany fund flows. By a process of netting interaffiliate payments, multinational companies can realize significant cost savings. It is no wonder why so many multinational companies use netting procedures to reduce transaction costs. A survey of 30 multinational companies by Venkat Srinivasan and Yong Kim (1986) found a number of interesting facts about netting practices. First, 82 percent of the respondents netted their intracompany payments. Second, multilateral netting was most frequently used. Third, 86 percent of the respondents netted payments between subsidiaries on a monthly basis. Fourth, most respondents developed the netting schedule by forecasting actual cash flows to and from subsidiaries.

Leads and Lags. Multinational companies can accelerate (lead) or delay (lag) the timing of foreign-currency payments in order to reduce foreign exchange exposure or to increase working capital available. These leads and lags can be achieved by modifying the credit terms extended by one unit to another. In order to reduce foreign exchange exposure, companies should accelerate the payment of hard-currency payables and delay the payment of soft-currency payables. If subsidiary X buys goods worth $10 million monthly from subsidiary Y on 60-day credit terms, Y is, in effect, financing $20 million of working capital for X. The extension of the terms to 120 days would enable subsidiary X to have an additional $20 million of working capital.

Most U.S. and non-U.S. multinational companies use leads and lags to minimize foreign exchange exposure and to shift the burden of financing from one unit to another. This technique has a number of advantages over direct loans. First, leading and lagging do not require a note that officially recognizes an obligation to the seller. Moreover, the amount of credit can be adjusted up or down by shortening or lengthening the credit terms. Second, indications are that governments interfere less with payments on intracompany accounts than on intracompany loans. Third, under Section 482 of the U.S. tax code, U.S. firms do not have to pay interest on intracompany accounts up to six months, but they have to pay interest on all intracompany loans.

Transfer Pricing. Transfer prices are prices of goods and services sold between a parent and its subsidiary. Increasing transfers of goods and services between related units in different countries are found as multinational companies have become larger and more diversified. Because transfer prices are frequently different from arm's length prices (fair market prices), there is obviously room for manipulation. Governments usually assume that multinational companies use transfer prices to reduce or avoid their taxes. For this reason, most governments have set up policing mechanisms to review the transfer pricing policies of multinational companies.

Multinational companies are also concerned with transfer prices because they affect direct cash flows for payments of goods and taxes, for cost structures, and for the evaluation of management performance. If companies have the discretion to set arbitrary prices, different conditions in each subsidiary country could lead to different transfer pricing decisions. For example, those countries with higher tax rates and tariffs are likely to induce higher transfer prices on flows from the parent and lower transfer prices on flows to the parent. On the other hand, those countries with lower tax rates and tariffs would induce lower transfer prices on flows from the parent and higher transfer prices on flows to the parent.

Multinational business executives are reluctant to discuss policies for transfer pricing. But in multinational cases, transfer pricing has been used to minimize income taxes and tariffs, to adjust for currency fluctuations, to avoid economic restrictions, and to present a favorable financial picture of a foreign affiliate. We will discuss all of these transfer pricing objectives in Chapter 19.

Reinvoicing Centers.   Some multinational companies circumvent or bypass governments' restrictions and regulations by setting up reinvoicing centers in tax-haven countries. Tax-haven countries are those nations which provide foreign companies with permanent tax inducements. It is possible for a reinvoicing center in the Bahamas to issue invoices for all goods sold by a U.S. parent to its subsidiaries or independent customers in different countries. In this case, the reinvoicing center takes titles of all goods sold by one corporate unit to its customers, even though the goods move directly from the seller in the United States to the buyer in Japan. The Bahamas center pays the U.S. seller and is paid by the Japanese buyer to complete the transaction.

Reinvoicing centers are often used to cope with foreign exchange exposures. Subsidiaries buy and sell goods in multiple currencies and must manage the resulting currency exposures. Mechanisms such as the reinvoicing center are necessary so that subsidiaries operate their business exclusively on a local currency basis without the active management of foreign exchange exposures. To see how the reinvoicing center works to minimize currency exposures, assume that the Canadian subsidiary purchases equipment from a Japanese firm and that payment should be made in Japanese yen. In this case, the reinvoicing center would buy the equipment in the name of the Canadian firm, pay the seller in Japanese yen, bill the Canadian firm in Canadian dollars, and receive Canadian dollars from the buyer. Thus, the objective of foreign exchange management based on the reinvoicing center is to centralize foreign exchange exposures in one unit—the reinvoicing center in a single country. To achieve this goal, the reinvoicing center buys on behalf of all related companies in various foreign currencies and then rebills those purchases to the buying units in their local currencies.

Intracompany Loans.

There are many different types of intracompany loans, but direct loans, credit swaps, and back-to-back loans are the most important. Direct loans involve straight dealings between the lending unit and the borrowing unit, but credit swaps and back-to-back loans normally involve an intermediary.

A credit swap is a simultaneous spot-and-forward loan transaction between a private company and a bank of a foreign country. For example, a U.S. company deposits a given amount of dollars in the Chicago office of a Mexican bank. In return for this deposit, the bank lends a given amount of pesos to the company's subsidiary in Mexico. The same contract provides that the bank return the initial amount of dollars to the company at a specified date and that the subsidiary return the original amount of pesos to the bank.

Credit swaps are, in fact, intracompany loans hedged and channeled through banks. These loans are also risk free from a bank's point of view because the parent's deposit fully collateralizes them. Credit swaps have several advantages over direct intracompany loans. First, credit swaps are free of foreign exchange exposures because the parent recovers the amount of its deposit in the original parent currency from the bank. Second, cost savings may be available with credit swaps because certain countries apply different tax rates to interest paid to the foreign parent and to interest paid to the local bank.

Back-to-back loans consist of two related but separate borrowings and typically involve four parties in two different countries. The U.S. parent lends an agreed amount in dollars to the American subsidiary of the Mexican parent. In return for this loan, the Mexican parent lends the same amount of money in pesos to the Mexican subsidiary of the U.S. parent. These loan arrangements involve the same amount for both loans and the same loan maturity. Certainly, each loan is paid in the subsidiary's currency.

Back-to-back loans are frequently used to effectively repatriate blocked funds by circumventing exchange control restrictions. To see how the back-to-back loan can be used to repatriate blocked funds, suppose that the Mexican subsidiary of IBM is unable to repatriate its peso profits. It may lend the money to the Mexican subsidiary of AT&T; AT&T would, in turn, lend dollars to IBM in the United States. As a result, IBM would have the use of dollars in the United States while AT&T would obtain pesos in Mexico.

Payment Adjustments.

There are many different forms of payments by foreign subsidiaries to the parent company. These payments can be adjusted to remove blocked funds. Dividend payments are by far the most important form of fund flows from foreign subsidiaries to the parent company, accounting for approximately 50 percent of all remittances to U.S. companies. Money-market countries recognize dividend payments as a method by which the earnings of a business firm can be distributed to the stockholders of the firm. Not all nations, however, allow dividends of local companies to be paid in hard currencies to the foreign parent companies. Countries characterized by balance-of-payments problems and foreign exchange shortages frequently place restrictions on the payment of dividends to foreign companies.

Two methods to adjust dividend payments in the case of these restrictions have become increasingly popular. They artificially inflate the value of the local investment base because the level of dividend payments depends on the company's capital. First, the parent company can magnify its subsidiary's registered capital by investing in used equipment whose value has been artificially inflated. Second, the parent company may acquire a bankrupt local firm at a large discount from book value and then merge it with its subsidiary on the basis of the failed firm's book value. Of course, this action would raise the subsidiary's equity base.

In addition to dividends, royalties and fees are also the important components of fund flows from foreign subsidiaries to the parent company. Royalties are paid to use certain technologies, patents, and trademarks. Fees are compensations for managerial services and technical assistance. Such royalties and fees are unique and thus do not have a reference in market value. Most host governments look with more favor on payments for royalties and fees than on payments for profit remittances. Hence, it is easier for multinational firms to repatriate blocked funds through inflated royalty and fee payments rather than through any other form of payment.

Unbundling Fund Transfers.

Multinational companies frequently unbundle remittances into separate flows for such purposes as technology fees and management fees rather than lump all flows under the heading of profit (dividend). Host countries are then more likely to perceive the so-called "remittance of profits" as essential purchases of specific services that would benefit the host country. Unbundling makes it possible for multinational companies to recover funds from their affiliates without irritating host country sensitivities with large dividend drains. This form of fund transfers is particularly useful for business operations in socialist and Islamic countries where interest and dividend profits are regarded unfavorably.

Cash Management

Cash gives a multinational company the ability to pay bills as they come due, but it is not an earning asset. Thus, it is very important to determine an optimal level of investment in cash. The major sources of cash inflows are dividends, royalties and fees, cash sales and collections on accounts receivable, depreciation, sales of new securities, loans from banks or nonbank financial institutions, and advance cash payments on contracts. In contrast, cash outflows are necessary for interest and dividend payments, retirement of debt and other securities, income tax payments, payments on accounts payable, wages and salaries, and purchases of fixed assets. The term **cash management** is used here to mean optimization of cash flows and investment of excess cash. International cash management is complex because of different laws among countries, exchange rate fluctuations, and many other constraints.

Companies prefer to hold cash rather than other forms of assets for three main reasons: the transaction motive, the precautionary motive, and the speculative motive. The transaction motive holds that cash balances are held partly in anticipation of day-to-day cash disbursements. The precautionary motive suggests that cash balances are held partly as protection against deviations from budgeted cash flows. The speculative motive relates to the holding of cash in order to take advantage of profit-making opportunities.

Objectives of Cash Management

General principles that apply to cash management on an international basis are frequently similar to those utilized by many companies domestically. The overall cash management objective of any corporation is to minimize the cash balance within the company with the goal of optimizing corporate fund utilization. However, the parameters within which multinational companies operate are broader and more complex than those of purely domestic companies. Furthermore, the relationships among these parameters are constantly changing. Hence, those responsible for cash management on an international basis must consider new variables such as tax concepts, governmental restrictions on intracompany fund flows, differences in cultures, and foreign exchange rates.

More specifically, international cash managers try to attain the traditional objectives of domestic cash management on a global basis: (1) to minimize the cost of funds, (2) to improve liquidity, (3) to reduce risks, and (4) to improve the return on investment.

First, with interest rates of more than 10 percent in many countries, considerable savings are possible when the cost of funds is lowered. Multinational companies should attempt to reduce their overall cost of funds by increasing internal funds and reducing borrowings.

Second, international cash managers must attempt to improve liquidity on a global basis. Certainly, it is difficult to improve liquidity on a worldwide basis because government regulations prohibit the free transfer of funds. But multinational firms could use centralized cash management and electronic fund transfers to improve their overall liquidity.

Third, international cash management involves a variety of risks such as political, economic, and exchange risks. Insurance, careful negotiations, forward contracts, and currency options may be used to reduce these risks.

Fourth, a variety of ratios, such as return on investment and return on net worth, are often used to measure performance. The improvement of financial performance is perhaps the most important aspect of treasury management.

Floats

To carry out its operations, a multinational company causes a steady flow of funds to take place among its family members. These fund flows cannot avoid the problem of float. Float refers to the status of funds in the process of collection. Float, from a domestic point of view, represents only the temporary loss of income on funds that are tied up in the process of collection. In international operations, however, the problem of float is twofold: (1) the loss of income on the funds tied up during the longer transfer process and (2) their exposure to foreign exchange risk during the transfer period. Nearly all aspects of both international and domestic cash management are associated with the concept of float. Thus, we ought to understand float to effectively evaluate the collection and disbursement procedures of any cash management system. For purposes of measurement and analysis, we can break down float into five categories:

1. Invoicing float refers to funds tied up in the process of preparing invoices. Because this float is largely under the direct control of the company, it can be reduced through more efficient clerical procedures.
2. Mail float includes funds tied up from the time customers mail their remittance checks until the company receives them.
3. Processing float consists of funds tied up in the process of sorting and recording remittance checks until they can be deposited in the bank. Like invoicing float, this float is under the company's internal control and thus can be reduced through more efficient clerical procedures.
4. Transit float involves funds tied up from the time remittance checks are deposited until these funds become usable to the company. This float occurs because it takes several days for deposited checks to clear through the commercial banking system.
5. Disbursing float refers to funds available in a company's bank account until these funds are actually disbursed by the company.

Collection and Disbursement of Funds

The overall efficiency of international cash management depends on various collection and disbursement policies. To maximize available cash, a multinational company must accelerate its collection process and delay its payments. Hence, it must consider these two policies simultaneously to improve its overall cash management efficiency. Significant benefits exist because long delays are possible in collecting accounts receivable and in paying accounts payable. Delays of seven to ten business days are common to allow for transit and other floats across national borders. Effective collection and disbursement policies have become even more important in recent years because of high interest rates, wide fluctuations in foreign exchange rates, and widespread credit restrictions.

Acceleration of Collections.
International cash managers should use every means in their power to gain control over incoming funds as quickly as possible after the collection process starts. The principal goals of speeding the collection process are to reduce floats, to minimize the investment in accounts receivable, and to reduce banking and other transaction fees.

A multinational company can use a number of useful techniques to speed the collection process: lock boxes, cable remittances, electronic fund transfers, and the use of the Society for Worldwide Interbank Financial Telecommunications (SWIFT). The SWIFT is an interbank communication network founded in 1973 to move messages for financial transactions.

Delay of Payments.
In addition to accelerating collections, international cash managers can produce a faster turnover of cash by controlling disbursements efficiently. By delaying disbursements, a company keeps cash on hand for longer periods. When the firm purchases goods on credit, it must delay its payments until the last day in order to have the additional funds for the extra time. A multinational company can delay its payments in a number of ways: (1) mail, (2) more frequent requisitions, and (3) floats.

First, in spite of the widespread availability of electronic fund transfer networks, a surprisingly large number of cross-border payments are still made by mail. It is not unusual for regular air mail to take seven days or more to reach its ultimate destination.

Second, a parent can use large sums of money on a temporary basis because of frequent requisitions of funds by foreign subsidiaries from the parent's central office and the centralized disbursements. For example, if a firm switches its requisition policy from monthly requisitions to weekly requisitions, it can keep cash on hand as much as three weeks longer.

Third, the use of float is yet another method used to maximize the availability of cash. At any given time checks written by a firm have yet to be cleared through the banking system because that process takes a number of days. Thus, it is possible for a firm to have a negative balance on its checkbook but a positive balance on its bankbook for a number of days.

The Cost of Cash Management.
A multinational company may use various collection and disbursement procedures to improve the efficiency of its cash management. Because these two types of procedures constitute two sides of the same coin, they have a joint effect on the overall efficiency of cash management. Accelerating collections and delaying disbursements involve additional costs. Hence, a company must determine how far it should go to make its cash operations more efficient. In theory, a company should adopt various collection and disbursement methods as long as their marginal returns exceed their marginal expenses.

The value of careful cash management depends on the opportunity cost of funds invested in cash. The opportunity cost of these funds in turn depends on the company's required rate of return on short-term investments. For example, assume that the adoption of a lock-box system is expected to reduce the investment in cash by $100,000. If a company earns 11 percent on short-term investments, the opportunity cost of the current system is $11,000. Hence, if the cost of the lock-box system is less than $11,000, it can be adopted to improve earnings performance.

Cash Centers

Cash management can be centralized, regionalized, or decentralized on a company level. Decentralization permits subsidiaries to use excess cash in any way they see fit. While this is popular among subsidiary managers, decentralization does not allow a multinational company to utilize its most liquid asset on a widespread basis. Effective cash management requires that executives predetermine cash flow centers. For example, a multinational company should not choose to hold cash in a country which has violent political upheavals and rampant inflation. Rather, it should transfer idle local cash balances as quickly as possible to a stable environment.

Centralized cash management calls for each local subsidiary to hold at the local level the minimum cash balance for transaction purposes. All funds not needed for transaction purposes are channeled to a central cash center. This cash center is responsible for placing a central pool of funds in those currencies and money market instruments which will best serve the needs of the multinational company on a worldwide basis.

Advantages of Centralized Cash Management.

Centralized cash management has a number of advantages over decentralized cash management:

1. The central cash center can collect information more quickly and make better decisions on the relative strengths and weaknesses of various currencies. Such information and decisions are necessary if we wish to invest a central pool of funds most profitably.
2. Funds held in a cash center can quickly be returned to a subsidiary with cash shortages by wire transfer or by providing a worldwide banking system with full collateral in hard currency. The central pool of funds eliminates the possibility that one subsidiary will borrow at higher rates while another holds surplus funds idle or invests them at lower rates.
3. By holding all precautionary balances in a central cash center, a multinational company can reduce the total pool without any loss in the level of production. This is due to a synergistic effect which is said to exist when the whole is worth more than the mere sum of its parts. This effect has been frequently defined as "2 + 2 = 5."

Before any cash is remitted to a central cash center, local cash needs must be properly assessed. The proper assessment of local cash needs in relation to the cash center involves the following steps:

1. Cash budgets should be prepared to know anticipated cash outflows and inflows at key future dates.

2. Each subsidiary must have effective cash collection procedures which would speed cash flows into the company.
3. Each subsidiary must also have systematic cash disbursement procedures which would delay cash flows out of the company.
4. Each subsidiary should estimate when and how much surplus cash it will have.
5. Each subsidiary should also estimate when and how much shortage it will have.
6. The multinational company must develop necessary steps for cash mobilization such as a management information system and a cash transfer system; it should have the clear responsibility for making cash transfer decisions.

Factors Affecting the Location of Cash Centers.

Many factors affect the location of cash centers. From an economic point of view, idle funds should move toward those locations which provide the highest profitability and safety. These funds are accumulated in cash centers for temporary investments prior to reassignment elsewhere. Thus, a multinational company must choose those locations from which funds can again be readily assigned to other places in the world.

Perhaps the most important factor affecting the location of cash centers is the local government's political stability and its attitude toward foreign-based companies. Local laws may require partial ownership of alien companies by nationals of the host country or by the government itself. Hostility of the courts toward foreign business claims and disclosure requirements may all work against a subsidiary operating as a cash center. Aggregate tax levels and penalty rates on excessive dividend remittances also play an important role in the selection of cash centers.

A multinational company must also consider several economic factors when selecting cash centers. These cash centers should be located in countries whose currencies are stable in value and readily convertible into other currencies. It is extremely difficult for financial managers to predict the exact timing of a change in the exchange rate. Most governments take all possible measures to avoid speculation against their currencies. It is critical, therefore, to engage in hedging operations to assure that foreign exchange losses can be minimized. Thus, the existence of an active forward market and the availability of suitable money market instruments for the deployment of temporary excess resources are important.

Cash centers are usually located in the major financial centers of the world such as New York and London. Brussels has become popular as a cash center for companies operating in Europe. Other popular locations for cash centers are tax-haven countries such as Luxembourg, the Bahamas, Bermuda, and the Netherlands. These countries offer most of the prerequisites for a corporate cash center: political and economic stability, freely convertible currency, access to international communications, and well-defined legal procedures.

Investing Excess Funds

Along with optimization of cash flows, the other key function of international cash management is to make certain that excess funds are wisely invested. This section discusses three types of portfolio management and portfolio guidelines.

Portfolio Management.   There are at least three types of portfolio management available to international cash managers. First, multinational companies can optimize cash flows worldwide with a zero portfolio. All excess funds of subsidiaries are remitted to the parent and then used to pay the parent's short-term debts. Second, they can centralize cash management in the third countries such as tax-haven countries and invest funds on marketable securities. Third, they can centralize cash management at headquarters with subsidiaries holding only minimum amounts of cash for transaction purposes.

Portfolio Guidelines.   Most surplus funds are temporary. Thus, if multinational companies invest funds in marketable securities such as Treasury bills, they should follow sound portfolio guidelines. First, instruments in the short-term investment portfolio should be diversified to maximize the yield for a given amount of risk or to minimize the risk for a given amount of return. Second, for companies that hold marketable securities for near-future needs of liquidity, marketability considerations are of major importance. Third, the maturity of the investment should be tailored to the company's projected cash needs. Fourth, the securities chosen should be limited to those with a minimum risk of default. Fifth, the portfolio should be reviewed daily to decide what new investments will be made and which securities will be liquidated.

Accounts Receivable Management

The level of accounts receivable depends upon the volume of credit sales and the average collection period. These two variables, in turn, depend upon credit standards, credit terms, and collection policy. As management moves from customers who are more likely to pay their bills to customers who are less likely to pay their bills, sales tend to increase. However, a lenient credit policy is also likely to increase bad debt losses and investments in accounts receivable. In theory, a company should liberalize its credit policy to the point where the marginal profit on its increased sales equals the marginal cost of credit.

Because money has a time value, accounts receivable have a cost in terms of foregone interest. Nevertheless, many multinational companies frequently decide to sell for credit in order to expand sales volume and profits. If sales are made on the basis of drafts on importers, trade acceptances or bankers' acceptances are created, and these may be discounted at banks or sold in the money market. In addition, in many countries the accumulation of accounts receivable is even highly desirable because government agencies extend export credit at preferential interest rates.

Multinational accounts receivable are created by two separate types of transaction—sales to outside the corporate group and intracompany sales. We must consider these two types of transactions separately because their economic consequences are different. One truly unique problem area of multinational accounts receivable management has to do with the risk of currency value changes. The accounts receivable manager should understand this risk and take all necessary actions to minimize it.

Sales to Independent Customers

Management of accounts receivable from independent buyers involves two types of decisions—the denomination of currency to be used for payments and the terms of payment. Domestic sales are always denominated in the local currency. In contrast, export sales can be denominated in the currency of the exporter, the currency of the importer, or a third country currency. The exporter would prefer to price and to invoice in the strongest currency, while the importer would prefer to pay in the weakest currency. Competition or custom will frequently resolve the problem, but the usual result is a trade-off between the terms of payment and the denomination of currency. For example, an exporter may grant a longer credit period in exchange for an importer's promise to pay for its purchase in a hard currency.

Many factors affect the terms of payment, but perhaps one of the most important is the strength of a currency denominated in a transaction. If payments are to be made in a soft currency, accounts receivable should be collected as quickly as possible in order to minimize the possibility of exchange losses between the sale date and the collection date. Sales made in a hard currency may be permitted to remain outstanding somewhat longer. If the devaluation of its home currency is imminent, an exporter might want to encourage slow payment of its hard currency receivables.

Currency Value Problems

Intracompany sales differ from sales to independent customers in that little concern is given to credit standing and that the timing of the payments may depend upon a company's desire to allocate resources rather than normal payment schedules. Such sales are necessary for many reasons. Subsidiaries produce different products and often sell to each other. Like the location of cash balances, the location of intracompany receivables and their amounts are a policy problem of the multinational company when it allocates its resources on a global basis. If a parent company desires to transfer funds to its affiliate, it may do so by having the affiliate delay the payment for intracompany purchases.

Because intracompany sales usually cross national boundaries, companies are concerned about currency values. Changes in exchange rates between the sales date and the collection date create accounts-receivable risks. There are several ways that the accounts receivable manager may reduce these risks.

Leading and Lagging. If subsidiaries are located in countries whose currencies are likely to devalue or to float downward, a parent company may instruct its subsidiaries to pay for their purchases more quickly (leading). In contrast, if subsidiaries are located in countries whose currencies are expected to upvalue or to float upward, the parent company may instruct its subsidiaries to delay payments (lagging). It is important to note that early payments and later payments in conjunction with intracompany sales are feasible only when the parent company owns 100 percent of its various affiliates.

Currency Denominations. A seller may require that all payments are to be made in hard currencies. This requirement assures the seller that payments are to be made in currencies likely to face little or no devaluation on the foreign exchange market. In certain instances, a multinational company refuses credit sales denominated in foreign currencies altogether. Multinational companies may buy currency credit insurance. For example, American exporters can purchase protection from the Foreign Credit Insurance Association or the Export-Import Bank described in Chapter 10.

Using Factors. Managers also use factors to minimize accounts-receivable risks from changes in exchange rates between the sale date and the collection date. Factoring is a process whereby a company sells its accounts receivable on a nonrecourse basis. Nonrecourse means that the factor takes the loss if the customers of its client do not pay their accounts. In addition to risk bearing, the factor performs a number of additional services such as credit checking, bookkeeping, and the collection of accounts. U.S. banks have been responsible for the rapid expansion of international factoring. In 1963, the Comptroller of the Currency ruled that factoring is a proper area for national bank expansion. Since then, many American banks have entered the factoring business not only in the United States but also in Europe and the rest of the world.

Inventory Management

The overall efficiency of inventory management is extremely important for two reasons. First, inventories represent a significant segment of total assets for most business firms. Second, they are the least liquid of current assets; thus, errors in inventory management are not quickly remedied. Hence, for the last few decades the greatest improvements within the area of current asset management have been made in inventory control and investment. The size of inventories in relation to sales has been greatly reduced with the application of computers and new inventory management systems.

Many U.S. and European multinational companies have recently adopted a Japanese inventory management system known as the "just-in-time" approach. This inventory management system requires that when orders are placed, specific goods are ordered along with an exact delivery date. The goal on the part of the company is to reduce inventory balances to practically zero. Under such an arrangement, it is not uncommon for suppliers to build facilities close to their major customers in order to ensure a ready supply of inventory. For example, many Japanese auto suppliers have established their production facilities close to Japanese transplants in the United States and Canada. In essence, the customer is passing the inventory balance problem back to the supplier.

Determining the Amount of Inventory

The level of sales, the length of the production cycle, and the durability of the product are major determinants of investment in inventory. In domestic or one-country operations, companies attempt to balance their inventory level in such a way that both carrying costs and stockout costs are minimized. However, differentials in the costs of production and storage in different countries allow the multinational company to maintain more flexible inventory policies. For instance, a multinational company can take advantage of lower costs in a particular country by shifting its production or storage function to that country. These advantages are offset by such disadvantages as tariff levels and other forms of import restrictions used by governments.

Given the fact that many foreign affiliates operate under inflationary conditions, a multinational company must determine whether to buy inventory in advance or to delay purchase until the inventory is actually needed. Advance purchases involve such carrying costs as interest on funds tied up in inventory, insurance premiums, storage costs, and taxes. Later purchases increase the possibility of higher costs either through inflation or devaluation. Inflation increases the costs of locally purchased items, and devaluation increases the costs of imported items.

Despite the desire for optimizing inventory levels, many companies which rely on imported inventories maintain over-stocked inventory accounts. The fears of continued inflation, raw materials shortages, and other environmental constraints induce companies to maintain high overseas inventory levels rather than risk curtailment of their overseas operations. Additional environmental constraints include anticipated import bans in foreign countries, anticipated delivery delays caused by dock strikes and slowdowns, the lack of sophisticated production and inventory control systems, and increased difficulty in obtaining foreign exchange for inventory purchases.

Protective Measures Against Inflation and Devaluation

Many foreign affiliates operate under inflationary economic conditions. Thus, it is important for multinational companies to determine the effects of an increasing local price level or devaluation on their inventory management policies. The type of inventory normally stocked by subsidiaries is of importance in this decision. Some subsidiaries rely heavily on imported inventories, while other subsidiaries depend heavily upon locally acquired inventories. Some other subsidiaries may rely almost equally on imported and locally acquired inventories.

If a subsidiary relies heavily on imported goods, it should seek to build its inventory of supplies, equipment, and components in advance of an expected devaluation because devaluation at a later date effectively increases the costs of imported goods. For example, if a host country declares a 10 percent devaluation of its currency in relation to the dollar, a subsidiary should pay 10 percent more local currency for the same amount of imported goods from the United States.

On the other hand, if a subsidiary depends heavily upon locally purchased goods, it should seek to minimize its inventory of supplies, equipment, and components because devaluation at a later date effectively reduces the dollar value of inventories acquired locally. If inventories are translated at current rather than historical exchange rates, a 10 percent devaluation of the local currency against the dollar would reduce the dollar value of its inventory by 10 percent.

Finally, if a subsidiary relies almost equally on imported inventories and locally purchased inventories, it should seek to reduce its locally acquired inventories and to increase its imported inventories in advance of an expected devaluation. However, if accurate forecasts of devaluation are not possible, a company should maintain the same amount of imported goods and locally purchased goods to avoid foreign exchange risks because a devaluation would affect both types of inventories equally, and thus the subsidiary would experience neither a gain nor a loss.

Pricing

Up to this point, our discussion has centered on preventive measures that multinational companies may take to reduce risks associated with devaluation. Additional action can be taken in pricing to reduce these risks.

Example 12-1.   Assume that 10 American-made radios have been imported into Korea which has subsequently devalued its currency by 100 percent. The original exchange rate was KW50 per $1, the original cost was KW1,000 per radio, and the original selling price was KW1,500 per radio.

The Korean subsidiary has a choice of two basic policies with respect to price: (1) it can maintain the original price of its inventory in an effort to undercut competition, or (2) it can increase the price of its inventory in order to earn all or part of the original dollar profit expected. Table 12-1 shows the effects of both policies on the Korean subsidiary. Maintenance of the old price will result in a dollar loss of $50 on the sale of the 10 radios even if local figures indicate a profit of KW5,000. If the subsidiary increases its selling price to the dollar equivalent of the original selling price, it will earn

Table 12-1
Effect of Pricing on Profits

Exchange Rate	(1) Maintain Old Price		(2) Adjust Price	
	Korean Currency	Dollars	Korean Currency	Dollars
KW100 (now) Sold for	KW15,000	$150	KW30,000	$300
KW50 (old) Cost	KW10,000	$200	KW10,000	$200
Profit	KW 5,000	($ 50)	KW20,000	$100

a profit of $100. However, it is important to note that this assumes the Korean government does not maintain price controls. Although there are no price controls imposed by the Korean government, a price increase of the magnitude indicated in policy 2 would perhaps discourage some sales. If the price elasticity of demand for the merchandise is extremely high, the local market may not bear the higher price. Nevertheless, a certain level of price rise is required to prevent a deterioration of converted earnings.

Another important question is whether a subsidiary should continue to import that type of merchandise. If local sales prices can be raised to cover the current higher dollar import prices, imports should continue. If not, imports could cease. Although the decision not to import merchandise does not cause any transaction loss, it may result in idle production and an eventual operating loss due to the surrender of that particular foreign market. If possible, multinational companies should price their inventory goods in such a way that sales revenues include the sum of the increase in replacement cost of the inventory sold, the loss in real value of the monetary profit expected, and increased income taxes.

Working Capital Practices

Current asset management is important not only because it involves the largest portion of a financial manager's time but also because current assets represent more than half the total assets of most companies. In addition, there is a close relationship between sales growth and the level of current assets. For example, increases in credit sales require more accounts receivable and inventories. Finally, companies may minimize their investments in fixed assets through leases, but it is practically impossible to avoid an investment in current assets.

Despite the importance of international working capital management, literature on this topic is rather limited for a number of reasons. First, decisions on working capital are relatively routine and frequent. Second, unlike capital investment decisions, these routine decisions on working capital are easily reversible. Third, working capital management requires cash flow projections; however, cash flows cannot be forecasted by the financial manager alone. In other words, financial aspects of a decision are sometimes concealed by marketing (credit policy) and production (inventory management) which have a major impact on a company's cash flows. Still, we can cite a few empirical studies on working capital practices.

Objectives of Working Capital Management.

James Gentry and others (1979) surveyed 579 top executives in Belgium, France, India, and the United States to collect information on working capital management. They isolated four objectives of working capital management and ranked them according to the responses of the 579 respondents. Approximately 55 percent of these managers reported that the most important objective of working capital management was to provide various current assets and short-term credit necessary to support anticipated sales. Another 21 percent indicated that the most important objective of working capital management was to minimize the investment in current assets. About 14 percent stated that it was to evaluate changes in current assets as an investment decision and to minimize the cost of short-term credit. The remaining 9 percent believed that working capital management should provide a financial buffer in order to minimize the effect of wide fluctuations in sales and production.

A review of the literature indicates a lack of consensus on the primary objective of working capital management. However, the study by Games Gentry (1979) and others indicated that an overwhelming majority of the respondents regard "supporting expected sales" to be the primary purpose of working capital management. No other objective rated close to this one in terms of a number one goal, thus making it a clear-cut choice as the primary objective of working capital management.

Working Capital Practices by U.S. and Japanese Firms.

Empirical studies revealed striking differences in working capital management between U.S. and Japanese manufacturing companies. The cost of short-term bank loans is lower in Japan than in the United States mainly because Japanese banks have more surplus funds than U.S. banks. Consequently, Japanese companies rely more heavily on short-term bank loans for working capital requirements than U.S. companies. In addition, Japanese companies tend to maintain lower levels of net working capital than U.S. companies because of unique practices such as the "just-in-time" inventory system.

A study by Sadahiko Suzuki and Richard Wright (1985) found that the interest rate of short-term bank loans in Japan is lower than that of short-term bank loans in the United States. First, the Bank of Japan provides major industries with loans at favorable rates through commercial banks. Second, the lenders know that the government protects business. Third, the size of Japanese banks is larger than that of U.S. banks. Fourth, Japan has more capital than the United States.

Another working capital study by Ravi Sarathy and Sangit Chatterjee (1984) revealed significant differences in financial structure between large U.S. and Japanese manufacturing companies. Japanese firms rely heavily on bank funded short-term debt. In addition, there are low levels of net working capital among Japanese firms. Japanese firms also differ in working capital management, with lower levels of inventory, higher levels of accounts receivable, and more than twice as much cash as U.S. firms.

Summary

Techniques of international working capital management are essentially similar to those employed domestically, but additional variables are involved. In domestic operations, all transactions are subject to the same rules of movement, accumulation, and reinvestment, but these rules vary when transactions occur across national boundaries. These additional variables include political, tax, foreign exchange, and other economic constraints.

To manage current assets from a global perspective, a multinational company must carefully evaluate various constraints such as foreign exchange rate fluctuations and base ultimate decisions about the transfer of funds on this evaluation. The company then must establish clear lines of accountability for asset deterioration and exchange losses. Finally, a workable system of controls must be developed to help measure the performance of working capital management.

Cash management can be centralized or decentralized on a company level. Although decentralization is popular among subsidiary managers, it does not permit the multinational company to use its most liquid asset on a widespread basis. Effective cash management requires the establishment of cash centers. This system calls for each local subsidiary to hold at the local level the minimum cash balance for transaction purposes. All funds not needed for transaction purposes are channeled to a central cash center. This cash center has responsibility for placing the central pool of funds in such currencies and money market instruments which will best serve the needs of the multinational company on a worldwide basis.

Multinational accounts receivable are created by two separate types of transactions: sales to independent customers and intracompany sales. Management of accounts receivable from independent customers involves the denomination of currency to be used for payments and the terms of payment. Intracompany sales differ from sales to independent customers in that little concern is given to credit standing and that the timing of the payments may depend upon a company's desire to allocate resources rather than normal payment schedules. One truly unique area of multinational accounts receivable management has to do with the risk of currency value changes. The accounts receivable manager should understand this risk and take all necessary actions to minimize such a risk.

The overall efficiency of inventory management is extremely important for two reasons. First, inventories represent a significant segment of total assets for most business firms. Second, they are the least liquid of current assets and thus errors in inventory management are not quickly remedied.

When foreign subsidiaries operate under inflationary conditions, it is important to determine whether to purchase inventory in advance or to delay purchase until the inventory is actually needed. Advance purchases involve such carrying costs as interest on funds tied up in inventory, insurance premiums, and storage costs. Later purchases involve the possibility of higher costs either through inflation or devaluation. Thus, the inventory manager should compute the optimal trade-off between high carrying costs and higher purchase costs for inventory.

Questions

1. What are the economic constraints of current asset management for multinational companies? Why do multinational companies face such constraints?

2. Why are various arbitrage opportunities available to multinational companies in their working capital management?

3. What techniques are available to a company with operating subsidiaries in many countries to optimize on cash and marketable securities?

4. What are the advantages of leads and lags over direct loans?

5. List the two major functions of international cash management.

6. Why is the problem of floats in international operations more serious than in domestic operations?

7. Explain the three types of portfolio management available to international cash managers.

8. Why should a firm invest in a portfolio of foreign currencies instead of just a single foreign currency?

9. Standard advice given to exporters is to invoice in their own currency or a strong currency. Critically analyze this recommendation.

10. Under what conditions should companies maintain over-stocked inventory accounts?

11. Explain the importance of current asset management.

12. Why is literature on international working capital management rather limited?

References

Anvari, M., "Efficient Scheduling of Cross-Border Cash Transfers," *Financial Management*, Summer 1986, pp. 40-9.

Bokos, W. J., and A. P. Clinkard, "Multilateral Netting," *Journal of Cash Management*, June/July 1983, pp. 24-34.

Cody, B. J., "Reducing the Costs and Risks of Trading Foreign Exchange," *Business Review*, Federal Reserve Bank of Philadelphia, November/December 1990, pp. 13-23.

Cotner, J., and N. Seitz, "A Simplified Approach to Short-Term International Diversification," *Financial Review*, May 1987, pp. 249-66.

Gentry, J. A., D. R. Mehta, S. K. Bhattacharyya, R. Cobbaut, and J. L. Scaringella, "An International Study of Management Perceptions of the Working Capital Process," *Journal of International Business Studies*, Spring/Summer 1979, pp. 28-38.

Madura, J., "Utilizing Currency Portfolios to Mitigate Exchange Rate Risk," *Columbia Journal of World Business*, Spring 1984, pp. 96-9.

Sarathy, R., and S. Chatterjee, "The Divergence of Japanese and U.S. Corporate Financial Structure," *Journal of International Business Studies*, Winter 1984, pp. 85-92.

Shapiro, A. C., *Multinational Financial Management*, Boston: Allyn and Bacon, 1992, pp. 326-53.

Smith, K. V., ed., *Readings in the Management of Working Capital*, St. Paul, MN: West Publishing, 1980).

Srinivasan, V., and Y. H. Kim, "Payments Netting in International Cash Management: A Network Optimization Approach," *Journal of International Business Studies*, Summer 1986, pp. 1-20.

Suzuki, S., and R. W. Wright, "Financial Structure and Bankruptcy in Japanese Companies," *Journal of International Business Studies*, Spring 1985, pp. 97-110.

13

International Portfolio Diversification

Harry Markowitz's (1959) and James Tobin's (1958) highly respectable mean–variance model employs two basic measures: an index of expected return (mean) and an index of risk (variance or standard deviation). The expected value for a portfolio of securities is simply the sum of the individual returns for securities that make up the portfolio. The standard deviation as a measure of risk for the portfolio is not easily measured. In many business situations, risks of individual securities tend to offset each other. Thus, with successful diversification, the investor may select a portfolio having fewer risks than the sum of the risks of individual securities.

There was a time when investment opportunities stopped at national borders. However, today we assume a unified and integrated world capital market when analyzing international finance and macroeconomics. Indeed, recent national policy discussions rely on this premise stimulated by global integration of capital markets. Thus, many countries have internationalized their capital markets since 1980.

National capital markets have changed to an integrated global capital market, often followed by widespread international multiple listings of securities. An economic revolution is taking place in many parts of the world as countries deregulate financial markets. Diversification among risky securities in a particular country reduces risk. Yet, this potential is rather limited because most companies usually earn more during booms and less during recessions, which suggests that international portfolio diversification reduces additional risk. In fact, gains from such diversification have become so commonplace in recent years that additional empirical studies are not needed to confirm the benefits of international diversification. Still this chapter describes key diversification terminologies and the gains from international diversification.

Key Terminologies

In the real world, no company or individual invests everything in a single asset. Accordingly, it is useful to consider the risk and return of a particular asset in conjunction with its counterparts in existing assets or new investment opportunities. Portfolio theory deals with selecting investment projects that minimize risk for a given rate of return or that maximize the rate of return for a given degree of risk.

Risk Analysis: Standard Deviation

Two conflicts from investment in assets are that: (1) very few financial variables are known with certainty and (2) investors are basically risk averters. Risk is variability in the return generated by investment in an asset. For example, investors buy common stock hoping to receive growing dividends and an appreciating stock price. However, neither the dividend stream nor price appreciation is certain or guaranteed. Thus, investors evaluate risk before they invest in common stock.

Risk may be measured by the dispersion of alternative returns around the average return. Standard deviation, being a measure of dispersion, fits nicely as a technique for measuring risk. To determine the standard deviation of, say, monthly returns for an asset, we may use the following formula:

$$\sigma = \sqrt{\frac{\Sigma (R - \overline{R})^2}{n - 1}} \qquad (13\text{-}1)$$

where:

σ = standard deviation
R = monthly returns
$\overline{R}$ = average monthly return

To illustrate, assume that the monthly returns of a common stock are 0.40, 0.50, and 0.60 for three months. The average monthly return is 0.50, and the standard deviation is 0.10.

Standard deviation is an absolute measure of dispersion. A relative measure of dispersion is the coefficient of variation, which is the standard deviation divided by the average return. In other words, it shows the amount of risk per dollar of average return when returns are expressed in dollars. In general, the coefficient of variation measures risk better than the standard deviation for assets whose returns are stated in dollars. Standard deviation should be used to measure risk only for those assets whose returns are stated as percentages.

Capital Asset Pricing Model

The capital asset pricing model (CAPM) assumes that the total risk of a security consists of systematic (undiversifiable) risk and unsystematic (diversifiable) risk. Systematic risk reflects overall market risk—risk that is common to all securities. Common causes of systematic risk include changes in the overall economy, tax reform by Congress, and changes in national energy supply. Because it is common to all stocks, systematic risk cannot be eliminated by diversification.

Unsystematic risk is unique to a particular company. Some causes of unsystematic risk include wildcat strikes affecting only the company, new competitors producing essentially the same product, and technological breakthroughs making an existing product obsolete. Because it is unique to a particular stock, unsystematic risk can be eliminated by diversification.

Within an international context, systematic risk relates to such global events as worldwide recessions, world wars, and changes in world energy supply. Unsystematic risk relates to such national events as expropriation, currency controls, inflation, and exchange-rate changes.

If a market is in equilibrium, the expected rate of an individual security (j) is stated as follows:

$$R_j = R_f + (R_m - R_f)\beta_j \qquad (13\text{-}2)$$

where:

R_j = expected rate of return on security j
R_f = riskless rate of interest
R_m = expected rate of return on the market portfolio, which is a group of risky securities such as Standard & Poor's 500 stocks
β_j = systematic risk of security j

This equation, known as the **security market line**, consists of the riskless rate of interest (R_f) and a risk premium [$(R_m - R_f)\beta_j$]. It is important to understand that beta—$\beta_j = [(R_j - R_f)/(R_m - R_f)]$—is an index of volatility in the excess return of one security relative to that of a market portfolio. In a portfolio context, the security market line constitutes various portfolios which combine a riskless security and a portfolio of risky securities.

Correlation Coefficients

Portfolio effect is defined as the extent to which unsystematic risks of individual securities tend to offset each other. Portfolio effect depends not only on the standard deviation of each security but also on the degree of correlation between two or more securities. The correlation coefficient measures the degree of correlation between two securities and varies from zero (no correlation, or independence) to ±1.0 (perfect correlation).

A correlation coefficient of −1.0 means that the two sets of returns for two securities tend to move in exactly opposite directions. Assume that a boom occurs. Security A is expected to earn $100, while security B is expected to earn nothing. In contrast, if a recession occurs, security A would earn nothing, whereas security B would earn $100. Consequently, these two securities are perfectly negatively correlated. Diversification can totally eliminate unsystematic risk when two securities are perfectly negatively correlated.

A correlation coefficient of +1.0 means that two sets of returns for two securities tend to move in exactly the same direction. Suppose that a boom occurs. Securities X and Y would earn an equal amount of $200. But if a recession occurs, they would yield an equal amount of $50. Then we can say that these two projects are perfectly positively correlated. In this case, diversification would not reduce unsystematic risk at all.

A correlation coefficient of zero means that the two sets of returns for two securities are uncorrelated or independent of each other. In this scenario, diversification would reduce unsystematic risk considerably.

Because the degree of correlation among securities depends on economic factors, most pairs of domestic securities have a correlation coefficient of between 0 and +1.0. Most stock prices are likely to be high during a boom, while they are likely to be low during a recession. But different product lines and different geographic markets tend to have a relatively low degree of correlation to each other. Thus, international diversification may eliminate unsystematic risk and reduce domestic systematic risk considerably.

Portfolio Return and Risk

Portfolio return is the expected return of a portfolio of securities. The expected portfolio return is simply a weighted average of the expected returns of the securities which make up the portfolio. One way to measure the benefits of international diversification is to consider the expected return and standard deviation of return for a portfolio which consists of U.S. and foreign portfolios. Such a portfolio return may be computed as follows:

$$R_p = x_{us}R_{us} + x_{fn}R_{fn} \qquad (13\text{--}3)$$

where:

R_p = portfolio return
x_{us} = percentage of funds invested in the U.S. portfolio
R_{us} = expected return on the U.S. portfolio
x_{fn} = percentage of funds invested in the foreign portfolio
R_{fn} = expected return on the foreign portfolio

The standard deviation of a portfolio measures the riskiness of the portfolio. The standard deviation of a two–security portfolio can be calculated as follows:

$$\sigma_p = \sqrt{x_{us}^2 \sigma_{us}^2 + x_{fn}^2 \sigma_{fn}^2 + 2x_{us} x_{fn} \sigma_{us,fn} \sigma_{us} \sigma_{fn}} \qquad (13\text{-}4)$$

where:

σ_p = portfolio standard deviation
σ_{us} = standard deviation of the U.S. portfolio
σ_{fn} = standard deviation of the foreign portfolio
$\sigma_{us,fn}$ = correlation coefficient between the returns on the U.S. and foreign portfolios

Example 13-1. Assume that an international portfolio consisting of a U.S. portfolio and a foreign portfolio calls for a total investment of $10 million. A U.S. portfolio requires an investment of $4 million and a foreign portfolio requires an investment of $6 million. The expected returns are 8 percent on the U.S. portfolio and 12 percent on the foreign portfolio. The standard deviations are 20 percent for the U.S. portfolio and 30 percent for the foreign portfolio; their correlation coefficient is –0.10.

The return on the international portolio is:

$$R_p = (0.4)0.08 + (0.6)0.12 = 10.4\%$$

The standard deviation of the international portfolio is:

$$\sigma_p = [(0.4)^2(0.20)^2 + (0.6)^2(0.30)^2$$

$$+ 2(0.4)(0.6)(-0.10)(0.20)(0.30)]^{1/2} = 3.6\%$$

Efficient Frontier

Suppose that A, B, and C are three exclusive portfolios which require the same amount of investment ($1,000). They have an equal return of 13 percent, but their respective standard deviations are 1.50 percent for A, 2.40 percent for B, and 4.10 percent for C. If we plot these three risk–return possibilities in Figure 13–1, we notice that A incurs the smallest risk for a

Figure 13–1
An Efficient Frontier

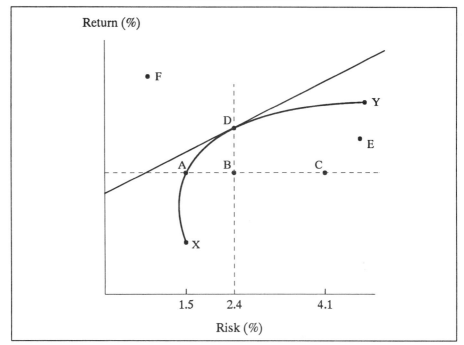

given level of return (13 percent). A is called an efficient portfolio. The efficient portfolio also exists when a particular portfolio (e.g., D) provides the highest return for a given level of risk (2.40 percent). If we compute more points such as A and D, we may obtain Line XADY by connecting such points. This line is known as the efficient frontier, which is the locus of all efficient portfolios. Portfolios B, C, and E are inefficient because some other portfolios could give either a lower risk for the same rate of return or a higher return for the same degree of risk. Portfolios, such as F, to the left of the efficient frontier, are unobtainable with the funds available for investment ($1,000).

There are numerous efficient portfolios along the efficient frontier. An efficient frontier does not tell us which portfolio to select but shows a collection of portfolios that minimize risk for any expected return or that maximize the expected return for any degree of risk. The objective of the investor is to choose the optimal portfolio among those on the efficient frontier. Thus, the efficient frontier is necessary but not sufficient for selecting the optimal portfolio. Given an efficient frontier, the choice of the optimal portfolio depends on the security market line.

If investors want to select the optimal portfolio from portfolios on a particular efficient frontier, they should land on the highest security market line. This optimal portfolio is found at the tangency point between the efficient frontier and the security market line. Tangency point D in Figure

13-1 marks the highest security market line that investors can obtain with funds available for investment. An optimum portfolio is the portfolio which has, among all possible portfolios, the largest ratio of expected return to risk. Once investors identify the optimal portfolio, they will allocate funds between the optimal portfolio and the risk-free asset to achieve a desired combination of risk and return.

Benefits of International Diversification

A rather convincing body of literature holds that internationally diversified portfolios are better than domestically diversified portfolios because they provide higher risk-adjusted returns to their holders. This section, based on several empirical studies, discusses (1) arguments for international diversification, (2) risk-return characteristics of national capital markets, and (3) selection of optimal international portfolios.

Risk Diversification Through International Investment

Table 13-1 provides correlations of stock market returns within each of ten major countries. First, the intracountry correlation is one for every country. On the other hand, the intercountry correlation is much less than one for every pair of any two countries. In other words, stock market returns have lower positive correlations across countries than within a country. Second, member countries of the European Community—Belgium, France, Italy, Germany, and the United Kingdom—have relatively high correlations because their currencies and economies are highly interrelated. Third, the intercountry correlation for the United States ranges from as high as 0.60 with the United Kingdom to as low as 0.30 with Norway.

Table 13–1
Correlations of Stock Market Returns

	AU	BE	FR	IT	JA	NO	SW	UK	US	GE
Australia	1.00									
Belgium	0.38	1.00								
France	0.38	0.69	1.00							
Italy	0.39	0.44	0.52	1.00						
Japan	0.34	0.36	0.31	0.37	1.00					
Norway	0.32	0.44	0.35	0.21	0.07	1.00				
Sweden	0.28	0.41	0.28	0.43	0.38	0.09	1.00			
U.K.	0.41	0.58	0.44	0.32	0.42	0.18	0.34	1.00		
U.S.	0.57	0.50	0.45	0.33	0.48	0.30	0.42	0.60	1.00	
Germany	0.39	0.49	0.48	0.37	0.37	0.01	0.39	0.45	0.51	1.00

Source: John E. Hunter and T. Daniel Coggin, "An Analysis of the Diversification Benefit from International Equity Diversification," *The Journal of Portfolio Management*, Fall 1990, p. 34.

Of course, a reason for low intercountry correlations is that much of stock market risk in an individual country is unsystematic and so can be eliminated by international diversification. Low international correlations may reflect different geographic locations, independent economic policies, different endowments of natural resources, and cultural differences. In summary, these results imply that international diversification into geographically and economically divergent countries may significantly reduce the risk of portfolio returns.

Figure 13-2 shows the total risk of domestically and internationally diversified portfolios as the function of the number of securities held. In this figure 100 percent of risk as measured by standard deviation represents the typical risk of a single U.S. security. As an investor increases the number of securities in a portfolio, the portfolio's risk declines rapidly at first, then slowly approaches the systematic risk of the market expressed in the broken line. However, the addition of more securities beyond 20 or 30 reduces risk a little.

Figure 13-2 illustrates a number of striking facts. First, the risk of a well-diversified U.S. portfolio is only 27 percent of the typical risk of a

Figure 13–2
Gains from International Diversification

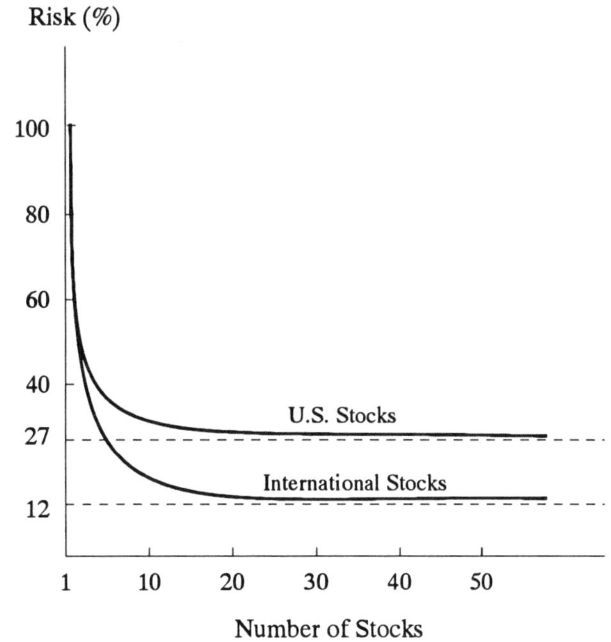

Source: Solnik, B. H., "Why Not Diversify Internationally Rather Than Domestical-ly?" *Financial Analysts Journal*, July/August 1974, p. 51.

single security. This relationship indicates that 73 percent of the risk associated with investing in a single security is diversifiable in a fully diversified portfolio. Second, the addition of foreign stocks to a purely domestic portfolio reduces risk faster, as shown in the bottom curve. Third, a fully diversified international portfolio is less than half as risky as a fully diversified U.S. portfolio. This and other studies have established that security returns are less highly correlated internationally than domestically. This argues a strong point for international diversification as a means of risk diversification.

It is important to note that a fully diversified portfolio or an efficient portfolio is one that has zero, or very little, unsystematic risk. As illustrated in Figure 13-2, an efficient international portfolio cut the systematic risk of an efficient domestic portfolio in half. Domestic systematic risk declines because international diversification offsets U.S.-specific reactions to worldwide events.

Risk–Return Characteristics of Capital Markets

In the previous section, we discussed the benefits from diversifying international portfolios in terms of risk reduction, but we ignored return, another important aspect of investment. Certainly, investors simultaneously consider both risk and return in making investment decisions. In other words, they want to maximize expected return for a given amount of risk and to minimize the amount of risk for a given level of return. Consequently, we ought to examine risk-return characteristics of stock markets.

Empirical studies conclude that international diversification pushes out the efficient frontier, thus allowing investors simultaneously to reduce risk and increase return. This benefit exists for a number of factors. First, more profitable investments are possible in an enlarged universe because faster-growing economies create higher returns or investors may see another advantage from currency gains. Second, the advantages of international diversification may occur because companies in different countries are subject to divergent cyclical economic fluctuations.

To ascertain the gains from international diversification, Mark Eaker and Dwight Grant (1990) constructed portfolios that began as 100 percent U.S. and then became increasingly international in increments of 20 percent. Switching from domestic to foreign investments was implemented by acquiring equally weighted portfolios of the five foreign indexes (Canada, Germany, Japan, Switzerland, and the United Kingdom). Table 13-2 shows the performance of these portfolios with the currency risk unhedged, hedged fully, and hedged selectively. As the proportion of the unhedged portfolio invested abroad increased, the return increased; in addition, the risk decreased until the proportion of foreign equities reached 60 percent of the portfolio. Hedged and selectively hedged international portfolios also displayed clear superiority over the U.S.-only portfolio.

Table 13-2
Investment Performance of Fixed-Allocation Portfolios

Proportion U.S. (%)	Hedged		Unhedged		Selective Hedge	
	Return	Standard Deviation	Return	Standard Deviation	Return	Standard Deviation
100	13.56	15.71	13.56	15.71	13.56	15.71
80	13.34	14.59	14.10	14.50	14.57	14.55
60	15.11	13.96	14.63	13.57	15.57	13.70
40	15.88	13.89	15.17	12.97	16.58	13.23
20	16.66	14.38	15.70	12.74	17.58	13.18
0	17.43	15.38	16.24	12.91	18.59	13.54

Source: Mark R. Eaker and Dwight M. Grant, "Currency Hedging Strategies for Internationally Diversified Equity Portfolios," *The Journal of Portfolio Management*, Fall 1990, p. 32.

The Selection of an Optimal Portfolio

Before we discuss the selection of an optimal international portfolio, let us review the basic concept of bonds and stocks. Bonds are less risky than stocks. The standard deviation of bond returns in any particular market is typically lower than the standard deviation of stock returns in that market. Certainly, lower risk implies lower mean rates of return for bonds compared with stocks. Table 13-3 shows risk-return statistics for bonds and stocks in

Table 13-3
Dollar-Adjusted Rates of Return and Standard Deviations

Country	Bonds		Stocks	
	Mean	Standard Deviation	Mean	Standard Deviation
Belgium	8.11%	9.66%	10.14%	14.19%
Denmark	6.99	13.14	11.37	24.83
France	5.99	12.62	8.13	21.96
Germany	10.64	9.45	10.10	20.34
Italy	3.39	13.73	5.60	27.89
Holland	7.90	8.28	10.68	18.24
Spain	5.17	11.52	10.35	20.33
Sweden	6.41	6.06	9.70	17.09
Switzerland	9.11	12.68	12.50	23.48
U.K.	6.81	15.30	14.67	34.40
Japan	11.19	12.21	19.03	32.20
Canada	3.52	6.44	12.10	17.89
U.S.	4.31	5.53	10.23	18.12

Source: Haim Levy and Zvi Lerman, "The Benefits of International Diversification in Bonds," *Financial Analysts Journal*, September/October 1988, p. 57.

various markets from the viewpoint of a U.S. investor. In terms of the mean-variance decision rule, both bonds and stocks were efficient investments in each market. All the bond means and standard deviations were lower than the corresponding stock statistics in each market, with the exception of Germany.

Haim Levy and Zvi Lerman (1988) compared the performance of various investment strategies for 13 industrial countries listed in Table 13–3. The right-hand curve of Figure 13–3 is the efficient frontier when investors are restricted to stocks only. The left-hand curve is the efficient frontier when investors can buy both stocks and bonds. The middle curve is the efficient frontier when investors are restricted to bonds only. M(bs), M(b), and M(s) represent the optimal international portfolios for stocks and bonds, bonds, and stocks, respectively.

Levy's and Lerman's study found several advantages to international bond and stock diversification. A U.S. investor who diversified across world bond markets could have earned almost two times as much as the mean rate of return on a U.S. bond portfolio, having the same risk level. Moreover, the U.S. stock market dominated the U.S. bond market in terms of risk–adjusted

Figure 13–3
Efficient International Portfolios

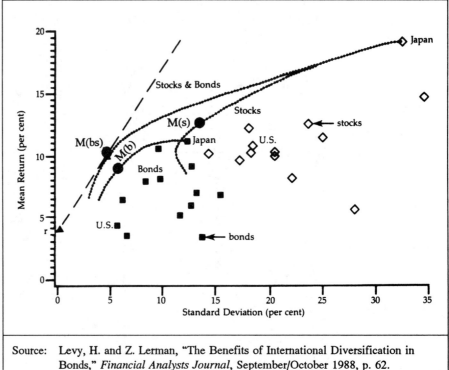

Source: Levy, H. and Z. Lerman, "The Benefits of International Diversification in Bonds," *Financial Analysts Journal*, September/October 1988, p. 62.

returns. However, internationally diversified bond portfolios outperformed internationally diversified stock portfolios. Finally, internationally diversified portfolios of stocks and bonds outperformed internationally diversified portfolios of stocks or bonds.

Investment in U.S. bonds is inefficient because as shown in Figure 13-3, its risk-return combination is deep inside the efficient frontier. The international bond portfolio M(b) in Figure 13-3 outperformed U.S. bonds in terms of mean rate of return at the same risk level. More specifically, U.S. bonds had a risk level of 5.53 percent and a mean return level of 4.31 percent. At about the same level of risk, the optimal international portfolio of bonds earned a mean return of about 8.5 percent—about twice the U.S.-only portfolio's return. This was achieved by investing in a portfolio of German, Swedish, and Japanese bonds with small amounts in U.S. and Spanish bonds.

Investment in U.S. stocks is also inefficient because, according to Figure 13-3, its risk-return combination is to the right of the efficient frontier. The performance of the international stock portfolio M(s) was better than that of U.S. stocks. Point M(s) had a standard deviation of 14.84 percent and a mean return of 15 percent. Compare this to the U.S. stocks whose standard deviation was 18.12 percent and mean rate of return was 10.23 percent. Consequently, U.S. investors could have earned more from international stock portfolios than from U.S. stock portfolios, and at a lower risk level. This was achieved by investing in a portfolio of German, Spanish, Japanese, and Canadian stocks with small amounts of Belgium and British stocks.

Figure 13-3 shows that the bond portfolios definitely outperformed the stock portfolios. At every level of mean return up to 11 percent, the bond portfolios had a lower risk level than corresponding stock portfolios. However, the efficient bond frontier stops at a mean return level of about 11 percent, while the efficient stock frontier extends up to a mean return level of about 19 percent. The upper bound represents investment in Japanese stocks, which had the highest risk and return of all the stocks. The higher range of risk-return combinations was not attainable with bond portfolios. Still, the stock portfolios played an efficient role on their own because of their upper bound.

As given in Figure 13-3, the efficient frontier of stocks and bonds dominated its counterpart of either stocks or bonds. This means that international portfolios of stocks and bonds outperformed both stock portfolios and bond portfolios. The optimal international portfolio of stocks and bonds is obtained at point M(sb) where the efficient frontier of stocks and bonds and the security market line intersect with each other.

Summary

Political and economic events in the 1980s underscored the growing importance of free flows of finance, trade, and investment among countries. These changes, along with improved ability to collect and analyze data, give us low cost information about foreign securities. As a result, U.S. investors are realizing substantial benefits from international investment. In this chapter, we saw that international stock and bond diversification can yield higher returns with less risk than investment in a single market.

In the last 20 years or so, researchers have convincingly argued in terms of mean-variance model the case for international portfolio investments, as opposed to purely domestic diversification. A major reason for such a case is that international investment offers a broader range of opportunities than domestic investment, even in a market as large as the United States or Japan. Studies have stressed the following two points: (1) adding foreign securities to a purely domestic portfolio reduces the total risk of the portfolio because of a low correlation between foreign securities and the domestic market; (2) in the past, international portfolios could have yielded both a higher return and a lower volatility than purely domestic U.S. portfolios.

Even though U.S. investors are increasingly interested in foreign securities, investment in foreign securities represents a small proportion of their total investment in stocks and bonds. Most commonly expressed barriers to international investment include: (1) excessive information and transaction costs, (2) double taxation of foreign investment profits, (3) foreign exchange regulations and currency risk, (4) greater rate-of-return volatility, (5) unfamiliarity with operating procedures of foreign stock exchanges, (6) unavailability of high-quality financial data for foreign companies, and (7) significant delays of transactions and settlements associated with foreign securities.

Questions

1. Discuss both unsystematic risk and systematic risk within an international context.

2. What is the market portfolio? Why is the market portfolio important?

3. Many studies found that intercountry correlations tend to be substantially lower than intracountry correlations. Explain some reasons for this fact. What significance does this finding have for international investment?

4. Describe the efficient portfolio, the efficient frontier, and the optimum portfolio.

5. Is the standard deviation of bond returns in any particular market typically higher or lower than the standard deviation of stock returns in that market? Does this information make any difference for investors?

6. Is it possible for an international portfolio to reduce the domestic systematic risk?

Problems

13-1 The expected rate of return on the market portfolio is 20 percent. The riskless rate of interest is 10 percent. The beta of a company is 0.5. What is the cost of this company's common equity?

13-2 At present, the riskless rate of return is 10 percent and the expected rate of return on the market portfolio is 15 percent. The expected returns for five stocks are listed below, together with their expected betas.

Stock	Expected Return	Expected Beta
A	0.22	1.5
B	0.30	1.3
C	0.12	0.8
D	0.15	0.7
E	0.14	1.1

On the basis of these expectations, which stocks are overvalued? Which stocks are undervalued?

13-3 The prices of a common stock were $40, $50, and $60 for the last three days. Compute the average stock price and the standard deviation.

13-4 A portfolio manager considers investing a total of $10 million on U.S. and German portfolios. The expected returns are 15 percent on the U.S. portfolio and 12 percent on the German portfolio. The standard deviations are 10 percent for the U.S. portfolio and 9 percent for the German portfolio. Their correlation coefficient is 0.33. What is the expected return and standard deviation of an international portfolio with 25 percent invested in the U.S. portfolio and 75 percent in the German portfolio?

References

Eaker, M. R., and D. M. Grant, "Currency Hedging Strategies for Internationally Diversified Equity Portfolios," *The Journal of Portfolio Management*, Fall 1990, pp. 30-2.

Eitman, D. K., and A. I. Stonehill, *Multinational Business Finance*, Reading, MA: Addison-Wesley, 1989, Chapter 12.

Eun, C. S., and B. G. Resnick, "Estimating the Correlation Structure of International Share Prices," *The Journal of Finance*, December 1984, pp. 1311-24.

Fatemi, A. M., "Shareholder Benefits from Corporate International Diversification," *The Journal of Finance*, December 1984, pp. 1325-44.

Hunter, J. E., and T. D. Coggin, "An Analysis of the Diversification Benefit from International Equity Investment," *The Journal of Portfolio Management*, Fall 1990, pp. 33-6.

Levy, H., and Z. Lerman, "The Benefits of International Diversification in Bonds," *Financial Analysts Journal*, September/October 1988, pp. 56-64.

Markowitz, H. M., *Portfolio Selection*, New York: John Wiley & Sons, 1959.

Rhee, S. G., "Securities Markets and Systematic Risks in Dynamic Asian Economics," Paris: Organization for Economic Cooperation and Development, 1992.

Shapiro, A. C., *Foundations of Multinational Financial Management*, Boston: Allyn and Bacon, 1991, Chapter 16.

Sharpe, W. F., "Capital Asset Prices: A Thoery of Market Equilibrium Under Conditions of Risk," *Journal of Finance*, September 1964, pp. 425-42.

Solnik, B., *International Investments*, Reading, MA: Addison-Wesley, 1988, Chapter 2.

Thomas, L. R., "The Performance of Currency-Hedged Foreign Bonds," *Financial Analysts Journal*, May/June 1989, pp. 25-31.

Tobin, J., "Liquidity Preference as Behavior Towards Risk," *The Journal of Economic Studies*, February 1958, pp. 65-86.

14
Foreign Direct Investment

Direct investments are equity investments such as the purchase of common stock, the acquisition of entire firms, or the establishment of new subsidiaries. The U.S. Department of Commerce defines foreign direct investment as investment in either real capital assets or financial assets with a minimum of 10 percent equity ownership in a foreign firm. Most multinational companies invest overseas directly for a variety of reasons. Chapter 2 discussed key economic motives for overseas direct investment

This chapter discusses several practical issues of foreign direct investment in four sections. The first section describes the overall concept of foreign direct investment. The second section covers inflows of foreign direct investment to developing countries. The third section discusses Japanese direct investment in the United States. The fourth section considers international mergers and acquisitions.

An Overview of Foreign Direct Investment

Decisions on capital expenditures involve the allocation and commitment of funds to investment projects whose returns are expected to extend beyond one year. Such investments usually require very large sums of money and are made in expectation of benefits over an extended period. Capital investment decisions are not readily reversible once they are made. Used plants and most used equipment in foreign countries have limited markets. In certain areas, production methods are rapidly outmoded by increasingly higher levels of technology. Moreover, foreign investments are much riskier than domestic investments. Thus, the rational use of capital resources is critical for the future well-being of a multinational company.

Benefits of Foreign Investment

Company Benefits.
Many multinational companies invest their capital abroad to utilize their oligopoly-created advantages. These advantages include proprietary technology, management know-how, multinational distribution network, access to scarce raw materials, production economies of scale, financial economies of scale, and possession of a strong brand or trade name. The use of such oligopolistic advantages could enable a multinational company to reduce its cost of capital and to increase its profitability, thereby increasing the value of the firm.

Host–Country Benefits.
Host countries can benefit from foreign direct investment in many ways:

1. Foreign investment induces the transfer of technology and skills which are frequently in short supply.
2. It increases both national employment and domestic wages.
3. It provides local workers with an opportunity to learn managerial skills.
4. It contributes to tax revenues and helps balance international balance of payments.

Arguments Against Foreign Investment

Although foreign investment tends to contribute much needed resources to host countries, and developing countries in particular, many view it with misgivings. There are many arguments against foreign investment. Most of these arguments have to do with conflicts between company goals and host-government aspirations:

1. Foreign investment brings about the loss of political and economic sovereignty.
2. It controls key industries and export markets.
3. It exploits local natural resources and unskilled workers.
4. It undermines indigenous cultures and societies by imposing Western values and lifestyles on developing countries.

It seems that, while foreign direct investment has the potential to contribute positively to development, there is no guarantee that it would have no harmful impact on host countries. But the question of foreign investment need not be a zero-sum game. A feasible framework for investment must be set up to define the rights and responsibilities of both parties. This framework should allow for a reasonable return to the investor and positively contribute to the development of a host country.

Licensing

Theory views direct investment, licensing, and international trade as foreign market-entry alternatives. Thus, licensing is an alternative to foreign direct investments. Multinational companies can set up their own production facilities abroad or license a local firm to manufacture their products in return for royalties. In other words, if a company has a differentiated product or proprietary technology, it usually seeks to exploit that advantage in foreign markets in two ways. First, it would make a capital investment and manufacture the product in foreign countries in order to earn dividends and other direct investment returns. Second, it would license its proprietary knowledge of products and intangible assets to a local company in order to earn royalties and licensing fees from the transfer of technology.

Advantages of Licensing.
Licensing has several advantages over direct investments:

1. It requires a relatively small amount of investment.
2. Companies have an opportunity to penetrate foreign markets.
3. It allows companies to reduce political and financial risks which might stem from their own foreign operations.
4. Many governments restrict autonomous foreign subsidiaries from operating within their borders; licensing is still an easy way to circumvent these restrictions.

Disadvantages of Licensing.
On the other hand, licensing may lead to establishing a competitor in third-country markets. Royalties and licensing fees are relatively small. It is frequently difficult to maintain product quality standards and to control exports by a licensee.

Benefits of Licensing for Local Companies.
Many local companies in developing countries are eager to have licensing agreements with multinational companies which have high-technology products. There are a number of good reasons for this sort of agreement:

1. Local companies need new technology to expand their business, but they cannot afford to acquire technology through their own research and development.
2. Local companies wish to diversify into other product lines beyond their saturated traditional geographic markets.
3. Local companies often control the channels of distribution, the financial resources, and the marketing know-how, but they do not have the products for marketing to capitalize on their unique market position.

Evaluation of Licensing.
Like all aspects of good business, successful licensing requires management and planning. Because there is no global clearinghouse for technology, the matching process stretches around the world with a wide variety of intermediaries. The process is further complicated

because of politics, international laws, different cultures, and global secrecy. Consequently, a continuous stream of profitable licensing agreements comes from hard thinking, good planning and, frequently, large outlays for research and development.

U.S. Foreign Investment Positions

U.S. multinational companies dominated foreign direct investment from World War II up until 1980. In fact, over much of the past two decades there were two familiar patterns. First, the multinational company tended to be based in the United States. Second, most foreign direct investment was made by these U.S. multinational companies. However, recent statistics indicate that these two familiar patterns may no longer exist. For example, in the early 1960s, U.S. multinational companies accounted for two-thirds of the world's 100 largest companies and for three-fifths of the 500 largest, but by 1985 their share had dropped to two-fifths of each category; by 1992 their share has dropped even further to one-third of each category. Moreover, the United States was the dominant direct investor abroad in the three decades (1950s, 1960s and 1970s), but since 1980 it has become the world's largest recipient of foreign direct investment funds. Consequently, in the 1980s U.S. policy makers focused on trade imbalances, but they now worry about investment imbalances.

Two Studies of Foreign Investment in the U.S.   In 1987, the U.S. Department of Commerce conducted a comprehensive study on foreign investment in the United States. This benchmark survey covered 8,260 fully consolidated U.S. businesses; these businesses represented 21,895 individual U.S. companies. The study found that (1) foreign investors increased their employment, assets, and sales primarily through acquisitions of U.S. companies, (2) while foreign investment in the United States was growing, it was relatively insignificant; (3) the foreign investors operated in basically the same way as domestic companies; and (4) existing U.S. laws were sufficient to protect U.S. interests. This survey of evidence suggests that U.S. affiliates of foreign companies look a lot like U.S.-based companies: they are comparable in terms of value added, compensation, research and development per worker, and many other areas. More specifically, the study found the following:

1. U.S. affiliates of foreign companies accounted for 3.6 percent of all U.S. business employment in 1987; the manufacturing sector accounted for almost one-half of total U.S. affiliate employment.
2. Their assets increased at an average growth rate of 18 percent per year from 1980 to 1987.
3. In 1987, they exported $48 billion worth of goods and imported $141 billion worth of goods; Japan accounted for 41 percent of their total exports and for 50 percent of their total imports.

4. Foreign investment was present in almost all sectors, even though the manufacturing sector took the largest share of all U.S. affiliates in assets, sales, and employment; foreign investment was concentrated in industrial states, but the more recent investors had located in the South and had come largely from Japan and Europe.

In 1989, Edward Graham and Paul Krugman conducted a similar survey on foreign direct investment in the United States. They concluded that there is nothing harmful about the increased role of foreign investment in the United States and that indeed the general economic effect is beneficial. Thus, there is no need from an economic perspective for new unilateral laws or policies specifically targeted toward greater regulation of foreign-controlled activities in the United States.

Comparative Analysis of Investment Positions. Available statistics indicate that foreign investment positions have dramatically changed in recent years. Foreign-owned business is becoming increasingly visible and important in all sections of the country.

Table 14-1 shows the U.S. foreign investment position and the foreign investment position in the United States for selected years. U.S. direct investment abroad increased 2.5 times, from $31.9 billion in 1960 to $78.2 billion in 1970. Foreign direct investment in the United States rose from $6.9 billion in 1960 to $13.2 billion in 1970, almost a two-fold increase. In contrast, U.S. direct investment abroad increased by almost three times from 1970 to 1980, and foreign direct investment in the United States rose by more than six times during the same period. While in the 1960s U.S. direct investment abroad increased at a faster rate than foreign direct investment in the United States, in the 1970s the trend reversed. This reverse trend had accelerated since 1980 until 1989; more specifically, U.S. investment abroad increased less than two times between 1980 and 1989, while foreign investment in this country increased almost five times during the same period. Consequently, foreign investment in the United States exceeded U.S. foreign investment abroad in 1989 for the first time in modern U.S. history.

However, some economists used to argue that U.S. foreign asset holdings were significantly undervalued because the United States estimated its direct investment position on the basis of book value (historical cost). The historical cost is the actual value of the investment when it occurred. Because inflation leaves book values far below market values, the true worth of the U.S. foreign holdings, which are far older than foreign-asset holdings in the United States, was greatly understated. To provide alternatives to this potentially misleading measure, in 1990 the U.S. Department of Commerce released two additional measures of U.S. foreign investment positions. The first measure, called current cost, is the current value of the net stock of direct investment capital. The second measure, called market value, is the market value of a firm's net worth; the net worth is the difference between assets and liabilities.

Table 14-1
United States: Foreign Investment Positions
(billions of dollars)

| | U.S. Investment Abroad | | | Foreign Investment in U.S. | | |
Year	Historical Cost	Current Cost	Market Value	Historical Cost	Current Cost	Market Value
1960	31.9			6.9		
1965	49.5			8.8		
1970	78.2			13.2		
1975	124.0			27.7		
1976	136.8			30.8		
1977	146.0			34.6		
1978	162.7			42.5		
1979	187.8			54.5		
1980	215.4			83.0		
1981	228.3			108.7		
1982	207.8	374.0	228.3	124.7	173.2	133.0
1983	207.2	357.9	273.3	137.1	181.3	157.5
1984	211.5	350.0	267.6	164.6	207.2	177.7
1985	230.3	379.6	380.5	184.6	227.2	227.9
1986	259.8	414.1	519.4	220.4	266.5	283.2
1987	314.3	485.2	577.6	263.4	316.0	315.7
1988	335.9	505.0	678.8	314.8	372.6	391.0
1989	370.1	536.1	807.7	373.8	433.7	533.5
1990	421.5	598.1	714.1	402.7	465.9	530.4

Source: U.S. Department of Commerce, *Survey of Current Business*, various issues.

As shown in Table 14-1, net direct investment and its trend over time are substantially different across all three measures. For example, the historical-cost and current-cost estimates indicate that the balance on direct investment declined by approximately $65 billion between 1982 and 1990 in contrast to an increase of approximately $88 billion for the market value measure. In addition, when direct investment is valued at market value, U.S. foreign investment abroad still exceeded foreign investment in the United States by $274 billion in 1989. Finally, current-cost and market-value estimates show that foreign direct investment in the United States actually declined in 1990. The U.S. government attributed this worrisome trend mostly to the U.S. economic slowdown and competing investment opportunities abroad.

Direct Investment in the Third World

It was not long ago that the flow of new money from industrialized nations to the Third World had slowed to a trickle, a victim of the debt crisis of the early 1980s. Bankers, multinational companies, individual investors—they all made investment in their home countries, or at least in those countries that were more like their own. For example, during the first half of the 1980s, money tended to move around primarily in the already developed countries. Japan and Europe invested heavily in the United States. The United States invested heavily in Western Europe. As the memory of the debt crisis began to fade, foreign capital began once again to move into the most promising developing countries. Today, multinational corporations and small entrepreneurs are building factories in Southeast Asia, Latin America, Eastern Europe, and the Commonwealth of Independent States (former Soviet Union).

Table 14-2 presents inflows of foreign direct investment to developing countries. Foreign direct investment in the developing countries rose by 22 percent a year between 1985 and 1989, reaching $30 billion in 1989; that compared with only 3 percent a year between 1980 and 1984. In Asia, the growth rate was 37 percent annually between 1985 and 1989. Argentina, Brazil, Egypt, Mexico, and other non–Asian nations also enjoyed a huge surge of outside capital.

Improved Investment Climate

Perhaps the best way for improving a country's investment climate is to remove obstacles which impede foreign investment, though many are

Table 14–2
Inflows of Foreign Direct Investment to Developing Countries
(Annual averages, in billions of dollars)

Regions	1980–1984	1985–1989	1988–1989
Africa	$1.29	$2.60	$3.20
Latin America and Caribbean	6.10	8.30	10.00
East, South, and Southeast Asia	4.70	10.70	15.20
Oceania	0.13	0.14	0.20
West Asia	0.37	0.40	0.54
Other	0.04	0.03	0.05
Largest Recipients			
Argentina	$0.44	$0.73	$1.09
Brazil	2.10	1.59	2.53
China	0.53	2.49	3.29
Colombia	0.40	0.56	0.39
Egypt	0.56	1.23	1.40
Hong Kong	0.68	1.65	2.04
Malaysia	1.13	0.83	1.28
Mexico	1.50	2.02	2.42
Singapore	1.39	2.50	3.29
Thailand	0.29	0.72	1.40

Source: Bernard Wysocki, Jr., "Returning to the Third World," *The Wall Street Journal*, September 20, 1991, p. R2.

unavoidable, inadvertent, or unintended. Bad roads, primitive port facilities, and the lack of local capital or qualified local technicians constitute unavoidable obstacles to investment. In some cases, the government of a country permits some obstacles to exist, but for reasons other than their effect on private foreign investment. As examples, the existence of a communist dictatorship in Cuba, the social orientation of Syria, and the South African policy of apartheid deter foreign investment. Finally, there are unintended obstacles which the government of the host country is anxious to avoid. These obstacles include a broad range of conditions from excessive red tape to corruption in the courts.

There are two broad groups of reasons why multinational companies will continue to invest heavily in developing countries: various incentive programs and emerging market-based capitalism. The shortage of capital in many parts of the world and an almost universal desire for economic growth have recently compelled many countries to institute incentive programs for private foreign investment. Several surveys found that developing countries have various incentive programs for foreign investors. These include tax incentives, tariff exemptions, financial assistance, remittance guarantees, administrative assistance, protection from competitive investments and imports, and protection from nationalization and political risk. These and other incentive programs undoubtedly motivate multinational companies to invest in those countries offering them.

Many developing countries are embracing market-based capitalism. Privatization, liberalization of trade, a positive attitude toward foreign investment, and a relaxation of the tight state control—these are all enthusiastically embraced by foreign investors. More concretely, these are the measures that make investment possible by putting companies on the block and allowing foreigners into the market.

Japanese Direct Investment in the United States

Several studies concluded that the increased role of foreign direct investment in the United States is not harmful but economically beneficial. However, Japan has penetrated American consciousness in ways which other countries have not. In some parts, a noticeable level of nationalistic sentiment against Japan was spurred by complaints about its trade practices and its growing direct investment. Data show that the British and the French are the leading buyers of American companies. Still, the issue of Japan's "buying America" is hotly debated throughout the nation. The debate is fueled by high-profile Japanese acquisitions: Columbia Pictures, CBS Records, Pebble Beach Golf Course in California, Universal Studios, and a major interest in New York's Rockefeller Center. Headline news of such acquisitions identified manifest examples of Japanese investment, as evidence of the Japanese economic threat to the United States.

Japan's direct investment has become uncomfortably large in recent years, but its firms still account for a small fraction of foreign presence in the United States. Still, concerns about foreign direct investment in the United States focused on Japanese firms. U.S. citizens and policymakers alike suspect that Japanese firms would behave differently than other firms with affiliates in the United States, for the following reasons:

1. Japanese firms are more sheltered from foreign competition in their home market than are firms in other industrial countries.
2. Japanese firms can be induced through "invisible handshakes" to act in ways their government believes serve the national interest.
3. Japanese firms participate in "keiretsu" (business groups) which tend to do business among themselves, thus constructing informal barriers to non-Japanese companies.

Direct Investment Positions

Table 14-3 shows the U.S. direct investment position in Japan and Japan's direct investment position in the United States. U.S. direct investment in Japan increased from $1.5 billion in 1970 to $6.2 billion in 1980, only 4.1 times, while Japan's direct investment in the United States increased from $0.2 billion in 1970 to $4.7 billion in 1980, a 23-fold increase. U.S. direct investment in Japan increased by about four times from 1980 to 1990, whereas Japan's direct investment in the United States increased by about 17 times during the same period.

Table 14-3
Direct Investment Positions
(billions of dollars)

Year	U.S. Investment in Japan	Japan's Investment in the U.S
1970	1.5	0.2
1975	3.3	0.6
1976	3.8	1.2
1977	4.1	1.7
1978	5.0	2.7
1979	5.8	3.4
1980	6.2	4.7
1981	6.8	7.7
1982	6.9	9.7
1983	8.1	11.1
1984	7.0	16.0
1985	9.2	19.3
1986	11.5	26.8
1987	14.7	35.2
1988	16.9	53.4
1989	19.3	69.7
1990	25.9	79.9

Source: The U.S. Department of Commerce, Bureau of the Census, *Statistical Abstract*, various issues; and Japan Economic Institute of America.

In 1981 Japan's direct investment in the United States exceeded U.S. direct investment in Japan for the first time. U.S. net investment (U.S. investment in Japan minus Japan's investment in the U.S.) was $1.3 billion in 1970, but it became negative in 1981. U.S. negative net investment increased from $0.9 billion in 1981 to $54 billion in 1990. In other words, Japan's 1990 net investment of plus $54 billion was almost 43 times the size of the 1970 discrepancy of minus $1.3 billion.

Japanese Automotive Transplants

Several studies showed that foreign investment in the United States was growing but not significantly. Nevertheless, in certain sectors foreign investment poses serious threats to industry and might imperil the stability of an entire industry. For example, consider the automobile industry. From 1914 to 1980, someone referring to automobiles would be speaking of GM, Ford, and Chrysler. Not so today. Even when we talk about American plants, we must account for Japanese transplants.

Japanese direct investment in the United States has attracted special attention for a number of reasons. Japanese automakers have been the most successful competitors against U.S. automakers. In semirural towns of the United States, the Japanese automakers set up ten transplants since 1982 through direct investment. Most of these are the most automated, most efficient, and least unionized auto plants in the United States. They have enormous cost advantages in capital, worker training, retirement benefits, and health care. Furthermore, they are expanding production of large cars and lightweight trucks, thus undermining the only sectors where American automakers make money. Transplants will enable the Japanese automakers to boost sales regardless of quotas, tariffs, or currency swings.

Japanese automakers have invested directly in the United States as a defensive measure. They felt it necessary to invest in this country to maintain the market position they initially developed. The move also gave them a foothold in a huge U.S. auto market. Because they produce within the territory of the U.S. market, they avoid taxes and export restrictions. Direct investment has also helped them to cope with competitive pressures from U.S. protectionist actions.

These Japanese transplants have already aggravated Big Three capacity problems and profitability. In 1992 Nissan doubled its Tennessee operations, and in 1993 Toyota built a second assembly plant next to the one in Georgetown, Kentucky. All these expansions took place at a time when Detroit's Big Three automakers were making sweeping cutbacks in their own operations. GM took a $3.3 billion charge that would cover the closing of seven North American plants, Chrysler was in the throes of a $2.5 billion cost-cutting effort, and Ford was struggling to maintain much-needed capital expenditures in the face of weakening sales and profit. In addition to all this bad news, GM announced in December 1991 that it would close 21 more factories, cut 74,000 jobs, and slash capital spending over the next four years in a broad retrenchment. By the end of 1995, it is clear that the GM will be a far smaller company. The projected North American work force--71,000 white-collar workers and 250,000 hourly workers--will be about half the size of GM's total employment in 1985.

The Japanese assembly plants in the United States enable Japanese companies to build more than two million cars a year in the United States, more than one-fourth of the total in a typical sales year. These latest developments highlight the historic shift of industrial wealth and power now under way in the U.S. auto industry. Japanese automakers are steadily taking over the U.S. auto industry. They captured a record one-third of U.S. auto sales in 1992. Analysts predict that by the late 1990s, their combined share could match that of the Big Three.

As shown in Table 14-4, GM and Chrysler ordered more than ten factories closed since 1987, while Japanese automakers have opened ten U.S. plants since 1982. The United Auto Workers Union (UAW) lost 500,000 members, one-third of the total, in the 1980s. The union has yet to organize a Japanese plant without its approval. The 1987 master agreement between the UAW and the Big Three prohibited plant shutdowns for the life of the contract. However, in response to UAW's grievances against their moves, GM and Chrysler had argued that shutdowns did not violate the contract because the plants were only indefinitely idled instead of being closed. So, the UAW filed a grievance with an arbitrator when GM shut down a Pontiac, Mich. assembly plant in 1988. Yet, in a binding decision announced on March 29, 1990, arbitrator Thomas Roberts sided with GM's contention that it acted within its right to lay off 1700 workers in Pontiac. Auto analysts said that this might be one of these cases where GM won the battle but started the war. That is why job security and income guarantee were a top priority when the UAW negotiated its new contract in Fall 1990. The Big Three spent billions of dollars to carry out a range of job and income security programs under a new contract for three years from 1990 to 1993 with the UAW.

Table 14-4
U.S. Plant Closings and Japanese Plant Openings

U.S. Plants Closed since 1987	Japanese Plants Opened since 1982
1987 GM, Norwood, Ohio	1982 Honda, Marysville, Ohio
1988 GM, Leeds, Mo.	1983 Nissan, Smyrna, Tenn.
1988 Chrysler, Kenosha, Wis.	1984 Toyota-GM, Fremont, Calif.
1988 GM, Pontiac, Mich.	1987 Mazda, Flat Rock, Mich.
1989 GM, Framingham, Mass.	1988 Mitsubishi-Chrysler, Normal, Ill.
1990 GM, Lakewoood, Ga.	1988 Toyota, Georgetown, Ky.
1990 Chrysler, Detroit, Mich.	1989 Subaru-Isuzu, Lafayette, Ind.
1990 Chrysler, St. Louis, Mo.	1989 Honda, East Liberty, Ohio
1992 GM, Lordstown, Ohio	1992 Nissan, Smyrna, Tenn.
1993 GM, Van Nuys, Calif.	1993 Toyota, Georgetown, Ky.
Three more GM plants will be closed before 1995	

The Power of Keiretsu

In Japanese, the word "keiretsu" stands for large, financially linked groups of companies that play a significant role in the country's economy. However, foreign critics translate it to mean something else: "economic barrier" to non-Japanese companies. They argue that, from production through distribution, keiretsu groups effectively construct informal barriers against foreign goods in Japan.

There are two types of keiretsu. The first type of keiretsu is a vertical production group most vividly exemplified by Toyota Motor Corp. and other major Japanese automakers. In the 1980s, Toyota-linked suppliers followed the car company to America; today they deliver components to Toyota's plant exactly when they are needed to support the company's "just-in-time" inventory system. The second type of keiretsu is a horizontal or financial group, embodied by Mitsubishi, Mitsui, and Sumitomo. Member companies own relatively small chunks of shares in one another, with a big bank at the core. The Sumitomo Bank, for example, owns chunks of 19 core Sumitomo companies.

Critics have frequently charged that Japanese firms participate in keiretsu to insulate themselves from outside competitors in all aspects of operations. They wag their fingers at keiretsu as barriers to everything: trade barrier, investment barrier in Japan, and financing barrier for Japanese firms in the United States and Europe. The Bush administration of the early 1990s feared that major Japanese companies were exporting the keiretsu system to the United States. Thus, the Federal Trade Commission and the Department of Justice have recently expressed concern about the possible violation of U.S. anti-trust laws by Japanese companies.

Impact of Japanese Investment

Some analysts say that Japanese-owned companies in the United States might save the American economy because they force U.S. companies to build new facilities and improve productivity, quality, and after-sales services. Those improvements, in conjunction with import restraints, will probably improve the U.S competitiveness in the world marketplace. Take the auto industry as an example. Japanese automakers have pressured GM, Ford, and Chrysler to improve car quality so much that several of their models are now as well-made as anything the Japanese offer. Through their discounts and financing deals, the Big Three now offer the lowest prices. And they are shifting emphasis away from styling and performance to safety, quality, and repairability issues.

International Mergers and Acquisitions

These days companies look for and need to explore growth opportunities on a global basis. In principle, growth of the foreign presence in any national economy could take place in either of two ways. Companies could grow primarily through the construction of new production facilities in a foreign country, financed either through establishment of new subsidiaries or through investment by their existing facilities in the foreign country. Alternatively, companies could grow through acquisition of existing foreign firms.

Obviously, both kinds of growth have recently taken place in the United States and other countries. For example, such ventures as the establishment of Japanese automobile plants in the United States have occurred simultaneously with such events as Japanese acquisition of Rockefeller Center in New York. In quantitative terms, however, acquisitions (external growth) are much larger than the construction of new production facilities abroad (internal growth). Statistics for international acquisitions involving U.S. firms show that in most years of the 1980s, the value of acquisitions had been several times that of new establishments. Although internal growth is usually natural and economical, the process of growth may be very slow. In recent years, a company's growth through merger with the existing business activities of a foreign firm has received substantial attention as an alternative to internal growth.

In Chapter 15, we consider the purchase of an individual asset as a capital budgeting decision. When a company is buying another company, it is making an investment. Thus, the basic principles of capital investment decisions apply. But mergers are often more difficult to evaluate. First, the financial manager must be careful to define benefits. Second, the financial manager needs to understand why mergers occur and who gains or loses as a result of them. Third, the acquisition of a company is more complicated than the purchase of a new machine because special tax, legal, and accounting issues must often be addressed. Finally, the integration of an entire company is much more complex than the installation of a single new machine.

International Acquisitions Involving U.S. Firms

There have been a number of major merger movements in the industrial history of the United States. The first merger movement took place in the late 1890s' with the development of the oil, railroad, tobacco, and steel industries. The second major movement happened in the 1920s with the consolidation of firms in a number of industries, such as utilities and communication companies. The third one was in the 1960s with the rage of conglomerate mergers. The latest one happened in the 1980s.

The major mania of the 1980s had been sparked by several factors: the relatively depressed condition of the stock market in the early 1980s; the

344   Chapter 14

unprecedented level of inflation during the 1970s and the early 1980s; the Reagan Administration's tolerant attitude toward mergers; and the general belief that it is cheaper to acquire other companies than it is to expand through new product development. One special feature of the latest merger movement involves U.S. acquisition of foreign firms and foreign acquisition of U.S. firms. Numerous U.S. multinational companies, such as Rockwell International, Ford Motor Co., and Dow Chemical Co. have recently engaged in international acquisitions. Numerous Japanese and European companies have also engaged in international acquisitions. In addition, many more international acquisitions are underway in Europe, mainly due to the economic integration of Western Europe and economic reforms in Eastern Europe.

Figures 14-1 and 14-2 show the volume and value of cross-border acquisitions involving U.S. firms. Both types of acquisitions have increased throughout the 1980s. However, foreign acquisitions of U.S. firms are clearly more than U.S. acquisitions of foreign firms. In fact, former acquisitions are several times larger than later acquisitions in terms of both volume and value. This difference is due to several reasons: (1) U.S. firms had less flexibility to borrow, (2) foreign countries had less favorable tax laws, (3) there were more stringent country barriers, and (4) there was a better investment climate in the United States. This trend, however, may change as European companies become the primary targets of international acquisitions in response to uniform regulations across Western Europe and the movement toward free enterprise in Eastern Europe.

Figure 14-1
Volume of International Acquisitions

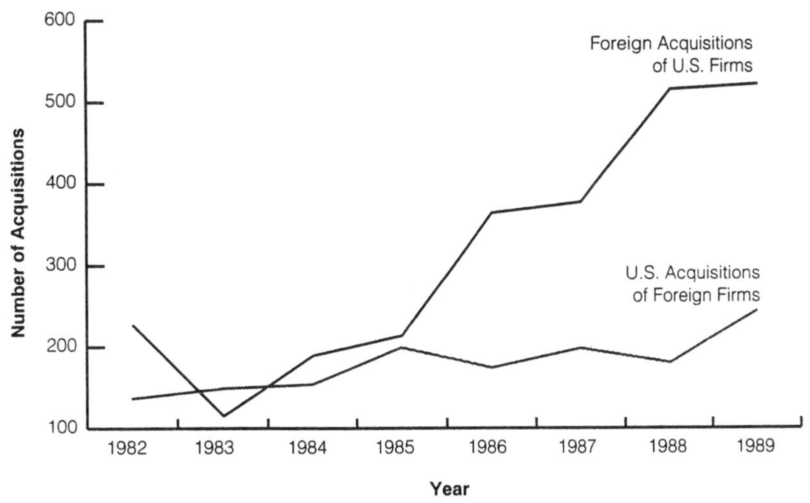

Source: *Mergers and Acquisitions,* May/June 1990.

Figure 14–2
Value of International Acquisitions

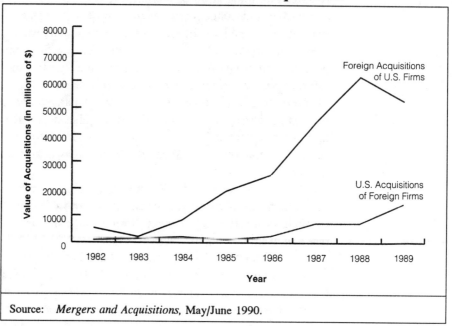

Source: *Mergers and Acquisitions*, May/June 1990.

Factors Affecting International Acquisitions

A company's acquisition of another firm is economically justified only if it increases the total value of a firm. The traditional capitalization to the valuation of the firm consists of four basic steps:

1. Determine the earnings after taxes the company expects to produce over the years or the earnings before taxes multiplied by (1 – tax rate).
2. Determine the capitalization rate (discount rate) for these earnings.
3. Determine the extent to which the company may be levered or the adequate amount of debt.
4. Compute the total value of the firm from the following formula:

$$Value\ of\ Firm\ =\ \frac{Earnings\ Before\ Taxes\ (1\ -\ Tax\ Rate)}{Capitalization\ Rate}\ +\ Debt$$

We can examine the effect of a merger on each of the factors that affect the total value of the firm.

Earnings Before Taxes.   A merger itself creates a larger physical size and opportunities for synergistic effect. The synergistic effects of business mergers are certain economies of scale from the firm's lower overhead. The merger allows the firm to acquire necessary management skills and to spread existing management skills over a larger operation. There are also opportunities to eliminate duplicate facilities and to consolidate the functions of production, marketing, and purchasing. These types of operating economies and better management can increase the profit margin and reduce risks as well.

A company is often able to improve its risk-return performance through international acquisition rather than through domestic acquisition. The key element here is the correlation coefficient between acquired firms and an acquiring firm. When firms with low degrees of correlation are combined with each other, the acquiring firm is able to reduce its risk of expected return. Companies from different countries tend to be less correlated with each other than domestic companies are. For example, the economic cycles of different countries do not tend to be totally synchronized. On the other hand, most domestic companies tend to be highly correlated with each other because they depend on the same state of economy.

Tax Considerations.

The tax benefit for mergers comes from the fact that the tax loss carryforward expires at the end of certain years (15 years in the United States) unless the firm makes sufficient profits to offset it completely. There are two situations where mergers could actually avoid corporate income taxes. First, when a profitable company acquires companies with a large tax loss carryforward, it can reduce its effective tax rate and, consequently, the merger increases its net operating income after taxes. Second, a company with a tax loss carryforward may acquire profitable companies in order to use its carryforward.

Accounting and tax laws may create even more competitive advantages for acquiring firms in some countries. If the acquiring company pays more than the net worth of the acquired company, the excess is treated as goodwill. Goodwill write-offs are not deductible for federal income taxes in the United States. This accounting treatment results in lower reported earnings for several years. However, in most industrialized countries, goodwill does not affect the acquiring company's earnings. Thus, foreign companies with more favorable accounting and tax laws may be able to bid higher prices for target companies.

Capitalization Rate.

An important advantage of mergers is the fact that earnings of larger companies are capitalized at lower rates. The securities of larger companies have better marketability than those of smaller companies. Larger companies are also better known among investors. An acquiring company can develop these factors, which leads to lower required rates of return and higher price-earnings ratios. Consequently, the value of the acquiring firm exceeds the values of the companies operating separately.

Another potential benefit of international acquisition is the lower required rate of return for the acquiring company. The required rate of return varies among countries because the cost of capital is different from country to country. As a result, companies in some countries may find acquisitions more attractive than companies in other countries.

Debt Capacity.

The appropriate mix of debt and equity reduces the overall cost of capital and thus raises the market value of the firm. There are two situations where a merger can raise the debt capacity for the acquiring company above the sum of debt capacities for the individual firms prior to merger. First, there are companies that fail to make optimum use of debt. Second, it is frequently possible for the acquiring company to borrow more than the companies were able to borrow individually.

Companies normally finance a portion of international acquisitions with borrowed funds. Companies in some countries have more flexibility to borrow, because investors and creditors in these countries are more receptive to higher debt ratios. The debt ratio for most companies in Denmark, Finland, Norway, and Sweden, for example, is higher than the comparable debt ratio for American companies. In other words, companies in Scandinavian countries have more flexibility to borrow than U.S. companies. Thus, U.S. companies may be more successful in international acquisitions because they can borrow in countries where higher degrees of financial leverage are tolerated than in the United States.

Other Considerations.

A variety of other factors affect international acquisitions: exchange rate movements, country barriers, and strategic choices, among others.

The ideal time for Japanese investors to buy a U.S. company is when the spot rate of the U.S. dollar is perceived to be very low and is expected to appreciate over time. Several studies confirmed that international acquisitions are influenced by exchange rate movements. A study by Felix Rohatyn (1989), for example, found that the combination of a relatively weak dollar and a strong Japanese stock market in the late 1980s encouraged Japanese acquisitions of U.S. firms.

Many country governments impose explicit and implicit barriers to foreign acquisitions of their domestic companies. These barriers prevent or discourage international acquisitions rather than offer advantages to specific acquiring companies. All countries have one or more agencies that monitor mergers and acquisitions, but they vary among countries. International acquisitions are tolerated more in the United States than in Japan. Consequently, it is much easier for Japanese investors to purchase a U.S. firm than for U.S. investors to purchase a Japanese firm.

To achieve corporate growth, companies these days view the world as a total business community. They consider international acquisitions as a viable alternative for achieving a corporate growth strategy. Lawrence Newman (1990) suggested that a growth-oriented company can globally close four types of growth gap between its sales potential and its current actual performance. A product-line gap can be closed by introducing improved or new products. A distribution gap may be reduced by expanding an existing distribution network. A usage gap is reduced by inducing current nonusers.

A competitive gap can be closed by making inroads into the market position of direct competitors. These strategic choices encourage companies to engage in international acquisitions.

Summary

Once companies decide to enter new foreign markets, their next concern is how to enter the foreign market. Some theories view direct investment, licensing, and international trade as foreign-entry alternatives. This chapter focused on direct investment as a foreign-entry alternative. More specifically, this chapter covered a number of practical issues in foreign direct investment, such as the benefits and drawbacks of foreign investment; the U.S. foreign investment position; inflows of foreign investment to developing countries; a comparative analysis of direct investment by the United States and Japan; and international acquisitions.

Questions

1. What are foreign market-entry alternatives?

2. Are U.S. government restrictions on imports likely to increase or decrease foreign direct investment in the United States?

3. It is fair to assume Chrysler and Ford are automobile manufacturers that desire to benefit from economies of scale. Suppose that Chrysler decides to establish distribution dealerships in foreign countries, while Ford decides to establish manufacturing subsidiaries in foreign countries. Which company is more likely to benefit from economies of scale? Which company has less to lose if the venture fails?

4. When people talked about foreign direct investment over much of the 1960s and 1970s, there were two familiar patterns. Explain these two familiar patterns.

5. What are the findings of major studies on foreign direct investment in the United States? Should the U.S. government place long-term restrictions on foreign direct investment in this country?

6. Discuss some reasons for the recent growth of foreign direct investment in the Third World.

7. How do Japanese firms, according to their critics, behave differently from other firms with affiliates in the United States?

8. Explain the Japanese word "keiretsu."

9. Explain why mergers are often more difficult to evaluate than the establishment of new production facilities.

10. What are factors affecting international acquisitions?

References

Blodgett, L. L., "Partner Contributions as Predictors of Equity Share in International Joint Ventures," *Journal of International Business Studies*, First Quarter 1991, pp. 63–78.

Chao, P., "Export and Reverse Investment: Strategic Implications for Newly Industrialized Countries," *Journal of International Business Studies*, Summer 1989, pp. 75–92.

Chernotsky, H. I., "The American Connection: Motives for Japanese Foreign Direct Investment," *Columbia Journal of World Business*, Winter 1987, pp. 47–54.

Contractor, R., "A Generalized Theorem for Joint-Venture and Licensing Negotiations," *Journal of International Business Studies*, Summer 1985, pp. 23–50.

Franko, L. G., "Use of Minority and 50–50 Joint Ventures by U.S. Multinationals During the 1970s: The Interaction of Host Country Policies and Corporate Strategies," *Journal of International Business Studies*, Spring 1989, pp. 19–40.

Geringer, J. M., "Strategic Determinants of Partner Selection Criteria in International Joint Ventures," *Journal of International Business Studies*, First Quarter 1991, pp. 41–62.

Gillis, J., *The Car Book*, New York: Harper & Row, 1991.

Globeman, S., "Government Policies Toward Foreign Direct Investment: Has A New Era Dawned?" *Columbia Journal of World Business*, Fall 1988, pp. 41–50.

Graham, E. M., and P. R. Krugman, *Foreign Direct Investment in the United States*, Washington, DC: Institute for International Economics, 1989.

Grosse, R., *Theory of Foreign Direct Investment*, Center for International Business Studies, The University of South Carolina, 1981.

Howenstine, N. G., "U.S. Affiliates of Foreign Companies: 1987 Benchmark Survey Results," *Survey of Current Business*, The U.S. Department of Commerce, July 1989, pp. 116–25.

Ingrassia, P., "Japanese Firms Come to Detroit, and City Is Glad to Have Them," *The Wall Street Journal*, May 7, 1991, p. A1 and p. A8.

Japan Economic Institute of America, *Foreign Direct Investment in Japan*, Washington, DC: Japan Economic Institute of America, September 20, 1991.

Madura, J., *International Financial Management*, St. Paul: West Publishing, 1992, pp. 517–25.

Newman, L. R., "Strategic Choices," in David J. Bendaniel and Arthur H. Rosenbloom, eds., *The Handbook of International Mergers and Acquisitions*, Englewood Cliffs, NJ: Prentice Hall, 1990, pp. 1–24.

Newman, R. G., and K. A. Rhee, "Midwest Auto Transplants: Japanese Investment Strategies and Policies," *Business Horizons*, April/May 1990, pp. 63–9.

Pitman, G. A., and S. T. Choe, "Attitudinal Variations Toward Japanese Investment in the United States," *Advanced Management Journal*, Summer 1989, pp. 15–18.

Rohatyn, F., "America's Economic Dependence," *Foreign Affairs*, Winter 1989, pp. 53–65.

Scholl, R. B., "The International Investment Position of the United States in 1990," *Survey of Current Business*, June 1991, pp. 23–7.

Taylor, A., III, "Can American Cars Come Back?" *Fortune*, February 26, 1990, pp. 62–5.

"World Business," *The Wall Street Journal*, September 20, 1991, Section R.

15
Multinational Capital Budgeting

The basic principles of analysis are the same for foreign and domestic investment projects. However, a foreign investment decision results from a complex process which differs in many aspects from the domestic investment decision.

Relevant cash flows are the dividends and royalties that would be repatriated by each subsidiary to a parent firm. Because these net cash flows must be converted into currency of a parent company, they are subject to future exchange-rate changes. Moreover, foreign investment projects are subject to political risks, such as exchange controls and expropriation. Normally, the cost of capital for a foreign project is higher than that for a similar domestic project. Certainly, this higher risk comes from two major sources, political risk and exchange risk.

This chapter is composed of three major sections. The first section describes the entire process of planning capital expenditures in foreign countries beyond one year. The second section examines how international diversification can reduce the overall riskiness of a company. The third section compares capital budgeting theory with capital budgeting practice.

The Investment Decision–Making Process

The foreign investment decision process involves the entire process of planning expenditures in foreign countries beyond one year. The one year time frame is arbitrary, but a one-year boundary is rather widely accepted. There are many steps and elements in the entire process of planning capital expenditures in foreign countries. Each element is a subsystem of the capital budgeting system. Thus, the foreign investment decision process may be viewed as an integral unit of many elements which are interrelated. Here we assume that the entire foreign investment process consists of 11 phases: (1) the decision to search for foreign investment, (2) an assessment of the political climate in the host country, (3) an examination of the company's overall strategy, (4) cash flow analysis, (5) the required rate of return, (6) economic evaluation, (7) selection, (8) risk analysis, (9) implementation, (10) expenditure control, and (11) post audit.

Search for Foreign Investment

The availability of good investment opportunities sets the foundation for a successful investment program. Hence, a system should be established to stimulate ideas for capital expenditures abroad and to identify good investment opportunities. Moreover, good investment opportunities come from hard thinking, careful planning, and frequently, large outlays for research and development.

The first phase in the foreign investment decision process is an analysis of the forces that lead some company officials to focus on the possibilities of foreign investment. If a company recognizes foreign investment as a legitimate program, its search for foreign investment opportunities will start. The economic and political forces in the host countries are largely responsible for the expansion of foreign investment. Many companies also desire foreign investment to seek new markets, raw materials, and production efficiency. Chapter 2 described these and other motives for foreign investment in detail.

It is not easy to pinpoint one motive for a decision to invest abroad in any particular case or to find out exactly who was the originator of a foreign project. The decision to search for foreign investment comes at the end of a series of events, and it is a combination of several motivating forces and activities of different persons. Typically, the decision to look abroad depends on the interaction of many forces. Considerations such as profit opportunities, tax policy, and diversification strategies are economic variables which may affect a decision to look overseas. In addition, environmental forces, organization factors, and a drive by some high ranking officials inside a company could be major forces leading a company to look abroad.

Essentially, advantages of superior knowledge and economies of scale determine foreign investment. These two types of advantages permit a multinational company to operate its subsidiary more profitably than local competitors. The term "knowledge" is used here to mean production technologies, managerial skills, industrial organization, and knowledge of product and foreign markets.

In addition to superior knowledge, foreign direct investment allows a multinational company to obtain economies of scale. Vertical foreign investment reduces costs and uncertainties that exist when subsequent stages of production are handled by different producers. Horizontal foreign investment gives the multinational company opportunities to eliminate duplicate facilities as well as to consolidate the functions of production, marketing, and purchasing.

Political Climate

Political risks may exist for domestic investment. Price controls may be established or lifted, some regulated industries may be deregulated, or quotas and tariffs on cheap imported components may be imposed. Certainly, there are more chances of political risks in foreign investment. For one thing, at least two national governments become involved in a foreign investment project—the home country of the parent company and the host country of the subsidiary. The goals of the two countries may differ; laws may change; rights to repatriate capital may be modified; and in an extreme situation, assets may be seized by a host government without adequate compensation.

One major concern of multinational companies is the possibility that the political climate of a host country may deteriorate. The multinational financial manager must analyze the political environment of the proposed host country and determine whether the economic environment would be receptive to the proposed project. In general, projects designed to reduce the country's need for imports and thus save foreign exchange are given the highest priority by the host government.

Political actions, such as government takeovers, exchange controls, and other operational restrictions adversely affect company operations. Thus, the analyst should emphasize such factors as the host government's attitudes toward foreign investment, the desire of the host country for national rather than foreign control, and its political stability. The analyst should also determine whether adequate and prompt compensation is guaranteed if a host country nationalizes alien assets in the public interest.

Company's Overall Strategy

If the initial screening of the political climate is favorable, the multinational company can move on to the next stage of the decision process. The analyst then assesses the usefulness of the company's overall strategy to determine how foreign operations may perpetuate current strengths or weaknesses. This approach allows a company to reduce alternatives to a manageable number. At this stage, the company must check whether the project conflicts with company goals, policies, and resources. The analyst must also evaluate whether the company has the experience to handle the project and how the project could be integrated into existing projects.

Overall Strategy. The company's overall strategy consists of objectives, policies, and resources. In capital expenditure analysis, there are objectives to be attained and policies designed to achieve these objectives. If a particular set of policies is not consistent with the stated objectives, either the policies or the objectives should be revised. The company must also have resources necessary to carry out its policies. If resources are not available, they must be acquired, or the policies and/or the objectives must be revised.

Company Goal.   The primary goal of the multinational company is to maximize its stock price. The market price of the firm's stock reflects the market's evaluation of its prospective earnings stream over time and the riskiness of this stream. Thus, the company must attempt to accept projects whose profits are higher and whose risks are lower. If the company has carefully established policies, it could overcome the threat of competitors and use its oligopolistic advantages. The company should systematically evaluate individual entry strategies in foreign markets, continuously audit the effectiveness of current entry modes, and use appropriate evaluation criteria.

Company Resources.   Resources are assets that enable the company to carry out its objectives and policies; they include marketing skills, management time and expertise, capital resources, technological capabilities, and strong brand names.

Cash Flow Analysis

The fourth stage of the screening process involves a standard cash flow analysis. The after-tax cash outflows and inflows directly associated with each project must be estimated to evaluate capital investment alternatives. A multinational company must forecast its expected expenditures for the proposed project. Ordinarily, it obtains these forecasts from data of similar ventures. A company may also make forecasts by such techniques as the percent-of-sale method or a linear regression analysis. An important difference in the application of cash flow analysis for foreign investment is that a company must make two sets of cash flow analysis, one for the project itself and one for the parent company.

Demand Forecast.   The first step in analyzing cash flows for any investment proposal is a forecast of demand. These estimates of usage are highly correlated with historical demands, population, income, alternative sources of products, competition, the feasibility of serving nearby markets, and general economic conditions.

There are a number of reasons for emphasizing market size in the investment decision process. First, the expected market size can be used as an indication of profit possibilities for the proposed investment project. Second, small markets tend to have high uncertainty. If a market is small, the multinational company has little or no leeway in case of an erroneous estimate. Third, small markets are not worth the effort. Because management is one of scarce resources in a company, the proposed project should be large enough to support management time on project analysis.

Duties and Taxes.   Because foreign investment cuts across national boundaries, a unique set of tax laws and import duties may be applicable. A multinational company must review the tax structure of the host country. In this analysis, the evaluator would include the definition of a taxable entity, statutory tax rates, tax treaties, treatment of dual taxation, and tax incentive programs. The multinational company should also know whether the host government imposes customs duties on imported production equipment and materials not obtainable from local sources.

Exchange Rate.

Another important feature of foreign investment analysis is that project inflows available to the investor are subject to foreign exchange rates and restrictions. When the host country has a stable exchange rate, no problems are presented. However, if the exchange rate is expected to change or allowed to float, cash flow analysis becomes more complicated because the analyst must forecast the exchange rate which may be applicable to convert cash flows into hard currencies.

It is equally important to recognize that many host governments have various exchange control regulations. Under these regulations, permission may be required to buy foreign exchange with local currency for payment of loan interest, management fees, royalties, and most other billings for services provided by foreign suppliers. Processing applications for permission to purchase foreign exchange may take a long time. Moreover, granting permission to buy foreign exchange does not guarantee that a related foreign exchange will be available in time because commercial banks can allocate only such amounts as are made available by a central bank.

Many factors affect the blockage of funds to nonresidents. They include an expected shortage of foreign exchange, a long-run deficiency of the foreign exchange, and certain types of domestic political pressures. If all funds are blocked in perpetuity, the value of a project is zero to the parent company. However, in actuality funds are likely to be only partially blocked because multinational companies have many ways to remove blocked funds. These methods include transfer price adjustments, loan repayments, royalty adjustments, and fee adjustments. Furthermore, most host countries limit the amount of fund transfers to nonresidents or block the transfer of funds only on a temporary basis. Nevertheless, multinational companies must analyze the effect of blocked funds on project return. It is critical that an analyst determine the amount of blocked funds, their reinvestment return, and ways in which funds can be transferred under the host country's law.

Project vs. Parent Cash Flows.

To yield after-tax profits from a proposed project, the multinational company must develop a demand forecast, forecast its expected expenditures, and review the tax structure of the host country. The estimated sales, less estimated expenses plus noncash outlays (such as depreciation), gives the cash inflows from operations.

Typically, a multinational company desires to maximize the utility of project cash flows on a worldwide basis. The multinational company must value only those cash flows which can be repatriated because only these funds can be used for investment in new ventures, for payment of dividends and debt obligations, and for reinvestment in other subsidiaries. Project cash flows would have little value if they could not be used for these alternatives.

Project cash flows and parent cash flows can be substantially different due to tax regulations and exchange controls. Moreover, some project expenses, such as management fees and royalties, are returns to the parent company. In general, incremental cash flows to the parent company are worldwide parent cash flows after investment minus worldwide parent cash flows before investment. These differences raise the question of which cash flows should be used as the relevant cash flows in project evaluation. Because the value of a project is determined by the net present value of future cash flows to an investor, a foreign investment analyst should use cash flows available for repatriation as the relevant cash flows. Hence, the multinational company must analyze the impact of taxation, expropriation, and exchange controls on cash flows to the parent company.

Capital Budgeting and Transfer Pricing. Cash flow analysis of a foreign investment project involves many unique environmental variables. They include (1) different tax systems, (2) foreign exchange risk, (3) project vs. parent cash flows, (4) restrictions on remittance of funds, and (5) political, financial, and business risks. In these five environmental variables, a transfer pricing policy is an integral part of each of the following three issues: First, multinational companies should know the amount of funds they can withdraw from their foreign investment. Transfer price adjustments, dividends, royalties, and management fees are the only techniques to withdraw funds where there are restrictions on fund flow movements. Second, transfer pricing policies are regarded as one of the best ways to reduce a variety of taxes, such as income taxes, tariffs, and other taxes. Third, transfer pricing policies are one of the better means to minimize foreign exchange losses from currency fluctuations because they enable multinational companies to shift funds from one country to another. However, it is important to understand that use of market-based transfer prices may lead to the better investment decision because transfer price adjustments may significantly distort the profitability of a foreign project.

The Cost of Capital

The cost of capital is the minimum rate of return that a project must yield in order to be accepted by a company. This minimum rate of return is sometimes called the discount rate or the required rate of return. The actual required rate of return applied by a multinational company may be the cost of capital adjusted for political and exchange risks.

The weighted average cost of capital is normally used as the firm's cost of capital for a number of reasons. First, if a single component cost is used as a criterion for acceptance, projects with a low rate of return may be accepted while projects with a high rate of return may be rejected. Some low return projects will be accepted because they can be financed with a cheaper source of capital such as debt. Some high-return projects will be rejected because they have to be financed with an expensive source of capital such as equity. Second, if a firm accepts projects that yield more than its weighted average cost of capital, it can increase the market value of its common stock. In this case, the market value of the common stock increases because these projects are expected to earn more on their equity-financed portion than the cost of equity.

The weighted average cost of capital is the cost for each type of capital multiplied by its proportion of the total amount of all capital issued by the firm:

$$k = \frac{S}{B + S}(k_e) + \frac{B}{B + S}(k_t) \qquad (15\text{-}1)$$

where:

k = weighted average cost of capital
k_e = cost of equity
k_t = after-tax cost of debt
B = market value of the firm's debt
S = market value of the firm's equity

Optimum Capital Structure.

The optimum capital structure is defined as the combination of debt and equity that yields the lowest cost of capital or that maximizes the overall value of the company. In this case, the amount of capital to be obtained is fixed, but the debt ratio is changed to determine the optimum capital structure. For instance, financial ratios published by Dun & Bradstreet, Robert Morris Associates, and other organizations show that the capital structures among companies in the same industry are similar.

We may not equally apply these considerations to the multinational cases because we cannot ignore the modifying effects of environmental variables peculiar to international operations. Evidence suggests that the capital structure of companies in the same industry varies widely from country to country. Many researchers point to high Japanese leverage as another source of their capital cost advantage. For example, a study by Sadahiko Suzuki and Richard Wright (1985) found that the debt ratio for most Japanese companies was higher than the comparable debt ratio for American companies. Because the tax deductibility of interest and the low risk of bonds make debt cheaper than equity, Japanese companies are said to have a lower weighted average cost of capital.

This conclusion suffers from one basic problem. Most researchers measure debt ratios using book-value weights instead of market-value weights. Book-value weights are derived from the stated values of individual components of the capital structure on the firm's current balance sheet. There are two major advantages to book-value weights. First, the proportions of the capital structure are stable over time because book-value weights do not depend on market prices. Second, book-value weights are easy to determine because they are derived from the stated values on the firm's balance sheet.

However, the book-value weights may misstate the weighted average cost of capital because the market values of bonds and stocks change over time and thus do not reflect the desired capital structure.

Market-value weights are based on the current market prices of bonds and stocks. Because the primary goal of the firm is to maximize its market value, market-value weights are consistent with the firm's objective. The market values of a company's existing securities depend on the expected earnings of the company and the risk of the securities as perceived by investors. In other words, market values reflect the assessments by current buyers and sellers of future earnings and risk. Thus, the weighted average cost of capital with market-value weights should be the valid average rate of return required by investors in the firm's securities.

Using market-value weights, the debt ratio for Japanese companies has declined since 1985 while the debt ratio for U.S. companies has remained stable (see Table 15-1). By 1987, the U.S. debt ratio has surpassed the Japanese debt ratio. James Poterba (1991) attributed this convergence of U.S. and Japanese leverage to two factors. First, U.S. companies purchased nearly $100 billion in equities each year between 1985 and 1990. Second, during the 1980s Japanese stock prices increased faster than bond prices. Consequently, the debt ratio of Japanese firms on a market value basis declined during the period.

William Sekely and J. Markham Collins (1988) compared debt ratios for 677 companies in nine industries from 23 countries. They concluded that cultural factors, such as political, legal, social, institutional, and tax environments cause debt ratios to cluster by country rather than by industry or size. They classified these 23 countries into seven cultural "realms" with similarities in capital structure norms:

Anglo-American   Australia, Canada, South Africa, United
                           Kingdom, and United States.
Latin American   Argentina, Brazil, Chile, and Mexico.

Table 15-1
Debt Ratios for U.S. and Japanese Corporations

Year	United States	Japan
1985	40.1%	57.0%
1986	40.0	50.2
1987	42.2	39.7
1988	42.4	37.5
1989	39.9	35.4
1990	45.1	39.7

Source: James M. Poterba, "Comparing the Cost of Capital in the United States and Japan: A Survey of Methods," *Quarterly Review*, Federal Reserve Bank of New York, Winter 1991, p. 28.

West Central Europe	Benelux, Switzerland, and Germany.
Mediterranean Europe	France, Italy, and Spain.
Scandinavia	Denmark, Finland, Norway, and Sweden.
Indian Peninsula	India and Pakistan.
Southeast Asia	Malaysia and Singapore.

They found low debt ratios in the Southeast Asian, Latin American, and Anglo-American groups of countries. They found high debt ratios in the Scandinavian, Mediterranean, and Indian Peninsula groups. The West Central European countries had debt ratios in the middle of the seven groups.

When companies raise funds for new investment projects, they are concerned with the marginal cost of new funds. Companies should always expand their capital budget by raising funds in the same proportion as their optimum capital structure. However, as their capital budget expands in absolute terms, their marginal cost of capital will eventually increase. This means that companies can tap only the capital market for some limited amount in the short-run before their marginal cost of capital rises, even though the same optimum capital structure is maintained.

A variety of factors affect a company's cost of capital: the size of the company, access to capital markets, diversification, tax concessions, exchange-rate risk, and political risk. The first four factors favor the multinational company, whereas the last two factors favor the purely domestic company. In other words, multinational companies usually enjoy a lower cost of capital than purely domestic companies for a number of reasons. First, multinational companies can borrow money at lower rates of interest because they are bigger. Second, they can raise funds in a number of capital markets such as the Euromarkets, local capital markets, and foreign capital markets. Third, their overall cost of capital may be lower than that of purely domestic companies because they are more diversified. Fourth, they may lower their overall taxes because they can use tax-haven countries, tax-saving holding companies, and transfer pricing.

Cost of Equity.   Interest and preferred dividends are directly measurable components of debt and preferred stocks, but we do not have such a measurable element for the cost of common equity. This is because dividend declarations on common stock are made at the discretion of the firm's board of directors. Consequently, the cost of common equity is the most difficult concept to measure.

The cost of equity for a firm is the minimum rate of return necessary to attract investors to buy or hold a firm's common stock. This required rate of return is the discount rate that equates the present value of all expected future dividends per share with the current price per share. If dividends per share are expected to grow at a constant growth rate indefinitely, we can measure the cost of equity by the following formula:

$$k_e = \frac{D_1}{P} + g \qquad\qquad (15\text{-}2)$$

where:

  D_1 = expected dividends per share to be paid at the end of one year
  P = current market price per share
  g = annual dividend growth rate

An alternative approach to the dividend valuation model for the cost of capital is the capital asset pricing model (CAPM). This model assumes that the total risk of a common stock consists of systematic risk and unsystematic risk. Systematic risk is a reflection of the overall market risk—risk that is common to all stocks. Some common causes of systematic risk include changes in the overall economy, tax reform by the Congress, and a change in the national energy situation. Because it is common to all stocks, systematic risk cannot be eliminated by diversification. Unsystematic risk is unique to a particular company. Some causes of unsystematic risk include a wildcat strike affecting only the company, a new competitor producing essentially the same product, and a technological breakthrough making an existing product obsolete. Unsystematic risk can be eliminated by diversification.

Within the international context, systematic risk relates to such global events as worldwide recessions, world wars, and changes in the world energy supply. Unsystematic risk relates to such national events as expropriation, currency controls, inflation, and exchange-rate changes.

If a market is in equilibrium, the expected rate of an individual security (j) is stated as follows:

$$R_j = R_f + (R_m - R_f)\beta_j \qquad\qquad (15\text{-}3)$$

where:

  R_j = expected rate of return on security j
  R_f = riskless rate of interest
  R_m = expected rate of return on the market portfolio, which is a group of risky securities such as Standard & Poor's 500 Stocks
  β_j = systematic risk of security j

This equation is known as the security market line, which consists of the riskless rate of interest (R_f) and a risk premium [$(R_m-R_f)\beta_j$].

One potential problem with using the CAPM is how to compute beta. Beta may be estimated solely on the basis of subjective probability distributions. But it is the common practice to use past data to estimate future betas. If the beta computed from historical data is a reliable surrogate for future beta, financial managers have an important new tool in formulating profitable investment decisions. Some empirical surveys indicate that past betas are useful in predicting future betas. Betas tend to have greater stability when the number of securities in a portfolio is larger and when the time intervals being studied are longer.

Another approach to measuring the cost of equity is the price–earnings ratio, which is the price per share divided by the earnings per share. More accurately, the earnings-price ratio can be used to determine the rate of return demanded by shareholders. Table 15-2 and the survey of previous studies suggest that the cost of equity based on the price-earnings ratio has been lower in Japan than the United States for most of the last two decades.

The main difference between the three approaches to the cost of equity is that the dividend valuation model and the price-earnings ratio emphasize the total risk of expected returns while the CAPM emphasizes only the systematic risk of expected returns. In any case, the cost of equity is some function of the market's preference for return and risk.

Cost of Debt.   The explicit cost of debt for a firm can be defined as the discount rate that equates the net proceeds of the debt issue with the present value of interest and principal payments. If we want to express all cost-of-capital rates on an after-tax basis, we must adjust this explicit cost of debt for taxes because interest charges are usually tax deductible. We denote the after-tax cost of debt by k_t, and determine this cost by the following equation:

$$k_t = k_i(1 - t) \qquad\qquad (15\text{-}4)$$

Table 15–2
Price–Earnings Ratios for the United States and Japan

Year	United States	Japan
1975	11.8	25.2
1976	11.2	22.0
1977	9.1	19.3
1978	8.2	21.5
1979	7.5	16.6
1980	9.6	17.9
1981	8.2	24.9
1982	11.9	23.7
1983	12.6	29.4
1984	10.4	26.3
1985	15.4	29.4
1986	18.7	58.6
1987	14.1	50.4
1988	12.9	54.3
1989	14.8	53.7
1990	15.9	36.6

Source: James M. Poterba, "Comparing the Cost of Capital in the United States and Japan: A Survey of Methods," *Quarterly Review*, Federal Reserve Bank of New York, Winter 1991, p. 25.

where:

k_i = before–tax cost of debt

t = tax rate

Multinational companies must account for a number of complicated factors to measure the cost of debt. First, multinational companies can borrow in Eurocurrency markets, international bond markets, or national capital markets. Hence, they must (in order to measure the before–tax cost of debt) estimate interest rates and the proportion of debt to be raised in each market. Second, multinational companies must (in order to measure the after–tax cost of debt) estimate tax rates in each market in which they intend to borrow and determine the deductibility of interest by each national tax authority. Third, the nominal cost of principal and interest in foreign currency must be adjusted for foreign exchange gains or losses when multinational companies issue debt denominated in a foreign currency.

The least controversial part of most studies on the cost of capital is the treatment of tax incentives for new investment. Different studies have reached different conclusions, however, regarding the net effect of tax provisions on the relative costs of capital. Table 15–3 shows the relevant tax parameters—the statutory corporate tax rate and the net tax–induced reduction in the price of capital goods. The tax benefits for the two examples of projects given here are greater in Japan than the United States. However, most studies of capital costs have argued that tax provisions in Japan are similar to those in the United States and that, therefore, the cost–of–capital differential between the two countries cannot be attributed to tax considerations.

The Appropriate Cost of Capital.   If multinational companies make a separate allowance for different levels of risk in foreign projects, they must use the weighted average cost of capital as an appropriate cost of capital. They have three choices in deciding their subsidiary cost of capital: (1) cost of capital to the parent company, (2) cost of capital to the subsidiary, and (3) some weighted average of the two.

Table 15–3
Tax Parameters in Cost–of–Capital Calculations

Parameter	United States		Japan	
	1980	1988	1980	1988
Statutory corporate tax rate	0.53	0.50	0.50	0.38
Present value of tax reduction for new investment				
Autos	0.46	0.47	0.53	0.33
Industrial plant	0.25	0.36	0.17	0.14

Source: James M. Poterba, "Comparing the Cost of Capital in the United States and Japan: A Survey of Methods," *Quarterly Review*, Federal Reserve Bank of New York, Winter 1991, p. 30.

If a parent company finances the entire cost of its foreign project by itself, the cost of capital to the parent company can be used as the appropriate cost of capital. If its foreign subsidiary obtains all of the capital for the project overseas, the foreign cost of capital can be used as the appropriate cost of capital. In most cases, however, the multinational company uses the whole world as a combined source of funds. Thus, the appropriate cost of capital is usually an overall weighted average of the two.

The inflation–adjusted discount rate may have to be used as an appropriate cost of capital if the analyst wishes to reflect local inflation for local projects. However, inflation tends to be built into the cost of debt and equity for a company because the weighted average cost of capital reflects such anticipated price changes. When lenders and equity holders anticipate price increase, they will demand a rate of return higher than in ordinary cases so that the weighted average cost of capital reflects inflation. Thus, the multinational company should not add an increase to the discount rate derived from the cost of capital in order to adjust for inflation.

The Cost of Capital in the United States and Japan.
Wide U.S. trade deficits with Japan during the 1980s prompted academicians, policymakers, and business people to search for the sources of declining U.S. competitiveness. Many argued that the cost of capital—the rate of return that firms must earn to produce the amount of profits demanded by shareholders and creditors—was significantly higher in the United States than in Japan. Thus, Japanese managers found it in their firms' best interest to undertake long–horizon projects that U.S. managers rejected. In other words, because U.S. managers took the short–run view, they forewent investment or market–development projects with high future yields to maintain their current profits.

Table 15–4 presents three sets of estimates from studies which assessed U.S. and Japanese capital costs. All of the studies conclude that the cost of capital is significantly higher in the United States than in Japan. The data given in Tables 15–1 through 15–3 suggest that differential costs of equity are

Table 15–4
Estimated Costs of Capital for the U.S. and Japan

Study	Year	United States	Japan
Hatsopoulos–Brooks	1980	14.1%	4.0%
	1988	9.7	3.8
McCauley–Zimmer	1980	11.5	8.8
	1988	11.2	7.8
Bernheim–Shoven	1980	18.7	11.0
	1988	11.1	4.1

Source: James M. Poterba, "Comparing the Cost of Capital in the United States and Japan: A Survey of Methods," *Quarterly Review*, Federal Reserve Bank of New York, Winter 1991, 30.

the single most important explanation of the cost-of-capital difference between the United States and Japan. Many institutional and economic differences between the two nations may contribute to this disparity—in particular, Japan's higher savings rate, higher debt ratio until the mid-1980s, larger tax benefits for new investment, and greater flexibility in spreading corporate risk.

Optimum Capital Budget.

The optimum capital budget is defined as the amount of investment that would maximize the value of the company. It is obtained at the intersection between the internal rate of return and the marginal cost of capital; at this point, total profit is maximized. Multinational companies can tap foreign capital markets when domestic capital markets are saturated; they have more investment opportunities than purely domestic companies. These two factors give multinational companies the optimum capital budgets which are higher than the optimum capital budgets of domestic companies.

Economic Evaluation

Once cash flows and the required rate of return have been determined, the company begins the formal process of evaluating investment projects. Many techniques have been developed for evaluating projects under conditions of certainty. They range from simple rules of thumb to sophisticated mathematical programming methods. The four most commonly used methods for an economic evaluation of individual projects are payback, average rate of return, internal rate of return, and net present value.

Literature on capital expenditure analysis favors the net present value and internal rate of return methods, which are sometimes called the discounted cash flow approaches. The two discounted cash flow approaches provide a more sophisticated basis for ranking and selecting investment projects because the payback and average-rate-of return methods have various limitations. They clearly recognize that money has a time value and that money in the near future is more valuable than money in the distant future. They also use the cash flows of a project over its entire life span. Analysts can avoid difficult problems underlying the measurement of income by using cash flows, thus eliminating such irrelevant influences as depreciation methods and inventory valuation.

The net present value of a project is the present value of its expected cash inflows minus the present value of its expected cash outflows. The decision rule tells us to (1) accept a project if its net present value is positive and (2) accept a project if its internal rate of return is greater than a firm's cost of capital.

The net present value and internal rate of return methods lead to the same decision in many situations. These two rules lead to the same decision if the following conditions hold:

1. Investment proposals under consideration are mutually independent and they are free of capital rationing considerations.
2. All projects are equally risky so that the acceptance or rejection of any project does not affect the cost of capital.
3. A meaningful cost of capital exists to the extent that a company has access to capital at this cost.
4. A unique internal rate of return exists; every project has just one internal rate of return.

In the absence of these assumptions, the two discounted cash-flow approaches may lead to different decisions, thus making the capital budgeting decision much more complex.

When the net present value and internal rate of return methods produce different answers, net present value is better for a number of reasons:

1. The net present value is easier to compute than the internal rate of return.
2. If the primary goal of a firm is to maximize the value of the firm, the net present value method leads to the correct decision, while the internal rate of return method may lead to an incorrect decision.
3. A single project may have more than one internal rate of return under certain conditions, whereas the same project has just one net present value at a particular discount rate.
4. Once computed, the internal rate of return remains constant over the entire life of the project. This assumption about static conditions is hardly realistic during a period of rising interest rates and inflation. Uneven discount rates present no problems when the net present value method is used.
5. In the net present value method, the implied reinvestment rate approximates the opportunity cost for reinvestment. But with the internal rate of return method, the implied reinvestment assumption does not approximate the opportunity cost for reinvestment at all.

Although the net present value method is theoretically superior, the internal rate of return method has certain advantages. First, internal rate of return is easier to visualize and interpret because it is identical with the yield to the maturity of bonds or other securities. Second, a required rate of return is not needed in the computation. In other words, the prior computation of the cost of capital is unnecessary. Third, business executives are more comfortable with internal rate of return because it is directly comparable to the firm's cost of capital.

Selection

Each of the capital budgeting techniques described in the previous section measures the rate of return on a uniform basis for all projects under consideration. A project or a set of projects will be chosen at this stage if the following three assumptions hold: first, the company has a definite cutoff point which all projects must meet; second, all cash outflows and inflows from each project are known with absolute certainty; third, the company's investment programs are not constrained by any lack of funds. The final selection of projects depends on the kinds of capital budgeting decisions: the accept-reject decision, the mutually exclusive choice decision, and the capital rationing decision.

The selected project must successfully pass the accept-reject decision. If projects under consideration are mutually independent and not subject to capital rationing constraints, the company must accept all projects whose expected rate of return exceeds its hurdle rate in order to maximize stockholder wealth. The hurdle rate may be based on the cost of capital, the opportunity cost, or some other arbitrary standard. However, it is important to recognize the possibility that (1) certain projects may compete with each other and (2) available projects may exceed available funds. Mutual exclusiveness and capital rationing constraints are two cases where otherwise profitable projects are rejected. Investment proposals are said to be mutually exclusive if the acceptance of one project means the rejection of all the other projects. Capital rationing refers to an upper ceiling on the size of capital expenditures during a given period of time.

Risk Analysis

Up to this point, we have assumed that the dollar cash flows will certainly occur. In reality, all foreign investment projects are subject to various risks—business and financial risks, inflation and currency risks, and political risks. A change in some of these risks may have a deciding impact on the financial consequences of a particular project. Furthermore, the risks vary widely from country to country.

Only a few of the financial variables are normally known with a fair degree of accuracy in advance. Investors are basically risk averters. If investors do not know in advance exactly which future events will occur, they will have to determine the risk-return trade-off in order to choose attractive projects.

Many multinational companies use the risk-adjusted discount rate and the certainty equivalent approach to adjust for project estimates. Assume that the cost of capital for a firm is 10 percent when the riskless rate of return is 7 percent. This 3 percent difference between the cost of capital and the riskless rate of return reflects the degree of risk for the company. The company may increase its discount rate by 2 percent to a total of 12 percent for a mildly risky project, by 5 percent to a total of 15 percent for a more risky project, and so on. Hence, the risk-adjusted discount rate accounts for the time value of money and the relative risk of the project in terms of a risk premium.

The certainty equivalent approach is an alternative to the risk-adjusted discount rate. It incorporates a manager's preference for return and risk directly into the capital budgeting decision. While the risk-adjusted discount rate adjusts for risk in the denominator of the net present value formula, the certainty equivalent approach adjusts for risk in the numerator of the same equation.

When an analyst uses the certainty equivalent approach, the annual cash flows are multiplied by a certainty equivalent coefficient, which is a certain cash flow divided by an uncertain cash flow. If the analyst is indifferent between a certain $140 and an uncertain $200, its coefficient is 0.70 ($140/$200). The coefficient assumes a value of between 0 and 1, and it varies inversely with risk. If a firm perceives greater risk, it uses a lower coefficient which would deflate the dollar return value. Once all the risky cash flows are adjusted downward to reflect uncertainty through the use of the coefficient, the analyst then discounts these certain cash flows at the risk-free rate of interest to determine the certain net present value.

Implementation, Control, and Post Audits

The last three steps of the capital budgeting system consist of implementation, expenditure control, and post audits.

Implementation.   Authorization to expend funds for the accepted projects may be obtained by submission of individual capital expenditure requests in accordance with formal procedures set forth by the budget director. These procedures typically cover the use of standard forms, the channels for submission and review, and the authority requirements and limits for approval.

Control.   There is a specific phase of the capital budgeting process during which the practical cost control of a foreign project becomes important. This is the time between the approval of the project and its completion. The expenditure control of a foreign project in process is designed to increase the probability that it is completed within the established guidelines. This phase is particularly important for foreign investment projects because operations are typically supervised from a distance.

Post Audit.   Because multinational capital budgeting decisions are made on the basis of assumptions in foreign countries, estimates and actual results may differ. Thus, when a foreign project is completed, the firm should perform a post audit on the entire project to determine its success or failure. The results of post audits enable the firm to compare the actual performance of a foreign project with established standards. If the capital budgeting process used by a multinational firm has been successful, the system is likely to be reinforced. If the system has been unsatisfactory, it is likely to be revised or replaced for future foreign projects.

Example 15-1.   In September 1994, the government of Jordan requested that the International TV Corporation establish a plant in Jordan to assemble television sets. The company wishes to invest 1,500 Jordanian dinars in the proposed plant in return for an increase in tariffs against other companies in the industry. The JD1,500 will be financed with only common stock, all of which will be owned by the parent company. The plant is to be depreciated over a five-year period on a straight-line basis for tax purposes. It expects to have a salvage value of JD750 at the end of five years. The company will pay income taxes at 20 percent on net income earned in Jordan and no withholding taxes on dividend repatriated. In this case, the United States also has a 50 percent tax rate with direct credit for Jordanian taxes. This means that net income earned in Jordan by U.S. companies will be subject to a total of 50 percent tax. Expected revenues, operating costs, and applicable exchange rates are given in Tables 15-5 and 15-6. There is no restriction on dividend repatriation, but depreciation cash flows may not be repatriated until the company is liquidated. These cash flows can be reinvested in Jordanian government bonds to earn tax-exempt interest at the rate of 8 percent. The company's cost of capital is 15 percent.

Table 15-5 shows the projected cash flows for the proposed plant. It is important to recognize that for the first year a total tax of 50 percent (JD225) will be levied: 20 percent of the Jordanian tax (JD90) and 30 percent of the U.S. tax (JD135).

Table 15-6 shows the depreciation cash flows and interest-compounded depreciation cash flows at the termination of the project at the end of five years. Thus, a total of JD880 will be repatriated to the United States along with the plant's fifth year earnings of JD375 at the end of five years.

The last two steps in the analysis are: (1) to convert the cash flows from dinars to dollars and (2) to determine the net present value of the plant. Table 15-7 shows these two computation steps. It should be noted that the fifth year

Table 15–5
Projected Earnings After Taxes for the Proposed Project

	Year 1	Year 2	Year 3	Year 4	Year 5
Revenues	JD1,500	JD1,650	JD1,800	JD1,950	JD2,100
Operating costs	900	900	1,050	1,050	1,200
Depreciation	150	150	150	150	150
Taxable income	JD 450	JD 600	JD 600	JD 750	JD 750
Total tax at 50%	225	300	300	375	375
Earnings after tax	JD 225	JD 300	JD 300	JD 375	JD 375

Table 15–6
Depreciation Cash Flows

Year	Depreciation	Interest Factor at 8%	Terminal Value Year 5
1	JD150	1.360	JD204
2	150	1.260	189
3	150	1.166	175
4	150	1.080	162
5	150	1.000	150
			JD880

Table 15–7
The Parent's Net Present Value

Year	Cash Flows	Exchange Rate	Cash Flows	Present Value at 15%	Cum. Net Present Value
0	–JD1,500	5.00	–$300	–$300	–$300
1	225	5.00	45	39	–261
2	300	5.25	57	43	–218
3	300	5.51	54	36	–182
4	375	5.79	65	37	–145
5	2,005	6.08	330	164	19

cash flow of JD2,005 consists of dividends (JD375), the estimated salvage value of the plant (JD750), and the interest–accumulated depreciation cash flows (JD880).

The current exchange rate of five dinars to the dollar is expected to hold during the first year. But the dinar is expected to depreciate at a rate of 5 percent per year after the first year. The expected cash flows in dollars are obtained by dividing the cash flows in dinars by the exchange rates. The dollar cash flows are then discounted at the firm's cost of capital (15 percent) to arrive at a present value figure for each year. Cumulative net present values are the final amounts given in Table 15-7. We see that from the parent's point of views, the plant would break even on a discounted cash flow basis during the fifth year. Because the net present value of the project is positive ($19), the International TV Corporation should accept the proposed plant in order to maximize the market value of the company. The project's internal rate of return is approximately 17 percent. Because the internal rate of return (17 percent) is greater than the cost of capital (15 percent), the internal rate of return criterion also indicates acceptance.

Portfolio Theory

In the real world, practically no company or individual invests everything in a single project. Thus, it is useful to consider the risk and return of a particular project in conjunction with its counterparts in existing assets or new investment opportunities. Portfolio theory deals with the selection of investment projects that would minimize risk for a given rate of return or that would maximize the rate of return for a given degree of risk. Such a portfolio is sometimes called the optimum portfolio.

Harry Markowitz (1959) and James Tobin (1958) developed a powerful technique for a simultaneous risk-return analysis of multiple projects. Although the technique was applied first for the selection of portfolios of common stocks, it is also applicable to the evaluation of capital investment projects. This approach employs two basic measures: an index of expected value and an index of risk. The expected value for a portfolio of investments is simply the sum of the individual present values for the projects that make up the portfolio. The standard deviation as a measure of risk for the portfolio, however, is not so easily measured. There are many business situations where the risks of individual projects tend to offset each other. Thus, successful diversification makes it possible for the company to have the risk of a portfolio less than the sum of the risks of the individual projects.

Example 15–2.   Project A has a cost of $800, while Project B has a cost of $1,000. These two projects are mutually independent and their possible net cash flows at the end of one year are given in Table 15–8. Assume that the cost of capital is 5 percent.

Because the expected net cash flow for both projects is $1,000 ($2,000 x 0.5 + $0 x 0.5), their net present values (NPV) are computed as follows:

$$NPV_A = \frac{\$1,000}{(1.05)^1} - \$800 = \$152$$

$$NPV_B = \frac{\$1,000}{(1.05)^1} - \$1,000 = -\$48$$

The standard deviation of a project (δ) is computed as follows:

$$\delta = \sqrt{\sum_{i=1}^{n} (R_i - R)^2 P_i} \qquad (13\text{-}5)$$

where:
R_i = net cash flow associated with the ith event (i.e., a particular economic condition such as boom or recession)
R = expected net cash flow
P_i = probability of the ith event

Table 15–8
Net Cash Flows Under Different Economic Conditions

Economic Condition	Probability	Net Cash Flows	
		Project A	Project B
Boom	0.50	$2,000	$ 0
Recession	0.50	0	2,000

Thus, the standard deviations of Projects A and B can be obtained as follows:

$$\delta_A = \sqrt{(\$2,000 - \$1,000)^2(0.50) + (\$0 - \$1,000)^2(0.50)} = \$1,000$$

$$\delta_B = \sqrt{(\$0 - \$1,000)^2(0.50) + (\$2,000 - \$1,000)^2(0.50)} = \$1,000$$

Project A has a net present value of $152 and Project B has a net present value of -$48. Both projects have an equal standard deviation of $1,000. Project B would have no chance to be accepted because its expected net present value is negative. Project A has a positive net present value of $152, but most investors are likely to reject the project because its risk is too high.

We can completely eliminate unsystematic risk by combining these two projects, because the unsystematic risks of individual projects tend to offset each other. Whether a boom occurs or a recession occurs, the expected net cash flow of this combination is $2,000 and their combined net present value is $104 ($152 - $48). The standard deviation of this two-project portfolio is zero (0) because the portfolio always produces a net present value of $104. When we consider Projects A and B separately, both projects are clearly undesirable. However, when we treat them as a portfolio, we find the portfolio acceptable.

Capital Budgeting Theory and Practice

A quarter of a century has passed since Arthur Stonehill and Leonard Nathanson (1968) surveyed 110 U.S. and non-U.S. multinational companies to determine their foreign capital budgeting practices. Since then, research on the subject has not only refined its theoretical base but also expanded the knowledge of actual practices used by multinational companies.

A review of the literature on foreign direct investment theory reveals the following:

1. Multinational companies should value only those cash flows which can be repatriated because only these funds can be used to reinvest in other subsidiaries, pay dividends, pay debt obligations, or invest in new ventures.
2. Multinational companies should use discounted cash-flow methods for ranking and selecting foreign investment projects because these methods clearly recognize the time value of money and also employ the cash flows of a project over its entire life span.
3. Multinational companies should use their weighted average cost of capital for evaluating foreign projects because those projects that yield more than the firm's weighted average cost of capital will increase the value of the firm.

4. Multinational companies should use either the risk-adjusted discount rate or the certainty equivalent approach in order to adjust project estimates for different levels of risk in foreign projects because these two methods are theoretically more sophisticated than other methods.

Independent surveys have shown that the art and science of foreign investment analysis have vastly improved since the Stonehill and Nathanson survey in 1966. A number of researchers surveyed U.S. companies and non-U.S. companies to determine how U.S. and non-U.S. companies fared when the above four principles are taken into account. These four principles are the computation of foreign income, the capital budgeting techniques used, the measurement of the discount rate, and the risk adjustment methods used.

These empirical studies found that, overall, U.S. firms use more sophisticated capital budgeting procedures than non-U.S. counterparts. When we compare these recent findings with the 1966 Stonehill-Nathanson study, we find that more multinational companies use discounted cash-flow methods and net cash flows than 25 years ago. However, no evidence suggests that multinational companies have changed how they measure the appropriate discount rate and how they adjust for risk.

These studies reported that multinational companies measure their foreign project income in terms of net cash flows, use discounted cash-flow techniques, compute the cost of capital in a variety of ways, and adjust for risk subjectively. Thus, there is reason to believe that large U.S. and non-U.S. multinational companies follow theoretically prescribed approaches in the areas of income measurement and capital budgeting techniques. But they have yet to adopt the techniques favored by academia in the selection of the discount rate and risk analysis.

Summary

This chapter focused on the capital investment decision-making process. Although we broke down the entire decision-making process for foreign investment projects into components and relationships for a detailed inspection, these stages should not be used mechanically. Some steps may be combined, some may be subdivided, and others may be skipped altogether without jeopardizing the quality of the capital budgeting system. It is likely, however, that several of these steps will be in progress simultaneously for any project under consideration. For example, if expenditure controls and post-audits are not planned until the economic evaluation of a project is completed, the capital budgeting process will hardly be realistic. Decisions for expenditure controls and post audits affect plans, just as planning decisions affect controlling decisions. Thus, the capital budgeting process consists of several related activities that overlap continuously rather than follow an ideally prescribed order. Because all steps in the investment decision-making process are interwoven, their relationships should not permanently place any one stage first or last in a sequence.

Foreign investment projects involve many complex variables which do not exist in domestic projects. Two major risks for foreign investment projects are political risk and foreign exchange risk. In Chapter 7, we considered the nature of foreign change risk and some methods to reduce it. In Chapter 16, we describe the nature of political risk and some techniques to minimize it.

Project cash inflows and outflows are analyzed after first identifying foreign investment alternatives. Parent cash flows are then obtained by dividing the project cash flows by the exchange rates. Within this context the net present value of parent cash flows must be positive for a foreign project to be acceptably profitable. In conjunction with the earlier stages of analysis, some adjustments should be made to facilitate risk.

Questions

1. List 11 phases of the entire decision-making process for a foreign investment project. Should the decision maker consider these stages one at a time or analyze several of them simultaneously?

2. Given the added political and economic risks that exist overseas, are multinational companies more or less risky than purely domestic companies in the same industry? Are purely domestic companies insulated from effects of international events?

3. Why should subsidiary projects be analyzed from the parent's perspective?

4. List additional factors that deserve consideration in a foreign project analysis but are not relevant for a purely domestic project.

5. Why are transfer pricing policies important in cash flow analysis of a foreign investment project?

6. What factors affect a company's cost of capital? Why do multinational companies usually enjoy a lower cost of capital than purely domestic companies?

7. All of the studies on U.S. and Japanese capital costs concluded that the cost of capital is significantly higher in the United States than in Japan. What is the single most important explanation of the cost-of-capital difference between these two countries?

8. Most academicians argue that net present value is better than internal rate of return. However, most practitioners say that internal rate of return is better than net present value. Present arguments of each side.

9. List popular risk-assessment and risk-adjustment techniques. What is the major difference between these two types of risk analysis?

10. What are theoretically prescribed capital budgeting techniques? Do foreign capital budgeting practices correspond to theoretically prescribed techniques?

Problems

15-1 Assume that the American Electrical Corporation (AEC) is considering the establishment of a freezer manufacturing plant in Spain. AEC wants to invest a total of 10,000 Spanish pesetas in the proposed plant. The Pts10,000 will be financed with only common stock, all of which will be owned by the parent company. The plant is to be depreciated over a five-year period on a straight-line basis for tax purposes. It is expected to have a salvage value of Pts5,000 at the end of five years. Spain has 35 percent corporate income tax and no withholding taxes on dividends paid. The United States has 50 percent corporate income tax with direct credit for Spanish taxes. Spain does not impose any restrictions on dividend repatriation, but it does not allow the parent company to repatriate depreciation cash flows until the plant is liquidated. These depreciation cash flows may be reinvested in Spanish government bonds to earn 8 percent tax exempt interest. The cost of capital used to analyze the project is 15 percent. The current exchange rate of Pts5.00 per U.S. dollar is expected to hold during year one, but the Spanish peseta is expected to depreciate thereafter at a rate of 5 percent a year. Assume the following revenues and operating costs in terms of Spanish pesetas:

	Year 1	Year 2	Year 3	Year 4	Year 5
Revenues	10,000	11,000	12,000	13,000	14,000

(a) Determine the projected earnings after taxes for the proposed plant.
(b) Determine the interest-compounded depreciation cash flows at the end of five years.
(c) Determine the net present value of the plant, the profitability index, and the internal rate of return for the plant in terms of the U.S. dollar.

15-2 The Wayne Company currently exports 500 calculators per month to Jordan at a price of $60. The variable cost per calculator is $40. In May 1990, the company was approached by the government of Jordan with a request that it establish a small manufacturing plant in

Jordan. After a careful analysis, the company decided to make an equity investment of $1 million, half of which would represent working capital and the other half fixed assets. The company would sell the plant to a local investor for the sum of $1 at the end of five years, and the central bank of Jordan would repay the company for the working capital of $500,000. In return for an increase in tariffs against other companies, the Wayne Company is willing to sell its calculators in Jordan for $50 per unit. In addition, the company will have to buy certain raw materials from local suppliers and use local managers. Total costs of local managers and materials would be $15 per calculator. Other materials would be purchased from the parent at $10 and the parent would receive a direct contribution to overhead after variable costs of $5 per unit sold. Under this arrangement, the company expects that it can sell 1,000 calculators per month. The fixed assets are to be depreciated on a straight-line basis over a five-year period. The company will have to pay income taxes at 50 percent on profits earned in Jordan. The United States also has 50 percent tax rate with direct credit for Jordanian taxes. The current exchange rate is ten Jordanian dinars per dollar and it is expected to stay the same for the next five years. There is no restriction on cash flow repatriation.

(a) Determine the net present value of the project at 10 percent.
(b) The Wayne Company has been informed that, if it decides to reject the project, it would lose its entire export sales. How does this affect the decision by the Wayne Company?

15-3 Problems 15-1 and 15-2 highlight the complexities involved in foreign investment decisions. Identify these problems.

15-4 A project with an initial cost of $15,000 is expected to produce net cash flows of $8,000, $9,000, $10,000, and $11,000 for each of the next four years. The firm's cost of capital is 12 percent, but the financial manager perceives the risk of this particular project to be much higher than 12 percent. The financial manager feels that a 20 percent discount rate would be appropriate for the project.

(a) Compute the net present value of the project at the firm's cost of capital.
(b) Compute the risk-adjusted net present value of the project.

15-5 A project has a cost of $1,400. Its net cash flows are expected to be $900, $1,000, and $1,400 for each of the next three years. The respective certainty equivalent coefficients are estimated to be 0.75, 0.55, and 0.35. With a 6 percent risk-free discount rate, determine the certain net present value.

15-6   Assume that a company wishes to sell $6 million worth of bonds and $14 million worth of common stock. The bonds have 13 percent before-tax cost of capital and the stock is expected to pay $1.4 million in dividends. The growth rate of dividends has been 8 percent and is expected to continue at the same rate. Determine the weighted average cost of capital if the tax rate on income is 50 percent.

15-7   Project F has a cost of $3,000 and Project G has a cost of $4,000. These two projects are mutually independent and their possible net cash flows are given below. Assume the cost of capital is 10 percent.

Economic Condition	Probability	Net Cash Flows Project F	Project G
Boom	0.50	$8,000	$ 0
Recession	0.50	0	$8000

(a) Determine the net present value of Projects F and G.
(b) Determine the standard deviation of Projects F and G.
(c) Determine the portfolio net present value and the portfolio standard deviation.
(d) Discuss the significance of the portfolio effect in terms of international context.

References

Bernheim, D. B., and J. B. Shoven, "Comparison of the Cost of Capital in the United States and Japan: The Role of Risk and Taxes," Stanford University, Center for Economic Research Center, 1989, mimeo.

Collins, J. M., and W. S. Sekely, "The Relationship of Headquarters Country and Industry Classification to Financial Structure," *Financial Management*, Autumn 1983, pp. 45-51.

Hatsopoulos, G. N., and S. H. Brooks, "The Gap in the Cost of Capital: Causes, Effects, and Remedies," in R. Landau and D. Jorgenson, eds., *Technology and Economic Policy*, Cambridge: Ballinger Publishing Co., 1986.

Kester, W. C., "Capital and Ownership Structure: A Comparison of United States and Japanese Manufacturing Corporations," *Financial Management*, Spring 1986, pp. 5-16.

Kim, S. H., and T. Crick, "Foreign Capital Budgeting Practices Used by U.S. and Non–U.S. Multinational Companies," *Engineering Economist*, Spring 1984, pp. 207–15.

Kim, S. H., and Y. K. Song, "U.S. Private Investment in Korea," *Columbia Journal of World Business*, Winter 1987, pp. 61–5.

Markowitz, H., *Portfolio Selection: Efficient Diversification of Investment*, New York: Wiley, 1959.

McCauley, R. N., and S. Zimmer, "Explaining International Differences in the Cost of Capital," *Quarterly Review*, Federal Reserve Bank of New York, Spring 1989, pp. 7–28.

Poterba, J. M., "Comparing the Cost of Capital in the United States and Japan: A Survey of Methods," *Quarterly Review*, Federal Reserve Bank of New York, Winter 1991, pp. 20–32.

Sarathy, R., and S. Chatterjee, "The Divergence of Japanese and U.S. Corporate Financial Structure," *Journal of International Business Studies*, Winter 1984, pp. 85–92.

Sekely, W. S., and J. M. Collins, "Cultural Influences on International Capital Structure," *Journal of International Business Studies*, Spring 1988, pp. 87–100.

Stanley, M. T., and S. B. Block, "A Survey of Multinational Capital Budgeting," *Financial Review*, March 1984, pp. 36–54.

Stonehill, A. I., and L. Nathanson, "Capital Budgeting and the Multinational Corporation," *California Management Review*, Summer 1968, pp. 39–54.

Suzuki, S., and R. W. Wright, "Financial Structure and Bankruptcy in Japanese Companies," *Journal of International Business Studies*, Spring 1985, pp. 97–110.

Tallman, S. B., "Home Country Political Risk and Foreign Direct Investment in the United States," *Journal of International Business Studies*, Summer 1988, pp. 219–34.

Tobin, J., "Liquidity Preferences as Behavior Toward Risk," *Review of Economic Studies*, February 1958, pp. 65–86.

16
Political
Risk Management

In the last few years massive changes have taken place in Central and Eastern Europe at a breathtaking pace. At the same time, the Iraqi invasion of Kuwait in August 1990 and the subsequent war with the U.S. allies have set off a chain of events that have significantly affected the conditions for international business in every region of the world. Moreover, the global business climate is also undergoing fundamental change triggered by such factors as continuing integration of the European Community, continuing disintegration of the former Soviet Union, the worldwide shortage of investment capital, the increasing tide of migration, and the growing pressure for protectionist trade measures. Rational business opportunities in a number of areas, such as Eastern Europe and the Commonwealth of Independent States, may be rare until political and economic conditions are stabilized; prospects of such stabilization are not good at the present time. Foreign investment projects have always been subject to political risks. However, these recent events have dramatized the importance of political risk assessment for foreign investment projects.

Foreign investment decisions must be made today based on the likely political climate for many years to come. Political risk is an assessment of economic opportunity against political odds. Thus, political risk assessment requires that multinational companies evaluate both economic and political indicators. Political risk management refers to steps taken by companies to protect against economic losses from unexpected political events.

When the goals of multinational companies and their host countries conflict, multinational companies face a variety of political risks. The primary goal of a multinational company is to maximize the wealth of its stockholders. On the other hand, most host countries desire to develop their economy through greater utilization of local factors of production in order to maintain more control over key industries through less reliance on foreign capital and know-how and to strengthen their international position through less imports and more exports.

Multinational investors should understand the forces at work when political uncertainty occurs so that they can forecast future business climates, establish appropriate objectives, and take precautionary measures when necessary. In this chapter, we discuss the nature of political risks, the types of political risks, political risk forecasting, and responses to political risks.

Nature of Political Risks

Traditionally, conflicts between multinational companies and host countries have occurred over such issues as conversion of an economy to the style of a specific political system, joint ventures, control of key industries, contribution to balance of payments, national sovereignty, and economic development. Such conflicts are not limited to developing countries. More subtle (yet very real) conflicts exist between multinational companies and developed countries.

It is frequently difficult to separate political and economic risks. While government decisions are political by definition, underlying forces behind the decisions may be purely economic. For example, funds to nonresidents may be blocked because of an unexpected shortage of foreign exchange or a long-run deficiency of the foreign exchange instead of certain types of domestic political pressures. Some government decisions are partly political and partly economic. For instance, the 1980 U.S. government decision to freeze all Iranian assets in the United States had two objectives: the release of American hostages held in Iran and the protection of U.S. economic interest in Iran. In another instance, the Carter Administration imposed a grain embargo against the Soviet Union when the Soviet Union invaded Afghanistan in 1979. The Reagan Administration imposed a variety of economic sanctions against South Africa in 1986 due to that country's official policy of apartheid. Finally, the United Nations imposed economic sanctions against Iraq in Fall 1990 because of Iraq's invasion of Kuwait.

Countrywide political risks depend on three broad groups of variables: political climate, economic climate, and foreign relations. The political climate may be measured by tendencies toward subversions, rebellion, or political turmoil. Multinational investors should consider such factors as levels of political violence, the existence of extreme tendencies among political parties, and recurring governmental crises.

Investment analysts should make an overall assessment of the economic climate to protect foreign investment from political risks. Relevant economic factors include the likelihood of government intervention in the economy, levels of interest and inflation rates, persistent balance-of-payments deficits, levels of foreign debts, and worsening monetary reserves.

Finally, multinational investors should determine the extent to which host countries manifest hostility toward other countries. Important factors here are incidence of conflict with their neighbors, evidence of an arms race, and size of defense budgets.

Types of Political Risks

Empirical studies have revealed some interesting findings about the attitudes of U.S. and U.K. multinational companies to political risk. Wicks Kelly and Michael Philippatos (1982) surveyed 67 U.S. companies to obtain the perceived importance of five variables in political risk. Scott Goddard (1991) surveyed 51 U.K. companies to determine the importance of six variables in political risk. Ranked in the descending order of importance, their findings appear in Table 16-1. Although there are several different types of political risk, these risks can be divided into two broad categories for all practical purposes: actions that restrict the freedom of a foreign company to operate in a given host environment and actions that result in the takeover of alien assets.

Operational Restrictions

Actions that restrict the freedom of a foreign company include operational restrictions such as employment policies; locally shared ownership; loss of

Table 16–1
Types of Political Risk and Their Importance

United States		United Kingdom	
Rank	Variable	Rank	Variable
1	Restrictions on remittances	1	Expropriation or nationalization
2	Operational restrictions on ownership, employment, and market shares	2	Political stability within the country
3	Expropriation or nationalization	3	Restrictions on remittances of dividends and royalties
4	Discrimination	4	Currency stability
5	Breaches in agreements	5	Tax changes
6	Others	6	Exchange controls

Source: Scott Goddard, "Political Risk in International Capital Budgeting," Robert W. Kolb, ed., *The International Financial Reader*, Miami: Kolb Publishing Co., 1991, p. 360.

transfer freedom; exchange controls, financial, personal, or ownership rights; breaches or unilateral revisions in contracts and agreements; discrimination through taxes or compulsory joint ventures; and damage to property or personnel from riots, revolutions, and wars.

Funds are usually blocked in the host country when operational restrictions are imposed. There are a number of ways to remove blocked funds. The most obvious way is to arrange swaps between corporations. Here each corporation lends to the other in the country where its own funds are restricted. Other methods include transfer price adjustments and other adjustments such as fees, royalties, and loan repayments. Of course, most of these methods raise some serious ethical and legal questions. Moreover, black market operations may not be available for relatively large transfers of money and highly visible transactions, such as an attempt to terminate company operations in a small developing country.

Expropriation

Expropriation includes sales of business assets to local shareholders, compulsory sales of business assets to local and federal government units, and confiscation of business assets with or without compensation.

Although there are many types of foreign environmental risks, much of the literature on this subject has concentrated on extreme cases of expropriation or nationalization. Donald Ball and Wendell McCulloch (1985) say that many governments nationalize both foreign and domestic companies and may do so for a number of reasons:

1. The government believes that it could run the business more efficiently.
2. The government believes that the company is concealing its profits.
3. Left-wing governments, often after being elected, nationalize business firms.
4. Politicians wish to win popular support as they save jobs by putting dying industries on a life-support system.
5. The government can control a company or industry by pumping money into the company or industry.

Business operations in foreign countries are subject to the power of host countries. It is customary to seize foreign assets for a public purpose without discrimination and with adequate compensation. Although these three rules are in accordance with traditional principles of international law, they have often been ignored by many less-developed countries.

No comprehensive listing of foreign takeovers of American companies exists because such records are not compiled by an official source at the time of the event. Nevertheless, several surveys of foreign takeovers shed some light on the number of expropriations and other features of American firms expropriated. According to a 1980 study by David Jodice (1980), since 1960 1,535 foreign companies from 22 industrial countries had been nationalized in 511 separate actions by 76 countries. Almost 12 percent of all foreign investment made in 1967 was expropriated in the subsequent nine years.

Perhaps the most comprehensive survey of this type was conducted by Robert Hawkins, Narman Mintz, and Michael Provissiero (1976). According to this survey, foreign governments took over 170 U.S. foreign affiliates from 1946 to 1973. Yet another survey conducted by David Bradley (1977) reported that governments in Latin America, Arabia, Africa, and Asia expropriated a total of 292 U.S. firms from 1960 to 1976. The breakdown of expropriations by region of host country shows that Latin America nationalized the largest number of U.S. firms (144) and that Arab States expropriated the largest percentage of U.S. firms in the region (20.4 percent).

Charles Kennedy (1991) analyzed the 79 countries in terms of political regimes and their expropriation policies. Over the 1960–1985 period, there were more than 300 regimes; these regimes were categorized as mass, selective, or non-expropriators. A mass expropriator was defined as a regime which had nationalized foreign investment in all sectors of the economy; a selective expropriator was specified as a regime which had seized foreign companies in several key sectors of the economy; and a non-expropriator was stated as a regime which had not expropriated a single foreign company. Consequently, 28 regimes were classified as mass expropriators; 95 regimes were categorized as selective expropriators; and 177 regimes were assorted as non-expropriators. As shown in Table 16-2, this study revealed that during the 1960–1985 period, 79 developing countries had nationalized 1,197 foreign companies in 598 separate actions. Twenty-eight regimes, identified as mass expropriators, accounted for 374 of these actions or 63 percent of the total.

Table 16-2
Number of Firms Expropriated by Regime Type and Industry

Type of Industry	Mass Exprop. (n = 28)	Selective Exprop. (n = 95)	Total
Oil Extraction	88	91	179
Oil Refinery	12	15	27
Oil Distribution	29	23	52
Metal/Ore Extraction	39	53	92
Utility	16	22	38
Communications	7	10	17
Transportation	15	16	31
Banks	260	27	287
Insurance	71	17	88
Retail/Wholesale Trade	95	8	103
Industrial Products	100	13	113
Consumer Products	148	22	170
Total	880	317	1,197

Source: Charles R. Kennedy, Jr., "International Banking and Expropriation Risk," in Thomas I. Kindel, ed., *Proceedings of the 1991 Conference*, Charleston, SC: Association for Global Business, 1991, pp. 235.

Forecasting Political Risks

Once a manager has examined political risks and their implications, the manager shifts attention to forecasting these risks in foreign countries where his or her company has business interests. As multinational companies have become more experienced and more diversified, they maintain political forecasting staffs on the same level as economic forecasting staffs.

In political risk analysis, a manager gives special attention to the "nationalism" of a host country. Nationalism represents loyalty to one's country and pride in it based on shared common features such as race, language, religion, or ideology. In other words, it is an emotion that can hinder or prevent rational dealings with foreigners. Some effects of nationalism on multinational firms are: (1) requirements for minimum local ownership, (2) reservation of certain industries for local companies, (3) preference of local suppliers for government contracts, (4) limitations on number and type of foreign employees, (5) protectionism based on quotas and tariffs, and (6) expropriation or confiscation.

Joseph Micallef (1981) suggests that in political risk assessment, multinational companies classify countries into three identifiable categories:

1. Countries which have potential to become the Cubas of tomorrow.
2. Countries whose political risks have decreased or which have been unnecessarily discounted for political risks.
3. Countries whose political risks are significant but not bad enough to automatically rule them ineligible for foreign investment.

The task of political risk forecasting involves four basic steps:

1. The multinational company investigates the present administration's attitudes and policies toward foreign investment.
2. It assesses the country's political stability.
3. It integrates the political risk assessment into the company's strategic planning.
4. It develops strategies to reduce the company's exposure to political risks.

Government's Attitudes Toward Foreign Investment

In forecasting political interference, forecasters must first understand the host government's attitudes toward policies on private foreign companies. The key here is to identify favorable or unfavorable trends affecting the climate in which the subsidiary will operate. A government will show changes in attitudes toward foreign direct investment prior to overtly confiscating alien assets. Other important factors include the dependency of a host country on the foreign investor's country for economic aid or political support, the types of pressures exerted on the chief governmental policymakers, the existence of leftist groups at the highest levels of government, and the government's economic development plan in relation to foreign investment.

Political Stability

The second step in evaluating a company's vulnerability to political risks is to understand the type of government currently in power, its patterns of political behavior, and its norms for stability. Political stability is, in fact, one of the principal preconditions for foreign direct investment by large multinational companies. Background information on the political environment of the host country goes far beyond understanding the administration's attitudes and policies toward foreign investment. Managers in a multinational company should understand the path along which all policies toward foreign investment have been made.

A Conference Board (1969) study of investors from the major capital exporting countries found that many investors had eliminated countries and even entire geographical regions from their investment for political reasons. Political instability was the most frequently cited political obstacle.

Because political factors are subject to change, it is also important to institute an intelligence system to monitor and evaluate political developments. The intelligence system should be concerned with two things: (1) reliable in-house expertise about the host country and (2) the collection and distribution of necessary information to all relevant parties.

Political Risk and Strategic Planning

The third step in the process of political risk assessment is to integrate the assessment into the company's strategic planning. A multinational company may establish cutoff points for foreign projects under different conditions of political risk. In addition, the multinational company may design capital budgeting plans to reflect changes in the level of political risk.

Various political risks require multinational companies to modify their investment analysis. Because political risks are extremely high in some countries, multinational companies may have to use a high risk premium in the cost of capital to compensate for these risks. This extra risk premium may eliminate new projects in these countries.

If foreign projects are divisible, different capital budget plans can be established to reflect different degrees of political risk. For example, oil companies may allocate their funds for oil exploration among countries with different levels of political risk. In addition, multinational companies can diversify their investment into projects with varying degrees of risk. For example, oil companies could invest a portion of their funds on safe projects such as pipelines and the remaining portion of the funds on risky projects such as oil exploration projects.

Strategies for Political Risks

The fourth step is to assess the relative strengths and security of the subsidiary itself. A multinational company must appraise the environment in which it operates as well as its bargaining power. This appraisal enables the multinational company to learn how its foreign affiliate can become a good citizen of the host country and to determine whether the host government will continue to need its presence.

To become a good citizen of a host country, the multinational company may use the greatest possible amount of locally supplied raw materials, hire local people for managerial positions, and make the equity of the subsidiary available to the host country's investors. The subsidiary's ability to retain an essential status in the host country depends on its competitive edge, the degree to which its product is valued by the host government, and the cost to the economy of local production of the product as opposed to importation.

Techniques to Assess Political Risk

A number of political-risk assessment techniques are available to multinational companies. Some popular techniques are the delphi technique, the grand tour, the old hand, and quantitative analysis.

Delphi Technique.   The delphi technique combines the views of independent experts in order to obtain the degree of political risk on a given foreign project or a particular foreign country. The opinions of these experts about political risk are collected and averaged. One advantage of this method is that political-risk assessment is made easily and quickly. However, its major disadvantage is that it is completely based on opinions rather than facts and analyses.

Grand Tour.   The grand tour relies on the opinions of company executives visiting the country where investment is considered. Their visit usually involves a series of meetings with government officials, local business people, and potential customers. This method places responsibility for political-risk assessment in the hands of those who must carry out the proposed investment project. But the results of such a visit can be very superficial and may produce only selected pieces of information.

Old Hand.   The old hand depends upon the advice of an outside consultant. Typically, such consultants are college professors, diplomats, local politicians, or business people. The knowledge and experience of the advisor determine the quality of the political-risk assessment.

Quantitative Analysis.   Some companies use statistical techniques to assess political risk. The basic purpose of these statistical methods is to supplement personal judgment and increase forecasting accuracy. The list of factors to be considered in quantitative methods varies from forecaster to forecaster. But all of these methods combine three major factors: external economic indicators, internal economic indicators, and political indicators.

Multiple Methods.   Any of the techniques described here may be used to assess political risk. Some companies may utilize a number of methods in an attempt to obtain a good picture of the situation. If these methods should all produce about the same results, more confidence may be placed in the findings. If they give widely divergent results, a more careful investigation is needed. Because political-risk assessment is extremely important for success or failure of a project, the multiple-method approach appears to be a sound policy.

Rating Risk

Lately, an enormous amount of attention has been focused on foreign direct investment in Eastern Europe and the Commonwealth of Independent States, although so far there has been a lot of talk and relatively little action. In part, that is because of uncertainty over the political environment. The failed coup of August 1991 in the Soviet Union and the dissolution of the Soviet Union in December 1991 served as a clear reminder of how difficult it is to assess the political risk. One minute, President Gorbachev was under house arrest, and the coup leaders appeared at a televised press conference. Investors shook. But the coup quickly failed, and suddenly the Soviet Union reappeared as a risky, but perfectly rational, investment opportunity. However, in December 1991 President Gorbachev accepted the end of the Soviet Union so that 11 former Soviet Republics could form a Commonwealth of Independent States.

Foreign investments in industrial countries are safe, but many investments in developing countries are risky. The list of things that could go wrong in these developing countries— political coups, currency devaluations, unreliable local partners, and others—is nearly endless. Is it a good idea to invest in Indonesia if you don't know whether the company is connected to the powerful Suharto family? Is it smart to invest millions of dollars in China, where memories of the 1989 crackdown in Tiananmen Square are still fresh? Will emerging nations turn out to be shooting stars bursting suddenly on the scene—bright and powerful—only to burn themselves out and fade quickly?

How risky are investments in developing countries? There is, of course, no easy answer. Political instability, limited track records, poor statistics—they all make it difficult for foreign investors to gauge their investment risk in developing countries. Nevertheless, a number of risk-rating models are available from academic journals or commercial sources. Perhaps International Country Risk Guide (ICRG) by International Business Communications Ltd., London, receives the most attention from foreign investors. Here we will look at how this consulting firm evaluates the risk in some of the countries. ICRG offers a composite risk rating, as well as individual ratings for political, financial, and economic risk. The political variable—which makes up 50 percent of the composite figure—includes factors such as government corruption and how economic expectations diverge from reality. The financial rating looks at such things as the likelihood of losses from exchange controls and loan defaults. And economic ratings take into account such factors as inflation and debt-service costs.

The maximum or least-risky score is 100 for the political category and 50 each for financial and economic risk. For the composite score, 85-100 is considered very low; 70-84.5, low risk; 60-69.5 moderate risk; 50-59.5, moderately high risk; and 0-49.5, very high risk. Table 16-3 shows a global risk ranking for 129 countries.

Responses to Political Risks

Forecasting political risk is critical to a multinational company deciding on a particular project. However, the multinational company can protect itself against political risk with government insurance policies and guarantee programs. Chapters 10 and 11 described these programs in some detail.

Defensive Measures Before Investment

There are three types of defensive measures before investment: concession agreements, planned divestment, and adaptation to host-country goals.

Concession Agreements.
Many host countries have recently increased their surveillance of foreign operations within their borders. A multinational company ought to negotiate concession agreements to minimize subsequent political risks. The concession agreement spells out contractual obligations of the foreign investor and the host government. Careful negotiations may result in contracts that address such critical issues as provision for arbitration of disputes, funds remittances, transfer prices, local equity participation, method of taxation, price controls, the right to exports, and limitations on nationality of personnel.

Planned Divestment.
Planned divestment has been frequently suggested as one of the most important preinvestment strategies in order to avoid subsequent expropriation. It provides for the sale of majority ownership in foreign affiliates to local nationals during a previously agreed-upon period of time. Planned divestment is often a necessary condition for entry into foreign markets or is imposed on already existing companies.

The major argument for planned divestment is that host countries benefit from foreign direct investment in the early years, but successful foreign firms replace potential local firms in the later years. These benefits include new capital, entrepreneurship, new management techniques, and new technology. Foreign investment makes it possible for local firms to develop their own capital, entrepreneurship, management, and technology. If successful foreign companies continue to dominate profitable growth areas, host countries tend to ask these companies the question, "What have you done for us?"

Table 16–3
Political Risk Rankings

Country	Political Risk	Financial Risk	Economic Risk	Composite Risk
Switzerland	93.0	50.0	39.5	91.5
Luxembourg	93.0	49.0	36.0	89.0
Norway	87.0	47.0	42.0	88.0
Austria	88.0	47.0	39.5	87.5
Germany	83.0	50.0	38.5	86.0
Netherlands	85.0	46.0	40.5	86.0
Brunei	81.0	48.0	41.5	85.5
Japan	80.0	50.0	39.0	84.5
Singapore	79.0	48.0	39.5	83.5
U.S.	78.0	49.0	39.5	83.5
Canada	81.0	48.0	37.0	83.0
Belgium	82.0	45.0	36.5	82.0
Denmark	86.0	41.0	37.0	82.0
Sweden	81.0	47.0	35.0	81.5
Taiwan	71.0	49.0	43.0	81.5
United Kingdom	76.0	50.0	36.0	81.0
Finland	85.0	44.0	32.0	80.5
France	79.0	46.0	34.5	80.0
Ireland	80.0	42.0	37.5	80.0
New Zealand	78.0	46.0	35.0	79.5
Australia	76.0	45.0	37.0	79.0
Iceland	82.0	42.0	33.5	79.0
Malaysia	71.0	45.0	38.5	77.5
Italy	72.0	47.0	25.0	77.0
Venezuela	75.0	40.0	36.0	75.5
Portugal	69.0	42.0	38.5	75.0
South Korea	63.0	47.0	36.5	73.5
Botswana	70.0	34.0	42.0	73.0
Cyprus	69.0	39.0	38.0	73.0
Bahamas	66.0	39.0	36.5	71.0
Spain	65.0	42.0	35.0	71.0
Malta	64.0	34.0	43.0	70.5
Mexico	71.0	41.0	28.5	70.5
Oman	65.0	34.0	42.0	70.5
Chile	67.0	42.0	30.5	70.0
Czechoslovakia	73.0	36.0	30.0	69.5
Costa Rica	71.0	35.0	32.0	69.0
Indonesia	57.0	44.0	35.5	68.5
Uruguay	66.0	39.0	32.0	68.5
Thailand	57.0	42.0	37.0	68.0
Colombia	60.0	41.0	34.0	67.5
Hong Kong	58.0	42.0	35.0	67.5
Paraguay	59.0	39.0	34.5	66.5
Qatar	56.0	33.0	42.0	65.5
Gabon	57.0	33.0	39.0	64.5
Mongolia	65.0	36.0	28.0	64.5
Greece	65.0	33.0	39.5	64.0
Jamaica	66.0	37.0	24.0	63.5

Table 16-3
(continued)

Country	Political Risk	Financial Risk	Economic Risk	Composite Risk
Saudi Arabia	60.0	31.0	35.5	63.5
Israel	58.0	33.0	34.5	63.0
Trinidad/Tobago	59.0	35.0	31.5	63.0
U.A.E.	53.0	33.0	39.5	63.0
Bahrain	54.0	30.0	40.5	62.5
Brazil	67.0	34.0	23.0	62.0
Hungary	68.0	32.0	24.0	62.0
Gambia	53.0	33.0	35.5	61.0
Poland	62.0	29.0	31.0	61.0
China	58.0	24.0	38.0	60.0
South Africa	56.0	30.0	32.5	59.5
Bolivia	52.0	34.0	32.0	59.0
Cote d'Ivoire	66.0	29.0	23.0	59.0
Algeria	54.0	30.0	32.5	58.5
Argentina	63.0	30.0	23.0	58.0
Senegal	53.0	29.0	33.5	58.0
Bulgaria	61.0	28.0	25.5	57.5
Ecuador	58.0	29.0	26.0	56.5
Egypt	54.0	30.0	29.0	56.5
Libya	52.0	27.0	34.0	56.5
Nigeria	49.0	29.0	35.0	56.5
Syria	53.0	23.0	36.0	56.0
Iran	56.0	28.0	26.5	55.5
Morocco	52.0	28.0	30.5	55.5
U.S.S.R.	53.0	36.0	21.5	55.5
Ghana	53.0	30.0	27.0	55.0
Namibia	47.0	24.0	38.0	54.5
Panama	47.0	28.0	34.0	54.5
Tunisia	54.0	23.0	32.0	54.5
Cameroon	47.0	27.0	34.0	54.0
Papua	54.0	26.0	28.0	54.0
Dominican Rep.	53.0	23.0	30.5	53.5
Congo	52.0	20.0	33.5	53.0
Tanzania	56.0	27.0	23.0	53.0
Angola	45.0	19.0	41.0	52.5
Honduras	49.0	28.0	28.0	52.5
Albania	55.0	33.0	16.0	52.0
Malawi	51.0	28.0	25.0	52.0
Madagascar	57.0	20.0	26.0	51.5
Togo	41.0	26.0	35.0	51.0
Guyana	51.0	29.0	20.5	50.5
Burkina Faso	41.0	23.0	36.0	50.0
Kenya	48.0	26.0	26.0	50.0
Zimbabwe	51.0	25.0	23.5	50.0
Romania	55.0	29.0	15.0	49.5
Turkey	52.0	19.0	27.5	49.5
Niger	45.0	24.0	29.0	49.0
Guinea	48.0	21.0	28.0	48.5
Guatemala	41.0	24.0	30.5	48.0

Table 16–3
(continued)

Country	Political Risk	Financial Risk	Economic Risk	Composite Risk
Jordan	45.0	20.0	30.5	48.0
Peru	45.0	28.0	21.5	47.5
Sri Lanka	36.0	26.0	32.5	47.5
Suriname	44.0	23.0	28.0	47.5
Philippines	41.0	22.0	29.5	46.5
Yugoslavia	45.0	24.0	23.5	46.5
Kuwait	38.0	24.0	29.5	46.0
New Caledonia	44.0	13.0	34.5	46.0
North Korea	59.0	15.0	16.0	45.0
Mali	40.0	19.0	30.5	45.0
Zambia	45.0	19.0	25.5	45.0
Nicaragua	44.0	27.0	17.0	44.0
Pakistan	34.0	22.0	32.0	44.0
Vietnam	50.0	18.0	20.0	44.0
El Salvador	37.0	18.0	32.0	43.5
India	34.0	25.0	27.0	43.0
Mozambique	44.0	26.0	15.5	43.0
Yemen	49.0	23.0	12.0	42.0
Cuba	54.0	16.0	12.0	41.0
Bangladesh	33.0	18.0	29.0	40.0
Lebanon	32.0	11.0	35.0	39.0
Sierra Leone	37.0	20.0	20.5	39.0
Guinea–Bissau	46.0	19.0	12.0	38.5
Zaire	30.0	18.0	20.0	34.0
Haiti	28.0	12.0	26.5	33.5
Ethiopia	22.0	16.0	25.0	31.5
Uganda	36.0	21.0	5.0	31.0
Burma	27.0	9.0	22.5	28.5
Iraq	19.0	4.0	25.5	24.5
Sudan	15.0	10.0	22.5	24.0
Somalia	22.0	12.0	5.0	19.5
Liberia	10.0	8.0	12.0	15.0

Source: "World Business," *The Wall Street Journal*, September 20, 1991, p. R4.

Adaptation to Host–Country Goals.   The concession agreement specifies specific rights and responsibilities of both the foreign company and the host country, but it is often revised to adapt to changing host-country priorities. When the foreign company sticks to the legal interpretation of its concession agreement, the host-country government uses pressures in areas not covered by the agreement. If these pressures do not work, the host-country government reinterprets the agreement to obtain changes from the foreign company. Thus, it is advisable for multinational companies to voluntarily adapt to changing host-country priorities whenever possible.

Defensive Measures After Investment

Once managers decide to invest and take preinvestment defensive measures, they can use several operating strategies to cope with political risks. We grouped them for convenience into two categories: strategies which are necessary to be a good citizen of the host country and strategies which make expropriatory actions difficult or unfeasible. In addition, joint ventures can be used to diffuse political risks.

Becoming a Good Citizen. Many foreign affiliates often attempt to harmonize their policies with their host-country priorities and goals. They may hire an increasing number of local persons for positions initially held by representatives of the parent company management. They may share ownership with host-country private or public companies. They may develop and use local sources of supply for their raw materials and component requirements. They may try to export their products to bolster host-country reserves of foreign exchange.

Making Expropriation Difficult. Many operational policies and organizational approaches make expropriatory actions extremely difficult or unfeasible. Multinational companies may maintain technological superiority over local companies and other competing foreign firms. The challenge here is to introduce into the host country technological improvements on a continuing basis. They may integrate individual subsidiaries into a worldwide production and logistical system through highly interrelated international operations. Under such an integration, a subsidiary alone could not operate or compete successfully, as is done in the petroleum industry. Control of key patents and processes, joint-venture arrangements, capitalization with a thin equity base and a large local debt proportion, and control of key export markets for a subsidiary's products are examples of policy actions in this respect.

Joint Ventures. Joint ventures with local partners have been frequently suggested as one answer to national demands for an ownership share in their own industries. They could improve the public image of a subsidiary, provide more capital, and deter nationalization. Joint ventures with investors from a number of different countries, such as the United States, Italy, and England, would make expropriatory actions extremely costly because nationalization could distress private investors in all three countries and thus impair good economic relations with these national groups of business executives.

Remedies After Expropriation

The resolution of a controversy prior to confiscation is far more attractive than a company's recovery of value for assets lost through expropriation. However, certain remedies or counteractions may be adopted after an expropriation has taken place. William Hoskins (1970) has suggested four action phases that follow an expropriation: rational negotiation, negotiation flavored with power tactics, exploration of legal remedies, and surrender by management.

Rational Negotiations.   Because most expropriations occur with some warnings for the involved enterprise, there are opportunities to dissuade the host-country government from its intended takeover. Once expropriation occurs, the value of further negotiations drops rather sharply. The multinational company uses this stage of the postconfiscation period to persuade the host government that its action was a mistake. The company may reiterate its earlier warnings of catastrophes resulting from the government action, in the hope that the government would reconsider. During this period, the company may well offer some concessions such as those in Table 16-4. Those concessions in Group A may not be sufficiently conciliatory for the host country, while those concessions in Group C may be too expensive for the company. Group B, therefore, offers the most likely area for post-confiscation negotiation.

Power Tactics.   If rational negotiations do not work, the multinational company may rely on power tactics. Power tactics on a political level consist of a negative-and-positive approach. The positive approach is designed to meet government needs (see Group B in Table 16-4). If this positive approach does not work, a company can concentrate on negative sanctions. Negative sanctions include the solicitation of political support from opposition parties or from friendly neighboring countries, and the intercession of the

Table 16–4
Types of Concessions During Phase 1

Group A: Steps Willing to Take	Group B: Steps Will Take Under Duress	Group C: Steps Will Not Take
Hire national managers	Invest more capital for expansion	Suspend payment of dividends
Raise transfer prices charged to U.S. parent	Contribute to political campaigns	Surrender majority control
Accept local company as minority partner	Release government from concession agreements	Remove all U.S. personnel
Change expatriate management	Support government programs	Distort global organization

Source: William R. Hoskins, "How to Counter Expropriation," *Harvard Business Review*, September/October 1970, p.104.

parent country's government on an informal basis. But these political tactics should be selected with caution because they may strengthen a government's resolve.

As a practical matter, economic pressures may be more efficient and effective than political tactics. Economic pressures include threats to cut off critical items—vital components, export markets, technological skills, and management skills. Essentially, economic power depends on several factors. First, a company may maintain technological superiority over local firms and other competing foreign firms. Second, the company may control export markets. Third, the subsidiary may be integrated into a worldwide production and logistical system. But such economic pressures may also produce political backlash and thus destroy any possibility of eventual salvage value. In many cases, a government assesses such threats before confiscation and concludes that they are not sufficiently harmful.

Legal Remedies.   The traditional view of capital exporting countries assumes that expropriation is valid if a host country provides the foreign company with full, prompt, and effective compensation. But this traditional view of expropriation has been mostly ignored by the less-developed countries. At some point following Phases 1 and 2, a foreign company may begin to explore legal redress of its grievances. It will first exhaust all local legal remedies. It will then seek legal redress in the parent country's court system. The government of the parent company often uses the promise of aid or the threat to withhold aid as a means of settling the dispute. The foreign company may have the government of its parent company present a claim through the International Court of Justice.

In addition to these legal remedies, multinational companies can take their grievances to the International Center for Settlement of Investment Disputes, which was established under the auspices of the World Bank in 1966. Most industrial countries, most African countries, and many Asian countries have signed the Convention of Settlement of Investment Disputes. Although the International Center was established to attract investment disputes, examples of settlement by the International Center are extremely rare. Because such settlements require that host governments relinquish sovereignty over activities within their own borders, there is considerable doubt about the extensive use of the organization in the future.

Management Surrender.   If Phases 1, 2, and 3 all fail to produce a satisfactory solution, management of an expropriated company will concede defeat and seek to salvage what it can from the situation. Hoskins suggests three possible avenues for a continued economic relationship without excessive concern for legal ownership:

1. The foreign company handles exports under a commission arrangement.
2. It signs a management contract to provide the host country with technical and managerial skills.
3. It sells raw materials and components to the host country.

Responses to Forced Equity Dilution

Many governments do not want to completely seize or confiscate foreign firms, but they pass legislation that requires multinational companies to dilute their equity in overseas subsidiaries. Most of these regulations restrict foreign equity participation in local operations to 49 percent or less so that these companies can become local companies for all practical purposes. At best, such legislation heralds shared ownership, and at worst it can mean a reluctant departure from the host country. But the consequences of such legislation are sometimes surprisingly favorable because multinational companies can enjoy benefits in the wake of the country's hostile equity laws. These benefits include new product lines and markets, risk diversification, and higher earnings.

Dennis Encarnation and Sushil Vachani (1985) studied India's Foreign Exchange Regulation Act and 12 foreign firms in India to explore the range of responses available to managers under pressure to dilute their equity ownership in local subsidiaries. This legislation restricted foreign equity participation in Indian operations to 40 percent. These two researchers found that no matter what the strategy, the 12 companies signaled their willingness to strike a balance between the company's goals and those of their host country. Multinational business executives who are compelled to reduce their foreign equity holdings have at least four options: preemptive action, negotiation, strict compliance, and departure.

Preemptive Action.   Multinational companies can initiate defensive strategies such as preemptive diversification, phased localization, and joint partnerships. Preemptive diversification may allow the multinational company to retain a majority ownership of subsidiaries whose business portfolios differ from its own. This strategy involves sustained efforts to increase high-technology production and export sales. If companies are not in high-priority industries or cannot increase export sales, it is unlikely that they will retain a majority ownership of their subsidiaries. They may then choose to look for new opportunities through voluntary but gradual divestment. Some multinational companies seek joint ventures with local investors from the beginning so that they do not have to worry about equity dilution legislation.

Negotiation.   Multinational firms may use the equity dilution requirements as a negotiating tool to further their own ends. By satisfying government demands for equity dilution, such companies often avail themselves of government concessions such as new licenses to expand or diversify, subsidized loans, and tariff protection. If companies operate in high-priority industries or export a significant portion of their output, they may retain a majority ownership of their subsidiaries because practically all equity dilution regulations have some exemptions.

Strict Compliance.   Multinational companies which seek to maintain existing operations usually sell a majority of their equity shares to local investors and keep total equity constant. By diluting its equity to 49 percent or less, a foreign subsidiary officially becomes a local company and could thereby maintain its dominant position in a profitable market, well protected by entry barriers.

Departure.   Some multinational companies may decide to leave a country rather than comply with local ownership requirements. Typically, exit is not the manager's first choice, but rather, the decision tends to follow a long process of negotiation with government officials. Managers might conclude that their company would lose more by setting up a precedent for shared control with local partners than it could gain from continuing operations under the new rules.

Summary

A company may incur losses from political risks because of governmental action which interferes with the completion of contractual obligations between the foreign company and its host government. Political risks cannot be predicted in the same way as credit losses and thus cannot be offset precisely in measurable ways. Thus, multinational companies must understand the types of political risks which they can expect to encounter, assess the likelihood of the encounter, and take various protective measures to minimize the risks.

Political risks range from moderate actions such as exchange controls to extreme actions such as expropriation. Although there are many types of foreign environmental risks, much of the literature on this subject has concentrated on extreme cases of nationalization. Business operations in foreign countries are subject to the power of host countries. Foreign assets can be seized for a public purpose, without discrimination, and with adequate compensation. Although these three rules are in accordance with traditional principles of international law, many less-developed countries have frequently ignored them.

Once the nature of political risks and their implications have been assessed, multinational companies should focus on forecasting these risks in foreign countries where they have business interests. The forecasting of political risks involves four basic steps. First, the multinational company examines the present administration's attitudes and policies toward foreign investment. Second, it assesses the country's political stability. Third, it integrates the political risk assessment into the company's strategic planning. Fourth, it develops strategies to reduce the company's exposure to political risks.

The multinational company is not helpless in the event of political risks because there are a variety of protections against them. These protections are grouped into three categories: protective measures before investment, defensive measures after investment, and remedies after expropriation. Protective measures prior to investment include concession agreements, planned divestment, and voluntary adaptation to host-country goals. Defensive measures after investment involve various actions for the foreign company to be a good citizen of the host country. After expropriation, the foreign company may use four-phase actions suggested by Hoskins: rational negotiation, negotiation flavored with power tactics, exploration of legal remedies, and surrender and decision to seek only salvage value.

Questions

1. Discuss the nature of political risk.

2. List two major forms of political risk.

3. What are the steps involved in determining the overall political rating of a host country?

4. What is nationalism? Why is nationalism important in assessing the political risk of a country?

5. Why do some multinational companies diversify their investment projects internationally?

6. Describe a company's strategic planning to deal with political risk.

7. Why does the multiple-method approach appear to be a sound forecasting policy?

8. List some forms of defensive measures against possible expropriation before investment.

9. How can multinational companies make expropriation difficult?

10. List the concessions that multinational companies are most likely to offer for post-confiscation negotiation.

11. What are responses to forced equity dilution?

References

Aggarwal, R., and L. A. Soenen, "Project Exit Value as a Measure of Flexibility and Risk Exposure," *The Engineering Economist*, Fall 1989, pp. 39-54.

Ball, D. A., and W. H. McCulloch, *International Business*, Plano, Texas: Business Publications, Inc., 1985, pp. 221-2.

Beaty, D., and O. Harari, "Divestment and Disinvestment from South Africa: A Reappraisal," *California Management Review*, Summer 1987, pp. 31-50.

Bradley, D. G., "Managing Against Expropriation," *Harvard Business Review*, July/August 1977, pp. 75-83.

Coplin, W. D., and M. K. O'Leary, "1991 World Political Risk Forecast," *The Banker*, April 1991, pp. 16-8.

Cosset, J., and J. Roy, "The Determinants of Country Risk Ratings," *Journal of International Business Studies*, First Quarter 1991, pp. 135-42.

Dow Jones and Company, Inc., "World Business," *The Wall Street Journal*, September 20, 1991, Section R.

Encarnation, D. J., and S. Vachani, "Foreign Ownership: When Hosts Change the Rules," *Harvard Business Review*, September/October 1985, pp. 152-60.

Ghertman, M., "Foreign Subsidiary and Parents' Roles During Strategic Investment and Divestment," *Journal of International Business Studies*, Spring 1988, pp. 33-46.

Goddard, S., "Political Risk in International Capital Budgeting," Robert W. Kolb, ed., *The International Financial Reader*, Miami: Kolb Publishing Company, 1991, pp. 357-62.

Hawkins, R. G., N. Mintz, and M. Provissiero, "Government Takeovers of U.S. Foreign Affiliates," *Journal of International Business Studies*, Spring 1976, pp. 3-15.

Hoskins, W. R., "How to Counter Expropriation," *Harvard Business Review*, September/October 1970, pp. 102-12.

Janah, M., "Rating Risk in the Hot Countries," *The Wall Street Journal*, September 20, 1991, p. R4.

Jodice, D. A., "Sources of Change in Third World Regimes for Foreign Direct Investment, 1978-1976," *International Organization*, Spring 1980, pp. 177-206.

Kelly, W., and M. E. Philippatos, "Comparative Analysis of Foreign Investment Evaluation Practices Used by U.S. Based Manufacturing Multinational Companies," *Journal of International Business Studies*, Winter 1982, pp. 19-42.

Kennedy, C. R., Jr., "International Banking and Expropriation Risk," in Thomas I. Kindel, ed., *Proceedings of the 1991 Conference*, Charleston, SC: Association for Global Business, 1991, pp. 228-38.

Kennedy, C. R., Jr., *Managing the International Business Environment: Cases in Political and Country Risk*, Englewood Cliffs, NJ: Prentice Hall, 1991.

Kim, W. C., "Competition and the Management of Host Country Intervention," *Solan Management Review*, Spring 1987, pp. 33-9.

Micallef, J. V., "Political Risk Assessment," *Columbia Journal of World Business*, Summer 1981, pp. 46-9.

National Industrial Conference Board, *Obstacles and Incentives to Private Foreign Investment*, New York, 1969.

Part Five
Reporting and Controlling

Part Five (Chapters 17 through 19) describes techniques for controlling the operations of a multinational company. Chapter 17 discusses multinational accounting theory and practices. It may be too early to recognize multinational accounting as a separate field of study. In recent years, however, substantial amounts of resources have been devoted to further development and refinement of international accounting. Meaningful financial reports are the cornerstone of effective management. Accurate financial data are especially important in international business where operations are typically supervised from a distance. Chapter 18 considers the significance of national tax systems on international business operations. Perhaps multinational taxation has the most pervasive effect on all aspects of multinational operations. Where to invest, how to finance, and where to remit liquid funds are just a few examples of management actions affected by multinational taxation. Chapter 19 covers international transfer pricing. Because transfers between business entities account for approximately 40 percent of total world trade, the multinational company must try to satisfy a number of objectives. This chapter examines some of these objectives, such as taxes, tariffs, competition, inflation rates, exchange rates, and restrictions on fund transfers.

17

Multinational Accounting

In order to achieve the firm's primary goal of maximizing stockholder wealth, the financial manager performs three major functions: (1) financial planning and control, (2) investment decisions, and (3) financing decisions. These financial functions cannot be performed effectively without adequate, timely information from the accountant. The two fundamental financial statements of any company are the balance sheet and the income statement. The balance sheet measures the assets, liabilities, and owners' equity of a business at a particular time. The income statement matches expenses to revenues in order to determine the net income or net loss for a period of time. In addition to these two financial statements, a control system is used to relate actual performance to some predetermined goal.

The actual and potential flows of assets across national boundaries complicate the accounting functions of a multinational company. The multinational company must learn to deal with different rates of inflation, changes in exchange rates, foreign exchange controls, possible expropriations, different customs, and local regulations. If a multinational company is to function in a coordinated manner, it must also measure the performance of its foreign affiliates. Equally important, managers of the affiliates must run operations with clearly defined objectives in mind.

This chapter consists of three major sections. The first section describes international accounting issues: accounting systems, financial reporting, and consolidation of accounts. The second section deals with multinational control system and performance evaluation. The third section examines the Foreign Corrupt Practices Act of 1977, its 1988 revision, and its impact on U.S. business firms.

Major Issues in Multinational Accounting

Two problems complicate multinational accounting. First, multinational companies face different economic conditions because they operate in many countries. Thus, satisfactory accounting practices in one country may not be satisfactory in other countries. Second, multinational operations have many special problems in accounting. These problems include transfer pricing, taxes and tariffs, varying rates of inflation, the significance of debt ratio in the context of different capital markets, inventory valuation, and currency translation. In this section, we discuss important issues in multinational accounting: different accounting systems, financial reporting, and consolidation of accounts.

Accounting Systems

Three basic types of economic systems are the free market system of most industrial countries, the controlled market system of developing countries, and the tightly controlled system of communist countries. If accounting is to maintain its social usefulness, each economic system should have a unique accounting pattern. Hence, essentially different economic systems should develop and employ different accounting systems. However, the accounting system adopted by a foreign subsidiary must be consistent with one established by host country reporting and tax regulations. It must also be consistent with the system established by the parent company for consolidation, tax, and managerial decisions.

Frederick Choi and Gerhard Mueller (1984) identified four possible approaches to accounting development in industrial countries with the free market system: the macroeconomic approach, the microeconomic approach, the independent–discipline approach, and the uniform accounting approach. Let us consider the philosophy behind each.

Macroeconomic Approach.

A group of countries, including Sweden, have adopted a macroeconomic approach to accounting. Its underlying hypothesis is that national economic policies lead rather than follow company goals. These countries have adopted policies designed to mitigate the disturbing effects of business cycles. Their accounting rules have been tailored to facilitate these policies through such requirements as some averaging of reported corporate income over the length of the typical business cycle.

Such accounting views are based on three postulates:

1. Business is an essential unit in the economic structure of a country.
2. Business best achieves its goals by closely coordinating its activities with the national economic policies of its environment.
3. To best serve the public interest, enterprise accounting must interrelate closely with national economic policies.

Under the macroeconomic approach, the purpose of accounting is to measure economic transactions of the business sector so that economic planners are prepared to monitor and direct national economic activities in desired directions. Thus, companies have been required to publish financial statements and information on their positions, future plans, employment, and total remuneration paid. In addition, many of our newer accounting concepts clearly fit into the macroeconomic framework of accounting development. Human resource accounting and accounting for corporate social responsibilities fit into the macroeconomic pattern of accounting.

Microeconomic Approach.

Accounting practices in another group of countries, including the Netherlands, have been heavily influenced by microeconomic theory. Under the free enterprise system, private business activities are the cornerstones of economic affairs, and accounting performs a service function for business and business enterprises. Thus, accounting should orient itself to the same micro considerations that reflect its environment:

A microeconomic-oriented accounting system depends upon four postulates:

1. Business companies are focal points of business activities.
2. Their policies are designed to ensure their continued existence.
3. The company's best policy for survival is optimization in an economic sense.
4. Because accounting is a branch of business economics, it derives its concepts and applications from economic analysis.

The most important concept of microeconomic-oriented accounting is that the accounting process must focus on maintaining the purchasing power of monetary capital invested in the firm. Replacement value accounting fits microeconomic concepts best. The value of goods is replacement value because the sale of something or its loss means the loss of a value that can generally be regained only by purchase or production of identical goods. The microeconomic approach to accounting also assumes that replacement costs are based on the present value of the income stream expected to be obtained from the use of an asset.

Independent–Discipline Approach.

The accounting systems in the United States, Canada, and the United Kingdom are treated as an independent discipline. Accounting and business practices have the same basis and follow the same pattern of development because there is a direct interrelationship between accounting and its environment. Accounting provides business with an effective service. Just as business can produce its concepts from experience and practice, accounting can develop its own concept from practice. Thus, existing accounting practices are the foundation for creating accounting concepts. Generally accepted accounting principles represent independent judgment and inductive reasoning from existing business practices. In other words, such principles are not clearly structured and defined, but instead there is a set of conventions that have evolved through years of practice.

Under the independent–discipline approach to accounting, the accounting principles used by a particular company must be consistent from year to year. However, the principles used by one company need not be used by another company. One company may use FIFO (first in, first out) to determine the cost of goods sold, while another may use LIFO (last in, first out). One company may depreciate an asset on a straight–line basis, while another company may depreciate the same asset on a double declining–balance method. Because accounting is regarded as an independent discipline with roots in the practical affairs of everyday business, a cohesive and complete conceptual structure of accounting is difficult to establish.

Uniform Accounting Approach. Germany, France, and Argentina have adopted uniform accounting systems using identical terminology and account classifications for all companies. Some countries have adopted a uniform accounting system for a number of reasons:

1. It seems to make accounting more scientific.
2. It presents itself as a convenient device for economic and business control by government.
3. It affords a relatively simple way to achieve uniformity among companies.

Typically, uniform accounting systems have been developed in countries where national corporate laws regulate various matters of company operations. These matters include rights of stockholders, rules concerning disclosure of financial information, and rules for preparation of financial statements. Unfortunately, uniform accounting systems do not recognize basic differences among different industries. Moreover, they tend to restrict the development of new accounting concepts and practices.

Financial Reporting

Multinational companies cross national boundaries in search for resources or markets. Thus, financial statements issued by companies in various countries differ in form of presentation and in degree of detail disclosed.

Dual Reporting System. In its 1975 study, the Accountants International Study Group recommended that primary and secondary financial statements be recognized as part of formal, generally accepted accounting standards and principles. Primary financial statements are prepared in accordance with the accounting and reporting standards of a company's country of domicile. They are also expressed in the language and currency of that country. Secondary financial statements are prepared according to the accounting and reporting standards of another country. Such secondary financial statements are translated into a foreign currency; they are expressed in a foreign language; and they accompany the independent auditor's report expressed in a form commonly used in a foreign country.

Secondary statements may not be necessary if primary statements satisfy information requirements of financial reporting audiences in other countries. However, most multinational companies with reporting audiences in more than a single country prepare secondary statements for interested parties in other countries. A dual reporting system may produce corporate financial information of a high quality, it may be more responsive to the perceived financial information needs of distinct users, and it may better serve international money and capital markets. The dual reporting system also has problems: (1) when mergers and investment decisions are made with an eye toward financial statement effects, and (2) when in the translation process the treatment of foreign exchange gains or losses and inventory valuation limit the validity of the secondary statements.

Areas of Major Differences.

Accounting standards and practices differ significantly from country to country. Despite some similarities, there are at least as many accounting systems as there are countries, and no two systems are exactly alike. These differences are important to business executives because accounting data and reports are a principal facet of business information and an integral part of management decision making. Underlying reasons for national differences in accounting standards and practices are essentially environmental. In other words, accounting and reporting standards evolve from and reflect the environments they serve. Accounting and reporting principles in any country of the world are the result of interactions of numerous environmental factors, such as educational systems, legal systems, political systems, and sociocultural characteristics.

Accounting principles worldwide differ in a number of ways. In some countries, such as the United States, the income statement is regarded as the most important statement, but in most European and Latin American countries, the balance sheet is regarded as the financial statement of prime interest. In the U.S. we focus on the income statement because most large U.S. corporations are publicly held. U.S. stockholders prefer increased wealth, which is measured by increasing stock prices and/or increased dividends. In contrast, stockholders in European and Latin American countries are primarily concerned with the ownership of wealth and the strength of the company in relation to claims of creditors.

Many European countries establish various reserves to smooth out income fluctuations from year to year because they are more conservative than the United States in their presentation of financial statements. Reserves for contingencies may be established in years when earnings are high, and they may be used in years when earnings are low. These reserves sometimes arise due to statutory requirements that a certain portion of annual profits be set aside as reserves.

Consolidation of accounts is another area of difference. Companies in such developed countries as the United States and the United Kingdom follow the practice of consolidated financial statements. However, many developing and European countries do not require companies to consolidate foreign subsidiaries. They are concerned that the parent company may decide to consolidate only profitable affiliates, and this would make it difficult for an outsider to evaluate the company's overall performance.

Financial Disclosure.   In the absence of uniform accounting standards on a global basis, many executives and investors believe that adequate disclosure of financial information is critical for purposes of proper and useful analysis. Normally, issuers of financial statements limit disclosure to avoid preparation cost and to preserve secrecy. But users of financial statements prefer greater disclosure than issuers are willing to make. Like general accounting standards and practices, disclosure standards and practices evolve from the educational, legal, political, sociocultural, and economic forces of each country.

One important purpose of financial reporting is to apply information for investment decision making. This purpose may be achieved by requiring companies to disclose proper financial data and other relevant information. Today, many multinational companies list their securities. In order to protect investors, most securities exchanges and governmental regulatory bodies impose disclosure requirements for both domestic and foreign companies that seek access to their securities markets.

Before companies disclose financial data, they should determine who will use the information, what amount of information will be disclosed, and for what purpose the information will be used. Users of disclosed financial data include stockholders, creditors, employees, customers, governmental agencies, and the general public. The amount of the information to be disclosed depends upon the expertise of the user and upon the desirable standard. Disclosure standards should be adequate, fair, and complete. The proper financial data are disclosed for investors so that they can use the information for investment decisions.

Because U.S. companies have financial reporting obligations to diverse audiences, multinational financial disclosure is required by Statement of Financial Accounting Standards (SFAS) No. 14 in cases where multinational operations account for at least 10 percent of total operations. Issued in 1977, SFAS No. 14, "Financial Reporting of a Business Enterprise," focuses on disclosures of information in four categories: industry, foreign operations, export sales, and major customers. But a disclosure may vary widely among countries. Most U.S. companies disclose their financial information to their stockholders and to the public as a whole because of the listing requirements of the U.S. Securities and Exchange Commission and the New York Stock Exchange.

European countries tend to disclose less financial data and provide less information about how assets are valued than U.S. companies. Income statements often fail to disclose sales or the cost of goods sold. A reader of the income statement has difficulty in determining the comparative strength of a company because trends in sales and in gross profit margins cannot be detected. In addition, methods of calculating depreciation and the degree of consolidation often are not explained.

European secrecy is traditional. Tradition aside, European companies disclose only a minimum amount of information because there may be the lack of legal requirements, of pressures from creditors such as banks and stockholders, of need for public equity financing, and of extensive equity markets. European companies also tend to understate earnings for several reasons. Higher reported earnings may encourage stockholders to demand higher dividends or unions to seek pay increases. Tax avoidance is another reason why European companies tend to hide earnings.

In fact, some U.S. executives charge that tougher U.S. accounting standards, such as disclosure requirements, have put U.S. companies at a competitive disadvantage. A number of surveys by the United Nations found that accounting standards of the United States are more strict and thorough than those of most countries around the world. In addition, there are some claims that foreign companies are reluctant to offer their securities in the U.S. stock markets because of the cost and time involved in complying with detailed and voluminous requirements of accounting standards.

Auditing.   Investors, creditors, regulators, and planners use published financial statements for a variety of purposes. Because managers, who have a vested interest in the statements, prepare financial statements, they could manipulate the figures to make them look better than they are. We can solve this problem of internal control and external reliability by an adequate system of internal controls and the opinion of independent, highly qualified external auditors.

The opinion of a competent, professional, and independent auditor is essential to maintain the high reliability of international financial statements because of the great diversity of accounting practices in various countries. Auditors review financial statements and then attest to their reliability and fairness. Thus, auditing establishes and maintains the integrity of published financial information.

Auditing standards differ country by country although they are less diverse than accounting standards. Auditing standards are pretty much alike in many countries—the United States, Canada, Germany, the Netherlands, the United Kingdom, Japan, Norway, and Sweden. The financial statements of most public companies in these countries are required to be audited by independent public accountants. However, companies in Belgium and France are required to appoint one or more statutory examiners who need not be independent public accountants. Moreover, some countries such as the Bahamas, Indonesia, Panama, and Uruguay have no auditing requirements for most companies.

Most U.S. public accounting firms have opened offices in many countries. Thus, U.S. subsidiaries in Kenya and Honduras may be audited by the same firms that audit parent books in the United States. The increasing use of their services by companies in foreign countries may lead to greater uniformity of auditing standards among countries. Another reason why auditing standards are more uniform than accounting standards is that professional auditors are the only parties involved in establishing such standards.

Auditing procedures are somewhat more diverse than international auditing standards. In the United States, trade accounts receivable are confirmed, and physical inventory counts are frequently taken. In contrast, these procedures are not practiced in many European countries. Trade accounts payable are not confirmed in United States, but they are confirmed in a number of other countries. Companies in many European and Latin American countries have difficulty in verifying their disbursements because cancelled checks become the property of the bank and are not returned to the issuing companies.

Consolidation of Accounts

Consolidated financial statements present the results of both foreign and domestic operations as if they were a single economic unit. Thus, these statements tend to disregard legal distinctions among separate corporate entities which have been organized under different national laws. However, consolidated financial statements are most useful to the shareholders and creditors of a parent company. The parent company consolidates its accounts with those of its subsidiaries on a line-by-line basis by adding assets, liabilities, net worth, revenues, and expenses.

Methods of Consolidation.
U.S. multinational companies are required to consolidate the financial statements of affiliates into those of a parent if the parent owns more than 50 percent of the affiliate's voting shares. Companies account for their foreign investments on the basis of the equity method if the parent owns between 20 and 50 percent of the affiliate. Under the equity method, the parent carries its affiliates at the initial cost of the investment plus its proportionate share of profits or losses. Companies are required to carry their foreign affiliates on the basis of the cost method if the parent owns less than 20 percent of the affiliate. Under the cost method, the parent carries its affiliates at the initial investment plus its dividends received.

Options of Consolidated Statements.
Though consolidation practices vary from country to country, there are basically three options for presenting the results of a company's operations: (1) consolidated financial statements only, (2) parent financial statements only, and (3) parent and consolidated financial statements. According to a survey by Price Waterhouse International (1988), only consolidated financial results are disclosed in the Bahamas, Bermuda, Canada, Panama, the Philippines, and the United States. Approximately ten countries, including Brazil and Spain, require their multinational companies to present only parent financial statements. Both parent and consolidated financial statements are required in most countries; these countries include France, Germany, Japan, the Netherlands, Sweden, and the United Kingdom.

Users of Consolidated Statements. Within every country, principal users of consolidated financial statements of multinational companies are stockholders and creditors of the parent company, stockholders and creditors of the affiliate, and management of the parent company. Stockholders of a parent company need consolidated financial statements to judge their share of total asset values and total income represented by the group of companies which they own through the medium of parent company stock. From a practical standpoint, however, the consolidated statement may distort the real position of the stockholder if a substantial portion of a particular firm's foreign assets and its earnings are in weak or nonconvertible currencies. Stockholders of an affiliate are not likely to have a direct interest in consolidated financial statements because their welfare depends upon the financial success of the single affiliate whose shares they hold. However, they may have an indirect interest in consolidated financial statements because such statements indicate the financial strength of the parent and its subsidiaries as a whole.

A parent's short-term creditors have a genuine interest in the financial statements of the parent alone because short-term obligations are paid from the cash flow of the parent. However, long-term creditors of the parent are primarily interested in consolidated financial statements because the satisfaction of their claims depends primarily upon the profitability of the enterprise as a whole. Creditors of a foreign subsidiary are concerned mainly with the financial statements of the subsidiary. However, consolidated financial statements are useful to creditors of the subsidiary in cases where the debts of the subsidiary are guaranteed by the parent.

Management uses consolidated financial statements for two purposes: (1) to report to stockholders on management's stewardship of the company; and (2) to set a foundation for internal judgment of its performance. Management also uses financial statements and other information to decide on production, marketing, pricing, and dividend policies.

Harmonization of Accounting Standards. The preceding sections pointed out that the accounting standards and practices of companies in different countries have major differences which create many complications for those who must prepare, consolidate, audit, and interpret published financial statements. In view of the many different accounting standards and practices in existence worldwide, we can hardly believe that any kind of harmony can take place. Although complete standardization would be impossible, many transnational organizations attempt to standardize or harmonize worldwide accounting standards. These efforts are being carried on a national, regional, and worldwide basis.

Worldwide, numerous bodies attempt to formulate international accounting standards. Perhaps the four most important sources of regional and international standards are the International Accounting Standards Committee (IASC), the International Federation of Accountants (IFAC), the United

Nations (UN), and the European Community (EC). In 1973, professional accounting organizations founded the IASC to harmonize regulations, accounting standards, and accounting procedures. In 1977, 63 professional bodies from 49 countries established the IFAC to work on accounting and auditing related issues other than standards. The UN has tried to develop international accounting and reporting standards since 1977. The EC is a form of regional economic integration comprised of 12 countries in Europe: Belgium, Denmark, France, Germany, Greece, Ireland, Italy, Luxembourg, the Netherlands, Portugal, Spain, and the United Kingdom. To facilitate the free flow of capital, the EC has issued a number of directives for harmonizing accounting standards among its member countries; the EC is expected to adopt a single accounting system sometime in the 1990s as it completes its economic integration.

There are a number of other organizations that attempt to harmonize accounting standards within certain regions. They inclue the Organization for Economic Cooperation and Development (OECD), an organization of 24 industrialized countries; the African Accounting Council (AAC), an organization of 27 African countries; and the Confederation of Asian and Pacific Accountants (CAPA), an organization of 20 Pacific Rim countries.

Control System and Performance Evaluation

A multinational company consists of the parent and its subsidiaries in foreign countries. To operate the multinational company as a system, the parent and its subsidiaries need continuing flows of data. Hence, the key element in the control system is the company's system for collection and dissemination of data on a worldwide basis. The company's information system between the parent and its subsidiaries generally consists of: (1) impersonal communications such as budgets, plans, programs, and regular reports; and (2) personal communications such as meetings, visits, and telephone conversations.

Communications essential to evaluating the performance of an enterprise usually follow established organization channels. An effective communication system requires an efficient reporting system for collecting information on the results of actual operations and for disclosing deviations from predetermined standards. The more efficient the system, the quicker managers may take corrective action.

Financial results of profits have traditionally provided a standard to evaluate the performance of business operations. However, as multinational companies expand their operations across national boundaries, the standard itself is affected by the environment in which they operate. Inflation and foreign exchange fluctuations affect all the financial measures of performance for multinational companies. To compare the results of various affiliates of a multinational company, multinational financial managers must understand the various ways in which inflation and exchange fluctuations affect operations as measured by traditional financial statements.

Inflation and Exchange Fluctuations

Every control system establishes a standard of performance and compares actual performance with the standard. The most widely used standards are budgeted financial statements. The preparation of the statements is a planning function, but their administration is a controlling function. We will compare budgeted financial statements with actual financial statements to determine the impact of inflation and exchange rate fluctuations on financial statements. Budgeted statements are prepared without anticipated inflation or exchange fluctuations, but the actual statements are prepared after these phenomena have occurred.

The Impact of Inflation on Financial Statements.

Table 17-1 presents the effects of a 10 percent and a 20 percent rate of inflation on the major accounts of the balance sheet and the income statement. If we assume that one unit is sold every month and that prices increase at an even rate throughout the year, the annual inflation rates reflected on sales would be 5 percent and 10 percent instead of 10 percent and 20 percent.

If we follow the results of a case having a total annual inflation rate of 10 percent or 0.83 percent per month, annual sales increase to 2,100—a 5 percent increase over the budgeted price. The cost of goods sold increases by only 4 percent from the budgeted cost of 1,500 to the actual cost of 1,560 because the cost of goods sold is based on historical costs. We assumed that interest expenses remain constant. The budgeted depreciation charges are based on historical costs. The combination of higher prices in sales and the use of historical costs in the two major accounts will increase the profits after taxes by 20 percent from 100 to 120.

The effects of inflation on the balance sheet accounts depend on the date when assets were acquired or liabilities incurred. Fixed assets and inventory are carried at cost, but accounts receivable and accounts payable are carried at the prices prevailing at the time of the transactions. The budgeted cash of 400 consists of profits after taxes (100), taxes payable (100), and depreciation (200).

The Impact of Exchange Fluctuation on Financial Statements.

Let us assume that a subsidiary purchases its raw materials from Country A and sells its finished products to Country B. Thus, both exports and imports are denominated in foreign currencies. In this case, exchange rate fluctuations affect the level of both revenues and costs measured in terms of the domestic currency. Table 17-2 shows that an appreciation in the revenue currency (Country B's currency) raises profits, assuming that costs remain constant. In contrast, an appreciation in the cost currency (Country A's currency) reduces profits after taxes unless selling prices are adjusted to reflect the increase in costs.

Table 17–1
The Impact of Inflation on Financial Statements

Income Statement
(in foreign currency)

		Budget	Actual with Annual Inflation Rate of:	
			10%	20%
Sales		2,000	2,100	2,200
Cost of goods sold		1,500	1,560	1,620
Gross margin		500	540	580
Depreciation		200	200	200
Operating income		300	340	380
Interest expense		100	100	100
Profit before taxes		200	240	280
Taxes (50%)		100	120	140
Profit after taxes		100	120	140

Balance Sheet
(in foreign currency)

	Initial	Budget	Actual with Annual Inflation Rate of:	
			10%	20%
Cash	0	400	440	480
Accounts receivable	200	200	220	240
Inventory	100	100	110	120
Total current assets	300	700	770	840
Plant and equipment	350	350	350	350
Less: Depreciation	—	(200)	(200)	(200)
Total assets	650	850	920	990
Accounts payable	300	300	330	360
Notes payable	300	300	300	300
Taxes payable	—	100	120	140
Total current liabilities	600	700	750	800
Equity	50	50	50	50
Retained earnings	—	100	120	140
Total liabilities & equity	650	850	920	990

There are similarities between the effect of inflation and the effect of exchange fluctuations on reported profits. If prices in the local currencies are increased by the same percentage as the increase in the cost of imports, the effect of exchange fluctuations on profits is identical with the effect of a comparable local inflation rate. A 10 percent increase in export prices, accompanied by a proportional increase in import prices, produces profits of 120; this is identical to the profit obtained when the local inflation rate was 10 percent in the example from Table 17-1.

We cannot determine the true impact of exchange fluctuations on foreign operations unless a parent's accounts and those of its subsidiaries are expressed in terms of a homogeneous currency unit. Any changes in the value

Table 17–2
Impact of Currency Fluctuations on Profits

	Budget	B's Currency Appreciate 10%	A's Currency Appreciate 10%	Both Currencies Appreciate 10%
Sales	2,000	2,100	2,000	2,100
Cost of goods sold	1,500	1,500	1,560	1,560
Gross margin	500	600	440	540
Depreciation	200	200	200	200
Operating income	300	400	240	340
Interest exp.	100	100	100	100
Profit before tax	200	300	140	240
Taxes (50%)	100	150	70	120
Profit after tax	100	150	70	120

of the local currency relative to the parent currency will affect the reported profits when financial statements expressed in the local currency are translated into the currency of the parent company. The translation procedure, already discussed in Chapter 7, is regulated by the accounting profession.

Performance Evaluation

Performance evaluation is a central feature of an effective management information system. A management information system is a comprehensive system to provide all levels of management in a firm with information so that production, marketing, and financial functions can be effectively performed to achieve the objectives of the firm. Management must plan its economic activities in advance, carry out its plans, and make sure that deviations are properly evaluated and handled. Thus, performance evaluation based on the concept of the management information system relates to the fundamentals of the management process: planning, execution, and control.

Criteria for a foreign subsidiary's successful performance are, first, cash flows and then standard profitability measures. Cash flows available for repatriation are widely used to evaluate the financial performance of overseas operations because the value of a project is determined by the net present value of future cash flows. A survey of 125 multinational firms by William Persen and Van Lessig (1979) identified four purposes of an internal evaluation system: (1) to ensure adequate profitability; (2) to have an early warning system if something is wrong; (3) to have a basis for allocation of resources; and (4) to evaluate individual managers. Of course, the performance evaluation system is designed to measure actual performance against budgeted objectives as well as the prior year's results. In the best of situations, the evaluation system should monitor and control performance on a year-to-date and regular basis.

Performance Criteria. Table 17-3 shows that there are many possible criteria to evaluate performance. Multinational companies use multiple performance evaluation criteria because no single criterion can capture all the facets of performance that interest management at the main headquarters. Moreover, no single basis of measurement is equally appropriate for all units of a multinational firm. For example, companies can appropriately evaluate their production unit on the basis of such measures as cost reduction, quality control, and meeting shipment targets. For a sales unit, however, cost reduction and quality control may be less appropriate than such measures as market share and number of new customers. Thus, it is highly desirable for companies to use multiple bases for performance measurement; that is, different ones for different kinds of operations in different countries.

Two broad groups of performance evaluation criteria— financial criteria and nonfinancial criteria—are used most widely by companies for evaluating their overseas operations. The return on investment relates enterprise income to some specified investment base such as total assets. Many companies compare their actual operating performance with their budgeted performance; budgets are pre-established standards to which operations are evaluated, compared, and adjusted by the exercise of control.

Many multinational companies do not define their performance criteria to financial considerations. Nonfinancial criteria complement financial measures because they account for actions that may not contribute directly to profits in the short run but may contribute significantly to profits in the long run. Important nonfinancial measures include market share and sales growth. The market share is measured by sales or orders received as a percentage of total sales in a market. The sales growth is measured by unit volume gains, selling price increases, and exchange variations.

Once questions of performance criteria have been resolved, companies should ascertain whether their criteria can be useful in comparing a foreign unit's performance against its competitors' performance, either in the same country or across different borders. But there are many pitfalls in such comparisons. For example, it is almost impossible to determine the transfer pricing of competitors as well as their accounting principles. Certainly, cross-border comparisons would compound the problem even further. Companies with many affiliates—at home or abroad—must also be cautious whenever questions of comparability arise. Differences in subsidiaries would automatically distort performance comparisons unless they are directly accounted for. Even if subsidiary objectives are the same, differences in country risk profiles, such as exchange controls and export subsidies, could distort performance comparisons.

Table 17–3
Evaluating Foreign Subsidiary Performance

Profitability Evaluation

1. Determine what shall constitute the investment figure; for example, total funds invested, net assets, or net fixed assets.
2. Determine the basis for computing profit. This may be actual dollar remittances or total book profits.
3. Adjust for distortions due to the position of a subsidiary in an international profit plan; tax factors may have pegged profits through artificial pricing, royalty, management, and interest arrangements.
4. Apply the standard financial ratios used in domestic evaluation: rate of return on investment, liquidity, sales and inventory turnover, return on sales, and sales margin analysis.
5. Check the disposition of funds available for acquisition and investment where the local manager is independent.
6. Watch the distribution of assets, especially in an inflationary economy. Has the local manager hedged properly?
7. Analyze performance against budgeted goals and determine why variances, if any, occurred.
8. Temper these considerations with the outlook for actual long-term dollar profits; be sure that immediate profitability does not hamper future performance.

Market Penetration and Product Performance Evaluation

1. Check percentage of market in total and by product.
2. Gauge the degree of competition, local and foreign.
3. Consider the impact of substitute products in the market.
4. Judge the treatment of export sales by the subsidiary, both of its own products and of those of related companies.
5. Weigh the reliance of the subsidiary on captive sales to related companies, to the U.S. parent, and to dependent local buyers.
6. Review the level of the sales effort (wholesale, retail, ultimate consumer). Do not penalize the subsidiary for an erroneous selection of distribution channels by the parent.
7. Analyze the subsidiary's advertising and promotion program.
8. Note the frequency of suggestions for new-product development and improvements of existing items.
9. Check the quality of after-sales servicing.
10. Appraise the performance and attitudes of distributors under the subsidiary's control.

Productivity Evaluation

1. Determine production per hour, without regard to cost.
2. Relate output costs, using either value added or sales billed.
3. Adjust for such variables as wage scales, volume of production, degree of automation, efficiency of equipment.
4. Express productivity in physical units when inflation and currency deterioration might distort a monetary figure.

Labor Relations Evaluation

1. Assess employee morale and attitudes.
2. Examine the general administration of personnel policies.
3. Consider the effectiveness of training programs.
4. Calculate work time lost through absenteeism, turnover.
5. Review union relations, especially for time lost owing to walkouts and strikes.

Table 17-3

(continued)

Personnel Development Evaluation
1. Count the number of promotions within departments.
2. Note the transfers to higher posts in other units of the company group.
3. Determine the number of promotable personnel available.
4. Assess the worth of the subsidiary's medium- and long-range personnel-need forecasts.

Public and Government Relations Evaluation
1. Appraise the degree of identification and national goals.
2. Assess the tenor of community relations.
3. Check relations with local and national business leaders.
4. Review relationships with government officials.

Planning Evaluation
1. Search for clear statements on future targets.
2. Weigh the balance between long-range goals and short-term requirements.
3. Examine the coordination of functional and staff planning at all levels in the foreign subsidiary.

Finally, temper these quantitative and qualitative factors with the judgment of an experienced international executive and the priority a particular company may place on one or more of these evaluation categories.

Source: Business International.

Performance Measurement Issues.

There are many crucial yet perplexing elements in the performance evaluation process. As described earlier, two measurement problems unique to multinational companies are exchange rates and inflation.

Perhaps the most critical element in the evaluation process is how to deal with results that are denominated in currencies other than that of the parent company. The financial performance of overseas operations can be measured in terms of local currency, home country currency, or both. The choice of currency can have a significant effect on the assessment of a foreign subsidiary's performance if major changes occur in the exchange rates. For example, a subsidiary could make a profit in local currency but could incur a loss in the parent company's currency. Most U.S. companies analyze the operating results of their foreign operations in dollar terms. But several of these companies also use different rates for budgeting and performance tracking because they recognize variations between actual and expected results which arise purely from exchange rate changes.

Fluctuating exchange rates may pose the most significant obstacle to proper evaluation, but this is certainly not the only environmental factor. Wide variations and rapid changes in inflation rates from country to country also complicate the evaluation process. Generally accepted accounting principles in the United States are based on the assumption of price stability. However, other countries have runaway inflation, thus making it essential to adjust local asset values for changing prices. Such restatements directly affect the measurement of various return on investment (ROI) components and performance statistics for budgeting purposes. Because failure to account for inflation may result in an overstatement of return on investment, company resources may not be channeled to their most promising use. Unfortunately, solutions to these problems are not readily formulated. Furthermore, multinational companies must consider two sets of laws, two competitive markets, and two governments. As a result, pricing considerations in international business are more numerous, more complex, and more risky than those in purely domestic business.

Organizational Structure

Many internal and external pressures strain a firm's existing organizational structure as strictly domestic companies evolve into multinational companies. Some responsibilities are changed, new ones are created, and some existing ones are eliminated. Furthermore, control and finance functions change over time as changes occur in countries' socioeconomic environments. Companies must constantly adjust their organizational structure to deal with new opportunities and challenges as they grow, diversify, and internationalize.

How should the financial staff of a company with foreign operations organize itself to carry out tasks that require the specialized expertise of multinational finance? There are three basic forms of organizational structure: centralization, decentralization, and hybrid structure. A centralized financial function has a strong staff at the parent company level which controls virtually all treasury decisions. The subsidiary financial staff only implements the decisions of its parent company. In a decentralized function, parent company executives issue a few guidelines, but most financial decisions are made at the subsidiary level. Many companies split responsibilities for international financial management between the corporate level and the regional level. The corporate level typically determines policy and grants ultimate approval on major financial decisions. But day-to-day decisions to implement policy are made at regional headquarters.

Both centralization and decentralization carry advantages. The advantages of a centralized financial function include close control of financial issues at headquarters, attention of top management to key issues, and an emphasis on parent company goals. A decentralized company may argue that these advantages could be disadvantages. Data collection costs may be enormous, centralized decision making may stifle flexibility, and many opportunities may be lost because of slow actions.

Decision Variables. The ultimate choice of a particular organizational structure depends largely upon the types of decisions one must make: (1) transfer pricing and performance evaluation, (2) tax planning, (3) exchange exposure management, (4) acquisition of funds, and (5) positioning of funds.

First, transfer pricing decisions made to minimize taxes may ruin the performance evaluation system for foreign subsidiaries. This problem sometimes forces a company to keep a second set of books for evaluation purposes. Many multinational companies may, in fact, keep three or more sets of books: one for taxes, one for financial reporting, and one for evaluation purposes. There may be a need for two transfer prices: one for tax purposes made at headquarters and one for evaluation purposes decided by direct negotiations between affiliates.

Second, the centralized organization usually works well to minimize worldwide taxes. When tax planning is centralized, it is easier to use tax-haven countries, tax-saving holding companies, and transfer pricing. Thus, it is more efficient for multinational companies to centralize their tax planning function rather than allow each region to create its own layer of tax havens and holding companies.

Third, most companies centralize their foreign exchange exposure management because it is difficult for regional or country managers to know how their foreign exchange exposure relates to other affiliates.

Fourth, many multinational firms borrow money from local sources for their working capital. On the other hand, cheap sources of funds depend upon alternatives in all capital markets and the cost of exchange gains of losses. Regional managers can hardly know all alternative sources of funds outside a local market.

Fifth, positioning funds involves paying dividends and making intracompany loans, thereby reducing consideration of total corporate tax liabilities, foreign exchange exposure, and availability of capital. Consequently, most companies tend to control positioning of funds from a centralized vantage point rather than from a regional viewpoint.

Foreign Corrupt Practices Act

The Securities and Exchange Commission (SEC) first investigated illegal foreign payments in 1974 with its probe of questionable contributions by U.S. companies to the reelection campaign of former President Nixon. Subsequent inquiries by the SEC, the Department of Justice, and the Senate Foreign Relations Committee disclosed questionable payments of $300 million by 450 companies. Revelations of such dubious payments by U.S. firms to foreign officials rocked governments in Japan and the Netherlands.

Congress felt that the U.S. corporate bribery (1) tarnished the credibility of American business operations, (2) caused embarrassment with allies and foes alike, (3) created foreign policy difficulties, and (4) generally tarnished the world's image of the United States. Consequently, they passed and signed the Foreign Corrupt Practices Act (FCPA) on December 19, 1977, as an amendment to the Securities Exchange Act of 1934.

Content of the FCPA

The FCPA consists of two separate sections, antibribery and accounting. The antibribery section was the first piece of legislation in U.S. history making it a criminal offense for U.S. companies to corruptly influence foreign officials or to make payments to any person when they have "reason to know" that part of these payments will go to a foreign official.

The accounting section establishes two interrelated accounting requirements. First, public companies must "keep books, records and accounts, which, in reasonable detail, accurately and fairly reflect the transactions and dispositions" of their assets. Second, corporations are also required to "devise and maintain a system of internal accounting controls sufficient to provide reasonable assurance" that transactions have been executed in accordance with management's authorized procedures or policies.

Congress concluded that the antibribery and accounting sections would effectively prevent payments of foreign bribes and off-the-book slush funds. Penalties for violations include fines of up to $1 million for corporations and $10,000 and/or five years in jail for individuals. Thus, both the antibribery section and the accounting section are enforced through civil and criminal liabilities.

Fate of the FCPA

From its inception in December 1977, the FCPA was the subject of extensive debate. Corporate executives and chief officers of accounting firms argued that the FCPA constituted an encroachment on legitimate and necessary management prerogatives. Some members of Congress and enforcement officers of government agencies, on the other hand, countered that the FCPA made U.S. executives aware of their responsibilities and immense influence in the international business community. There were three basic positions about the fate of the FCPA: (1) repeal the law, (2) retain the law in its original form, and (3) amend the law to make it less onerous.

Repealing the FCPA.   Critics of the FCPA argued for its repeal for a number of reasons:

1. It forced U.S. companies to increase their audit cost substantially.
2. The Department of Justice and the SEC had failed to establish a set of clear guidelines.
3. It had put U.S. companies at a competitive disadvantage.
4. In many countries, foreign payments are not outlawed, but instead encouraged.
5. It was unnecessary because U.S. law enforcement agencies already had many statutes to prevent illegal foreign payments by U.S. companies.

Retaining the FCPA.

Proponents of the FCPA contended that if U.S. companies are allowed to corrupt foreign officials, in all likelihood they would wish to do the same in the United States. The FCPA encouraged U.S. companies to introduce corporate policies against corrupt foreign payments and to improve internal controls because the FCPA bans illegal payments to foreign officials, monitors accounting procedures, and levies heavy penalties for violations.

An overwhelming majority of the companies have undertaken positive steps to prevent illegal payments to foreign officials and to improve their internal controls. Some believe that the reduction of questionable foreign payments by U.S. companies is essential to upgrade the image of U.S. business. Thus, a strong argument can be made for the retention of the FCPA because the basic purpose of the FCPA was to improve the image of U.S. business and institutions tarnished by Watergate and related scandals. In addition, it is extremely difficult, if not impossible, to find documented evidence that U.S. companies have lost a substantial amount of export sales as a direct result of the FCPA.

Modifying the FCPA.

The Reagan Administration and U.S. Senators, John Chafee among them, launched a major effort to amend the FCPA in January 1981. Those who advocated modifying the FCPA argued that the United States should not completely scrap the law as we awaited an international solution to a worldwide problem of corrupt business practices. In order to make the FCPA more effective, understandable, and equitable, they suggested that the U.S. Congress remove criminal sanctions from the FCPA, end dual enforcement by the SEC and by the Department of Justice, end the dual burden of record keeping for both domestic and foreign transactions, eliminate the "reason to know" provision in the antibribery section, and limit accounting requirements.

President Reagan signed the FACP amendment of 1988 into law as part of an omnibus trade bill. Most proponents of its changes affirmed the original purposes of the FCPA. They found that the FCPA had been effective in curtailing bribes, kickbacks, and other unethical activities by U.S. companies. Still, the 1988 amendment removed one of the statute's strongest export disincentives: the threat of statutory criminal liability based on accidental or unknowing negligence in the retention of certain accounting records. So, only corporate employees who "knowingly" circumvent corporate accounting controls or falsify records of corporate payments are now subject to criminal liability. In fact, the old law and the new law differ in notable ways:

1. The old law assessed both civil and criminal sanctions on both deliberate and negligent violators of the accounting section. The new law assesses only civil (no criminal) penalties on negligent or unintentional violators of the accounting section.

2. The old law did not define "reasonable detail" in the accounting section and "reason to know" in the antibribery section. The new law defines them as those which would satisfy a "prudent individual" under similar circumstances.

3. The old law did not define "grease payments" and virtually precluded all forms of grease payments to foreign officials. In fact, grease payments were enforced via both civil and criminal sanctions. The new law specifically permits such grease payments if: (1) they help expedite routine governmental action; (2) they are legal in that foreign country; or (3) they demonstrate gratitude or reimbursement for expenses incurred in connection with a contract.

4. The old law had been severely criticized from its inception on the ground that it was vague and difficult to interpret. Still, no government agency issued interpretative guidelines. The new law specifies that a set of clear guidelines will be issued by the government if the business community wants further clarification of the new law.

5. The old law did not require any government agency to give its opinion on the legality of a contemplated transaction. The new law requires the Department of Justice to give its opinion on the legality of a planned transaction within 30 days after receiving the necessary information.

The international business community will experience dramatic fluctuations and keener competition in the rest of this century. Many U.S. executives believe that the huge U.S. trade deficit and the weakening competitive advantage of the United States are signals that this country cannot afford to ignore. To overcome such problems, there must be a process of mutual cooperation and involvement between the federal government and the business community. Such cooperation has taken place since the U.S. Congress began its deliberations on the possible revision of the FCPA in 1981 and on removal of other U.S. export disincentives in recent years. The 1988 amendment to the original FCPA could enable U.S. companies to increase their export sales.

Summary

Accurate financial reports on operations must be prepared for stockholders and creditors to make decisions about the value of existing operations. They are especially important in international business where operations are typically supervised from a distance. Hence, meaningful financial reports are the cornerstone of effective international financial management. Financial control systems must fit international circumstances to check performance against standards on a worldwide basis.

World accounting systems can be classified into four basic types. A macroeconomic approach assumes that the accounting system should facilitate government economic policies. A microeconomic approach assumes that accounting performs a service function for business and thus it should orient itself to the same micro considerations that reflect its environment. An independent-discipline approach assumes that accounting can develop its concepts from practice. A uniform accounting system involves identical terminology and account classifications for all companies.

Because multinational companies cross national boundaries in search of markets or resources, their financial statements differ in the form of presentation and in the degree of detail disclosed. In the United States, the income statement is more important than the balance sheet, while in Europe, the balance sheet is treated as the financial statement of prime interest. European companies establish various reserves to smooth out income fluctuations from year to year. In contrast, such reserves are quite rare in the United States. The United States follows the practice of consolidation, but many European countries do not do so for foreign operations.

Companies must disclose proper financial data and other relevant information for their stockholders and other potential investors. The amount of disclosure depends on the expertness of the user and the desirable standard. The three major standards generally proposed are adequate, fair, and full disclosure. U.S. multinational companies are required to disclose appropriate financial data if their foreign operations account for more than 10 percent of total operations. European companies tend to disclose less financial data than U.S. companies.

Consolidated financial statements present the results of both foreign and domestic operations as if they were a single economic unit. U.S. multinational companies are required to consolidate the financial statements of the parent and those of its subsidiaries if the parent owns more than 50 percent of the subsidiary's voting shares. Principal users of consolidated statements are stockholders of the parent company, stockholders of the foreign subsidiaries, and managers of the parent.

A financial control system is used to make sure that financial goals and objectives are being met. Control decisions affect financial plans, just as planning decisions affect controls. Budgeted financial statements are the most widely used standards. Thus, it is important to measure the impact of inflation and exchange fluctuations on financial statements.

The major purpose of performance evaluation is to assure adequate profitability. Normally, companies use multiple measures of performance evaluation because their objectives and operating environments differ. Still, companies use return on investment and budgeted performance as two main criteria for evaluating their overseas operations.

The financial staff of a multinational company should be organized to carry out tasks that require the specialized expertise of multinational finance. A centralized company has a strong staff at the parent company level which controls practically all financial decisions. In a decentralized company, parent company executives issue a few guidelines, but the majority of financial decisions are made at the regional level. The ultimate choice of a particular organizational structure depends upon a number of important decision variables, such as transfer pricing and performance evaluation, tax planning, and exchange exposure management.

The Foreign Corrupt Practices Act of 1977 intended to stop the erosion of international confidence in U.S. business and institutions. The FCPA made it unlawful for U.S. companies to influence foreign officials through payments and required these firms to maintain strict accounting controls over their assets. Many U.S. executives would have liked the U.S. Congress to repeal the FCPA because (1) it compelled U.S. companies to increase their audit cost substantially; (2) the Department of Justice and the SEC failed to establish a set of clear guidelines; (3) it placed U.S. companies at a competitive disadvantage; (4) many foreign countries encouraged and legalized foreign payments; and (5) many other laws may be used to prevent illegal foreign payments by U.S. companies. Congress amended the FCPA in 1988 to make U.S. companies more competitive in the world market.

Questions

1. Explain two major problems that make multinational accounting complicated.

2. Why are accounting systems shaped by the environment in which they operate?

3. Why do financial statements issued by companies in various countries differ?

4. Describe some reasons for the recognition of primary and secondary financial statements as part of generally accepted accounting principles.

5. What is the difference between accounting standards and auditing standards? Why are auditing standards less diverse than accounting standards from country to country?

6. What is the conflict of interest in terms of financial disclosure between users and issuers of financial statements? Why does such a conflict arise?

7. Discuss the rationale behind the movement by numerous bodies to harmonize international accounting and auditing standards.

8. Explain why multinational companies are required to prepare consolidated financial statements.

9. Why are budgets and the return on investment in performance evaluation systems more frequently used than any other indicators?

10. Discuss centralization vs. decentralization as it impinges on decisions relating to transfer pricing and performance evaluation, exchange exposure management, acquisitions of funds, positioning of funds, and tax planning.

11. What is the Foreign Corrupt Practices Act? What are the two sections of this law?

References

American Institute of Certified Public Accountants, *The Accounting Profession in Japan*, New York: AICPA, 1988.

Arnold, J. L., and M. A. Diamond, *Corporate Financial Policies: A Review and Analysis of Existing Literature*, Morristown, NJ: Financial Executives Research Foundation, 1989.

Arpan, J. A., and L. H. Radebaugh, *International Accounting and Multinational Enterprise*, New York: Wiley, 1985.

Choi, F. D. S., *Frontiers of International Accounting: An Anthology*, Ann Arbor, MI: UMI Research Press, 1985.

Choi, F. D. S., and G. G. Mueller, *International Accounting*, Englewood Cliffs, NJ: Prentice-Hall, 1984.

Fox, S., and N. G. Rueschhoff, *Principles of International Accounting*, Austin, TX: Austin Press, 1986.

International Accounting Standards Committee, *Comparability of Financial Statements*, London: IASC, 1990.

International Accounting Standards Committee, *Survey of the Use and Application of International Accounting Standards 1988*, London: IASC, 1988.

Kim, S. H., "On Repealing the Foreign Corrupt Practices Act," *Columbia Journal of World Business*, Fall 1981, pp. 75–80.

Mouzin, D. J., and M. B. Solomon, "Practical Means of Promoting International Standards," *The CPA Journal*, December 1989, pp. 38–48.

Mueller, G. G., H. Germon, and G. Meek, *Accounting: An International Perspective*, Homewood, IL: Irwin, 1991.

Organization for Economic Cooperation and Development, *Harmonization of Accounting Standards: Achievements and Prospects*, Paris: OECD, 1987.

Pasztor, A., and B. Ingersoll, "Recent Charges of Payoffs by Companies Coincide with Bid to Relax Law Barring Overseas Bribes," *The Wall Street Journal*, July 10, 1986, p. 46.

Persen, W., and V. Lessig, *Evaluating the Performance of Overseas Operations*, New York: Financial Executive Institute, 1979.

Price Waterhouse, *Doing Business in Germany*, New York: Price Waterhouse, 1988.

United Nations Center on Transnational Corporations, *International Accounting and Reporting Issues*, New York: United Nations, 1990.

18

International
Taxation

Usually one of the most important variables in multinational operations is taxation. Perhaps no other environmental variable, with the possible exception of foreign exchange, has such a pervasive influence on all aspects of multinational operations. Taxation influences (1) the choice of location in the investment decision, (2) the form of the new enterprise, (3) the method of finance, and (4) the method of transfer pricing.

International taxation is complicated because tax laws differ among countries and are constantly changing. Hence, it is not accidental that international taxation still remains somewhat of a mystery for many international executives. For example, multinational financial managers need to understand the following:

1. Shareholders of foreign and domestic corporations are subject to different rules.
2. Accounting for foreign taxes on foreign operations is not identical to that on domestic operations.
3. Bilateral tax treaties and foreign tax credits exist to avoid double taxation of income.
4. Many countries offer a number of tax incentives to attract foreign capital and know-how.
5. Tax savings realized in low tax countries may be offset by taxes on undistributed earnings.

There are many such added complexities because governments have failed to come to any general agreement on tax policies. Each country has its own tax philosophies, tax incentives, transfer pricing policies, and the like. Multinational financial managers must sort them out in order to maximize profitability and cash flow. To attain this end, they must acquaint themselves with the overall tax environment. Thus, this chapter covers such general topics as national tax environments, parent country taxation of multinational operations, tax incentives, and taxation of U.S. citizens abroad.

National Tax Environments

Each country has its own array of taxes. This makes it imperative for the multinational company to seek local tax counsel in each country it operates. Differences among national tax systems include assessment philosophies, collection purposes, tax computations, and tax procedures. This section describes various manifestations of these differences such as tax philosophies, types of taxes, tax morality, and tax burdens.

Tax Philosophies

A country can claim the right to tax income either on a global basis or on a territorial basis. Global claims assume that countries have the right to tax a firm and all its foreign subsidiaries. Such a firm may be domiciled, incorporated, or otherwise headquartered within their borders. Under this system, overseas earnings could be taxed twice. A German subsidiary of an American company may have to pay both U.S. and German taxes on income earned in Germany. Fortunately, most countries whose tax systems are based on global claims grant some relief from double taxation. Nevertheless, most multinational companies feel that global claims put them at a competitive disadvantage. Tax treaties and/or tax credit for taxes paid to foreign governments do not completely eliminate double taxation, while local companies pay only local taxes.

Unitary taxes are a special type of tax based on a global tax principle. The unitary method of taxation used by the state of California and by several other states of the United States was designed to tax a company's worldwide income. The unitary tax method applies to U.S. companies with foreign operations as well as to foreign firms with operations in the unitary tax state. In a case brought before the U.S. Supreme Court, Container Corporation tried to avoid tax payments on its foreign source income. But the Supreme Court ruled that California had the right to pursue its tax concept. Shell Petroleum, N.V., the Dutch parent of Shell Oil Company, tried to argue that the unitary tax concept did not apply to foreign corporations, but the Supreme Court again ruled in favor of California.

The unitary tax debate has surfaced in recent years as a source of strong controversy between the U.S. government and other governments such as the United Kingdom and the Netherlands. A popular compromise to the worldwide concept of the unitary tax is the water's edge concept. Under this compromise, taxable state income is defined as income earned in the United States only rather than income earned worldwide. This method was adopted quickly by most states that had used the unitary tax method.

Under the principles of national sovereignty, countries claim the right to tax income earned within their own territory. These territorial claims are very popular with multinational companies, but not as popular with governments. Such financial centers as Hong Kong and Switzerland, plus many Latin American countries, do not tax their firms' income earned overseas.

Types of Taxes

Multinational companies face a variety of direct and indirect taxes. Direct taxes include corporate income and capital gains taxes. Indirect taxes include value-added taxes, tariffs, and withholding taxes. In addition to these direct and indirect taxes, multinational companies may have to pay property taxes, payroll taxes, stamp and registration taxes, taxes on registrations of agreements of various types, sales and excise taxes (excluding value-added taxes), and taxes on undistributed earnings.

Income and Capital Gains.

As with individual income taxes, corporate income taxes are an important source of revenue for many countries. Because most developing countries have low per capita income, individual income taxes or sales taxes are not very appropriate. Thus, developing countries obtain a larger share of government revenues from corporate income taxes than industrial countries.

Gains and losses on sales of capital assets are called capital gains and losses. Capital assets are those assets that are not primarily for resale and not acquired in the ordinary course of business. These assets include stocks and bonds. If capital assets are held longer than a specified period of time, gains on sales of these assets may be subject to preferential tax treatment.

Value-Added Taxes.

Value-added taxes are a special type of sales tax. Sales taxes are those taxes assessed at one or more stages in the production process. In Canada, sales taxes are levied when production is complete; in England, when products are wholesaled; in the United States, when products are retailed; and in Germany, at all stages in the production cycle. Many European countries have adopted the value-added tax as the major source of revenue to avoid the compounding effect of sales taxes. For example, if a car dealer purchased a car for $10,000 from a car manufacturing company and then sold it for $15,000, the value added would be $5,000 and the tax would be levied on this $5,000 increment.

Tariffs.

Tariffs are simply taxes assessed on imported goods which parallel excise and other indirect taxes paid by domestic producers of similar goods. They may be imposed for purposes of revenue or protection. When tariffs are employed to increase revenues, they are usually modest. However, when tariffs are used to protect domestic companies from foreign competition, they are typically high. Although protective tariffs do not eliminate the importation of foreign products completely, they clearly put foreign sellers at a comparative disadvantage. In this instance, consumers must pay more for foreign goods, which in turn would reduce their consumption of imported commodities.

Withholding Taxes.   Withholding taxes are those taxes imposed by host governments on dividend and interest payments to foreign investors and debtholders. These taxes are collected before receipt of the income. In other words, they are usually withheld at the source by the paying corporation. For example, a 20 percent withholding tax on $10,000 interest payments to foreigners means that the tax proceeds of $2,000 are deducted from the interest payment made to the lender and collected by the borrower on behalf of the government. Hence, the purchaser of the bonds would receive only $8,000, or 80 percent of the $10,000 interest payment. Withholding taxes are generally modified by bilateral tax treaties because they frequently restrict the international movement of long–term investment capital.

Tax Morality

The issue at stake is the conflict between economics (profits) and ethics (corporate morality). Some business executives think that profits are one thing and corporate morality is another; thus, they conclude that they have to make a choice. It is well known that in many countries both corporate and individual taxpayers are not completely honest with their tax authorities. Multinational companies must decide whether to comply with the tax laws voluntarily. Although most multinational companies comply fully with the tax laws, some companies feel that they should evade taxes to the same extent as their competitors in order to protect their competitive position. Ethical standards vary greatly among people, companies, and societies because business ethics are partly a function of cultural patterns and historical development. Therefore, there is obviously no universally accepted answer to the problem.

Host governments also have a similar moral problem. Two basic tax principles are that taxes should be equitable and neutral. In other words, taxes should be fair to everyone, and they should not affect decisions in the economic system. Nevertheless, many countries have imposed some arbitrary tax penalties on multinational companies for presumed violations of local tax laws. Many developing countries have various tax incentive programs for private foreign investments. These tax incentive programs abandon the principle of an economically neutral system. Under a neutral tax system, supply and demand should be left alone to determine prices and economic activity if we want the most efficient economic system.

Tax Burdens

Because different countries have varying statutory rates of income tax, differences in overall tax burdens are another natural feature of international business operations. The corporate tax rate ranges from zero in such tax-haven countries as the Bahamas to 60 percent in such countries as Libya.

Differences in definitions of taxable corporate income create greater disparities than differences in nominal corporate tax rates. Thus, differential tax rates tell us only part of the story. In one country taxable income may be computed on a cash basis while in another country it may be determined on an accrual basis. Investment allowances and credits, reserves, the timing of depreciation deductions, and asset valuations vary greatly from country to country. Some countries provide companies with full credit for taxes on the income paid in other countries.

Tax systems also affect relative tax burdens internationally. In general, there are three classes of systems: single tax, double tax, and partial double tax. Under the single tax system, income is taxed only once. If corporations pay no taxes, their stockholders pay taxes on dividends. Under the double tax system, corporations pay taxes on profits at a given rate and dividends are then taxed as income to stockholders at their personal income tax rates. Under the partial double tax system, taxes are levied on corporate income, but dividends are taxed at a lower rate than other forms of personal income, or distributed corporate earnings are taxed at a lower rate than undistributed earnings (retained earnings).

Table 18-1 lists statutory income and withholding tax rates that foreign investors may be subject to if they conduct a business or make an investment in the named countries. All listed corporate income and withholding tax rates represent the highest possible tax rate in each category. All these tax rates were in effect as of December 31, 1991.

Carrybacks and Carryforwards.

An operating loss is the excess of deductible expenses over gross income. Operating losses can often be carried back or forward to offset earnings in other years. Tax provisions for carrybacks and carryforwards vary among countries. Most countries do not permit operating losses to be carried back. But virtually all countries allow companies to carry their losses forward for a limited number of years.

U.S. companies may carry their excess foreign-tax credit back two years and carry it forward five years to offset U.S. tax on foreign-source income. The choice depends largely upon whether a company has had foreign-source income in those two years immediately prior to the excess foreign-tax credit. If this is the case, the company must carry the excess foreign-tax credit back in order to expedite the refund of tax payment.

The purpose of this provision is to allow corporations to average their operating results, which fluctuate widely from year to year. However, some profitable multinational companies have used the carryback and carryforward feature as a means of reducing their taxable income by merging with other firms that have considerable operating losses or excess foreign-tax credits.

Table 18–1
Foreign Income and Withholding Tax Rates
(in percent)

Country	Domestic Income	Foreign Income	Dividends	Interest	Royalties
Europe					
Belgium	39	19	25	25	10
Denmark	40	40	30	0	0
France	34	34	25	45	33
Germany	35	35	35	35	35
Greece	34	34	30	30	30
Ireland	43	43	0	30	30
Italy	36	36	32	12	21
Netherlands	35	35	25	0	0
Norway	51	51	25	25	0
Spain	35	35	20	20	20
Sweden	30	30	30	0	0
Switzerland	27	27	35	0	0
U.K.	35	35	0	25	25
The Americas					
Argentina	20	36	20	14	29
Brazil	30	30	25	25	25
Bahamas	0	0	0	0	0
Canada	29	25	20	30	38
Colombia	30	30	30	38	38
Mexico	25	25	55	42	42
U.S.A.	34	34	30	30	30
Venezuela	50	50	20	20	20
Others					
Australia	39	39	30	10	39
Hong Kong	16	16	0	0	0
Japan	37	37	20	20	20
Korea	34	34	0	10	0
Singapore	31	31	0	31	31
South Africa	50	50	15	0	15

Source: *Worldwide Corporate Tax Guide and Directory*, New York: Ernst & Young, January 1992.

Parent Country Taxation of Multinational Operations

Countries differ with respect to their tax treatment of foreign source income earned by their multinational companies. Major differences include varying interpretations of tax neutrality, the method of granting credit for foreign income taxes already paid, and concessions gained in bilateral tax treaties.

Tax Neutrality

A neutral tax is one that would not affect the location of the investment or the nationality of the investor. Tax neutrality is justified on the ground that world welfare would be increased if capital is free to move from countries whose rate of return is low to those whose rate of return is high.

Tax neutrality consists of domestic neutrality and foreign neutrality. Domestic neutrality means the equal treatment of Americans who invest at home and Americans who invest abroad. This neutrality involves equalization of all taxes on profits.

Foreign neutrality indicates that the tax burden imposed on each foreign subsidiary of a U.S. company should equal the tax burden placed on its competitors in the same country. The firm owned by residents of the host country and the foreign subsidiary of a non-U.S. company are the two basic types of competitors faced by the foreign subsidiary of a U.S. firm.

Tax neutrality is designed to achieve a status of equality within the tax system. In practice, however, it is difficult to define and measure tax neutrality. The issue of tax equity is also difficult to define and measure. Many governments claim that they tax foreign income at the same rate as domestic income. However, most countries in the world have many important departures from the theoretical norm of tax neutrality.

Tax Treaties

Countries enter into bilateral tax treaties to avoid double taxation and thus to encourage the free flow of investments internationally. Treaty countries agree on how taxes will be imposed, shared, or otherwise eliminated on business income earned in one taxing jurisdiction by nationals of another.

Over the last 50 years, international organizations have drafted models to standardize the treaties. The League of Nations drafted the first model in 1929, and this model was followed by the so-called Model Conventions of Mexico (1943) and London (1946). The Organization for Economic Cooperation and Development (OECD) developed the recent model called the "Draft Double Taxation Convention on Income and Capital" in 1963, and this model was revised in 1974. The OECD is a governmental body which consists of 24 member countries, most of which are industrial. The purpose of the OECD is to encourage economic growth of its members and nonmembers in the field of international trade and investment. The 1963 Draft Model Convention has become an essential document in guiding tax treaty negotiators and tax advisors.

Most tax treaties now in effect are agreements between industrial countries. Because most industrial countries are both capital exporting and importing countries, they have common interests in such areas as reduction of withholding taxes on corporate foreign income and royalties. Fewer treaties have been signed between developed and developing countries. In 1967 the United Nations established a "Group of Tax Experts on Tax Treaties" to overcome this problem. In 1974 they issued Guidelines on Tax Treaties between developed and developing countries. Recent U.S. tax treaties are based on the OECD model. In May 1976 the U.S. Treasury Department published its own Model Income Tax Treaty, which represents the provisions of future U.S. tax treaties.

The provisions of most tax treaties override the provisions of national income tax laws. For example, Section 8894 of the U.S. Internal Revenue Code states that "income of any kind, to the extent required by any treaty obligation of the United States, shall not be included in gross income and

Table 18–2
Foreign Withholding Rates and U.S. Income Tax Treaties
(in percent)

Country	Dividends	Interest	Patent and Know–How Royalties
Australia	15	10	10
Austria	15	0	0
Belgium	15	15	0
Canada	15	15	10
China	10	10	10
Cyprus	15	10	0
Denmark	15	0	0
Egypt	15	15	15
Finland	15	0	0
France	15	0	5
Germany	15	0	0
Greece	30	0	0
Hungary	15	0	0
India	25	15	15
Indonesia	15	15	15
Ireland	15	0	0
Italy	15	15	10
Jamaica	15	12.5	10
Japan	15	10	10
Korea (South)	15	12	15
Luxembourg	15	0	0
Malta	15	12.5	12.5
Morocco	15	15	10
Netherlands	15	0	0
New Zealand	15	0	0
Norway	15	0	0
Pakistan	30	30	0
Philippines	25	15	15
Sweden	15	0	0
Switzerland	15	5	0
Trinidad & Tobago	30	30	15
United Kingdom	15	0	0
Russia	30	0	0

Source: *Worldwide Corporate Tax Guide and Directory*, New York: Ernst & Young, January 1992.

shall be exempt from taxation under this subtitle." Thus, U.S. tax treaties provide that profits earned by U.S. companies in a foreign country are exempt from taxation unless they have permanent establishment in the foreign country. Tax treaties also reduce withholding taxes on dividends, interest, and royalties.

Table 18-2 shows various rates of withholding taxes imposed by countries with which the United States has a tax treaty. The withholding tax rates may not apply if the U.S. corporation has a permanent establishment in the treaty country. Moreover, all withholding tax rates were in effect as of December 31, 1991, and these withholding tax rates are considerably lower than the statutory rates of Table 18-1.

Foreign Tax Credit

The purpose of the foreign tax credit is to avoid international double taxation when profits earned abroad become subject to the full tax levies of two or more countries. Under the foreign tax credit system, the United States relinquishes tax on profits earned abroad up to the amount of the foreign tax. Thus, the foreign government takes the first bite of profits earned in its jurisdiction. In addition, taxes subject to these credit provisions include withholding taxes on dividends, interest, and other income.

Example 18-1. Assume: (1) a U.S. corporation has $1,000 of foreign income; (2) the foreign country's tax rate is 40 percent; and (3) the U.S. tax rate is 50 percent. The net U.S. tax of $100 is computed as follows:

Foreign income	$1,000
Foreign tax (40%)	400
Net income after tax	$ 600
U.S. taxable income	$1,000
U.S. tax (50%)	$ 500
Foreign tax credit	400
U.S. tax payable	$ 100
Total foreign and U.S. taxes	$ 500
Effective tax rate	50%

As this example illustrates, the purpose of the foreign tax credit is to limit the total tax on foreign income to the higher tax rate of the two countries. If the foreign tax on income earned abroad and remitted to the United States is less than or equal to the U.S. tax rate, that income will be subject to a total tax of 50 percent. Thus, if the foreign tax rate is lower than the U.S. rate, the U.S. government receives some tax revenues on the foreign income. If the foreign tax rate is higher than the U.S. rate, the U.S. government receives no tax revenues on the foreign income.

As an alternative to the foreign tax credit, U.S. companies can treat any foreign tax paid directly as a deductible expense. Because both a credit and deduction cannot be claimed in the same year, the U.S. company must decide whether to claim the credit or deduction for foreign income taxes. In general, it is advantageous to claim a credit against federal income tax rather than a deduction.

Example 18–2.   Assume: (1) a U.S. corporation has $1,000 of foreign income; (2) the foreign country's tax rate is 50 percent; and (3) the U.S. tax rate is 50 percent. The following computation shows that the credit is better than the deduction:

	Foreign Tax Credit	Foreign Tax Deduction
Foreign income	$1,000	$1,000
Foreign tax (50%)	500	500
Net income after tax	500	500
U.S. taxable income	$1,000	$ 500
U.S. tax (50%)	$ 500	$ 250
Foreign tax payable	500	0
U.S. tax payable	$ 0	$ 250
Total foreign and U.S. taxes	$ 500	$ 750
Effective tax rate	50%	75%

Foreign Companies in the U.S. and Their Tax Payment

The United States was the dominant direct investor abroad in three decades (1950, 1960s, and 1970s), but since 1980 it has become the world's largest recipient of foreign direct investment funds. Consequently, foreign-owned businesses are becoming increasingly visible and important in all sections of the country.

A fundamental economic premise is that there should be a reasonable relationship between the amount of assets owned and the amount of taxes collected. Evidence indicates that this goal is not met with respect to foreign investors in the United States. The U.S. House Ways and Means Oversight Subcommittee recently found that many foreign companies in the United States had not paid their fair share of U.S. taxes. An investigation by the subcommittee found that more than half of the foreign companies paid little or no income taxes. One of the 36 foreign companies investigated by the subcommittee reported gross profits of about $600 million on sales of over $3.5 billion but paid only $500 of Federal income taxes. These foreign companies have used a variety of techniques to avoid U.S. income taxes, such as tax treaties, foreign tax credit, different tax schemes, and transfer pricing policies.

Tax Incentives for Foreign Investment

Many countries, especially developing countries, offer tax incentives to attract foreign capital and know-how to their countries. The two basic forms of tax incentive programs are government concessions and tax havens.

Government Concessions

Developing countries offer many concessions to attract multinational companies. Most concessions are in the form of a complete tax exemption for the first few years, known as "tax holidays." Some other forms of temporary tax concessions include reduced income tax rates, tax credits on new investments, tax deferrals, and reduction or elimination of various indirect taxes. These concessions, along with lower labor costs in relation to developed countries, have made many developing countries attractive for assembly and manufacturing operations.

Tax Havens

Some countries promise permanent tax inducements in order to attract multinational companies. Known as tax havens, these nations have few natural resources. In addition to low tax rates, tax havens must have (1) a stable government, (2) good communication facilities, (3) freedom of currency movements, and (4) the availability of financial services. Tax havens may be classified into four broad categories:

1. Countries with no income taxes, such as the Bahamas, Bermuda, the Cayman Islands, and Vanuatu.
2. Countries with very low taxes, such as Switzerland, Liechtenstein, Hong Kong, and the Channel Islands.
3. Countries which tax income from domestic sources but exempt income from foreign sources.
4. Countries which allow special privileges to make them suitable as tax havens for very limited purposes.

A large number of non-U.S. multinational companies have foreign affiliates which act as tax havens for corporate funds. These corporate funds are held in the tax havens until they are reinvested or repatriated elsewhere. Tax-haven affiliates are the outgrowth of tax-deferral features on foreign earnings allowed by some parent countries to their multinational companies. Normally, parent companies can defer taxes on their foreign earnings until these earnings are received as dividends.

Subpart F of the U.S. Internal Revenue Code

The U.S. government originally permitted U.S. companies to defer taxes on their foreign earnings so that they could invest abroad and compete on an equal footing with foreign companies. Unfortunately, these tax-deferral features were frequently used by U.S. companies to avoid U.S. taxes. Typically, a U.S. parent company established a foreign holding company with a tax-haven domicile. The major purpose of such a tax-haven corporation was to receive tax free the profits earned by its operating subsidiaries. For example, this holding company would receive the exclusive right to export the products of the parent company. This makes it possible for a portion of the profits to shift from the parent to the foreign holding company. Similar mechanisms were often used by some U.S. companies to avoid taxes on royalties and other foreign-source income.

The U.S. Revenue Act of 1962 introduced Subpart F to prevent U.S. multinational companies from using tax havens in order to avoid U.S. and foreign taxes. Subpart F of the 1962 Revenue Act subjects all U.S. foreign affiliates to U.S. tax obligations whenever they engage in intracompany transactions across national boundaries. The Revenue Reduction Act of 1975 and the Revenue Reform Act of 1976 tightened the Subpart F rules. The Tax Reform Act of 1986 retained the basic concept of Subpart F income, but the 1986 Act expanded the categories of income subject to taxation and reduced exceptions.

Under this provision taxes are imposed on Subpart F income of controlled foreign corporations or undistributed foreign base company income. A controlled foreign corporation is a foreign corporation in which more than 50 percent of the voting shares are owned by U.S. shareholders. Only shareholders holding more than 10 percent of the voting power are counted for the purpose of arriving at the percentage of control.

The term "foreign base company" describes a corporation whose base or registration is in a country in which it does not conduct active operations. Foreign base company income includes foreign personal holding company income, foreign base company sales income, foreign base company service income, and foreign base company shipping income.

There are a number of exceptions to the general rule:

1. If controlled foreign corporations domiciled in developing countries reinvest their earnings in these countries, Subpart F provisions do not apply.
2. If the combination of U.S. and foreign taxes paid on all income of the controlled foreign corporation is close to the U.S. tax rate, Subpart F provisions do not apply.
3. If foreign base company income is less than 10 percent of the controlled foreign company's gross income, Subpart F provisions do not apply.

U.S. Tax Incentives

The United States has introduced a number of tax incentives into its tax provisions over the years to encourage certain business activities in specific areas of the world. But many of these tax incentives have been phased out since the Revenue Reform Act of 1976. The United States still has two types of tax incentive programs: operations in U.S. possessions (Possessions Corporations) and export promotions (Foreign Sales Corporations).

Possessions Corporation.

A U.S. firm engaged in business within a United States possession obtains tax advantages if it meets certain requirements:

1. It is a domestic U.S. corporation.
2. At least 80 percent of its gross income for the last three years is derived from sources within a possession of the United States.
3. At least 75 percent of its gross income results from the active conduct of a trade or business.

A possessions corporation is a U.S. corporation that conducts its business in a U.S. possession. Possessions of the United States include American Samoa, Guam, the Panama Canal Zone, Puerto Rico, Wake Island, the Virgin Islands, and Midway Island.

However, the Virgin Islands are not counted as a U.S. possession for this particular purpose because of their peculiar tax situation. Under the Virgin Islands' incentive legislation, a qualifying company would receive a 75 percent subsidy of the tax paid from the Island. Consequently, qualifying companies would pay tax of only 8.5 percent (0.25 x 0.34) on Virgin Island income. In order to qualify, the company must meet above requirements 2 and 3.

Possessions corporations exclude from U.S. gross income amounts earned outside the United States unless the income is received in the United States. Hence, they would arrange to receive their income initially outside the United States even though they may subsequently transfer the income from foreign bank accounts to bank accounts in the United States. When possessions corporations pay dividends to their U.S. parent company, the parent company treats the dividends as if they were received from foreign corporations and can claim direct and deemed paid foreign tax credits.

Possessions corporations are treated in most ways as foreign corporations, but there are two important exceptions. First, they are treated as domestic corporations for purposes of organization, reorganization, and liquidation. Second, they are not treated as controlled foreign corporations for Subpart F purposes.

Foreign Sales Corporations.

To provide a tax incentive for U.S. companies to increase their exports, the Revenue Act of 1971 introduced a system of tax deferral for a new type of U.S. corporation called a Domestic International Sales Corporation (DISC). Under these rules, the DISC's earnings were not taxed but, instead, were taxed to the stockholders when distributed or deemed distributed. Essentially, the DISC could defer U.S. tax on 50 percent of its taxable income while the other half was deemed distributed and taxed as a dividend to the shareholders. The shareholders of a DISC were entitled to the foreign tax credit for foreign taxes on the DISC.

The Foreign Sales Corporation Act of 1984 was signed into law on July 18, 1984, as a part of the Deficit Reduction Act of 1984; it became effective as of January 1, 1985. This law largely replaced DISC with the new Foreign Sales Corporation (FSC). The DISC was the object of complaints by major U.S. trading partners on the grounds that DISCs violated subsidy rules laid down by the General Agreement on Tariffs and Trade (GATT). GATT rules require that countries do not use taxes as a form of subsidy. The FSC is designed to comply with GATT rules while still promoting U.S. exports. Unlike its DISC predecessor, the FSC must satisfy the following eight requirements:

1. It must be incorporated in a U.S. possession or in a foreign country.
2. There can be no more than 25 shareholders at any time.
3. There can be no preferred stock.
4. Its records must be kept at a non-U.S. office.
5. The board of directors must have at least one non-U.S. resident.
6. It cannot be a member of a controlled group of corporations which also include a DISC as a member.
7. It must elect to be a FSC.
8. Foreign management and economic process requirements must be met.

There are three rules for meeting the foreign management requirement. First, the FSC must hold all director and stockholder meetings outside the United States. Second, it must hold the principal bank account outside the United States. Third, it must pay all dividends, legal and accounting fees, and management salaries out of foreign bank accounts.

There are two rules for meeting the foreign economic process requirement. First, the FSC or its agent must participate in solicitation, negotiation, and contracting the transaction outside the United States. Second, foreign direct costs must be either at least 50 percent of the total direct costs for the transaction or at least 85 percent of two or more of these costs: advertising and sales promotion, processing costs, transportation costs, accounting and collection costs, and assumption of credit risk.

If a company meets FSC requirements, a portion of its income is exempt from U.S. corporate income tax. From the standpoint of exporters, a major advantage of FSC over DISC is that the tax exemption is permanent. There is no recapture of the benefit in future years if dividends are paid or the FSC no longer satisfies its requirements. The FSC's other feature is the permanent forgiveness of taxes deferred under DISC provisions.

Taxation of U.S. Citizens Abroad

U.S. multinational companies must offer their overseas employees a significant salary to induce them to move abroad. Their salary usually consists of the base salary plus additional compensation in the form of housing allowance, hardship allowance, educational allowance for their children, and cost-of-living difference. These additional allowances can escalate an overseas employee's salary significantly and subject it to a higher income tax in the foreign country as well as in the United States.

Every country has the right to tax earnings of its citizens. But the United States goes far beyond most industrial countries by taxing the worldwide income of its citizens. According to a 1979 survey of Business International, the United States was the only industrial country that taxed its expatriates on worldwide income. This has compelled U.S. multinational companies to pay their expatriates more or to replace their expatriates with local people.

The U.S. policy of taxing the foreign income earned by U.S. citizens abroad has changed significantly throughout history. Some tax relief for U.S. citizens abroad was provided by the Foreign Earned Income Act of 1978, which allowed deductions for cost of living, housing, schooling, home leave travel, and hardship. These deductions were repealed for 1982 and thereafter, because the Economic Recovery Tax Act of 1981 completely overhauled the U.S. tax treatment of U.S. citizens working abroad.

Perhaps the most significant feature of the 1981 Act was the reintroduction of an exclusion of foreign earned income which existed prior to 1978. The new earned income exclusion was equal to $75,000 beginning in 1982 and increased $5,000 annually to $95,000 in 1986. However, the Tax Reform Act of 1986 changed the law considerably and has made it more costly for U.S. companies to send employees abroad. For example, the 1986 law reduced the maximum annual exclusion of foreign earned income from $95,000 to $70,000. The 1986 tax law also allows U.S. citizens abroad to exclude the excess of housing expenses over a base amount of $70,000.

Summary

Multinational taxation has a significant impact on the choice of location in the initial investment decision, form of the new enterprise, method of finance, and many other international financial decisions. Tax planning for multinational operations involves complex problems such as national tax environments, double taxation, and various tax incentive programs. Thus, it is highly desirable that multinational companies seek the inputs of experienced tax and legal counsel in both parent and host countries. Nevertheless, to preserve profit opportunities abroad and receive special tax incentives, it is important for the financial manager of a multinational company to be acquainted with the national tax environments and other tax problems in the host countries in which the company operates.

Questions

1. Why is taxation one of the most important variables in multinational operations?

2. In what general ways do countries differ with regard to their tax systems?

3. Explain tax morality from viewpoints of both multinational companies and host governments.

4. What is double taxation? How can its effect be lessened?

5. What types of tax incentives are given to U.S.-based multinational companies by the U.S. government? What is the purpose of these tax incentives?

References

Arpan, J. S., and L. H. Radebaugh, *International Accounting and Multinational Enterprises*, New York: Wiley, 1985.

Bannock, G., *VAT and Small Business: European Experience and Implications for North America*, Washington, DC: Canadian Federation of Independent Business Research and Education Foundation, 1986.

Choi, F. D. C., and G. G. Mueller, *International Accounting*, Englewood Cliffs, NJ: Prentice Hall, 1984.

Deloitte Haskins & Sells, "Foreign Parent Denied Standing to Challenge California Unitary Tax," *The Week in Review*, December 7, 1983, p. 6.

"DISC/FSC Legislation: The Impact of the Phantom Profits," *Journal of Accountancy*, January 1985, pp. 83-97.

Ernst & Young, *Worldwide Corporate Tax Guide and Directory*, New York: Ernst & Young, January 1992.

Hartman, D. G., "Tax Policy and Foreign Direct Investment in the United States," *National Tax Journal*, December 1984, pp. 475-87.

Kaplan, W. S., "Foreign Sales Corporations: Politics and Pragmatics," *Tax Executive*, April 1985, pp. 203–20.

Price Waterhouse, *Corporate Taxes: A Worldwide Summary,* New York: Price Waterhouse, January 1992.

Watt, G. C., R. M. Hammer, and M. Burge, *Accounting for the Multinational Corporation*, New York: Financial Executive Foundation, 1977.

19

International
Transfer Pricing

Transfer prices are prices of goods and services bought and sold between parent companies and subsidiaries. Internal transfers include raw materials, semifinished goods, finished goods, allocation of fixed costs, loans, fees, royalties for use of trademarks, and copyrights. International transfer pricing policies become increasingly complex as companies increase their involvement in international transactions through foreign subsidiaries, joint ventures, and parent-owned distribution systems. Discrepancies between transfer pricing methods used by companies and those allowed by taxing agencies take place because taxing agencies and companies have different objectives. For example, multinational companies try to maximize profits and improve performance evaluation by manipulating internal transfer prices. Taxing authorities, on the other hand, try to allocate through fair market prices the profit of a sale between their country and other countries. Thus, multinational financial managers must understand transfer pricing objectives and their impact on transfer prices.

This chapter has four sections. The first section discusses the major objectives of transfer pricing. The second section describes Section 482 of the Internal Revenue Code and its implications for international transfer pricing. The third section describes two new regulations on Section 482 transfer pricing rules. The fourth section covers foreign sales corporations because Section 482 affects them and because they have significant tax advantages.

Transfer Pricing Objectives

Transfer pricing strategies are sensitive internal corporate issues, because successful pricing is a key element in achieving profits. Transfer pricing also helps multinational companies determine how company profits are allocated across divisions. Governments show interest in transfer pricing, because these prices will decide tax revenues and other benefits. So, many host governments have policing mechanisms to review the transfer pricing policies of multinational companies.

Transfer pricing has the following objectives:

1. Income tax minimization
2. Import duty minimization
3. Avoiding financial problems
4. Adjusting for currency fluctuations

Income Tax Minimization

A number of researchers such as Jeffrey Arpan and Lee Radebaugh (1985) singled out tax minimization as the most important variable influencing international transfer pricing decisions. Their finding is not surprising because transfers between related business entities account for approximately 40 percent of total world trade. Economic benefits are immediate if transfer prices can shift profits from a country with a higher tax rate to a country with a lower tax rate. Yet, a company using transfer pricing for maximizing profits must balance this approach by having prices consistent with regulations of taxing authorities.

Example 19–1. To illustrate the tax effects of a change in transfer prices on corporate earnings, assume the following: (1) Affiliate A is in a low tax country (20 percent tax rate) and affiliate B is in a high tax country (50 percent tax rate). (2) Affiliate A produces 100 radios for $5 per unit and sells them to affiliate B. (3) Affiliate B sells these radios for $20 per unit to an unrelated customer. Table 19–1 shows the tax effects of low versus high transfer price on company earnings.

Under the low transfer price, A pays taxes of $60 and B pays taxes of $300 for a total tax bill of $360 and a consolidated net income of $540. Under the high transfer price, A pays taxes of $160 and B pays taxes of $50 for a total tax bill of $210 and a consolidated net income of $690. Earnings before taxes are the same at $900 despite the different prices at which the radios transfer from A to B. Still, the higher transfer price reduces total taxes by $150 ($360 - $210) and increases consolidated net income by the same amount ($690 - $540).

Table 19–1
Tax Effect of Low versus High Transfer Price

	Low Tax (A)	High Tax (B)	Combined (A + B)
Low Transfer Price			
Sales price	$1,000	$2,000	$3,000
Cost of goods sold	500	1,000	1,500
Gross profit	$ 500	$1,000	$1,500
Operating expenses	200	400	600
Earnings before taxes	$ 300	$ 600	$ 900
Taxes (20%/50%)	60	300	360
Net income	$ 240	$ 300	$ 540
High Transfer Price			
Sales price	$1,500	$2,000	$3,500
Cost of goods sold	500	1,500	2,000
Gross profit	$1,000	$ 500	$1,500
Operating expense	200	400	600
Earnings before taxes	$ 800	$ 100	$ 900
Taxes (20%/50%)	160	50	210
Net income	$ 640	$ 50	$ 690

Import Duty Minimization

Affiliate A sells goods to affiliate B. The rule of thumb for income tax minimization is: (1) set the transfer price as high as possible if A's tax rate is lower than B's rate and (2) set the transfer price as low as possible if A's tax rate is higher than B's tax rate. The introduction of import duties complicates this rule because multiple objectives could conflict. For example, a lower transfer price reduces import duties, but it increases income taxes. A higher transfer price reduces income taxes, but it increases import duties. Suppose that B must pay import duties at the rate of 10 percent. Import duties are normally levied on the invoice (transfer) price. The higher transfer price raises tariffs by $50 ($1,500 x 0.10 - $1,000 x 0.10), thus offsetting tax effects of $50 in terms of increased tariffs.

Import duty minimization is easy, but tax reductions, which have offsetting effects, may complicate it. Also, a country with low import duties may have high income taxes, while a country with high import duties may have low income taxes. If multinational companies use low or high transfer prices in certain countries, they have to balance import duties and income taxes to maximize a combined benefit from tariff and income tax reductions.

Avoiding Financial Problems

Transfer prices can avoid financial problems or improve financial conditions. Transfer pricing often avoids economic restrictions and exchange controls that host countries place on multinational companies. For example, some developing countries restrict the amount of profits that can leave the country. An obvious way around this restriction is to charge high prices for imports. So, countries with such restrictions watch import and export prices closely.

Some countries do not allow multinational companies to charge certain expenses against taxable income. For instance, they do not permit expenses for research and development done elsewhere. Royalty fees a parent company charges against its subsidiary income are often not allowed. Because the host country does not allow them, they can be recaptured by increasing the transfer price of goods shipped into the country.

Transfer prices also channel profits into an affiliate to bolster its financial condition, thus presenting a favorable profit picture to satisfy earnings criteria set by foreign lenders. So, the parent company does not need to commit much capital to its foreign subsidiary even though the subsidiary may be required to secure the loan. Besides, low transfer prices give the subsidiary a competitive edge it might need starting a new venture or reacting to an economic downturn.

Adjusting for Currency Fluctuations

A wide range of currency fluctuations may influence the performance reports of foreign subsidiaries. Many U.S. multinational companies evaluate the performance of foreign subsidiaries with reports stated in U.S. dollars. If currency exchange rates fluctuate, it may be difficult to evaluate the performance of the subsidiary. Management of the subsidiary often prefers to evaluate its performance with reports stated in local currency rather than U.S. dollars. Adjusting transfer prices for currency fluctuations can solve this performance evaluation problem. But, performance evaluation is difficult when the objective is tax minimization or when currency fluctuates. One subsidiary's profit in one country may be greater than another subsidiary's profit in another country, not because of better management but because of the transfer price. One way to solve this problem is to maintain two sets of books: one for foreign authorities and another set for performance evaluation purposes.

Summary of Transfer Pricing Objectives

This section discussed several transfer pricing objectives such as minimizing income taxes and import duties, avoiding financial problems, and adjusting for currency fluctuations. Minimizing income taxes and import duties is important. Taxing agencies in many countries usually pay close attention to companies transferring profits to countries with lower taxes. As some unfortunate companies discovered, overzealousness may have short-run gains but long-run losses. Many multinational companies have also manipulated transfer prices to avoid financial problems of a foreign affiliate. They adjust for currency fluctuations to evaluate affiliate performance. Based on our discussion, changes in transfer prices seem to attain transfer pricing objectives easily. Yet, rules in many countries regulate how transfer prices must be set. A company should balance its transfer pricing objectives by making its transfer pricing policies consistent with regulations of host countries.

As this discussion shows, international transfer pricing must meet the objectives of management control and other objectives. These other objectives are sometimes so important that goal congruence (profit maximization) and performance evaluation are secondary or unachievable. Thus, multinational companies must establish an efficient transfer pricing system. Wagdy Abdallah (1989) suggests five criteria for an efficient international transfer pricing system:

1. The transfer pricing system should measure profits of subsidiaries and their managers, including controllable divisional contributions.
2. The transfer pricing system should supply top management information for guidelines in managerial decision making.
3. The transfer pricing system should improve company performance.
4. The transfer pricing system should motivate subsidiary managers to increase efficiency and maximize divisional profits in harmony with the objectives of top management.
5. The transfer pricing system should minimize international transaction costs by reducing border and income tax liabilities, foreign exchange losses, and currency manipulation losses.

Empirical studies reveal some interesting findings about the practices of U.S. companies in international transfer pricing. Researchers single out income tax minimization as the most important objective of transfer pricing. Still, other studies find that the influence of a given variable differs according to environments. For example, Jane Burns (1980) surveyed 62 U.S. companies with subsidiaries in industrialized countries to identify the importance of 14 variables influencing transfer pricing decisions. Seung Kim and Stephen Miller (1979) surveyed 342 U.S. companies with subsidiaries in eight developing countries to obtain the perceived importance of nine variables in transfer pricing decisions. According to Burns, the five most important influences on transfer pricing decisions were: (1) market conditions in the foreign country, (2) competition in the foreign country, (3) reasonable profit for foreign affiliates, (4) U.S. federal income taxes, and (5) economic conditions in the foreign country. Kim & Miller found that the five most important objectives were: (a) profit repatriation restrictions within the host country, (b) exchange controls, (c) joint-venture constraints within the host country, (d) tariffs/customs duties within the host country, and (e) income tax liability within the host country.

Minimizing income tax ranked fourth highest in Burns' survey and fifth highest in Kim-Miller's survey. One problem with making a transfer pricing decision is that multiple objectives could conflict with each other. Therefore, multinational financial managers must understand transfer pricing objectives and their effect on transfer prices.

Section 482 and Transfer Pricing

International transfer pricing decisions have a major impact on global sales, tax liabilities, and profits of multinational companies. Tax authorities of most countries require multinational companies to use fair market prices as the transfer pricing policy. Their objectives are: (1) to prevent multinational companies from reducing tax liabilities by shifting profits from one country to another; (2) to allow tax authorities to adjust income and deductions to reflect the correct taxable income within territories; and (3) to counter abusive transfer pricing policies.

Few governments are similar. Nor are they all equally concerned about the effects of transfer prices. The United States, Canada, and developing countries show the most concern. In the United States, for example, Section 482 of the Internal Revenue Code (IRC) permits the Internal Revenue Service (IRS) to "distribute, apportion, or allocate gross income, deductions, credits, or allowances" between related companies to prevent tax evasion. The IRS prefers that all transfers among related parties take place at an "arm's-length" price, which is the price that would take place between unrelated parties. Section 482 of the 1986 Internal Revenue Code compares intragroup transfer prices with arm's-length prices. The IRS monitors transfers in the following five areas:

1. Loans and advances.
2. Performance of services.
3. Use of tangible property.
4. Use of intangible property.
5. Sale of intangible property.

This chapter deals with only (3), which covers transfer pricing of tangible property.

Section 482 assumes that subsidiaries are legally and economically separate from their parent corporation. On the other hand, it fails to consider that multinational companies may base their intracompany prices on the assumption that the organization is one economic unit. This fundamental difference—the source of recent controversy—has caused severe discrepancies between the transfer pricing methods the IRS will accept and those U.S. multinational companies use.

An important feature of minimizing taxes is the assurance that transfer prices reflect arm's-length transactions as much as possible. Section 482 and other regulations allow U.S. companies to use four pricing methods in determining the arm's-length price for the sale of tangible property. These methods are the comparable uncontrollable price method, the resale price method, the cost-plus method, and other acceptable methods.

Comparable Uncontrolled Price Method

Under this method, uncontrolled sales are comparable to controlled sales if their physical property and circumstances are nearly identical with the physical property and circumstances of controlled sales. This method most accurately approximates an arm's-length standard, because it reflects (1) the price of sales made to unrelated customers, (2) the price of sales from unrelated sellers to the company, and (3) the price of sales between other unrelated parties. The comparable uncontrolled price is similar to the prevailing market price when markets are perfectly competitive. Section 482 allows an adjusted market price if markets are less than perfectly competitive.

Though simple in theory, the comparable uncontrolled price method is often impractical. Perfectly competitive markets rarely exist for products transferred between related entities. There are many cases where no useful evidence of uncontrolled transactions is available. The goods transferred between related parties are so special to the group that there is no open market for them. This may be the case for semifinished products or for transfers of technology. Without perfectly competitive markets, adjustments can be made easily for such items as freight and insurance. But they cannot be made accurately for other items such as trademarks and brand names.

Resale Price Method

Under this method, an arm's-length price is obtained by subtracting an appropriate markup from the applicable sale price. The applicable sale price is the price at which a buyer resells goods obtained in a controlled sale. A company must use the resale price method only when the following three conditions exist: First, there are no comparable uncontrolled sales. Second, an applicable resale price is available. Third, the buyer adds only an insubstantial amount to the value of the property.

Markup percentages should be derived from the uncontrolled purchases and resales of a reseller who acts in the controlled sale. But, markup percentages may be obtained from the resale of other resellers if the same reseller makes the sale. Although the resale price method is applicable to most market operations, the IRS may reject it on the basis that it is difficult to find which markups are appropriate. In other words, the IRS may reject this method when a reseller adds to the value of the product.

Cost-Plus Method

Under this method, an arm's-length price is determined by adding an appropriate markup to the seller's cost. Markup percentages are determined by referring to similar transactions with or between unrelated entities. The IRS stipulates that costs must be determined on the basis of accounting practices that neither favor nor burden controlled sales. The IRS selects the cost-plus method instead of the resale-price method if the cost and profit of a seller are easier to evaluate than the cost and profit of a reseller. Thus, the cost-plus method is useful when a reseller adds a substantial value to property before resale. Such situations occur when related parties sell semifinished products or when one entity acts as a subcontractor for a related entity.

As some court cases show, the cost-plus method is arbitrary. It is difficult to assess the cost of the product and to figure out the appropriate markup percentage. The Internal Revenue Code does not define full cost given. It also does not give a uniform formula for prorating shared costs over joint products. Thus, multinational companies manipulate the markup percentage over cost.

Other Methods

The IRS had allowed companies to use only these three transfer pricing methods. In 1968, however, it permitted a fourth choice in cases where the three other methods did not apply. The fourth alternative may be entirely distinct from the three already described in the regulations. How far the IRS wishes to allow other methods is unknown. But it is likely that the taxpayer's method will be analyzed to see whether it results in an arm's-length price. Some of these methods are the rate-of-return on investment, the proportionate profit method, and the appraisal method. The rate-of-return method is a variation of the resale price and the cost-plus methods. Under the rate-of-return method, the markup percentage depends on a certain rate of return on total assets. The proportionate profit method allows companies to allocate total profits among segments, using full cost as the allocation basis. Under the appraisal method, the arm's-length price is the price at which an unrelated party would agree to buy the products in an uncontrolled sale.

Summary of Transfer Pricing Methods

The Tax Reform Act of 1986 reduced U.S. corporate tax rates from 40 percent to 34 percent on domestic corporations and branches of foreign corporations. These U.S. tax rates fall below those of other industrial countries. Thus, most accounting practitioners and international business executives believe that these lower rates would encourage U.S.-based multinational companies to bring more taxable income to the United States. Section 482 still insists on the use of arm's-length prices for intracompany transactions.

The IRS may decide that the price for merchandise sent to an affiliate is below an arm's-length price—the amount that unrelated parties would charge in an independent transaction. As a result, the agency would adjust upward the taxable income of the parent company to reflect this higher arm's-length price. The affiliate, in effect, incurs double taxation since it would have used the lower price when computing the cost of goods sold in estimating its foreign tax. Foreign tax credit provisions of the United States partially offset this problem. Foreign income is taxed at the same rate as domestic income, and credit is given for any taxes paid to a foreign government according to domestic tax neutrality. Not many cases of double taxation are completely resolved, however, because there are many departures from this theoretical norm of tax neutrality.

The threat of double taxation is no longer as great as it was before the U.S. government agreed to many bilateral tax treaties. In a fashion similar to Section 482 of the Internal Revenue Code, many foreign governments have recognized the principle of allocating income and deductions among related parties. The IRS allocates income and deductions among related parties when it thinks that intracompany dealings are not at arm's-length. The provisions also recognize the right of another country to make allocations that will reflect arm's-length dealings based on its domestic laws.

The IRS requires that companies must follow a specific order for finding arm's-length prices. No pricing method can be used unless a preceding one is unsuitable. According to the Internal Revenue Code, the first method is the comparable uncontrolled price method, followed by the resale price method. The third method is the cost-plus method if the first two are unsuitable. If none of these three options apply in a particular case, another method, including a variation of the first three, may be used.

Comparison of Transfer Pricing Methods in Use

Suk Kim (1988) surveyed business executives from 168 U.S. firms to find out how the IRS applied the methods outlined in Section 482. His findings reveal that many firms did not practice the pricing methods they should have used. As Table 19-2 shows, approximately 69 percent of exports to subsidiaries were products sold to unrelated customers while 31 percent were sold to related customers. Two-thirds of the products were either components or semifinished, and one-third were finished goods.

Though 69 percent of export sales qualified for a comparable uncontrolled price, only 17 percent of the respondents used it for intracompany exports. Furthermore, while only 10 percent of exports to subsidiaries seemed to qualify for a resale price, 27 percent of the respondents used it for

Table 19-2
IRS Transfer Pricing Methods and Their Uses

	Comparable Uncontrolled Price	Resale Price	Cost-Plus Price	Other Price
Pricing methods that seem most appropriate, according to types of intracompany sales	69%	10%	21%	
Pricing methods used by 168 sample companies	17%	27%	47%	9%

intracompany sales. The variation is more dramatic for the cost-plus method: 47 percent of the respondents used it even though only 21 percent of exports to subsidiaries seemed to qualify for the cost-plus method. Jane Burns (1980) has found that about 10 percent of the IRS audits on intracompany prices was based on the resale price method, 25 percent depended on the comparable uncontrolled price method, and the remaining 65 percent relied on the cost-plus or other method. These studies suggest that the IRS does not follow regulations when assessing additional taxes or settling disputes.

Several arguments support the popular cost-plus method. Being liberal, this approach can be easily justified to tax authorities. In perfectly competitive markets, a company can justify its departure from prevailing prices because of product differentiation. When there is no identical market price, a company can argue for its transfer prices on available data. Next, the cost-plus method avoids internal friction of arbitrary systems. Most multinational companies are highly decentralized. So, each unit's manager is in the best position to estimate the cost of products and their appropriate profit markup. This method also safeguards against manipulation in transfer pricing.

New Regulations on Transfer Pricing

The U.S. government has recently conducted a series of studies about transfer pricing practices used by U.S. affiliates of foreign-based companies. Their findings include:

1. About two-thirds of U.S. imports can be traced to two factors. Roughly one-third of U.S. merchandise imports are products manufactured abroad by affiliates of U.S. companies. Another third consists of foreign-made products imported by U.S. affiliates of foreign companies.
2. In 1987, foreign firms in the United States paid taxes on less than one percent of their gross receipts—well below the tax levels of domestic companies.
3. The IRS should collect more than $12 billion in additional taxes from about 30 foreign companies.
4. U.S. sales by Japanese owned-companies in the United States rose nearly 50 percent in 1987, but their reported taxable income dropped by two-thirds.
5. In 1990, Japanese auto transplants in the United States produced 1.3 million cars and trucks with an estimated value of $22 billion, but they paid about $12 million in taxes.
6. The IRS should have the authority to inspect financial records of foreign parent companies, not just their U.S. subsidiaries.
7. Foreign companies have hired many former IRS and Treasury-Department officials to help fight the government's efforts to collect billions of dollars in additional taxes from them.

At issue are so-called questionable "transfer pricing" policies employed in intracompany transactions between foreign companies and their U.S.

subsidiaries. The government claims that foreign-based companies underpaid taxes on the profits of their U.S. subsidiaries by inflating the prices they pay to their foreign parents for goods and services. These findings spurred the IRS to step up its audits of foreign companies. They also pressed the IRS to toughen the reporting and record-keeping requirements for foreign corporations. In this section, we discuss two new rules on transfer pricing: Section 482 White Paper and New Section 6038A Regulations.

Section 482 White Paper

On October 18, 1988, the IRS issued its findings and recommendations from its study of intracompany pricing—the so-called Section 482 White Paper. The study outlines five key concepts:

1. At the time a tax return is filed, the taxpayer should document contemporaneous pricing or significant mispricing.
2. The IRS should aggressively pursue pricing information through administrative summons and Section 482 formal document requests. IRS economists and counsel should become involved early in the case.
3. The procedures for determining the appropriate transfer price of intangibles should be revised, and appropriate pricing readjustments should be made over time.
4. The rules for acceptable cost-sharing agreements should be made more specific. They should require an arm's-length "buying" charge for pre-existing unshared research.

The full impact of the paper will not be known for years. Still, renewed IRS interest in intracompany pricing may be the most significant tax issue that U.S. and non-U.S. multinational companies will confront for the rest of this century. Foreign countries have already expressed concern over proposals in the White Paper. First, these proposals fail to recognize that an arm's-length price is not a single specific number. The IRS is trying to require one specific price. Second, taxpayers must involve tax economists/Section 482 specialists early on when making their pricing decisions. Third, the IRS will create a confrontational climate with tax payers and foreign fiscal authorities. Fourth, the proposals may ultimately result in final outcomes of intracompany pricing disputes which are not any different from solutions before the White Paper.

New Section 6038A Regulations

On October 4, 1990, the IRS released new regulations with respect to information which must be reported and information which must be maintained by certain foreign-owned corporations under Section 6038A. Foreign companies have expressed two major concerns about these new regulations. First, the new regulations are broader than old record-retention policies. Second, penalties for no-compliances are too strict.

Reporting Requirements.

The revised Section 6038A requires foreign-owned companies to file a separate form 5472 for each foreign-related party with whom the reporting corporation had a "reportable transaction" during the taxable years. Reporting transactions include:

1. Sales and purchase of inventory.
2. Sales and purchase of other property.
3. Rent and royalties.
4. Use of intangible property.
5. Technical, managerial, and other services.
6. Commissions.
7. Amounts loaned and borrowed.
8. Interest.
9. Premiums for insurance.
10. Other amounts paid or received.

Reporting and Record-Keeping Responsibilities.

The revised Section 6038A regulations specify reporting and record-keeping responsibilities for the reporting corporation, the domestic related party, and the foreign related party. The reporting and record-keeping responsibilities for the reporting corporation include:

1. File a Form 5472 with respect to each related party with which it has had reportable transactions during the taxable year.
2. Maintain relevant records with respect to all related party transactions.
3. Act as limited agent for foreign related parties for purposes of receiving summons and IRS information requests.
4. Be subject to all penalties for noncompliance with Section 6038A.

The domestic related party must maintain relevant records with respect to all related party transactions. The foreign related party: (1) must maintain relevant records with respect to all related party transactions attributable to U.S.-connected products or services; (2) may designate the reporting corporation as its limited agent; and (3) must use Form 5472 to report transactions with the reporting corporation.

Monetary Penalties.

There are two types of monetary penalties for noncompliance with Section 6038A. The first set of penalties has to do with the failure of reporting and record-keeping duties. The second set of penalties is related to the continuous noncompliance after 90-day notification about the violation of Section 6038A regulations. Tables 19-3 and 19-4 show these two types of monetary penalties.

A Treasury Department Study on Transfer Pricing Compliance.

A U.S. Treasury Department study, mandated under the Revenue Reconciliation Act of 1990 and released in March 1992 shed light on the effectiveness of new transfer pricing compliance rules. The Treasury Department analyzed four directives mandated by Congress in the 1990 law.

Table 19–3
Penalties Under Section 6038A Regulations

Reason	Liability Imposed On	Time Period	Penalty Applies Separately To	Amount
Failure to file information returns	Reporting Corporation	Annually	Each related party	$10,000
Failure to maintain the requisite records	Reporting Corporation	Annually	Each related party	$10,000
Failure to produce records within time prescribed	Reporting Corporation	Annually	Each related party	$10,000

Table 19–4
Penalties Where Failure Continues After 90–Day Notification

Reason	Liability Imposed On	Time Period	Penalty Applies Separately To	Amount
Failure to file information returns	Reporting Corporation	Every 30 days after the 90 day period in which information is requested	Each related party	$10,000 every 30 days after notification period
Failure to maintain the requisite records	Reporting Corporation	Every 30 days after the 90 day period in which information is requested	Each related party	$10,000 every 30 days after notification period

As part of the Revenue Reconciliation Act, Congress directed the Treasury Department to:

1. Assess whether 1991 changes have increased taxpayer compliances with Section 482 transfer pricing rules.
2. Study the use and effectiveness of advance pricing agreements between the IRS and taxpayers.
3. Recommend future legislative and administrative changes.
4. Examine facilitating cooperation between the U.S. and foreign governments to resolve disputes from the outset and avoid double taxation.

The findings of this study would lead the U.S. government to take further actions on transfer pricing rules in the next few years.

Foreign Sales Corporation (FSC)

Although this chapter does not discuss foreign sales corporations in detail, we mention them because they are affected by Section 482 and have significant tax advantages. As mentioned in Chapter 18, the purpose of a FSC is to encourage U.S. manufacturers to increase exports by providing them with substantial tax benefits. The basic tax advantage is the exemption of federal income tax on a significant portion of the FSC's earnings.

The difficult part of the 1985 FSC Act is determining the FSC's income. Because the parent company usually owns the FSC which sells its merchandise, the price of the merchandise is a transfer price. Transfer prices are subject to artificial manipulation. According to this legislation, the price should be an actual arm's-length transfer price or a formula price designed to fit the definition of a transfer price set forth by the General Agreement on Tariffs and Trade.

Thirty-four percent of the income from transactions is exempt from federal taxes if the transfer price of the merchandise is an arm's-length price. Seventy-four percent of the income from the transaction is exempt if the transfer price is based on the special administered pricing rules.

Administrative pricing guidelines allow two pricing methods: the combined taxable income method and the gross receipts method. Under the combined taxable income method, the transfer price to the FSC is the sales price less the FSC expense and 23 percent of the combined taxable income. Under the gross receipts method, the transfer price to the FSC is the sales price less the FSC expense and the lesser of 1.83 percent of foreign trading gross receipts or twice the allowable FSC profit under the combined taxable income method.

Assume that an FSC buys export property from a related supplier and sells it for $1,000. The FSC incurs expenses of $200 and the supplier's cost of goods sold is $600. In selling the export property to the FSC, the supplier incurs a cost of $100. Table 19–5 shows transfer prices under the two administrative pricing guidelines.

Foreign trading gross receipts include the sales of export property, the lease or rental of export property, services related to the sale or lease of export property, engineering and architectural services, and export management services. These transactions must take place outside the United States in order to qualify. If 50 percent of the direct costs for a transaction takes place in a foreign location, the transaction qualifies as a foreign trading gross receipt.

Summary

Many international transactions take place between members of a group—sales of goods, the provision of services, the licensing of patents and

Table 19–5
Administrative Pricing Guidelines

(a) Combined taxable income:	
FSC foreign trading gross receipts	$1,000.00
Cost of goods sold of related supplier	−600.00
Combined gross income	$ 400.00
Direct expenses of related supplier	−100.00
Direct expenses of FSC	−200.00
Combined taxable income	$ 100.00
(b) Transfer price under combined taxable income method:	
Sales price	$1,000.00
Direct expenses of FSC	−200.00
FSC profit (23% of combined taxable income)	−23.00
Transfer price to FSC	$ 777.00
(c) Transfer price under gross receipts method:	
The allowable FSC profit is 1.83% of foreign trading gross receipts	
($18.30) or twice the amount in (b) above ($46).	
Sales price	$1,000.00
Direct expenses of FSC	−200.00
FSC profit	−18.30
Transfer price to FSC	$ 781.70

know-how, and the granting of loans. The prices for such transfers do not necessarily result from the free play of market forces. They may diverge considerably from the prices that unrelated parties would agree on. Although minimizing income tax is the most persuasive objective influencing transfer prices, other objectives often dominate. Among these objectives are import duty minimization, avoidance of financial problems, and adjustment of currency fluctuations for performance evaluation.

Minimizing income tax takes place by an allocation of profits among the countries involved in the production and sale of the product. In the United States, Section 482 of the Internal Revenue Code regulates the allocation of profits. Section 482 specifies three methods of determining transfer prices: the comparable uncontrolled price method, the resale price method, and the cost-plus method. In addition, taxpayers may be allowed to use any other method if they can convince the IRS that the other method is more appropriate than any of these three methods.

The Foreign Sales Corporation Act became effective as of January 1, 1985. The Act encourages U.S. companies to increase exports by giving them substantial tax benefits. Foreign sales corporations have major tax advantages if they meet certain conditions in Section 482 of the Internal Revenue Code and other regulations.

Questions

1. Explain the possible conflict of interests between a parent company and its foreign subsidiaries.

2. List some key objectives of transfer pricing policies.

3. Is it possible for a multinational company to minimize both income taxes and import duties simultaneously?

4. How do multinational companies use transfer prices to avoid financial problems faced by their subsidiary?

5. Why do tax authorities of most countries require multinational companies to use fair market prices as the transfer pricing policy?

6. Describe some situations where market-based transfer prices are better than cost-based transfer prices for multinational companies.

7. How does Section 482 of the U.S. Internal Revenue Code affect transfer pricing?

8. Why is the cost-plus method most popular in practice?

References

Abdallah, W. M., *International Transfer Pricing Policies: Decision Making Guidelines for Multinational Companies*, New York Quorum Books, 1989.

Arpan, J. S., and L. H. Radebaugh, *International Accounting and Multinational Enterprises*, New York: Wiley, 1985, pp. 261–3.

Benke, R. L., and J. D. Edwards, *Transfer Pricing: Techniques and Uses*, New York: The National Association of Accountants, 1980, Chapter 6.

Burns, J. O., "How the IRS Applies the Intercompany Pricing Rules of Section 482: A Corporate Survey," *Journal of Taxation*, May 1980, pp. 308–14.

Burns, J. O., and R. S. Ross, "Establishing International Transfer Pricing Standards for Tax Audits of Multinational Enterprises," *Journal of International Business Studies*, Fall 1980, pp. 23–39.

Eccles, R. G., *The Transfer Pricing Problem: A Theory for Practice*, Lexington, MA: Lexington Books, 1985.

Kim, S. H., "International Transfer Pricing for Tangible Property and Section 482 of the Internal Revenue Code," *The Journal of Business Issues*, Fall 1988, pp. 23–6.

Kim, S. H., and S. W. Miller, "Constituents of the International Transfer Pricing Decision," *Columbia Journal of World Business*, Spring 1979, pp. 69–77.

Knowles, L. L., and I. Mathur, "Designing International Transfer Pricing Systems," *Managerial Finance*, Summer 1985, pp. 21–4.

Mueller, G. G., H. Gernon, and G. Meek, *Accounting: An International Perspective*, Homewood, IL: Irwin, 1991.

Price Waterhouse, *Section 6063A Workplan*, Washington, DC: Price Waterhouse, 1991.

Pugel, T., and J. L. Ugelow, "Transfer Pricing and Profit Maximization for the Multinational Firm," *Journal of International Business Studies*, Spring/Summer 1982, pp. 115–19.

Schindler, G., "Intercompany Transfer Pricing After the Tax Reform Act of 1986," *Tax Planning International Review*, November 1987, pp. 9–10.

Tang, R. Y., "Environmental Variables of Multinational Transfer Pricing: A U.K. Perspective," *Journal of Business, Finance, and Accounting*, Summer 1982, pp. 179–89.

Part Six

Case Problems in Global/Corporate Finance

Case 1:
U.S. Steel Imports[1]
(Trade Protectionism for a Single Product)

In 1950, the United States accounted for almost 50 percent of raw steel production in the world, but this share fell to below 20 percent in 1976. The U.S. share of steel production in the world declined even further to about 10 percent in 1992. The number of jobs in the U.S. steel industry dropped from 453,000 in 1979 to 180,000 in 1992. More shocking is the fact that, while the U.S. world share of steel production has fallen, the United States has become a net importer of steel. Total imports of both steel and products using steel increased from 23.9 percent of the U.S. steel market in 1980 to more than 30 percent in 1992. Two of the nation's eight top producers and 23 smaller ones have been forced to file for bankruptcy-law protection in the past 15 years. The industry had been insulated from imports for so long (from 1969 to March 1992) that it had become thoroughly addicted to Washington-style industrial policy.

However, the steel industry has adjusted dramatically in recent years: costs have been slashed; the number of production workers dropped sharply; the industry has embraced continuous casting; technology and management links have been forged with Japanese firms; and efficient minimills are flourishing. All this adjustment has enabled the industry to turn the corner from a string of losses; steel companies had earned billions of dollars since 1987 until 1991. Also vital to this cyclical industry's recovery have been the weak dollar, the general economic rebound, and help from the government.

Steel analysts predict that this upturn may not last too long. Pension liabilities, overcapacity, high labor costs, outdated manufacturing facilities, and low-priced imports may hamper U.S. companies' return to long-term profitability. Their prospects for survival are threatened by tougher competition, falling demand, and rising imports. First, leading overseas producers have lower labor costs and more efficient equipment than U.S. counterparts; many foreign steelmakers also benefit from government subsidies and unfair trade practices. Second, U.S. steel consumption will continue to fall because: (1) small cars continue in popularity; (2) alternative materials—plastics, ceramics, and high-tech metal composites—are increasingly used in manufacturing; and (3) the farm equipment industry is depressed. Third, foreign imports have accounted for about 20 percent of the U.S. consumption in recent years, excluding steel in imported goods. Steel companies in the United States have argued that this figure underestimates the inroads of foreign competition because so much additional steel enters in finished products such as cars and pipes. By some estimates, as much as half the steel consumed in the United States is foreign made.

A number of factors are important for understanding a worldwide competitive situation. Many developing countries such as Brazil, Korea, and Taiwan feel that steel mills are essential for their industrialization. These countries have increased steel producing capacity because technology is well established and quite mobile. It may be argued that for mature industries such as the steel industry, the most important factors of competition are product price, economies of scale, consumer perception of quality, and flexible production processes rather than product innovation and process technology. Some countries have placed an extremely high priority on steel; they have foregone other development projects to build mills or have received financial assistance from outside for construction. Since the early 1970s the largest capacity increase has been among Third World countries; as a result, they have an excessive capacity for production.

Given the high costs of steel production, much of the world's production is government-owned, and government-owned companies tend to continue operations even though they might not cover short-term costs. State-owned steel companies in such countries as England, Spain, and Argentina have been reporting substantial losses but continue operations. Because of both employment pressure in these countries and the political implications of unemployment, it is difficult to cut back production rapidly in the state facilities. Export markets have been employed as an instrument of sustaining more output. In addition, U.S. steel companies have faced a competitive disadvantage, because foreign steelmakers often benefit from government assistance through tax incentives, low-interest loans, and waiving of environmental requirements.

Furthermore, leading overseas producers have better production locations than U.S. steel companies. Most U.S. steel mills were built many years ago in the corridor of states around the Great Lakes. These locations minimized transportation costs for both raw materials and finished steel because raw materials suppliers and industrial users of steel were located in this same corridor. These locations are no longer practical because suppliers of raw materials and users of steel are widely dispersed. Because most foreign mills are situated at deep-water ports, they have a cost advantage on purchases of raw materials even though they are imported.

Several competitive responses offer some hope for the future of the steel industry in the United States. First, so-called minimills are profitable and competitive because they run modernized plants, have good cost controls, and produce specialized products that big steelmakers leave alone. The minimills have already captured 25 percent of the domestic steel market. These efficient minimills are expected to increase their combined capacity and sales for years to come. Second, some foreign steel companies have infused funds and technology into the U.S. industry. Japanese steelmakers want access to the U.S. market; U.S. steelmakers want access to Japanese technology; and so seven Japanese and U.S steel producers have come together to make metal in recent years. Third, U.S. steel producers have been buying semifinished steel from abroad, thus cutting costs at an important level of production. Fourth, the U.S. steel industry has reduced its capacity by about 40 million tons since

1980 and is expected to reduce its capacity further. Operators of major integrated mills now understand that they must reduce cost structures, improve quality, and have better value-added product mixes.

In spite of these competitive responses, steel corporations and the United Steelworkers of America (USA) have repeatedly sought more stringent protection from the government, insisting that they have taken major actions on their own. They stress that the U.S. steel industry cannot successfully compete with foreign steel makers without further government help. On the eve of the 1984 elections, Big Steel—knee-deep in red ink—marshaled forces behind quotas on foreign steel. Under the Reagan relief plan, the U.S. government carved up the U.S. market in an effort to roll back imports of finished steel to around 18.4 percent from 26 percent. In recent years, U.S. steel makers have supplied about 80 percent of the 100 million tons of steel used annually by the nation. Of the remaining 20 percent needed, the steel-quota negotiations allocated 15 percent to foreign suppliers, with the difference supplied mainly by Canada.

These quotas were not scheduled to expire until September 30, 1989. But new campaigns in the battle to maintain walls around the U.S. market into the 1990s started as early as mid-1987. In an election-eve letter to Senator John Heinz (R., Pa.), candidate George Bush promised to extend the voluntary restraint agreement (VRA) on steel imports. Mr. Bush's letter, written just before the election on November 8, 1988, came at a time when economic facts said protection was no longer needed; domestic steel mills were running at 90 percent of capacity, the industry was expected to earn $1.5 billion in 1989, and many steel products were scarce. Advocates of protectionism rested their case mainly on two premises. The first appealed to the commonsense notion that high-wage countries such as the United States cannot compete with low-wage countries such as Korea. The second appealed to self-interest, asserting that the United States plays by the rules of a free market while foreign governments support targeted industries such as steel with subsidies, selective procurement, and trade protection. In July 1989, President Bush extended the nation's steel quotas for 30 months until March 31, 1992. But he emphasized that he would seek in the meantime to negotiate an end to all such trade-distorting practices in the world steel market.

On the other hand, some critics contend that the steel industry too often runs to Washington for help. Critics of protectionism have pointed to U.S. Steel's acquisition of Marathon Oil even though the steel producer lacked funds for technological improvements. Critics also blame steel-industry executives for spending funds at hopelessly obsolete plants rather than targeting outlays to efficient facilities. Furthermore, they argue that the steel industry does not need government protection any more because VRAs had accomplished their intended objectives. Consequently, President Bush terminated the VRAs on steel on March 31, 1992.

Questions

1. Do you think that the U.S. government should allow foreign steelmakers to export steel to the United States at prices below cost?

2. Do you think that the United States should maintain the steel industry though it can not compete with foreign steel?

3. List and discuss the types of government assistance which would make the U.S. steel industry more competitive with foreign steel producers.

4. What are the steel industry's options in the absence of government assistance?

5. Why have U.S. and Japanese steel makers decided to form joint ventures?

6. Describe the impact of VRAs on the U.S. steel industry.

Note

[1] John D. Daniels and Lee H. Radebaugh, *International Business*, Reading, MA: Addison-Wesley, 1989, pp. 179-82; Nathaniel Gilbert, "Foreign Firms' Resources Drive U.S. Steel Revival," *Management Review*, September 1989, pp. 52-56; Gary Hufbauer, "Wean the Steel Barons from Protection," *The Wall Street Journal*, December 27, 1988, p. 16A; Gloria T. LaRue, "Graham Offers Three Options to Finance Steel Restructuring," *American Steel Market*, May 20, 1987, pp. 21-22; Gloria T. LaRue, "U.S. Steel Capacity Hits 2nd Largest Drop in Decade," *American Metal Market*, January 16, 1987, p. 29; George McManus, "A Tariffic Disappointment for Steelmakers," *Iron Age*, October 1991, pp. 32-34; Robert J. Samuelson, "Goodbye to the Age of Steel," *Newsweek*, November 3, 1986, p. 55; "Statistical Highlights: U.S. Iron and Steel Industry," *Iron and Steel Engineer*, September 1991, p. 48; Rick Wartzman, "Japan, U.S. Steelmakers Link Up," *The Wall Street Journal*, November 18, 1988, p. 12A; Richard Wartzman and Carol Hymowtiz, "Big Steel Is Back, But Upturn Is Costly, and May Not Last," *The Wall Street Journal*, November 4, 1988, p. 1A and P. 7A; and Richard Wartzman and Peter Pae, "USX-Pohang Steel Venture Is Launched, Pointing to New Era for Industry in U.S.," *The Wall Street Journal*, April 1989, p. B2: "World Steel in Figures," *Iron and Steel Engineer*, September 1991, pp. 38-39.

Case 2:
Trade Friction Between the U.S. and Korea[1] (Trade Argument Between Countries)

Korea's closed-door policy refused commerce with the Western world until the late 19th century. Then in 1871, American naval units seized the forts on Kangwha Island of Korea and demanded that the Korean government sign an agreement with the United States, backing these demands with even more warships. These events, framed by a show of force, persuaded Korea to sign a Treaty of Peace, Amity, Commerce and Navigation with the United States in 1882.

Now more than one hundred years later, the United States hopes to accomplish a similar feat. It has charged in recent years that Korea maintains unfair trade barriers and undervalues its currency to generate large trade surpluses. In a show of economic force, the United States revoked on January 29, 1988, duty-free privileges enjoyed by Korea. Effective January 2, 1989, Korea was graduated from the U.S. Generalized System of Preferences (GSP). Although Korea barely avoided the U.S. primary "hit list" of countries with trade barriers under the 1988 Trade Act, it has been placed on "a watch list" since May 1989. Along with this listing came a warning to remove its trade barriers to U.S. goods and services if it wished to avoid trade retaliation. The 1988 Trade Act also requires the U.S. Department of Treasury to identify those countries which manipulate their exchange rate to gain a competitive advantage. The U.S. Department of Treasury has singled out Korea as a currency manipulator two times since the enactment of the 1988 Trade Act. Furthermore, U.S. imports under protectionism have risen from 10 percent in 1980 to more than 20 percent in 1991.

Since the end of the World War II, the United States and Korea have moved from a beneficial relationship to a full-fledged partnership. Their bilateral trade, which grew to almost $50 billion in 1991, created problems because of Korea's large trade surpluses with the United States for 10 years from 1981 to 1990. Though easing trade relations best serves the political and economic interests of both countries, trade imbalances have become worrisome.

Table C2-1 underscores the reasons for U.S. trade protectionism. The U.S overall trade deficit increased from only $25 billion in 1980 to a record $160 billion in 1987, an increase of 540 percent. Its trade balance with Korea shifted from a surplus of $252 million in 1980 to a deficit of almost $10 billion in 1988. Korea moved from being the 14th largest trading partner of the U.S. in 1981 to its seventh largest in 1988; on the negative side of the ledger, Korea was the source of the fifth largest bilateral trade deficit of the U.S. in 1988. Access to the U.S. market is crucial to Korea because the

Table C2–1
U.S. Merchandise Trade Balances

Year	Overall Balance (billion dollars)	Balance with Korea (million dollars)
1980	− 25.5	+ 252
1981	− 28.0	− 358
1982	− 36.4	− 483
1983	− 67.1	−1,732
1984	−112.5	−4,319
1985	−122.1	−6,887
1986	−145.1	−7,142
1987	−159.5	−9,402
1988	−127.2	−9,691
1989	−109.0	−6,359
1990	−106.0	−4,263
1991	− 66.0	−1,651

Source: United States International Trade Commission, *The Operation of the Trade Agreements Program*, various issues.

United States has been its number one export market since the early 1970s. For example, the United States took 33 percent of Korea's total exports in 1989, while Japan, Korea's second largest trading partner, accounted for only 21 percent of Korea's export market in the same year.

The United States and Korea have maintained for more than four decades a mutually beneficial relationship based on several economic, political, and military factors. This remarkable friendship has been forged through close cooperation in war and peace. In recent years, however, U.S.–Korean economic relations have been strained by a growing number of conflicts over trade and macroeconomic policies.

Even though Korea had enjoyed considerable trade surpluses with the United States from 1981 until 1990, its overall trade surplus of $4.5 billion for 1986 was the first real surplus in its modern history. Korea's economic development, from a war–devastated economy into a newly industrialized economy, is impressive. Korea, along with Hong Kong, Singapore, and Taiwan, are frequently called newly industrialized countries (NICs). Often overlooked, however, is that until the mid–1980s, Korea had a massive foreign debt (ranked the fourth largest debtor nation in the world as late as 1985) and chronic trade deficits. Fortunately, the situation turned around in the mid–1980s as a result of external factors mostly beyond the country's control. A decline in interest rates, the devaluation of the U.S. dollar, and the decline of world oil prices all combined to significantly reduce Korea's real debt burden, improve its trade balance, and strengthen the competitiveness of its products in the world market. Ironically, Korea's economic success has strained U.S.–Korean relations mainly because of uncharacteristically large trade imbalances between the two countries.

Spurred by specific concerns expressed by its trading partners, most notably the United States, Korea began in the mid–1980s to accelerate internalization of its economy, restructure its industry, and pursue the basic framework of a free market system. However, these steps have been cautious and slow. In the meantime, Korea's bilateral trade surpluses with the United States skyrocketed from 1983 until 1988. Understandably, U.S. critics have accused Korea of maintaining unfair trade barriers and manipulating its exchange rates, thereby contributing to its trade surpluses in the 1980s. Consequently, the United States has demanded that Korea remove its trade barriers and revalue its currency.

Currency Manipulation. Since the mid-1980s the United States has argued that Korea has manipulated exchange rates to prevent balance of payments adjustments or to gain unfair competitive advantage in international trade. The U.S. decision in 1988 to strip Korea of its tariff-free status stemmed from the U.S. Treasury Department's anger over Korea's refusal to float its currency freely against the dollar. The U.S. Treasury Department assumed that Korea would have been far less competitive and its trade surpluses smaller if strategic manipulation of the currency had not prevented its appreciation.

While currency manipulation is difficult to establish and its effectiveness more so, we can gain a few insights into a government's exchange rate objectives by examining policy statements, capital controls, and indicators of intervention in exchange markets. Up to the late 1970s, Korea officially pegged its currency to the U.S. dollar, but it abandoned this strategy in January 1980. It now uses a new managed-floating system based on a basket of currencies to reflect changes in its external position. While the composition of the basket of currencies has not been disclosed, Korean authorities have been somewhat explicit about their exchange objectives in this decade. In 1980, the Korean government devalued its currency by 20 percent against the dollar to dampen growth in external deficits. After 1985, authorities apparently adjusted their exchange rate target to maintain an annual trade surplus of about $5 billion to reduce Korea's large outstanding foreign debt.

Certainly, it is impossible to determine what the exchange rates of Korea would have been in the absence of government intervention in exchange markets. Ramon Moreno (1989) used regression analysis to weigh the relative contributions of the explanatory variables to changes in Korea's trade balances from 1975 to 1987. Susan Hickok and Thomas Klitgaard (1988) also used regression analysis to identify the extent to which exchange rate movements directly explain improvements in competitiveness and changing trade surpluses in Korea from the second quarter of 1987 to the same quarter of 1988. These two recent studies found that exchange rate movements improved Korea's competitiveness and thus contributed directly to its trade surpluses in the 1980s.

Market Opening Requests. President Reagan brought on his visit to Korea in November 1983 the first of a series of market-opening request lists. Since then, high-profile bilateral trade negotiations have continued, and trade liberalization under pressure from the United States has become a key objective in the economic reform efforts of the Korean government. In the last few years, Korea has taken a variety of unilateral initiatives to ease trade friction with the United States. For example, Korea's average tariff rates fell from 22.6 percent in 1983 to 12.7 percent in 1991; the Korean government is scheduled to reduce its average tariff rates to 7.9 percent by 1993. In addition, the share of importable commodities enjoying automatic licensing approval rose from 80.4 percent in 1983 to more than 96 percent in 1992; this share had been about 50 percent in 1977. Nevertheless, U.S. imports from Korea grew rapidly, and U.S. exports to Korea grew slowly through 1988, thereby widening trade imbalances.

Dissatisfied with Korea's unilateral initiatives along with its own rising trade deficits, the United States has submitted a request list covering goods and services for additional or accelerated import liberalization by Korea. The United States, in quest of fair trade, has taken or threatened to take retaliatory actions under Section 301 of the 1974 Trace Act and Super 301 of the 1988 Trade Act unless these requests are met. Section 301 of the 1974 Trade Act covers proceedings against unfair trading practices. The so-called Super 301 covers proceedings against "consistent" unfair trade practices. These trade tensions have been compounded by growing anti-Americanism in Korea.

In addition to Super 301, the U.S. government has used two more types of policy to remove Korea's trade barriers: voluntary arrangements for export restraints and regulations covering unfair practices. A case in point, Korea's two major export products—textiles and steel—have recently experienced discriminatory quantitative restrictions. In 1986, the two governments renewed a textile agreement covering multi-fibers. A crucial feature of this agreement is the inclusion of silk, ramie, linen, and other natural fiber products. Based on a policy of voluntary arrangements, Korea and the Unites States signed a steel agreement in February 1985. This agreement limited Korea's share to 1.9 percent of the total U.S. steel market until September 1989; a new agreement signed in October 1989 limited Korea's share to about 2 percent of the U.S. market until March 1992. The negotiated voluntary export restraints are only part of the controls placed on Korea's exports. Korea has also voluntarily and unilaterally restrained exports primarily to prevent even tougher U. S. protectionism. The number of products covered by Korea's unilateral export restraints for the United States has increased from only two products in 1979 to 14 products in 1987.

Actions under unfair trade statutes in the United States have surged alarmingly in recent years. Anti-dumping duties, countervailing duties, and the application of Section 337 of the 1930 Tariff Act were three such steps. More ominous after 1984, petitions and affirmative findings under Section 337 of the 1930 Tariff Act escalated. This act defines infringements of patent and other intellectual property rights as unfair import practices. As a result of the courts' rulings, about ten Korean products have been excluded from the U.S. market.

Is Korea Another Japan?

Korean authorities frequently complain that the United States treats Korea as if it were another Japan. Japan has felt the thrust of U.S. protectionist pressures for the past two decades (1970s and 1980s) on the ground that it has taken full advantage of the open U.S. market but without reciprocity. U.S. measures against Japanese export surges and Japan's reaction to the U.S. pressure have established instructive precedents for U.S.-Korean trade relations. For instance, the United States has demanded that Japan open its market to U.S. products, to restrain Japanese growth in the U.S. market, and to invest in the United States. At the same time, U.S. companies have used unfair trade laws to harass Japanese exporters. Unfortunately, these measures have not been successful.

Admittedly, U.S. trade relations with Korea and Japan differ, but U.S. officials tend to point more to similarities than to differences. U.S. officials and business executives cite parallels between the close relationship of Korea's and Japan's major industrial groups. Korean exports have recently made strong inroads in certain sectors of the U.S. market such as steel and autos, markets where the Japanese have long dominated. Korea has closely imitated the Japanese response to U.S. protectionist pressures. It has accepted voluntary export restraints, selectively liberalized import barriers, and promoted one-time buying missions. However, following the Japanese model has not been successful because the United States has not repeated its failed policy.

Summary

Economic relations between the United States and Korea are of increasing importance. In spite of that notion, their relations have become strained as Korea's role in the world economy has grown and as the United States has become concerned about its international economic position. Many Americans charge that Korea maintains unfair trade barriers and undervalues its currency to produce huge trade surpluses. On the other hand, many Koreans believe that the United States has built barriers of its own and perceive that U.S. criticism is unfair. Koreans also believe that the U.S. does not recognize that Korea is still a net debtor nation with $30 billion in debt and that its struggles to reduce this debt occur amid monumental social and political turmoil.

Questions

1. What is the U.S. Generalized System of Preferences?

2. What are the key elements of the U.S. Trade Act of 1988?

3. Is Korea another Japan?

4. Does the Korean managerial style resemble the Japanese or the American style?

5. Why have the same measures, designed to reduce the U.S. trade deficit with both Japan and Korea, been unsuccessful with Japan but highly successful with Korea?

Note

[1] Thomas O. Bayard and Soo-Gil Young, eds., *Economic Relations Between the United States and Korea: Conflict or Cooperation?* Washington, DC: Institute for International Economics, January 1989; Chan Sup Chang, "Chaebol: The South Korean Conglomerates," *Business Horizons*, March/April 1988, pp. 51-57; Kae H. Chung and Hak Chong Lee, *Korean Managerial Dynamics*, New York: Praeger, 1989; Susan Hickok and Thomas Klitgaard, "U.S. Trade with Taiwan and South Korea," *Quarterly Review*, Federal Reserve Bank of New York, Autumn 1988, pp. 60-66; Larry M. Hyson, *Doing Business with South Korea*, Westport, CT: Quorum Books, 1990; T. W. Kang, *Is Korea the Next Japan?* New York: The Free Press, 1989; Youn-Suk Kim, "Korea's Export-Managed Industrialization and Its Lessons," *Human Systems Management*, 1990, pp. 173-185; Youn-Suk Kim, "Korea-U.S. Trade Friction and the Japan Factor," *Asian Profile*, February 1990, pp. 79-87; Korea Foreign Trade Association, *Korea's Exchange Rate Policy*, Washington, DC: Reid & Priest, September 1989; Nina J. Lahoud, "The Non-Discriminatory United States Generalized System of Preferences: De Facto Discrimination Against the Least Developed Countries," *Harvard International Law Journal*, Spring 1982, pp. 3-20; Ronald I. Meltzer, "The U.S. Renewal of the GSP: Implications for North-South Trade," *Journal of World Trade Law*, September/October 1986, pp. 513-535; Ministry of Trade and Industry, Republic of Korea, *Free and Fair Trade: Korea's Record and Commitment*, March 1989, pp. 58-59; Ramon Moreno, "Exchange Rates and Trade Adjustment in Taiwan and Korea," *Economic Review*, Federal Reserve Bank of San Francisco, Spring 1989, pp. 30-47; Walter S. Mossberg, "U.S. Removal of Trade Benefits Is Tied to Currency Rates of Four Asian Nations," *The Wall Street Journal*, February 1, 1989, p. A10; Chwee H. Ow-Taylor, ed., *U.S.-Korea Economic Relations*, Bloomington, IN: The East Asian Studies Center of Indiana University, 1992; and The United States International Trade Commission, *Operation of the Trade Agreements Program*, July 1992.

Case 3:
A North American Free Trade Area[1]
(Trading Blocs)

On September 26, 1990, after months of informal and often secret discussions, President Bush requested authority from the U.S. Congress to open trade talks with Mexico that were to begin formally in 1991 and to culminate in a U.S.-Mexico Free Trade Agreement. However, both the Canadians (who already have a free trade agreement with the United States) and the Americans were questioning the wisdom of such a move.

The new market would be large, as shown in Table C3-1, with much of its economic strength coming from the United States. In fact, the population and GNP of the free trade area would exceed that of the European Community and help offset some of Japan's strength in Asia.

It is interesting to note that the population in the United States is 69 percent of the total population of the proposed free trade area. Germany, the largest country in the EC, is only 19 percent of the total population of the EC.

The United States, Canada, and Mexico already enjoy a large amount of international trade. Trade between the United States and Canada is by far the largest bilateral trading relationship in the world, and this would likely increase in the future. The exports from the United States to Canada in 1989 were $80.451 billion, and the U.S. Imports from Canada were $88.960 billion. The bilateral trade between the U.S. and Mexico in 1989 was $58.6 billion. However, Canadian trade with Mexico was only $2.6 billion in 1989.

A free trade area involving these three countries could make them totally self-sufficient in energy. In addition, manufacturers in the three countries would have unrestricted access to each other's markets. Canadian and Mexican agricultural and industrial sectors would benefit from U.S.- developed technology. The infusion of modern technology could be especially beneficial to Mexico in helping to alleviate high unemployment.

Table C3-1
Vital Statistics for the U.S, Canada, and Mexico

Variables	United States	Canada	Mexico
Population	250 million	26 million	86 million
GNP	$5.23 trillion	$483 billion	$201 billion
Per Capita GNP	$20,920	$17,808	$2,337

The United States–Canadian Free Trade Agreement. In the past 30 years, a variety of forms of economic cooperation have emerged between the United States and Canada. Since 1965, an Automotive Products Trade Agreement has existed between the two countries. It provides for qualified duty-free trade in specified automotive products between the United States and Canada. In the early 1980s there was discussion about developing free trade in specific sectors, such as steel and textiles, which gave way to a broader discussion of free trade. Negotiations were held in 1987 to open up trade even more between the United States and Canada. The United States was concerned about the amount of governmental subsidies given Canadian businesses and also about gaining greater access to investment opportunities in Canada. The Canadians, on the other hand, sought exception from U.S. laws protecting U.S. producers from Canadian competition. Canadians preferred dealing with an international tribunal to resolve trade disputes rather than having to deal with U.S. antidumping and countervailing duty legislation. Canadian manufacturers would be able to cut costs by an estimated 20 percent due to economies of scale that would follow from freer access to the U.S. market.

Preliminary discussions gave way to the Canada-U.S. Free Trade Agreement (FTA), which went into effect on January 1, 1989. Canadians were concerned that Canada would: (1) lose its cultural identity, (2) become too closely integrated with a violent society, (3) be hitching its wagon to a declining economic power, (4) forfeit its independence in foreign policy, and (5) be overwhelmed politically and economically by the United States. Some U.S. politicians, especially in the Midwest, worried that their states would lose production to Canada. However, the dynamic effects of the expansion of the two markets in a freer environment were expected to create an additional 750,000 jobs in the United States and 150,000 jobs in Canada. Some experts predicted that high-volume production lines would be shifted to the United States and small-volume specialty lines would be shifted to Canada. The expansion of these two markets, with fewer trade barriers than exist currently in the EC, will result in a market that is 15 percent larger than the EC. As mentioned earlier, the U.S.-Canadian trade relationship is the largest bilateral relationship in the world. Canada is the United States' largest trading partner, supplying 20 percent of U.S. imports, a percentage just slightly smaller than that of the entire European Community. The United States is Canada's largest supplier, sending across the border 70 percent of Canada's imports and receiving 78 percent of Canada's exports.

The FTA eliminates all tariffs on bilateral trade by 1998, although 73 percent of all U.S. exports to Canada were free from tariffs before the signing of the FTA. Each country retains its own external tariffs, however. In order to maintain the integrity of the bilateral relationship, the FTA established rules of origin, which means that cross-border trade must identify where the goods were produced. That keeps non-FTA goods from entering the United States through Canada and vice-versa. The FTA also expands the amount of government procurement that will be open to exporters from each country.

Although there is a significant two-way flow of foreign invest-ment—approximately $79 billion in 1988—and a large amount of services trade, the FTA liberalizes flows in both areas and allows firms from each country to gain greater market access. A new dispute–settlement mechanism was also set into place which should allow for a more efficient settlement of disputes in the future. FTA established a Canada–U.S. Trade Commission to deal specifically with disputes arising from the application and interpretation of the FTA. The Commission can deal with any trade dispute issue except for antidumping and countervailing duty actions and financial services, but the dispute mechanism should result in actions taking no longer than eight months from start to finish to resolve.

The FTA is expected to have important ramifications as time goes on, but it is still too early to tell what the overall effects will be. Many Canadian industries are among the most efficient in the world, but many are also very inefficient. There will probably be plant closings and mergers as firms attempt to establish their market niche. Parent companies in both countries are struggling to determine how to serve both markets and whether or not to rationalize production facilities. Americas' 25 largest corporations already control 35 percent of Canada's corporate assets, so there is some concern there that too much industrial concentration might emerge.

The Mexican Connection.

Mexico has undergone some important changes in recent years. In 1986 Mexico joined GATT and began the process of dismantling tariff and nontariff barriers. Prior to that, tariffs ranged from 35 to 100 percent.

When Carlos Salinas de Gortari became President of Mexico, he decided to revolutionize the economic structure of the country so that Mexico would be better prepared to enter the twenty-first century. He cut down the size of the government bureaucracy, diversified the Mexican economy from oil, and started to privatize the economy. Then he liberalized foreign- investment rules in 1989 and renegotiated Mexico's large international debt. However, it was not until he made a trip to Eastern Europe that Salinas realized how much had to be done to compete with the opening of Eastern Europe as well as the exploding growth in Asia. As a result, he decided that he needed to reform even faster.

The discussions on free trade began quietly in 1990. However, they are progressing rapidly, and Canada is a formal part of the process. Mexico has much to offer both Canada and the United States. Mexico is tied with Iran as the fourth-largest oil producer in the world, after the Common Wealth of Independent States, the United States, and Saudi Arabia. However, foreign investment in the oil industry is prohibited by the Mexican constitution. In spite of that problem, Mexico's large oil reserves and production base would help to make North America relatively self-sufficient in oil.

In addition, Mexico has a huge consumer market. The population in 1989 was 83.7 million people, although the per capita GNP was only $2,337, which makes Mexico a lower-middle-income country. As wages continue to rise, Mexico will become a potent consumer market.

Another strength of Mexico is its low wages. Table C3-2 summarizes the hourly labor costs for Canada, the United States, and Mexico, and it is easy to see why low-skill unions in Canada and the United States feel threatened by Mexico.

As the executive of a large U.S. apparel company said, "Are we going to move all U.S. production to a place where there are no employee rights or benefits? Is it right to lay off the U.S. employee who has been with the company for 20 years and go down to Mexico and hire a 16-year-old?"

Even without the FTA, there are a number of companies that have taken advantage of the low labor rates of Mexico, with mixed blessings on the U.S. economy. When Jerrold Electronics closed its plant in Kansas City, it eliminated 190 jobs that paid $9 per hour. The company relocated in Mexico, where it is paying $1 per hour. However, in an Ohio division of General Motors, workers are making parts and components that are shipped to low-cost assembly facilities in Mexico, thus keeping 8400 people employed. Thus, the FTA with Mexico would allow large, labor-intensive firms, where 30 percent or more of product value comes from labor, to get access to cheaper labor and parts. Foreign investment should also rise, especially in previously protected industries and possibly oil. The development of more job opportunities could also help stabilize the political situation in Mexico.

However, there are bound to be losses in low-wage jobs. Some industries, such as agriculture, might undergo painful restructuring. Mexico is the largest avocado-producing nation in the world, but it does not ship a single avocado to the United States because of protectionist legislation. Organized labor in both Canada and the United States will suffer as low-paying jobs disappear and downward pressure is put on wages. Competition will also increase, which will be good for consumers but scary for producers, and the impact on trade will be uneven—border communities will be enhanced more than those far away. Another issue surrounding the free trade talks is the concern over environmental damage. There is serious pollution in Mexico City itself and in the Mexican towns bordering the United States where significant foreign investment is taking place. The

Table C3-2
Hourly Labor Costs for Production Workers

Year	Canada	United States	Mexico
1989	$14.72	$14.31	$2.32
1988	13.53	13.85	1.99
1987	11.95	13.40	1.57
1986	11.00	13.21	1.50
1985	10.80	12.96	2.09

concern is that an upsurge of investment in Mexico will lead to even greater environmental damage.

For a while, the Canadians were very tense about the negotiations between the U.S. and Mexico, because they felt that they were being left out. As one journalist pointed out, "The United States prefers to deal with its North American neighbors separately: bargaining for Canada's natural resources first, then for Mexico's cheap labor. To have both of its junior trading partners at the same table at the same time would only complicate matters."

Questions

1. List the benefits that would accrue to all three members of the new common market.

2. List the major economic problems that could arise from such a union.

3. Discuss the political and nationalistic ramifications of such a union.

4. How would this union compare with some other economic unions, such as the EC?

5. If you were a U.S. manager looking at the newly created market, what strategies might you employ to serve all three markets? What factors would you consider in making your choice?

6. What are the major elements of the U.S.-Canadian Free Trade Agreement?

7. What is the U.S.-Canadian Auto Pact (Automotive Products Trade Agreement) of 1965?

Note

[1] John D. Daniels and Lee H. Radebaugh, *International Business,* © 1992, Addison-Wesley Publishing Co., Reading, Massachusetts. Reprinted with permission of the Publisher. **Data for this case were taken from:** Stephen Baker, "Mexico: A New Economic Era," *Business Week*, November 12, 1990, pp. 102+; William J. Holstein, David Woodruff, and Amy Borrus, "Is Free Trade with Mexico Good or Bad for the U.S.?" *Business Week*, November 12, 1990, pp. 112–113; Fred Blaser, "Benefits of Mexican Trade Deal," *Financial Post*, December 6, 1990; Clyde H. Farnsworth, "Preliminary Trade Pact with Mexico Is Shaped," *New York Times*, October 7, 1989; John Saunders, "Trade with Mexico Has Winners and Losers," *Globe and Mail*, November 14, 1990; Alan Freeman, "Free-Trade Pact with Mexico Creates Winners, Losers," *The Wall Street Journal*, February 7, 1989, p. A14; Ann H. Hughes, "United States and Canada Form World's Largest Free Trade Area," *Business America*, January 30, 1989, pp. 2–3; Louis Kraar, "North America's New Trade Punch," *Fortune*, May 22, 1989, pp. 123–127; Lee H. Radebaugh and Earl H. Fry, eds., *Canada/U.S. Free Trade Agreement: The Impact on Service Industries* Provo, UT: Brigham Young University, 1988.

Case 4:
The Colombian Peso[1]
(Foreign Currency Forecasting)

The Colombian government had pegged its peso to the U.S. dollar since its system of fixed, but adjustable, exchange rates (based on the 1944 Bretton Woods Agreement) collapsed in 1973. However, on June 2, 1993, Colombia unexpectedly announced its decision to devalue the peso close to 100 percent and to float the peso. This announcement was accompanied by more elaborate foreign exchange controls. The peso devaluation and the peso float, at first glance, seemed to have caused some serious problems for the International Products Corporation whose manufacturing facilities in Colombia depend heavily upon raw materials and components from the United States. An emergency meeting of the International Finance Committee was called on June 4 at 7:30 a.m. to deal with the consequences of the devaluation and the float. Kevin Redlin, Vice President of Finance for South American operations of International Products, knew that all of the company's top executives would be attending the meeting and felt certain that he would be asked why the devaluation and the float had caught the company off guard. He decided to analyze economic statistics for both Colombia and the United States along with the news clippings in his file on the Colombian peso.

Concern over the possibility of a devaluation had existed for years because, from 1973 to June 1, 1993, the exchange rate of 20 pesos per dollar had been artificially maintained through a variety of mechanisms. Exchange controls, import controls, and intervention were employed extensively to make the peso appear more stable than it was. These controls frustrated multinational companies with manufacturing operations in Colombia because many could not import crucial raw materials and components. Nevertheless, many analysts had not expected a devaluation until after the July 1993 meeting of Colombia's finance minister with representatives of a consortium bank. On the agenda was a discussion to reschedule $1 billion in overdue Colombian loan payments. Moreover, some observers felt that a bumper coffee crop and higher coffee prices might improve the country's balance of payments to such an extent that devaluation would not be necessary.

Mr. Redlin was, therefore, not the only person caught off guard by the size of the devaluation and by the timing of the float. When Colombian Central Bank opened on Tuesday, June 2, it began quoting pesos at about $0.0263 per peso or 38 pesos per dollar as compared with the June 1 value of $0.05 per peso or 20 pesos per dollar. By Wednesday, foreign exchange experts had become sharply divided on how far the peso might fall. Some said that the foreign exchange market had already overreacted, while others saw no end in sight to the peso's depreciation. Analysts also disagreed whether the devaluation and the float would be sufficient to correct the country's balance-of-payments difficulties. All these conflicting and perplexing points of view made it more difficult for Mr. Redlin to assess the effects of the float and of the newly imposed exchange controls on his company's operations in Colombia.

By March 1993, rumors of an imminent devaluation of the peso were widespread. Although the same exchange rate of $0.05 per peso had been maintained for about 20 years, this was not the first time that rumors of a devaluation had surfaced; rumors had cropped up periodically for years, especially around the spring time. But this time, there were a number of reasons for apprehension. Colombia's growing trade deficits and an inflation rate (at least twice the rate of the United States) had prompted international treasurers and bankers to conclude that a devaluation of the peso was inevitable. The annual growth rate of the country's money supply had been more than three times that of the United States in recent years. The spread between official and free market exchange rates had skyrocketed since November 1992. Many wealthy Colombians had moved large sums of money from Colombia into the United States and other foreign countries. Finally, for 1992 the difference between the U.S. interest rate and the Colombian interest rate ranged up to 8 percent in favor of the peso, but the forward discount rate for the peso ranged up to 20 percent.

Market analysts, including Mr. Redlin, agreed that the peso was overvalued in dollar terms. However, the size of the devaluation and the timing of the float came as a surprise to even the most sophisticated international treasurers and bankers. Colombia's ongoing success in obtaining large sums of money to finance its huge current account deficits indicated that the country could defend the exchange rate of 20 pesos per dollar. In May 1993, for example, Colombia borrowed $200 million from a group of European banks, thus making its total foreign debts close to $10 billion. In fact, the country's international reserves had recently increased though its current account had been consistently negative. Second, many international treasurers and bankers said that Colombia did not have unused productive capacity sufficient enough to capitalize on a lower exchange rate. Moreover, favorable international economic conditions and reasonably promising growth for Colombian exports (higher-value exports of coffee in particular) had steadily narrowed the discounts on forward pesos since early April 1993. The country's finance minister had repeatedly denied rumors that a devaluation of the peso was imminent: in fact, the latest denial was issued on May 28, just a few days before the government announcement to float the peso on June 2.

Table C4–1
Colombia's Balance of Payments
(millions of U.S. dollars)

Accounts	1973	1979	1984	1988	1989	1990	1991	1992
Goods and Services	-30	-41	-75	-90	-98	-150	-300	-400
Unilateral Transfers	1	1	2	6	6	7	11	13
Current Account	-29	-40	-73	-84	-92	-143	-289	-387
Errors & Omissions	13	-1	4	-10	-15	-15	-30	-80
International Reserves*	-45	-40	-60	-90	-120	-130	-140	-150

*Remember that a negative sign means an increase in international reserves.

Table C4–2
Selected Economic Indicators for the U.S. and Colombia
(1984 = 100)

	The United States		Columbia	
	Consumer Prices	Money Supply	Consumer Prices	Money Supply
1973	70	60	50	40
1978	70	65	57	60
1983	76	70	76	80
1988	81	75	83	90
1990	100	100	100	100
1992	140	130	180	200

Questions

1. Do you think that the peso has fallen far enough or that it will continue to lose value? (Hint: answer this question using the purchasing power parity theory.)

2. Could the peso float have been forecasted? (Hint: answer this question using such economic indicators as the balance of payments, international reserves, inflation, money supply, and official versus market rates.)

3. How can you be sure that many wealthy Colombians had moved large amounts of money out of their country? (Hint: One of the items in Table C4–1 may shed some light on this question.)

4. The discrepancy between the interest differential and the forward discount rate for the peso in 1992 seemed to open incentives for arbitrage. Could it have been possible to take advantage of the opportunity for covered interest arbitrage?

5. What alternatives are available to the Colombian government for dealing with its balance-of-payments problems?

6. Briefly outline courses of action that International Products should take to cope with the foreign exchange controls. (Remember that the company's manufacturing facilities in Colombia depend heavily on raw materials and components from the United States.)

Note

[1] **This is a fictitious case and draws heavily upon the following two cases:** Richard Moxon, "The Mexican Peso," in Gunter Dufey and Ian H. Giddy, ed., *50 Cases in International Finance*, Reading, MA: Addison-Wesley, 1987, pp. 138-149; and John D. Daniels and Lee H. Radebaugh, "The Mexican Peso," *International Business*, Reading, MA: Addison-Wesley, 1992, pp. 259-264.

Case 5:
Olivetti's Exposure[1]
(Foreign Exchange Risk Management)

Carlo De Benedetti took over as CEO of Olivetti in 1978 and turned the company, known primarily as a typewriter company, into the leading European-based office automation company and one of the largest manufacturers of IBM-compatible computers. De Benedetti's aggressive strategy thrust Olivetti into the international marketplace and forced management to re-examine its exposure to foreign exchange risk and determine whether or not the policies and procedures designed to protect against risk were adequate in light of its new international strategy.

The Company. When De Benedetti was offered the CEO spot at Olivetti in 1978, the company was losing $8 million a year, had a debt position in excess of liquid assets by more than $600 million, and had a management team that was very discouraged. "We had only a few products and a local culture" recalls Elserino Piol, executive vice-president for corporate strategies. "We were sort of a country-boy company. As soon as De Benedetti came on board, he instituted massive layoffs, increased the research and development budget significantly, introduced new products, and replaced most of Olivetti's top management.

By 1986, sales were $4.9 billion, and earnings were $380 million. Of Olivetti's sales, approximately 50 percent are in Italy, 32 percent in other European countries, and 18 percent in non-European countries. Olivetti manufactures computers under the AT&T name and has struck strategic alliances with a number of multinational companies, including AT&T, Matsushita Electrical Industrial Co., and Toshiba. As noted by De Benedetti, "The traditional multinational approach is obsolete. Corporations with international ambitions must turn to a new strategy of agreements: alliances and mergers with other companies."

However, Olivetti's fortunes began to wane in the late 1980s. As the Italian economy began to slow in 1989, so did the growth of Olivetti. Profits in 1989 were down 40 percent from their level in 1988, and the company's market share in Europe dropped from 9 to 8 percent. Layoffs in 1990-1991 were expected to reach 5 percent of Olivetti's labor force. De Benedetti and Managing Director Vittorio Cassoni realized that mergers or alliances would be necessary to catapult Olivetti into a solid position in Europe, but they have had trouble finding the right partner. It looked like the 1984 joint venture with American Telephone & Telegraph would do the trick, but the venture fell apart in 1989.

In spite of these failures, De Benedetti wanted to move away from the narrow niche of being a hardware manufacturer to being a firm that solves business problems through hardware and software. Olivetti entered into an arrangement with GM's Electronic Data Systems Corp. to provide computer services in Europe. Currently, Olivetti is the top computer maker in Italy, but it is struggling in Europe and the United States. Given the size and strength of the U.S. Market, especially in the hardware and software industry, De Benedetti is determined to improve Olivett's position there, even though the venture with AT&T was not successful.

The Olivetti Risk Management Strategy.

Olivetti has production and distribution facilities scattered around the world. As a result, it has tried to establish good strategies for managing foreign exchange risk. Olivetti's strategy is developed by a committee made up of the group controller, the international treasurer, the chief economist, and a member of the operational planning department.

The first thing that the committee does is consider the relationship among three currencies: the local currency (the currency of the country where the operation is located); the currency of denomination (the currency in which a transaction actually is denominated); and the currency of determination (currency used to determine the global price of products). The committee tries to see how fluctuations in the three currencies will affect Olivetti's competitiveness in the markets where it operates. Once a year, the committee simulates the effect of different exchange rate scenarios on the profitability of each unit and the company as a whole.

There is a strong interrelationship between the exchange rate and the economic environment. As noted by Angelo Fornasari, Olivetti's vice-president of finance: "To maintain market share and satisfactory profit levels, Olivetti must constantly consider the problems of sourcing product input, of funding in different currencies and markets, of reorienting marketing efforts, of seeking higher productivity levels, of shifting from one currency of invoicing (i.e., of denomination), to another, etc." Currently, Olivetti develops its economic exposure scenario three years into the future.

Although the major exposure for Olivetti is economic exposure, management also is concerned about translation and transaction exposure. The hedging strategy is centralized at the corporate level so that local managers can concentrate on operating decisions. Transaction exposure is centralized, and hedging activities are carried out for the balances of transactions actually booked, as well as for forecasts of what the balances are expected to be four months into the future.

A major event likely to have an impact on discussions at Olivetti was the currency scandal at Volkswagen in 1986. Burkhard Junger, the former chief currency trader of Volkswagen AG confessed to complicity with fugitive currency trader Joachim Schmidt, the owner of a small foreign-exchange brokerage in Frankfurt. Apparently, Junger and Schmidt entered into fraudulent forward contracts with the National Bank of Hungary to sell the bank U.S. dollars for German marks at a rate just under three marks per dollar. When the contracts turned up fraudulent, Volkswagen was left with dollars worth less than two marks each, and it lost $260 million, which was 80 percent of its net income in 1986. VW currency traders were allowed to trade contracts for a profit, a policy that many shareholders felt was inappropriate. They felt that foreign exchange conversion should only take place to support manufacturing operations, not to gain a profit. In addition, VW had adopted a policy not to hedge against foreign currency fluctuations, since it felt that those fluctuations would balance themselves out over the medium term.

Questions

1. Given the nature of Olivetti's products, markets, and strategic alliances, what different types of foreign exchange risks do you think it will encounter?

2. In terms of foreign exchange risk management, what difference does it make what the currency of determination is for Olivetti products?

3. Why do you think Olivetti does not look into the future more than three years to develop its economic exposure scenario?

4. Evaluate Olivetti's programs of production, marketing, and finance for economic exposure management. Do you think that Olivetti's hedging strategy is more realistic than VW's?

5. What is your opinion of Olivetti's policy of centralizing hedging strategies at the corporate level? What role should local management play in developing and implementing those strategies?

Note

[1] John D. Daniels and Lee H. Radebaugh, *International Business,* © 1992, Addison–Wesley Publishing Co., Inc., Reading, Massachusetts. Reprinted with permission of the publisher. **Data for this case were taken from:** Olivetti Annual and Extraordinary General Meeting, 1985; "How Olivetti Manages Foreign Exchange Risk To Protect Long–Term Profits," *Business International Money Report*, New York: Business International, November 2, 1987, pp 349–351; Olivetti's *Annual Reports*, various issues; William C. Symonds, Thane Peterson, John J. Keller, and Marc Frons, "Dealmaker De Benedetti," *Business Week,* August 24, 1987, pp. 42–47; and Terrence Roth, "Former Trader at VW Admits Role in Fraud," *The Wall Street Journal*, September 14, 1987, p. 16.

Case 6:
Who Is No. 1: The U.S. or Japan?[1]
(Global Financial Leadership)

In the late 1980s the United States reached a climax in its fifth wave of decline since the 1950s, a phenomenon largely triggered by its foreign debt as well as financial threats from Japan. The first wave occurred in 1957 and 1958 when the Soviet Union launched the Sputnik, the first manned satellite. The second wave came at the end of 1960s when President Nixon began to prepare Americans for a multipolar world because American decline economically and militarily was inevitable. The third wave followed immediately after the OPEC oil embargo of 1973 and the dramatic increase in oil prices. The fourth wave took place in the late 1970s because of Vietnam, Watergate, continued development of Soviet nuclear forces, and the expansion of Soviet power in a half-dozen countries such as Afghanistan.

Every single empire and great nation of history has been destroyed or greatly diminished in world influence. Why should we assume that the United States, today's great nation, can defeat the pattern of history? If we accept for the moment America's decline, no other financial leader in the world, with the possible exception of Japan, seems likely to emerge in the coming century. "The American century is over," Clyde Prestowitz, a former Deputy Assistant Secretary of Commerce in the Reagan Administration, has said. "The big development in the latter part of the century is the emergence of Japan as a major superpower."

We can base the current wave of decline on three bodies of evidence: (1) mounting U.S. budget and trade deficits, (2) continuing declines in U.S shares of global economic power; and (3) declining U.S. leadership in science and technology.

Fading America and Emerging Japan.   Is the United States really passing its baton in the race for world financial leadership to Japan? We can find several appealing arguments that such a switch is already under way. Banking surveys rank Japan as the world's most creditworthy nation, the yen being the strongest major currency since September 1985. By Spring 1987, the Tokyo stock exchange traded nearly $3 trillion and overtook its U.S. counterpart as the world's largest stock market. The world's largest creditor nation, Japan stands today in the same position as other nations which dominated the world at the height of their economic power. Historically, its rule rivals the domination of Great Britain from 1851 to 1890 and the supremacy of the United States from 1946 to 1970.

Table C6-1 underscores a new reality. Japan has become a rich uncle, the chief source of foreign capital in the United States. Japanese net overseas

Table C6–1
Net Overseas Investment
(in billions of U.S. dollars)

Year	Japan	U.S.
1980	$ 11.5	$106.3
1981	10.9	141.1
1982	24.7	137.0
1983	37.3	89.6
1984	74.3	3.6
1985	129.8	–111.9
1986	180.4	–269.2
1987	240.7	–378.3
1988	291.7	–532.5
1989	293.2	–727.8
1990	328.0	–700.4

Source: The U.S. Department of Commerce, *Survey of Current Business*; and Japan Economic Institute of America.

investment (net external assets) has climbed from $11 billion in 1981 to $328 billion in 1990. Most of that money went to the United States.

This dramatic reversal in the international position has awakened economists and the American public to the significance of global capital flows. The United States was a net creditor nation until February 1985. In just a few years it then took an opposite role, becoming the world's biggest debtor nation. Huge trade and budget deficits for ten years (1981–1990) are two major reasons for this shift. Foreign debt grew at such a breathtaking pace that few people were aware of its potential impact until it was too late. By 1990 the U.S. foreign debt reached $700 billion; it is more than half of the combined total debt of 114 developing countries.

History shows that no country has managed to be a great power and a great debtor at the same time. Two great powers—Spain in the 16th century and England in the 19th century—lost stature as world leaders when their status moved from creditor to debtor. Can the United States as the world's largest debtor nation remain the world's leading power? Can the United States continue to lead its alliances as it increases its debt to the countries that are supposed to be its followers? Can it demand allegiance from those countries on issues of global strategy while pushing them to follow U.S. economic imperatives? The U.S. external debt also jeopardizes the dollar's status as a reserve currency and limits the U.S. efforts to address Third World debt problems.

In the past few years, international operations in Japanese securities houses have increased beyond all expectations thanks to Japan's widening trade surplus and Tokyo's booming capital markets. Their biggest gains have come in Eurobonds due to a new freedom from regulation on London's international capital markets. Japanese firms have recently replaced U.S. companies as the leaders in the Eurobond underwriting market. The next area for confrontation will center on equities; British and U.S. companies will struggle to keep their leadership in this market.

Until not too many years ago the United States was the world leader in almost every field of science and technology. To retain its leadership position in the world economy and to support a high-wage and high-consumption society, the United States had to remain ahead of other countries in the most vital research areas simply because modern industry is knowledge driven. Manual labor was the norm until recently. In the 1950s, 70 percent of all employed people in Western Europe and America were use-of-hands workers, while only 30 percent were use-of-brain workers. That ratio has almost reversed. However, since the early 1970's the U.S. loss of vital scientific ground in a number of important areas has had major economic consequences. Today the Unites States has less money available, and certainly less political will, than in the past to catch up to other world leaders. U.S. dominance in old manufacturing such as textiles, iron and steel, shipbuilding, and basic chemicals has long gone. In addition, the United States has also suffered relative industrial decline in global shares of high technology products such as robotics, aerospace products, automobiles, machine tools, and computers.

America's fall from leadership is nothing new in the eyes of the world. Great Britain, for instance, was the world's wealthiest and most technologically advanced nation until the eve of World War I. History has shown, as in Britain's case, that such leadership can shift; with it goes technological, economic, political, military and cultural dominance. British power vanished in large part because few Britons understood or helped to preserve two foundations of the empire, science and technology. Unfortunately, many leading U.S. universities neglect these areas of study; likewise, U.S. leaders in recent years seem unconcerned about this lack of development.

Japan is a strong country with a huge trade surplus, saving more than it spends and sending excess money abroad. Lists which rank the world's top industrial companies, banks, and securities firms resemble the Tokyo phone directory. The flow of Japanese cash into the United States had helped fuel eight years of U.S. economic expansion and had enabled the United States to become an engine of world economic growth until 1990. Japan no longer can be ignored in important financial issues such as Third World debts, international monetary reform, and global trade negotiations.

New waves of Japanese wealth have reached American shores. Contrary to public beliefs, most of it has little to do with government/corporate securities and real estate investments. Uneasy about a growing image problem with the U.S. public, Japanese companies are spending huge sums of money here designed to ease complaints about unfair trade practices and the purchase of American landmarks such as Rockefeller Center in New York and the Pebble Beach golf course in California. Donations from Japanese businesses to U.S charities have increased 17 times from $30 million in 1986 to $500 million in 1991. The Japanese are not just giving more money but are giving to more types of organizations. While in the past they almost exclusively gave to elite institutions—endowing chairs at major universities and supporting high-brow cultural icons—the Japanese are increasingly making donations to grass-roots groups, such as U.S. education, museums, public television stations, think tanks, political action groups, and public relations firms.

Many economists compare Japan's ascendancy with the changing of the guard after World War I when the United States emerged supreme and Britain began its long decline. Of course, lessons of history are more complicated than this sort of generalization. True switches in financial leadership happen infrequently, usually only after a catastrophic event such as a war. Merchants from Venice, to cite a clear lesson from history, ruled economically in the 1500's until the Dutch built larger fleets and circulated their currency, the *thaler*, throughout the known world. Great Britain had a leading financial role from the late 1700's until after World War I because of its markets throughout the British empire and its stable economic system. Then the United States supplanted England as European nations engaged in long and destructive combat.

The undisputed financial powers of earlier centuries distinguished themselves for more reasons than their money. Venice's wealth in the 16th century was also due to its breakthrough in accounting and credit techniques. Great Britain in the last century had an empire on which the sun never set—and an extensive overseas market to match its colonial territories. Just as important as this vast market was England's ability to give the world what it wanted—the stability of a freely convertible gold-backed currency. The United States had enjoyed a political and military strength, making the dollar a stabilizing currency around the world. Now the Japanese yen is the strongest major currency, though foreign banks still hold most of their reserves in dollars. Even top Japanese managers concede that the dollar is their last-resort currency.

In our contemporary context, several nations have gained temporary dominance, but they are like shooting stars bursting suddenly on the scene—bright and powerful—only to burn themselves out and fade quickly. Most notable in recent times were the oil-producing Arab nations in the 1970's. Saudi Arabia and other Mideastern countries were huge capital exporters, like Japan. Their seemingly endless ability to buy U.S. Treasury bills, New York real estate, and European equities made daily headlines or leading stories on television. However, the influence of these Arab nations waned after oil prices collapsed in the 1980's.

Certainly, Japan's economy is much more broadly anchored than those of the Arab countries which relied on a single product. Japan has a huge industrial base in electronics, steel, autos, and a host of other businesses. Japan's economic output of $3 trillion ranks it second only to the United States. Furthermore, Japanese companies are establishing manufacturing facilities abroad to shield themselves from fluctuations of exchange rates or worries of trade wars—issues they would face if solely exporting from Japan.

U.S. Foreign Debt.
America's investment surplus evaporated as the country amassed huge budget and trade deficits during the 1980s. The rise of foreign investment in the United States sounded alarms and prompted calls for Congress to curb foreign purchases of U.S. companies and real estate. The United States was a net debtor nation for most of the 19th century with no bad effects as European capital helped to build railroads and factories. However, some private economists contend that there is a marked difference between the 19th century net debtor period and the present. In the last century, America was a developing country and needed foreign capital to become an industrial power. But during the 1980s, much of the foreign money went to finance Federal and consumer deficits rather than being invested in ways that would boost American productivity.

Declining U.S. Economic Share.
Some skeptics insist that America's economy is shrinking relative to others, and they have a valid point. For a time in the 1950s the United States produced about 50 percent of the gross world product, a far larger proportion than now. However, such a situation was clearly a temporary product of World War II because Japan and Europe were still devastated by the war. By the mid-1960s, with the world fully recovered, the United States accounted for 25 percent of the gross world product and has consistently remained at that level ever since. Economically, America remains the world's largest producer; this pattern is unlikely to change drastically in the future. In fact, a number of studies indicate that the U.S. share of global product will remain remarkably stable— between 20 percent and 25 percent until 2010. In short, if leadership means having 50 percent of the world's economic activity, American leadership disappeared long ago. If leadership means producing 25 percent of the world product, American leadership looks quite secure.

During the 1980s U.S economic performance improved significantly compared to that of other industrialized countries. During the 1960s Japan's economy grew at 11 percent a year, compared to America's average growth rate of 3 percent a year. No country's economy will grow indefinitely at 11 percent per year. As the Japanese economy has matured, its growth rate is not be expected to be much higher than that of the United States. As shown in Table C6-2, in 1989 the U.S. Gross National Product (GNP) was almost two times as much as Japan's GNP.

Technology.
Many Americans have been concerned in recent years about the country's loss of competitiveness. They conclude that the United States is no longer dominant because its technological superiority has slipped. Although Japan has caught up with the United States in most older technologies, it is struggling and will continue to struggle to pass the United States in the new growth industries of the 1990s and beyond—computer software, genetic engineering, exotic material manufacturing, and others. In the new phase, Japan will still depend on the United States and Europe even though its technological borrowings will be mostly at the pre-commercial stage. In spite of all the high-powered programs and money spent on blue-sky

Table C6–2
Vital Statistics of Two Nations

Variables	U.S.	Japan
Population (in millions)	250.4	123.3
Gross National Products (in billions)	$5,234	$2,835
Inflation (in percent)	4.8%	2.3%
Unemployment Rate (in percent)	5.3%	2.3%
Gross Private Investment (in percent of GNP)	14.8%	25.7%
Savings (percent of household-after-tax income)	5.4%	16.8%
Per Capita Income	$20,938	$23,031
Budget Deficit (in billions)	$152	$51.5
Merchandise Trade Balance (in billions)	–$109	+$59.7

Source: Urban C. Lehner and Alan Murray, "Strained Alliance: Selling of America to Japanese Touches Some Very Raw Nerves," *The Wall Street Journal*, June 13, 1990, p. A8.

research, Japan still does not have a strong base of homegrown advanced technology. According to a study by the National Science Foundation, the United States is ahead of Japan in basic and undirected research on most of 12 key areas, whereas Japan clearly leads in development work having specific commercial applications in most of these areas. Strong in development and weak in research—this has been a Japanese problem for a long time. These 12 areas of research and development are: artificial intelligence, automated factory assembly, biotechnology, compact-disk technology, computer design, computer integrated manufacturing, computer software, fiber optics, high-strength construction plastic, integrated circuits, mobile radio systems, and telecommunication networks.

Americans held the lead in research but let foreigners use this technology to develop products, selling their ideas to Japan and other countries for small royalties. Much of Japan's success has been based on rapid commercialization of technology developed in America. However, Japanese will find it increasingly difficult to buy or copy U.S. high technologies from now on because U.S. manufacturers belatedly took steps to protect product lines from imitators. U.S. companies are working hard to protect their patents, to cooperate in the development of new technologies, and to turn their discoveries into products more quickly. For example, they are using American lawyers more skillfully to tie up adversaries in legal knots at home and abroad. Computer companies are learning to cover their design tracks and to make their new machines almost clone-proof. Computers themselves are beginning to revolutionize more and more American factories, allowing people to make things faster, better, and cheaper. Government and industry have begun to work together on research too.

The superior research environment, along with the encouragement of creative thought and stimulating nature of a melting-pot society, enables the

United States to stay ahead of Japan in basic science and technology. Japan is a closed, conformist, and homogeneous society which does not tolerate mavericks and original thinkers. In other words, Japanese may learn more facts, but unruly Americans learn to think. The Japanese problem is with pure science—the kind that solves nature's secrets and wins Nobel prizes. This pure science produces economic gain only later. Specifically, only five Japanese scientists have ever won Nobel prizes, compared with about 150 Americans. "Japan's science is definitely inferior to America's in terms of real creativity," Nobel laureate Susmu Tonegawa told a Tokyo audience early in 1988. "It is clear that Japan is making money by taking and applying the fruits of science that the West creates at great expense." Mr. Tonegawa, a MIT professor who won 1987's Nobel prize in medicine, has not worked in Japan since 1963. He claims he could not have done his ground-breaking work if he had stayed in his homeland. Japanese money and programs will not buy all the changes it needs. The culprits are deeply ingrained traditions, the same ones that made Japan an industrial powerhouse: submission to authority, strict seniority, a stable but immobile work force, and little debate.

Japanese industrial-style hierarchy extends to the chair system in which professors and lab managers in their 40s and 50s hold absolute power. Japan's best and brightest young scientists continue to find their creative urges stifled by a social fabric that seems to idolize seniority, hate individualism, and suppress debate. The social conventions that dominate Japan's research system have often discouraged innovation. Much basic work is thwarted by a calcified bureaucracy, poorly equipped universities, and a conservative educational system. Young scientists are often barred from going to conferences and do not dare to engage in free scientific discussion which criticizes other scientists' work. Promotions are based on seniority, not ability. Young scientists find it almost impossible to find money for research projects.

Questions

1. Estimate Japan's and the U.S. net overseas investment for seven years from 1990 to 1995. Use the following two approaches to obtain your estimate: (1) assume that their net external assets will increase at the four year average (1985–1989) per year and (2) use a trend line for an annual series on net external assets during the same period (1985–1989).

2. Discuss the following: (1) the causes of the U.S. foreign debt and (2) the burdens of the U.S. foreign debt.

3. Some scholars such as Peter Drucker argue that Japan practices "adversarial trade," which means that a nation sells but does not buy. Elaborate this theory in some detail.

4. Has Japan paid its dues to be No. 1 in international financial affairs?

5. Which country will be the world financial leader in the 21st century?

Note

[1] **Data for this case were taken from:** Suzanne Alexander, "Japanese Firms Embark on a Program of Lavish Giving to American Charities," *The Wall Street Journal*, May 23, 1991, p. B1 and p. B5; The Council of Economic Advisors, *Economic Report of the President*, Washington: United States Government Printing Office, various issues; Peter F. Drucker, *The Frontiers of Management: Where Tomorrow's Decisions Are Being Shopped*, New York: Truman Talley Books, 1986; Japan Economic Institute of America, *Foreign Direct Investment in Japan*, September 20, 1991; Samuel Huntington, "The U.S.: Decline or Renewal?" *Foreign Affairs*, Winter 1988/89, pp. 79–87; Norris S. Hetherington, "British Empire's Sad Lesson for America," *The Wall Street Journal*, September 31, 1987; Karen Elliott House, "The 90s & Beyond: For All Its Difficulties, U.S. Stands to Retain Its Global Leadership," *The Wall Street Journal*, January 23, 1989, p. A1; The Joint Economic Committee, Congress of the United States, *The Economy at Midyear: A Legacy of Foreign Debt*, August 5, 1987; Paul Kennedy, *The Rise and Fall of the Great Powers: Economic Change and Military Conflict from 1500 to 2000*, New York: Random House, 1987; Youn-Suk Kim, "Prospects for Japanese-U.S. Trade and Industrial Competition," *Asian Survey*, May 1990, pp. 493–504; Joel Kurtzman, *The Decline and Crash of the American Economy*, New York: Norton, 1987, Section 4; Urban C. Lehner and Alan Murray, "Strained Alliance: Will the U.S. Find the Resolve to Meet Japanese Challenge?" *The Wall Street Journal*, July 2, 1990, p. A1 and p. A4; Urban C. Lehner and Alan Murray, "Strained Alliance: Selling of America to Japanese Touches Some Very Raw Nerves," *The Wall Street Journal*, June 19, 1990, p. A1 and p. A12; Urban C. Lehner and Alan Murray, "Strained Alliance: U.S., Japan Struggle to Redraft Relations," *The Wall Street Journal*, June 13, 1990, p. A1 and A8; Jacob M. Schlesinger, "MITI Vision for 1990s Seeks a Mellow Japan Others Shouldn't Fear," *The Wall Street Journal*, July 3, 1990, p. A1 and p. A5; The Staff of Fortune, "An American Vision for the 1990s," *Fortune*, March 26, 1990, pp. 14–16; Bernard Wysocki, Jr., "Technology," *The Wall Street Journal*, November 14, 1988, p. R35; Stephen K. Yoder, "Japan's Scientists Find Pure Research Suffers Under Rigid Life Style," *The Wall Street Journal*, October 31, 1988, p. A1 and p. A10; and Stephen K. Yoder, "Native Son's Nobel Award Is Japan's Loss," *The Wall Street Journal*, October 14, 1987, p. A26.

Case 7:
LSI Logic Corp[1]
(Investment Financing)

In the late 1970s, Wilfred Corrigan, the British-born chairman and president of Fairchild Camera & Instrument Corp., sold the company to Schlumberge Ltd. Approximately one year later, in November 1980, he started LSI Logic Corp., a manufacturer of custom-made microchips based in Milpitas, California. Although Mr. Corrigan's idea of custom-made microchips sounded unconventional at the time, he was able to use his record at Fairchild to convince some U.S. venture capitalists in January 1981 to invest nearly $7 million in the new firm.

The company had only four employees at that point, but since Corrigan had solved two key issues—the nature of the product and the initial infusion of cash—there was a solid foundation for growth. Corrigan then had to decide how LSI Logic should service its customers worldwide, and how and where it would raise capital to keep expanding.

Global Strategy. Mr. Corrigan learned from his experience at Fairchild that a producer of microchips had to think globally in terms of the location of production and the consumer. He quickly decided that in order to be successful, he needed to concentrate on being in three key geographic areas—Japan, the United States, and Europe. He coined this his "global triad strategy." The key organizational strategy was to establish firms incorporated in the producing and consuming countries that would be jointly owned by LSI Logic and local investors. However, LSI Logic would hold a controlling interest in the firm. Although the operations in each country would be relatively independent of each other, they would still be linked by technology, money, and management. This would allow the synergy of interdependence to take place, but it would also permit local freedom in meeting the demands of the market.

Initial European Thrust. Once Corrigan got operations underway, he began to look for more cash. The key was to find the right amount, at the right price, with the least number of problems. In February 1982, slightly more than a year after U.S. venture capital gave the company a start, LSI Logic turned to Europe in search of venture capital. It found a European investing community hungry for U.S. high-tech stock, so it was able to raise $10 million, mostly—but not exclusively—in Britain. That offering brought LSI Logic an average of $7 a share, compared with only $0.90 per share when it was set up only a year earlier.

At that point LSI Logic was growing rapidly. In May 1983, Corrigan took the firm public in the United States and raised over $162 million, an average now of $21 a share. That was a significant improvement over its European experience and demonstrated the size of the appetite in the United States for new high-tech companies.

The Japanese Strategy.

In spite of the success in Europe and in the United States, Corrigan still had not been able to complete the third part of his triad—Japan. However, Corrigan learned that Nomura Securities, the largest brokerage house in Japan and subsequently the world, had purchased large blocks of LSI stock for its clients in Japan. Encouraged by this information, Corrigan traveled to Japan to meet with Nomura officials and try to decide what LSI Logic's next move should be. As a result of the visit and discussions, Corrigan decided that the time was right for starting operations in Japan. Following the strategy he had used elsewhere, Corrigan established a Japanese subsidiary of LSI Logic (called LSI Logic Corp. K.K.) in which the parent company owned 70 percent, and 25 local Japanese investors owned 30 percent. The investors were not small operations, however. Nippon Life Insurance Company, the third largest insurance company in the world, just behind Prudential and Metropolitan Life, became a major shareholder in the new venture. The new investment was just right for LSI Logic. Not only did Corrigan then have access to the Japanese consumer market, but he also had access to the Japanese capital market. As a Japanese company, LSI Logic Corp. K.K., and its manufacturing affiliate, Nihon Semiconductor Inc., could establish lines of credit with Japanese banks. In order to help LSI Logic penetrate the capital markets better and to develop more of a local image in Japan, Corrigan hired Keiske Awata, a senior executive of NEC Corp. who was working outside of Japan at the time. Mr. Awata gave a Japanese image to LSI Logic in Japan and helped open the right doors to the financial world. LSI Logic was able to get a local line of credit at only 6 percent, compared with 9 percent in the United States at the time.

Second European Thrust.

Once that business in Japan was underway, Corrigan turned his attentions again to Europe. He was planning to set up a new European company and he needed to decide on its structure. The company could be set up as a branch of the U.S. parent that would use U.S. capital and be totally controlled and protected by the parent; or it could be set up as a European company. Corrigan decided to do the latter, so he used Morgan Stanley & Co., the largest U.S.-based securities firm, to set up LSI Logic Ltd. The parent company retained an 82 percent stake in the new company, and the rest was sold to European investors in a private offering. One of the investors was the venture capital arm of the five West German banks. Corrigan was convinced that by setting up a European company, he was able to get more money by selling shares at a higher price than would have been possible otherwise, and that LSI Logic Ltd. was better placed to service European customers than a branch of the parent company would have been.

Convertible Bonds.   In 1985 and again in 1987, Corrigan returned to European capital markets, but this time LSI floated a bond issue. The first issue of $23 million was put together by Swiss Bank Corp., one of the largest banks in the world. The second issue, a bond issue with securities convertible into common stock, was floated by Morgan Stanley and Prudential-Bache Capital Funding. There were two main attractions to the bond market for LSI Logic: a decent price (lower interest rates than would have been offered in the United States), and a quicker time frame. Since LSI did not have to worry about all of the listing regulations of the Securities and Exchange Commission in the United States, it was able to get the offering together and out to the investing public faster.

Although significant amounts of funds were raised in foreign markets (over $200 million since 1982), there was no real exchange risk. LSI Logic operations worldwide were earning revenues that could be used to pay off the financial obligations. In addition, LSI Logic subsidiaries had access to local credit markets because they were organized as local corporations rather than branches of a foreign corporation.

Questions

1. What were the different ways that LSI Logic used international capital markets? Discuss specifically the nature of the instruments (i.e. local, foreign, euro, etc.).

2. Why did LSI Logic use those foreign and U.S. markets rather than just the U.S. market?

3. How did its organizational strategy fit with its capital acquisition strategy?

Note

[1] John D. Daniels and Lee H. Radebaugh, *International Business*, © 1992, Addison-Wesley Publishing Co., Inc., Reading, Massachusetts. Reprinted with permission of the publisher. **Data for this case were taken from:** Udayan Gupta, "Raising Money the New-Tangled Way," in "Global Finance & Investing: A Special Report," *The Wall Street Journal*, September 18, 1987, p. 14D; Nick Arnett, "LSI Lands Former NEC Chief to Head Affiliated Company," *Business Journal–San Jose*, January 14, 1985, p. 17; "LSI Gets A Circuit-Supply Pact," *The Wall Street Journal*, January 6, 1987, p. 7.

Case 8:
NUMMI[1]
(International Joint Venture)

In 1983, General Motors of the United States and Toyota Motor Corporation of Japan announced a joint venture, New United Motor Manufacturing, Inc. (NUMMI), to build automobiles in Fremont, California. Japanese managers shocked GM executives when they persuaded the UAW local, one of GM's most troublesome workforces, to build top-quality cars, using the team concept in the Fremont plant. First of all, in a few years the UAW local had changed from a militant, anti-management union to one that placed the health of the company among its top priorities. Second, the Chevrolet Nova produced by the plant had been known to have the lowest rate of warranty repairs in the United States. Third, absenteeism had fallen from 25 percent (just before GM shut down the plant in 1982) to 3 percent in 1991. The plant makes about the same number of cars with about half the GM workers. NUMMI has been so successful that U.S. automakers have adopted the team approach for operations of their factories. However, this modern-day experiment faced its toughest struggle so far in 1988. According to NUMMI officials, sales of the Nova dropped to about 100,000 units in 1988; that was about half the company had hoped to sell; breakeven point was said to have been about 200,000 units.

Because of continued sales erosion from foreign competition, the U.S. automotive industry had considered a variety of strategies for recovery—outside importation of models wholly produced abroad; use of major foreign components in U.S. assembled models; and finally, collaboration with the Japanese in the production of automobiles on U.S. soil. Ultimately, two of the world's largest and successful corporations, General Motors and Toyota, agreed to a joint venture. NUMMI was more than an opportunity for mutual financial gain, although that cannot be denied. It was, in fact, a commitment to experiment with a new approach to managing a business. NUMMI may be regarded as a learning laboratory in which GM, Toyota, and the United Auto Workers (UAW) developed innovative ways to manage a corporation for the 1990s and beyond. The venture created a fundamental change in traditional organizational structure as well as in the behavior and expectations of NUMMI's management, workers, and their union. The key element of this new approach was the exchange of job security for worker cooperation.

Reasons for A Joint Venture.   NUMMI, a cross-cultural venture, operates in a charged-up atmosphere that encourages change and adaption to new working environments. Its challenge is to create a harmonious fit between the values and the technical and social systems of East and West that will fulfill the promise of the "best of both worlds."

The overwhelming environmental pressure for change on the participants—GM, Toyota, and the UAW—in the early 1980s suggests why NUMMI was formed. GM and other U.S. automakers faced a crisis caused by their declining share of the world auto market. The U.S. government and labor unions put a great deal of pressure on the U.S. auto companies to retain jobs for U.S. workers rather than to increase outsourcing. Relations in the industry between labor and management remained adversarial, oftentimes inflexible. Roger Smith, the chief executive officer of GM, realized that it was essential to transform the organization of GM's manufacturing operations if it was to compete successfully with Japan and other foreign entrants in the global market. The company needed a model on which to base its transformation, one which would also provide much needed hands-on learning on how to deal with the newly emerging system. With astute perception, contrary to GM managers who thought they knew everything, Smith chose to learn directly from Toyota, GM's most formidable competitor.

There was increasing pressure on Toyota from both the U.S. and Japanese governments to address balance-of-payments issues by shifting manufacturing activities to the United States. Japanese automakers, such as Honda, Nissan, and Mazda, were developing subsidiary operations in the United States. Toyota had little experience in overseas manufacturing and needed to establish a manufacturing presence in the United States as quickly as possible. The joint GM-Toyota venture provided Toyota management with an opportunity to learn how to work with U.S. suppliers, managers, workers, and their unions.

The UAW was no less frustrated with its threatening environment than the two corporations. Thousands of UAW members were already unemployed, and prospects for the future were bleak. U.S. auto manufacturers threatened to increase the outsourcing of parts or to manufacture automobiles entirely in cheaper labor markets abroad. Japanese manufacturing plants in the United States continued to resist unionization. The union needed an environment free from the adversarial roles of the past so that the U.S. auto industry would retain its world leadership. The potential to shape future contracts and share in the rewards of operating and rebuilding an ailing industry were indeed powerful incentives.

By way of background, GM's plant in Fremont, California was considered to be a representative of automobile production facilities in the United States. It began production in 1963 and attained peak employment in 1978. By this time, approximately 5,000 workers were employed at the plant, but continuous decline in productivity eventually led to its closing in 1982.

Internal problems contributed heavily to the plant's decline in productivity. Some of them were a lack of discipline, high absenteeism, sabotage, drug abuse, and low morale. These problems were considered to be characteristic of production facilities within the automotive sector. In its history, the plant had shut down four times because of strikes or sickouts. It had a poor record of productivity when compared to a typical Japanese manufacturing facility.

For example, GM's Fremont plant averaged 34-man hours per vehicle while the Japanese averaged only 20-man hours per vehicle. A tremendous amount of effort would be required to equate American and Japanese productivity.

New Management Style.   On February 17, 1983, GM and Toyota agreed to build subcompact vehicles, based on Toyota's Corolla design, at the GM's Fremont plant. The vehicle was eventually named the "Nova." According to this agreement both parties entered into a 12-year venture which would terminate in 1996; each owns a 50 percent stake. After 12 years of production, either side could buy out the other's interest in the venture. NUMMI's goal was to produce automobiles in an adaptive and innovative environment, different than the traditional American environment, because it purported to increase productivity and improve quality. The modernized Fremont plant was managed by senior members of Toyota. NUMMI management was even granted considerable freedom in the decision-making process. While the Japanese tackled problems of how to manage the venture, GM assumed responsibility for the marketing and distribution of the finished product.

The labor agreement between the UAW and NUMMI was historic. Not only did the agreement lack complicated legal jargon, it also displayed an overt influence of Japanese labor-management relations. Mutual trust and good faith were stressed, two qualities not often found in traditional U.S. labor agreements. Traditional work rules, narrow job classifications, and rigid seniority were abolished. The new agreement provided for one job class for production workers and three classifications for tradesmen. Workers were given control over more job responsibilities. The UAW made it clear from the start that it would no longer tolerate chronic absenteeism or practices which caused poor quality.

The UAW and NUMMI management agreed that workers would receive U.S. wages and benefits. However, NUMMI's costs were actually lowered because it was not required to have pensions or supplemental unemployment benefits. New workers were selected from the laid-off Fremont workforce; however, "militants" of the past were eliminated in the selection process, which combined both Japanese and U.S. methods.

Workers were organized into teams of six to eight members. Three teams would comprise a group, each team having a leader with the ability to perform all functions required of the team. Team members tended to rotate jobs frequently; moreover, this process could occur even within a single shift. There was no need for relief workers because team leaders replaced workers on breaks. Workers in conjunction with engineers determined the pace of the assembly line, thereby allowing workers to control their environment and ultimately to monitor the quality of performance. Team problems were solved by a majority vote, thus eliminating the need for the filing of grievances.

Initially, many work group members and group leaders traveled to Japan for in-depth training. Later in the training process, Japanese technicians visited the United States to oversee the start-up of the NUMMI plant. The

Japanese approach emphasized quality obtained through training, team building, and reinforcement of systems and values. Management practices at the NUMMI facility stressed a cooperative interaction of employees and management to obtain efficiency. Every employee was responsible for creating innovative procedures to improve efficiency. For example, groups frequently evaluated the methods and procedures utilized to improve productivity.

"Jikoda," the quality principle, cannot be overstressed at NUMMI. Many information systems had been set in place to improve quality. Line managers were given the responsibility of strict financial control. This authority was given at lower levels in the management structure because these individuals, being close to the problems, would grasp the implications of potential solutions. Assembly line workers were even allocated the authority to stop production when they believed quality was compromised.

NUMMI stressed performance and continued development. It was believed that individuals, working toward common goals of quality, efficiency, and productivity, would benefit both the corporation and the workers in the organization. In addition, a team effort from the highest level of management down through the assembly line would utilize all the human resources available to the firm.

NUMMI management stressed that every employee was a manager. As such, each employee was expected to accept responsibility for issues which could affect the performance of the organization. Corporate information was made available at all levels to encourage or stimulate creativity in solving problems relating to internal operations. Each worker had the authority and responsibility to order parts and supplies to meet requirements of job performance. This process would reduce inventories while generating pride and commitment.

Transitional Problems.   NUMMI's highest priority was job security, followed by opportunities for growth and advancement. Moreover, the agreement covered alternatives to layoffs. Contracted personnel would be relieved, and management compensation would be slashed before the workforce was reduced. The procedure aimed to maintain morale in difficult periods, but it was very unusual in the United States because equality between labor and management hardly existed in this particular area. Still, the extensive restructuring of the Fremont plant had its share of problems. By late 1986, as the assembly line reached full speed, the atmosphere of trust began to diminish. Although NUMMI produced about 50 percent more cars per person than other U.S. plants, Japanese principles of teamwork, of constant improvement, and of quality became increasingly difficult to maintain. Initial setbacks were due to poor quality, low efficiency, and excessive inventory.

Quality was considered poor because of high absenteeism and continual equipment repairs. Besides that, parts obtained from suppliers lacked quality. Inefficient operations were attributed to excessive inventory and poor utilization of equipment, and poor parts management was identified as the reason for excessive inventory. Workers would thus have a greater variety of parts at their work stations than necessary. Assembly line workers were also slow in responding to the inventory problems.

Management discovered that workers, in general, were slow in evaluating the cause of bottlenecks; thus the team concept needed to be developed further. These problems have been corrected since then, and the plant is still operating at a very high level of efficiency. The quality of parts received from U.S. suppliers have also been approaching that of Japanese suppliers. Since November 1988, when Geo Prizm production cranked up, local content has risen by five points to 65 percent by the end of 1989. NUMMI increased its local content to 75 percent by the end of 1991. Nevertheless, American auto parts suppliers insist that they have been shut out of Japan's $60 billion auto parts market because of the cozy, interlocking relationship between Japanese automakers and their suppliers. American suppliers charge that the Japanese have exported the same system—called keiretsu—to the United States, where it may violate anti-trust laws. They note that dozens of Japanese auto parts suppliers have set up plants clustered around the Japanese auto and truck transplants in the United States.

In addition, union grievances and absenteeism have been drastically reduced. The plant's productivity has met the expectations of all parties when the agreement was signed. Apparent success of this venture has encouraged GM to spread teams to all its 175 plants in early 1987. GM has started teams in a dozen or more components plants. Since January 1987, 30–odd assembly plants have sent groups of managers and UAW officers to study NUMMI. GM also set up an executive task force to develop a "common" GM production system involving everything from materials handling to teamwork. GM has already decided to use NUMMI's five-member teams as its model instead of existing teams which averaged 15 people.

Some UAW members feel that teams are a company trick to get them to work harder, though many welcome teams as a way to insulate themselves from cutbacks. The largest complaint is that union officials no longer act as representatives for workers but rather as mediators between workers and management. As a result, some workers reluctantly go to the union for help. Lower-level managers resist changes because they are reluctant to give up power. Most team systems replace foremen with team leaders who are union members. Those managers who still remain must suggest actions and discuss problems rather than issue orders—a major cultural change for many on the lower rungs of the management ladder.

Unlike conventional auto companies, NUMMI had pledged from the beginning not to lay off any of its 2500 employees; its officials showed good faith in the summer of 1986 when they decided against layoffs after sales of the Nova dropped. Although production decreased from 950 cars a day to 650 cars, the company created new tasks for employees rather than put them out of work, but it still had to face more struggles. NUMMI officials shut down the line for three extra days during the 1987 Christmas holidays and asked workers to take off the time without pay. The slide in sales as well as the threat of layoffs continued unabated as matters were expected to stay the same, at least through 1990. NUMMI lost about $50 million in 1988. Although its production increased from 130,000 units in 1988 to 190,000 units in 1989, the plant also incurred a considerable amount of a net operating loss in 1989. Car sales continued their slump in summer 1992. Analysts started to blame heavy competition, a weak advertising campaign, and an uninspiring design of the Nova for the car's disappointing performance.

Although the first Nova models were produced in 1984, the Nova model was introduced to the public in June 1985 with an advertising theme of "Best of Both Worlds." Market analysts predicted that annual sales of the car, in its fourth year without a style change, would be 250,000 units, but its actual sales decreased more than 50 percent of company expectations to 100,000 units in 1988. General Motors dropped Nova at the end of the 1988 model year. The Nova was replaced in Spring 1989 by a new model called the Geo Prizm. Like the Nova, Prizm is based on Toyota's Corolla model, but with sportier outside styling. As nova sales dropped, the joint venture introduced a Toyota vehicle called the Corolla FX in 1986 and another Toyota vehicle called the 300,000th Car in 1987. The plant added a Toyota pickup truck to the line in August 1991. Toyota spent $350 million to add this second assembly line to build trucks at the joint venture plant. The other assembly line assembles Corollas for Toyota and the similar Geo Prizm for GM.

Table C8-1
NUMMI Milestones

Old GM Plant Opened	1962
Old GM Plant Closed	1982
Joint Venture Announced	February 17, 1983
Company Formed	February 21, 1984
First Nova Produced	December 10, 1984
Second Shift Added	December 10, 1985
Toyota Corolla FX Introduced	September 4, 1986
Toyota 300,000th Car Introduced	February 21, 1987
Nova Production Ended	December 31, 1988
GM Geo Prizm Introduced	Spring, 1989
Toyota Pickup Truck Introduced	August, 1991
12-year Agreement Ends	February 21, 1996

Questions

1. What are the advantages and disadvantages of a joint venture between a multinational company and host–country companies?

2. Why did Japanese auto companies such as Toyota decide to invest in the United States?

3. Compare key characteristics of an American organization with those of a Japanese counterpart.

4. What were the key elements of the 1987 UAW contract with GM, Ford, and Chrysler? Discuss the 1990 UAW contract with the Big Three.

5. Discuss how the Japanese government supports and encourages its businesses.

6. Describe the keiretsu system.

Note

[1] **Data for this case were taken from:** Aaron Bernstein and Wendy Zellner, "Detroit vs. the UAW: At Odds Over Teamwork," *Business Week*, August 24, 1987, pp. 54-55; Clair Brown and Michael Reich, "When Does Union-Management Cooperation Work? A Look at NUMMI and GM-Van Guys," *California Management Review*, Summer 1989, pp. 26-41; Berry Bryan, "What Makes the NUMMI Different," *Iron Age*, September 5, 1986, pp. 27-34; Peter F. Drucker, "What We Can Learn from Japanese Management," *Harvard Business Review*, March-April 1971, pp. 110-122; Melinda Guiles, "GM Puts Captive Imports to New Test," *The Wall Street Journal*, September 16, 1988, p. 21; Richard T. Johnson and William G. Ouchi, "Made in America Under Japanese Management," *Harvard Business Review*, September-October 1974, pp. 61-69; Richard G. Newman and K. Anthony Rhee, "A Case Study of NUMMI and its Suppliers," *Journal of Purchasing and Materials Management*, Fall 1990, pp. 15-20; William G. Ouchi and Alfred M. Jaeger, "Type Z Organization: Stability in the Midst of Mobility," *Academy of Management Review*, April 1978, pp. 305-374; John E. Peterson, "U.S. Parts Firms Fear Japan's Keiretsu," *Detroit News*, July 2, 1990, p. 3E and p. 4E; Bill Powell and Rich Thomas, "Japan: All in the Family," *Newsweek*, June 10, 1991, p. 35 and p. 39; Robert Rehder, "NUMMI, The Best of Both Worlds?" *Management Review*, December 1985, pp. 35-41; Jacob M. Schlesinger, "Job-Security Contracts Are Catching On," *The Wall Street Journal*, June 29, 1987, p. 6; Paul D. Staudohar, "Labor-Management Cooperation at NUMMI," *Labor Law Journal*, January 1991, pp. 57-63; and Stephen E. Weiss, "Creating the GM-Toyota Joint Venture: A Case in Complex Negotiation," *Columbia Journal of World Business*, Summer 1987, pp. 23-35.

Case 9:
Ford Disinvestment in South Africa[1]
(Political Risk Analysis)

Since it left the British Commonwealth in 1961, South Africa's official policy of apartheid has been a principal cause of foreign apprehension about investing in that country. Nevertheless, U.S. direct investment in South Africa had steadily increased over the years, expanding direct investment from $490 million in 1966 to $2.6 billion in 1981. A number of reasons accounted for this rapid expansion. First, relatively high incomes of four million whites provided a fairly large and concentrated local market for the sophisticated goods which U.S. multinational companies wished to sell. Second, instead of risking their capital by direct investment in what they considered to be unstable African-governed countries, U.S. companies hoped to gain a foothold in Africa through what they perceived to be a businesslike, rapidly growing economy run by people very much like themselves. Third, wages of African workers were only between a tenth and a sixth what they were in factories owned by the same companies in the United States. Finally, South Africa provided U.S. companies with a variety of incentive programs for direct investment, such as tax incentives, financial assistance, and protection from nationalization.

Since 1981, however, the value of U.S. investment has dropped because of several nonapartheid factors: the South African economy declined; government regulations changed; and the American dollar gained strength. Decreases in U.S. and other countries' investment in South Africa produced only a few changes in South African racial policy. In 1983 the two-tier exchange-rate system which had been used since 1979 was abolished and exchange controls relaxed; the two-tier exchange-rate system was reintroduced in 1989. Dividends and branch profits could be repatriated without restriction provided that available cash funds financed them.

Apartheid has been a part of South Africa for several decades; changes have been slow in coming. However, opposition has gravitated to the concept of one man, one vote. Black nationalists have repeatedly said that they would settle only for total voting rights, whereas the white government has refused that principle at all costs. Rioting has left thousands dead and has heightened the uncertainty of South Africa's political future. The African National Congress (ANC), the black majority's largest representative body, publicly stated that it opposed capitalism and might nationalize domestic as well as foreign companies. On the other hand, Afrikaner Weerstandsbeweging (AWB), South Africa's far right wing, has warned against the day of black majority rule, and party officials have declared that they are prepared for war to secure a whites-only state.

Massive U.S. corporate withdrawals from South Africa started in 1984 due mainly to the U.S. policy of trade sanctions and disinvestment aimed against that country. This policy was designed to persuade the white-minority government to end apartheid by bringing economic pressure on South Africa. Furthermore, in 1986 Leo H. Sullivan, the author of the Sullivan principles and member of the General Motors Board of Directors, encouraged U.S. companies to withdraw their remaining investments in South Africa. Seven U.S. companies sold or closed down their operations in 1984, 40 followed in 1985, 50 in 1986, 57 in 1987, and 25 in 1988. Goodyear Tire and Rubber Company, one of the largest U.S.-based employers in South Africa, sold its operations in June 1989 and pulled out of the country. The number of U.S. companies with direct investment or employees in South Africa (about 130) is now only two-fifths what it was in 1984.

In 1977 Sullivan authored a Statement of Principles, formerly known as the Sullivan Principles, by which companies pledge to work for equal employment opportunity for blacks and use their influence to end apartheid. Many U.S. companies had used this conduct for more than ten years. Sullivan recognized that too many social injustices existed in South Africa, most revolving around a white minority's rule over a black majority.

In 1986, the United States and the European Community imposed economic sanctions against South Africa along with embargoes on many imports and some exports. Many states have also adopted divestiture laws to pull their pension fund holdings out of companies doing business in South Africa. Everybody admits that sanctions and disinvestment failed to budge the South African government.

The end of communism in Eastern Europe and the dissolution of the Soviet Union had an unexpected result in the view of South African government officials; it accelerated the movement toward a black majority rule. In February 1990, the South African government released Nelson Mandela from prison after 28 years and legalized the African National Congress. In December 1990, the European Community lifted a ban on new investment in South Africa and said it would phase out other embargoes when the white-led government introduces laws to abolish land segregation. In July 1991, the Olympic Committee readmitted South Africa into the Olympic movement after a 21-year suspension; this reinstatement cleared the way for South African athletes to compete in the 1992 games. In August 1991, the United States removed the economic sanctions imposed on South Africa in 1986.

South Africa supports one of the most sophisticated auto markets in the world. The country's multi-lane highways are packed with a variety of automobiles equal to any in the world. About ten major automobile manufacturers—mostly foreign-controlled—assemble cars in 40 models with more than 250 variations. Those people who can afford them—and very few blacks can buy new cars—can select an Alfa Romeo, BMW, Fiat, Ford, Nissan, Toyota, Chevy, or Mercedes. The automotive industry is critical to South Africa's economy; it dominates the country's manufacturing sector.

The Big Three in South Africa. Until recently, the three largest automobile companies in the United States—General Motors, Ford, and Chrysler—had come to play a crucial role in the South African economy. They were among the oldest dominant auto companies in South Africa until the late 1970s. They competed for government contracts to sell vehicles to the army and police. Ford built the first assembly plant in South Africa in 1923, and General Motors entered the market three years later. Chrysler established its first plant in South Africa in 1958 outside Cape Town. The automobile companies in South Africa were criticized about their labor practices and the economic support their operations gave to the South African government.

In 1977, church groups affiliated with the Interfaith Center on Corporate Responsibility asked Ford and other U.S. companies to terminate their South African operations unless apartheid ended. Ford emphasized its opposition to apartheid and its intention to obey completely both the Sullivan Principles and the letter of U.S. law. However, until the mid-1980s the company resisted suggestions that it withdraw from South Africa on the ground that its continued participation in the South African economy could significantly affect social and economic changes.

Ford in South Africa. In 1923 Ford Motor of Canada began operations in South Africa. The structure of Ford in South Africa changed in 1985 when Ford merged with Anglo American Corporation to form the South African Motor Company (SAMCOR). There is no official printed data available on the profitability of SAMCOR because it is a non-reporting entity. The purpose of the merger was to reduce the overcapacity of production in the country.

Ford Motor's 1981 Annual Report summarized sales in South Africa:

Ford of South Africa sold a record 66,700 cars and trucks in 1981, up 13 percent from 1980. New car sales were 50,640 surpassing the 50,000 mark for the first time. Contina remained the best selling car in its segment with sales of 22,000. Sales of the new Escort introduced in the Spring of 1981 were 21,600, up 37 percent from 1980.

From 1972 to 1981 Ford remained an automotive power in the South African market. Table C9–1 shows that sales of vehicles in South Africa were actually moving counter cyclical to those in the North American market from 1979 to 1981.

In the 1981 Annual Report, the Ford Motor Company announced that it was among 135 U.S. companies endorsing the Sullivan Principles. It considered itself to be in the highest category of companies making progress toward fulfilling the goals of these principles.

In 1987 Ford officially withdrew its 42 percent stake in SAMCOR; 24 percent of SAMCOR was given to an employee-controlled trust owned by its 4,900 workers. This transaction was valued at $52 million to Ford. The remaining 18 percent of SAMCOR was sold to Anglo American Corporation for $1. Ford also committed to placing $4 million of its own funds into

Table C9-1
Auto Sales of Ford Motor Company

Year	In South Africa	In North America
1972	33,178	3.8 million
1973	35,473	4.1
1974	40,155	3.6
1975	36,378	3.0
1976	33,638	3.5
1977	34,156	4.4
1978	46,201	4.5
1979	40,447	3.6
1980	52,671	2.4
1981	66,962	2.3

community trusts. Anglo American Corporation threatened to shut down operations of SAMCOR and thus forced Ford to forgive $61 million in debt to preserve the 4,900 jobs.

Ford's disinvestment produced some positive results. First, it saved 4,900 jobs. Second, two seats on SAMCOR's Board of Directors were to be represented by the 4,900 workers. Third, Ford donated $4 million to community projects. Fourth, Ford agreed to provide technical assistance to insure the continued success of SAMCOR. On the other side of the scale, some members of Congress have accused Ford of violating the 1986 Anti-Apartheid Act by forgiving $61 million to ensure the future of SAMCOR.

Ford Motor issued its official statement on South Africa in its 1987 annual report:

> After complex negotiations Ford completed an agreement to divest its 42 percent share of South African Motor Corporation. Ford of Canada is donating a 24 percent equity interest in SAMCOR to a trust that will be controlled by SAMCOR's 4,900 employees. The remaining 18 percent equity is being transferred to the majority stockholders, Anglo American Corporation and its associates. The plan which preserves as many as 17,000 jobs and the livelihood of about 100,000 people, gained support of black labor and political leaders in South Africa as well as many concerned Americans.

Table C9-2
Timeline

1923	Ford begins South African operations.
1961	South Africa leaves British Commonwealth and establishes apartheid.
1977	Sullivan Principles established.
1981	American investment reaches its peak of $2.6 billion.
1983	South Africa abolishes its two-tiered exchange-rate system.
1984	America begins push of economic pressure to end apartheid.
1985	Ford creates SAMCOR. South Africa eases exchange controls.
1986	U.S. Congress outlaws any new South African investment and bans most imports from the country.
1987	Ford officially withdraws from SAMCOR.
1989	South Africa adopts a two-tier exchange-rate system.
1990	South Africa releases Nelson Mandela from jail and legalizes the African National Congress.
1991	The United States and the European Community removed most economic sanctions against South Africa.
1991	The Olympic Committee reinstated South Africa.
1992	South Africa ends apartheid.

Questions

1. Discuss some of the major risks that foreign companies face in their operations in South Africa.

2. Why has Ford pulled out of South Africa?

3. Discuss the impact of the two-tiered exchange-rate system on a company's cash flow projections.

4. In his 1991 article on South Africa's futures, Francis Fukuyama suggested three scenarios: the future South Africa will be (1) something like Germany, (2) the nightmare of Lebanon, and (3) a Latin American model. Summarize this article: Francis Fukuyama, "South Africa's Alternative Futures," *The Wall Street Journal*, June 17, 1991, p. A10.

5. Discuss some case examples in political risk using the following articles: Richard Borsuk, "Investing in Indonesia: Bring Patience and Be Prepared for Risks," *The Wall Street Journal*, September 20, 1991, p. R6; Thomas Kamm, "Brazil Deposit Freeze Jars Foreign Firms," *The Wall Street Journal*, May 8, 1990, p. A20; and Sue Shellenbarger, "Off the Blacklist: Did Hospital Supplier Dump Its Israel Plant to Win Arab's Favor," *The Wall Street Journal*, May 1, 1990, p. A1 and p. A10.

Note

[1] **Data for this case were taken from:** David Beaty and Oren Harari, "Divestment and Disinvestment from South Africa: A Reappraisal," *California Management Review*, Summer 1987, pp. 31-48; Thomas F. O'Boyle, "Few U.S. Businesses Plan to Reenter South Africa Despite Promised Reforms," *The Wall Street Journal*, February 6, 1990, p. A6; William D. Coplin and Michael K. O'Leary, "1991 World Political Risk Forecast," *Planning Review*, April 1991, pp. 16-18; Francis Fukuyama, "South Africa's Alternative Futures," *The Wall Street Journal*, June 17, 1991, p. A10; John E. Peterson, "Free at Last: Mandela," *Detroit News*, February 17, 1990, pp. 6A-7A. "They're Getting Out of S. Africa," *USA Today*, Tuesday, June 14, 1988, p. 7B; "Sanctions Bite Back," *The Wall Street Journal,* Thursday, September 8, 1988, p. 28; and David Versical and Jeremy Sinek, "Ford Sheds S. Africa Holdings; Workers to Benefit," *Automotive News*, November 30, 1987.

Case 10:
World Electric Corporation[1]
(International Finance Function)

The World Electric Corporation is one of the world's leading electronics companies. The scope of its activities has changed dramatically since Robert Guin started the company in Southland, England, in 1960. Product diversification and geographic dispersion of manufacturing facilities have occurred more or less continuously. World Electric manufactures a broad line of electronically oriented consumer and industrial goods ranging from small transistor radios to complete cyclotron installations; it now produces more than 7,000 different products. Although the company is headquartered in London, England, a substantial part of its manufacturing activity is carried out in other countries. Its product line, in whole or in part, is sold and serviced in virtually every country around the world. World Electric has maintained a strong financial staff at the parent company level for a quarter of a century. The parent company has controlled virtually all international treasury decisions. Under this highly centralized system, the company achieved a high growth rate in total assets, earnings, and stock prices in the last 25 years.

However, these favorable trends were reversed in 1985. Faced with major problems, the company expected an uncertain future. Unfavorable trends started when its major competitors reported record earnings and major expansion programs. This unfavorable situation persisted to early 1990, at which time a new president, Thomas Hart, was appointed by the board of directors. Mr. Hart graduated from a major private university in Michigan with an M.B.A. in finance. After five years of experience in international banking with one of the major banks in New York, he joined the international finance staff of Westinghouse and served in a variety of positions within the international division of the company for 20 years. Mr. Hart knew that most major companies in the field decentralized their operations even further some years ago as they became larger and more diversified. His intuition was that the principal reason for the poor performance of World Electric was its outdated organizational structure in international finance. He could not believe that the company had maintained such a highly centralized financial organization for so long in spite of 30 years of steady growth and diversification into new products and foreign markets.

Before Mr. Hart took over, he knew that his predecessor had been fired for inept international treasury management. For his part, he decided to analyze "A Set of New Operational Guidelines" issued by his predecessor in January 1992 but never implemented. This plan was designed to improve planning, budgeting, and control; it had five major provisions:

1. Growth rate targets for each foreign subsidiary's sales and earnings would be set by the central headquarters' staff in accordance with the corporate strategic plan. The foreign subsidiary would then be required to develop programs to meet these targets.

2. To improve the quality of the foreign subsidiary's budgets, the foreign subsidiary manager would be informed that the continuance of wide variances between the projected and actual budget figures would result in dismissal.

3. A system would be instituted under which funds would be allocated to foreign subsidiaries on the basis of their average return on investment (ROI) during the last four quarters. Because funds are short, foreign subsidiaries with high ROI would get most of the available cash.

4. Only about two-thirds of each subsidiary manager's present compensation would be received as salary. The rest would be in the form of a bonus related to the subsidiary's average ROI for the quarter.

5. Each foreign subsidiary would have to submit all capital expenditure requests, production schedules, and price changes to the central office for approval.

After studying the operations of the company for a number of weeks, Mr. Hart developed three propositions: (1) The treasury's function had become too complex and diffuse to be managed effectively from the center; (2) the treasurer was too much preoccupied with tax savings and too little with reducing the cost of funds; (3) the financial data essential for use by the treasurer's office was considerably different from the data needed for the performance of the controller's function. On the basis of these findings, he proposed major organizational changes: break up the international division into several foreign area divisions, each of which would have status on a par with a U.S. product division and create a new layer of treasurers, controllers, and tax attorneys at the area division level. However, he decided to postpone the ultimate choice of a particular organizational structure for the company until the treasurer further analyzed a number of important decision variables, such as transfer pricing and performance evaluation, exchange exposure management, acquisition of funds, positioning of funds, and tax planning.

Questions

1. Do you think that the new procedures issued by Mr. Hart's predecessor would improve the accuracy of budget forecasts? Should all foreign subsidiaries be expected to maintain the same degree of accuracy? In what other ways might the budgets be made?

2. What problems would be associated with the use of ROI criterion for allocating funds among foreign subsidiaries and rewarding foreign subsidiary managers?

3. Discuss centralization vs. decentralization as it impinges on decisions relating to transfer pricing and performance evaluation, exchange exposure management, acquisition of funds, positioning of funds, and tax planning.

4. What do you think about the three propositions developed by Mr. Hart?

5. Digital Equipment Corporation undertook a major reorganization in 1982 and decentralized its finance functions in 1984. Discuss Digital Equipment's reorganization as a case study. (See references.)

Note

[1] **This is a fictitious case and draws heavily upon the following two cases:** Raymond Vernon, "Sola Chemical Company," in Gunter Dufey and Ian H. Giddy, eds., *50 Cases in International Finance*, Reading, MA: Addison-Wesley, 1987, pp. 419–434; and Roy L. Crum and Eugene F. Brigham, "Moseley Vault and Alarm Company, Inc.," *Cases in Managerial Finance*, Chicago: Dryden, 1987, pp. 43–50. **For Question 5,** see: "A New Strategy for No. 2. in Computers," *Business Week*, May 2, 1983, pp. 66–75; ; David A. Buchanan and James McCalman, *High Performance Work Systems: The Digital Experience*, London: Routledge, 1989; Jagannath Dubashi, "Hitting the Dirt," *Financial World*, April 18, 1989, pp. 68–69; Susan Fraker, "How DEC Got Decked," *Forbes*, September 22, 1986, pp. 160–161; Michael Goold, "Strategic Control in the Decentralized Firm," *Solan Management Review*, Winter 1991, pp. 69–81; Diane Harris, "The Infatuation with DEC," *Financial World*, February 28, 1983, pp. 14–20; Dyan Machan, "DEC's Democracy," *Forbes*, March 23, 1987, pp. 154–156; Bruce J. Ryan, "DEC's Decentralized Financial System Puts Strategy Above Controls," *Financial Executive*, July/August 1989, pp. 42–46; Harold Seneker, "Mid-Life Crisis," *Forbes*, May 21, 1984, pp. 32–34; and "What Next for Digital?" *Business Week*, May 16, 1988, pp. 88–96.

Case 11:
Advanced Technology Company[1]
(Ethics in International Finance)

The Executives Committee of Advanced Technology (AT)—Robert Smith, President; Linda Humphrey, Vice President of Finance; Sam Miller, Vice President of Marketing; and Susan Crum, Vice President of Production—scheduled a luncheon meeting on September 1, 1993, to discuss two major problems for the welfare of the company: (1) how to finance the rapid expansion of its production facilities and (2) how to cope with a growing competition in its major overseas markets. In addition, the Department of Justice requested AT to answer several questions about bribes, gifts, slush funds, and grease payments in relation to its foreign sales. This inquiry started in response to a 100-page complaint by its overseas competitor which alleged that AT violated the Foreign Corrupt Practices Act of 1977.

AT has recently enjoyed a rapid growth in business. The company anticipated substantial increases in sales for the next few years. However, it must solve two major problems—capacity and strong competition in foreign operations—if it is to maintain fast sales growth for years to come.

AT produces office automation systems and equipment. In addition to introducing a newly designed mainframe computer, the company aggressively increased research in mini-computers and word processors. These products are in high growth markets, and the firm's expenditures for these projects have more than proven their worth. In fact, the company's major problem has been to increase production fast enough to meet demand of its Asian customers. The company's capacity has expanded steadily since 1980, but it has often lost sales because of insufficient production.

The industry recognizes AT as one of the fastest growing companies in the market. Experts in the high-tech industry have projected for the next ten years a potential bonanza for mini computers and word processors. Thus, the company plans to invest heavily in research and development for the next five years. It also plans to increase production quickly by acquiring existing computer manufacturing firms and by establishing new production facilities.

AT is a multinational company with headquarters in Los Angeles, California. The company has five manufacturing locations in the United States and three abroad, with offices in 13 countries. Approximately 40 percent of its sales came from foreign operations in 1992—primarily South America and Asia where the company had recently faced stiff competition from its larger rivals, such as IBM, Digital Equipment, and Olivetti. The company depended on distributors for most of its overseas sales.

Conflict of Interest in Financial Affairs.

Thomas Nickerson is a Special Assistant to the Vice President of Finance, Linda Humphrey. He graduated from a major university in St. Louis, Missouri with an MBA in Finance. After two years of experience with one of the Big Eight CPA firms in St. Louis, he joined the accounting staff and served in a variety of accounting and finance positions for five years. He was appointed two years ago as Special Assistant to Ms. Humphrey at an unusually high salary mainly because of his outstanding financial and communication talents. Thomas Nickerson has a wife, five children, and a home with a $450,000 mortgage. His deep debt and huge financial needs hardly matter to him because he has a promising future at the company.

Ms. Humphrey approached Thomas with a special task on August 1, 1993. She informed him that she met with other vice presidents and decided to purchase Computer Engineering to alleviate the capacity problem. She further stated that the acquisition will be highly advantageous for AT, but she needs to convince two members of the Board of Directors. Then she instructed him to prepare a report justifying the acquisition of the company. Under the terms, AT will offer Computer Engineering two million shares of its stock. The market price of the stock is $20 per share.

Normally Thomas would have welcomed the assignment, but this one made him uneasy. Computer Engineering's financial statements indicated poor performance as compared with comparable companies in the field. He knew that Ms. Humphrey and other vice presidents helped current top executives of Computer Engineering set up their company. He suspected that vice presidents of AT owned sizable blocks of Computer Engineering stock which was not publicly traded. To establish a fair market price for Computer Engineering, he has compiled the statistics presented in Table C11-1. High Tech is more similar to Computer Engineering than any other company whose stock is traded in the public market.

Ethics Versus Profits in Global Business.

The Foreign Corrupt Practices Act of 1977 (FCPA) has encouraged U.S. companies to introduce policies against corrupt foreign payments and to improve internal controls. The FCPA bans illegal payments to foreign officials, monitors accounting procedures, and levies heavy penalties for violations. The FCPA forced AT to think about its way of doing business overseas. The company had expanded its foreign operations very quickly. In the 1960s, less than 1 percent of its sales came from foreign operations, but by the late 1970s its foreign operations accounted for 30 percent of total sales.

Just like many other companies, AT had undertaken positive steps to prevent illegal payments to foreign officials and to improve internal control. In 1978, the company published its first corporate code, along with two separate area codes: one for the U.S. and another one for the foreign area. The code of business conduct for overseas employees reflected most provisions of the FCPA so that the company would not have any trouble with the law.

Table C11-1
Key Statistics for Computer Engineering and High Tech

Variables	Computer Engineering	High Tech
Earnings per share	$1.00	$2.00
Dividend per share in year 1	$0.75	$1.00
Annual dividend growth rate	0.04	0.07
Price per share	?	$20.00
Book value per share	$8.00	$10.00
Cost of equity	?	0.15
Number of shares outstanding	1.0 million	1.2 million

Marketing Vice President Miller has been under heavy pressure from President Smith to increase the company's foreign sales by 30 percent per year for the next five years. Mr. Miller thought that when in Rome, some do as the Romans do. In other words, he did not hesitate to call the FCPA "bad business" and "unnecessary." Miller felt that the FCPA should be repealed for several reasons. First, it forced U.S. companies to increase audit costs substantially. Second, the Department of Justice and the SEC failed to establish clear guidelines. Third, it put U.S. companies at a competitive disadvantage. Fourth, in many countries, foreign payments are not outlawed, but instead are encouraged. Fifth, the FCPA was unnecessary because U.S. law enforcement agencies already had many statutes to prevent illegal foreign payments by U.S. companies.

Mr. Miller reflected on the report he would present to the Executive Committee. The purpose of this report was to make certain that AT was complying with its corporate code of conduct. There was, however, one situation that required a tough decision. This particular situation was considered an acceptable practice in the countries where it occurred, but he did not know how he would handle specific questions if they should come up.

Kevin Hart is the exclusive distributor for Advanced Technology products in South American countries. He has a reputation for reliability and efficiency. But the most recent audit suggested that he has corruptly influenced customs officials to obtain lower duty rates for AT's products. In doing so, he violated both the FCPA and the company's code of conduct.

AT had asked Kevin to agree in writing to abide by the code, but he refused to do so. He argued that these "grease payments" were customary in these countries. He insisted that he could not compete effectively without them. Kevin had represented AT for many years and generated approximately $10 million worth of business per year for the company. His exclusive dealership contract would be up for renewal in a few months. AT suggested that it might refuse to renew its contract unless he agreed to abide by the code. Mr. Miller knew that it would be difficult to resolve this problem while he was under heavy pressure to increase the company's overseas sales by 30 percent per year.

Questions

1. Use the data in Table C11–1 to estimate the market value of Computer Engineering in the following three ways: (1) price–earnings ratio, (2) market value/book value, and (3) dividend growth model.

2. List and discuss options available to Thomas Nickerson.

3. Discuss the two major sections of the FCPA—antibribery and accounting.

4. List and discuss pros and cons concerning corporate codes of conduct.

5. If you were Sam Miller, what would you do about the situation in these South American countries?

Note

¹ **This is a fictious case. Data for this case were taken from:** Arthur Aronoff, "Complying the Foreign Corrupt Practices Act," *Business America*, February 11, 1991, pp. 10–11; General F. Cavanagh, *American Business Values*, Englewood Cliffs, NJ: Prentice Hall, 1984; Suk H. Kim, "On Repealing the Foreign Corrupt Practices Act: Survey and Assessment," *Columbia Journal of World Business*, Fall 1981, pp. 16–21; Catherine C. Langlois and Bodo B. Schlegelmilch, "Do Corporate Codes of Ethics Reflect National Character?" *Journal of International Business Studies*, Fourth Quarter 1990, pp. 519–540; Manuel Velasquez, "Unicomp, Inc.," St. Charles, Illinois: Center for Professional Education, Arthur Anderson & Co., 1990; and David Whiteside and Kenneth E. Goodpaster, "Dow Corning Corporation: Business Conduct and Global Values," in Kenneth E. Goodpaster and Thomas R. Piper, eds., *Managerial Decision Making and Ethical Values*, Boston: Publishing Division/Marketing Department, Harvard Business School, 1991.

Glossary

Accommodating (Compensating) Transactions: Those transactions necessary to account or compensate for differences between international payments and receipts. These transactions are used to eliminate international disequilibrium.

Accounting (Translation) Exposure: Financial statement items to be exposed to foreign exchange risk whenever a change in exchange rates alters their value.

Acquisition: The purchase of one company by another company.

Advising Bank: A bank which notifies the beneficiary of a letter of credit without adding its own commitment to that of the issuing bank.

Affiliate: A foreign operation formed as either a branch or a subsidiary.

African Development Bank (AfDB): A regional development bank for Africa established in 1964 and located in Abidjan, Ivory Coast.

Agency: An office established by a foreign bank to offer a limited range of banking services such as loans in that area.

Agency for International Development (AID): An office within the U.S. State Department established in 1961 to carry out nonmilitary U.S. foreign assistance programs.

Agency Theory: A theory that deals with a conflict of interest between managers and stockholders.

Agreement Corporation: A bank chartered by a state to operate in international banking under an agreement with the Board of Governors of the Federal Reserve System.

Allocation Efficiency: The apportionment of resources among firms and industries to obtain the production of goods and services most wanted by society (consumers).

Antidumping Duty: A custom duty imposed on an imported product whose price is lower than that of the same product in the home market.

Arab League: A political organization of 22 North African and Middle Eastern Arab countries.

Arm's–Length Price: The price that would take place between unrelated parties.

Appreciation: A rise in the value of a currency against other currencies.

Arbitrage: The purchase of something in one market and its sale in another market to take advantage of price differential.

Asian Development Bank (ADB): A regional development bank for Asia formed in 1966 by several Asian countries in partnership with the United States, Canada, and a number of European countries.

Asian Dollar Market: Market in Asia where banks accept deposits and make loans denominated in U.S. dollars.

Ask Price: Price at which a trader of foreign exchange is willing to sell a particular currency.

Association of South East Asian Nations (ASEAN): An economic integration agreement among a group of Asian countries.

Autonomous Transactions: Those transactions that occur due to self-interests. They include exports, imports, unilateral transfers, and investments.

Average Rate of Return: The ratio of the average annual profit after taxes to the average net investment.

Back-to-Back Loan: A loan in which two companies in two different countries borrow each other's currency for a given period of time and repay the other's currency at maturity.

Balance of Payments: A financial statement that records all transactions between a given country and the rest of the world during a specified period of time.

Balance Sheet Hedge: A method designed to protect the value of a company's exposed assets. It involves the selection of the currency in which monetary assets and liabilities are denominated so that an exchange rate change would make exposed assets equal to exposed liabilities.

Bank of International Settlements (BIS): A bank in Switzerland which facilitates transactions among central banks.

Bankers' Acceptance: A draft accepted by a bank. When a bank accepts a draft, it promises to honor the draft at maturity.

Barter: An exchange of goods and services between two countries without the involvement of finance.

Basis Point: One-hundredth of one percent or 0.0001.

Bearer: The person who holds an instrument.

Benelux Countries: The countries of Belgium, the Netherlands, and Luxembourg.

Beta: Second letter of Greek alphabet, used as a statistical measure of systematic risk in the capital asset pricing model.

Bid Price: The price at which a trader is willing to buy a given item such as foreign exchange.

Big Bang: The October 1986 liberalization of the London capital markets.

Bilateral Netting: Netting method used for transactions between two related units.

Bill of Exchange (draft): An order written by an exporter that requires an importer to pay a specified amount of money at a specified time.

Bill of Lading: A shipping document issued to the exporting firm or its bank by a common carrier that transports the goods.

Black Market: An illegal foreign exchange market.

Bloc: A group of countries tied by treaty or agreement for mutual support or interest.

Blocked Funds: Financial assets which cannot be repatriated because the local monetary authorities forbid their conversion into foreign exchange.

Book Value: The asset value recorded at historical cost.

Branch: A foreign bank that provides a full range of banking services under the name and guarantee of the parent bank.

Bretton Woods Agreement: An agreement signed by the representatives of 44 countries at Bretton Woods, New Hampshire, in 1944 to establish a system of fixed exchange rates.

Broker: An intermediary in the foreign exchange market.

Buy–American Policy: A policy that requires the recipients of American aids to buy goods and services from American companies.

Call: An option to buy a foreign currency or other financial assets.

Capital Account: In the balance of payments, the section that records the net changes in loans, investments, and other transfers of financial assets. The capital account consists of two major sections: long-term flows and short-term flows.

Capital Asset Pricing Model (CAPM): A theoretical model implying that the total risk of a security consists of systematic (undiversifiable) risk and unsystematic (diversifiable) risk.

Capital Budgeting: The entire process of planning expenditures whose benefits are expected to extend beyond one year.

Capital Gains and Losses: Gains and losses on sales of capital assets such as stocks and property.

Capital Market: The market for long-term funds such as bonds, common stock, and preferred stock.

Capital Structure: The combination of long-term debt, preferred stock, common stock, paid-in surplus, and retained earnings.

Cartel: A formal written or oral agreement among firms or countries to set the price of the product and the outputs of individual cartel members or divide the market for the product geographically.

Cash Center: A geographic location where all idle funds from the subsidiaries of a multinational company are maintained until they are needed.

Cashier's Check: A bill of exchange (draft) issued by the cashier of a bank, for the bank, upon the bank.

CBD: Cash before delivery.

Central Bank: The official bank of a government, such as the Federal Reserve Bank in the United States or the Bank of Japan.

Centrally Planned Economy: An economy where resources are controlled and allocated by the central government.

CEO: The chief executive officer of a company.

Certainty Equivalent Approach: A method used to adjust for project risk. It adjusts for risk in the numerator of the net present value formula.

Certificate of Deposits (CDs): A time deposit with a specific future maturity date.

CHPAS: Clearing House Payments Assistance System. It is used to move funds between London offices of most financial institutions.

CHIPS: Clearing House Interbank Payments System. A computerized clearing system used by banks in New York to settle interbank foreign exchange obligations.

Closed Economy: An economy which neither exports nor imports goods and services.

COD: Cash on delivery.

Collecting Bank: Any bank that handles an item for collection.

Common Market: A form of regional economic integration in which countries abolish internal tariffs among themselves, levy common external tariffs, and eliminate restrictions on the flow of factors of production.

Comparable Uncontrolled Price Method: The method allowed by the Internal Revenue Service to determine the arm's-length price of intracompany transactions. Under this method, uncontrolled sales are comparable to controlled sales if their physical property and circumstances are identical with the physical property and circumstances of controlled sales.

Comparative Advantage: The relative advantage of a country in producing goods or services.

Compensation (Buy–Back) Agreement: A form of countertrade. Under this form of countertrade, the initial seller receives compensation in products that arise out of the original sale.

Competitive Trade: A practice whereby two countries buy from each other similar goods which both can produce.

Confirmed Letter of Credit: The letter of credit confirmed by a bank other than the opening bank. Thus, the confirmed letter of credit is a firm obligation of two banks.

Confirming Bank: A bank that confirms a letter of credit issued by another bank.

Consignment: The delivery of goods into the possession of another for the purpose of sale.

Consolidation: An accounting process in which financial statements of related entities are added together to produce a unified set of financial statements.

Consortium Bank: A bank formed by a group of banks from different countries to handle large international loans.

Controlled Corporation: A foreign corporation in which more than 50 percent of the voting shares are owned by U.S. shareholders.

Convertibility: The ability to exchange one currency for another currency. The second currency must be convertible without restrictions.

Convertible Currency: The currency which may be converted into other currencies without government restrictions.

Cooley Amendment Funds: Local currency funds received in payment for agricultural products sold by the United States under U.S. aid programs.

Correlation Coefficient: Measures the degree of correlation between two securities.

Correspondent Bank: A bank located in any other city, state, or country that provides a service for another bank.

Cost of Capital: The required rate of return that the company must earn on its projects for the market value of its common stock to remain unchanged.

Cost and Freight (C&F): The FOB (free on board) and the cost of transportation to the named point of destination.

Cost, Insurance and Freight (CIF): The FOB (free on board) value, the cost of transportation, insurance premiums, and other costs incurred in connection with the shipment from the time of loading in the export country to its arrival at the named port of destination.

Cost Method: The method used in consolidating the financial statements of affiliates into those of a U.S. parent when the parent owns less than 20 percent of the affiliate. Under this method, the parent carries its affiliates at the initial investment plus its dividends received.

Cost Plus Method: The method allowed by the Internal Revenue Service to determine the arm's-length price of intracompany transactions. Under this method, an arm's-length price is obtained by adding an appropriate markup to the seller's cost.

Council for Mutual Economic Assistance (COMECON): Economic integration arrangement among East-bloc countries.

Counterpurchase: A form of countertrade that involves a standard hard-currency export but where the seller agrees to a return purchase with a minimum quantity of specified goods from the buyer.

Countertrade: International trade arrangements that are variations on the idea of barter.

Countervailing Duty: An import charge used to offset an export subsidy by another country.

Covered-Interest Arbitrage: Portfolio investment in a foreign country "covered" by forward sale of the foreign currency to eliminate foreign exchange risk.

Covering: The purchase or sale of foreign exchange forward to protect a foreign exchange loss in the conversion from one currency to another.

Crawling Band: A proposal under which each parity level would be adjusted upward or downward once a year and which the actual exchange rate would be allowed to fluctuate within a wider band from this parity level.

Crawling Peg: A proposal for regular change in the par value according to an agreed upon formula.

Credit Swap: A hedging device that involves a simultaneous spot and forward loan transaction between a private company and a bank of a foreign country.

Credit Tranche: The amount that a member country of the International Monetary Fund can borrow from the IMF above the gold tranche.

Cross Rate: The exchange rate between two currencies when it is obtained from the rates of these two currencies in terms of a third currency.

Culture Shock: A generalized trauma one experiences in a new or different culture.

Currency Cocktail Bond: Bond denominated in a basket of currencies.

Currency Futures: An obligation to buy and sell a specified amount of a foreign currency for delivery at a specified date.

Currency Futures Options: The right, but not the obligation, to buy or sell a futures contract of a foreign currency at any time through a specified period.

Currency Options: The right, but not the obligation, to buy or sell a specified amount of a foreign currency at a specified price through a specified date.

Currency Swap: An agreement made between parties to exchange one currency with another for a specified period of time and then exchange the latter currency with the former currency.

Current Account: In the balance of payments, the section which includes merchandise exports and imports, earnings and expenditures for invisible trade items (services), and unilateral transfer items.

Current/Noncurrent Method: A method that translates the financial statements of a foreign affiliate into the parent reporting currency. All current items are translated at the current exchange rate, and all noncurrent items are translated at their historical exchange rates.

Current Rate Method: A method that translates the financial statements of a foreign affiliate into the parent reporting currency. All assets and liabilities are translated at the currency exchange rate.

Customs Union: A form of regional economic integration which eliminates tariffs among member countries and establishes common external tariffs.

Customs Valuation: The value on which customs authorities charge tariffs. If values are set arbitrarily high, tariffs will also be higher.

Debit: In the balance of payments, the part of an international transaction that increases assets of a country and reduces liabilities or net worth of the country.

Debt–Equity Swap: An exchange of foreign debt for equity in local companies.

Delphi Technique: A technique which combines the views of independent experts in order to obtain the degree of political risk on a given foreign project or a particular foreign country.

Depreciation: A decrease in the foreign exchange market value of a currency.

Devaluation: An official reduction in the par value of a currency by the government of that currency.

Development Bank: A bank established to support the economic development of underdeveloped areas through long-term loans.

Direct Investment: Equity investment such as the purchase of stock, the acquisition of an entire firm, or the establishment of a new subsidiary. The U.S. Department of Commerce defines direct investment as investment in either real capital assets or financial assets with a minimum of 10 percent equity ownership in a foreign firm.

Dirty (Managed) Floating System: A system in which exchange rates are allowed to change according to market forces but governments intervene to prevent undesired fluctuations. The monetary system since 1973 is sometimes called a dirty floating system because most industrial countries have permitted their currencies to fluctuate with frequent government intervention in the foreign exchange market.

Discounted Cash Flow Approaches: Net present value and internal rate of return methods which take into account the time value of money.

Diversification Strategy: A term used in international business to mean that a company produces or sells in many countries.

Divestment: Reduction in the amount of investment.

Division of Labor: An economic theory which allows each person or nation to utilize any peculiar differences in skills and resources in the most economic manner. Division of labor is frequently called specialization of function.

Documentary Draft: A draft which accompanies such documents as bills of lading, commercial invoices, and other documents.

Domestic International Sales Corporation (DISC): A subsidiary of a U.S. corporation which is allowed to defer its tax.

Double-Entry Accounting: An accounting principle that requires each transaction to be recorded as debits and credits of an equal amount.

Draft (Bill of Exchange): An order written by a seller that requires a buyer to pay a specified amount of money at a specified time.

Drawee Bank: A bank upon which a draft is drawn and which thus must pay. Such a bank is often called a paying bank.

Drawer Bank: A bank which draws (writes) a draft offering payment.

Dumping: A practice of selling a product in a foreign market at a price lower than that of the same product in the home market.

Duty: A government tax (tariff) levied on goods shipped internationally.

Eclectic Theory: A theory that tries to combine both trade and investment theories.

Economic Exposure: Expected future cash flows whose real values may be changed because of exchange rate changes.

Economic Integration: Cooperation among different countries: eliminating trade barriers among member countries and bringing separate economies together to form one large market.

Economic Union: A form of regional economic integration which combines common-market characteristics with harmonization of economic policy.

Economies of Scale: A reduction in average cost per unit as sales volume or output increases.

Edge Act Corporation: A subsidiary of a U.S. commercial bank created under the Edge Act of 1916.

Efficient Exchange Market: The exchange market where exchange rates reflect available information and market prices adjust quickly to new information. In the efficient exchange market, market participants buy and sell foreign currencies in a way that eliminates all profits in excess of the minimum required to sustain their continued participation.

Efficient Frontier: The locus of all efficient portfolios.

Efficient Portfolio: A portfolio that provides the highest return for a given level of risk or the smallest amount of risk for a given level of return.

Elasticity: The degree of responsiveness in one variable to changes in another. For example, in international trade the price elasticity measures the degree of responsiveness in exports or imports to changes in prices.

Embargo: A practice that prohibits all trade.

Equilibrium Exchange Rate: The exchange rate at the intersection of the demand curve for and the supply curve of foreign exchange.

Equity Method: The method used in consolidating the financial statements of affiliates into those of a U.S. parent when the parent owns between 20 and 50 percent of the affiliate. Under this method, the parent carries its affiliates at the initial cost of the investment plus its proportionate share of profits or losses.

Eurobond: A bond that is sold in a currency other than that of the country of issue.

Eurocurrency: A currency deposited in a bank located in a country other than the country issuing the currency.

Eurodollar: Dollar-denominated deposits in banks outside the United States. These banks may be foreign banks or foreign branches of a U.S. bank.

European Bank for Reconstruction and Development (EBRD): A regional development bank established in 1990 by 42 countries for emerging democracies in Eastern Europe.

European Community (EC): An organization formed in 1957 by France, Germany, Italy, Belgium, the Netherlands, and Luxembourg to remove trade barriers among the member countries. The United Kingdom, Ireland, Denmark, Greece, Portugal, and Spain joined later.

European Currency Unit (ECU): An artificial currency unit fixed in terms of the currencies of the nine EC countries.

European Free Trade Association (EFTA): A form of regional economic integration involving a group of central European countries which are not members of the EC.

European Investment Bank (EIB): A regional development bank established in 1958 by members of the European Community.

European Monetary System: A complex exchange rate and intervention system adopted in 1978 by EC countries to replace the snake.

Exchange Rate: The price of one currency expressed in terms of another currency.

Exchange Rate Risk: The variability of a company's earnings that may occur due to uncertain exchange rate changes.

Excise Tax: A tax on various commodities within a country, such as tobacco and alcoholic beverages.

Exercise Price (Strike Price): The price at which the owner of a currency call option is allowed to buy a foreign currency or the price at which the owner of a currency put option is allowed to sell a foreign currency.

Expatriates: Noncitizens of the country where they are working.

Export–Import Bank (Exim Bank): A U.S. government agency established to promote U.S. exports.

Export Trading Company: A trading company sanctioned by law to become involved in international trade as an agent or a direct outlet. The U.S. Trading Company Act of 1982 relaxed the anti–trust law and the bank holding company act.

External Debt: Public debt owed to foreign citizens, firms, and institutions.

Factor: A financial institution which buys a company's accounts receivable on a nonrecourse basis.

Factors of Production: Those things necessary for producing finished goods. Factors of production consist of land, capital, labor, and technology.

FASB No. 8: Under this rule, monetary items of a foreign affiliate are translated at the current exchange rate, and nonmonetary items are translated at the historical exchange rate.

FASB No. 52: Under this rule, the current exchange rate is used in translating foreign-currency financial statements into U.S. dollars.

Financial Accounting Standards Board (FASB): The private-sector organization in the United States that sets financial accounting standards.

Financial Assets: Claims on such wealth as stocks, bonds, and other securities.

Financial Market: The market that deals in financial assets.

Financial Risks: In international finance, those risks which may occur because of varying exchange rates, divergent tax laws, different interest and inflation rates, and balance-of-payments problems.

Fisher Effect: This theory assumes that the nominal interest rate consists of a real interest rate and an expected rate of inflation.

Fixed Exchange Rate: An exchange rate which does not fluctuate or which changes within a predetermined band.

Flexible (Floating or Fluctuating) Exchange Rate: An exchange rate which fluctuates according to market forces.

Foreign Base Company: A corporation whose base or registration is in a country in which it does not conduct active operations.

Foreign Bond: Bond sold outside the borrowing country but in the country of the currency in which the bond is denominated.

Foreign Corrupt Practices Act: U.S. law that makes it illegal for American companies and managers to make payments to foreign government officials for the purpose of obtaining business.

Foreign Credit Insurance Association (FCIA): An association of insurance companies in the United States which provide credit insurance to export sales.

Foreign Currency Swap: An agreement between two parties to exchange local currency for hard currency at a specified future date.

Foreign Currency Translation: The expression of balance-sheet items denominated in a foreign currency into a local currency.

Foreign Direct Investment: The acquisition of physical assets in a foreign country to be managed by the parent company.

Foreign Exchange: Any currency other than the currency used internally in a given country.

Foreign Exchange Exposure: The possibility that a firm will gain or lose due to changes in exchange rates.

Foreign Sales Corporation (FSC): Under the U.S. Foreign Sales Corporation Act of 1984, a type of corporation that provides tax-exempt or tax-deferred income for its export-oriented activities.

Foreign Tax Credit: The amount by which a domestic company may reduce domestic income taxes for income tax payments to a foreign government. This credit is used to avoid international double taxation.

Forfaiting: The purchase of financial obligations such as promissory notes with no recourse to the exporters. This technique is used to finance medium-term export financing.

Forward Discount or Premium: An annualized percentage by which the forward exchange rate is less or more than the spot rate.

Forward Exchange Rate: An exchange rate for a currency to be delivered at a future date.

Free Alongside (F.A.S.): A price that includes the delivery of the goods alongside overseas vessel within reach of its loading tackle.

Free Float: An exchange rate system characterized by the absence of government intervention.

Free on Board (FOB): The price of the goods to the foreign buyer which includes all costs, charges, profits, and expenses accruing up to the point where the goods are deposited on board the exporting vessel or aircraft.

Free Trade: The absence of artificial barriers to trade among individuals and firms in different countries.

Free Trade Area: A form of regional economic integration which eliminates tariffs among member countries and establishes common external tariffs.

Free Trade Zone: An area within a country into which foreign goods may be brought duty free for purposes of additional manufacture, inventory storage, or packaging.

Freely Floating Exchange–Rate System: A system which allows exchange rates to move on the basis of market forces without government intervention.

Functional Currency: The currency of the primary economic environment in which the entity operates.

Fundamental Analysis: A forecast based on fundamental relationships between economic variables and exchange rates.

Futures Contract: A contract that specifies an exchange rate in advance of the future exchange of the currency.

Futures Options: The right to buy or sell the futures contract of a specified currency at a specified price by a specified expiration date.

Gap Analysis: A tool used to estimate why a market potential for a given product is less than a company's sales in a country.

General Agreement on Tariffs and Trade (GATT): An agreement signed in 1947 by 23 countries to liberalize world trade.

Generalized System of Preferences: Arrangements through which industrialized countries grant preferential import duty rates to products from developing countries.

Geographic Arbitrage: A practice which buys a currency in a market where its price is lower and then sells the currency in another market where its price is higher.

Glasnost: A Russian term referring to openness in political policies.

Gold Exchange Standard: A system in which a country is prepared to convert its currency into gold.

Gold Export Point: The rate of exchange for a foreign currency above which the foreign currency will not be purchased and gold will be sent (exported) to the foreign country to make payments there.

Gold Import Point: The rate of exchange for a foreign currency below which a nation's own currency will not be purchased and gold will be sent (imported) into that country by foreigners to make payments there.

Gold Standard: A system where a country uses gold as a medium of exchange and a store of value.

Gold Tranche: The amount that each IMF member country contributes in gold or dollars as a part of its membership quota in the IMF. The gold tranche is usually 25 percent of a country's quota.

Gramm–Rudman Act: Legislation enacted in 1985 by the U.S. federal government requiring annual reductions in federal budget deficits and mandating an automatic decrease in expenditures when Congress and the President cannot agree on how to meet the targeted reductions.

Grand Tour: A political-risk forecasting technique which relies on the opinions of company executives visiting the country where investment is considered.

Grandchild Subsidiary: A so-called second-tier subsidiary, which is under a tax-haven subsidiary.

Gross National Product (GNP): The total market value of all final goods and services produced in the economy during a year.

Group of Five: Five industrial countries: France, Germany, Japan, the United Kingdom, and the United States.

Group of Seven: Group-of-five countries plus Canada and Italy.

Group of Ten: Ten major industrial countries which pledged in 1962 to lend their currencies to the IMF under the so-called General Agreement to Borrow. These ten countries are the Group of Seven countries plus Belgium, the Netherlands, and Sweden.

Group of Twenty: The group of countries established to develop a proposal for reform of the international monetary system when the IMF felt that the Group of Ten countries did not sufficiently represent its entire member countries. The United States, the United Kingdom, Germany, France, Japan, and India had individual representation in the Group of Twenty and 14 additional countries each represented a group of countries.

Group of Twenty-Four: Twenty-four countries formed to ensure that interests and economic conditions of less-developed countries are taken into account in reform of the international monetary system. These 24 countries include eight countries each from Africa, Asia, and Latin America.

Hard Currency: Currency that may be used in international trade.

Hedging Device: An approach designed to reduce or offset a possible loss. For example, the multinational company may sell forward exchange or use other means such as credit swap to offset or reduce possible losses from exchange rate fluctuations that affect values of assets and liabilities.

Horizontal Expansion: A combination of firms engaged in the same line of business.

Host Country: The nonheadquartered country in which an international firm operates.

Import Quota: The maximum amount of a given product to be imported during a specified period of time.

Import Substitution: An industrialization policy whereby new industrial developments emphasize products that would otherwise be imported.

Indexing: The practice of adjusting assets, liabilities, or payments by some measure of inflation to preserve the purchasing power of the original amounts.

Infant Industry Argument: An argument that protective measures are essential for newly begun domestic industries to establish themselves.

Inflation: The overall rate of increase in prices for a group of goods and services in a given country.

International Monetary Reserves: Assets held by central banks or governments which can be used to settle international payments.

Inter-American Development Bank (IDB): A regional development bank founded in 1959 by the United States and 19 Latin American countries to further the economic development of its member countries.

Interbank Market: The foreign exchange market among banks.

Interbank Transactions: Foreign exchange transactions that take place between banks as opposed to those between banks and nonbank clients.

Interest Arbitrage: A practice of lending or investing in another currency to take advantage of higher interest rates.

Interest Equalization Tax: A tax imposed on U.S. residents who bought foreign securities between 1963 and 1974 in order to reduce after-tax yields on such bonds to the level of the yield on U.S. bonds.

Interest Parity Line: A line that describes the equilibrium position for the relationship between interest differentials and forward premium or discount. Every point on the line represents a situation in which the interest differential equals the forward premium or discount.

Interest Parity Theory: A theory stating that the difference between the spot rate and the forward rate equals the difference between the domestic interest rate and the foreign interest rate.

Internal Rate of Return: The discount rate that equates the present value of expected net cash flows to the present value of the net investment.

Interest Rate Swap: Under this swap, companies exchange cash flows of a floating rate for cash flows of a fixed rate or exchange cash flows of a fixed rate for cash flows of a flexible rate.

International Accounting Standards Committee: The international private–sector organization established to set financial accounting standards that can be used worldwide.

International Bank for Reconstruction and Development (IBRD): The World Bank which is a companion institution to the IMF.

International Banking Facilities (IBFs): Vehicles that enable bank offices in the United States to accept time deposits in either dollars or foreign currency from foreign customers, free of reserve requirements and of other limitations.

International Bonds: Those bonds that are initially sold outside the country of the borrower.

International Development Association (IDA): An affiliate of the IBRD established to make long-term "soft" loans for development.

International Finance Corporation (IFC): An affiliate of the IBRD established to make development loans in forms which could be sold to other investors and converted into equity.

International Fisher Effect: A theory that the spot exchange rate should change by an amount equal to the difference in interest rates between two countries.

International Monetary Fund (IMF): An international monetary organization created at the Bretton Woods conference to make the new monetary system feasible and workable.

International Monetary System: A system of such elements as laws, rules, institutions, instruments, and procedures which include international money.

Intervention: The buying and selling of currencies by central banks to influence the exchange rate.

Intrinsic Value: The difference between the exchange rate of the underlying currency and the strike price of a currency option.

Irrevocable letter of credit: A letter of credit that cannot be changed without consent of all parties involved in the letter.

Issuing Bank: The bank which issues a letter of credit, usually the importer's bank.

J-Curve: Following a currency devaluation, an initial decrease in the trade balance followed by an increase.

Joint Venture: A business venture in which two or more parties, for example, a foreign firm and a local firm, have equity interest.

Just-in-Time (JIT) Inventory System: A manufacturing system that reduces inventories by having components and parts delivered as they need to be used in production.

Keiretsu: A Japanese word which stands for large, financially linked groups of companies that play a significant role in the country's economy.

Kennedy Round: The trade negotiations concluded in 1967 to reduce trade barriers between the United States and the EC countries.

Law of One Price: A law stating that all goods sell for the same price worldwide when converted to a common currency.

Leads and Lags: Payment of a financial obligation earlier (leads) or later (lags) than is expected or required.

Less Developed Countries (LDCs): Countries characterized by relatively low levels of economic output and income per capita, limited industrial activity, and lack of adequate health, educational, and other social services.

Letter of Credit: A document issued by a bank at the request of the importer. In the document, the bank agrees to honor a draft drawn on the importer if the draft accompanies specified documents.

Leveraged Buy Outs (LBO): A large loan to buy a controlling interest of a company.

Lifetime Employment: A customary Japanese situation in which workers are effectively guaranteed employment with the company for their working lifetime.

Licensing Agreement: An agreement whereby one firm gives rights to another for the use of such assets as trademarks, patents, or copyrights.

Link Financing: An arrangement that commercial banks in strong-currency countries help subsidiaries in weak-currency countries obtain loans by guaranteeing repayment on the loans.

Local Currency: The currency of the country to which reference is made.

London Interbank Offered Rate (LIBOR): The arithmetic average of the interest rates offered by six major banks in London on six-month Eurodollar time deposits at a certain time during the morning.

Long Position: An agreement to buy a futures contract.

M1: The most common measure of money supply which consists of currency in circulation, demand deposits at commercial banks, balances in NOW accounts, and other transaction accounts at financial institutions.

M2: Another common measure of money supply which consists of M1 plus savings and small-denomination time-deposit accounts, plus money market mutual fund shares.

Mail Float: Mailing time involved in payments sent by mail.

Managed Float: Also known as dirty float, a system that floats exchange rates with central bank intervention to reduce currency fluctuations.

Margin: Money deposited with a broker to finance futures trading.

Margin Call: A broker's request for additional deposit when funds in his client's account fall below the minimum amount.

Market Economy: An economic philosophy in which resources are allocated and controlled by consumers who "vote" by buying goods.

Market Portfolio: A well-diversified group of risky securities with little or no unsystematic risk.

Marshall Plan: The European Economic Recovery Program established by the United States in 1948 to restore the productive capacity of European industry and agriculture destroyed during World War II.

Merchandise Trade Balance: The net of merchandise imports and exports within a country's balance of payments.

Merger: A situation where two companies combine their operations to form a new company.

Monetary/Nonmonetary Method: Under this method of translation, all monetary accounts are translated at the current exchange rate, and all nonmonetary accounts are translated at the historical exchange rate.

Money Market: Financial market where short-term securities such as commercial paper and bankers' acceptances are sold and bought.

Money Market Hedge: A hedging device which involves a contract and a source of funds to carry out that contract. If an American firm has a German mark import payable in 60 days, it may borrow in dollars, convert the proceeds into German marks, buy a 60-day German Treasury bill, and pay the import bill with the funds derived from the sale of the Treasury bill.

Most–Favored Nation: A nation which receives the most favored treatment in application of duties from another country.

Multicurrency Clause: A clause that gives a Eurocurrency borrower the right to switch from one currency to another when the loan is rolled over.

Multinational (Transnational) Corporations: Companies that conduct business operations in several countries. They usually consist of a parent firm and a number of affiliates.

Multiple Exchange–Rate System: Under this system, a government sets different exchange rates for different transactions.

Negotiable Order of Withdrawal (NOW) Account: An account in savings and loan associations or mutual savings banks against which a check may be written and which pays interest to the depositor.

Negotiating Bank: A bank which negotiates such things as discounts or purchases of drafts drawn by exporters.

Net Exposure: The difference between exposed assets and liabilities.

Net Present Value: The present value of future net cash flows minus the present value of the net investment for a project.

Netting: A method designed to reduce the foreign exchange transaction cost through the consolidation of accounts payable and accounts receivable. For example, if subsidiary A buys $1 million worth of goods from subsidiary B and B in turns buys $3 million worth of parts from A, the combined flows are $4 million. But on a net basis, subsidiary A would pay subsidiary B only $2 million.

Newly Industrialized Countries (NICs): Third world countries in which the cultural and economic climate has led to a rapid rate of industrialization and growth since the 1960s.

Nikkei Index: A measure of the level of stock prices on the Tokyo Stock Exchange, based on the prices of a group of Japanese securities.

Nominal Interest Rate: The rate of interest that consists of a real interest rate and an expected rate of inflation.

Nonmarket Economy: An economy in which resources are allocated and controlled by government decision.

Nontariff Barriers: Restrictive practices in trade other than custom duties used by governments or by private firms. Nontariff barriers used by governments include import quotas, voluntary restrictions, exceptional customs valuation procedures, and health regulations. Nontariff barriers used by private firms include price control, division of markets, restriction of supplies, patent agreements, or control of technology.

Notifying (Advising Bank): A bank which notifies the beneficiary of the opening of a letter of credit.

Offer Price: The price at which a trader is willing to sell a given item.

Office of Foreign Direct Investment (OFDI): A U.S. government agency created in 1965 to impose controls on U.S.-financed foreign direct investment. Its regulations were voluntary between 1965 and 1967 and became mandatory from 1968 until they were abolished in 1973.

Official Reserves: Government-owned assets which consist of gold, SDRs, and convertible foreign exchange.

Offshore Banking: Banking activities that accept deposits and make loans in foreign currency—the Eurocurrency market.

Offshore Funds: Funds which use the currency of a country but are located outside that country for tax and other purposes.

Oligopoly Model: This model assumes that business firms make foreign investments to exploit their quasi-monopoly advantages.

Opening Bank: A bank which opens a letter of credit.

Opportunity Cost: The rate of return that funds could earn if they were invested in the best available alternative project.

Optimal Portfolio: A portfolio found at the tangency point between the efficient frontier and the security market line. This is the portfolio which has, among all possible portfolios, the largest ratio of expected return to risk.

Optimum Capital Budget: The amount of investment that will maximize a company's total profits.

Optimum Capital Structure: The combination of debt and equity that yields the lowest cost of capital or maximizes the overall value of the company.

Option: The right to buy or sell a given amount of foreign exchange or other financial asset at a fixed price for a specified time period.

Option Premium (Price): The price the option buyer must pay the option seller.

Organization for Economic Cooperation and Development (OECD): An organization established in 1961 to replace the Organization for European Economic Cooperation (OEEC). The OECD includes Group-of-Ten countries, Austria, Denmark, Luxembourg, Norway, Switzerland, Finland, Greece, Iceland, Ireland, Portugal, Spain, Turkey, and Australia. The OECD encourages cooperative efforts among its member countries in economic studies, economic policy formulation, and economic aid to developing nations.

Organization of Petroleum Exporting Countries (OPEC): An organization established by a number of oil exporting countries to formulate uniform policies such as selling prices on their oil export sales. Full members with vote and veto include Algeria, Ecuador, Indonesia, Iran, Iraq, Kuwait, Libya, Nigeria, Qatar, Saudi Arabia, the United Arab Emirates, and Venezuela.

Outright Forward Rate: A forward exchange rate expressed in terms of the amount of one currency required to buy a unit of another currency.

Outsourcing: A situation in which a domestic company uses foreign suppliers for components or finished products.

Overdraft: A line of credit which permits the customer to write checks beyond deposits.

Overseas Private Investment Corporation (OPIC): A U.S. government agency established in 1969 to insure American overseas investors against political risks.

Par (Mint) Value: The value of a currency specified by the government of the currency.

Parallel Loan: A loan which involves an exchange of currencies between two parties, with a promise to re-exchange the currencies at a specified exchange rate and future date.

Parent: A company that controls another (its subsidiary).

Payback Period: The number of years required for the net cash flows of a project to return its cost.

Payee: The party to whom payment is made. The drawer may also be a payee of a draft.

Paying Bank: The drawee bank on which a draft is drawn.

Peg: To fix the value of a currency to some benchmark such as the U.S. dollar.

Petrodollars: OPEC deposits of dollars in the Eurocurrency market.

Piracy: The unauthorized use of property rights protected by patents, trademarks, or copyrights.

Planned Divestment: The sale of majority ownership in foreign affiliates to local nationals during a previously agreed upon period of time.

Political Risk: Potential changes in political conditions that may cause company operating positions to deteriorate.

Portfolio Effect: The extent to which the variations or risks of individual assets tend to offset each other.

Portfolio Investment: Investment in foreign financial assets without significant management control of the real assets.

Portfolio Theory: A theory that indicates a company is often able to improve its risk-return performance by holding an internationally diversified portfolio of assets as opposed to a domestically diversified portfolio.

Possessions Corporation: A U.S. firm engaged in business within U.S. possessions such as Guam and American Samoa. The possessions corporation obtains tax advantages if it meets certain requirements.

Premium: The excess of the forward exchange rate over the spot exchange rate.

Private Export Funding Corporation (PEFCO): A corporation established in 1970 at the initiation of the Bankers' Association for Foreign Trade to mobilize private capital in order to finance U.S. exports of big-ticket items.

Privatization: A situation in which government-owned assets are sold to private individuals or groups.

Product Differentiation: Development of a product that is different from those produced by competitors to maintain or improve market share.

Product Life-Cycle Theory: A theory that attempts to explain both world trade and foreign investment patterns on the basis of stages in a product's life. Product life-cycle is the time it takes to bring new and improved products to markets.

Production Efficiency: The production of goods in the least costly way.

Protectionism: A political attitude or policy intended to prohibit the import of foreign goods and services.

Public Law 480: The U.S. law that permits less developed countries to purchase surplus American agricultural products and to pay for them with their own currencies rather than with dollars.

Purchasing Power Parity Theory: An economic theory postulating that, in the long-run, exchange rates reflect the relative purchasing power of currencies.

Put: An option to sell foreign exchange or financial contracts.

Quality Control Circle: A production system whereby small groups of workers meet regularly to detect and solve problems in their area.

Quota: A limit set on the import of a product.

Real Interest Rate: Nominal (quoted) interest rate minus the inflation rate.

Recourse: A right of an intermediary to claim reimbursement from a drawer of a draft if the drawee fails to pay.

Regional Development Bank: A development bank that makes loans only to countries in particular regions.

Regulation M: A regulation of the U.S. Federal Reserve System which requires U.S. banks to keep a stipulated percentage of their deposits at a Federal Reserve Bank or in vault cash.

Regulation Q: A regulation of the U.S. Federal Reserve System which limited the interest rate that U.S. banks could pay on time deposits. This regulation was phased out by 1986 under the Monetary Control Act of 1980.

Reinvoicing Center: A subsidiary that takes title to all goods sold by one corporate unit to other affiliates or independent customers. The center pays the seller and in turn is paid by the buyer.

Resale Price Method: The method allowed by the Internal Revenue Service to determine the arm's-length price of intracompany transactions. Under this method, an arm's-length price is obtained by subtracting an appropriate markup from the applicable sale price.

Reporting Currency: The currency in which the parent firm prepares its own financial statements.

Required Rate of Return: The minimum rate of return required by the investors.

Reserve Country: A country whose currency is held as a reserve asset by central banks or governments of other countries.

Reserve Currency: A currency held as a reserve asset by central banks or governments of countries other than the country of the currency.

Reserve or Official Reserve Account: In the balance of payments, the section that represents the changes in official reserves such as SDRs and convertible foreign exchange.

Return on Investment (ROI): Profits divided by the amount of investment, usually total assets.

Revaluation: Either an upvaluation or a devaluation.

Revocable Letter of Credit: A letter of credit that can be canceled at any time without prior notification to the beneficiary.

Risk: The variability of return associated with a project.

Risk–Adjusted Discount Rate: A rate which consists of the riskless rate of return plus a risk premium.

Risk Analysis: An analysis of the different outcomes under different assumptions that each of these outcomes will occur.

Royalties: The payment for use of assets abroad.

Safe Harbor: A rule set in legislation which guarantees favorable treatment to the party.

Safeguard Clause: A clause for conditions under which tariffs and nontariff barriers may be reintroduced.

Section 482: A provision of the U.S. Internal Revenue Code regulating transfer pricing practices.

Securities and Exchange Commission (SEC): A U.S. government agency that regulates securities brokers, dealers, and markets.

Semistrong–Form Efficiency: When related to foreign exchange markets, this theory implies that current exchange rates reflect all publicly available information, thereby making such information useless for forecasting exchange-rate movements.

Short Position: An agreement to sell a futures contract.

Sight Draft: A draft payable on demand (at sight).

Smithsonian Agreement: An agreement reached in December 1971 to widen the band up to 2.25 percent on either side of the par value.

Snake Within Tunnel: A system that EC countries agreed on to allow their currencies to fluctuate a maximum of 2.25 percent against one another and permitted a 4.5 percent band against other countries. The tunnel disappeared in 1973 and the snake ended in 1978.

Society for Worldwide Interbank Financial Telecommunications (SWIFT): An interbank communication network that carries messages for financial transactions.

Sovereign Risk: The risk of a country that will impose foreign exchange regulations or the risk of government default on a loan made to it or guaranteed by it.

Sovereignty: The power of a country to act as it wishes within its own borders.

Specific Duty: A duty imposed as a fixed charge per unit, such as $2 per ton.

Special Drawing Rights (SDRs): A reserve asset created in 1967 by the IMF. SDRs are rights to draw on the IMF.

Spot Rate: A foreign exchange rate paid for delivery of a currency within two days from the date of the trade.

Spread: The difference between the bid and ask prices in a price quote, or the difference between the spot rate and the forward rate.

Strike Price: The price at which a currency can be sold or bought in an option contract.

Strong–Form Efficiency: When related to foreign exchange markets, this theory suggests that current exchange rates reflect all pertinent information, whether publicly available or privately held.

Subpart F: Foreign-source "unearned income" taxed by the Internal Revenue Service whether or not it is remitted to the United States.

Subsidiary: A foreign-based affiliate which is separately incorporated under the host country's law.

Subsidies: Direct or indirect governmental assistance to companies, thereby making them more competitive with imports.

Super 301: A section in the 1988 U.S. Trade Act that covers proceedings against consistent unfair trade practices.

Swap Loan: A loan made by a local bank based on deposit of funds in offices of that bank in another country.

Switch Trading: A practice where payments for exports to the East-bloc and nonmarket countries are made through clearing units whereby sales are balanced with purchases from other countries.

Syndicated Loan: A credit in which a group of banks makes funds available on common terms and conditions to a particular borrower.

Synergistic Effect: A situation where the combined company is worth more than the sum of its parts.

Systematic Risk: The risk common to all assets or all countries, which cannot be diversified away.

Tariff: A duty or tax imposed on imported commodities.

Tariff Harmonization: The process of making tariffs more homogeneous by eliminating disparities in tariff rates on the same commodity.

Tax Haven: A country which promises permanent tax inducements to attract multinational companies.

Tax Holidays: The form of a complete tax exemption for the first few years given by a country when multinational firms invest their money in that country.

Technical Analysis: A currency forecasting technique that uses historical prices or trends.

Temporal Method: A method that translates the financial statements of a foreign affiliate into the parent reporting currency. Monetary assets and liabilities are translated at current exchange rates; nonmonetary assets, nonmonetary liabilities, and owners' equity are translated at historical exchange rates.

Third World: A term used to mean those countries other than the industrial countries and the centrally planned economies.

Time Draft: A draft payable a specified number of days after presentation to the drawee.

Trade Acceptance: A draft accepted by an importer or a business enterprise.

Trademark: A name or logo which distinguishes a company or product.

Translation Exposure: Exchange gains or losses that will occur when a company translates its foreign-currency operations into its home currency.

Transaction Exposure: The possibility that gains or losses may result from the settlement of transactions whose terms are stated in foreign currency.

Transfer Price: The price of goods and services sold between related parties such as parent and subsidiary.

Triangular Arbitrage: The process of buying and selling foreign exchange at a profit due to price discrepancies where three different currencies are involved.

Unilateral Transfer: In the balance of payments, the account which covers gifts by domestic residents to foreign residents, or gifts by the domestic government to foreign governments.

Unit of Account: A benchmark on which to base the value of payments.

Unitary Tax: A method of taxing a company's worldwide profits rather than on profits in the area where the taxing authorities are located.

Unsystematic Risk: The risk unique to a particular company or country, which can be diversified away.

Upvaluation: An official increase in the par value of a currency by the government.

U.S.-Canada Free Trade Agreement: A 1988 agreement between the United States and Canada to remove their trade barriers.

Value-Added Tax (VAT): A sales tax assessed at one or more stages in the production process but only on the value added during that production stage.

Vertical Integration: The integration of different stages in which the special drawing rights of a product move from the earliest production to the final distribution.

Weak–Form Efficiency: This theory implies that all information contained in past exchange-rate movements is fully reflected in current exchange rates.

Withholding Tax: A tax collected from income to employees, stockholders, and others; it is collected before receipt of the income.

World Bank: A multinational financial institution established in 1944 to enhance economic development.

Yield: The actual rate of return on a financial asset. It depends on the price paid for the security and the stated rate of interest or dividend.

Name Index

Marrinan, J., 136
Mathur, I., 461
McCalman, J., 512n
McCauley, R. N., 244, 378
McCulloch, W., 22, 382
McCulloch, W. H., 36, 398
Mcelravey, J. N., 15, 225
McGeady, M., 271
McManus, G., 465n
Meek, G., 426, 461
Meek, G. K., 225
Mehta, D. R., 315
Meltzer, A. H., 136
Meltzer, R. I., 469n
Melvin, M., 225
Micallef, J., 384
Micallef, J. V., 399
Miller, S., 449
Miller, S. W., 243, 461
Mintz, N., 383, 398
Mirus, R., 272
Mishkin, F. S., 136
Moreno, R., 471
Morgan, J. B., 243
Morris, F. E., 244
Mossberg, W. S., 469n
Mouzin, D. J., 426
Moxon, R., 481n
Mueller, G. G., 404, 426, 443, 461
Mulroney, B., 26
Murray, A., 488n, 493

N

Nathanson, L., 372–73, 378
Nehrt, L., 31, 37
Newman, L. R., 348, 351
Newman, R. G., 351, 499n
Nigh, D., 290

O

O'Boyle, T. F., 506n
Obstfeld, M., 136
O'Leary, M. K., 398, 506n
O'Reilly, A. J., 290
Orr, J., 67

Ott, M., 198
Ouchi, W. G., 499n
Ow-Taylor, C. H., 469n

P

Padebaugh, L., 446
Pae, P., 465n
Paris, D. G., 10
Park, Y. S., 225, 244
Parsons, M., 103
Pasztor, A., 427
Pavel, C., 15, 225
Perry, M., 58
Persen, W., 427
Peterson, J. E., 499n, 506n
Peterson, T., 485n
Philippatos, M. E., 381, 399
Piper, T. R., 515n
Pitman, G. A., 351
Poterba, J. M., 359, 362, 363, 364, 378
Powell, B., 499n
Provissiero, M., 383, 398
Pugel, T., 461

Q

Quelch, J. A., 37
Quijano, A., 244

R

Rabino, S., 272
Radebaugh, L. H., 15, 426, 443, 460, 465n,
    475n, 481n, 485n, 496n
Reagan, R., 26, 265, 380, 471
Rehder, R., 499n
Reich, M., 499n
Resnick, B. G., 330
Rhee, K. A., 351, 499n
Rhee, S. G., 330
Robock, S. H., 15
Rogalski, R. J., 198
Rohatyn, F., 348, 351
Rojas-Suarez, J., 244
Root, F. R., 15
Rose, R. L., 15
Rosensweig, J. A., 67

Rosenweig, J. A., 137
Ross, R. S., 460
Rossman, M. L., 272
Roth, T., 485*n*
Roy, J., 398
Rueschloff, N. G., 426
Ryan, B. J., 512*n*

S

Salama, E. R., 37
Samuelson, R. J., 465*n*
Sarathy, R., 312, 315, 378
Sarnat, M., 30, 37
Saudagaran, S. M., 225
Saunders, A., 225
Saunders, J., 475*n*
Scaringella, J. L., 315
Schindler, G., 461
Schlegelmilch, B. B., 515*n*
Schlesinger, J. M., 488*n*, 499*n*
Scholl, R. B., 351
Seberger, D. P., 272
Seitz, N., 315
Sekely, W. S., 359, 377, 378
Seneker, H., 512*n*
Seringhaus, F. H. R., 67
Seth, R., 244
Shah, K., 272
Shapiro, A. C., 15, 164, 183, 315, 330
Sharpe, W. F., 330
Shoven, J. B., 377
Simmons, K., 15
Sinek, J., 506*n*
Smith, K. D., 290
Smith, K. V., 315
Smith, R., 500
Soenen, L. A., 14, 397
Solnik, B., 164, 323, 330
Solomon, M. B., 426
Song, Y. K., 378
Srinivasan, V., 297, 315
Stanley, M. T., 378
Staudohar, P. D., 499*n*
Stern, J. M., 164
Sternand, J. M., 137
Stiff, R., 271

Stockman, A. C., 137
Stoffel, J., 272
Stone, N., 37
Stonehill, A. I., 15, 164, 330, 372-73, 378
Stultz, R. M., 137
Sullivan, L. H., 507
Suzuki, S., 312, 315, 358, 378
Swanson, P. E., 198
Sweeney, R. J., 198
Symonds, W. C., 485*n*

T

Tallman, S. B., 378
Tang, R. Y., 461
Taylor, A. III, 351
Thatcher, M., 27
Thomas, L. R., 331
Thomas, R., 499*n*
Tobin, J., 316, 331, 370-71, 378
Triffin, R., 100, 103
Truell, P., 37
Turner, P., 201, 225, 244

U

Ugelow, J. L., 461

V

Vachani, S., 395, 398
Van Horne, J. C., 164
Veazey, R. E., 198
Velasquez, M., 515*n*
Vernon, R., 512*n*
Versical, D., 506*n*
Veugelers, P. T., 198
Vinso, J. D., 198

W

Wartzman, R., 465*n*
Watt, G., 444
Watt, G. C., 444
Weiss, S. E., 499*n*
Whiteside, D., 515*n*
Whitt, J. A., 97, 103, 137
Williamson, J., 243

Wolff, C., 198
Woodruff, D., 475*n*
Wright, R., 312, 358
Wright, R. W., 315, 378
Wysocki, B., Jr, 15, 37, 338, 488*n*

Y

Yeager, L. B., 103
Yoder, S. K., 488*n*
Yoffie, D. B., 273
Young, B., 272
Young, S.-G., 469*n*

Z

Zellner, W., 499*n*
Zimmer, S., 378
Zimmer, S. A., 244
Zwick, J., 15, 244

Subject Index

short-term capital in, 43-44
unilateral transfer in, 42-43
Japanese international transactions
current and capital account overview, 57
as key economic indicator, 172
restoring international equilibrium, 62-65
income mechanism, 63-64
price mechanism, 62-63
public control, 64-65
trade friction between U.S. and Japan, 58-62
as a whole, 44-45
Balance on capital account, 48
Balance on goods and services, 45, 48
Balance sheet accounts, effects of inflation on, 413
Balance-sheet hedge, 182-83
Bank. *See* Commercial banks; International banking operations
Bankers' acceptances, 306-7
discounting, 306
in financing foreign trade, 264
marketability of, 253
Bank financing
bankers' acceptances, 253, 264, 306-7
for foreign trade, 263-64
loans to exporters and importers, 264
trust receipts, 264
Bank for International Settlements (BIS), 80
Banking subsidiaries, foreign, 228
Bank of Credit and Commerce International (BCCI), western regulator seizure of, 209-10
Bank of England, backing of sterling by, 71
Bank of Japan, participation of, in exchange market, 108
Bank trading rooms, 107-8
Barter, 259-60
Beta, computation of, 361-62
Bilateral netting, 296-97
Bilateral trading agreement, 260
Bills of lading, 254-55
clean, 255
definition of, 251
foul, 255
on-board, 255

order, 254
received-for-shipment, 255
straight, 254
Black market, participation of, in exchange market, 109
Boeing Aircraft, 9
Bonds
international, 215-19
zero-coupon, 219
Book-value weights, 358-59
Branch banks, foreign, 228
Brazil, and international debt crisis, 230
Break-even point, 156
Bretton Woods Agreement (1973), 207
Bretton Woods System, 74-76
basic defects in, 95
breakdown of, 75-76
Bridge loans, as source of funds for foreign investment, 278
Bullion, 69
Buy-back agreement, 261

C

Call option, currency, 48-49, 153-55
Call options market
hedging in, 153-54
speculating in, 154-55
Call option price, graphic analysis of, 155
Capital
cost of, 357-65
appropriate, 363-64
long-term, 46
short-term, 47
Capital account, 46-47
Japanese, 57
Capital asset pricing model (CAPM), 318, 361-62
and computation of beta, 361-62
Capital budget, optimum, 365
Capital budgeting. *See also* Multinational capital budgeting
in cash flow analysis, 357
control in, 368
implementation in, 368
post audit in, 368-70
in theory and practice, 372-73

inventory management, 308-9
    determining amount of inventory, 309
    pricing, 310-11
    protective measures against inflation
        and devaluation, 309-10
    positioning of funds, 295
    working capital practices, 311-13
        objectives of, 312
        practices by U.S. and Japanese firms,
            312-13
Current/noncurrent method, 175
Current rate method, 175

D

D/A (documents against acceptance) draft,
    254
Daimler-Benz AG, 9
Debt, cost of, 362-63
Debt capacity, in international mergers and
    acquisitions, 348
Debt ratios
    in country-risk assessment, 236-37
    for U.S. and Japanese corporations, 359
Default risk, 209
Deficit, measurement of, 48-49
Deficit Reduction Act (1984), 441
Delphi technique to assess political risk, 386
Demand forecast, in cash flow analysis, 355
Devaluation, protective measures against, in
    inventory management, 309-10
Developed countries, labor-intensive
    industries in, 21-22
Developing countries, debt ratios of, 236
Development banks, as source of funds for
    foreign investment, 282-88
Direct investments, 46. *See also* Foreign
    direct investment
    definition of, 332
Direct loans, 299
    as source of funds for foreign investment,
        275
Dirty floating system
    international policy coordination, 79-80
    multiple exchange rates, 77, 78-79
        future of, 79
Disbursing float, 302

Discount rates, risk-adjusted, 367, 373
Distribution gap, 348
Diversified financing, 191-92
Diversified marketing, 191
Dividend valuation model for the cost of
    capital, 361
Documentary drafts, 254
Domestic International Sales Corporation
    (DISC), 440-41
Domestic loans, comparison of, 235
Double-entry accounting, 41-45
    long-term capital in, 43
    merchandise trade in, 42
    services in, 42
    short-term capital in, 43-44
    unilateral transfer in, 42-43
Diversified production, 191
Dow Chemical Co., 345
D/P (documents against payment) draft, 254
Drafts, 252-54
    clean, 254
    definition of, 251, 252
    D/A, 259
    documentary, 254
    D/P, 254
    parties in, 253
    sight, 253
    time, 253, 254
Drawee, 253
Drawer, 253
Dual reporting system, in financial reporting,
    406-7
Dun & Bradstreet, 358
Duties, in cash flow analysis, 355-56

E

Eastern Europe
    economic reforms in, 8
    hard-currency debt in, 233-34
Eclectic theory, 33-34
Economic cooperation, types of, 24-25
Economic effects of market integration,
    28-29
Economic exposure, 168
Economic exposure management, 190-92
    diversified financing, 191-92

Futures options, 158-59
Future spot rate, and forward rate, 123

G

G-5, and international policy coordination, 80
G-7, and international policy coordination, 80
GATT. *See* General Agreement on tariffs and trade
General Agreement on Tariffs and Trade (GATT), 23, 49, 441
 Kennedy Round, 24
 stabilization of currencies through, 23
 Tokyo Round, 24
 Uruguay Round, 24
Geographic arbitrage, 126
Germany, role on the world economic stage, 8
Global competition, implications of, for the finance function, 11-12
Global financial leadership, case study in, 488-95
Gold standard, 69-70
 gold export and import points, 70-71
 international adjustments, 71-72
 London's dominance in international finance, 71
Gold tranche, 81
Goods and services, balance on, 45
Government attitudes, toward foreign investment, 384-85
Government concessions, in tax incentives, 438
Government financing of foreign trade, 267-69
 Export-Import Bank in, 267
 Foreign Credit Insurance Association in, 268-69
 Private Export Funding Corporation in, 268
Grand tour, to assess political risk, 386
Grantor of an option, 149
Group of Tax Experts on Tax Treaties, 434-35
Group of Ten
 and establishment of Smithsonian Agreement, 75-76

and use of Eurodollars, 208
Growth gaps, closing, 348-49
Guidelines for adequate capitalization, 282

H

Hard currencies, 182
Hard-currency debt, of East Europe, 233-34
Hedging
 in the call options market, 153-54
 in the currency futures market, 140, 146-48
 in the forward exchange market, 184
 in the money market, 184-85
 in the options market, 185-87
 translation exposure, 181-83
Holder of a call option, 149
Horizontal foreign investment, 353-54
Horizontal investments, for foreign production, 31
Host-country benefits, of foreign investment, 333
Hyundai Group of Korea, 281

I

IBM, 281
IMF Survey, 84-85
Import duty minimization, in transfer pricing, 447
Importers, bank loans to, 264
Import quotas, impact on domestic production, 22
Income mechanism, 63-64
Income taxes, 430
 minimization of, in transfer pricing, 446-47
Independent customers, sales to, 307
Independent-discipline approach to accounting, 405-6
Infant industry argument, logic of, 22
Inflation
 impact of, on financial statements, 413
 as key economic indicator, 173
 protective measures against, in inventory management, 309-10
Initial margin, 145

Insurance documents, 257
Inter-American Development Bank, as source
   of funds for foreign investment, 285
Interbank clearinghouse systems, 228-29
Interest Equalization Tax (1963-74), 207, 215
Interest-rate parity theory, 122-23, 125, 171
Interest rates, for Eurodollar instruments,
   211-13
Interest rate swaps, 189
Internal rate of return, 365
Internal Revenue Code Section 482 of, and
   transfer pricing, 450
International Accounting Standards
   Committee (IASC), 411
International adjustments, and fluctuating
   exchange rate, 73-74
International Bank for Reconstruction and
   Development (World Bank)
   creation of, 74
   as source of funds for foreign investment,
      283-84
International banking facilities (IBFs), 107,
   227
   as source of funds for foreign
      investments, 280-81
International banking market, 227
International banking operations, 226-34
   country risk
      debt ratios in, 236-37
      nature of country-risk assessment,
         235-36
      overall-country creditworthiness,
         237-38, 239
   interbank clearinghouse systems, 228-29
   international banking market, 227
   international loans, 229
      East Europe's hard-currency debt,
         233-34
      evaluation of international loans, 233
      international debt crisis of 1982-84,
         230-32
      rise of Japanese banking operations,
         229-30
      syndicated loans, 232-33
   types of foreign banking offices, 227-28
      agencies, 228
      banking subsidiaries, 228

branch banks, 228
consortium banks, 228
correspondent banks, 227
representative offices, 227
U.S. debt crisis, 238-42
   causes of, 240-41
   lower living standards, 241
   and policy constraints, 241
   and reduced international influence,
      241-42
International bond
   currency denomination of, 216-17
   types of, 218-19
International bond market, 215-16
   Eurobonds in, 216
   foreign bonds in, 215
   size of, 216
International capital market, 214-20
   currency denomination of international
      bonds, 216-17
   international bond market, 215-16
   international equity market, 219-20
   market size of international bonds, 216
   types of international bonds, 218-19
International CD Market Association, 211
International Center for Settlement of
   Investment Disputes, 394
International Country Risk Guide (ICRG),
   387
International debt crisis of 1982-84, 230-32
International Development Association, as
   source of funds for foreign investment,
   284-85
International equilibrium, restoring, 62-65
International equity market, 219-20
International Federation of Accountants
   (IFAC), 411
International finance
   case study in ethics in, 515-18
   London's dominance in, 71
International Finance Corporation, as source
   of funds for foreign investment, 284
International finance function, case study in,
   512-14
International financial markets
   Asian currency market, 213-14
   Eurocurrency markets, 202

balance of, 45
Mergers, international, 344-49
Mexican connection, 477
Mexico
    and international debt crisis, 230
    Model Convention of (1943), 434
Microeconomic approach to accounting, 405
Mitsubishi, 9, 343
Mitsui, 343
Model Conventions of Mexico (1943) and
    London (1946), 434
Model Income Tax Treaty, 435
Monetary disorder, 72-74
    fluctuating exchange rate and international
        adjustments, 73-74
Monetary/nonmonetary method, 175
Monetary union, definition of, 88
Money market approach, to covering foreign
    exchange risk, 186
Money market hedge, 184-85
Money supply, as key economic indicator,
    173
Morris, Robert, Associates, 358
Multilateral Investment Guarantee Agency of
    the Bank, as source of funds for foreign
    investment, 284
Multilateral netting, 296-97
Multinational accounting
    consolidated statements, 410
        methods of consolidation, 410
        options of, 410
    control system and performance
        evaluation, 412-20
        inflation and exchange fluctuations,
            413-15
        organizational structure, 419-20
        performance evaluation, 415-19
    financial reporting, 406
        areas of major differences, 407-8
        auditing, 409-10
        dual reporting system, 406-7
        financial disclosure, 408-9
        harmonization of accounting standards,
            411-12
        users of consolidated statements, 411
    Foreign Corrupt Practices Act, 420-23
        content of, 421

fate of, 421
modifying, 422-23
repealing, 421
retaining, 422
independent-discipline approach to
    accounting, 405-6
macroeconomic approach to, 404-5
microeconomic approach to, 405
uniform accounting approach, 406
Multinational capital budgeting, 352-78
    capital budgeting theory and practice,
        372-73
    investment decision-making process,
        352-53
    cash flow analysis, 355-57
    control, 368
    cost of capital, 357-65
    economic evaluation, 365-66
    implementation, 368
    optimum capital structure, 358-60
    overall strategy, 354-55
    and political climate, 354
    post audit, 368-70
    risk analysis of projects, 367-68
    search for foreign investment, 353-54
    selection of projects, 366-67
    portfolio theory, 370-72
Multinational companies
    access to international capital markets, 68
    conflicts of interest in, 6
    environmental differences in, 5-6
    multiple environments in, 6
    risks in, 5-6
    types of, 11-12
Multinational financial managers,
    environmental constraints on, 5
Multiple exchange rates, 77, 78-79

N

National development banks, 286-88
    Agency for International Development,
        287, 286-87
    Export-Import Bank, 286-87
    Overseas Private Investment Corporation,
        287-88
National Industrial Conference Board, 32

NEC Corporation, 9
Negotiation, in response to political risk, 395
Net capital flows to the U.S., 54
Net present value of a project, 365-66
New Asian Industries Development Plan, 28
New United Motor Manufacturing, Inc., 499–505
New York, as international financial center, 201
Nomura Securities, 191-92
Noncompletion risk, in foreign trade, 252
Nonresidents, blockage of funds to, 356
Nontariff trade barriers
    classes of, 22
    impact on international trade, 23
North American Free Trade Area (NAFTA), 7, 26-27, 475–80
Northern Telecom, 7

O

Office of Foreign Direct Investment Regulations (1968), 207
Official reserve account, 47-48
Official versus market rates, as key economic indicator, 173-74
Old hand, to assess political risk, 386
Oligopoly model, 31
Olivetti, and foreign exchange risk management, 485–87
Omnibus Trade and Competitiveness Act, 58
On-board bills of lading, 255
Open accounts, 262
Operational restrictions as political risk, 381-82
Optimal portfolio, selection of, 325-27
Options, versus forward contracts, 186-87
Options market hedge, 185-87
Order bill of lading, 254
Organization for Economic Cooperation and Development (OECD), 80, 412, 434
Out-of-the-money option, 152
Overall-country creditworthiness, in country-risk assessment, 237-38, 239
Overdrafts, as source of funds for foreign investment, 278

Overseas Private Investment Corporation, as source of funds for foreign investment, 287-88

P

Parallel loans, 189-90
Parent cash flows, in cash flow analysis, 356-57
Parent corporations, as source of funds for foreign investment, 275-76
Parent country taxation of multinational operations, 433
    foreign tax credit, 436-37
    tax neutrality, 434
    tax treaties, 434-36
Parent currency, 177-78
Parent guarantees, as source of funds for foreign investment, 276
Payback, 365
Payee, 253
Payment mechanism, operation of, by commercial banks, 106
Payments
    double-entry accounting for, 41-45
        long-term capital in, 43
        merchandise trade in, 42
        services in, 42
        short-term capital in, 43-44
        unilateral transfer in, 42-43
    as a whole, 44-45
Pebble Beach Golf Course, 339
Percent-of-sale method, 355
Performance evaluation, 415-19
Planned divestment, in response to political risks, 388
Political climate, and foreign investment, 354
Political risk, 5
    case study in analyzing, 506-11
    definition of, 379
    forecasting, 384-88
        government's attitudes toward foreign investment, 384-85
        political risk and strategic planning, 385
        political stability, 385
    for foreign investment projects, 352

Revolving letter of credit, 256
Risk
 commercial bank rate in reduction of, 107
  diversification through international
    investment, 322-24
  of participating banks in Eurocurrency
interbank market, 209
  systematic, 361
  types of, as environmental constraint, 5-6
Risk-adjusted discount rate, 367, 373
Risk analysis, of foreign investment projects,
  367-68
Risk management, foreign-exchange, 10
Risk-return characteristics of capital markets,
  324-25
Rockefeller Center, 339, 344
Rockwell International, 345S

S

Securities and Exchange Commission (SEC),
  and investigation of illegal foreign
    payments, 420-23
Security market line, 318, 361
Semi-strong form efficiency, 170
Services, 42, 45
Service trade, 52-53
Settlement risk, 209
Short-term capital, 43-44, 47
Short-term Eurodollar loans, 211
Sight draft, 253-54
Singapore Interbank Offered Rate (SIBOR),
  212, 214
Single European Act (1987), 25
Smithsonian Agreement, 75-76, 88
Society for Worldwide Interbank Financial
  Telecommunications (SWIFT), 228, 229,
    303
Soft currency, 182
Sony, 10
South Africa, Ford disinvestment in, 506-11
Sovereign risk, 209
Special drawing rights (SDRs), 47-48, 79,
  217
  creation of, 7, 48, 82-85
  as currency peg, 88
  definition of, 47

interest rate for, 86-87
 as international reserve, 87
 modifications in the provisions relating to,
   104
 as unit of account, 88
 use of, 85-86
Specialization, goods and services provided
  by, 16-17
Specialized markets, 109-10
Speculation
  in the call options market, 154-55
  in the currency futures market, 140,
    145-46
  in the foreign exchange market, 115-16
  in the forward market, 116
  in the spot market, 115-16
Spot market, speculating in, 115-16
Spot rate, 110-16
Standard deviation, 316
  in risk analysis, 317-18
Statistical discrepancy, 53-54
  errors and omissions, 47
Steel imports, protectionism for, 465-68
Sterling crisis, chronology of, 92
Stockholders, versus financial management,
  4-5
Straight bill of lading, 254
Strategic planning, and political risk, 385
Strike price, 149
Strong form efficiency, 170
Subsidiaries
  evaluating performance of foreign, 417-18
  loans from sister, 277
Sumitomo Bank, 343
Super 301, 58
Surplus, measurement of, 48-49
Survey of Current Business, 49
Swap agreements, 187-90
  back-to-back loans, 189-90
  credit swap, 188-89
  currency swaps, 187-88
  interest rate swaps, 189
Switch trade broker, 260
Switch trading, 260
Syndicated loans, 232-33
Systematic risk, 361

T

Taiwan Aerospace Corp., 9
Tariffs, 430-31
Taxes. *See also* International taxation
    capital gains, 430
    in cash flow analysis, 355-56
    income, 430
        minimization of, in transfer pricing, 446-47
    types of, 430-31
Tax-haven countries, 298, 306, 438
    cash centers in, 305
Tax holidays, 438
Tax incentives, treatment of, for new investment, 363
Tax Reform Act (1986), 439, 452
Tax treaties, 434-36
Technical analysis forecasting, 171-72
Technical and health regulations, impact on imports, 23
Temporal method, 175
Third World, foreign direct investments in, 337-39
Three-point arbitrage, 127
Time deposits, 210
Time draft, 253, 254
Time value, 152
Tokyo, as international financial center, 201
Tokyo Round, 24
Toyota Motor Corp., 281, 343
Trade. *See also* Foreign trade
    merchandise, 51-52
    service, 52-53
Trade acceptances, 263, 306-7
Trade argument between countries, case study in, 469-74
Trade controls, 64
    forms of, 22-23
Trade financing, in foreign trade, 252
Trade friction, between the U.S. and Japan, 58-62
Trading blocs, case study in, 475-80
Transaction exposure, 167
Transaction exposure management, 183-90

forward exchange market hedge, 184
money market hedge, 184-85
options market hedge, 185-87
swap agreements, 187-90
Transfer prices. *See also* International transfer pricing
    in cash flow analysis, 357
    in current asset management, 297-98
    definition of, 445
    and Internal Revenue Code Section 482, 450
Transit float, 302
Translation exposure, 166-67
    hedging, 181-83
Translation exposure management, 174-83
    translation rules, 175-77
Treaty of Rome, 25
Trend analyses, 171-72
Triangle arbitrage, 127
Tripolar economic system, 7
Trust receipts, in financing foreign trade, 264
Two-point arbitrage, 126-27

U

Unbundling fund transfers, 300
Unconfirmed letter of credit, 256
Uniform accounting approach to accounting, 406
Unilateral transfer, 42-43, 46
Unitary taxes, 429-30
United Nations, and accounting standards, 412
United States
    balance of payments in, 51-55
    cost of capital in, 364-65
    debt crisis, 238-42
        causes of, 240-41
        and lower living standards, 241
        and policy constraints, 241
        and reduced international influence, 241-42
    debt ratios for corporations in, 359
    direct investment positions in, 340-41
    foreign investment positions in, 335-37
    international investment position in, 55-56
    Japanese automotive transplants in,

341-42
Japanese direct investments in, 339-40
net capital flows to, 54-55
price-earnings ratios for, 362
trade deficit with Japan, 23
trade friction between Japan and, 58-62
trade friction between Korea and, 469-74
working capital practices by firms in, 312-13
U.S.-Canada Auto Pact (1965), 27
U.S.-Canada Free Trade Agreement (FTA), 24, 26-27, 476
Universal Studios, 339
Unsecured short-term loans, as source of funds for foreign investment, 278
Unsystematic risk, elimination of, by diversification, 361
Uruguay Round, 24
Usage gap, 348-49

V

Value-added taxes, 430
Value of exchange-rate volatility, 153
Vertical foreign investment, 31, 353
Volatile exchange rates, 10
Voluntary Foreign Credit Restraints (1964), 207

W

Wall Street Journal, 110-11
    currency option quotes in, 150
    reading currency futures quotes in, 142-43
Water's edge concept, 429-30
Weak form efficiency, 170
Weighted average cost of capital, 357-58
Wider band alternative, 98
Withholding taxes, 431
Working capital practices, 311-13
World balance of payments, 49-51
World Bank. *See* International Bank for Reconstruction and Development
World Bank Group
    International Bank for Reconstruction and Development, 283-84

International Development Association, 284-85
International Finance Corporation, 284
    as source of funds for foreign investment, 282-83
World economy, 6-11
    Asian Pacific Rim economies, 7-8
    countertrade, 9
    economic integration in, 6-7
    economic reforms in Eastern Europe, 8
    international joint ventures in, 9
    tripolar economic system in, 7
    volatile exchange rates in, 10
World Electric Corporation, 512-14
World trade. *See* Foreign trade

Y

Yen Trading Bloc, 27

Z

Zenith Electronics Corp., 27
Zero-coupon bonds, 219